William Wisheart

Theologia

Vol. II

William Wisheart

Theologia
Vol. II

ISBN/EAN: 9783337160104

Printed in Europe, USA, Canada, Australia, Japan

Cover: Foto ©ninafisch / pixelio.de

More available books at **www.hansebooks.com**

OR,

DISCOURSES OF GOD.

DELIVERED IN CXX

SERMONS.

IN TWO VOLUMES.

CONTAINING,

VOL. I.	VOL. II.
DISCOURSES	DISCOURSES
Of the Neceffity and Excellency of the KNOWLEDGE of GOD; of his BEING—INCOMPREHENSIBILITY—KNOWLEDGE—WISDOM—POWER—HOLINESS—GOODNESS—JUSTICE—PATIENCE—MERCY—TRUTH.—ETERNITY and GLORY.	Of making the glorifying GOD our Chief End, and our great Employment and Bufinefs; of GOD's Bleffednefs; of his Decrees; of the Unity of the Divine Effence; of the Trinity of Perfons in the Godhead; of beholding the Glory of GOD in the Glafs of the Gofpel; and of propagating the Knowledge of GOD.

By Mr. WILLIAM WISHEART, Senʳ.
Principal of the Univerfity of EDINBURGH,
and one of the Minifters of that City.

VOL. II.

———

PAISLEY:
PRINTED BY JOHN NEILSON,
FOR *ROBERT REID*, THE PUBLISHER.
M.DCC.LXXXVII.

TO THE HONOURABLE

Sir GEORGE WISHEART,

OF *CLIFTON-HALL*, BARONET;

AND

Sir JAMES WISHEART,

LATE ADMIRAL OF THE WHITE.

HONOURED AND DEAR BRETHREN,

THE bonds of nature, and the many endearing passages that, for so many years, have glued our affections so intimately, easily induced me to believe it would not offend that your names were prefixed to this Volume of my Discourses.

Amidst all the changes that have befallen us, BROTHERLY-LOVE hath continued: and though I am confident you are too firmly persuaded of my sincere affection and respect to you, to need any such memorial to assure you of it; yet I judge it proper for me to take this occasion of testifying it to the world. I am the rather inclined to this, that I may hereby bear testimony against the great want of natural affection that so much prevails in this corrupt age, a notorious instance whereof we had in the late HORRID and PERFIDIOUS REBELLION,

DEDICATION.

tion, whereby, as all our sacred and civil interests were boldly threatened, so the strictest bonds of nature were most shamefully violated.

Though many defects and weaknesses will be found in these Discourses, yet the subjects treated of in them are so excellent and necessary, that they are of general concern to all Christians, and as such deserve your most serious consideration.

I conclude with my hearty prayers to God, That he would multiply his best blessings upon you and your families; that his good Spirit may be your constant guide; that he may ever compass you with his favour as with a shield; that BROTHERLY LOVE may still continue amongst us; and that what I now offer you, in testimony of it on my part, may, through the divine blessing, be a mean to promote your eternal salvation, which will be matter of great joy, and a crown of rejoicing to,

HONOURED AND DEAR BRETHREN,

Yours, in the entirest bonds of brotherly affection,

WILL. WISHEART.

OR,

DISCOURSES OF GOD.

DISCOURSE XV.

Of making the Glory of God our Chief End.

SERMON LXI.

1 Cor. x. 31. *Whether therefore ye eat or drink, or whatsoever ye do, do all to the glory of God.*

THE apostle, in the preceding verses, had been discoursing concerning the eating things offered to idols, and in this and the following verses, he concludes this subject by laying down some general rules that are of use in the whole course of our life. Of these rules this is one in my text, wherein we may notice these two things.

1. That which should be a Christian's great end and scope, viz. The glory of God: that is, the declaring and manifesting his glory. Let this be that you chiefly and ultimately aim at. Have this chiefly in your eye, and level at this mark. Let your hearts be chiefly set upon this, as that which you aim at and design above and beyond all other things.

2. Wherein it is that this should be our chief end and aim. This is, 1. Laid down more generally, in these words, *Whatsoever ye do;* in all your actions, whether natural, civil, or religious; so that this is a general rule. No man, in any action or business, is free from the obligation of it. Though there be many things in their own nature indifferent; yet in none of these things is any man so at liberty, as that he should not consult what may be most for the glory of God, which he ought chiefly to aim at in all that he doth. 2. He doth particularly mention *eating and drinking.* It might be thought sufficient to his main scope to have satisfied himself with that general rule, *Whatsoever ye do, do all to the glory of God :* But he speaks particularly of *eating and drinking,* for three reasons,

(1.) Be-

(1.) Because the apostle had been directing the Christians at Corinth about eating and drinking with the pagan idolaters, and how to ease their consciences of real or supposed guilt in eating things sacrificed unto idols; so that it was apposite to mention *eating and drinking* for applying this general rule to that special case. (2.) Because in these natural actions we are in great danger to offend. Therefore it was that Job sacrificed when his sons feasted (*a*). Among other dishes that come to our table, the devil brings his; therefore we need to watch and feed with fear. We are in greatest danger of sinning, when the thing we are about is not in itself sinful. Men usually startle at evident and known sins; but in the use of lawful and allowed comforts, we are often overtaken unawares. (3.) For the greater emphasis, as an argument from the less to the greater; for, if even in these natural actions, we are to aim at the glory of God; much more in other actions that are not so common.

The doctrine I propose is this.

Observ. *The glory of God should be our chief end in all that we do.*

In prosecuting this doctrine, I shall shew,

1. *What it is to make the glory of God our chief end.*
2. *Wherein, or in what things we should do so.*
3. *Why we should do so.*
4. *I shall apply the doctrine.*

First, What it is to make the glory of God our chief end.

It is here implied, that we may have other subordinate ends in what we do; but nothing else must be our chief end. As for example; we may eat and drink, and sleep, for this end, that we may refresh, nourish, and strengthen the body and natural spirits: But our chief end in this must be the glory of God. Again, men may be diligent in their worldly employments, for this end, that they may provide for themselves and their families the good things of this life that are convenient for them: But that which they ought chiefly to aim at in this is, that they and their families may be in the better capacity for serving and glorifying God; so that we may have other subordinate ends. There are other lawful ends we may propose to ourselves in what we do: But it must be in a due subor-

(*a*) Job i. 5.

subordination to the glory of God, as that which we aim at and design above and beyond all other things.

But what is it to make the glory of God our chief end? Or, when may we be said to do so? I answer, We make the glory of God our chief end in these cases, 1. When our hearts are chiefly set upon this. When our chief cares, desires and endeavours, are levelled at this, to have God glorified; and the bent of the heart is towards God. 2. When other lawful ends we propose to ourselves in lawful things, are eyed and designed as means in order to this. As for example, I may eat and drink for this end, to nourish and refresh the body: Now, when I eye this lawful end, to wit, the nourishing and refreshing my body, as a mean to enable me the more to glorify God, then I make the glory of God my chief end. 3. When our desires after other lawful things are subordinate to our desires after the glory of God; so that we desire these other things with submission to his will, if he shall see it meet for his glory and our good to deny them. As for example, when we pray, "Lord, grant me success in such and such a "design and business, or grant me such and such a blessing, "if it may be for thy glory; and if it be not for thy glory, "then I desire humbly to submit to thy will in the denial of "it." In such cases we make the glory of God our chief end. 4. When there is nothing beyond the glory of God that we aim at. We stop here, designing nothing further. If God may have glory, then the heart is at rest and ease. The man hath no further design; he aims at nothing beyond that. 5. When we renounce and forsake all inferior interests and enjoyments, so far as they come in competition with the glory of God. To this purpose is that warning our blessed Lord hath given to all his followers, *Whosoever he be of you that forsaketh not all that he hath, he cannot be my disciple* (b). When we are in a readiness to part with our dearest earthly comforts and enjoyments, rather than dishonour God; when our hearts and affections are so far weaned from all things here below, that we are ready to part with them all, yea, with our own lives also, so God may have glory by it; then we make his glory our chief end.

Second, I proceed to shew, wherein we are to make the glory of God our chief end. We are to do so, in every thing, in all our actions, affairs, and business: *Whatsoever ye do, do all to the glory of God.* Particularly, 1. In all our actions. 2. In all conditions of life.

1. We

(b) Luke xiv. 33.

1. We are to make the glory of God our chief end, in all our actions, natural, civil, and religious.

(1.) In all our natural actions, eating, drinking and sleeping. Works of nature become acts of grace, when we singly eye the glory of God in them. Your eating and drinking is idolatry, and your table the table of devils, if you design merely or chiefly the satisfying your appetite, or the pleasing and gratifying self. Hence, we read of some whose *god is their belly* (*c*).

(2.) In all our civil actions: In your trading, buying and selling, in your honest labour in your callings; all must be done with an eye to the glory of God. If you go about these things merely or chiefly to get wealth, then you make Mammon your God, your good and last end. So, in servants their doing service to their earthly masters; the glory of God must be the end of it. This is the apostle's direction to them; *And whatsoever ye do, do it heartily, as to the Lord, and not unto men* (*d*). We are to mingle in any worldly business, only in so far as we may be serviceable to the glory of God.

(3.) In all our religious and sacred actions, whether internal or external. 1. In the internal acts of religion; such as, desires after grace, pardon, peace, comfort, &c. You should desire grace for this end, that God may have the glory of his grace. You should seek grace, mercy, peace, and pardon, for the same end for which God gives them, to wit, *The praise of the glory of his grace* (*e*). So also, in your desires after salvation: You may lawfully desire your own salvation; yet you should not rest there, but your utmost end should be, that God may be glorified in your salvation. 2. In the external acts of religion. Duties of worship must be performed with an eye to the glory of God. Hence, he is said to *inhabit the praises of Israel* (*f*); that is, the temple, where God was praised and honoured by his worship.

2. We are to make the glory of God our chief end in all conditions of life; by a holy indifference as to any state or condition, so God may be glorified by it. Hence the apostle says, *According to my earnest expectation, and my hope, that—Christ shall be magnified in my body, whether it be by life or by death: for to me to live is Christ, and to die is gain* (*g*). Life and death was all one to him, so Christ might be magnified by either of them. Whatever your condition be, prosperous or adverse, high

---

(*c*) Phil. iii. 19.　(*d*) Col. iii. 23.　(*e*) Eph. i. 6.　(*f*) Psal. xxii. 3.　(*g*) Phil. i. 20, 21.

high or low, rich or poor, it should be all one to you, so it be for the glory of God.

But here it may be enquired, are we bound actually to intend the glory of God in every action? I answer, in these three particulars.

1. We should actually intend the glory of God in every action, so far as possibly we can. For, 1. We are obliged to this in point of gratitude: For God doth always remember us, and look after and care for us; *In him we live, and move, and have our being.* Why then should we forget God at any time? Not a good thought of thine, not a word spoken for God, is forgotten. 2. Such actual intentions are no great trouble to the soul. Thoughts are quick and sudden; therefore it would be no great labour or burden, to be often lifting up the eye of the soul unto God. And if we were, through grace, accustomed to this, it would become our very nature, pleasant and delightsome to us. 3. Such actual intentions of the glory of God would be of great profit and advantage. For, (1.) This would be as a golden crown upon the head of every action, to render it the more acceptable and pleasing to God. (2.) In this lies the vigour of the spiritual life, when our very natural actions are thus raised to a supernatural intention. (3.) This would be a mean to keep the heart the more upright, that we may not act like blind archers that shoot at random. But,

2. Because it is not possible to have such actual intentions in every particular action, therefore in the lesser actions of our lives a habitual intention is sufficient. A habitual intention is, when we have a habitual purpose of glorifying God in every thing. This may be, and many good actions may proceed from the force of such an intention, though there be no actual, distinct, and explicit thoughts about it. A traveller on his journey intends home, though he be not always thinking on home: So, the heart of a Christian may be set on glorifying God, though he hath not always actual and explicit thoughts about it. Yet,

3. It is sometimes necessary to renew our actual intentions of glorifying God, and to have actual, distinct, and explicit thoughts this way. As, 1. In duties of immediate worship, such as, prayer, praise, reading and hearing the word, &c. The Lord's prayer is a pattern of our daily worship, and there we are taught to pray, that the name of God may be glorified: *Hallowed be thy name.* 2. In all the more noble actions of our lives, when about any eminent piece of service for

God and our generation. I say, in such cases we should actually intend the glory of God. The reason is, because then Satan is most busy, and seeks to blast the duty and service, by turning the soul aside to carnal and corrupt ends.

Third, I come, in the next place, to shew, why we should make the glory of God our chief end in all our actions and business. I give these following reasons.

Reas. 1. Because God is the first cause: Therefore his glory ought to be our chief end. God is the alone independent Being. It is his royal prerogative, that he is *of himself*, and *to himself*; but *of him* and *to him* are all things. He is the *Alpha and Omega, the Beginning and the End* of all things. He is *the First, and the Last* (h); the first cause, and the last end. But dependence is the proper notion of a created being; dependence on God, as the first cause, and the last end. As God is *of himself*, and *to himself*; so the creature is *of another*, and *to another*. The creature hath its rise from the fountain of God's infinite power and goodness, and therefore must run toward that again, till it empty all its faculties and excellencies into that same ocean of goodness. It is as plain and evident, that man should act *for* God and his glory, and for no other ultimate end, as that he is *from* God, and from no other first cause. We have our life and breath, and all the comforts of life, from God; therefore it is highly reasonable that we should live to him, making his glory the chief scope and end of our lives.

Reas. 2. Because the glory of God is the chief end of our creation and being. It was this God chiefly intended and aimed at in making man. For seeing every rational agent proposeth some end to himself in what he doth; therefore God, being an infinitely wise agent, must have some end in the creation of man; and there being nothing higher or better than his own glory, he could propose no other end to himself. The end must be more worthy than the means, something higher and better than all created beings, which can be no other than his own glory. Hence it is said, *The Lord hath made all things for himself* (i). And if all things, then man especially, who is the master-piece of the visible creation. Hence it is that God hath given man a soul capable of glorifying him above other creatures. Now, seeing the glory of God was the chief end of our creation and being, therefore it should be the chief end and scope of our lives. Seeing his glory was the

---

(h) Rom. xi. 36. Rev. i. 8, 17.   (i) Prov. xvi. 4.

the chief end which he proposed to himself in making man, it must needs be the chief end which every man ought to propose to himself.

Reas. 3. Because the glory of God is the end of all his works. It is the end of creation; for *God made all things for himself.* It is the end of election and predestination: For he hath *predestinated us unto the adoption of children, to the praise of the glory of his grace* (*k*). It is the end of redemption: *Ye are bought with a price,* says the apostle, *therefore glorify God* (*l*). It is the end of regeneration: Hence the Lord says, *This people have I formed for myself; they shall shew forth my praise* (*m*). Believers are adopted into God's family, and made a royal priesthood for this end: They *are a chosen generation, a royal priesthood, that* they may *shew forth the praises of him who hath called* them (*n*). And it is the end of all providences, whether joyous or grievous; *I will deliver thee,* says the Lord, *and thou shalt glorify me* (*o*). And says our Saviour concerning Lazarus's sickness, *This sickness is not unto death, but for the glory of God, that the Son of God might be glorified thereby* (*p*). It is not ambition, nor sinful self-seeking, but the glorious excellency of the divine nature, that God doth all things for himself, for his own glory. Indeed, for men to seek their own glory, is not glory, but rather matter of shame: Self-seeking in creatures is monstrous and incongruous. But for God to seek his own glory, is his eminent excellency: It is indeed his glory, because *he is, and there is none else*. Now, if the glory of God be his chief end in all his works, why should it not be our chief end in all our works? Certainly, we cannot act more nobly, than by prosecuting according to our capacity, the chief end and purpose of God.

Reas. 4. Because his glory is most excellent. *O Lord our Lord,* says the Psalmist, *how excellent is thy name in all the earth! who hast set thy glory above the heavens.* And, *His name alone is excellent, his glory is above the earth and heaven* (*q*). The glory of God transcends the thoughts of men and angels. It is of more worth than heaven, of more value than the salvation of the souls of all men. It is dear to God. He hath bestowed many excellent gifts upon his people, but *his glory he will not give to another* (*r*). And if his glory be dear to him, why should it not be dear to us? Man being a rational creature,

---

(*k*) Prov. xvi. 4. Eph. i. 5, 6. (*l*) 1 Cor. vi. 20. (*m*) Isa. xliii. 21. (*n*) 1 Pet ii. 9. (*o*) Psal. l. 15. (*p*) John xi. 4. (*q*) Psal. viii. 1. and cxlviii. 13. (*r*) Isa. xlii. 8.

ture, should act for some end; and here is the most noble and worthy end, the glory of God.

SERMON LXII.

Fourthly, I COME in the last place to apply this doctrine.
Use 1. For reproof. To them that do not singly eye the glory of God in what they do, but have other ends they chiefly aim at. Self is the great idol in the world: And it is chiefly seen in this, that men aim at themselves, their own profit, or their own glory and praise, in what they do. All is to advance self. Men set self at the end of every action, and justle out God.

Particularly, men's aiming at themselves, is seen in their actions, both natural, civil, and religious.

1. You make self your end in your natural actions, when you eat and drink, merely to nourish the body, or to gratify the sensual appetite. In this case your eating and drinking is idolatry; it is a meat-offering and drink-offering to appetite. You make self your last end, and *your belly your god* (*a*); and your table is the table of devils.

2. You make self your end in your civil actions, when you trade merely that you may grow rich and wealthy, and get portions to your children. When you have no further aim, this is to make Mammon your God, and to set the world in God's room. Again, when you seek after places of profit and preferment, merely that you may make up yourselves, and raise your families. Grace will teach a man to do otherwise. It is very remarkable, that, though Joseph had a great trust in Egypt, yet he had made no provision for himself. It is the glory of a man in public place, rather to depart from his own right, than to seek to make up himself by preying upon his brethren.

3. Men's aiming at themselves is seen in their religious actions, both external and internal. And,

(1.) You make self your end in your external acts of religion, when you are moved to take up a profession by a regard to your own interest, or a regard to the countenance that is given to religion in the times wherein you live; or when you make any public appearances for God or religion, that you may get glory and praise from men; as Jehu did (*b*). Many times

(*a*) Phil. iii. 19. (*b*) 2 Kings x. 16.

times men have base ends in their seeming zeal for religion: As Demetrius and the craftsmen, who cried up the greatness of Diana, not out of any true zeal for her, but for their own gain. Again you make self your god, when you attend ordinances, or pray, or give alms, to be seen of men, that you may get a name, and advance your repute; and when in prayer, you desire health for your own ease, and success for your own plenty, and gifts for your own applause, and children for the increase of your family; and when family-duties are performed, to beget in others a good opinion of you, and to support your reputation among your godly neighbours.

(2.) You make self your end in the internal acts of religion, when in your desires after heaven you aim only at your own happiness: When you make this the ultimate end of your desires, this is to respect self more than God. We should aim at the glory of God in our salvation; so that his glory should be our chief and ultimate end. But when you aim only at your own happiness, this is a motion of mere nature. Again, when you desire pardon of sin, only for your security from eternal damnation; and sanctification, only to fit you for everlasting blessedness; and peace of conscience, only that you may live the more comfortably: Then you make self your end. I confess, seeing God urgeth us to seek after these blessings, by motives from the great advantages that will redound by them unto ourselves; therefore we may lawfully desire them with respect to ourselves: Yet this respect must be contained in its due bounds, in a due subordination to the glory of God, not above it, nor in an equal balance with it. But when in your desires after such spiritual blessings, your thoughts of God's glory and honour are over-topt by aims at your own advantage; this is to make self your end.

I shall, in prosecuting this purpose a little further, 1. Assign some evidences of men's aiming at themselves, their own profit, or their own glory and praise in what they do. 2. Hold forth the great evil thereof.

First, Men's aiming at themselves, or making self their end, appears in these things.

1. In being much troubled for what disgraceth themselves, but nothing troubled for what dishonours God. When you cannot put up what you apprehend to be an affront offered to yourselves, but do easily pass what is evidently dishonourable to God without any just resentment; this plainly shews that that your own honour is more dear to you than the glory and honour of God.

2. In envy at others. Many would gladly make a monoply of religion, and shine alone; therefore they envy the gifts and graces of others, and endeavour to blast their repute. They are pleased when God is glorified by themselves, but grieved when it is done by others. This is a sign that their hearts are more set upon their own repute, than upon the glory of God. Thus the Pharisees envied Christ: *Behold,* say they, *the world is gone after him* (c). Men are envious, because they think the gifts and graces of others derogate from their esteem.

3. In mens' being careless of the public interests, so it go well with themselves. If their own private interests prosper, they care not what become of the public. On the contrary, the children of God are ready to sacrifice their own private interests for the public good. Jonah was content to be cast into the sea, that it might be calmed for the safety of those that were in the ship with him (d). And we have an eminent instance in Moses. God offers him a composition, as it were: " *Let me alone,* Moses, do not plead with me in behalf of this " people, *and I will make of thee a great nation,* the holy feed " shall be continued in thy line instead of Abraham's line (e):" Yet Moses would not let him alone, but still wrestled with him in the behalf of that people; that is, No matter what become of me, if thou wilt pity and spare thy people.

4. In mens' seeking their own private benefit with the public loss. Many seek to make merchandise of the calamity of the times. They trouble the waters that they may fish in them, and set on foot innovations that they may promote themselves. Many care not how much they embroil a nation, so they themselves may be set up in place and power; and regard not what miseries people are brought under, so they may make up themselves. But good Nehemiah was of a far other temper; because of the calamity and distress of the people, he would not take what the king of Persia had allowed for supporting the greatness of his place (f).

5. In men's taking up a profession of religion for their own temporal good and conveniency. As many followed Christ for the loaves (g); so many own religion for worldly advantage: Thus the Shechemites yielded to circumcision, in hopes that all the cattle of the children of Israel would be theirs (h). This is usual in times of public changes. It was an old complaint,

(c) John xii. 19. (d) Jonah i. 12. (e) Exod. xxxi. 10, 11. (f) Neh. v. 14. (g) John vi. 26. (h) Gen xxxiv. 23.

plaint, *That it was not piety but covetousness that prompted many to overturn idolatry* †.

6. In mens' being able to endure trials and persecutions for religion. When troubles arise, many are ready to quit their profession. Their lamp will not burn, unless it be fed with the oil of praise or profit. Oh, how many are loth to be losers by religion? Now, when men are so tender and delicate that they cannot endure to suffer for religion, it is a sign they had other aims in it than the glory of God.

7. In mens' carrying on their carnal designs under the pretence and vail of religion, as these corrupt teachers in Corinth, who would take no maintenance, that they might gain credit and applause (*i*). Herod pretended he would worship Christ, when really he intended to destroy him. Jezebel ordered a fast to be proclaimed, that she might destroy Naboth. Simeon and Levi urged circumcision on the Sechemites, that they might have an opportunity for revenge. Absalom pretended to go and pay a vow at Hebron, that he might carry on his unnatural rebellion against his father. Carnal ends, yea, wicked ends, are many times carried on under religious pretences.

Second, I come next to hold forth to you the great evil of making self your end, or aiming at your own profit, or your own glory and praise, in what you do. To make self your end is a woful evil. For,

1. It is an invading of God's prerogative. It is his prerogative to be his own end, and to act for his own glory: Therefore to make self your end, is to usurp the rights of the Deity, and to set yourselves in the throne of God. When you mind chiefly your own glory and praise, you rob him of his honour, and take the crown off his head.

2. It is base and unworthy. Such as aim at themselves are men of low and base spirits. Self is an unworthy mark to aim at: And all actions savour of their end. If the end be base and unworthy, the action is so too.

3. It is to act against self and your own interest. No man doth less enjoy himself, and more lose himself, than he that doth most aim at and seek himself; for God useth to disappoint mens' carnal and selfish aims.

4. It tends to the dishonour of God and disgrace of religion. We read of some who are *enemies to the Cross of Christ, whose god is their belly, who mind earthly things* (*k*). There are no greater enemies to Christ than such as profess religion for their self-interest.

† *Non pretate everterunt idola, sed avaritia.*
(*i*) 2 Cor. xi. 12.   (*k*) Phil. iii. 18, 19.

interest. It is an honour to God, when men serve him out of pure love to him, and not for hire and wages: But when you make a market of religion, and under the name and profession of Christianity, mind nothing but your own profit and gain; this is dishonourable to God, and creates great prejudices against religion. As Satan said of Job: *Doth Job fear God for nought* (*l*)? So are carnal men ready to say of professors, do they profess religion and follow the duties thereof for nought? They hunt after places of profit and preferment; and God may have abundance of servants at this rate.

5. When your end in religion is your own glory and praise, then *you have your reward* (*m*), as our blessed Lord saith of the Pharisees. When your utmost aim in taking up a profession and performing duties is, that you may have praise and glory of men, you do thereby give God a solemn discharge, and have no other reward to look for.

6. It exposeth to *greater damnation* (*n*). It is a great sin to take up a profession, and make a fair shew and appearance of being godly, when in the meanwhile you are quite naught and rotten at the heart: But this being done for a corrupt end, for a pretence and cloke only, your sin is the greater, and so will your judgment be.

Use 2. For exhortation. Make the glory of God your chief and ultimate end in all you do. Whatever you are about, in all your actions, natural, civil, and religious, let it be your chief aim to have God glorified. Have this always in your eye. Let your hearts be chiefly set upon this, that God may have glory.

For exciting and engaging you to this, consider,

1. True Christian sincerity lies chiefly in this. The great difference between hypocrites and sincere Christians, lies in their different ends and aims. They are both employed in religious duties; but the one aims at his own glory and profit, the other at the glory of God. When you prostitute your religious duties to base ends, all your acts are acts of sin and folly, how splendid soever they are in outward appearance.

2. A right end ennobles a man. Low spirits have low designs, and base ends are usually pursued by base means. But when your chief end is to glorify God, this will ennoble your soul, and put you upon noble employment. To this purpose our Lord says, *The light of the body is the eye: If therefore thine*

eye

(*l*) Job i. 19.   (*m*) Matth. vi. 2, 5.   (*n*) Matth. xxiii. 14.

eye be single, thy whole body shall be full of light. But if thine eye be evil, thy whole body shall be full of darkness (o). What poor lives do they live, far below the dignity of men, whose chief end is to gratify the sensual appetite? Beasts eat and drink, and sleep as they do. And when men aim at earthly things as their chief end, then they themselves become earthly; earthly in their frame, thoughts, desires, designs, projects, employments, &c. But when God is your chief end, all will be heavenly and God-like.

3. This will make you faithful, watchful, and diligent in the duties incumbent on you, both in your general, and in your particular callings. Whence is it that many are so unfaithful and negligent in their respective duties, and fill up their lives with many things inconsistent with their great end? It is because they do not set the right end before them. But when the glory of God is your chief end, this will cut off many impertinencies and extravagancies in your practice: For you will reason with yourselves thus; What respect hath this to my great end? Is this the way to glorify God?

4. To make the glory of God your chief end will sweeten and facilitate your work amidst all these difficulties and hardships wherewith your duty to God may be attended. It is hard to pinch the flesh, to deny its lustings and cravings, to row against the wind and tide of corrupt nature, and to expose yourselves to many troubles and inconveniences, in the way of duty: But this will make all easy, when you consider that this is the way to glorify to God.

But what shall we do that we may have the glory of God for our chief end in all that we do? Take these directions.

1. Get a new nature. An old unrenewed nature can never raise up itself to a supernatural intention. Carnal men have always carnal and corrupt ends. They cannot aim at the glory of God: For they hate God, and are enemies to him; there is an utter averseness to God rooted in their natures; yea, an unrenewed nature is *enmity against God* (p). Therefore, get a new nature. Get a deep humbling sense of the depravation and corruption of your natures: Lament and mourn over the same: Cry to God for the new heart and new spirit: And wait for his renewing and regenerating grace in the use of the means and ordinances he hath appointed.

2. Get a saving interest in Christ. You cannot aim at the glory of God, till you are at peace with him: And you can-

(o) Matth. vi 22, 23.   (p) Rom. viii. 7.

not have peace with God, but through Chrift; he is the only peace-maker between God and finners. Again, you cannot bring glory to God in an active way, but by virtue of grace and ftrength communicated to you through this bleffed Mediator. Therefore, ftudy your abfolute need of Chrift, and his tranfcendent worth, and the gracious terms on which he is offered; and be earneft with God for grace to make you able and willing to clofe with Chrift, by confenting heartily to thefe terms.

3. Get much love to God. Men's aims are as their affections are. Love to God is the great principle that draws us off from felf to God. Self-love makes you mind and pleafe yourfelves: But love to God would bend and incline you heart to him. When you love God, then his glory will be dear to you, above any enjoyment or intereft of your own.

4. Study much felf denial and mortification to the world. The more dead you are to felf and the world, you will be the more alive unto God. Therefore, labour to get your heart weaned from all things here below; and ftudy to be denied to your eafe and liberty, your credit and reputation, your wealth and outward eftate, &c. You muft down with felf and the world in your hearts, if you would fet up God.

5. Think often on the end of your creation and being. In this we have our bleffed Saviour for a pattern: *To this end was I born,* fays he, *and for this caufe came I into the world* (q). Alas, many men live like beafts: They eat, and drink, and fleep, but never mind for what end they were born But it would be of great advantage to you to be often thinking thus with yourfelves, " Why hath God fent me into the world, and " given me a reafonable foul? Do I live up to the end of my " creation?"

(q) John xviii. 37.

DISCOURSE

DISCOURSE XVI.

Of making it our great Employment and Business to Glorify God.

SERMON LXIII.

1 Cor. vi. 19, 20.——*And ye are not your own: For ye are bought with a price: Therefore glorify God in your body, and in your spirit, which are God's.*

IN this and the preceding verses, the apostle is arguing against that filthy sin of fornication, that some of the Corinthians had fallen into: And here he argues against it from the redemption of believers by Christ. That the apostle is here speaking to and dealing with sincere believers in Christ, is plain, not only from these words, but from the preceding verses. He speaks to such as were *saints*, verse 2d. To such as were *sanctified and justified*, verse 11th. To such as were savingly *united to Christ*, verses 15th, 17th, and had *the Spirit of Christ dwelling in them*, verse 19th.

In the words read, we have these three things,

1. A denial of any right of propriety in themselves. *Ye are not your own.* That is, not at your own disposal; not so your own as to have it in your power to use and dispose of yourselves at your own pleasure.

2. An assertion of God's propriety in them upon the account of their redemption by Christ: *Ye are bought with a price.* There is no buying, properly, without a price; but the word *price* is added for the greater emphasis, to shew that it was a great price, and a full price that Christ paid. He did not compound our debt with the Father: He paid the uttermost farthing. The price was that of his own *precious blood* (a). And with this price Christ bought both the bodies and spirits of believers, their whole man; as is implied in what follows: *Therefore glofy God in your body, and in your spirit.* And from this the apostle infers God's propriety in them *who are his*. Both the bodies and spirits of believers are his, not only by a right of creation and preservation, but also by right of purchase, as here, and by right of covenant-resignation.

3. The

(a) 1 Pet. i. 18.

3. The duty of believers, inferred from all this: *Therefore glorify God in your body, and in your spirit.* Seeing both are his, both ought to be used and employed for his glory and honour. From these words I shall speak to this doctrine.

> *Observ.* The consideration of this, that our bodies and spirits are not our own but God's, should engage us to make it our great employment and business to glorify him in both.

Here I shall shew,

1. *What it is to glorify God in our bodies and spirits.*
2. *What force there is in this argument to engage us to glorify God in our bodies and spirits, that both are his, and that we are not our own.*
3. *I shall apply the doctrine.*

First, What is it to glorify God in our bodies and spirits? We glorify God, not by adding any glory to him; for being infinitely glorious, he is not capable of any additional glory: nothing can be added to his essential glory. Nothing we do can be of any advantage to him. So Elihu tells us, *If thou be righteous, what givest thou him? Or what receiveth he of thine hand?——Thy righteousness may profit the son of man* (b). But we glorify God by declaring and manifesting his glory. We may here observe a very great difference between God's glorifying us, and our glorifying him. His glorifying us is creative; he makes us glorious: But our glorifying him is only declarative, by declaring him to be what he is, and what he ever will be, without any shadow of turning. We are to be witnesses of his glory, and to give testimony to the appearances and out-breakings thereof. The inanimate creatures glorify him passively or objectively; we are to do it actively: They do it necessarily; but we are to do it voluntarily and out of choice. Our proper work is to acknowledge in our hearts inwardly, and to express in our words and actions outwardly, what a glorious Majesty he is: So that we are to glorify him *inwardly*, and *outwardly; in our spirits,* and *in our bodies.*

1. Inwardly in our hearts and spirits. And that, 1. By owning and acknowledging his infinite perfection, and his transcendent glory and excellency; that there is none like him, and that he is the only true God. So doth the prophet: *There is none like unto thee, O Lord; thou art great, and thy name is great*

(b) Job xxxv. 7, 8.

in might: And the psalmist, *Among the gods there is none like unto thee, O Lord.* And, *Thou art God alone* (c). 2. By an high and honourable esteem of him; prizing him highly, and counting all things but loss and dung in comparison of him: As the psalmist, *Whom have I in heaven but thee? and there is none upon the earth that I desire besides thee* (d). 3. By an holy admiration of his matchless excellency and glory. To this purpose are these and the like expressions: *O Lord our Lord, how excellent is thy name in all the earth! Who is like unto thee, O Lord, among the gods! who is like thee!* And again, *Who is a God like unto thee* (e)! 4. By such high and reverend thoughts of him as become his greatness and majesty; meditating on him, till our souls receive the impression and stamp of all the letters of his glorious name. 5. By believing on him through Christ the Mediator, and as he hath manifested himself in Christ. So it is said, *He that hath received his testimony, hath set to his seal, that God is true* (f). This is a compendious way of glorifying God, when upon the credit we give to his testimony concerning Christ, we receive and close with Christ by faith in all his mediatory offices, and make choice of God in him for our God and portion. 6. By an entire resignation of ourselves soul and body to him, to be wholly, fully and for ever his. As it is said of the believing Macedonians, that they *gave themselves to the Lord* (g). We glorify God, when we give ourselves to him as the most worthy Being, and dedicate and devote ourselves to him and his service as the best of Masters. 7 By a sincere love to him, and ardent desires after him; giving him the chief room in our hearts: When our love to him and desires after him are such as do plainly declare that there is none like him in our esteem (h). 8. By trusting him upon his bare word, even contrary to human appearances and probabilities. Hereby we give him the glory of his faithfulness. Hence it is said of Abraham, *He was strong in faith, giving glory to God* (i). 9. By a holy fear of his blessed name, on the account of his greatness, power, holiness, justice, and goodness. Hence we are bidden *fear this glorious and fearful name, THE LORD THY GOD;* and *fear God, and give glory to him* (k) 10. By a heart-burning zeal for him and his interests. *My zeal hath consumed me,* says the psalmist; *because mine enemies have forgotten thy words* (l). Never was

(c) Jer. x. 6 Psal. lxxxvi. 8, 10. (d) Psal. lxxiii. 25. (e) Psal. viii. 1. Exod. xv. 11. Mic. vii. 18. (f) John iii. 33. (g) 2 Cor. viii. 5. (h) Psal. lxxiii. 25. (i) Rom. iv. 20. (k) Deut. xxviii. 58. Rev. xiv. 7. (l) Psal. cxix. 139.

was there a more zealous parcel of men than the primitive Chriſtians. But, alas, in our days primitive zeal is almoſt gone. Oh what deteſtable neutrality and indifferency in the matters of God is there this day among profeſſors of religion! O that primitive zeal were again revived; ſuch a zeal as might make us tender of God's honour, and grieved for his diſhonour. We have the pſalmiſt for a pattern in this: *The zeal of thine houſe hath eaten me up,* ſays he; *and the reproaches of them that reproached thee are fallen upon me* (m).

2. We are to glorify God outwardly in our bodies, and that both in word and converſation: Yet not without the heart; for even in theſe things whereby we are to glorify God outwardly, the heart muſt go along, elſe all is done in hypocriſy.

Firſt, We are to glorify God in word. And that, 1. By aſcribing glory to him; of which I ſpoke formerly. 2. By ſpeaking to his commendation. We ſhould be trumpeters of his praiſe, and as heralds to proclaim his glory and riches, his beauty and goodneſs: *Sing forth the honour of his name,* and *make his praiſe glorious* (n). 3. By declaring and publiſhing the glorious and wonderful works of God to the glory of his name. As the pſalmiſt exhorts: *Declare his glory among the heathens; his wonders among all people* (o). Particularly, by declaring in due circumſtances the great things he hath done for us. *Come and hear,* ſays the pſalmiſt, *all ye that fear God, and I will declare what he hath done for my ſoul* (p). Of this there are many inſtances, eſpecially in the book of Pſalms. 4. By bleſſing and praiſing his glorious name, as the people of God did: *Bleſſed be thy glorious name, who is exalted above all bleſſing and praiſe* (q). Hence is that exhortation, *Let them praiſe the name of the Lord: For his name alone is excellent; his glory is above the earth and heaven. Whoſo offereth praiſe, glorifieth him* (r). The nine lepers that went away without giving thanks, are ſaid *not to return to give glory to God.* As all the beaſts have their own peculiar ſounds and voices, ſo this is the natural ſound of a man. It is as proper to us to praiſe God, as to a bird to chant. 5. By pleading for his name, his cauſe and intereſts. When we are called to ſpeak for God, our ſilence may coſt us dear. Let us ponder Mordecai's meſſage to queen Eſther: *If thou altogether holdeſt thy peace at this time, thou and thy father's houſe ſhall be deſtroyed* (s).

It

(m) Pſal. lxix. 9.   (n) Pſal. lxvi. 2.   (o) Pſal. xcvi. 3.
(p) Pſal. lxvi. 16.   (q) Neh. ix. 5.   (r) Pſal. cxlviii. 13. and l. 23.   (s) Eſth. iv. 14.

It is dangerous to be tongue-tacked when we are called to speak for God. 6. By a humble confession of sin under afflicting providences, to the glory of God's justice; thus justifying God, and taking shame to ourselves. To this Joshua exhorts Achan: *Give glory to the Lord of Israel, and make confession unto him* (*t*).

Second, We are to glorify God in our conversation,

(1.) By departing from all iniquity; renouncing, abandoning, and forsaking whatever is dishonourable to his name, and strikes against his glory. God is much dishonoured by the vicious lives of men, especially of such as profess his name. Hence the Lord saith of the Jews that were carried captive to Babylon, and there lived profanely and viciously: *They profaned my holy name, when they said to them, These are the people of the Lord, and are gone forth out of his land* (*u*). And, says the apostle, of the Jews who professed to be the people of God, *Thou that makest thy boast of the law, through breaking the law dishonourest thou God? For the name of God is blasphemed among the Gentiles through you* (*x*). Alas! many professors of religion glorify God in profession, but pollute him in conversation. Therefore it is necessary for the glory of God, that you who are called by his name, seperate yourselves from the abominations of the time, and keep yourselves unspotted of the world.

(2.) By positive holiness of conversation. Hence God saith, *He that offereth praise glorifieth me; and to him that ordereth his conversation aright, will I shew the salvation of God* (*y*). You glorify God, when you are fruitful in holiness and obedience. *Herein is my Father glorified,* says our Lord, *that ye bear much fruit* (*a*). And the apostle prays, that the Philippians might *be filled with the fruits of righteousness, which are by Jesus Christ unto the praise and glory of God* (*b*). You ought to live and walk so as you may in a sort express the glorious perfections of God in your conversation, and that the image of God may be seen stamped on your very lives. *Ye are an holy nation,* says the apostle, *a peculiar people, that ye should shew forth the praises* (or, virtues) *of him who hath called you out of darkness into his marvellous light* (*c*). We should be as so many clear glasses wherein the glory of God doth evidently shine forth. But, alas, the best of us are but dim glasses; it is but little of God's glory that we shew forth to the world. Your lives should be a con-

stant

(*t*) Josh. vii. 19. (*u*) Ezek. xxxvi. 20. (*x*) Rom. ii. 23, 24.
(*y*) Psal. l. 23. (*a*) John xv. 8. (*b*) Phil. i. 11. (*c*) 1 Pet. ii. 9.

stant hymn to the glory and praise of God, by proclaiming to the world a deep sense of the omniscience, infinite justice, and holiness of that God whom you profess to serve. And you should walk so sweetly, both in your general and in your particular callings, as others may be induced to glorify God: *Let your light so shine before men, that they may see your good works, and glorify your Father, who is in heaven* (d).

(3.) By diligence in the duties of his worship. So it is said, *Fear God, and give glory to him.* And, *Give unto the Lord, the glory due unto his name: Worship the Lord in the beauty of holiness* (e). We glorify God by acts of worship, and a diligent attendance on his ordinances. He hath instituted duties and ordinances for his glory and honour. The worship of God is an homage which we owe to him on the account of his sovereignty. On this ground the psalmist calls for it: *Serve the Lord with gladness; come before his presence with singing. Know ye that the Lord he is God* (f). Thereby we own our allegiance to him as our Sovereign, and our absolute dependence on him for all things; and this glorifies him.

(4.) By an open profession and confession of his name. Our blessed Lord presseth this: *Whosoever shall confess me before men, him will I confess also before my Father who is in heaven* (g). You glorify God, when you are not ashamed of him, nor of his way, but are ready to declare on all proper occasions whose servants you are, and whom you own as your Lord and Master. The glory of God is greatly concerned in this. God is much dishonoured by professors of religion, when they dissemble their religion and profession, and their respect to his work and cause, for fear of men, or out of love to this present world.

(5.) By being active in your place and station for his kingdom and interests; standing up and contending for his cause and gospel, and advancing and promoting his interests, to the glory and honour of his name. You should be often devising how you may lay out yourselves in your several stations for Christ, by advancing his interests, and enlarging his kingdom. As this will be honourable to Christ, so it will be a great honour to yourselves to be thus employed. "To do for Christ," said Ignatius, "is more honourable than to be monarch of all "the world."

(6.) By suffering for him and for his cause and gospel, when
called

(d) Matth. v. 16. (e) Rev. xiv. 7. Psal. xxix. 2. (f) Psal. c. 2, 3. (g) Matth. x. 32.

called to it. God is glorified by patient sufferings. Hence God's remnant are exhorted to *glorify the Lord in the fires* (*f*). And the apostle doth hereby encourage us to suffering for Christ: *If ye be reproached for the name of Christ, happy are ye—On their part he is evil spoken of, but on your part he is glorified* (*g*). He is glorified when such as serve him are ready to suffer for him even unto death. Therefore you should not only bear testimony to his truths, but be ready to seal your testimony with your blood. It brings much glory to him, when in the face of all dangers, and under the greatest trials and discouragements, you are neither afraid nor ashamed to cleave to him and his cause and gospel. You do thereby manifest the power of his grace in you. Therefore, dear Christians, let not this be grievous to you : Let *glory to God* be written, though it should be written with your blood.

(7.) By walking chearfully and comfortably in the good ways of the Lord. God is dishonoured when such as serve him are dejected in spirit, and give way to despondency and discouragement. The Persian kings would not suffer such to abide in their presence; they thought it a disparagement to them. It is much for the glory of God that you who are his children walk chearfully. This brings up a good report on him, and on his way. Hereby you give him the glory of his goodness, and proclaim to the world what a good God and Master you serve.

(8.) By holy Christian contentment in all conditions: And particularly by a chearful and humble submission to the will of God under afflicting providences, without murmuring or complaining. Hereby you give him the glory of his wisdom, that he knows what is good for you, and how to carve out your lot for you, better than you do yourselves.

SERMON LXIV.

Second, I Proceed, in the next place, to shew what force there is in this argument, to engage us to glorify God in our bodies and spirits, that both are his, and that we are not our own. Justice requires that every man should be served of his own, and that what a man hath an interest and propriety in, should be at his command and disposal. So here, seeing both our bodies and spirits are God's, it is just that both be employed in his service, and for his honour and glory.

Vol. II. N°. 5.   D   Par-

(*h*) Isa. xxiv 15. (*i*) 1 Pet. iv. 14.

Particularly we are God's by creation, by preservation, by redemption, and by covenant-resignation; and being his, by a manifold right, we should not live to ourselves, but to him whose we are.

1. We are God's by creation. *It is he that hath made us, and not we ourselves* (a). He not only made the first man and woman, but all other men and women in the world. Our bodies were formed by him in the womb. *Thy hands,* says the Psalmist, *have made me, and fashioned me.* And, *My substance was not hid from thee, when I was made in secret, and curiously wrought in the lowest parts of the earth* (b). That is, in my mother's womb, a place as secret and remote from human eyes as the lowest parts of the earth. And our souls were created by him: For he is *the Father of Spirits,* and he *formeth the spirit of man within him* (c). Now, seeing we are made by him, he hath an absolute propriety in us. We are wholly and only of him and from him, and from none else: Therefore we should be wholly and only for him, and for none else. Being his creatures, we should be entirely devoted to his interest, and forthcoming for his glory; especially considering these two things.

(1.) That the glory of God is the end of our creation. For *of him, and through him, and to him are all things;* and he *made all things for himself* (d): But man in a special and peculiar manner. Man was made for God, and other creatures for man. It is true, the other creatures were made ultimately for God, but nextly for man. Hence the psalmist falls a wondering, *What is man that thou art mindful of him? Thou madest him to have dominion over the works of thy hands; thou hast put all things under his feet* (e). So that man is placed in the middle between God and the other creatures. Therefore, it is from man that all the excellency and perfection of the other creatures should reflect toward God again. Seeing man was made for the glory of God, therefore it should be his business to advance and promote his glory. Yea, it is the beauty and perfection of a man, and the greatest accession that can be to his being, to glorify God in that being. We are not else answerable to the great end of our creation.

(2.) As the glorifying God is the end of our creation, so in our creation God put us in some meet capacity for this. He hath

(a) Psal. c. 3. (b) Psal. cxix. 73. and cxxxix. 15. (c) Heb. xii. 9. Zech. xii. 1. (d) Rom. xi. 36. Prov. xvi. 4. (e) Psal. viii. 4, 6.

hath given us noble souls, and excellent faculties, that are specially suited hereunto. Other creatures are the books wherein the glorious perfections of God are written; but man only is made capable of reading them: They are a well tuned instrument; but man is to make the music. Therefore Epictetus said well, † "If I were a lark, I would sing as a lark; but now seeing I am a man, what should I do but praise and glorify God without ceasing."

2. We are God's by preservation. He hath *made the earth, and all things that are therein, and preserveth them all.* He *preserveth man and beast* (*f*). We are continued and preserved in being by the constant influence of his providence: *In him we live, and move, and have our being* (*g*). We cannot hold either soul or body one moment longer than God pleaseth. We depend on him wholly for the being and preservation of both; so that we cannot lay claim to either of them for one moment, but are wholly his. We cannot preserve one member or faculty by our own power: So that we are not our own to dispose of. Our absolute and continual dependence on God, gives him a full right to both body and spirit; so that both are to be employed according to his will, and for his glory.

3. We are God's by redemption. This is the argument specially pleaded in my text: *And ye are not your own; for ye are bought with a price: Therefore glorify God, &c.* Believers in Christ are redeemed by him from sin and wrath by the price of his own *precious blood* (*h*). Under the law, when a man was bought with another's money, his time, strength, and all he had, belonged to his master; so that his master might freely employ him in any piece of lawful service. Therefore he was called *his money* (*i*). His master might freely use him as his own money. But you who are sincere believers in Christ are bought at a far higher rate, even with his own precious blood; and you are redeemed from the worst slavery, even that of sin and Satan: So that you are not your own, but his. Therefore, unless you mean to defraud God of his right, you should mind this more than you do, to live, not to yourselves, but to him that bought you. Especially considering that you were redeemed for this very end, that you might serve God, and live to his glory. Hence it is that believers are said to be

redeemed

---

† *Si Luscinia essem, canerem ut Luscinia; cum autem homo sim, quid agam? laudabo Deum, nec unquam cessabo.*

(*f*) Neh. ix. 6. Psal. xxxvi. 6.   (*g*) Acts xvii. 28.   (*h*) 1 Pet. i. 18.   (*i*) Exod. xxi. 21.

redeemed TO *God* (*k*): That is, not only to his favour and fellowship, but to his service and obedience. And we read, that *Christ died for all, that they who live, might not henceforth live unto themselves, but unto him that died for them, and rose again:* And that he *died that he might be Lord both of the dead and living* (*l*). True it is, that believers only have an interest in Christ's redemption; yet for as much as you all profess to be of that number, that you are Christ's, and that he died for you, and redeemed you; therefore I may plead this argument with you all. You profess that you are bought with a price; and if you are really so, then you are not your own but his; so that your profession obligeth you to live as his, by glorifying him both in body and spirit.

4. You are God's by covenant-resignation, viz. As many of you as have covenanted with him through Christ. *I entered into a covenant with thee, saith the Lord God, and thou becamest mine.* And, says the prophet, *One shall say, I am the Lord's; and another shall call himself by the name of Jacob; and another shall subscribe with his hand unto the Lord, and sirname himself by the name of Israel* (*m*). When you covenanted with God, you solemnly resigned yourselves to him and his service; you consecrated both soul and body to him to be wholly and forever his: So that you are no more your own, but his, by your own voluntary consent and covenant-resignation. You *gave yourselves to the Lord* (*n*), as it is said of the believing Macedonians. You gave your hearty consent to God's right to you and propriety in you: And therefore are obliged to employ yourselves for his glory. If you use either soul or body, or any faculty or member, according to your own pleasure, after all that you have done, this is perjury, and breach of covenant, which exposeth to dreadful wrath. When Ananias and Sapphira kept back a part of what they dedicated to God, they were struck dead upon the place: How much sorer vengeance will you deserve, if you alienate yourselves from him, after such a solemn dedication of yourselves to him and his service.

Third, I go on to the application of this doctrine.

Use 1. For lamentation. Alas, that God is so little glorified by us. And,

1. Many, instead of glorifying God, live to his dishonour. Herein chiefly lies the great evil of sin that it is dishonourable to God, and strikes against his glory. It is a practical denial and

con-

(*k*) Rev. v 9.   (*l*) 2 Cor. v. 15. Rom. xiv. 9.   (*m*) Ezek. xvi. 8. Isa. xliv. 5.   (*n*) 2 Cor. viii. 5.

contempt of God, an affronting and abusing of him and all his glorious attributes. It is a contempt of his sovereignty, as if his laws were not to be regarded; and a disgrace to his holiness, when we cast our filth before his face. The truth is, it cannot be conceived what a dishonour sin is to God. Yet, alas, how many live in their sins? How much is God dishonoured in the generation wherein we live? How should it cut us to the heart, when we see his glory trampled upon by wicked and profane men? How much is he dishonoured by the vicious lives of many that profess his name, whereby they give occasion to others to blaspheme that worthy name by which they are called? How many live pagan lives, under a Christian name and profession, and are called Christians to the dishonour of God and Christ?

2. There are others, who, though they do not openly dishonour God, or act against his glory, yet are not active in advancing and promoting his glory. What carelessness is there of improving advantages and opportunities of glorifying God? How little zeal is there for his glory? What lukewarmness and indifferency in any thing wherein the glory of God is concerned? Alas, though we have the light of former times, yet we want the heat and life. How many are careless of the interests of Christ, so their own interests flourish and prosper? Many profess to be well affected to the interests of religion, but are slack and remiss in their endeavours to promote the same.

But whence is it that men are not active in glorifying God? I assign these causes.

(1.) Laziness and love of carnal ease. Hence it is that men are loth to be troubled with the faithful performance of their duty. But you can be active and diligent in things of a worldly concern; and should you not much more be hard at work for God? Therefore, shake off this laziness and ease of the flesh. God is at work for you, and sets all the creatures at work for you; and should not you be much more at work for him?

(2.) A sinful modesty. Some have a modest sense of their own meanness and weakness, and want of gifts and parts, and are ready to cry out, What can I do? And so they lie by, and do not what they might do and ought to do. But this should not be. When God calls out any of you to be employed for his glory, you should not, like Saul, hide yourselves among the stuff; nor should you draw back, like Moses, when an opportunity is put in your hand of glorifying God, and doing good in your generation. God can help the stammering tongue, and bless mean gifts, when you sincerely obey his call.

(3.) Shame: Many are ashamed to speak or act for the glory of God; they cannot endure scoffs, and taunts, and scorns. But as it is true fortitude to despise shame in the cause of God; so it is an argument of a base spirit, when you cannot endure a disgraceful word for him. Christians should not be ashamed to speak or act for God, before any sort of men in the world. *I will speak of thy testimonies before kings*, says the psalmist, *and will not be ashamed* (*o*).

(4.) Fear: Some are afraid to put forth themselves for the glory of God in their place and station, lest they lose the favour of men, and incur their hatred and displeasure. But what is this but to prefer the favour of men to the favour of the great God? Some are brow-beaten with frowns, and cannot venture a little worldly loss, and therefore are afraid to own God and his despised cause and interests. But is this not a Christian frame. It is contrary to what the apostle requires: *Strive together for the faith of the gospel; in nothing terrified by your adversaries* (*p*).

3. Many formal professors make a fair shew of glorifying God, but do it not sincerely. They do that which for the matter tends to his glory, they speak and act for his cause and interests, but without any intention of glorifying him: Their end is, to get a name to themselves, or to advance themselves, and promote their own interests. Jehu made a shew of *zeal for the Lord* (*q*); but it was indeed a zeal for himself and his own interests. Some are publicly active in promoting the interests of religion, but are really hunting after their own interests; therefore they are no longer active that way, than they can carry their own interests along with it.

4. Alas, even the children of God are not so active and forward in glorifying God as they ought to be. What cause have even the best among us to lament, that we have come so far short of what we ought to have done, and might have done, for advancing the glory of his blessed name? Alas, that God hath so little glory by us. Some of you who are truly gracious would have God glorified, but you do not lay out yourselves this way as it becomes you.

Use 2. For exhortation. Seeing your bodies and spirits are not your own, but God's, therefore make it your great employment and business to glorify him, both in body and spirit. Dear friends, I am come to proclaim and assert God's right to you and

(*o*) Psal. cxix. 46.   (*p*) Phil. i. 27, 28.   (*q*) 2 Kings x. 16.

and all that is yours. Indeed, he hath best right to you. He hath an absolute right to you, and propriety in you; so that you are not your own, but wholly his. And I do in his name lay claim to you all, to your souls, and to your bodies; to all your faculties, abilities, and interests; all are his. Will you acknowledge his title? Are you his, or are you not? Dare any of you deny his right to you? If not, as I hope there are none, then I have one thing to demand of you, to wit, that you would give God his own: Render to God the things that are God's: Let your bodies and spirits, all your powers and faculties, all your abilities, be employed in promoting the glory and honour of his name. It is not enough that you do not act against his glory, and that your gifts and abilities are not employed as weapons of unrighteousness; but you must act positively for his glory. In the parable (r), the man that hid his talent, is condemned as a wicked servant, though he did not misemploy it, or waste it in riotous living. It is fault enough to hide your talent, though you do not abuse it. You must be active for the glory of God. And,

1. Improve all the advantages you have for glorifying God; such as time, health and strength, wealth and riches, power and authority over others; all your gifts, parts, graces; all that God hath given you, must be employed in his service, and for his glory and honour. Each of these are a price put in your hand; and, in a scriptural sense, God must be a gainer by every one of them. Therefore, look within you, without you, and round about you, and consider how much you are entrusted with, and improve all for God. Let him have glory by all that you have received. The meanest gifts must not be idle. If you have but one talent, God requires a faithful improvement of it.

2. Improve all for his glory with your utmost diligence. To do a little good by the bye, will not be accepted. You must shake off your sloth and laziness, and bestir yourselves, that you may be hard at work for God. There must be labour and diligence. A lazy and loitering profession will bring no glory to God.

3. Your improvement must be proportionable to what you have received. If you have more wit than others, if you have better parts, or greater plenty, or be higher in place and power than other men, you must bring the more glory to God. The greater advantages and opportunities you have for glorifying God, he requires and expects the more. *Unto whomsoever much*

(r) Matth. xxv.

is given, of him shall much be required: And to whom men have committed much, of him they will ask the more (s). God will accept of that from others, that he will not accept of from you whose opportunities and advantages are greater.

Well then, let it be your great business to glorify God, and to improve all advantages and opportunities that way. To quicken you to this, consider,

1. As you yourselves are not your own, so nothing you have is your own. Your gifts, parts, wealth, power, all that you have; nothing thereof is absolutely your own, but God's. He hath absolute right to you and yours. All your possession is but a *stewardship*. They were rebels against God, who said, *Our lips are our own* (t). Therefore you must not use your gifts, or parts, or wealth, or power, as your own; but use all as his.

2 All that you have received is a trust committed to you. They are talents to trade with: A trust given you to employ. And this calls for faithfulness.

3. All is entrusted to you for this end, that you may bring glory to God. All your gifts, time, strength, wealth, power and authority; all are given you, that you may be in the greater capacity for promoting the glory of God. All that you have received is for the Master's use.

4. You are answerable to God how you manage this trust, how you employ what you have received. A day of reckoning will come, and an account will certainly be required of you. *Every one of us shall give account of himself to God* (u). On that great day you must give account to God, how you employed all his good gifts, and the advantages you had for glorifying him; if you honoured the Lord with your substance; and what advantage you made of your worldly honour and power for the glory and honour of God. And it will be a most exact and accurate account that will be required of you: For on that day the *books will be opened*, wherein there is an exact account kept, what number of talents were entrusted to you, and what return of gain you made to your great Lord and Master. And your quality will not exempt any of you: For the glorious sunshine of that day will extinguish the candles of all worldly glory; so that all shall stand upon the same level, as to their outward worldly circumstances. O, what will you answer, when God shall reckon with you, what glory

(s) Luke xii. 48. (t) Luke xvi. 2. Psal. xii. 4. (u) Rom. xiv. 12.

ry he hath had by you, as magistrates, as counsellors, as deacons of crafts, as constables, as masters of families, as private Christians; and what use you made of your time, strength, parts, wealth, and power. O think deeply and seriously on that day's reckoning, that you may be thereby quickened to more activity and diligence in your proper work †.

SERMON LXV.

IN prosecuting this purpose yet further, I shall,

1. *Branch out the exhortation.*
2. *Propose some considerations to press it.*
3. *Conclude with some directions.*

First, In branching out this exhortation, let me exhort you to glorify God, 1. In your more public station and capacity. 2. In your more private station.

1. In your more public station and capacity. Some of you being in public place, and having power and authority over others, have more access to speak and act for the glory of God than other men have. You have more special advantages and opportunities for it: and these you ought to improve with diligence and faithfulness, as you will be answerable to God in the day of your accounts.

Particularly, magistrates are under a special obligation to glorify God in their place. They are called *gods.* They are his substitutes on earth, by whom he governs and judges. They are *the ministers of God;* his vicegerents that *judge for* him. He hath stamped upon them that image of his, which consists in glory and honour, authority and power (a). He hath cast on them a beam of his glory (b), and invested them with power and authority (c). Therefore the glory of God should be very dear them. Bearing his name, they should be active for his glory. Being his vicegerents, they should rule for him. Being clothed with power by him, they should employ it for his honour:

† This sermon and the following were preached before the Honourable Magistrates and Council of Edinburgh, in the Tron-Church, when they were going their circuit through the churches of the city, before the annual election.

(*a*) Exod. xxii. 28. Psal. lxxxii. 6. Rom. xiii. 4. 2 Chron. xix. 6.
(*b*) Psal. xxi. 5. Deut. v. 18, 19.   (*c*) Rom. xiii. 1. Prov. viii. 14, 15.

nour. The power given unto them by God should be employed for the Giver.

I shall therefore address myself to you the honourable Magistrates of this city. I have a word to speak to you on God's behalf; and I bless the Lord that I have such ground of hope that it will be acceptable to you. As you are from God, so you ought to be for God. Being appointed by him, you are to be employed for him. The glory and honour of God ought to be the great and chief end of your government. Good king Jehoshaphat well understood this, and therefore speaks thus unto the judges: *Take heed what ye do; for ye judge not for man, but for the Lord, who is with you in the judgment* (d). And so doth the Spirit of God speak to you. You rule and judge, consult, vote and act, not so much for men, as for God. It is not your own advancement, your own honour or wealth, that should be the end of your government; but the glory and honour of God as supreme, and the good of men as subordinate thereunto. Therefore, let me lay these three things before you.

(1.) Let the glory of God be singly eyed and designed by you in the ensuing election. This will be a mean to direct you to a happy choice: therefore I do earnestly recommend it, not only to the honourable Magistrates, but also to all that have a vote in this election. Chuse such as are best fitted and qualified to act for the glory and honour of God, in their respective places and offices, and particularly in the office of the magistracy. Jethro, in his advice to Moses, directs you whom to chuse: *Moreover*, says he, *thou shalt provide out of all the people, able men, such as fear God, men of truth, hating covetousness; and place such over them* (e). Chuse *able men*, for wisdom and understanding; and *able men*, that is, men of might, to wit, for courage, resolution and constancy of mind. Chuse *such as fear God*, who will be faithful in acting for the glory of God and the public interests. Chuse *men of truth;* such as love the truth, and prize it, and deal truly and uprightly with God and men; and who will search out the truth, and prefer it in all causes that come before them. And chuse such as *hate covetousness*, of whom it may be expected, that they will not convert the public treasure or revenue to their own private use. In a word, vote, not for such as are most ambitious of the place, but such as best deserve it. They are but brambles that catch hold of preferment. Courting for places bewrays sordid and base ends. The most worthy to govern are often they that think themselves most unworthy. It is a disgrace to magistracy, when

such

(d) 2 Chron. xix. 6. (e) Exod. xviii. 21.

such are advanced, not who deserve it best, but who court it most. Let me also exhort you singly to design the glory of God in the election of men to other places and offices, besides that of the magistracy. Still consider what choice may be most for the glory of God. Remember that your vote is not your own, to give it to whom you please, or to gratify any man or party with it. No, your vote is more God's than yours; and therefore must be given according to his will, and for his honour and glory.

(2.) Let the glory of God be aimed at with a single and honest heart in your entrance into public places, and particularly that of the magistracy. Take heed of sordid self-seeking. See that your aim be not your own honour or wealth, the advancing or enriching yourselves. This is base and unworthy: And base ends, in entering into the magistracy, put men upon base practices in their deportment in it: for base ends are usually pursued by base means. But let your end be, your greater capacity to promote the glory and honour of God, and the good of the city in subordination thereunto. When this is your end, then your management is like to be such as will commend you to God, and to all good men. Such a noble end will put you upon noble employment. And when the glory of God is singly eyed by you, then may you with the more confidence expect his counsel, assistance and blessing, in following the duties of your office.

(3.) Let it be your great scope and business to glorify God when you are in office. When God advanceth you to place and power, make it your business to lay out yourselves for him in that place, and to employ your power for his glory, and for the public good in subordination thereunto. So did Nehemiah; he *sought the welfare of the children of Israel* (*f*). He improved his place for God when he was in it. Particularly, magistrates are to glorify God in their place,

First, By suppressing and punishing whatever is openly dishonourable to his blessed name. Magistrates are the *shields of the earth* (*g*), and should defend the glory of God. Two things are recommended here.

[1.] The suppressing and punishing vice and profaneness. You are the *ministers of God*; not to reprove and threaten only, but *to execute wrath upon him that doth evil* (*h*). It is not enough that you frown upon vice, and discountenance it, and express your displeasure against it; but there ought to be a vigorous

(*f*) Neh. ii. 10. (*g*) Psal. xlvii. 9. (*h*) Rom. xiii. 4.

gorous execution of the good laws against it. Careless magistrates, who are negligent of their duty in this matter, as they do thereby often bring down wrath upon the places where they bear office: so they do thereby become partakers of the guilt, and may bring down heavy wrath on themselves and their families. Notable to this purpose is that passage concerning Eli and his sons. Eli was a good man, and was the high-priest and judge of the land; but his sons greatly dishonoured God by their profaneness and wickedness; and Eli reproved them, and very sharply too. But because he did no more, God severely threatened him and his house; even because *his sons made themselves vile, and he restrained them not* (*i*). Mark, it was because *he restrained them not;* he did not curb them by drawing the sword of justice against them. This exposed him to God's severe displeasure, and brought heavy wrath upon his house and family, though he was a good man. If you suffer profane men to go on openly in their profane courses without just puishment, this may bring a curse upon your families, even though you be truly godly. Therefore let not the sword of justice lie rusting in the scabbard, but draw it out to execute judgment, and that impartially, let men make what figure they will; that *judgment may run down as water, and righteousness as a mighty stream* (*k*). And, for this end, take care that in the ensuing election the sword of justice be put into the hands of able and faithful men, men of zeal, courage, and boldness for God.

[2.] A zealous concern for the glory of God should also engage magistrates to lay an effectual restraint upon such, who, pretending to a spirit of prophecy and immediate revelation, most blasphemously personate the great JEHOVAH in delivering their pretended prophecies, which some of them value as of equal authority with the holy scriptures, crying down and despising a gospel ministry: All which are to me convincing proofs and evidences that they are actuated and agitated by an evil spirit, if it be by any spirit but their own. Yet they draw away many into their gross and damnable delusions and blasphemies. I shall not express what abominations and blasphemies I have heard to be among them: nor are all reports to be laid hold on; though I wish some search were made into the truth of these things. But this I am persuaded of, that the suppressing such abominations requires a very zealous concern. I know that by many these things are despised, as what will of themselves come to nothing. But, oh, few consider

the

(*i*) 1 Sam. iii. 14.   (*k*) Amos v. 24.

the great power of delusion, when God in his just judgment gives up people to it (*l*): And how many things there are that may justly provoke God to give up this generation to strong delusion, I have elsewhere declared.

Second, Magistrates are to glorify God in their place, by promoting and encouraging piety and righteousness, that people *may live under them*, not only *in* peace and *honesty*, but also *in all godliness* (*m*). It is foretold as one of the great blessings of Solomon's government, that, *In his days the righteous should flourish* (*n*). How much is it for the glory of God, that religion and righteousness flourish and prosper? These you are to promote by your own good example; and by your countenance and encouragement, having a due regard to such as are truly pious, and of a Christian conversation, in distributing your rewards and favours, and in promoting men to beneficial and honorary places and offices.

Third, Magistrates are to glorify God in their place, by promoting the interest of the gospel in the city. How much the glory of God is concerned in this, is so evident that I need not insist to declare it. In order to this, it is necessary that the city be planted with a competent number of faithful and prudent ministers, and that all due encouragement be given to them. Blessed be God, that you have given proof and evidence of your inclination to these things, and of your affection to a gospel ministry: And it may be thought improper for me to speak any thing on this head; therefore I shall be very modest in it. My personal concern is very small: But the glory of God, and the good of precious immortal souls, are so much interested in it, that I cannot say, that in a time when so much spite and malice is vented against a gospel ministry by a profane generation, it concerns you so much the more, to maintain and keep up the credit of the ministry by all proper means. And thus I have shewed how you are to glorify God in your more public station and capacity.

2. You are to glorify God in your more private station and capacity. There are none of you but have received some gift from God, some talent or other, which being rightly employed, may render you useful in promoting the glory of God. You have some advantages and opportunities of glorifying God, which are to be improved with diligence. None must lie by or be idle. You may be instrumental for the glory of God, even in your private station: And when less is required of

---

(*l*) 2 Thess. ii. 10.   (*m*) 1 Tim. ii. 2.   (*n*) Psal. lxxii. 7.

of you, your negligence will be the more aggravated: And seeing you are not exposed to such dangers and temptations as men in public place are, your neglect will be the more culpable. Well then, let it be your great business to glorify God, both inwardly, in your hearts, and outwardly, in your lives, and that both in word, and in deed, as I shewed in clearing the doctrine.

So much I thought necessary in branching out this exhortation. Now,

Secondly, I proceed to propose some considerations that may be of use, through grace, to excite and quicken you to make it your great business to promote the glory of God, both in your more public, and in your more private capacity. And,

1. He is worthy for whom you should do this. God is infinitely glorious in himself; and his incomprehensible glory deserves this at your hand. *His name alone is excellent: His glory is above the earth and heaven* (o). He is the most worthy Being, the Being of beings. O, will you not glorify him?

2. It is God's admirable condescension that he will employ such vile unworthy creatures as you are this way. It is most honourable employment to glorify God. It is God's own work: he glorifies himself; and it is the work of angels and glorified saints: So that it is admirable condescension that he should call vile sinful dust to be employed herein, and that he hath put you in some capacity for such work, and that you have so many advantages and opportunities put in your hand for this end. Admire his condescension, and let the consideration thereof gain upon your hearts.

3. It is your interest to glorify God, considering your absolute dependence on him. All your hopes hang upon him, your happiness lies in him, and you depend on him for all things. *In him you live, and move, and have your being* (p). From him you have your being and well-being. Your life and breath, and all your ways are in his hand. It is in his power, to kill you, or to keep you alive; to damn you, or to save you. Your business lies more with God than with all the world besides. So that it is your interest to glorify him.

4. It will be your great advantage to glorify him. For, 1. God will *honour them that honour* him. *If any man serve me*, says Christ, *him will my Father honour* (q). God can procure you public and visible honour among men: And you shall be

honour-

(o) Psal. cxlviii. 13.   (p) Acts xvii. 28.   (q) 1 Sam. ii. 30. John xii. 26.

honourable in the eyes of them that fear God: And God will honour you, in making you his friends and favourites, and granting you near access to, and communion with him. 2. It will be comfortable at death. How sweet will it be in a dying hour, when you can say, *I have glorified thee on earth* (r). There is nothing more comfortable to a dying Christian than the conscience of a well spent life. 3. If you glorify God on earth, he will glorify you in heaven. It is Christ's argument, *I have glorified thee on earth: And now, O Father, glorify thou me with thine own self* (s). The day is coming when he will put such glory upon you as shall be admired by all beholders. *Christ will come to be glorified in his saints, and admired in all them that believe* (t). To glorify God is the sure way to the eternal enjoyment of him.

5. Your conformity to Christ requires this. He made it his great business to glorify God. *I honour my Father*, says he, *and I seek not mine own glory*. And in his prayer to the Father, he says, *I have glorified thee on the earth* (u). He sought not his own ease, peace, and quiet, but the honour and glory of God. Now, it is ridiculous to own Christ for your Master, and not to conform to his example. Such as live to themselves, and not to the glory of God, have another master than Christ.

6. Consider the example of the saints, who have been scholars at Christ's school. The apostle gives us their character, when he says, *None of us liveth to himself; and no man dieth to himself: For whether we live, we live unto the Lord; and whether we die, we die unto the Lord: Whether we live, therefore, or die, we are the Lord's* (x). Weak and strong, all agree in this. Paul is a great instance: *For I could wish*, says he, *that myself were accursed from Christ, for my brethren, my kinsmen according to the flesh* (y). And Moses, when he pleads thus with God, *If thou wilt, forgive their sin; and if not, blot me, I pray thee, out of thy book which thou hast written* (z). Whatever be the meaning of these texts, it is plain that they are two such great instances, of men denied to themselves, and entirely devoted to the glory of God, that it is a wonder how Christians now-a-days can look upon them without shame and blushing.

7. All other creatures glorify God according to their capacity; even the brute and inanimate creatures. *The heavens declare the glory of God, and the firmament sheweth his handi-*

(r) John xvii. 4. (s) John xvii. 4, 5. (t) 2 Thess. i. 10. (u) John viii. 49, 50. and xvii. 4. (x) Rom. xiv. 7, 8. (y) Rom. ix. 3. (z) Exod. xxxii. 32.

work (*a*). Every pile of grass proclaims the glory of the Maker. It is true, they do it only passively or objectively; but their capacity reacheth no further: And shall man only of all the creatures, devils excepted, come short of improving his capacity for glorifying God?

8. This is all he seeks, and all we can give, for all his mercies and blessings. It is God's bargain, *I will deliver thee, and thou shalt glorify me* (*b*). This is all his rent and revenue. When you consider the great things God hath done for you; when you think on your glorious privileges, the great blessings you enjoy, and all your gracious receipts; your hearts should and will be ready to cry out, *What shall I render unto the Lord for all his benefits toward me* (*c*). Now, you can render nothing to God as a valuable recompence for his favours and blessings. But this is all he seeks, and all that you can give, and that which he will be well satisfied with, that you glorify him. He lets out to you all the blessings you enjoy for the rent of glory.

9. God can never be sufficiently glorified. Such is his matchless and transcendent glory and excellency, and the invaluable worth of these blessings and benefits we have from him, that when we have done our best, we shall still come short. Hence the saints bind themselves to this, as their eternal employment: *I will glorify thy name*, says the psalmist, *for evermore* (*d*). And it is usually added in doxologies, *for ever and ever;* or, *both now and ever.* The saints take a long day to pay a great debt. There is no less required than a succession of ages to ages, and eternity's leisure. Therefore let us not grudge to employ this short life in glorifying God; let us begin early, and be diligent, and hard at work. It is but little we can do in it, when we have done our best.

10. Your not glorifying God will come to a sad account at last. For, 1. God will one day reckon with you about it. So it is said in the parable of the talents, *After a long time the Lord of these servants cometh, and reckoneth with them* (*e*). He will call you to an account, what revenues of glory you have brought to him. It will not bring you off on that day, that you have not dishonoured God by open gross sins; but, what good have you done? What glory have you brought to God? Oh, how will you be able to look God in the face, if this be neglected? 2. If God get no glory by you, he will have glory upon you. So he says of the great oppressor of his people, *I will get me honour*

(*a*) Psal. xix i. (*b*) Psal. l. 15. (*c*) Psal. cxvi. 12. (*d*) Psal. lxxxvi. 12. (*e*) Matth. xxv. 19.

honour upon *Pharaoh*: And he tells us, *I will be sanctified in them that come nigh me, and before all the people I will be glorified* (*f*). God is resolved to be no loser by you. He will have his glory. If he be not glorified by you, he will be glorified upon you. If you do not glorify him actively, you shall glorify him passively, whether you will or not. And, O how sad will your case be, when you shall serve for no other end, but to set forth the glory of vindictive justice to all eternity?

Thirdly, I shall now shut up this discourse, by giving a few directions what to do, that you may glorify God in your place and station.

1. Resign and give yourselves to God to be his, and to serve him, and live to him. *Yield yourselves unto God* (*g*). You must cordially own his right to you, and power over you. Give your hearty consent to be his. None can lay such claim to you as God can do; you can never serve a better Master; and you are never more your own than when given up to him. Therefore, resign yourselves to him deliberately, and to his whole will in all things. Resign yourselves to him wholly, soul and body, to be wholly and for ever his. Resign yourselves to him absolutely, without reserve, for life or death, for better or worse. And resign yourselves to him through Christ.

2. Get an interest in the blessed Mediator: For you are in no meet capacity for glorifying God, till you are reconciled to him through Christ, and the breach be made up that sin hath made between God and you; and neither your persons, nor any thing you do, can be acceptable to God, but upon the account of Christ's mediation.

3. Be earnest for much sanctifying grace, that you may be vessels meet for the Master's use. Till you are sanctified, you are like salt that hath lost its savour, meet for nothing. It is the proper work of the Spirit, to cleanse and purge, fit and prepare you for every good work.

4. Often consider God's right to you and in you. He hath a natural right to you all as his creatures. And he hath a superadded right to you who believe in Christ, as by your own resignation, so also by Christ's purchase. He bought you with the price of blood, even the blood of his own dear Son: So that you are not your own to dispose of, but wholly his, by a manifold right. Ponder this deeply and frequently; and labour to have the sense of it always upon your heart.

5. Study much self-denial. Many are discouraged in acting

(*f*) Exod xiv. 17 Lev. n. 3. (*g*) Rom. vi. 13.

for the glory of God in their place, by incumbrances, inconveniencies, and worldly losses they are put to, and scoffs and scorns they meet with. Therefore study to be denied to your own ease, credit and profit, and all your own interests. Lay all down at God's feet. Count nothing too dear to you, so you may be instrumental in promoting the glory of God.

6. Get much love to God in exercise. There is no constraint like that of love. *The love of Christ constraineth us* (*h*). When you love God, you will count no cost or labour too much, so you may glorify him; and you will be glad when an opportunity of glorifying him is put in your hand. Love to God will put strength and life in your soul, and add wings and feet to the body. Keep this grace lively, and then you have an over-ruling bent in your own hearts.

7. Think on your last accounts at death and judgment. We are all hastening to the other world, and know not how soon we shall arrive there. Ponder seriously what you will do or say, when it shall be said to you, *Give an account of your stewardship?* Death may suddenly sift you before the tribunal of God, to give an account what hath been your great work and business in the world. Ponder this seriously; and urge your hearts with the thoughts of an after-reckoning. *O that they were wise,* says the Lord, *that they understood this, that they would consider their latter end* (*i*).

(*h*) 2 Cor. v. 14. (*i*) Deut. xxxii. 29.

DISCOURSE XVII.

Of God's Blessedness.

SERMON LXVI.

Psal. cxix. 12. *Blessed art thou, O Lord; teach me thy statutes.*

DAVID is supposed to have been the penman of this psalm. His scope therein is to set forth the excellency and usefulness of God's word, from his own experience of the benefit of it. It is indeed a long psalm; but the matter of it is so spiritual and heavenly, that, as one says, the longer it is, it is the better. There is seldom any coherence between the verses in it.

In this verse we have these two things,

1. An acknowledgement of God's blessedness. *Blessed art thou, O Lord.* That is, being possessed of all fulness, thou hast an infinite complacency in the enjoyment of thyself; and thou art he alone in the enjoyment of whom I can be blessed and happy; and thou art willing and ready to give out of thy fulness, so that thou art the Fountain of blessedness to thy creatures.

2. A request or petition. *Teach me thy statutes.* As if he had said, Seeing thou hast all fulness in thyself, and are sufficient to thine own blessedness, surely thou hast enough for me; there is enough to content thyself, therefore enough to satisfy me; this encourages me in my address. Again, Teach me that I may know wherein to seek my blessedness and happiness, even in thy blessed self; and that I may know how to come by the enjoyment of thee, that so I may be blessed in thee. Further, Thou art blessed originally, the Fountain of all blessing; thy blessedness is an ever-springing fountain, a full fountain, always pouring out blessings: O let me have this blessing from thee, this drop from the Fountain.

The doctrine is, *God is Bless'd; or, blessedness is one of the attributes of the divine nature.*

I shall here shew,

1. *That God is blessed*
2. *In what sense blessedness is attributed to him; or, how he is blessed.*
3. *I shall make application.*

First, Blessedness is attributed to God in scripture. Hence the gospel is called *the glorious gospel of the blessed God* (a). In which text it is applicable, either to the first, or to the second person of the Godhead. However it is elsewhere expresly attributed to the *second* person. He is called *the blessed and only Potentate* (b). It is true, there are other texts also wherein *blessedness* is ascribed to God (c) and Christ (d): But in these texts the word * is not that which properly signifies *blessed* or *happy*, as an attribute of God; but the word † is of a quite different notion. It properly signifies to be *worthy of all glory and praise*, to be *praised*, *extolled*, *celebrated*; and so indeed it may
import

(a) 1 Tim. i. 11.   (b) 1 Tim vi. 15.   (c) Mark xiv. 61. Rom. i. 25.   (d) 2 Cor. xi. 31. Rom. ix. 5.

* Μακάριος.   † Εὐλογητός.

import his bleſſedneſs and happineſs in himſelf, though that be not the proper ſenſe of the word. I do not remember of any text of ſcripture, where it is expreſsly, and in ſo many ſyllables, attributed to *God the Holy Ghoſt*. Yet there are ſeveral divine perfections attributed to *the Spirit*, which do very plainly import his bleſſedneſs. He is called the *good Spirit of God, the holy Spirit; the Spirit of grace;* and *the Spirit of glory* (g): And conſequently he is *the bleſſed Spirit.*

And God muſt needs be bleſſed, 1. Becauſe he is an abſolutely perfect Being; an Ocean of all perfection. All theſe perfections that are ſcattered among all the creatures, centre and meet in him after an infinite manner: So that nothing is or can be wanting to his infinite bleſſedneſs and happineſs. 2. Becauſe he is the Fountain of all bleſſedneſs to his creatures. Whatever bleſſings they enjoy, come originally from him. He makes others bleſſed, therefore he himſelf muſt be moſt bleſſed, ſeeing nothing can give or communicate what it hath not. 3 Hence either God is bleſſed and happy, elſe there can be no bleſſedneſs and happineſs at all; which is contrary to the natural deſires and appetites of all rational creatures; for all ſeek to be happy. Either bleſſedneſs is to be found in God, the firſt and beſt Being, and the cauſe of all other beings; elſe it can be found in no being whatſoever. Therefore the very heathens aſcribed bleſſedneſs to their gods. Nothing is more frequent in heathen authors, than to call God *the moſt happy and moſt perfect Being* *. Even the Epicureans uſually deſcribed God to be *that bleſſed and eternal Being* †. Hence they denied to God a providence; becauſe, as they apprehended, the care and trouble of preſerving and governing the creatures and their actions, would derogate from and diſturb his bleſſedneſs and happineſs. But herein they bewrayed their ignorance of God, and their perverſe notions of the divine power and wiſdom.

Secondly, I proceed to ſhew in what ſenſe bleſſedneſs is attributed to God. God may be ſaid to be bleſſed ‡,

1. Subjectively; as he is bleſſed in himſelf, and the Fountain of all bleſſedneſs to his creatures.

2. Objectively; as he is the object of our bleſſedneſs.

1. God

(g) Neh. ix 20. Eph. iv. 30. Heb. x. 29. 1 Pet. iv. 14.

* *Beatiſſimam & perfectiſſimam naturam.* † Cic. de Nat. Deor. L. 1.

‡ *Cum ſolo vero Deo, & in ſolo, & de eo ſolo, anima humana beata eſt.* Aug. de. C. D. L. 9. C. 2.

Of God's Blessedness. 45

1. God is blessed subjectively: As he is, 1. Blessed in himself. And, 2. The Fountain of all blessedness to his creatures.

(1.) As he is blessed in himself. And that I may, in some measure, clear to you, according to our capacity, how God is blessed in himself, I shall first shew what blessedness is, in general; and then apply the same to God's blessedness.

Blessedness lies in a freedom from all evil, and the possession and enjoyment of all good in the Chief Good.

1. There is in blessedness a freedom from all evil. Therefore the Greek word * which signifies *blessed*, is by some derived † from a privative or negative particle, and a word which signifies *death;* importing, that in blessedness there is a freedom and immunity from death and miseries. The less liable any person is to any evil or misery, the more blessed he is.

2. There is in blessedness a possession of all good. Therethe Hebrew word, *ashrei* (*h*), which signifies blessed, is used in the plural number; importing, that it is not enough to a person's blessedness that he hath this or that or the other good, unless he abound with all good things. Therefore, some define blessedness, *a perfect state and condition of life, consisting in the abundance of all good things* ‡. The more good things any possesseth, and the fewer wants and needs he hath, he is the more blessed.

3. I added, that in true blessedness, there is a possession of all good IN THE CHIEF GOOD: For happiness lies but in *one thing* (*i*), and that must be the chief good; a sufficient good, which contains all good in it, so that it is able to yield content, and to satisfy the appetite without satiety. Now, God alone is this Chief Good. Believers possess all good things in him. Hence it is said, *He that overcometh shall inherit all things* (*k*). How *all things?* This is accounted for, in the words following, *and I will be his God.* In him they have all things.

4. There is necessary to true blessedness, not only the possession, but the enjoyment of the Chief Good. The one is not sufficient to blessedness without the other, as appears in believers under spiritual desertion. They possess the chief Good; God

---

* Μακαριος   † Μὴ *non, and* κὴρ *Mors.* Favorinus.
(*h*) Psal. xxxii. 1. and elsewhere.
‡ *Ille beatus est, qui omnia quæ vult habet, nec aliquid vult quod non decet.* Aug. de Spiritu & Lit.
(*i*) Psal. xxvii. 4.   (*k*) Rev. xxi. 6.

God is theirs, and they have him: But they know it not; they are in the dark, and under doubts, about their interest in him; so that they do not possess him with joy and delight. Therefore, I say, it is necessary to blessedness, that we not only possess the Chief Good, but have the enjoyment thereof, which lies in the knowledge and sense of what we possess, with joy and complacency. Though a man possess all that is good and desirable, all that is necessary to happiness, yet if he doth not think so, he cannot be happy. Hence philosophers and divines distinguish between objective and formal blessedness. Objective blessedness is the great God; for he alone is the Chief Good, and consequently the only object of our blessedness. But formal blessedness lies in the intellectual vision of God, and the fruition and enjoyment of him with complacency and delight. And this is the blessedness and happiness of the saints, here in part, and hereafter fully and perfectly.

Now, let me apply what hath been said about blessedness in general, to God's blessedness. God's blessedness in himself, is that attribute, whereby, being for ever free from all evil, and having all fulness of perfection and sufficiency in himself, he doth most perfectly and unchangeably enjoy himself. So that God's blessedness in himself, implies these things,

1. That he is for ever free from all evil. *God is light, and in him is no darkness at all* (*l*). As there is no mixture of any evil or imperfection in his nature; so he is not liable to any evil from without. He is above the malice of sin and Satan, and all the injuries of his creatures. As their holiness cannot help him, so their sin cannot hurt him. *If thou sinnest,* says Elihu, *what doest thou against him? Or if thy transgressions be multiplied, what doest thou unto him? Thy wickedness may hurt a man as thou art* (*m*). All these darts of sin that wicked men shoot up against heaven, fall short of God, and come down upon their own heads.

2 That he hath all fulness of perfection and sufficiency in himself. For, he is an infinitely and absolutely perfect Being. *Your Father who is in heaven is perfect* (*n*), says Christ. *He is perfect in knowledge* (n): And so also in his power, wisdom, mercy, goodness, and other attributes. He is God *all-sufficient* (*o*), as that word may be rendered. He is sufficient

of

(*l*) 1 John i. 5. (*m*) Job xxxv 6, 8. (*n*) Matth. v. 48.
(n) Job xxxvii. 16. (*o*) Gen. i. 17.

of himself to his own happiness. So that there is no want of any thing in him; nor doth he need any thing from us: *Seeing he giveth to all life, and breath, and all things* (*p*). We need one another; the greatest stand in need of the meanest; the meanest members have their use in the body: But he hath no need of us. He neither needs nor desires the creature, nor any thing from the creature, as if any benefit could redound to him thereby. He hath enough in himself to his own blessedness. He is above our benefits as well as our injuries; as Eliphaz declares, *Can a man be profitable unto God, as he that is wise, may be profitable unto himself? Is it any pleasure to the Almighty, that thou art righteous? Or is it gain to him, that thou makest thy ways perfect* (*q*)? And to the same purpose is that of Elihu; *If thou be righteous, what givest thou him? Or what receiveth he of thine hand?——Thy righteousness may profit the son of man* (*r*). Our goodness extendeth not unto him (*s*). As the sun gains nothing by the shining of the moon and stars; so the self-sufficient God gains nothing by all the services, praises, and prayers of his creatures: For, he is *exalted above all blessing and praise;* and *who hath first given to him, and it shall be recompensed unto him again* (*t*). The whole world cannot add any thing to his blessedness: For, he hath enough in himself, and was sufficient to his own happiness, before the world was made; so that he created the world, not that he might be happy, but that he might be liberal. He requires obedience and service from us, not for any good or advantage to himself, but for our own good and happiness. And he useth means and instruments in his works both of nature and grace; not out of necessity, as if he needed them; but out of his abundant goodness, that he may impart the dignity of a kind of efficiency to his creatures.

3. His most perfect enjoyment of himself. God's blessedness lies not in the enjoyment of the creature, but in the enjoyment of himself. We enjoy a thing for itself, but use it for another: So that God cannot be properly said to enjoy the creature; he only useth it in a subserviency to his own glory, for he *made all things for himself* (*u*). And as God's blessedness lies in the enjoyment of himself; so, he enjoys himself in the most perfect manner. Men enjoy themselves by the help and benefit of some other thing besides themselves; but God doth, by, in, and of himself, most perfectly enjoy himself; and this is his perfect blessedness and happiness.

Par-

(*p*) Acts xvii. 25.   (*q*) Job xxii. 2, 3.   (*r*) Job xxxv 7, 8.
(*s*) Psal. xvi. 2.   (*t*) Neh. ix. 5, Rom. xi. 35.   (*u*) Prov. xvi 4.

Particularly, God's enjoyment of himself takes in these three things. 1. His most exact knowledge of himself. The apostle tells us, *The Spirit searcheth all things, yea, the deep things of God* (x). Where, by *the Spirit*, we are to understand the Holy Spirit of God. He SEARCHETH *the deep things of God;* the word denotes such an exact knowledge as men have of a thing after diligent search. God exactly knows, and thoroughly understands, the depths of his own essence and perfection. He hath a perfect and comprehensive knowledge of the same. And without this knowledge of himself he could not be blessed: For nothing can in a rational manner enjoy itself, without understanding itself. So that this is one thing wherein the blessedness of God consists, his perfect knowledge of himself, of his own excellency, all-sufficiency and infinite perfection. 2. His infinite contentment and satisfaction: His condition being such that he can neither desire it should be better, nor hath any cause to fear it shall be worse. 3. His infinite complacency, joy and delight in himself. So some divines understand that text, *In thy presence is fulness of joy* (y). Orig. *in thy face:* and by *the face of God*, they understand the essence of God, or God himself, as it is taken in God's answer to Moses, *Thou canst not see my face* (z). So that they take the meaning to be, in God's own essence, there is full joy and complacency. Hence we read of the infinite delight and complacency that the divine Persons took in each other from all eternity: As in that text, wherein Christ, the personal Wisdom of the Father speaks, *Before the mountains were settled, &c. Then was I by him, as one brought up with him; and I was daily his delight, rejoicing always before him* (a). The Father had an infinite complacency in the Son, as *the brightness of his glory, and the express image of his Person* (b): And the Son had an infinite complacency in that *glory which he had with* the Father *before the world was* (c): and the Holy Spirit had an infinite complacency in the love and communion of the Father and the Son. So that God had an infinite complacency in Christ, and Christ in God, and both in the Spirit, and the Spirit in both; all in each, and each in all; before the world was.

4. The impossibility of any change. A state of blessedness is a fixed and unmoveable state; any thoughts and fears of a change cannot but cause great disquiet: So that if God's perfection, fulness and sufficiency, might be diminished, or his per-

---

(x) 1 Cor. ii. 10.　(y) Psal. xvi. 11.　(z) Exod. xxxiii. 20.
(a) Prov. viii. 25, 30.　(b) Heb. i. 3.　(c) John xvii. 5.

perfect enjoyment of himself fail in any sort, this would derogate from his perfect blessedness †. But he is for ever possessed of that fulness of perfection that he hath in himself, and secure in the enjoyment of himself, without the least possibility of any change. As he cannot create any trouble or disquiet to himself, or any disturbance to his perfect blessedness, by doing any thing contrary to his own nature, or unbecoming his glorious perfections: So he is of infinite power, to secure his own happiness against all attempts whatsoever, and to check and controul whatever would be a disturbance to it; and of infinite wisdom to direct his power, and manage it in such a manner as may be most effectual for this end.

From what is said, it appears that God is incomparable in blessedness. Angels and glorified saints are blessed; but they are not blessed, in comparison of God; not blessed as he is. For, 1. God is blessed in and of himself; and not in or from another. He is blessed in himself, being sufficient to his own happiness. And he is blessed of himself: He hath his being and perfections of himself, and consequently his blessedness. The blessedness of angels and glorified saints is derivative, derived from the blessed God: But God's blessedness is originated in his own nature, so that he is not beholden for it to any other. 2. God is immutably and unchangeably blessed. His blessedness doth not admit of any increase or decrease. Nothing can be added to it, nor any thing taken from it: For, *with him there is no variableness, neither shadow of turning* (d). His blessedness is still the same, without any change. 3. God is eternally blessed. This follows from what hath been said. He could not be blessed in and of himself, and immutably blessed, if he were not eternally blessed. He is *blessed for evermore* (e). It is an inseparable adjunct of true blessedness, that it lasts for ever: For, it would disturb and disquiet the blessedness of any to have thoughts and fears of its finite duration: So that it is not perfect blessedness, that is not eternal and without end. 4. God is essentially blessed. His blessedness is inseparable from his essence; yea, it is his very essence. He is not only blessed, but Blessedness itself. 5. He is infinitely blessed. As he is without bounds and limits of perfection, so he hath a boundless blessedness. None can set limits to it, and say, He is so blessed

† *Beatitudo vera non est, De cujus æternitate dubitatur.* Aug. de Civ. Dei. Lib. 3.

Nisi stabili & fixo & permanente bono, beatus esse nemo potest. Cic. 5. Tusc.

(d) James i. 17. (e) 2 Cor. xi. 31.

sed and no more. He is blessed above all measure, *exalted above all blessing* (*f*). 6. He is communicatively blessed. He communicates his blessedness to his creatures, according to their capacity; but of this afterward. 7. It follows from all this, That God is incomprehensibly blessed. Even the blessedness of the glorified saints, though it be but finite, is such as *eye hath not seen, nor ear heard, nor* hath *entered into the heart of man* (*g*). And if our our hearts cannot conceive the finite blessedness of the saints in heaven, how much less can we conceive the infinite blessedness of God? God alone doth perfectly know and comprehend his own blessedness, seeing he alone hath the perfect and comprehensive knowledge of his infinite and glorious perfections.

Thus I have shewed that God is blessed in himself.

(2.) God is subjectively blessed, as he is the fountain of all blessedness to his creatures. He is *the fountain of life; and the fountain of living waters* (*h*). He is so blessed, that his blessedness doth, as it were, overflow and run out to the creatures. His blessedness is like an ever-springing fountain. He fills every living thing with his blessing. *He opens* his *hand, and satisfies the desire of every living thing:* But especially of his saints; for *he will fulfil the desire of them that fear him* (*i*). It is a part of God's blessedness, that he is still of the giving hand. *It is more blessed to give than to receive* (*k*). This is God's happiness, that he gives to all, and receives of none.

Particularly, God communicates himself and his blessedness, according to the capacity of the creature. 1. Mediately, in this life. 2. Immediately, in the life to come.

1. Mediately, in this life; by the interposition of means and second causes between him and us. And thus he communicates himself, 1. In common blessings. The earth is filled with his blessings. *The earth, O Lord,* says the psalmist, *is full of thy mercy* (*l*). This is seen especially in his providence toward man. O, how many blessings flow to us from this blessed Being and fountain of blessedness! Such as food and raiment, health and strength, daily preservation, &c. and all these by the interposition of second causes. He feeds us with his good creatures, and cherishes us by the influences of the sun, &c. So that we have our blessings at second or third hand, as is imported in that prophecy: *And it shall come to pass in that day, I will hear, saith the Lord, I will hear the heavens, and they shall hear the earth; and the earth shall hear the corn,*

and

(*f*) Neh. ix. 5. (*g*) 1 Cor. ii. 9. (*h*) Psal. xxxvi 9. Jer. ii. 13. (*i*) Psal. cxlv. 16, 19. (*k*) Acts xx. 35. (*l*) Psal. cxix. 64.

and the wine, and the oil; and they shall hear Jezreel (*m*). God hath communicated influences to the heavens; he causes the heavens send forth these influences upon the earth; he makes the earth to bring forth corn and wine: and he makes corn and wine nourish and refresh our bodies and spirits. Whatever good the creatures convey to us, they have the same first from God. The creatures are but empty pipes through which the blessing runs; and it passeth from pipe to pipe, till it come to us. 2. In spiritual and saving blessings. And thus he communicates himself to his own. He hath promised such blessings to them: *In blessing*, says he, *I will bless thee* (*n*). And he is as good as his word, in *blessing them with all spiritual blessings in heavenly places in Christ* (*o*). He blesses them with pardon and peace, access to him and communion with him, his favour and the light of his countenance, and rich communications of grace, &c. and sometimes affords such abundance of these blessings that their *cup runneth over* (*p*). Believers are vessels into which God is still pouring more, till they be completely filled up. And all this he doth by the means of the word and sacraments. These are the conduits through which spiritual blessings are conveyed into the souls of the elect; narrow conduits from a full fountain.

2. Immediately, in the life to come, by immediate influences from God himself. And this is the blessedness of the glorified saints above. In heaven God shall be *all in all* (*q*). There is no temple, no ordinances there; but God communicates himself immediately. Here we see God veiled in ordinances: But then *face to face. In* his *presence* (Orig. *in* his *face*) *is fulness of joy* (*r*). In heaven, God supplieth all immediately from himself.

We see then, what variety and abundance of blessings spring from this blessed Being. O, he is a full, ever-springing, and inexhaustible fountain. His store is nothing diminished by giving. Though he hath been giving out blessings from the beginning of the world till now, yet there is not the less behind. O, what a blessed Being must he be!

Thus I have shewed you that God is blessed subjectively, as he is blessed in himself, and the fountain of all blessedness to his creatures.

II. God is objectively blessed; as he is the object of our bles-

---

(*m*) Hos. ii. 21, 22.   (*n*) Gen. xxii. 17.   (*o*) Eph. i. 3.
(*p*) Psal. xxiii. 5.   (*q*) 1 Cor. xv. 28.   (*r*) 1 Cor. xiii. 12.
Psal. xvi. 11.

blessedness. He is so blessed that the enjoyment of him makes us blessed. And a greater blessedness than this there cannot be. *Blessed is that people whose God is the Lord* (s). Seeing he is an infinitely blessed Being, what happiness can there be comparable to this, to enjoy him? He is an all-sufficient Being, sufficient of himself to his own blessedness and happiness, much more to ours: So that it is the height of happiness to enjoy him. Now, believers enjoy him in part, even in this world. God hath promised this to them, even his gracious presence, access to and communion with him. And it is this that the saints long for; as the psalmist did; *As the hart panteth after the water brooks,* says he, *so panteth my soul after thee, O God; my soul thirsteth for God, for the living God:* And, *My soul thirsteth for thee, to see thy power, and thy glory* (t). And the saints do sometimes enjoy him in such a measure and manner, that they are apt to cry out with the psalmist, *The lines are fallen unto me in pleasant places; yea, I have a goodly heritage* (u). But in heaven they shall enjoy him fully. There they shall have the highest enjoyment of God that their capacity can admit of, when they shall be filled with all the fulness of God, and he will communicate himself to them in the utmost latitude they are capable of.

SERMON LXVII.

Third, I COME now to the Application.

Use 1. For instruction; in several particulars.

Instr. 1. Is God infinitely blessed in himself? Then he cannot be properly wronged or hurt by sin. True it is, that sin, interpretatively, and in the intention of the thing, doth wrong him; it is a contempt of his Majesty, an affronting him to his face, and strikes against all his glorious attributes: Yet, the blessed God cannot, by the sins of men, suffer any hurt or damage, in his Being, or in his essential glory and perfection. He is *over all God blessed for ever* (a); so that it is not in the power of all the sinners in the world to hurt him in the least. All the hurt and misery that cometh by sin redounds to sinners themselves.

Instr. 2. Is God infinitely blessed in himself? Then, how admirable and astonishing is it that he should seek after such poor nothings as we are, and be at so much pains to engage

our

(s) Psal. cxliv. 15.   (t) Psal. xlii. 1, 2. and lxiii. 1, 2.
(u) Psal. xvi. 6.   (a) Rom. ix. 5.

our hearts to him and his service! It is evident, that he doth doth seek or aim at his own blessedness and happiness herein; for he is infinitely blessed and happy in and of himself, and hath no need of us. O then, what cause have we to cry out, *What is man that thou art mindful of him?* And, *Lord, what is man, that thou takest knowledge of him? Or the son of man, that thou makest account of him* (b)? What would God lose, though you were all damned; and what would he gain, though you were all saved? He hath no more need of you, than of devils and damned reprobates; and he knows how to make use of you for his glory, as he doth of them, if you wilfully reject the offers of his grace. So that he seeks to win your hearts, not that he may be blessed in you, but that you you may be blessed in him. O what astonishing condescension is here!

Instr. 3. It follows from this doctrine, that Atheists are, of all men in the world, the greatest enemies to mankind; seeing they cut off from men all hopes of blessedness and happiness, by taking away the spring and fountain of it. For, if there is not a God, how can any man be blessed and happy in the enjoyment of him? And other happiness there is none; for unless we suppose that God is, we cannot possibly frame any true idea of happiness. All the enjoyments and comforts in the world are not so necessary to our happiness as God is: Without him, there can be none; and without them, he alone is sufficient. So that in nothing can a man shew himself a greater enemy to mankind, than by endeavouring to banish the belief of a God out of the world. That is true of the atheist, *His hand is against every man;* therefore every man's hand should be against him, in so far as he is such. Further, the Atheist is the greatest enemy to himself. He that wishes there were no God, cannot wish worse to himself: So that he that *says in his heart there is no God,* must be a *fool* indeed (c). Seeing there is no happiness but in the enjoyment of God, no man can shew himself a greater enemy to himself and his own happiness, than by endeavouring to raze the impressions of the being of a Deity out of his mind.

Instr. 4. We see from this doctrine, that blessedness and happiness is attainable by us poor creatures; even such happiness as our finite capacity can admit of, the perfection whereof is reserved for the life to come. Two things here offer themselves to our consideration. 1. That God can make us happy. There can be no doubt of this, if we consider God's infinite

---

(b) Psal. viii. 4. and cxliv. 3.   (c) Psal. xiv. 1.

infinite blessedness and happiness in himself. Certainly, he who is possessed of it after an infinite manner, and hath all the treasures of it in himself, can communicate it to us according to our finite capacity. 2. That he is willing to make us happy, providing we take the right way to attain to happiness, and to be qualified and made meet for it. This plainly appears from his infinite goodness, which is the propension and disposition of his nature to make others happy by letting out of his fulness to them. It cannot in the least impair his own happiness, to make others happy. On the contrary, his goodness, which inclines him to it, is a part of his happiness; so that it is the happiness of the divine nature to communicate himself to his creatures. Noble and generous spirits are free and bountiful; they cannot be happy themselves, unless, according to their capacity, they make others so: Now, certainly God is not of a niggardly and envious nature, as Satan represented him unto our first parents to be; but of a most generous disposition: So that it is his glory and delight, and the highest expression of his goodness, to communicate happiness to his creatures. Hence he is represented as rejoicing in the conversion of a sinner, because thereby the sinner becomes capable of this happiness (*d*).

Instr. 5. This doctrine discovers to us wherein it is that we should seek our blessedness and happiness, and wherein it consists: Not in earthly enjoyments and comforts, but in the enjoyment of the blessed God. He only is the object of our blessedness. He is the alone all-sufficient Being: So that it is the enjoyment of him alone that can make us happy.

But here it may be enquired, What is it to enjoy God? It implies these things, 1. A saving interest in God as our God in Christ. That which we enjoy is our own. And indeed we cannot be blessed but in what is our own. Hence the psalmist says, *God, even our own God, shall bless us: Blessed is the nation whose God is the Lord* (*e*). 2. A saving union with God through Christ. Hence believers are said to *dwell in God, and he in them* (*f*). This is a glorious mystery, and shall never be fully understood till we come to heaven. *At that day*, says our Lord, *ye shall know that I am in my Father, and you in me, and I in you* (*g*). 3. Familiar communion and fellowship with God: For *truly our fellowship is with the Father, and with his Son Jesus Christ* (*h*). When God manifests and communicates himself to the soul in a gracious way, then we enjoy him.

(*d*) Luke xv. (*e*) Psal. lxvii. 6. and xxxiii. 12. (*f*) 1 John iv. 15. (*g*) John xiv. 20. (*h*) 1 John i. 3.

Of this our Lord speaks: *I will love him, and will manifest myself to him* (i). 4. The saving knowledge of God, his perfection, fulness, and all-sufficiency: *When God gives us an heart to know him; and shineth into our hearts, to give us the light of the knowledge of the glory of God in the face of Jesus Christ* (k). We cannot be said to enjoy that whereof we have no knowledge: So, we do not enjoy God, unless we have some knowledge of his excellency and all-sufficiency, that so we may see our own happiness and blessedness in the enjoyment of him. 5. Complacency and delight in God. We do not enjoy that wherein we do not joy †. He that enjoys God takes pleasure and delight in him. This the psalmist requires, *Delight thyself also in the Lord:* And the spouse tells us, that she *sat down under his shadow with great delight* (l) 6. The soul's acquiescing and resting in God as its Chief Good. The man sees himself happy in God: Therefore he rests here; now he would change no more. He seeks after no object to make up his happiness, but is ready to cry out with the psalmist, *The lines are fallen unto me in pleasant places:* And, *Whom have I in heaven but thee? and there is none upon the earth that I desire besides thee* (m).

Use 2. For reproof: To two sorts of persons.

Repr. 1. To such as do what in them lies to disturb God's infinite blessedness and happiness, by offending, provoking, and dishonouring him, and grieving his Spirit by sin. The Lord complains, *I am broken with their whorish heart, which hath departed from me: Thou hast made me to serve with thy sins; thou hast wearied me with thine iniquities: Behold, I am pressed under you, as a cart is pressed that is full of sheaves* (n). You that indulge yourselves in a liberty to sin, do what in you lies, to deprive God of his blessedness, and to make him a miserable Being. It is true, this is labour in vain; for God is *blessed for evermore* in spite of all the sinners in the world: Yet it plainly shews the wickedness of your hearts, and your enmity and madness against God. This will cut you off from all hope of blessedness; for, when you do what in you lies to disturb the blessedness of God, or to spoil him of it, how can you expect he will be a fountain of blessedness to you?

Repr. 2. To them that seek blessedness and happiness in other things besides the blessed God. Some seek it in sensual pleasures,

---

(i) John xiv. 21.   (k) Jer. xxiv. 7. 2. Cor. iv. 6.
† *Frui est cum Gaudio uti.*   August.
(l) Psal. xxxvii. 4. Cant. ii. 3.   (m) Psal. xvi. 6. and lxxiii. 25.
(n) Ezek. vi. 9. Isa. xliii. 24. Amos ii. 13.

pleasures. But this is brutish: And though sinful pleasures go down sweetly, yet they come up again bitter as gall: And, O, how bitter will they be in the latter end; and what bitterness will they cause in the other world? Others seek blessedness and happiness in worldly comforts and enjoyments, riches, and wealth and honour. But, 1. This is most dishonourable unto God. It is to *forsake the fountain of living waters, and to hew out to yourselves broken cisterns, that can hold no waters* (*o*). It is a great contempt of God, and undervaluing of this blessed Being; as if other things had more sufficiency in them to your blessedness and happiness, than the blessed God hath. 2. It is great folly: For these things cannot make you blessed and happy, so that you lose your labour. As they are but transitory and perishing things; so they are empty and unsatisfactory †. *He that loveth silver, shall not be satisfied with silver; nor he that loveth abundance, with increase* (*p*). They are not proportioned to the desires and cravings of a rational soul. We cannot have full happiness and contentment in any thing, till we are filled with it, and have as much of it as we can hold: But, the soul of man is so boundless and restless in its desires, that it can never be filled but with the infinite God.

Use 3. For exhortation to all, but more especially to such as are strangers to God, and live without him in the world. My exhortation to such is twofold.

Exhort. 1. Is God infinitely blessed? O then, seek to be blessed in him, to be happy in the enjoyment of this blessed Being. It is God's own happiness to enjoy himself; and he is willing to communicate his blessedness to poor creatures, according to their capacity: Therefore seek to be blessed in the enjoyment of the blessed God.

To quicken and excite you this, I propose these considerations.

1. You cannot else be blessed and happy but in the enjoyment of God. You cannot be happy but in the enjoyment of the greatest good you are capable of, and such a good as is able to supply all your wants, and answer all your necessities, and satisfy all your desires and longings: But God alone can do this. All other enjoyments are nothing without the enjoyment of him. Earthly enjoyments may vex, but cannot satisfy. Yea, ordinances are nothing without it: The word and sacraments are valuable only as means of the enjoyment of

(*o*.) Jer. ii. 13. (*p*) Eccl. v. 10.
† *Beatus qui post illa non abiit quæ possessa onerant, amata inquinant, amissa cruciant.* Bern. in Epist.

of God and communion with him. Therefore gracious souls can take no pleasure in the best ordinances, if God be not there. When they long after the public ordinances, it is not bare ordinances, but God in the ordinances they long for: And when they miss God in the ordinances, they are to them as clouds without rain, or pipes without water, poor empty things. I say then, there is no happiness but in the enjoyment of God.

2. The enjoyment of God is sufficient to your blessedness and happiness, though you had no more: For he is an infinitely blessed and all-sufficient Being, sufficient to the necessities both of this life and of that which is to come. There is a want annexed to all other things, but God alone sufficeth. He can suit all your faculties, and fill up all the capacities of your immortal soul. He is sufficient to his own blessedness, much more to ours. He hath enough for himself, much more for us. He finds infinite satisfaction in himself, much more may we find satisfaction in him. That which will fill a tun, is it not enough to fill a little bottle? That which will satisfy a prince, may it not content a beggar? Is God blessed in himself, and may not a poor creature be blessed in him? Indeed, you need no more but God, to content, satisfy, and delight your soul. There is enough in him to make your heart run over. The enjoyment of God is a solacing and satisfying thing. It is this that makes ordinances sweet. How is the heart enlarged in prayer, inflamed in meditation, refreshed in hearing and communicating, when God is enjoyed in these ordinances! The enjoyment of God can sweeten all your other enjoyments, and make every condition of life sweet to you.

3. You may be blessed and happy in the enjoyment of God, if you be not wanting to yourselves. Though the enjoyment of God be the height of happiness; yet blessed be he, it is attainable by the vilest and most unworthy sinners among you. Others have attained it, who were as vile and unworthy as any of you can be. God hath made you capable of this blessedness, capable of the enjoyment of himself; and he is an infinitely blessed Being, the fountain of all blessedness, and willing to communicate his blessedness to poor creatures, according to their capacity. This he takes great delight and pleasure in. For this end he makes offer of himself to you on terms of free grace: *I am the Lord thy God*, says he, *open thy mouth wide, and I will fill it* (q). Though your sins have separated

(q) Psal. lxxxi. 10.

between God and you, yet it is good news that you may meet again in Christ. The blessed Son of God stept in, and purchased peace with and access to God for poor sinners. O, it is glad tidings, that *God was in Christ reconciling the world to himself* (r). So that the greatest sinners among you may have access to God and communion with him through Christ on gracious terms.

4. This is the way to improve your excellency above the beasts. What is man's excellency above other creatures? Even this, that other creatures were made to glorify God, but man only, of all visible creatures, was made to enjoy him. Therefore, that man might be capable of so high an elevation, God breathed into him a soul or spirit from heaven; and this soul hath such unlimited, vast, and restless desires, that it can be satisfied with nothing but the enjoyment of the blessed God. Well then, *remember and shew yourselves men* (s): When you do not seek your blessedness and happiness in the enjoyment of the blessed God, you do not act like men: You degrade yourselves, and abase and abuse a noble soul, in not acting according to the excellency of your natures; you act like beasts and not like men. He is but a beast in the shape of a man that can satisfy his soul with the world; and he is a devil incarnate that can satisfy his soul with sin. You never shew yourselves men, till you seek your blessedness in the enjoyment of the blessed God.

5. The enjoyment of God is the very happiness of heaven. The glorified saints enjoy God fully and immediately; and this is their blessedness. They see God *face to face* (t), and behold his glory immediately, and not by reflection, as in a looking-glass. Now if the full enjoyment of God be the happiness of heaven, then the enjoyment of God, in this life, tho' but in part, is heaven begun upon earth. The enjoyment of God in ordinances, will set you, as it were, in the suburbs of glory; so that you will have cause to say, as Jacob said, *This is the gate of heaven* (u). Your enjoyment of God here will be a sure pawn and pledge of the eternal enjoyment of him in heaven. On the other hand, unless you enjoy God here, you cannot enjoy him hereafter. What should they do with the enjoyment of God in heaven, who are careless of his company on earth.

But it may be enquired, What shall we do that we may be blessed in the enjoyment of God? The gospel shews the way: Therefore it is called *the glorious gospel of the blessed God* (x). In the

(r) 2 Cor. v. 19. (s) Isa. xlvi. 8. (t) 1 Cor. xiii. 12.
(u) Gen. xxviii. 17. (x) 1 Tim. i. 11.

the gospel God is discovered as ready to bless us, and there the way is laid down how we may come to be blessed in him. From this gospel I give these directions. 1. Get a deep sense of your misery while you are without God. This is the sad case of all that are in an unconverted state. While you are *without God*, your misery is inexpressible (*y*). All your other enjoyments cannot supply this want. This is the misery of the damned in hell. As the heaven of heaven lies in the enjoyment of God, so the hell of hell lies in the loss of him. 2. Renounce all earthly vanities, riches and wealth and honour. Whatever your earthly enjoyments and comforts are; renounce them so as not to regard them as your chief good, and so as not to set your heart upon them, or seek your happiness in them in less or more. 3. Flee to Christ. Receive and close with him as he is offered to you in the gospel. You cannot have friendship with God, till you make peace with him through Christ; and till you have his friendship, you cannot have his company, either here or hereafter. *Can two walk together, except they be agreed?* You cannot enjoy God but in Christ. He must *bring you to God*, and is the only *way* to the Father (*z*). 4. Chuse God in Christ, for your chief good, portion, and happiness: For, he cannot be yours but by your own choice. Chuse him deliberately: Think seriously if you can be content to have God for your all, and to have all your happiness in him. And chuse him absolutely: There must be no ifs nor ands, no reserves, no conditions, in your choice of God; nor any place left for repentance: And chuse him wholly, in all that he is, God the Father, Son, and Holy Ghost, to be your portion. 5. Think on death. Then all your earthly comforts and enjoyments will fail you, and your worldly happiness will come to an end. O, how sad will your case be in a dying hour, if you do not enjoy God! For then must you take your last farewell of all your earthly enjoyments, never more to return to them. 6. Wait on God in the duties and ordinances of his appointment. This is the way wherein he is to be found, and wherein others have met with him. Especially be diligent in attending the public ordinances. In the due use of them, you are in God's way for a blessing. *Blessed is he that heareth me,* says Christ, *watching daily at my gates, waiting at the posts of my doors: For, whoso findeth me, findeth life, and shall obtain favour of the Lord* (*a*). 7. Go to God for the light and power of his Spirit: Light, to discover

---

(*y*) Eph. ii. 12.   (*z*) Amos iii. 3. 2 Pet. iii. 18. John xiv. 6.
(*a*) Prov. viii. 34, 35.

ver the vanity of all worldly things, and God's own excellency and all-sufficiency; and power, to take your heart off the world, and draw it in to God. Cry to him for a day of his power; and be earnest with him that he would take your heart in his hand, and counsel you effectually to make a happy choice for your own souls. When David declared his choice of the Lord for his Lord, he owns that it was the Lord himself that had given him counsel so to do: *O my soul,* says he, *thou hast said unto the Lord, Thou art my Lord;* and then he adds, *I bless the Lord who hath given me counsel* (b).

Exhort. 2. Is he the blessed God, the fountain of blessedness? Then go to him for all needful blessings. In this imitate the example of Jabez: *Oh that thou wouldest bless me indeed* (c), says he. The words express a vehement wish and desire. His heart was much set upon this, to have God's blessing. In the original text the words are expressed in the form of a vow; *If thou wouldest in blessing bless me.* If thou wouldest do so, then I would— What wouldest thou do? O what would I not do, or suffer, or part with, to have thy blessing? If thou wouldest bless me, then I would be thine, and love, and fear, and serve thee.

I say then, go to this blessed Being for all needful blessings. Bring your empty pitcher to this fountain, that you may be filled with his blessing.

Go to him even for temporal blessings, supply of bodily wants, outward provision and maintenance, food and raiment. You are warranted to go to him even for these. 1. Because you need them. *Your heavenly Father knoweth that ye have need of all these things* (d). You have a body as well as a soul; and the one hath its necessities, as well as the other. 2. Because we are directed to pray for them, in that perfect pattern of all prayer; *Give us this day our daily bread.* Upon these accounts, you may warrantably go to God, even for temporal blessings. But seek to have them, not in a way of common providence, but in way of covenant mercy; not as fruits of God's common bounty, but as fruits of special love. And seeing such blessings are not absolutely necessary, nor absolutely promised in the covenant, but only conditionally, so far as it may serve for God's glory, and the good of his people: Therefore be not too peremptory in seeking them, but seek them with much humble submission; for you may be as happy without them, and sometimes it is a greater blessing to want them, than to have them.

(b) Psal. xvi. 2, 7.   (c) 1 Chron. iv. 10.   (d) Matth. vi. 32.

them. Only, ye who are the children of God are warranted confidently to expect, that God will not let you want necessary maintenance, so long as he hath use and service for you in the world: And when he hath no more use and service for you, you should be glad to go hence and bid adieu to all earthly blessings.

But especially, go to this infinitely blessed Being for spiritual and saving blessings (e). Gracious hearts are most set upon these. Consider what blessings you need, and go to the Fountain of blessedness for supply.

SERMON LXVIII †.

LET me here shew you what blessings ye are to seek, especially in order to your preparation for the Lord's supper. And, 1. Seek the sanctification of your natures: That you may be renewed by grace, and cleansed from your filthiness, and get your souls adorned with the graces of the Spirit. The sanctifying work of the Spirit is necessary to fit you for communion with God. It is a part of the apostolical benediction: *The communion of the Holy Ghost be with you all* (a). That is, all the gracious communications of the Spirit of grace. Till you are sanctified, you are unfit guests for the Lord's table. Our blessed Lord prefigured this, by washing his disciples feet before the supper (b). 2. Seek a covenant-interest in God as your God. We find this in Isaac's blessing Jacob: *God Almighty bless thee,* says he, *and give thee the blessing of Abraham, to thee, and to thy seed with thee* (c). The *blessing of Abraham;* What was that? Even the blessing which God promised to Abraham in these words, *And I will establish my covenant between me and thee, and thy seed after thee, in their generations, for an everlasting covenant, to be a God unto thee, and to thy seed after thee* (d). It is a great blessing to have the Lord for your God, to be in covenant with him. Till then you have no right to the seal of the covenant. 3. Seek the pardon of your sins. *Blessed is the man whose transgression is forgiven, whose sin is covered: Blessed is the man unto whom the Lord imputeth not iniquity* (e). Sin unpardoned will separate between God and you, and obstruct your communion with him. It will petition against you, at the Lord's table, as Esther

(e) Eph. i. 3.

† This sermon was preached on the Sabbath before the sacrament was administered.

(a) 2 Cor. xiii. 14.   (b) John xiii.   (c) Gen. xxviii. 3, 4.
(d) Gen. xvii. 7.   (e) Psal. xxxii. 1, 2.

Esther did against Haman at the banquet of wine. But pardon of sin will make way for and usher in all other covenant blessings. 4. *Seek the favour of God in Christ.* This is a great blessing: For, *in his favour is life; and his loving kindness is better than life* (*f*). And seek the sense of his favour, the light of his countenance, and the shinings of his blessed face, that your hearts may rejoice and be glad in him. 5. *Seek the gift of the Spirit.* This is a necessary and excellent blessing: For, the maintaining, strengthening, and quickening the spiritual life, depend upon his gracious influence; and it is only by his assistance that you can do or suffer any thing for God. 6. *Seek fresh supplies of grace.* You have great and difficult work before your hand; solemn humiliation work, covenanting and communicating work: And such is your insufficiency of yourselves, that you will surely miscarry in these solemn duties, to the dishonour of God, and the hurt of your own souls, if you be not supplied with grace from above. Therefore seek quickening, strengthening, and assisting grace, 7. *Seek the wedding-garment,* viz. The imputed righteousness of Christ, and inherent righteousness and holiness. This is the garment that becomes the solemnity of the marriage-feast of the King's Son. It is a royal feast, a spiritual feast, a costly feast; and the Lord and Master of the feast is *a great King, the King of kings, and Lord of lords, and the Prince of the kings of the earth.* It is a disgrace to the feast, and an affront to the Master, to come in your old or ordinary apparel. Put on the Lord Jesus, and the garments of sanctification and holiness; then are you welcome guests, and not intruders. 8. Seek the accomplishment of that promise, *And they shall look upon me whom they have pierced; and they shall mourn for him, as one mourneth for his only son, and shall be in bitterness for him, as one that is in bitterness for his first-born* (*g*). Seek such a sight of a crucified Christ by faith, as you may remember his sufferings with suitable affections, and the exercise of suitable graces 9. Seek so much light, and life, and love, as you may with holy seriousness and resolution devote yourselves to God through Christ. O what a blessing would it be, if that were the language of all your souls, *Come, let us join ourselves to the Lord in a perpetual covenant never to be forgotten* (*h*). 10. Seek to be made partakers of Christ and his benefits, sealed in the sacrament, and dispensed there to worthy receivers. Seek communion with him, and to have virtue and grace communicated from him

---

(*f*) Psal. xxx. 5. and lxiii. 3.   (*g*) Zech. xii. 10.   (*h*) Jer. L. 5.

him to your soul in the right use of that blessed ordinance. 11. Seek the inward seal of the Spirit, to accompany the outward seal of the covenant; that so you may attain to the assured persuasion of your interest in God through Christ, and of the pardon of all your sins; that your doubts and fears may evanish, and you may cry out with Thomas, *My Lord, and my God* (i).

Go to God for these blessings, and seek them with holy seriousness and earnestness. To excite and quicken you to this, I propose these considerations.

1. These are necessary blessings. You may want other blessings, and yet be happy; but you are undone for ever, if you get not these blessings. Without spiritual blessings, all your other blessings are cursed, and you will fall under the curse of God for evermore. Hence is that dreadful threatening, *I will even send a curse upon you, and I will curse your blessings* (k).

2. These are excellent blessings. They are blessings for the soul, which is the better part. They are dear bought blessings, purchased by the blood of God. They are discriminating blessings, the favours of God's peculiar people (l). They are fruits and effects of special love, and pledges of eternal blessings. They are substantial blessings: Other blessings are but the shadows of blessings; but these are blessings indeed. They are durable blessings: Temporal blessings are transitory and perishing things; but these are the better part, that shall not be taken away; they are secured to believers by an everlasting and sure covenant. They are such blessings as will turn all your curses into blessings, and all your miseries into mercies. They are enough to swallow up all the grievances of affliction, and all the contempt and scorn of the world.

3. These blessings are attainable, even by the vilest sinners. Remember, you have to do with an infinitely blessed God, who delights to communicate of his blessedness. It is a part of his blessedness to be still giving out blessings. And he is more ready to bless than to curse. He doth not curse, but when it is, as it were, extorted from him: But he blesseth freely, without any merit or desert on our part. God's great end in sending Christ was, that he might bless poor sinners: As the apostle Peter declares to his hearers, *God having raised up his Son Jesus, sent him to bless you* (m). In the days of Christ's flesh, we never read that he formally cursed any man: But he was much

---

(i) John xx. 28.   (k) Mal. ii. 2.   (l) Psal. cvi. 4.   (m) Acts iii. 26.

much in blessing. He began blessing, in his excellent sermon upon the Mount: *Blessed are the poor in spirit; blessed are they that mourn*, &c (*n*). And he went on blessing: *Yea, rather,* says he, *blessed are they that hear the word of God, and keep it: And he took* little children *up in his arms, put his hands upon them, and blessed them* (*o*). And he died blessing: He prayed on the cross, *Father, forgive them, for they know not what they do.* And he went off the world blessing: *He led* his disciples *out as far as to Bethany, and lifted up his hands and blessed them* (*p*). And never any that came to him for a blessing, was sent away without it; and he hath pledged his word that never any shall: *Him that cometh to me*, says he, *I will in no ways cast out* (*q*). Seriousness and earnestness in seeking to God for these blessings, is the sure way to obtain them; For he hath not *said unto the seed of Jacob, seek ye me in vain;* but *is good to the soul that seeketh him*. And others have prevailed, and have gotten the blessing; as Jacob and Jabez (*r*).

But some serious soul may say, I cannot think that ever God will bestow such excellent and glorious blessings on the like of me, I am such a vile worthless wretch. I answer, 1. God hath already conferred such blessings on some of the vilest wretches that ever were; such as Manasseh, Paul, Mary Magdalene, and divers others. And as their sins were great in their nature, so who can tell what hainous aggravations they were attended with? 2. These blessings are free gifts. God gives them without a regard to any worth in men. His end in bestowing spiritual blessings is the glory of his rich and free grace: And the glory of his grace is that which he takes great delight and pleasure in. He delights to magnify his grace on them that are most unworthy: So that your vileness and unworthiness, if you have a deep humbling sense of it, shall not come between you and the best of blessings.

But it may be enquired, What shall we do that we may obtain such excellent blessings from God? Take these directions. 1. Get a deep sense of the need you have of these blessings. Your natural state is a cursed state. Till you are renewed by grace, you are lying under the curse of the first covenant, and are excluded from the blessings of the second covenant. A deep sense of this is necessary to awaken and rouze your soul. 2. Study the excellency and worth of spiritual blessings. The worth

(*n*) Matth. v. (*o*) Luke xi. 28. Mark. x. 16. (*p*) Luke xxiii. 34. and xxiv. 50. (*q*) John vi 37. (*r*) Isa. xlv. 19. Lam. iii. 25. Gen xxxii. 26. 1 Chron. iv. 10.

worth of them is inexpreffible. All other bleffings are nothing in comparifon of them. 3 Seek them in and through Chrift the bleffed Mediator. You cannot elfe obtain them. All fuch as are made fharers of fpiritual bleffings are *bleffed* only *in* Chrift (*s*). As Jacob got his father's bleffing in the garments of his elder brother Efau: So, you cannot obtain fpiritual bleffings from God, unlefs you come to him in the garment of Chrift's unfpotted righteoufnefs. Therefore put on Chrift and his righteoufnefs by faith. 4. Seek thefe bleffings in the way of repentance. It was by fin that man forfeited all fpiritual and faving bleffings: Therefore, this forfeiture cannot be taken off, till you are engaged to renounce all iniquity with grief and fhame, and to refign yourfelves obedientially to God as your Lord and Sovereign 5. Diligently attend the public ordinances: For they are the pipes through which thefe bleffings run. *Bleffed is he that heareth me,* fays Chrift, *watching daily at my gates,* &c (*t*). The ordinances are the chariot of the Spirit, the means by which God conveys fpiritual bleffings into the fouls of his people. It is good to wait on God in his own way. 6. Pray much for thefe bleffings, as Jabez did: *Oh, that thou wouldeft blefs me indeed* (*u*). And be very earneft in prayer, and wreftle for the bleffing. Whatever difcouragements, and feeming denials and repulfes you may meet with; yet do not give over, but perfevere, and be very importunate, and fay with Jacob, *I will not let thee go, except thou blefs me* (*x*). Such is God's admirable condefcenfion, that he allows you to be importunate, to prefs hard, and not to let him go without a bleffing. And your own neceffity fhould quicken you: *Either I muft prevail, or I fhall go to hell*. God is well pleafed with your importunity. He feems to put you off, that he may quicken you to more earneftnefs. And this is the way to prevail: Importunity is prevalent, both with God and with men. Therefore, ftir up yourfelves to take hold of God, and wreftle with him; and refolve, through grace, that you will never give over, till you get the bleffing.

Ufe 4. For exhortation, to believers in Chrift, who have a faving intereft in this infinitely bleffed Being. From the doctrine I have been upon, I exhort fuch of you to feveral duties.

Exhort. 1. Admire God's grace and condefcenfion, in communicating his bleffednefs to you, according to your capacity.

(*s*) Eph. i. 3. (*t*) Prov. viii. 34. (*u*) 1 Chron. iv. 10. (*x*) Gen. xxxii. 26.

It is God's own blessedness to enjoy himself; and this blessedness he hath communicated to you, according to your measure. Consider who he is, what you are, what blessedness this is that he hath conferred upon you, and what moved him to it. O, how admirable and astonishing is it, that the blessed God, who is sufficient of himself to his own blessedness, would bless such vile wretched sinners as you are, who can neither hurt him nor help him; and that with no less than the enjoyment of himself; and that most freely, not being induced to it by any hope of recompence: For, *who hath first given to him, and it shall be recompenced to him again* (y). O, admire the riches and freedom of his grace.

Exhort 2. Bless the name of God. Bless him, as and because he is blessed in himself, sufficient of himself to his own happiness. And bless him, as he is the Fountain of your blessedness. Bless him for all blessings: but especially for spiritual blessings. *Blessed be the God and Father of our Lord Jesus Christ*, says the apostle, *who hath blessed us with all spiritual blessings in heavenly places in Christ* (z). But what is it to bless God? Though we cannot bless God, as he blesseth us, by bestowing blessings on him; nor as one man blesseth another, by wishing for blessings to him, seeing he is infinitely blessed in and of himself: Yet we should keep up a thankful remembrance of his benefits; and esteem highly of him on the account of them, counting him *worthy* of all *honour, and praise, and blessing* (a); and declare and publish his blessedness before others, as the psalmist doth in my text, *Blessed art thou, O Lord;* and applaud his b'essedness, speaking of it with thanksgiving and praise; and wish well to him, wishing that he may ever be what he is, and what we know he ever shall be. To will God's blessed and glorious being, is one of the most excellent acts of the creature: And in so doing, we bless him as much as a creature can bless him.

Exhort. 3. Bless yourselves in him. *He who blesseth himself in the earth, shall bless himself in the God of truth:* And, *The nations shall bless themselves in him* (b). You are compleat in him: He is an infinitely blessed and all-sufficient Being: Therefore you may well count yourselves blessed and happy in the enjoyment of him, whatever your outward wants and straits be; for, in him you may find every want abundantly supplied.

Exhort. 4. Rejoice in God. So the apostle exhorts: *Rejoice in*

(y) Rom. xi. 35. (z) Eph. i. 3.
(a) Rev. v. 12. (b) Isa. lxv. 16. Jer. iv. 2.

in the Lord away: And again, I say, Rejoice. And the psalmist: *Rejoice in the Lord, O ye righteous* (c). Your interest in this infinitely blessed Being is sufficient matter and ground of joy. Nothing can be such cause of grief to you, as your interest in him is cause of joy. Let the men of the world see that you judge yourselves well provided for in an all-sufficient God; and that you have enough in him, though you were deprived of all your other enjoyments.

Exhort. 5. Rest content with him alone. Is the infinitely blessed and all-sufficient God yours? Then you have cause enough to be content, whatever your wants and losses be: For, you have enough in him. O, do not disgrace your God by a discontented spirit. Let your Christian contentment proclaim before the world, *that the lines are fallen unto you in pleasant places, and that you have a goodly heritage* (d).

Exhort. 6. Let the consideration of God's infinite blessedness engage and quicken you to a chearful obedience to his commands: For he doth not lay such commands on you, for any profit or advantage to him, seeing he is sufficient of himself to his own blessedness; but for your own good and happiness. So Moses tells the children of Israel, *The Lord commanded us to do all these statutes; to fear the Lord our God for our good always.* This is often urged, *That it may be well with you* (e).

Exhort. 7. Seek to be more and more blessed in this infinitely blessed Being, in a more full enjoyment of him. Consider, 1. You are as yet blessed only in part. You have not the full and perfect enjoyment of God in this life: And you cannot have perfect blessedness, till you have perfect enjoyment. Therefore, you should be always aiming at, and pursuing after, further degrees of enjoyment, till you come there where you shall be filled with all the fulness of God. 2. A more full blessedness, and further degrees of enjoyment, are attainable, even in this life. You never enjoy so much of God, but more may be enjoyed. 3. It is the temper of the saints, to pursue after the enjoyment of God. They would be more and more blessed in him. This was the temper of the church: *With my soul have I desired thee in the night; yea, with my spirit within me will I seek thee early* (f). The saints pant and long after God: most gladly would they have more and more of him. If you have the temper of gracious souls, you will reckon that you cannot enjoy

---

(c) Phil. iv. 4. Psal. xxxiii. 1. (d) Psal. xvi. 6. (e) Deut. vi. 24. (f) Isa. xxvi. 9. See Psal. xxvii. 4. and xlii. 1, 2. and lxiii. 1, 2.

enjoy God enough, and you cannot rest fully satisfied till you have the full enjoyment of him in glory.

Well then, seek to be more and more blessed in this infinitely blessed God. Pursue after further degrees of the enjoyment of him; greater nearness to him, and more intimate and familiar communion with him, in all duties and ordinances, and especially in that great ordinance of the Lord's supper. To excite and quicken you to this, consider, 1. This is the great end of the ordinances, that in them you may enjoy God, and have communion with him. Particularly, this is the end of the sacrament. Therefore it is called *the communion* (g); because in it we have more near communion with God than in other duties and ordinances. We come to the sacrament, that we may get more of God and Christ, and feast with him at his own table. 2. This renders the ordinances beautiful and amiable. It made the psalmist cry out, *How amiable are thy tabernacles, O Lord of Hosts* (h)? What a glory is there in the ordinances, when we enjoy God in them? The beauty and glory of the ordinances comes and goes with it. 3. All the saving efficacy and blessed fruit of ordinances depends on it. When you enjoy God in the sacrament, it will be a soul-reviving, soul-strengthening, and soul-refreshing ordinance to you. 4. This will make the ordinances a heaven upon earth unto you. It is the enjoyment of God in heaven that makes heaven to be what it is, a place of unspeakable blessedness and happiness: Therefore the enjoyment of God, in the sacrament, will set you, as it were, in the suburbs of glory. This would render the communion-day one of the best days of your lives; and you would have cause to say with the psalmist, *This is the day which the Lord hath made: we will rejoice and be glad in it* (i).

But, what shall we do, that we may enjoy much of God, and have near and intimate communion with him in that great sealing ordinance? Take these directions. 1. Get sin removed out of the way. See that there be no standing ground of controversy between God and you. Any known sin unrepented of will seperate between him and you, and mar your communion with him: For he is *of purer eyes than to behold evil, and* cannot *look on iniquity.* Therefore, *if iniquity be in thine hand, put it far away; and let not wickedness dwell in thy tabernacles* (k). 2. Employ Christ the Mediator, For it is *in him that*

(g) 1 Cor. x. 16.   (h) Psal. lxxxiv. 1.   (i) Psal. cxviii. 24.
(k) Hab. i. 13. Job xi. 14.

that *God is well pleased* (*l*). All your access to and communion with God, is only through him, and on the account of his mediation. *In him we have boldness and access with confidence by the faith of him* (*m*). 3. Get much love to God. This will bend and incline your heart toward him. When you love God, you cannot want his company; your heart will be set upon the enjoyment of him, and you cannot live without him. You will be ready to cry out with the spouse, *Saw ye him whom my soul loveth* (*n*)? 4 Quicken your desires after him. Long *to see* his *power and glory in the sanctuary* (*o*). Let your desires after God be ardent, vehement, and burning desires. God hath promised to fill and satisfy the hungry and longing soul. 5. Let nothing satisfy you without God. Account that duty or ordinance to be but empty, in which you do not find and meet with him; and count all other enjoyments but loss and dung in comparison of him.

Exhort. 8. Go to this blessed Being, the fountain of blessedness, for an increase of all spiritual blessings; more sanctifying grace, more faith, more love, more spiritual strength, &c. And to excite you to this, consider, 1. You need an increase of spiritual blessings. You never receive so much, but that you still need more. Consult what your spiritual wants and necessities are. 2. In God there is all fulness. He is an infinitely blessed and all-sufficient Being. He is a full fountain, that is always running, and yet never diminished. Esau cried out, *Hast thou but one blessing, my father* (*p*)? This cannot be said of God. Though he hath given out inumerable blessings to needy souls, he hath not the less behind: He is an ocean of blessings. 3. He is most willing and ready to give out blessings to you who are his own. Consider, (1.) His relation to you. He is your Father, and fathers use to bless their children. Surely, the near and dear relation wherein you stand to him, gives you ground with confidence to seek and expect your Father's blessing. (2.) Consider his love to you. Such was his love, that he gave Christ to and for you; what then will he not give! *He that spared not his own Son, but delivered him up for us all; how will he not with him also freely give us all things* (*q*)? (3.) Consider his promise. He hath promised to bless you. In the covenant there are promises of all kinds of blessings. There his truth and faithfulness is laid in pawn. (4.) Consider your own experience. You have already received

---

(*l*) Matth. iii. 17.   (*m*) Eph. iii 12.   (*n*) Cant. iii. 3.
(*o*) Psal. lxiii. 1, 2.   (*p*) Gen. xxvii. 38.   (*q*) Rom. viii. 32.

ed manifold blessings, suited to your various wants and exigencies, and these are pawns and pledges of more. 4. The more you seek, the more you shall have. God is willing to multiply his blessings upon you, and to bless you abundantly. *Open thy mouth wide*, says he, *and I will fill it*. *Eat and drink abundantly.* Christ *came that you might have life, and that you might have it more abundantly* (*r*) You are not straitened in him: Why should you be straitened in yourselves? *Ask, and ye shall receive, that your joy may be full* (*s*).

Particularly, seek an increase of spiritual blessings in the right use of the Lord's supper; for that sacrament is a mean that God is pleased to use in communicating such blessings to the souls of his people; therefore own God as the fountain of blessings, and the sacrament as the mean of conveyance. And in order to your improving the sacrament for an increase of spiritual blessings, I give these directions. 1. Get a deep sense of your spiritual wants and necessities. Consider what blessings you need, and wherein you are most defective. 2. Be often taking fresh views of God's blessedness and all-sufficiency, and of the fulness that is in Christ. O there is enough in him. In your Father's house there is bread enough and to spare. 3. Get a firm persuasion of the excellency and usefulness of that precious ordinance, as a blessed channel of the communication of all needful blessings. There, believers have been recruited with new strength, have gotten nourishment to the spiritual life, and have had their smoking flax blown up into a flame. 4. See that you come to the sacrament in faith, looking to and resting upon Christ in that ordinance, for all the blessings you need. It is by faith you must eat his flesh, and drink his blood. Therefore rouze up your faith, and labour to have it in a lively exercise. 5. Come with enlarged desires. *Open thy mouth wide*, says the Lord, *and I will fill it* (*t*). There is enough in God to fill and satisfy the most enlarged desires of your souls. He needs no more but your empty vessels. You may be too full for God, but you cannot be too empty. Therefore enlarge your desires. 6. Come to the sacrament with large expectations. There are large supplies of grace, and an increase of all spiritual blessings, to be had in the right use of that ordinance. Christ hath promised that worthy receivers shall *eat his body and drink his blood:* So much is implied in the words of institution: Therefore come with large expectations to have
this

(*r*) Psal. lxxxi. 10. Cant. v. 1. John x. 10. (*s*) John xvi. 24. (*t*) Psal. lxxxi. 10.

this promise made good to you. Do not say, I look for no good at the sacrament: For, as this will weaken your heart and hand in duty; so it will provoke God to withdraw his hand from working. Many times you get but little, because you look for little. Therefore enlarge your expectations. You have to do with an infinitely blessed Being, who delights to communicate of his fulness, to needy sinners that come to him by Christ. When you are entertaining thoughts of drawing near to God in the Lord's supper; or it may be when you are come to his table; you may meet with something like a storm in your face: But go on, resting upon Christ, and the still small voice will come. Believe, hope and wait, and you shall see the glory of God.

DISCOURSE XVIII.

Of the Decrees of God.

SERMON LXIX.

Eph. i. 11.—*Who worketh all things after the counsel of his own will.*

HAVING spoken formerly of the Being of God, and of his nature and attributes; I shall next discourse to you of his Decrees, which are the original spring and first rise of all his external works. I am aware that there are not a few who are against ministers meddling with the decrees of God in their sermons to the people. I confess we ought not to pry curiously into what God hath kept secret; and many things in in God's decrees are so, till they appear by the event. Yet it is our duty to study the knowledge of what God hath revealed; for *things revealed belong to us* (a). Now, the doctrine of God's decrees is plainly revealed in the holy scriptures; and it is a doctrine of great practical use, as will appear when I come to the practical part of this discourse.

In this chapter, after the inscription, the apostle treats of the causes and means of salvation, and ascribes all to the free grace of God in Christ. He speaks of them, 1. More generally, by way of thanksgiving to God, verse 3. 2. More particularly; and that, (1.) As they are prepared by the eternal decree of election, verses 4, 5, 6. (2.) As they are purchased by

(a) Deut. xxix. 29.

by Chrift, verfe 7. (3.) As they are applied to the elect in their effectual calling, by the means of the revealing and publifhing the gofpel, verfes 8, 9, 10. And then he gives inftances of this in the effectual calling both of the Jews and of the Gentiles. Of the Jews, verfes 11, 12. In verfe 11. he fhews that the reafon why they had obtained the heavenly inheritance, was not their own worth and merit, but God's predeftinating them to it, in his unchangeable purpofe and decree of election: And, in my text, he proves this particular by a general, he *worketh all things after the counfel of his own will;* and confequently thefe alfo I have been fpeaking of.

In thefe words, the apoftle, being to explain the nature of God's working, expreffeth thefe two things.

1. God's working itfelf: *Who worketh all things.* The pronoun *who* refers to God, fpoken of all along in the preceding verfes. WORKETH ALL THINGS—The word rendered *working* fignifies to work powerfully and effectually, fo as to overcome all contrary refiftance, and all rubs and difficulties in the way: And God's way of working is plainly fuch; he works mightily, againft all oppofition and lets in his way. *I will work,* fays he, *and who fhall let it* (*b*)? ALL THINGS—This cannot be reftricted to the beft bleffings the apoftle had been fpeaking of, but is to be underftood of all things whatfoever, all beings, and all natural motions and actions as fuch. For, as I faid, the apoftle here argues from the general to the particular; he worketh *all things* fo, and confequently thefe alfo: And from the lefs to the greater: he worketh *all things* fo, even in the meaneft creatures, much more thefe things that concern the falvation of finners.

2. The rule of God's working—*After the counfel of his own will*—It is God's decree that is here called *the counfel of his will.* This is, as it were, the rule and pattern according to which all things are brought to pafs in time. God's decree is called *the counfel of his will,* to denote his wife and free determination therein. As God's decree is an act of his will, and fo moft free, being confidered in relation to the creatures; fo his decree and will are never without counfel. He willeth or decreeth things to be done, with the greateft reafon and judgment, moft wifely, as well as freely.

The doctrine I propofe is this:

There hath been an eternal purpofe or counfel of the divine will concerning all things that come to pafs in time. Or thus, God

(*b*) Ifa. xliii. 13.

Of God's Decrees.

God by the most wise and holy counsel of his will hath decreed or fore-ordained whatsoever comes to pass.

In prosecuting this Doctrine, I shall,

1. *Prove the general truth of the doctrine.*
2. *Shew what is the general nature of God's decrees, and in what sense they are attributed to him.*
3. *Speak of the extent of God's decree.*
4. *Assign some properties thereof.*
5. *Speak of the end why he hath decreed these things that come to pass.*
6. *Make application of the whole.*

First, I shall prove this general truth, that God hath decreed or fore-ordained these things that come to pass in time. This is a truth about which the holy scriptures are very plain and positive. He *worketh all things after the counsel of his own will.* What comes to pass in time is by his appointment. *I appointed the ancient people,* says he, *and the things that are coming and shall come* (c). We read expressly of God's decree. *I will declare the decree: This is the decree of the most High:* And, *Before the decree bring forth:* And Christ is said to be *fore-ordained before the foundation of the world* (d). That is, By God's decree appointed to the work of redemption. And things that are come to pass are said to be *established by God* (e). His decree is sometimes called his counsel, to denote the wisdom of it. *My counsel shall stand* (f), says the Lord. So, it is called in my text, *the counsel of his will;* and elsewhere, his *determinate counsel*: And things are said to be done as *determined before by the counsel of God* (g). Sometimes his decree is called his pleasure, to denote the freedom of it in relation to the creatures. *I will do all my pleasure* (h), says the Lord. So, we read of his *good pleasure* and *the good pleasure of his will* (i). Sometimes again, his decree is called his purpose, to denote the immutability of it: As in that of the prophet, *This is the purpose that is purposed upon the whole earth; and this is the hand that is stretched out upon all the nations. For the Lord of hosts hath purposed, and who shall disannul it* (k)? So we read of *his good pleasure which he purposed*

(c) Isa. xliv. 7. (d) Psal. ii. 7. Dan. iv. 24. Zeph. ii. 2. 1 Pet. i. 20. (e) Gen. xli. 32. (f) Isa. xlvi. 10. (g) Acts ii. 23. and iv. 28. (h) Isa. xlvi. 10. (i) Eph. i. 5, 9. (k) Isa. xiv. 26, 27.

in himself; and *his eternal purpose which he purposed in Christ:* And believers are said to be called and saved *according to his own purpose and grace* (*l*).

This truth is evident also, 1. From God's omniscience. He knows all things, past, present, and to come, by one simple act of intuition from eternity. *Known unto God are all his works from the beginning of the world* (*m*). He foresees all things that come to pass in time, so that he cannot be surprised by any event. Now, it cannot be imagined whence he should have such a foreknowledge but from his own decree. He foreknew such and such events, because he decreed they should come to pass. As he sees all things possible, in his own power; so he sees all things future, in his own will and decree; and he sees the nature of things, in the eternal ideas in his own mind. 2. From God's independency. All second causes depend in their being and operation upon the First Cause, and all things and events upon the supreme Being; so that nothing could give a certainty of future being to any thing, save only the will and decree of God determining the event. Therefore all things and events must be reduced to this as their proper spring and fountain. 3. From God's immutability. He is *the Lord that changeth not,* and *with whom is no variableness, neither shadow of turning* (*n*). The actual providence of God is extended to all events, motions, and actions of the creatures: For, *he worketh all things,* says my text; and, says our Lord, *My Father worketh hitherto, and I work* (*o*). Now, God works nothing in time, but what he decreed from eternity to work, else there would be a change in him. As every rational agent first thinketh and purposeth, and then worketh: So God, the highest rational agent, doth nothing but what he first purposeth and determineth to do; and this purpose must be eternal, seeing there can be no new thoughts or purposes in God, because of his immutability. Hence, 4. The very heathens, under the conduct of nature's light, owned the doctrine of the divine decrees. Seneca, writing to his friend, prescribes the belief of it, as a remedy against impatience under affliction: " Losses," says he †, " wounds, pains, fears, " have made an incursion upon you: These things are usual:
" That

(*l*) Eph. i. 9. and iii. 11. 2 Tim. i 9.   (*m*) Acts xv. 18.
(*n*) Mal. iii. 6. James i. 17.   (*o*) John v. 17.

† *Damna, Vulnera, Labores, Metus incurrerunt, solet fieri: Hoc parum est: Debuit fieri: Decernuntur ista, non accidunt.* Sen. Ep. 96.

" That is little: Thefe things muft needs come to pafs: They
" are decreed, and do not come by chance."

Ufe. Then, let us afcribe nothing to chance or fortune, but all events to God's appointment and ordination. The word *fortune*, in the fenfe of the Gentiles, is a blafphemy which the devil hath fpit upon the decree and providence of God: Therefore Auguftine repented that he had fo often ufed that word. But, doth nothing fall out by chance? Doth not the preacher fay, *Time and chance happeneth to them all* (*p*). I anfwer, it is not an uncertain chance that is there intended, or an event falling out befides the intent of the Firft Caufe: But any *occurrent* (*q*), as the fame word is rendered elfewhere. Even thofe things that are moft cafual with refpect to us, are under the decree and providence of God. *The lot is caft into the lap: But the whole difpofing thereof is of the Lord* (*r*). That blind goddefs, Fortune, holds her deity only by the tenure of mens ignorance. Becaufe we could not forefee fuch an event, or could not fee it in its caufes, therefore it is faid to fall out by chance. But with refpect to God, nothing is cafual. That which is cafual to us, is decreed and appointed by him. Things cafual to us, are counfels to him. Therefore learn to own and acknowledge the eternal will and counfel of God, in all that befals you, and particularly in afflicting providences; and do not entertain afflictions as the paftimes of fortune, as too many do. One great caufe why many of you are not ferioufly concerned to know and comply with the mind and will of God, in afflicting difpenfations, is becaufe you do not look upon them as ordered and appointed by him. Hence is that exhortation, *Hear ye the rod, and who hath appointed it* (*s*). When you meet with afflictions, you look upon them as cafual and fortuitous things; this is bad luck, or bad fortune, fay ye, and fo ye pafs it over. But that opinion that afcribes any event merely to chance or fortune, ought to be exploded from among Chriftians. *Affliction cometh not forth of the duft, neither doth trouble fpring out of the ground* (*t*). It comes not by chance, nor by a ftated courfe in nature, but by God's appointment and ordination.

Secondly, I proceed to fhew what is the general nature of of God's decrees, and in what fenfe they are attributed to him.

God's decree is varioufly expreffed in the holy fcriptures. It
is

(*p*) Eccl. ix. 11.   (*q*) 1 Kings v. 4.   (*r*) Prov. xvi. 33.
(*s*) Mic. vi. 9.   (*t*) Job v. 6.

is called his *decree*, his *purpose*, his *will*, his *pleasure*, his *counsel, the counsel of his will, his determinate counsel*, as I shewed already. Now, when decree or counsel are attributed to God, we must carefully advert, that we do not ascribe to him any thing favouring of imperfection, which attends the decrees and counsels of men; as if he consulted and deliberated concerning things to be done, as men use to do from ignorance or hesitation of mind. Such things can have no place in God, because of his infinite wisdom and knowledge, his immutability, and the simplicity of his essence. But decree and counsel are attributed to God, as they denote his wise and immutable determination concerning the after-being of things; as the most wise and stable determinations among men, are usually after much consultation and deliberation. The will and pleasure of God is alone instead of all counsel and deliberation, seeing it hath infinite wisdom joined with it. Therefore, in my text, the apostle doth not say, *after the will of his counsel*, as if counsel and deliberation went before, and the choice of his will followed after; but *after the counsel of his will:* To shew that his willing a thing to be done, is in place of all consultation about it. His will is his counsel.

But what are the decrees of God? They are well described in our Shorter Catechism, "The decrees of God are his eter-
"nal purpose, according to the counsel of his own will, where-
"by, for his own glory, he hath fore-ordained whatsoever
"comes to pass." Or, more briefly thus, "God's decree is
"his determinate purpose, whereby he hath fore-ordained
"whatsoever comes to pass." In it two things are usually distinguished by divines. 1. The act of his will purposing or decreeing: And so God's decree doth not differ really from his essence, being nothing else but the divine essence willing or decreeing. In this respect, God's decree is but one and necessary; of which after. 2. The respect, tendency, and relation it hath to things without God, or things to be brought to pass; which tendency or relation makes no change in God, nor adds any thing to him. In so far, God's decree differs from his essence, which involves no such tendency or relation. In this respect, God's decree is free, and considered as manifold.

Further, according to our manner of conceiving, God's decree implies these three things, 1. His knowledge of all things possible, called his "Knowledge of simple intelligence." From eternity he knew and saw all things possible in his own power. He had a perfect knowledge of his own power, and consequently of all things possible to be wrought by it. 2. His
free

free choice of some of these possible things, to be brought into a state of futurition or after-being. Whence is it that of all things possible, only such and such are future, or to come to pass? This is to be referred, not only to God's will, but also to his wisdom Hence, his decree is called his counsel. He had all things possible in his view, and pitched on such and such of them to be brought to pass, rather than others, as in his infinite wisdom he saw meet for his own glory 3. His determinate purpose to bring them to pass. And not only their being, but their manner of being and various circumstances, fall under the decree and purpose of God. Not only Christ's death, but the manner of it, and various circumstances, by what instruments, when, where, &c. All were determined by God's eternal counsel. His enemies did to him *whatsoever God's hand and counsel determined before to be done* (*u*).

SERMON LXX.

FROM what is said, and from my text, it appears that God's decree is, 1. The original spring and first rise of all things without himself. And, 2. The original copy or pattern of them.

1. It is the original spring and first rise of all things without himself. It is the decisive vote of God's everlasting decree and purpose, that translated such a number of beings and events, from the state of pure possibility, into a state of futurition; so that their futurition, or the certainty of their after-being, is founded in his decree, and to this they must be reduced as their proper spring and fountain. It is easy to conceive that there are a great many things possible, which yet will never be. Now, whence is it that of all things possible only such and such come to pass? That there is such a number of men, and no more? That there are such and such events of providence rather than others? All this is from the will and pleasure of God, his fixed decree and purpose: This determines his power. So that nothing comes to pass in time, but what was first conceived in the womb of God's everlasting purpose and decree. All the creatures, and all their actions, that have been, are, or shall be, all events of providence, take their rise originally from the eternal counsel of God's will, appointing such things to come to pass in time. *I appointed the ancient people*, says the Lord, *and the things that are coming, and shall come* (*x*).

2. God's

(*u*) Acts iv. 27, 28.   (*x*) Isa xliv. 7.

2. God's decree is the original copy and pattern of all things. He *worketh all things after the counsel of his own will,* as men do after a pattern or idea. So that whatever comes to pass in time, doth in all its circumstances and manner of being, exactly answer to God's eternal decree, as the impression made upon the wax answers to the engraving upon the seal. God's decree is, as it were, the idea according to which all things that come to pass are exactly expressed in time. Let me explain this a little. An idea is an imagination or conception in one's mind, representing the figure or pattern of a thing. Now, as every wise and free agent works according to some idea or pattern; so the ideas of all things may be said to be in the mind of God from everlasting, and that not only of things future, but even of all things possible. These ideas are nothing else but the very essence of God knowing his own perfections, and willing that such and such vestiges of them should be in the creatures, if ideas of things future; or not be, if they be ideas of things purely possible. Hence, as the divine essence is but one, so there is but one idea in God; yet because of the respect and relation it hath to things without God, it is considered by us as divers and manifold. Now, I say, the ideas of all things future are exactly expressed in the things themselves when they are brought into being. They are exactly according to the eternal ideas in the mind of God. As Moses was commanded to make the tabernacle and all the instruments thereof, *after their pattern, which was shewed* him *in the Mount:* So God *worketh all things after the counsel of his own will* (*y*). Another expression that may also serve to clear this, is that of the prophet: *Gather yourselves together — before the decree bring forth* (*z*). Where the divine decree is resembled to a pregnant woman. The child of the creature is first conceived in the womb of God's eternal decree, and then is in time brought forth into the light of actual being. God's decree is, as it were, with child of beings: They have an objective being in the will and decree of God, before they have an actual being in the world: And this objective being in God's decree is what we call the divine idea. All things that come to pass in time do exactly answer to the divine decree, or to the eternal ideas in the mind of God; as the tabernacle answered to the pattern, or as the birth answers to the conception. As the actual fashioning of David's body exactly agreed with the plat-form thereof laid down in God's book (*a*): So all things that come to pass are exactly framed

---

(*y*) Exod. xxv. 9, 40.   (*z*) Zeph. ii. 2.
(*a*) Psal cxxxix. 16.

ed and fashioned, as the draughts and lineaments were proportioned in God's decree. There is nothing in the works of his hand, but what was in the ideas in his mind from all eternity.

Use. Well then, let us not be stumbled at any event, especially when the providence of God seems to cross and contradict his promises. Sometimes great opposition is made to the gospel by such from whom better things were expected: Sometimes religion suffers by them that seem to be most zealous for it, and the church is wounded in the house of her friends: Sometimes the ruin of the church is threatened by a sad aspect of providences, &c. But let not these things offend you. All are ordered according to the counsel of God's will: They are under his wise appointment and ordination. And he that fore-ordained and determined those things to be done, could have determined quite otherwise, if he had not intended his own greater glory and the church's greater good by them. Therefore do not charge God foolishly, when things do not fall out according to your mind. When you see strange things come to pass, you wonder greatly at them: You wonder, how many worthy instruments of the Lord's work, and of public good, should be laid aside, or removed by death: You wonder how the enemies of the church should prosper in their wicked devices and enterprises. But all these were in the mind and heart of God from everlasting. And seeing you know from the holy scriptures, that such things are ordered and appointed for the glory of God and the good of the church; therefore be not stumbled at them. These are the accomplishments of the wise decrees and counsels of heaven. God knows what he is doing, and what he hath to do. Men have their ends, and God hath his. Whatever seeming confusions there are here below, yet all is clear and serene in his wise counsels. This made Luther, in the troubles of the church, to cry out, That it was far otherwise concluded in heaven than at Nurenburg.

Thirdly, I come in the next place to speak of the extent of God's decree. And, 1. It extends to all things that come to pass in time. For he *worketh all things after the counsel of his own will*: And, *known unto God are all his works from the beginning;* for *of him, and through him, and to him are all things;* and *who is he that saith, and it cometh to pass, when the Lord commandeth it not* (b). Nothing comes to pass but what he hath decreed; and nothing can come to pass otherwise than he hath decreed it should come to pass. His decree is of universal extent. It is past

upon

(b) Acts xv. 8. Rom. xi. 36. Lam. iii. 37.

upon every being and action in the world. There is a counsel or purpose of his will touching all things that have been, are, or shall be. He hath determined what number of men should live upon the earth, and fixed the times and places of their abode. So the apostle tells us, that he *hath made of one blood all nations of men, for to dwell on all the face of the earth, and hath determined the times before appointed, and the bounds of their habitation* (c). 2. It extends even to such possible things as shall never come to pass. As the eternal counsel of the divine will determined concerning such and such possible things, that they should be brought to pass; so the same eternal counsel hath determined, concerning all other possible things, that they shall remain in the state of pure possibility, and never come forth into being: So that the glory of all things that are not, as well of those that are, is due unto God. 3. It seems to extend to all possible connections between possible things, though God hath determined that neither of these possible things shall come to pass. I adduce two passages in the holy scriptures for clearing this. One is concerning David's being at Keilah when Saul was pursuing him: *Then said David, Will the men of Keilah deliver me and my men into the hand of Saul? And the Lord said, They will deliver thee up* (d). Whence I observe, that there was a certain connection between David's staying at Keilah, and the Keilites delivering him up; and this connection could be founded in nothing but a positive decree of God: Yet it appears from the event, that God had also decreed, that neither should David stay at Keilah, nor the Keilites deliver him up. The other passage is concerning the king of Israel's smiting on the ground at the command of the prophet Elisha: The king *smote thrice and stayed;* whereupon the prophet said, *Thou shouldest have smitten five or six times, then hadst thou smitten Syria till thou hadst consumed it; whereas now thou shalt smite Syria but thrice* (e). If the king of Israel had smitten on the ground five or six times, then he had smitten Syria as many times, or, till he *had consumed it.* This connection was certainly founded on a positive decree of God: Yet God had decreed that the king should smite on the ground but thrice, and so overcome the Syrians but thrice. The absolute perfection of the divine decree seems to require that it should be extended to all things capable of an act of his will and pleasure, and consequently that it should be extended, not only to those things that come to pass in time, but even to such possible things as shall never come

(c) Acts xvii. 26.   (d) 1 Sam. xxiii. 12.   (e) 2 Kings xiii. 19.

come to pass, and to all possible connections between them. And this seems to be agreeable to what God hath revealed, as appears from the scripture instances I have adduced.

But God's decree, as it extends to these things that come to pass, is most proper for our consideration. Therefore that I may be a little more particular here, know that, according to our manner of conceiving, God's decree is either general or special. When we consider it as extended universally to all things that come to pass, we call that his general decree: But when we consider some things particularly, and what is decreed concerning them, we call that his special decree. And so there is, 1. The decree of creation. 2. The decree of providence. And, 3 The decree of predestination, which is most commonly called by divines, God's special decree. But this last requiring a more special consideration, I shall here speak only of the decree of creation, and the decree of providence.

1. The decree of creation. From all eternity God decreed to make such a number of creatures originally of nothing, to the glory of his power, wisdom, and goodness. *He hath created all things, and for his pleasure they are and were created* (*f*). Nothing is made without his will and pleasure. And this will and pleasure doth not only respect the works of creation in general, but also the manner of them, in which also his will and pleasure is accomplished. It was his will and pleasure to make them: And whereas he might have done it in this manner, or in another; by that same good pleasure it was concluded to be done as it hath now come to pass. And this is his end in so doing, that his good pleasure, which hath wisely moulded means for his own glory, might be accomplished.

2. The decree of providence. From all eternity God decreed to preserve the creatures so made by him, and to rule and govern them and all their actions. He did not, as some men dream, once create the creatures in a good state, and put them in capacity henceforth to preserve themselves, or exercise their own virtue and power, without dependence on him. He is not only the general original of motion and action; but he appoints and orders all immediately, and disposeth of all the particular actions of his creatures, and that according to the counsel of his own will. His decree extends even to inanimate creatures: According thereunto they are regulated in all their motions toward man. This is mentioned by the psalmist as matter of praise to God's name: *Let them praise the name of the Lord,* says

(*f*) Rev. iv. 11.

says he: *For he commanded and they were created: He hath also established them for ever and ever: He hath made a decree which shall not pass* (g). So, we read of *a decree made for the rain*: And of *a decree given to the sun* (h).

But let us especially consider God's decree concerning the government of his rational creatures. It extends to greater matters, as the incarnation and coming of Christ: *Lo, I come,* says he, *in the volume of the book it is written of me* (i). That is, it is written in the roll of God's eternal decree and counsel: And we read of the decree concerning the stability of Christ's kingdom (k). It extends itself also to small er matters as well as greater. Even the very *hairs of* our *head are all numbered:* And *in* his *book all* our *members are written* (l). All events of providence are under appointment by God's eternal decree. Our wives are appointed for us. *Let the same be the woman,* says Abraham's servant, *whom the Lord hath appointed out for my master's son* (m). That such a woman, rather than any other, should be wife to such a man, is by the decree and appointment of Heaven. Our children are appointed: Hence Eve says, God *hath appointed me another seed instead of Abel, whom Cain slew* (n). Death is appointed: *It is appointed unto men once to die* (o). And the season and time of it is appointed: Job puts the question, *Is there not an appointed time to man upon earth* (p)? The day of judgment is under an appointment: *He hath appointed a day in which he will judge the world in righteousness* (q). All our comforts are under appointment: Comforts temporal as well as spiritual; the summer seasons of our lives: Hence the prophet says, *Salvation will God appoint for walls and bulwarks* (r). All our afflictions are appointed for us: *Hear ye the rod,* says the prophet, *and who hath appointed it:* And says the apostle, *No man should be moved by these afflictions: For yourselves know that we are appointed thereunto* (s). The nature, the measure and degree, the season and continuance; all the ounces and grain weights of your cup, were all weighed in the scales of God's eternal counsel.

Yea, the most certain and necessary things, according to the course of nature, have no certainty in them but from the appointment of God, who hath established such a course in the creatures, and can suspend the same when he pleaseth.

And

(g) Psal. cxlviii. 5, 6. (h) Job xxviii 26. Prov. viii 29. (i) Psal. xl. 7. (k) Psal. ii. 7. (l) Matth. x. 29. Psal. cxxxix. 16. (m) Gen. xxiv. 44 (n) Gen. iv. 25. (o) Heb ix. 27. (p) Job vii. 1. (q) Acts xvii. 31. (r) Isa. xxvi. 1. (s) Mich. vi. 9. 1 Thess. iii. 3.

And there is nothing that falls out by chance to you, whether of greater or lesser moment, but what falls out by God's decree and appointment. Even the most casual and contingent thing, though it surprise the whole world, is no surprisal to him: An act of his eternal will and pleasure passed upon it. Yea, the most free actions of rational creatures, these wherein men exercise the power of their free-will, were fore-ordained by God's decree. Yet the decree of God doth not offer any violence to man's free-will, nor take away the liberty or contingency of second causes, but rather establish the same: Seeing God decreed so to order all things by his providence, that they should fall out according to the nature of second causes, either necessarily, or freely, or contingently.

Use. See here and admire the majesty of God's dominion. He is *wonderful in counsel, and excellent in working: Great in counsel, and mighty in work* (t). His dominion is of universal extent to all things, so that whatever he hath willed and decreed must needs come to pass, in spite of all opposition. *My counsel shall stand,* says the Lord, *and I will do all my pleasure* (u). And nothing can come to pass but what he wills: For, *who is he that saith, and it cometh to pass, when the Lord commandeth it not* (x)? The whole government of the world doth entirely depend on the determinate counsel of his will as supreme and absolute Sovereign: For *he doth according to his will, in the army of heaven, and among the inhabitants of the earth; and none can stay his hand.* And, *Who hath known the mind of the Lord, or who hath been his counsellor? For of him, and through him, and to him are all things.* He *gives kingdoms to whom he will:* He *divideth* gifts *to every man severally as he will:* And *he hath mercy on whom he will* (y). All is according to his will and pleasure. God's good pleasure is the supreme and satisfactory reason of all his administrations. He is absolute Lord, and hath no rule but his own will.

Well then, let us admire the majesty of his dominion. The prophet, when he contemplates the extent of divine providence to some of the creatures, cries out, *Who hath measured the waters in the hollow of his hand? And meted out heaven with the span, and comprehended the dust of the earth in a measure, and weighed the mountains in scales, and the hills in a balance* (z)? Now, these things

(*t*) Isa. xxviii. 29. Jer. xxxii. 19. (*u*) Isa. xlvi. 10. (*x*) Lam. iii. 37. (*y*) Dan. iv. 35. Rom. xi. 34, 36 Dan. ii. 21. 1 Cor. xii. 12. Rom. ix. 19. (*z*) Isa. xl. 12.

things he speaks of concerning the waters, the heaven, the dust of the earth, the hills and mountains, are but one small part of the execution of his decree: How much more cause then have we to be rapt up in holy admiration, when we contemplate the decree itself, which eminently containeth all; and to say, Who is this, that doth not only measure the waters, mete out the heavens, comprehend the dust, weigh the mountains and hills; but doth also exactly and infallibly comprehend and dispose of all things, of all events which have been, are, or shall be, in this world, or in the world to come, yea, and in hell itself, in one eternal act? Let us improve the consideration of these things, to raise in us high and admiring thoughts of the great God, a holy fear of his glorious name, and a deep reverence of his sovereign will and pleasure in all events of providence, and particularly in these events that are cross and afflicting to us: For all are according to the counsel of his will: And it is meet that our wills should stoop to his, and most unbecoming that foolish creatures should censure or find fault with infinite wisdom.

SERMON LXXI.

BUT there are two things in God's decree of providence that require a more special consideration, because of difficulties and controversies moved about them. As, 1. His decree about the futurition or after-being of sin. 2. His decree about the fixed and unmoveable term or period of the lives of men.

I shall at this time speak of the first of these. This is a subject wherein there is danger in speaking even that which is true; and great caution is necessary that we give no just occasion for any unworthy or unbecoming thoughts of the infinitely holy God. I shall, 1. Prove that God hath decreed the futurition of sin. 2. Shew why he hath done so. 3. Endeavour to clear this truth of some difficulties it seems to lie under; and then, 4. Make some practical improvement of the whole.

I. I prove that God hath decreed the futurition of sin. All sinful actions fall under the divine decree. Though sin itself flow from transgressing the law, yet the futurition of it is from the divine decree. No such thing could have been in the world, if it had not been determined by the eternal counsel of God for a holy and just end. This is most plainly asserted by the apostle Peter, with respect to Christ's death and sufferings at the hands of men; *Him*, says he, *being delivered by the*
deter-

determinate counsel and foreknowledge of God, ye have taken, and by wicked hands have crucified and slain (a)   And the church gives this account; *For of a truth against thy holy child Jesus, whom thou hast anointed, both Herod and Pontius Pilate, with the Gentiles, and the people of Israel, were gathered together, for to do whatsoever thy hand and thy counsel had determined before to be done* (b).   There never was nor can be a higher act of wickedness commited, than the murdering the Lord of glory: Yet it appears from these texts, that in this horrid scene, wicked men did no more but what God's hand and counsel determined before to be done.   Indeed, it cannot be conceived how sin should enter into the world, and disorder the whole creation, without the will and pleasure of God determining the event. That Adam should certainly fall, and that Christ should certainly suffer by the hands of wicked men, these were truths from eternity: Now these things being in themselves only possible, could not pass from a state of possibility to a state of futurition and after-being, and that from eternity, but from some cause without the creature, and consequently in God; to wit, his holy and wise decree and appointment concerning them. I might argue also from the actual providence of God. His providence in time is extended even to the sinful actions of men; he hath a holy and spotless hand of providence in them: And he doth nothing in time but what he did from all eternity decree to do, else there would be a change in him. So that it is evident that God hath decreed the after-being of sin. Hence it is that the futurition of sinful actions is spoken of as necessary. *It must needs be that offences come,* says our Lord; and, *Ought not Christ to have suffered these things* (c)? The rise of Antichrist, and the persecution of the church under his reign, are of the number of these things of which it is said, that *they must come to pass* (d).   There is a *must be,* a necessity, in respect of God's decree determining the event.

II. I proceed to shew why God hath decreed the futurition or after-being of sin   Indeed, it cannot be conceived that an infinitely holy Majesty should decree the futurition of sin, but for some great and glorious end.   True, sin in its own nature hath no tendency to a good end: If it end in any good, it is from the the over-ruling providence of God, and that infinite divine skill that can bring good out of evil, as well as light out of darkness.   Now the great and glorious end for which God
decreed

(a) Acts ii. 23.   (b) Acts iv. 27, 28.   (c) Matth. xviii. 7. Luke xxiv. 26.   (d) Rev. i. 1.

decreed the after-being of sin, is his own glory; and the ends subordinate thereunto are very many. Particularly, God decreed the futurition of sin, 1. That he might have occasion of glorifying his infinite wisdom, love, and grace, in the redemption and salvation of a company of lost sinners, through the death and sufferings of his own dear Son. 2. That his long-suffering patience, in bearing with and forbearing sinners, might be magnified, admired, and adored. 3. That he might be glorified by the repentance of his people, by their believing on Christ, and by their walking humbly with him. 4. That his justice might be glorified in the eternal damnation of reprobate sinners for their own sins; sin being the cause of their damnation, though not of their reprobation. Thus, I say, God decreed the futurition of sin for these holy and wise ends, that he might glorify his wisdom, in bringing good out of so great an evil, and a greater good than the evil he decreed to permit. Hence, an old father says †, " God judged it better " to bring good out of sin, than not to permit sin to be com- " mitted."

III. I shall next endeavour to clear this truth of some difficulties it seems to lie under. God's decree is distinguished by divines into that which is effective, and that which is permissive ‡: Not that his decree doth properly effect any thing, seeing it is an immanent act; but because there is an eternal decree, according to which he purposed, that in time he would effect some things and permit other things. 1. His effective decree respects all the good that comes to pass: Whatever hath any goodness in it, whether it be moral goodness, or natural goodness, as all actions and motions of the creatures as such, and even sinful actions, considered abstractly from any irregularity, obliquity, or deformity cleaving to them. True it is, there is a further goodness in spiritual and gracious actions: Yet even sinful actions have a goodness in them so far as they are actions; they have a goodness of being, considering them purely as natural, and abstractly from any irregularity in them. Concerning all these, God decreed to work and effect them; yea, even sinful actions, considered purely as natural: For he is the first and universal cause of all things, the fountain and original of all good. Hence it is said, even with respect to the

---

† *Deus judicavit melius de malis bene facere, quam mala esse non permittere.* August.

‡ *Non fit aliquid, nisi Omnipotens fieri velit, vel sinendo ut fiat, vel ipse faciendo.* Aug. Enchir. C. 95.

the oppression of the church by wicked men, *Our God is in the heavens; he hath done whatsoever he pleased (e)*. 2. His permissive decree doth only respect the irregularity and pravity that is in sinful actions: God decreed to permit the same; or he decreed it to be, himself permitting it. Hence it is said, *He suffered all nations to walk in their own ways* (*f*): And God doth nothing in time but what he did from all eternity decree to do. So that the futurition of sin is from the decree of God. God hath determined that it shall be. He did not determine to have any efficiency in sin, considered as such: But he willed that it should be done, himself permitting it. The counsel of God did not determine to do it, but that it should be done (*g*).

We see from what hath been said, that our doctrine doth not make God the author of sin. The sinful action, considered purely as a natural action, God decreed to effect by his providential influence: and so decreed to be the author of the action as such But as for the evil cleaving to the action, God decreed only to permit that. And he decreed to permit it, or willed it to be through his permission, for a better end, viz. The manifestation of his own glory; of the glory of his mercy on the elect, and the glory of his justice on the reprobate. Now, though sin as sin be evil, yet the being of sin for a better end is good: And God's decree is not the cause of sin, but only of the futurition of it; as indeed it is not the cause of any thing that comes to pass, but only of the futurition of things; the decree being an immanent act, which can have no influence, physical or moral, upon any thing without God. Though the decree be the antecedent or foregoer of sin, yet it is not the cause of it; and though sin be the consequent of the decree, that is, something infallibly following upon it, yet it is not the effect thereof.

But it may be said, If sin follow necessarily upon the decree, then sinners cannot be blamed, because God's decree lays them under a necessity of sinning. I answer, Sin doth not follow the decree by a necessity of co-action or compulsion, which indeed would destroy human liberty; but by a necessity of infallibility, which is very consistent with it. It is sufficient unto human liberty, or the freedom of man's will, that a man act without all constraint, and out of choice: Now, this is not taken away by the decree: Men sin as freely as if there were no decree, and yet as infallibly, as if there were no liberty:
And

(*e*) Psal. cxv. 3.   (*f*) Acts xiv. 16.   (*g*) Acts iv. 28.

And men fin not to fulfil God's decree, which is hid from them; but to ferve their lufts and corrupt affections.

To conclude, I confefs there are great difficulties here, and it is hard to loofe all knots. Yet this muft not incline us to deny or part with what is plain and evident truth. I have proved the univerfal extent of God's decree even to the finful actions of men; and it is plain that God neither is nor can be the author fin Now, fhall we deny either of thefe plain truths, becaufe we cannot folve all the difficulties about them? This is contrary even to reafon itfelf: For it is a received rule, even amongft philofophers, that when a man hath once embraced an opinion upon juft grounds and reafons, he ought not to defert it, merely becaufe he cannot anfwer every objection made againft it. There are a great many things in nature, of the truth whereof we are well affured, and yet we cannot untie all the knots and intricacies about their natures, properties, and operations: And muft it not be much more fo in the fublime truths of God? Hence a learned divine faith, that in this matter we are now upon, † "It is certain there
" are many things in which we ought humbly to acknowledge
" the weaknefs of our underftanding, retaining what we have
" certain out of the fcripture, notwithftanding difficulties, the
" folution and perfpicuous underftanding whereof we find by
" experience is not given to man in this life." And an ancient Father * fays, " Shall we therefore deny that which is
" manifeft, becaufe we cannot comprehend that which is hid-
" den? Shall we fay, that which we fee to be fo, is not fo,
" becaufe we cannot find why it is fo?"

IV. I come to make fome practical improvement of this truth.

Ufe 1. For caution, in two particulars.

1. Take not occafion from this doctrine to entertain any unworthy or unbecoming thoughts of the infinitely holy God, as if he were a favourer of fin, or any way approved of it.

Men

---

† *Certiſſimum eſt in hac materia multa eſſe in quibus humiliter agnoſcere debemus Mentis noſtræ Imbecillitatem; Retinentes quod ex Scriptura certum habemus, non obſtantibus difficultatibus, quarum ſolutionem & perſpicuam intelligentiam homini in hac vita datam non eſſe experimur.* Rivet. Carth. Orth. Tom 2. Tract. 4. Qu. 6.

* *Nunquid ideo negandum eſt quod apertum eſt, quia comprehendi non poteſt quod occultum eſt? Nunquid, inquam, propterea dicturi ſumus, quod ita eſſe perſpicimus, non ita eſſe, quoniam cur ita ſit non poſſumus invenire.* Auguſt. de Perſever. L. 2. Cap. 14.

Men are naturally apt to entertain blasphemous notions of God, as if he were not so holy as indeed he is, but some way approved of their sinful and wicked course. But though God decreed the permission of sin, yet this doth not infer his approbation of it in any sort: For he did not decree to give any indulgence to it by a moral permission: But he decreed to permit it by withholding from men that help and grace which is necessary to prevent it. And God was not obliged to prevent the commission of sin. His supreme and absolute dominion and sovereignty exempts him from any such obligation. There is nothing in the nature of God that could oblige him to hinder the entrance of sin into the world. And then, he did not decree to permit sin as sin, or barely for itself, but for a greater good, his own glory.

2. Let none of you abuse this doctrine, by taking liberty to sin. Think not that you are warranted to commit sin, because God decreed to permit it for his own glory. Do not take liberty to sin for this end, that God may have glory by it. Consider, 1. No man can sincerely intend or will the glory of God by sinning. The reason is, because sin is in its own nature, directly opposite to his glory; it is most dishonourable to him. Now, will you pretend to design the glory of God, by doing that which is directly contrary to his glory? How absurd is this? Hence, 2. No thanks to you if God have any glory by your sin. For sin doth not glorify him in its own nature, but dishonour him: So that when you sin, all your activity is spent in dishonouring him and acting against his glory. Therefore, if he get any glory by your sin, you are only passive instruments of his glory: You do not bring glory to God by your sin, but God brings glory to himself out of your sin: So that God is not at all beholden to you for any glory he gets by it. 3. Our actions are not to be measured by the event of them, but by the divine rule. Though God decreed to permit sin for his own glory; yet you are not to measure your actions by his decree, or by the intended event, but by the rule of his word. Now sin is contrary to the rule of his word: You do thereby violate God's holy law, and break his commandment. 4. Though God decreed to bring glory to himself out of the sins of wicked men, yet he decreed also take vengeance on their persons: As wise politicians make use of the treasons of others, but do not reward the traitors. God got glory to himself by the death and sufferings of Christ; yet doubtless many that were the murderers of him were turned into hell. God will glorify himself in the eternal salvation of

many thousands, by the effusion of that blood, for the shedding whereof many will be eternally damned. What encouragement can it be to you to commit sin, that God will get glory by it, when you are not assured that he shall have the glory of his pardoning mercy, but have cause rather to fear that he shall get the glory of his vindictive justice, by taking vengeance on you for sin? As God said of Pharaoh, *I will get me honour upon Pharaoh, and upon all his host* (h). How was that? Even by breaking him in pieces, and destroying him and his army in the Red-Sea. 5. Though God decreed to bring glory to himself and good to his people out of their sins, yet it is never without a great deal of grief and sorrow of heart to themselves. They are *saved, yet so as by fire* (i). Sometimes God makes use of the sins of his people, to make them more humble and watchful for the time to come: But they first suffer a great deal of loss in the peace of their own souls, so that they go to heaven ordinarily with broken bones and bleeding hearts. Upon these grounds, I say, that God decreeing to permit sin for his own glory, gives no encouragement to any of you to commit sin.

Use 2. Is it so that God hath decreed to permit sin for his own glory? Then labour ye to make such use of the sins that abound in the world, and of your own sins, as by occasion of them God may be more glorified by you. And, 1. As to the sins of others: Take occasion from them to give God the glory of his admirable patience in bearing so long with wicked sinners, and forbearing the execution of deserved wrath, notwithstanding of their hainous provocations. And you that are believers in Christ would take occasion from the sins of others, to admire and praise the free grace and mercy of God toward your own souls. O bless God that he hath given you another heart than he hath given to the wicked of the world. Had it not been for free grace, you had been as bad as they. 2. As to your own sins: Give glory to God by a humble confession of them. Let the sense of them drive you to Christ, that God may have glory by your believing on him. Let the remembrance of your sins beat down your pride, and your rash and uncharitable judging and censuring others, and engage you to humble walking with God. And let believers in Christ, take occasion from their sins, to admire and praise the free grace of God in pardoning them, and in renewing and changing their hearts. Thus, I say, take occasion from your own

and

(h) Exod. xiv. 17.   (i) 1 Cor. iii. 15.

and other mens sins, to bring glory to God. This is to join issue with God, in a way proper to you, for bringing about the glorious end for which he decreed to permit sin, to wit, the glory of his own name.

SERMON LXXII.

ANOTHER thing in God's decree of providence that requires a special consideration, is his decree about the fixed and unmoveable term of the lives of men. That I may speak a little on this head from clear scripture ground, see Job vii. 1. *Is there not an appointed time unto man upon earth?* Job having, in the preceding chapter, expressed his desire to die, doth here confirm and justify his desire from the common condition of man's life in this world. As if he had said, seeing man's life in this sinful and miserable world, is limited to a certain and short time; is it any crime for me to desire that God may bring my life to a happy period? *Is there not an appointed time unto man upon earth?* This question imports a strong affirmation, *Is there not an appointed time?* Surely, there is. AN APPOINTED TIME, or *a warfare:* So it is rendered in the margin of some Bibles. The word in the original signifies both *a warfare* and *an appointed time.* The reason is, because wars, of all other actions and affairs, have their seasons and appointed times. So that the plain meaning is, there is a set and appointed time for the troublesome and warfaring life of man. It is added, *upon earth;* because in heaven all variety and distinctions of times and seasons evanish.

From these words you may take this doctrine, The time of man's life in this world is determined and appointed by the Lord.

Because this truth is denied by the Socinians and Arminians, that they may the more easily maintain the mutability of the divine decrees, and the independent indifferency of the free-will of man; therefore I shall, at this time, insist a little upon it; and shall, 1. Clear this truth a little. 2. Confirm it. 3. Make some practical improvement of it.

I. For clearing this truth, I observe these things. *Obs.* 1. We must distinguish between the common term of man's life in general, and the particular term of each individual man's life. As to the first, it is granted by all that there is a common term of man's life, and that this is variable in particular men; many come short of it, and some exceed it. Of this common term of man's life the psalmist speaks; *The days of our years are threescore and ten, and if by reason of strength they be fourscore years, yet is their strength labour and sorrow* (a). Seventy or eighty years is the common date of the life of man, which few exceed, and multitudes never come near.

Obs. 2. The question is not, if every man shall die, or if his life shall come to a period at one time or other; for this also is granted by all: But the question is, if God hath determined how long every man shall live in this world, and at what time he shall die, even to a moment; and if the term of the lives of men be unmoveably fixed and determined in God's eternal decree and purpose; which is that we assert.

Obs. 3. The term of man's life may be considered, either absolutely, or respectively. Considered absolutely, it is unmoveably fixed and determined by God's decree. But if we consider the term of man's life respectively, and that either with respect to what is common among men, or with respect to the course of nature, and the particular temper and constitution of mens bodies, or with respect to what either they themselves or others expected; in these respects, the term of man's life may be either lengthened or shortened; though this also be only according to the will and pleasure of God. Accordingly, we read often in scripture, of *God's lengthening the days* of the godly, and *shortening the days* of the wicked. The fifth commandment hath a promise of long life: And God promised to Solomon, that he would *lengthen his days*. On the other hand, it is said, *That bloody and deceitful men shall not live out half their days* (b). Now, these and the like expressions in scripture are not to be understood of lengthening or shortening the term of life decreed by God; but of lengthening or shortening the time that the ordinary course of nature might bring men unto, and which they or others expected they might arrive at. Some live a much shorter time than otherwise they might have lived by the course of nature, God having determined to cut them off by an untimely death: And others live longer than either they themselves or others expected. But we speak here of the term of man's life considered absolutely; and so we say, that God hath, in the eternal counsel of his will, determined and appointed, how long every man shall live upon the earth, so that he shall assuredly live so long, and no longer: And when mens days are either lengthened or shortened, in either of these respects I mentioned, this is nothing else

but

(a) Psal. xc. 10.   (b) Exod. xx. 12. 1 Kings iii. 14. Psal. lv. 24.

but what God determined and appointed in the eternal counfel of his will. And fo I come,

II. To confirm this truth: And I fhall do it in thefe three propofitions.

Propof. 1. The time of our life is determined and appointed by the Lord. *His days are determined,* fays Job; *the number of his months are with thee; thou haft appointed his bounds that he cannot pafs* (*c*). The time of our life is bounded and limited, our days determined, and our months numbered by the Lord. He hath determined what number of days and months every man fhall live. *He hath determined the times before appointed* (*d*). The time of every man's life. Hence the pfalmift prays, *Lord, make me to know mine end, and the meafure of my days, what it is* (*e*). Our days are meafured. They are *as the days of an hireling,* faith my text. As an hireling hath a fet time for work, fo every man and woman hath an appointed time for work in this world. We are but pilgrims and ftrangers on the earth, and in a little time muft be gone hence; and the time is fixed and determined. We are here like men upon a ftage, to act our parts; and in a little time we muft go off, and others will come in our room. Our glafs is always running, and the day and hour when it will be run out is fixed by a divine decree.

Propof. 2. We cannot live beyond the time that God hath fixed and determined. We have an *appointed time upon earth,* and beyond that we cannot go. Our *days and months* are *numbered* by the Lord (*f*): When that number is fulfilled, then we muft die. God hath *appointed our bounds that we cannot pafs.* As the raging fea cannot pafs the bounds that God hath fet to it, fo neither can the life of man. Our *days* are *meafured* (*g*): When we have filled up our meafure, we muft prefently be gone to another world. When the time is come that the Lord hath appointed for putting a period to our life, we can live no longer. Kings and emperors muft die at the time appointed, All angels and men cannot keep us in life one moment beyond the Lord's appointed time; nor can we ourfelves do it †. *There is no man that hath power over the fpirit,*

(*c*) Job xiv. 5. (*d*) Acts xvii. 25. (*e*) Pfal. xxxix. 4. (*f*) Job xiv. 5. (*g*) Pfal. xxxix. 4.

† *Certa quidem finis Vitæ Mortalibus adftat:*
  Nec Devitari Lethum pote quin obeamus. Lucret. L. 3.

Nemo nimis cito moritur, qui victurus diutius quam vixit non fuit.

rit, to retain the spirit; neither hath he power in the day of death, and there is no discharge in that war; neither shall wickedness deliver those that are given to it (h). There is no bribing of death when it cometh to our door with a summons to remove.

Propos. 3. Our life shall not come to a period, till the Lord's appointed time come. Till the number of our days and months be fulfilled, death cannot surprise us. Every man shall fill up his measure before death come. True it is, our life is threatened by manifold accidents we are liable unto, both from within and from without: But † even these things that are merely accidental in respect of us, are are all ordered by a supreme over-ruling hand of divine providence; so that nothing can fall out without the will, pleasure, and providence of God. Says our Lord to his disciples, *Are not two sparrows sold for a farthing? And one of them shall not fall to the ground without your Father. But the very hairs of your head are all numbered. Fear ye not therefore, ye are of more value than many sparrows* (i). If God hath an over-ruling hand of providence even in these accidents that may reach the life of a sparrow, much more in these that may reach the life of a man. Therefore it is often given as a reason why our Lord's enemies did not apprehend him, that his *hour was not yet come* (k). We have a clear instance for the proof this, in Isaiah xxxviii. 1—5. where we read that God added fifteen years to Hezekiah's days: Not to the days that God had decreed he should live, but to the days he had already lived. Now, Hezekiah had been sick unto death; his disease was in its own nature mortal; and he would have certainly died, if God had left him to the strength of his disease, verse 1. There was no hope of his recovery, unless God had wrought a miraculous cure, which the Lord accordingly did, that he might not die till these fifteen years were expired. Whence I observe, that God will rather work miracles for the preservation of a man's life, than that he should die before his appointed time. God will so over-rule all accidents, that death shall not come sooner than the time appointed by himself.

I shall add some general reasons or arguments, for the confirmation

---

fixus est cuique Terminus, manebit semper ubi positus est, nec illum ulterius Diligentia aut Gratia promovebit.

Sen. de Consol. ad Marc. C. 20.

† *Et pace & bello cunctis stat terminus ævi.*

Extremumque Diem primus tulit. Sil. Ital.

(h) Eccl. viii. 8. (i) Matth. x. 29, 30, 31. (k) John vii. 30. and viii. 20.

firmation of this truth. And, 1. I argue from scripture prophecies. In scripture God hath often foretold the term of particular men's lives. He set 120 years to the lives of those that lived in the old world before the flood came upon them. He foretold the term of Moses's life, of the life of Jeroboam's child, of the life of Ahaziah king of Israel, and of divers others (*l*). Now, if God certainly foretold the term of some particular mens lives, then he certainly foreknew the same; and it cannot be imagined whence he should have such a foreknowledge, but from his own eternal decree. 2. Even the most casual deaths among men are determined by God's immutable decree and purpose. I give instance in Ahab, whose fall at Ramoth-Gilead, was foretold by the prophet Micajah: And yet it is said to be casual; *A certain man drew a bow at a venture, and smote the king of Israel* (*m*). 3. I argue from God's absolute and sovereign dominion over men, and his irresistible and incontestible power to dispose of them as he pleases, particularly with respect to life and death; for he is Lord of life and death. Hannah tells us in her song, *The Lord killeth, and maketh alive: He bringeth down to the grave, and bringeth up* (*n*). And says the Lord, *I kill, and I make alive* (*o*). It is God that directs the arrows of death: Death is his messenger, and strikes whom and when he bids: He *turneth man to destruction, and says, Return, ye children of men* (*p*). 4. Many things depend on the lives of men being shorter or longer. Now, if there were no certainty of the term of mens lives, there could be no certainty of the futurition or after-being of the many things that depend upon the same; and this would exempt a great variety and multitude of events from the decree and purpose of God, contrary to the doctrine that I have formerly proved from the holy scriptures.

But it may be and is objected, that if this doctrine be true, then the use of means for the preservation of life and health, would be utterly unnecessary: For carnal men reason thus, If God hath appointed and determined how long I shall live, then I shall not die sooner, though I neither eat nor drink. But this is a wrong way of arguing, as appears from what the apostle Paul says to the mariners and others in the ship with him. He had assured them from God that there should be no loss of any of their lives; yet when some were about to flee

out

(*l*) Gen. vi. 3. Deut. xxxi. 14. 1 Kings xiv. 12. 2 Kings i. 4, 16. (*m*) 1 Kings xxii. 20, 34. (*n*) 1 Sam ii. 6. (*o*) Deut. xxxii. 39. (*p*) Psal. xc. 3.

out of the ship, he says to the centurion, *Except these abide in the ship, ye cannot be saved;* and he exhorts them to take some meat, telling them that this was for their health (*q*). Whence it appears, that as God had decreed to save their lives, so he had decreed to save them in the due use of ordinary means; so that they were to use the means for the preservation of life and health. The plain reason is, because God's decree about the end, includes the decree about the means necessary for obtaining that end. Though God hath decreed how long we shall live; yet, seeing it is his ordinary way to work by means, and he hath commanded the use of them; therefore it is still our duty to use lawful means for preserving life and health, and to wait on God in the use of them, refering the event to his wise determination.

SERMON LXXIII.

III. I Shall now make some practical improvement of this truth.

Use 1. For instruction. It follows from this doctrine, that God is the only Lord and Master of time. Time is his, and not ours. He gives time, and denies it, at his pleasure. Hence the Lord says of Jezebel, *I gave her space to repent* (*a*). Whatever time we have, it is his gift. Our *times are in* his *hand* (*b*).

Use 2. For reproof to them that live so as if they were absolute masters of their own time. It is certainly a great affront offered to God, when men live so as if their times were in their own hand, and not in his. But who do so? 1. Such as promise to themselves more time and days, without respect had to the purpose and appointment of God. Here is the reason why many are surprised by death †; they are still expecting and promising to themselves more time, but in a moment they and all their *thoughts perish* (*c*). Hence Solomon adviseth, *Boast not thyself of to-morrow: for thou knowest not what a day may bring forth* (*d*). 2. Such as boast of their undertakings and enterprizes, and the great things they will do, without a reservation of the will and pleasure of God. Sennacherib, king of Assyria, sent Rabshakeh to rail upon Hezekiah and the men of Jerusalem; and he threatened to make them *eat their own dung,*
and

(*q*) Acts xxvii. 22, 23, 24, 31, 34.
(*a*) Rev. ii. 21.   (*b*) Psal. xxxi. 15.
† *Multos vitam differentes mors incerta prævenit.* Jo. Benedict, Parif. in Annot. in Luc. 12. ex Senec.
(*c*) Psal. cxlvi. 4.   (*d*) Prov. xxvii, 1.

and drink their own piss, &c. but what followed? An hundred eighty and five thousand of Sennacherib's army were killed by an angel in one night, and Sennacherib himself was murdered by his two sons. Many boast that they will do such and such things, but forget that their time and breath is in the hand of the Lord; as Pharaoh, Exod. xv. 9, 10. Against such the apostle speaketh, James iv. 13, 14. 3. Such as promise to themselves great outward plenty, peace, and prosperity, for many years to come. *Their inward thought is, that their houses shall continue for ever, and their dwelling-places to all generations* (e). The rich man, in the parable, did thus abandon himself to sensuality: *Soul, thou hast much goods laid up for many years; take thine ease, eat, drink, and be merry* (f). But see what follows, verse 20 *But God said unto him, Thou fool, this night thy soul shall be required of thee: then whose shall these things be which thou hast provided.* Carnal men would enjoy their earthly comforts, without any thoughts of death: but death will be a sad messenger to them. 4 Such as delay repentance upon a presumptuous hope that they shall have time to repent afterward. I may, say some, follow carnal pleasures while I am young: I hope I may have time enough to repent before I die †. But remember that your times are in the hand of the Lord; and many candles have been put out before they were half burnt. How suddenly may the number of your days be fulfilled, and then you must be gone.

Use 3. For exhortation; in two branches.

Exhort. 1. To you all in general.

1. Do not seek earthly things as your portion. Why will you have your portion in this life, when God hath set a period to it? Your enjoyment of earthly things is limited to a certain time and day, after which you can enjoy them no longer. God hath appointed your time upon the earth: therefore live as pilgrims and strangers in it. Do not set your hearts upon the world, but labour to have your affections weaned from all things here below. And if God give you plenty of outward good things, learn to use and possess them as being shortly to part with them; and protest, as an eminent holy man did, that you will not be put off with these things.

2. Own and acknowledge God as the Lord and Master of your time. It is he that hath determined the number of your days,

---

(e) Psal. xlix. 11.   (f) Luke xii. 19.

† *Alienus est a fide, qui ad agendam pænitentiam tempus expectat senectutis.* Jo. Benedict. Parif. in Annot. in Luc. 12.

days, and appointed your time upon earth. Therefore, if you have time and days continued to you, acknowledge him thankfully, especially considering that time is a precious talent.

3. Labour to improve the time that God gives you. To excite and quicken you to this, consider, 1. You have much and great work to do. The work of your salvation is no easy work, but very difficult, and will prove an uptaking work to you, if you be rightly employed about it: And how diligent soever you be, you will have enough to do when you come to die. 2. The time of this present life is the only time you have for this work: For, *There is no work, nor device, nor knowledge, nor wisdom, in the grave whither thou goest* (g). In the grave there is no contriving or acting for the honour of God, or promoting your own eternal happiness; therefore be diligent: *Whatsoever thy hand findeth to do, do it with thy might.* 3. The time of this present life will come to an end. Your days and years are numbered, and your time is appointed. You cannot live one moment beyond the time appointed by the Lord. Your time for work is limited and fixed, *as the days of an hireling* (h). 4. Your time will shortly come to an end. God hath *made your days as an hand-breadth*, and your *age is as nothing before* him. What is your life, but as *a vapour that appeareth*, and suddenly *evanisheth* (i); even like that puff of breath that goeth out of our mouth? It is but a few days, and then comes your last day. 5. Your time is not only short but uncertain. It may be, you shall not live one day longer. The Lord may come when it is yet midnight with you, when you are most secure, and least expecting his coming †. Death may surprise you on a sudden. This day, for ought you know, you may throw your last cast for eternity. 6. You must give an account to God how you spend your time. God keeps an exact account what time he gives you. *I gave her space to repent*, says the Lord: And, *These three years I come, seeking fruit on this fig-tree, and find none* (k). And there is a day of reckoning coming, when God will say to you, *Give an account of thy stewardship* (l). O, what will you answer to God on that day? 7 Misspent time will one day be more bitter to you than death. If ever God open your eyes, and awaken your conscience, and give you grace to repent, then the thoughts of misspent time will be matter of bitter grief and sorrow to you.

(g) Eccl. ix. 10.   (h) Job vii. 1.   (i) Psal. xxxix. 5. James iv. 14.

† *Nihil tam firmum cui periculum non sit, etiam ab invalido.*

(k) Rev. ii. 21. Luke xiii. 7.   (l) Luke xvi. 2.

You will be apt to cry out, *How have I hated instruction, and my heart despised reproof; and have not obeyed the voice of my teachers, nor inclined mine ear to them that instructed me* (m). But if misspent time be not bitter to you within time, yet it will be so at death and judgment. How will it gall you to the heart then, that you wasted your time upon vanity, and spent it idly and unprofitably: And you would then give ten thousand worlds if you had them at command, for another lease of your time, but shall never have it. 8. Well spent time will be sweet to you in the last review. When you are about to launch forth into the depths of eternity, O how sweet and refreshing will the conscience of well spent time be to you! How sweet will it be, when you can say with the apostle, *I have fought a good fight, I have finished my course, I have kept the faith: Henceforth there is laid up for me a crown of righteousness* (n).

But what shall we do that we may improve time well? I give these following directions. 1. Make the glorifying God, and the saving your own soul your great business in the world. This is the end of your creation, the great errand upon which God sent you into the world; and that which is the great end of your creation, ought to be the great scope and business of your lives. Let all your other lawful business be directed to this as your great end, how you may glorify God, and be most useful and serviceable in your generation, and save your own soul, and the souls of others, in your place and station. 2. Lament misspent time. You have already had many days and years; but, alas, how little have you done for God, and for your own soul? Lament this before the Lord. The more you lament the misspending of time past, you will be the more concerned how to improve the little bit of time that may be yet before your hand. 3. Often call yourselves to an account how you spend your time. Your deceitful heart, like an unfaithful servant, will be apt to take the more liberty, when it is not called to a reckoning. Many take so much liberty to waste their time upon vanity, because they consider not what they are doing. Therefore sit yourselves often before the bar of your own conscience. 4. Think deeply and frequently upon your last accounts. Think on that day when we must all stand before the judgment-seat of Christ, and give an account of our time. And if you be not able now to answer your own conscience, how much less will you be able to answer the great God on that day? 5. Redeem some competent time from your worldly affairs and business, to be

(m) Prov. v. 12, 13.   (n) 2 Tim. iv. 7, 8.

be spent in the duties of God's immediate worship. It is very sad, when your other lawful business swallows up the time that ought to be spent in religious duties. Time may be ill spent, even in business that is in itself lawful, yea, necessary. Labour therefore to redeem some time for reading and hearing the word, for prayer, meditation, self-examination, &c.

Exhort. 2. To believers in Christ. 1. Learn to be content with your lot. Study a humble submission to the will of God under all the troubles and afflictions you meet with in this present life. God hath appointed your time upon earth, and consequently the time of your trouble. Your life will come shortly to an end, and that will be the end of all your misery. It is but winking, as the martyr said, and then in heaven. Therefore submit to God, to be long in trouble, and short while at ease, as he pleaseth. 2. Be faithful in your duty to God, notwithstanding of all the threatenings of men. Do not fear them that threaten your life for his sake; for they shall not be able to take it away, till his appointed time come. Our Lord's enemies had no power to apprehend him, because *his hour was not yet come* (*o*). And see what he saith to his disciples, Matth. x. 28, 29, 30, 31. The psalmist, upon this ground, encouraged himself to trust in God: *They devised to take away my life*, says he: *But I trusted in thee, O Lord: I said, thou art my God; my times are in thy hand* (*p*). In the greatest dangers, he trusted in God, because he knew that life and death were in his hand, and not in the power of cruel and bloody men. You may therefore go boldly on in your duty to God, being firmly persuaded that the most blood-thirsty enemies shall not be able to anticipate his time. Till the time appointed by the Lord, he himself will be a guard to you, so that the malice of men shall not be able to reach you. 3. Learn to use the means for the preservation of life and health without anxiety. Your life being a trust committed to you, it is your duty to use lawful means, and to take care of your health; but guard against anxiety and perplexity of mind. Be not anxious about more time, but rest confidently on him who hath times and seasons in his hand. He will allow you time, so long as he hath use and service for you: And when he hath no more service for you, you should be content to be gone. 4. Live in a constant expectation of the end of your time and days. Be always waiting and looking for death till it come, as Job resolved to do: *All the days of my appointed time*, says he, *will I wait till my change come* (*q*).

SER-

(*o*) John vii. 30.   (*p*) Psal. xxxi. 13, 14, 15.   (*q*) Job xiv. 14.

SERMON LXXIV.

Fourthly, I come in the next place to speak of the properties of the divine decree. God's decree is eternal, most wise, most free, absolute and independent, immutable, effectual, one and simple. And because these are generally controverted, and the right understanding of them contributes not a little to give light in a great many controversies with the Jesuits, Socinians, and Arminians, therefore I shall insist a little upon them.

Propert. 1. God's decree is eternal: Without beginning, from everlasting. His foreknowledge of what comes to pass is eternal: *Known unto God are all his works from the beginning of the world* (a): Therefore his decree must be eternal; seeing he could not foresee things that come to pass but in his own decree. As they were known from the beginning, so they were decreed from the beginning: As they are known at once so are they decreed at once. Hence the wisdom of the gospel is said to be *ordained before the world* (b). The apostle expressly asserts the decree of election to be eternal, when he says, *He hath chosen us in him before the foundation of the world:* And, *He hath saved us, and called us, —— according to his own purpose and grace, which was given us in Christ Jesus, before the world began* (c): And heaven is called *the kingdom prepared* for Christ's people, *from the foundation of the world* (d). And if election be eternal, all God's other decrees must be so too; for they are all of the same nature, and there is the same reckoning to be made of them. True, God is often spoken of as deliberating and consulting in time, after the manner of men; to denote the wisdom of his administrations; as the wisest administrations among men are usually after much consultation and deliberation. But there can be no new thoughts or purposes in God, because of his eternity and immutability. It cannot be imagined of him, that he should afterward conceive some purpose which formerly he had not; or, that he should attain to a certainty of some events, which once he was destitute of †. Nor is it consistent with his wisdom, to ascribe new purposes
on

(a) Acts xv 18. (b) 1 Cor. ii. 7. (c) Eph i. 4. 2 Tim. i. 9. (d) Matth. xxv 34.

† *Non est in Deo accidens motus, nec nova voluntas, nec temporale Consilium, nec Cogitatio ejus cum rerum mutabilium inæqualitate variatur.* Ambros. L. 2 de Voc. Gent. C. 10.

or decrees to him; seeing nothing can occur to him which he did not foresee, to put him upon consulting and advising, as it is among men. So that all God's decrees and purposes must be from everlasting.

And as in eternity there is no succession; so, with God there is no succession of counsels and purposes. He did not first decree one thing, and then another, but all at once. It is true, there is an order in the divine decrees, according to our manner of conceiving, in respect of the things decreed, which have an order in the execution. But God's decree concerning all things that come to pass, considered as it is in him, is but one simple act; as I shall shew you afterward. He comprehends all things together, and at once, in one moment of eternity. There is a succession in the execution; as in the decree of election, first grace, and then glory: But the decree to bestow both, was in one and the same moment of eternity.

Let me apply this head. And,

1. Hence we see, that it must be unaccountable boldness and folly for us, to censure the counsels of God; because we are but creatures, and receive a being in time; but God's decrees and counsels are eternal. The eternity of the divine decrees sets them above all our bold inquiries and censures. Shall we who are but of yesterday, presume to measure the eternal motions of the divine will in our shallow understandings? We cannot understand the reasons of many things within time; and shall we dare to censure the eternal counsels of an infinite Being? Therefore, when any unworthy notion of the counsels of God is suggested to you by Satan, or by your own corrupt hearts, look backward to the eternity of them, and silence yourselves with that question, whereby the Lord put a stop to Job's reasonings, *where wast thou when I laid the foundations of the earth* (e)?

2. Here is matter of comfort to you who are believers in Christ. You may take comfort in the thoughts and purposes of God toward you. His gracious promises are declarations of his purposes; they shew what his thoughts and purposes are toward you, that they are purposes of love, mercy, and grace. Now, these his purposes are eternal; so that his love toward you is of an ancient date. He *hath loved thee with an everlasting love* (f). And his love to you, and gracious purposes toward you, being eternal, are also unalterable. Having once loved you, he will love you for ever; so that you need not

(e) Job xxxviii. 4.   (f) Jer. xxxi. 1.

not fear he will caft you off. Surely God will not forget you, nor caft you off, feeing he hath borne a good will to you from eternity.

Again, it is comfortable, that his gracious promifes to you are fure promifes, and cannot fail of an accomplifhment. They are ftrong grounds of confidence, being the fruits of God's eternal counfel. They are unalterable, and ftand faft for ever. As nothing can intervene to hinder, or to make a change in his eternal counfels; fo nothing can intervene to hinder the accomplifhment of his promifes.

Further, here is ground of comfort with refpect to the church. The holy fcriptures declare what are the counfels and purpofes of God in reference to the church, to wit, to build and eftablifh her, to protect and defend her againft the power and policy of hell: And as we have heard thefe counfels and purpofes are eternal, and confequently they ftand to all generations. All the powers of darknefs, all the wicked potentates of the earth, fhall not be able to put God upon any new purpofes or counfels about his church. There may be variations and changes in our fight; the winds may tack about, and every day new and crofs accidents may happen, which may threaten the church with fhipwreck: But this is comfortable, he whofe counfels and purpofes are eternal, fits at the helm, and the winds and waves obey him.

Propert. 2. God's decree is moft wife. Hence it is called in my text, *The counfel of his will.* His will is always one with wifdom. His will doth, as it were take counfel and advice of wifdom, and difcern according to the depth and riches of his underftanding Thefe two, Will and Wifdom, are often feparated among men: And indeed there is nothing fo diforderly and uncomely, as when Will is feparated from Wifdom, when men follow the dictates of their own will againft reafon and confcience. But the counfels and purpofes of the divine will are depths of wifdom unfearchable. As for example, There is infinite wifdom in decreeing to bring about all things in the moft convenient order, fo as may conduce moft to God's fupreme and chief end, to wit, his own glory; in appointing fubordinate ends to his glory; in chufing and appointing fuch means as moft conduce to thefe ends, and difpofing and ordering them in fuch a way as is moft fuitable thereunto. Some dark fhadow and refemblance of this is to be obferved in the wife counfels of men: But O the unfearchable depth that is in the counfels and purpofes of God! He is *a God of judgment* (g).

He

(g) Ifa. xxx. 18.

He acts judiciously and rationally; so that he decreed nothing without reason, though his wise reasons are often hid from us.

The wisdom of the divine decrees is manifest in the execution of them, though oft-times it is not observed or attended unto by men. It is seen, 1. In creation: For the world is established in an excellent order. Hence the psalmist cries out, *O Lord, how manifold are thy works! In wisdom hast thou made them all* (*h*). When we consider how God hath disposed variety of excellencies in the world, our hearts are struck with reverence and admiration, in contemplating the wisdom of the contrivance. If we consider the glorious fabric of the world, the beautiful order established in it, and the sweet harmony it keeps in all its motions; O it must be an infinitely wise counsel that contrived it. Man now, having the idea of this world in his mind, might imagine many other worlds bearing some proportion and resemblance to this: But if we had never seen nor known this world, we could never have imagined the thousandth part of what is in it. Creatures must always have some example or copy given them: But what was his pattern in framing the world? *Who hath been* HIS *his counsellor* (*i*)? Who gave him the first rudiments and principles of that art? None at all. He had no pattern of the world given to him, but it is absolutely and solely his own wise contrivance. 2. In providence. The administration of all things is ordered in perfect wisdom; for he *worketh all things after the counsel of his own will*. The counsel of God runs throughout his providence. There is an excellent contexture of occurrences that renders the whole frame the more beautiful. *He hath made every thing beautiful in his time* (*k*). Indeed, at first view, there are seeming confusions in the government of the world, and the events that happen in it: But when the whole work is done, and all is viewed together, O then it is full of beauty. One part of providence taken out of the frame seems very uncomely; and providences viewed singly and apart, seem to be full of confusion and disorder; but viewed together and in their contexture, there is admirable beauty, and a depth of wisdom seen in the contrivance. Yea, the wisdom of God is to be seen even in the follies of men; and the disorders of second causes fall under the order of the First Cause. 3. In redemption. Men and angels could never have contrived any possible way of salvation for lost sinners: But when all creatures were non-plused with the case of fallen man, and none of

---

(*h*) Psal. civ. 14.   (*i*) Rom. xi. 34.   (*k*) Eccl. iii. 11.

of them could entertain one thought of a remedy, then infinite wisdom contrived a way of salvation for us. And O the depth of wisdom that is in this contrivance! Here is *hidden wisdom*, and *the wisdom of God in a mystery*, and *the manifold wisdom of God* (*l*). Though the glorious angels pry into this depth, yet they are not able to search it to the bottom.

From all this it appears, that there is an unsearchable depth of wisdom in the divine decrees; so that we may cry out with the apostle, *O the depth of the riches both of the wisdom and knowledge of God! How unsearchable are his judgments, and his ways past finding out! For who hath known the mind of the Lord, or who hath been his counsellor* (*m*)?

For application of this head,

1. Let us contemplate with holy admiration the wisdom of the divine decrees and counsels in the execution of them, and particularly in creation and redemption. Can we behold such a glorious and beautiful fabric as this world is, and the exact harmony and temperament in all the creatures, one creature answering the ends and designs of another? Can we view the distinct beauties of the several creatures, and all together, like different strings in an instrument, giving forth diverse sounds, and yet all reduced to a delightful order and harmony. And especially can we behold the glorious work of redemption, wherein such different interests are reconciled? I say, can we contemplate these things, and not admire the wisdom of the contrivance? The wisdom of men and angels is worse than nothing and vanity, in comparison of this vast ocean: Therefore let us adore and reverence the great God on the account thereof.

2. Let us reverence this infinitely wise God in all his ways of providence. There is no case wherein he doth not direct all the acts of his will by counsel. Nothing is done by him in a rash way, but all is the result of his wise counsel: Therefore reverence his determination. Do not quarrel or murmur, whatever your lot in the world be: It is the lot that infinite wisdom hath carved out for you. Do not censure God in any of his ways. There are secrets of widom beyond your reach, and depths of wisdom that you cannot fathom. You are bound to believe that he hath infinitely wise reasons for what he doth, though your shallow capacity cannot comprehend

---

(*l*) 1 Cor. ii. 7. Eph. iii. 11. 1 Pet. i. 12. (*m*) Rom. xi. 33, 34.

hend them. Therefore acquiesce in his proceedings, and learn to adore, rather than censure.

Propert. 3. God's decree is most free. He is a most free agent, discerning, appointing, and ordaining concerning his own works, as he pleaseth. *Is it not lawful for him to do what he will with his own* (n)? He is not liable to any account. He hath power to determine concerning the work of his hands, as he sees meet, as *the potter hath power over the clay* (o). It is true, God cannot be conceived to have been at any time indifferent to decree or not decree; because then his decree had not been eternal. It is true also, that it is necessary that he decree and will something in general: And some things in God's decree are necessary, in regard of his own perfections, as to punish sin once permitted by him.

Yet in decreeing these things that come to pass, he is free,

1. From a necessity of nature, or a necessity in respect of the objects: So that there is no necessary connection between his being and the being of the things decreed by him. He had no need of them; he might have been without them. He had been blessed for ever, though they had never been. But † how the divine will and appointment doth freely go out to the objects, is a mystery too deep for us to search into. Yet this we can warrantably and safely say, that if God had never resolved to create any thing without himself, he had been infinitely blessed then as now, because of his infinite self-sufficient perfection. God needs not go out of himself for any additional happiness to his being, as we poor finite creatures must do. Such is our want and indigence, that we must needs go out of ourselves for the happiness of our being: But God's own glorious being yields him infinite content and satisfaction. He comprehends in himself all possible perfection, infinitely beyond what can be conceived by any creature; so that he needs not go without himself to seek love and delight; for it is all within him. Having all imaginable perfections in himself, in an infinite and transcendent manner, his decreeing to make the world, and his doing of it, adds nothing to his inward blessedness and contentment.

SER-

(n) Matth xx. 15. (o) Jer. xviii. 6.

† *Objecta a Deo nequaquam necessario volita esse demonstrare possumus: Quomodo tamen nutus divinus libere transeat ad objecta, perscrutari non est nostrum.* Twis. pref. in lib. de Sc. Med.

SERMON LXXV.

2. FROM any moral obligation. God had done the creature no wrong, though he had never decreed or willed it to be. He was under no obligation from the creatures, to appoint or determine so or so concerning any of them. He cannot become a debtor to any creature, further than he is pleased to make himself a debtor by his own promise: For *who hath first given to him, and it shall be recompenced unto him again* (a).

3. From any motive or cause besides or without himself. Nothing † can move him but his own will and pleasure. This is the only cause and reason, why he hath disposed and ordered all things thus, and no otherwise. Thus it is in his eternal appointments with reference to the immortal souls of men, as the apostle tells us: *He hath mercy on whom he will have mercy; and whom he will he hardeneth* (b). And this is the cause assigned by our blessed Lord; *I thank thee, O Father*, says he, *Lord of heaven and earth, because thou hast hid these things from the wise and prudent, and hast revealed them unto babes. Even so, Father, for so it seemed good in thy sight* (c). His own will and pleasure is the cause of all. And if it be so in matters of the deepest concern, it must needs be so in all other things. We may find many inferior causes, many peculiar reasons, of this or that way of administration of things, and many ends or uses for which they serve; for there is nothing that the infinitely wise God hath appointed, but is for some reason and use: Yet we must rise above these inferior causes, and ascend at last to the sovereign will and pleasure of God, as the supreme reason and cause of all, and the original of all the order, administration, and use of the creatures. Herein lies a great difference between the purposes of God and the purposes of men. Something is presented to us as good and convenient, that moves our will to purpose and determine, that we will seek after it, and use the means to obtain it; so that the end which we propose to ourselves hath an influence upon our purposes. But

‡ no

(a) Rom. xi. 35. (b) Rom. ix. 18. (c) Matth. xi. 25, 26.

† *Causas Voluntatis Dei sine fine quærunt, cum voluntas Dei omnium quæ sunt ipsa sit causa —Compescat ergo se humana temeritas, & id quod non est non quærat, ne id quod est non inveniat.* Aug. L. 1. de Genes. contr. Mani. c. 2.

‡ no created thing can thus determine the great God: Nothing in the creature can move him: But himself, his own glory, is the great end, which he loves for itself, and for which he loves other things. The creature having no actual being, could not move him. That which is the effect of the decree, could not be the cause or motive thereof. It is true, † God willeth one creature to be for the use of another, and he willeth one thing in order to another: Yet that other is not the cause of his so willing. As for example, God willed other creatures here below for the use and service of man, so that man is the subordinate end of their being: Yet man is not the cause of God's willing their being to that subordinate end. It was not man's goodness and perfection, but merely God's own will and pleasure, that moved him to appoint the other creatures for his use, that both he and they might be for the glory of God. Again, he willed effectual calling in order to justification, and both in order to glory: Yet his will and pleasure is the original and cause of this order; he doth not find this order, but make it.

4. From all co-action and compulsion. No force could be put upon him, considering his absolute power, dominion, and independency: For *who hath resisted his will* (d)? He decreed and willed other things besides himself, and determined and appointed so and so concerning them, out of his mere good pleasure. It is *lawful for him to do what he will with his own:* And he hath *predestinated us unto the adoption of children by Jesus Christ to himself, according to the good pleasure of his will;* and hath *made known unto us the mystery of his will, according to his good pleasure which he hath purposed in himself* (e). Considering his infinite wisdom, he decreed nothing but with reason and judgment, and consequently with infinite complacency.

For application of this head,

1. Let me exhort you all to admire and praise God's free goodness to each of you in particular. As, 1. That it was his eternal will and pleasure, that you should have a being, and such

---

‡ *Qui causam quærit voluntatis divinæ, aliquid majus ea quærit, cum nihil major sit.* Lombard. Lib. 1. Dist. 45 post August. L. 1. de Genes contr. Mani. c. 2.

† *Deus vult hoc esse propter hoc, sed non propter hoc vult hoc.*
                                    Thom. P. 1. Q. 19 Art. 5.
Deus hoc vult esse et hoc, et hoc propter hoc. Hoc est, Deus vult et effectus esse et causas, non tamen propter Causas vult effectus.
                            Twiss Lib 1. De Elect. part 2.

(d) Rom. ix. 19. (e) Matth. xx. 15. Eph. i. 5, 9.

such a being; that you should be rational creatures, capable of glorifying God, and enjoying him as your portion. God was under no necessity to will so concerning you; he had been blessed for ever, though you had never been. Therefore admire and praise his free goodness. How admirable is it, that he would from all eternity entertain any thought of such worthless nothings as you are. 2. That it was his will and pleasure, that you should be born and brought up in such a part of the world, wherein you hear the joyful sound of the gospel, and the glad tidings of salvation by Christ, and have the rich offers of Christ and salvation through him tendered to you on most gracious terms. God was under no necessity, no obligation lay on him, so to appoint and determine concerning you: Nothing moved him to it but his own will and pleasure. O, how admirable is it, that God should of his own good pleasure dispose and order your lot under a clear gospel-light, when so many thousands are left to walk and wander in darkness, and know not whither they are going! To conclude, 3. All the mercies you receive, and all the blessings you enjoy, are the fruits of God's eternal purpose and counsel concerning you. His own will and pleasure is the original spring of them. It was merely of his good pleasure that he appointed such blessings for you. Admire his free goodness, and praise his name.

2. More particularly, let me exhort you who are the children of God, to admire and praise his free-love, grace, and mercy toward you. All your gracious receipts and enjoyments, all your spiritual blessings and privileges, all are free in the original spring and fountain of them, to wit, the eternal decree and purpose of God. That you should be effectually called and converted, and drawn to Christ; that you should be brought into favour with an offended God through him; that you should have access to and communion with God; and that your souls should be refreshed and satisfied with the goodness of his house: All this is *after the counsel of his own will*. It was from all eternity that he purposed to be thus gracious unto you. And he was under no necessity nor obligation to discern and appoint such blessings for you; nothing moved him to it, but his own will and pleasure. O then, what cause have you to admire the freedom of his grace! " Who and what am I, that the " blessed God should have had such purposes of love and grace " from eternity for the like of me!" O bless and praise his name. His will, his own will, is the fountain of all the love and grace that is let out upon you. Nothing but the will and pleasure of God, made the difference between you and the

vilest sinners in the world. And it is not the will of ministers, but the will and pleasure of God, in every ordinance, that doth you good: You are *born, not of the will of man, but of God* (*f*). All the grace and blessings you have received, are conveyed to you originally from his own hand, and are dispensed according to his free and gracious purpose. O then, admire his grace, and bless his name.

Propert. 4. God's decree is unchangeable. He *resolves the end from the beginning*, and *his counsel stands* (*g*). The psalmist tells us, *The Lord bringeth the counsel of the heathen to nought; he maketh the devices of the people of none effect: The counsel of the Lord standeth for ever; the thoughts of his heart to all generations* (*h*). And, says Solomon, *There are many devices in a man's heart; nevertheless the counsel of the Lord, that shall stand* (*i*). It stands unmoveable. Hence we read of *the immutability of his counsel* (*k*). His counsel is immutable; his decrees unalterable. This follows from the eternity of them. That which is eternal is unalterable; one and the same, yesterday, to-day, and for ever. † He cannot lay aside his eternal purposes, and form new ones. This appears also from the wisdom of his decrees. The Medes and Persians boasted of their decrees, that they altered not: But doubtless their folly was often seen in this; for even the wisest among men may err in their decrees, and in this case, it is a great point of wisdom to alter them. But there can be no blots or blemishes in the counsels of infinite wisdom to occasion a change. If God could change his purposes, it must be either to the better or to the worse: But he cannot change to the better, because then he was not wise in his former purpose; nor to the worse, because then he would not be wise in his present purpose. There are many things that may occasion a change of purposes among men; but nothing can be imagined that should occasion any alteration in the counsels and purposes of God. 1. Men alter their purposes sometimes out of a natural levity that is in them. But he is *the Lord that changeth not:* And *with him is no variableness, neither shadow of turning* (*l*) Being unchangeable in his nature, therefore his decree and counsel is unalterable. 2. Among men, sometimes some impediment falls out, which they did

---

(*f*) John i. 13. (*g*) Isa. xlvi. 10. (*h*) Psal. xxxiii. 10, 11. (*i*) Prov. xix. 21. (*k*) Heb. vi. 17.

† *Statuerunt, quæ non mutarunt; nec unquam primi consilii Deos pœnitet.* Sen. de benef. L. 6

(*l*) Mal. iii. 6. James i. 17.

did not foresee, and this makes them alter their purposes. But nothing can fall out but what God himself decreed, and foreknew from the beginning; therefore he may come to a fixed resolution from all eternity: and being resolved, he can see no reason of change, because nothing can appear to him which he did not perfectly discover from the beginning. 3. Men change their purposes sometimes through a defect of power; they are not able to do what formerly they intended to do. But God being Almighty, cannot be forced to a change. *He is in one mind, and who can turn him* (m)? Devils and men cannot do it. They cannot force him to change his mind. *There is no wisdom, nor understanding, nor counsel against the Lord* (n). No created power hath strength enough to be a bar against God. He can break through all impediments in his way. 4. Men do oft-times change even their good purposes, because such is the perverseness of their wills, that they cannot be constant in any thing that is good. But no such thing can be imagined of the infinitely perfect and infinitely blessed God. He is infinitely pure and holy, and there is *no iniquity or unrighteousness in him* (o).

True it is, God is often said to repent: But that is said of him after the manner of men. God is pleased to speak to us of himself in borrowed terms, and useth our own dialect, to point out to us our great ignorance of him, and our utter incapacity to conceive of him as he is in himself. Because men use not to change their manner of dealing, without some repentance and change of mind; therefore, when God changeth his outward dispensations, he is said to repent. Yet when he changeth all things about him, he is not changed; for all these changes were at once in his mind from eternity. All these various changes of dispensations, with respect to which God is said to repent, were decreed and determined by him from everlasting: So that, though he change his dispensations, yet he never alters his counsels. In this sense he cannot repent, cannot change his mind. *God is not a man, that he should lie: neither the son of man, that he should repent: And, the strength of Israel will not lie nor repent: For he is not a man, that he should repent* (p).

For application of this head,

1. Here is matter of terror to such of you as live and go on in sin. It is the purpose of God declared in his word, to take vengeance

(*m*) Job xxiii. 13.   (*n*) Prov. xxi. 30.   (*o*) Deut. xxxii. 4. Psal. xcij. 15.   (*p*) Numb. xxiii. 19. 1 Sam. xv. 29.

vengeance on all unbelieving impenitent sinners. *He that believeth not, shall be damned. Except ye repent, ye shall likewise perish* (q). And his purpose is immutable and unalterable. It is not to be expected that God will alter his purpose, and change his mind, to gratify your lusts: You may as soon expect that he will cease to be God, that you may continue to be wicked. Therefore, there must either be a change in you, and a gracious change, else the wrath and vengeance of God will unavoidably overtake you.

2. Here is great encouragement to believe in Christ. The counsel of God declared in his word, is that *whosoever believeth on Christ*, whatever difficulties he meet with from within or from without, *shall certainly be saved* (r). And the immutability of his counsel herein is made so evident, that there is no place left for any objection against it. The apostle tells us, that *God willing more abundantly to shew unto the heirs of promise the immutability of his counsel, confirmed it by an oath: That by two immutable things, in which it was impossible for God to lie, we might have a strong consolation, who have fled for refuge to lay hold upon the hope set before us* (s). A greater encouragement to believe there cannot be. Your salvation is sure and certain upon your believing. There is a certainty of the event, because of the immutability of God's counsel; so that it cannot miscarry.

3. Here is ground of comfort to you that believe in Christ. The assurance of your present comforts, and of your future glory, depends on the counsel of God, and that is immutable. True, you are to use your own earnest endeavours, to attain all necessary grace, and to persevere in grace that you may come to glory: You are to *give all diligence to make your calling and your election sure* (t). Yet, it is comfortable that your perseverance in grace, and your future glory, do not depend on your own endeavours, but upon the immutable will and purpose of God. And indeed, this alone is able to bear the charges of so great a work.

4. Here is a ground of patience under afflictions. The time of your trial is appointed by the immutable purpose and counsel of God; so that you yourselves cannot shorten it, and wicked men cannot lengthen it. Therefore do not strive against God, by giving way to murmuring and discontent. God is stronger than you, to make good his own purpose. Hence Job says, *He is in one mind, and who can turn him? And what his soul desireth*

(q) Mark xvi. 16. Luke xiii. 5.   (r) John iii. 15, 16.
(s) Heb. vi. 17, 18.   (t) 2 Pet. i. 10.

fireth even that he doth. *For he performeth the thing that is appointed for me* (*u*). It is spoken by him with reference to his afflicted condition. God's counsel shall stand: In vain is all your struggling against it. Therefore be patient under affliction, and wait God's appointed time for your deliverance. *In your patience possess ye your souls* (*x*).

SERMON LXXVI.

Propert. 5. GOD's decree is absolute and independent; not depending on any doubtful condition of an uncertain event. Our adversaries say that God decreed to save such and such men, upon condition they would believe and repent; leaving it in the power of their own free-will, to believe or not, to repent or not, as they please. But all God's decrees and appointments are peremptory, not depending on the variable will of man, but only on his own will and pleasure. *Even so, Father,* says Christ, *for so it seemed good in thy sight* (*a*). And the apostle tells us, he hath *predestinated us according to the good pleasure of his will;* and hath *made known unto us the mystery of his will, according to his good pleasure, which he hath purposed in himself* (*b*). All is according to his own will and pleasure, and not the will and pleasure of man. His decrees are eternal and immutable, and therefore can have no dependence on temporary and variable conditions. And it is not agreeable to his infinite wisdom, so to work as to determine nothing concerning the end of his work; to make man, and not to appoint what shall become of him. Nor is it consistent with the love he bears to his own glory, to have creatures more beholden to themselves than to their Maker. And if any of the divine decrees did depend upon uncertain and doubtful conditions, thence it would follow that he were not the first and universal cause of all things, nor certain of future events, and that all things did not depend on him. How absurd is it, to make the great God depend upon a poor creature, and the will of God upon the will of man.

It cannot be denied, that there are means of the execution of the divine decree, God having decreed to bring about such and such ends by certain means subordinate thereunto. But, 1. Such means cannot, by any propriety of speech, be called conditions. It is one thing, to decree a thing upon a certain condition;

(*u*) Job xxii. 13, 14. (*x*) Luke xxi. 19.
(*a*) Matth. xi. 26. (*b*) Eph. i. 5, 9.

and another thing, to decree a thing to be brought to pass by such means. 2. The means for attaining the end, are under an absolute and peremptory decree, as well as the end itself. 3. Admit that these means might be called conditions; yet they could not be called conditions of the decree, but only of the execution thereof, or of the things decreed. So, if faith and perseverance be called conditions of decreed salvation, because salvation cannot be expected without them: Yet they are not conditions of God's eternal decree to save this or that man. It was not upon condition of their faith and perseverance, that God decreed to save them; but by decreeing to save them, he decreed to give them faith, and grace to persevere, and all other necessary means of salvation; so that both the necessary conditions or means of salvation, and salvation by these means, are decreed absolutely. It is not doubted, but that God by his eternal decree, ordained that in the execution, this or that event should not follow, but upon this or that going before. As for example, That the salvation of such as come to ripeness of years, should depend on their believing, repenting, and persevering: That the safety of Paul and these in his company, should depend on the mariners staying in the ship. Yet this is not to make God's eternal decrees to depend on the contingent acts of man's free-will; but only to make temporal events or things, to depend conditionally one upon another, for their being or not being in time.

As for conditional promises and threatenings, these being annexed to divine commands, do not pertain to God's will of decree, but to his will of command; and so do not infer any conditional decrees: But they depend on God's absolute decree concerning the connection of the end with the means. As for example, *Believe, and thou shalt be saved:* The truth of this conditional promise depends on an absolute decree, whereby faith is inseparably connected with salvation. Again, when the apostle says to believers, *If ye live after the flesh, ye shall die* (c): The truth of that conditional threatening, depends on an absolute decree of God, whereby living after the flesh is inseparably connected with eternal death.

We see then that all God's decrees are absolute and independent. Men have such imperfect desires, "I would do such " a thing, or have such a thing done, if it were not for this or " that:" But there are no imperfect or half-wishes in God. Again, men have conditional purposes and resolutions, "I resolve " to speak to such a man, if I meet with him in such a place, or if
" I

(c) Rom. viii. 13.

"I find him in a good disposition." But it is impossible that an eternal, unchangeable and independent Being should waver thus in suspense. What he wills and decrees, he wills and decrees absolutely and peremptorily, that it shall be.

This doctrine of the absoluteness and peremptoriness of God's decree, doth not discourage the use of means; because in his decree the end and the means are inseparably knit together, in so far as God decreed to bring about the end by such means, and no otherwise; so that the use of the means is necessary for attaining the end. And the use of the means being a part of the decree, and the effect of it, the knowledge of this cannot but be an obliging and encouraging motive to the use of them, yea, an effectual motive to all that fear God.

For application of this head,

Let me exhort you who are belivers in Christ, to admire and praise the free love and grace of God toward you. God hath promised eternal salvation to you that believe in Christ: This promise is a declaration of his eternal counsel and purpose: and that is absolute and peremptory. This is that which I would have you to bless God for, that his purpose of salvation to you that believe, is absolute and peremptory, and is not suspended on any uncertain conditions left in the power of your own free-will. It is true, as it is necessary that you believe in Christ, so it is necessary that you persevere in grace to the end; for only such as endure to the end shall be saved: Yet it is not left in the power of your own free-will, to persevere or not, as you please; but your perseverance is that which God hath absolutely undertaken for in the new covenant, by that promise, *And I will make an everlasting covenant with them, that I will not turn away from them, to do them good; but I will put my fear in their hearts, that they shall not depart from me* (d). God hath promised that he will not turn from you, and that you shall not turn from him for ever. And this promise is absolute and peremptory, and consequently is a declaration of an absolute and peremptory purpose of God. Indeed, if it were left in the power of your free-will, you are such changeable and mutable creatures, that you might soon chuse to depart from God totally and finally. But God hath promised so to determine your will, that you cannot chuse but persevere. Not only your salvation, but also your perseverance in order to it, is decreed absolutely; so that your salvation cannot miscarry.

Propert. 6. God's decree is effectual. As he himself cannot change it, so none can hinder the execution of it. What he purposes

(d) Jer. xxxii. 40.

purposes doth infallibly come to pass, as is evident from these texts: *The Lord of hosts hath sworn, saying, Surely as I have thought, so shall it come to pass; and as I have purposed, so shall it stand.* And, *The Lord of hosts hath purposed, and who shall disannul it? And his hand is stretched out, and who shall turn it back? He is in one mind, and who can turn him? And what his soul desireth, even that he doth. Hath he said, and shall he not do it? Or hath he spoken, and shall he not make it good? Yea, I have spoken it, I will also bring it to pass; I have purposed it, I will also do it* (e). Whatever his will and pleasure is, that he doth. So the psalmist tells us, *Our God is in the heavens; he hath done whatsoever he pleased:* And, *Whatsoever the Lord pleased, that did he, in heaven, and in earth, in the seas, and all deep places* (f). He is almighty, and carries on the pleasure of his will, by his efficacious providence, without controul. His decree and counsel obtains the effect, by his wisdom directing, and his power executing. Hence, God's hand and counsel are joined together. It is said of Christ's enemies, that they were *gathered together, to do whatsoever* God's hand and his *counsel determined before to be done* (g). His will in due time applies almighty power to fulfil the desires of it; and almighty power being set a-work by his will, cannot but *work all things after the counsel of his will.* His counsel cannot be frustrated, seeing he wants neither skill, nor will, nor power, to bring it to pass † Whatsoever he hath purposed and decreed, either with respect to whole nations in general, or with respect to private persons in particular, shall certainly be accomplished. This is clear from variety of experiences, especially these recorded in the holy scriptures. When God hath manifested or declared his purpose, as sometimes he was pleased to do by the prophets; this purpose and counsel of his, hath still been exactly and infallibly accomplished. We have an instance of this, in the relief of Samaria, in the time of a terrible famine. The prophet Elisha foretels that there would be great plenty on a very sudden. But a certain nobleman looked on that as incredible, and said, *Behold, if the Lord would make windows in heaven, might this thing be* (h)? Yet it came to pass, as the prophet had foretold it, and that in all its circumstances.

(e) Isa. xiv. 24, 27. Job xxiii. 13. Numb. xxiii. 19. Isa xlvi. 11.
(f) Psal. cxv 3. and cxxxv. 6. (g) Acts iv 28.
† *Impossibile est ista non fieri, quia nec incerta præscientia Dei est, nec mutabile consilium, nec inefficax voluntas.*
Ambr. L. 1 de Voc. Gent. C. 3.
(h) 2 Kings vii. 1, 2, 18, 19, 20.

circumstances. Another instance is the Lord's bringing the children of Israel out of Egypt. God had declared his counsel and purpose in that matter unto Abraham: *Know of a surety,* says the Lord, *that thy seed shall be a stranger in a land that is not theirs, and shall serve them, and they shall afflict them, four hundred years* (*i*). The four hundred years are to be computed from the beginning of the affliction there mentioned, which began with Isaac in the land of Canaan: But there were four hundred and thirty years from the first promise made to Abraham, or from the confirmation thereof by the gift of Isaac. Now, this purpose was exactly accomplished, as Moses tells us: *And it came to pass, at the end of the four hundred and thirty years, even the self same day it came to pass, that all the hosts of the Lord went out from the land of Egypt* (*k*). From these and other instances, it appears, that the decree and purpose of God never fails of its accomplishment †.

And who can hinder him to perform what he hath purposed? What power will attempt it? Good angels neither can nor will resist his will. Devils, though they would, yet they cannot: For he hath them chained, and sets bounds and limits to them. Good men, who know his will, and love it, are willingly led by it, and yield themselves to his disposal. Wicked men, even the highest and mightiest, cannot hinder it: For their breath is in their nostrils, so that they soon perish at his will and pleasure: And all their power and wisdom, is but weakness and folly comparatively to his. He can unhinge the best laid counsels of men, so that no counsels nor endeavours of theirs can frustrate his purposes. This the psalmist declares; *The Lord bringeth the counsel of the heathen to nought: He maketh the devices of the people of none effect. The counsel of the Lord standeth for ever; the thoughts of his heart to all generations* (*l*). Balaam attempted to curse Israel; but he could neither do nor speak any thing against the purpose of God. As his counsels ar settled and established; so according to this establishment, he settles or unsettles all the purposes and projects of the sons of men. He *frustrateth the tokens of the liars, and maketh diviners mad. He turneth wise men backward, and maketh their knowledge foolish* (*m*). We see then that no created power can hinder the execution of the divine decrees. Yea, suppose the

(*i*) Gen. xv. 13.   (*k*) Exod. xii 41.

† *Quod statuit Deus, nulla potest ratione non fieri.*
Ambr. L 2. de Voc. Gent. C. 10.

(*l*) Psal. xxxiii. 10, 11.   (*m*) Isa. xliv. 25.

the power and strength of all creatures were united together in one; yet, being finite, it could lay no bar in the way of Omnipotency. And then the creatures can do nothing without God, much less against him: And all of them, angels, devils, and men, are subject to him as their supreme Lord; they are all at his beck: So that he can lead them on by an invisible hand, and apply them, quite contrary to their own purpose, to execute the counsel of his will.

But it may be said, If the decrees of God do necessarily obtain the effect, then whatever cometh to pass, cometh to pass necessarily? Indeed it is so; and yet some things come to pass freely, and other things contingently, according to the nature of second causes. For God's decree doth not impose a necessity upon the things themselves, but only infer a necessity of of the event, which is very consistent with the liberty and contingency of second causes. In the last place, let us advert, that man's disobedience to God's will of command doth not frustrate his intention or purpose; because his commands do not express or signify what he purposes or intends to have done, but what is man's duty to do. But there is nothing he intends or purposes to be done, but he will certainly do it, or make it to be done. If it be a work of his own power alone, himself will do it alone: But if he require the subordinate working of creatures in it, as means and instruments; then he will effectually apply them to their work, and not wait in suspense for their determination.

For application of this head,

1. Here is matter and ground of comfort to you who are the children of God. And that, 1. With respect to yourselves in particular. God's counsel and purpose, about your salvation; which is declared in the promises of the covenant, shall be infallibly accomplished: So that not all the devils in hell, nor all the wicked men in the world, nor all the corruptions that are in your own hearts, can hinder or obstruct your salvation. 2. With respect to the church in general. God hath declared in his word what his counsels and purposes are with reference to his church; to wit, that *she shall be established;* that *the gates of hell shall not prevail against it;* that *no weapon formed against her shall prosper;* that *he will make her a burdensome stone for all people;* that *kings shall be her nursing-fathers, and queens her nursing-mothers* (n): And these counsels and pur-

---

(n) Psal. lxxxvii. 5. Matth. xvi. 18. Isa. liv. 17. Zech. xii. 3. Isa. xlix. 23.

purposes shall certainly be accomplished, in spite of all the gates of hell. Wicked men may have contrary counsels; the powers of the world may combine together, and consult and plot the ruin of the church: But *he that sitteth in the heavens shall laugh; the Lord shall have them in derision* (o). He will infatuate and blast the counsels of men, that he may establish and accomplish his own. Hence the prophet gives a defiance to all wicked affociations against the church: *Affociate yourselves, O ye people, and ye shall be broken in pieces: And give ear, all ye of far countries: Gird yourselves, and ye shall be broken in pieces: Gird yourselves, and ye shall be broken in pieces. Take counsel together, and it shall come to nought: Speak the word, and it shall not stand: For God is with us* (p).

2. Take heed of opposing yourselves to any of the counsels and purposes of God declared in his word. Men are guilty of doing so divers ways. Seeing God hath appointed the gospel and ordinances thereof, to be the ordinary means of salvation; therefore when men oppose themselves to the planting or spreading of the gospel, or endeavour to extirpate it, or labour to corrupt God's pure ordinances with the inventions of men; this is to oppose themselves to God's counsel. Again, God hath declared his counsel and purpose concerning Antichrist; that he shall fall, and that the kingdom of the beast shall be overturned: Therefore when men endeavour to support the antichristian kingdom, to spread popery, to promote the interest of a popish pretender to the throne, and thereby to bring the Romish yoke again upon our neck; this is to oppose the counsel of God. I beseech you, search the holy scriptures, and labour to discover what God's counsel is: And when you see and know his counsel, O take heed of opposing it. For, 1. It is a great sin: For you thereby fight against God, and grapple with Omnipotency, as if you thought to be stronger than he. 2. It is in vain; it will be to no purpose; your labour will be lost: For the counsel and purpose of God shall infallibly be accoplished, in spite of you and all the world.

SERMON LXXVII.

Propert. 7. GOD's decree is one and simple. *He is in one mind* (a). His mind is one; his purpose and decree is one, of all, and concerning all. By one simple act and resolution of his holy will, he hath determined all

---

(o) Psal. ii. 4. (p) Isa. viii. 9. 10. (a) Job xxiii. 13.

all thefe things that come to pafs in all ages, with all their times, conditions, and circumftances. Whatever God willeth, he willeth by one fimple act. Hence he calls himfelf, *I AM* (*b*). In him there is nothing paft, nothing to come, but all is prefent. This is further evident from the fimplicity of God, which is God confidered, as one pure perfect act, without all compofition. True it is, his decree, in refpect of the things decreed, is confidered by us as manifold. Hence it is that *thoughts* and *counfels* (*c*), in the plural number, are attributed to him. And when we confider God's decrees thus, we conceive a beautiful and wife order in them, fuch as the fubordination of the means to the end: And fo we rightly conceive, that God firft willed or decreed the end, and then the means in order to it. Yet this is not to be fo underftood, as if there were different decrees in God; but with refpect to the things decreed: For by one act of his holy will he decreed and appointed that order, which we find in the things decreed, when they come to pafs. There is one decree about the end and the means. By one act of his will he decreed to bring about the end by fuch means. But we view thefe things feparately that are joined together in one decree, that we may the more diftinctly conceive the wifdom of God's eternal counfel.

But it may be faid, Is not the will of God twofold, his will of decree, and his will of command? I anfwer, Thefe are not diverfe, or contrary wills, but one and the fame will in God, though confidered by us as diverfe, with refpect to the different object. His decree determines what fhall be done; his command fhews, not what fhall be done, but what is man's duty to do; and both are from the fame will of God. As for example, God decreed that Pharaoh fhall not let Ifrael go; yet he commanded him to let them go. But that command did not fhew that God willed that he fhall let them go, but only that he willed to make it his duty to let them go: And this alfo was decreed by God. Though God decreed that Pharaoh fhall not let Ifrael go, yet he decreed alfo to make it Pharaoh's duty to let them go, by giving him a command fo to do. Again, God decreed that Abraham fhall not actually offer up Ifaac: Yet he decreed to try Abraham in that matter, and to make it Abraham's duty to apply himfelf to the offering him up, by giving him a command to that purpofe.

I fay then that God's will and decree is but one: So that all the various changes of his difpenfations in time, all the revolutions of affairs in the world in all ages, all thefe ftrange and

new

(*b*) Exod. iii. 14. (*c*) Ifa. xxv. 1. and lv. 8.

new things that fall out in our days, were at once in his mind; he had one thought and purpose concerning them all from eternity. This is that which we poor creatures cannot comprehend. Therefore the consideration of this should humble us. What a humble sense should we have of our own nothingness, when we compare ourselves with God? How brutish is our knowledge and understanding in these things? as wise Agur says of himself (*d*). But let us admire that in God which we cannot comprehend. Our poor narrow and limited minds cannot think of many affairs at once, nor have many purposes at once; we must have one thought and purpose for this, and another for that. But it is not so with an infinite Being. As he sees all things distinctly at one view, by one intuitive act: So by one nod of his will he hath appointed all things; by one simple and undivided act of his holy will, he hath past a determination on all things, in their times and orders.

Fifthly, I proceed to speak a little of the end why God decreed these things that come to pass. His own glory is the supreme and ultimate end: For *of him, and through him, and to him are all things* (*e*). As all things are of him, so all are to him: As he is the first cause of them, so he is the last end of them: For he *hath made all things for himself* (*f*); that is, for his own glory. The apostle tells us expresly, that this was his great end in the eternal decree of election; *He predestinated us unto the adoption of children—to the praise of the glory of his grace.* And, *We are predestinated according to the purpose of him, who worketh all things after the counsel of his own will: That we should be to the praise of his glory* (*g*). The end that we propose to ourselves, hath an influence upon our purposes: But nothing without God can have any influence on him; for being independent, he cannot be moved by any thing without himself. He is God all-sufficient; sufficient to himself for all things; and so must be his own end. And being the first cause and first principle of all things, he must also be the last end of them. Hence our Lord says, *I am Alpha and Omega, the Beginning and the End, the First and the Last* (*h*). All things are ordered in the eternal counsel of God's will in infinite wisdom, and therefore must be ordered to his own glory: For infinite wisdom directeth the best means in order to the best end; and this is the highest and best end, the glory of God. The end must be more worthy than the means, something

(*d*) Prov. xxx. 2. (*e*) Rom. xi. 36. (*f*) Prov. xvi. 4.
(*g*) Eph. i. 5, 6, 11, 12. (*h*) Rev. xxii. 13.

thing higher and better than all created beings, which can be no other than the glory of God. As, *because God could swear by no greater, he sware by himself* (i) : So, because he could act for no higher end, he acts for himself, for his own glory. To this all things that come pass are subservient, in their own way and order, which the only wise God hath appointed. All things are ordered so in his eternal counsel, as may conduce most to his own glory. This is a justice whereby God gives himself that which is his due. His justice requires that he appoint such means as most conduce to his own glory, and dispose of them in such a way as is most suitable thereunto. In his own glory, the good of his elect is included, as that wherein he chiefly designs his glory.

For application,

1. It follows from what hath been said, that the glory of God should be our chief and ultimate end, in all that we do. We cannot act more nobly than by prosecuting, according to our capacity, the chief end and purpose of God. To this the apostle exhorts, *Whether therefore ye eat or drink, or whatsoever ye do, do all to the glory of God* (k). As man is from God, and from no other first cause : so he ought to act for God and his glory, and for no other ultimate end : and the glory of God being the chief end of our creation and being, ought also to be the chief scope and end of our lives. To make self our end, to act for our own glory and praise, as it is base and unworthy, so it is an invasion of God's prerogative, and an usurping a peculiar right of the Deity; for it is God's peculiar and eminent excellency, to be his own end, and to act for his own glory. Well then, in all that you do, study to be single and sincere in your aims at the glory of God, as your chief and ultimate end.

2. Here is a ground of a deep reverence of God in all his dispensations, how cross soever they may be to your desires and inclinations; and that whether these dispensations respect the church in general, or yourselves in particular. All was established in the eternal counsel of God's will for his own glory; and infinite wisdom set all in the best order imaginable for this great end. Therefore your will should acquiesce chearfully in the will and pleasure of God, without murmuring or disputing : For the infinitely wise God could not be deceived in contriving, choosing, and appointing means for his own glory. O how dear should the glory of God be to you ? If he be glorified, this should yield you heart's content and satisfaction,

(i) Heb. vi. 13. (k) 1 Cor. x. 31.

faction, how cross soever his dispensations be. This is, or should be, the sum of all your prayers, that God may be glorified. If he be glorified, a gracious person hath his highest wish, and utmost design and desire. Therefore, when afflicting providences befal you or the church, you should reason with yourselves thus, "This is that which the infinitely wise God "ordered in his eternal counsel for his own glory: Why then "should I murmur, or dispute, or find fault? If God be glo- "rified, that is enough; his holy will be done." Life or death, prosperity or adversity, should be all one to you, so God get glory by it. And though you cannot understand how such an event can tend to the glory of God; yet God is infinitely wiser than you, and such a thing did not slip his eternal counsel; for he *worketh all things after the counsel of his own will.*

Sixthly, I come, in the last place, to the general application of this doctrine.

Use 1. For instruction. Hence we may infer God's certain fore-knowledge of all things to come. He knows them, because he decreed them. He decreed all things that come to pass; therefore knowing his own decreee, he must needs know all future things. All things were in God, from eternity; not really, in their own nature; but in him, as a cause; in him, as a model is in the mind of a workman. He sees all things in the eternal ideas of them in his own mind; for he hath the idea of all things in himself, and doth not receive it from the things themselves. As he sees all things possible, in the glass of his own power; so he sees all things to come, in the glass of his own will: Of his effecting will, if he hath decreed to produce them; of his permitting will, if he hath decreed to suffer them. Hence, his declaration of things to come is founded on his appointing them: *And who, says he, as I, shall call, and shall declare it, and set it in order for me, since I appointed the ancient people, and the things that are coming, and shall come* (*l*). He knows his own decree, and therefore must know all things he hath decreed to exist in time, else we must say that God decrees he knows not what. He foreknows the most necessary things according to the course of nature, because he decreed that such effects should necessarily flow from such and such causes. And he knows all future contingents, all things that shall fall out by chance, and the most free actions of rational creatures; because he decreed that such things should come to pass contingently or freely, according to the nature of second causes: So that what is casual or contingent

(*l*) Isa. xliv. 7.

in regard of us, is certain and necessary in regard of God. It follows also from this doctrine about the decrees of God, that God's foreknowledge of things is most certain; seeing his decree is effectual, so that the things decreed do infallibly come to pass. To ascribe unto him a conjectural knowledge, is most unworthy of him; for we must then conceive him wavering in his decrees and purposes: But all his decrees and purposes are absolute and peremptory, not depending on any doubtful conditions of an uncertain event. Again, if God's decrees and resolves were from eternity, his foreknowledge must be so too. As he decreed from eternity, so he knew from eternity what he decreed, else he decreed he knew not what, which were blasphemous to imagine. He hath at once a view of all successions of times, and of all things to come, so that they are always present with him. They were all present to his knowledge, as if they were in actual being; as fresh in his mind from eternity, as in any instant of their being.

We see then that God hath from all eternity a certain foreknowledge of all things to come. Let us, therefore, honour and adore his majesty on the account of this perfection. We use to honour and reverence men that have the spirit of prophecy. The very heathens regarded this as a character and mark of divinity. Hence it was that the devils and pagan oracles gained so much credit, though their oracles were usually very ambiguous, and oft-times false. There is something more ravishing in the knowledge of things to come, than in any other kind of knowledge. Therefore let us adore the ever blessed God for this perfection, whereby he infinitely surmounts the understandings of men and angels. Because of his foreknowledge, he can give check to all the resolves, and undermine all the counsels, of wicked enemies against his church and people: For he sees their intentions, and their clandestine plots and contrivances, long before they are, and so can provide against them. They cannot come on him by way of surprise. We poor short-sighted creatures are often so surprised with dangers, that we have no time for the use of means to avoid them: But the blessed God cannot come into such straits; he foresees all the dangers his church and people can come into, and therefore can order and direct means for their defence and rescue. So that the consideration of God's foreknowledge affords much matter of comfort to believers.

Use 2. For reproof, to several sorts of persons.

Repr.

Repr. 1. To them that abuse the divine decrees. Men do so divers ways. As,

1. By pleading God's decree to excuse their sins. Wicked men, when they have committed some villany or wickedness, will plead thus, "Who can help it? God would have "it so; this was appointed for me, so that I could not avoid "it." But this implies a perverse conceit of the decrees of God, as if they constrained men to sin; whereas the decree is an immanent act of God, and so can have no influence, either physical or moral, upon the wills of men, but leaves them to the liberty and free choice of their own hearts. It is a horrid wickedness to cast the blame of your sin upon God's decree. This is to charge your sin upon God, as if he were the author of it. It is a great folly to cast your sin upon Satan who tempted you, or upon your neighbour who provoked you; but it is horrid blasphemy to cast it upon God himself. A greater affront cannot be offered to the infinite holiness of God.

2. By separating the end from the means; as if God's decree about the end, rendered the use of lawful means for attaining that end altogether unnecessary. Satan thus abused the divine decree, when he tempted our blessed Lord (*m*). God had declared his purpose, by a promise, to keep Christ, by giving his angels charge over him. From this Satan tempted him to a neglect of the ordinary means of his preservation, as if it were needless for him to go down the stairs of the temple, but that he might throw himself headlong, seeing God had purposed and promised to keep him. So, some wicked men will argue thus, "If I am eternally chosen to salvation, then I "shall be certainly saved, though I neither believe, nor re- "pent, nor be holy." And men may as well argue thus, "If "God hath decreed that I shall live a year longer, then I shall "certainly live so long, though I neither eat nor drink." But this is a horrid abuse of God's decree, whereby the end and the means are joined together; God having decreed to bring about the end by such means, and not otherwise. So that it is utterly false, to assert, even upon the supposition of a divine decree, that we shall attain the end, though the means be neglected. I clear this from that passage in the xxviith chapter of the Acts. God had decreed and determined to save all that were in the ship, and Paul had declared this decree and purpose of God: Yet none might infer from this, then let the mariners do what they will, they shall be saved; for the contrary is asserted by Paul, verse 31st, *Except these abide in the ship*,

ye

(*m*) Matth. iv. 6.

ye cannot be saved. The reason is, because as God had decreed to save them, so he had decreed to save them by the means of the mariners abiding in the ship, and no otherwise. So it is in other cases. Though God hath decreed to save all that believe in Christ; yet no believer may hence infer, Then though I live after the flesh I shall be saved: For this is false; the apostle asserts the contrary, when he is speaking to believers: *If ye live after the flesh, ye shall die* (n). The reason is, because in God's decree, living after the flesh is inseparably connected with eternal death, as holiness is inseparably connected with eternal happiness. So that it is contrary to scripture truth, for an elect person to say, Though I live after the flesh I shall be saved. And so it is contrary to truth in other cases, for a man to say, that he shall attain the decreed end, though the use of lawful means be neglected. God having joined the end and the means together in his decree. This is, 1. A strong motive to the use of them: For I cannot attain the end, unless I use such means. And, 2. A great encouragement to use them. Seeing God hath decreed such an end to be attained by such means, then it will not be in vain to use them.

3. By a curious search and inquiry into that which God hath kept secret. God's decrees about things to come to pass are his cabinet counsels, hidden secrets, except in so far as he is pleased to reveal or declare them. But O, how curious are men to pry into these divine secrets; to know future things which he hath not discovered in natural causes, nor by supernatural revelation! What a curiosity is there in men, to find out and discover the events of their own and other mens lives, and the disposal states of and kingdoms? The horrors of magic, and the vanities of astrology, have sprung from this. And hence also arose these many ways of divination that have been too commonly practised among men. But, 1. This curious searching and prying into God's hidden decrees is vain; for they are secrets that God hath kept to himself. The psalmist cries out, *Thy judgments are a great deep;* and the apostle, *How unsearchable are his judgments, and his ways past finding out* (o)! And if his works and judgments are a great deep, and unsearchable, his eternal decrees and purposes must be much more so: For it is the secret and hidden purpose of God, that is, the very depth of his way and judgment. 2. It is a bold invading God's prerogative, to whom secret things belong: For, *The secret things belong*

(n) Rom. viii. 13.   (o) Psal. xxxvi. 6. Rom. xi. 33.

long unto the Lord our God (*p*). They belong to him; they are none of our bufinefs. It is certainly intolerable boldnefs, to attempt to know that which God hath kept fecret, and would not have you to know. It is an ambition to be of his cabinet counfel. Hence our Lord reproves his difciples: *It is not for you to know the times or the feafons, which the Father hath put in his own power* (*q*). It is *not for you:* This doth not belong to you. And what a check did our Lord give to Peter, when he defired to know the fate of John? *If I will*, fays he, *that he tarry till I come, what is that to thee* (*r*)? That is none of your concern; it is not my pleafure to reveal it; therefore lay afide your curiofity. Chrift abhors curiofity even in the beft of his people.

SERMON LXXVIII.

Repr. 2. TO fuch as contemn the decrees of God. Men fhew their contempt,

1. By vilifying his decrees and counfels, and fcoffing at them. As that wicked people did, who faid, *Let him make speed, and haften his work, that we may see it: And let the counfel of the holy One of Ifrael draw nigh and come, that we may know it* (*a*). Where, by God's *counfel*, we are to underftand his judgments, which are the fruits of his eternal counfel (*b*). The prophets had declared the counfel and purpofe of God to execute judgment on that wicked generation: But they fcoffed and jeered at this; as if they had faid, You have often told us, that God had taken counfel againft us, and purpofed and determined to pour out his judgments upon us; but let him execute his counfel and purpofe if he can; we would gladly fee it once done. Much the fame language with that of *the fcoffers in the laft days, Where is the promife of his coming* (*c*)? Many look on the threatenings of the word as bugbears to frighten fools and children, and fo contemn the counfel and purpofe of God againft wicked finners.

2. By refifting and oppofing his counfel. It is faid of the Pharifees, *They rejected the counfel of God againft themfelves* (*d*). By *the counfel of God* there, we may underftand, even his eternal counfel and decree, to give them the means of eternal life and falvation, and particularly the miniftry of John, which in

its

(*p*) Deut. xxix. 29.   (*q*) Acts i. 7.   (*r*) John xxi. 22.
(*a*) Ifa. v. 19.   (*b*) Ifa. xiv. 24, 26. and xix. 17.   (*c*) 2 Pet. iii. 4.   (*d*) Luke vii. 30.

its own nature was a proper means in order to eternal life. But they rejected this counsel of God; they despised it, and opposed the proper end of it. So, when men reject and disobey the gospel, and refuse Christ offered in it; they thereby oppose themselves to the eternal counsel of God, for the salvation of elect sinners: If they can have their will, God's counsel in that matter shall be rendered vain and ineffectual. Again, when there is a work that is evidently of God, and about which he hath declared his counsel and purpose to establish it; if men set themselves in opposition to it, they thereby oppose the counsel of God. This is that from which Gamaliel dissuaded the counsel of the Jews: *If this counsel, or this work, be of men,* says he, *it will come to nought: But if it be of God, ye cannot overthrow it, lest haply ye be found to fight even against God* (*e*).

3. When men are full of projects, and confident of their success, without any reservation of the will and pleasure of God, or so much as minding his decree and counsel. Against such the apostle speaks: *Go to now, ye that say, To-day or to-morrow we will go into such a city, and continue there a year, and buy, and sell, and get gain. Whereas ye know not what shall be on the morrow.——For that ye ought to say, If the Lord will, we shall live, and do this, or that* (*f*). How often do men promise to themselves a happy accomplishment of their carnal projects, without any sense or thought of the will and counsel of God. This is done, 1. When men undertake things without prayer. You may speak of success, when you have owned God; according to Eliphas' advice to Job, *Thou shalt make thy prayer unto him, and he shall hear thee.——Thou shalt also decree a thing, and it shall be established unto thee* (*g*). But when you undertake things without prayer, this is to promise to yourselves great things without God's leave, as if you meant to have success, whether it be God's pleasure or not. 2. When men are too confident of future events and contingencies, and boast of mere human liklihoods. So, Pharaoh boasted, that he would overtake and ruin the children of Israel; and Benhadad boasted that he would plunder and ruin Samaria; and carnal men often project how to spend their days, in buying, and selling, and getting gain. Men are often confident of three things. (1.) Of the continuance of their lives. They dream of many days and years to come; as that rich man did in the parable (*h*).

(2.) Of

(*e*) Acts v. 39. (*f*) James iv. 13, 14, 15. (*g*) Job xxii. 27, 28. (*h*) Luke xii. 17, 18.

(2) Of their endeavours. Men are full of thoughts and projects, that they will do this and that, go to such a place, &c. as if their actions were in their own power, and exempted from the decrees and counsels of Heaven. (3.) Of the success of their endeavours: That they shall gain so much by such a merchandise, and promote their interest so and so. Thus men set up and rest on their own endeavours, and neglect God, as if all depended on the course of sublunary causes.

Thus I have shewed, wherein it is that men shew too great confidence of their own understandings, without any thought of the counsel and purpose of God. But this is a great evil: For, 1. It is to invade the rights of the God-head, and to encroach on the prerogative of God, on whose will and pleasure all events depend. When you are confident of your own purposes and projects, and the success of them; this is to set yourselves in the room and place of God, as if your purposes must stand, whatever the counsels and purposes of God may be. 2. It is utterly vain: For you are not lords of your own lives, nor of your own actions, nor doth the success of them depend on your will and pleasure. Remember that God hath, in his eternal counsel, past a determination on all that shall befal you. He hath determined concerning your time in the world, and all your affairs and business, and the success of all your endeavours: And his counsel shall stand, whatever your projects and purposes be. You know not what may be in the womb of God's eternal counsel concerning you and your affairs. You know not what may be in the womb of the next morning. As your lives, so your works are in the hand of God; the performance, and the success of them. Therefore, it is a mere vanity for you to be so confident of your own purposes and endeavours. It is true, you may lawfully provide for the time to come. The Spirit of God remits us to the ant, to learn a piece of provident care (*i*). You may lawfully have purposes and projects for your own and your families welfare. But all this must be with a reservation of, and submission to the will and pleasure of God: For he may soon disappoint all your projects.

Repr. 3. To them that reproach and affront the divine decrees. This is done,

1. By censuring any of God's decrees or administrations. He *worketh all things after the counsel of his own will*: Therefore, in censuring any of his administrations, you censure his eter-

---

(*i*) Prov. vi. 6, 7, 8.

nal counsels. When you will not submit to his plain will, without penetrating into the hidden reasons of it; nor adore his counsels without controuling them; but are apt to think this or that wrong, or that this or that might have been better ordered: This is, 1. To reproach the decrees and counsels of God, as if he had not ordered matters wisely. 2. It is to affect a wisdom superior to his. When you cite God to answer at your bar, and are apt to find fault with this or that; it implies a secret conceit that you are wiser than he. 3. It is to usurp an authority beyond your ability. For his ways and counsels are too deep for you. What presumptuous boldness is it, for poor empty nothings to make themselves God's judges? How unbecoming is it, for such as are but of yesterday, to censure the resolves and counsels of eternity? What intolerable arrogance is it, for poor blind creatures to censure the methods and counsels of infinite wisdom? We are too short-sighted to judge of the ways of God. Man cannot understand his own way, much less the ways of an infinite Being.

2. By being peremptory for our own will, and to have God acting in such and such a method. He *worketh all things after the counsel of his own will.* But many times you would have him working after your own will and counsel, following your humour, and gratifying your desires and appetites. This is to impeach the wisdom of his counsels, as if he had not laid down right measures for the administration of affairs. You will not let God act after the counsel of his own will, but will be directing him, and *teaching him knowledge* (*k*); as if you could contrive and order things, and dispose and appoint concerning your affairs, better than God. How often do you pray for this and that, without a due submission to the will and pleasure of God, and are peremptory for such and such mercies, and to have your lot and condition so and so ordered? All these are encroachments on God's wise disposal of affairs. You prescribe to God, as if you were *his counsellors* (*l*). As if he had not wisely ordered matters in his eternal counsel, you would direct him how to dispose of you, and would have the only wise God taking his measures from your passions. This imposing on God is a hellish disposition. We find it in hell: The rich glutton would direct God a way to prevent his brethrens ruin, as better than the means of God's appointment (*m*).

3. By discontent and murmuring under cross and afflicting providences.

(*k*) Job xxi. 22.   (*l*) Rom. xi. 34.   (*m*) Luke xvi. 29, 30.

providences. How apt are you to quarrel with God, as if he were in the wrong to you, when his dealings with you are not according to your fancies and wishes? You demand a reason, and call God to an account, "Why am I thus? Why so much "afflicted? And why so long afflicted? And why with such "an affliction rather than another?" Thus your hearts rise many times against God. Yea, there is a secret discontent that often arises in the hearts even of the best men, whence they sometimes mutter impatient and discontented expressions, and vent their anger and displeasure against God; as we see in Jonah, when the gourd was withered (*n*). This is to defame the counsels of infinite wisdom, as if God had not ordered your affairs wisely in his eternal counsel. For this the Lord reproves Job: *Shall he that contendeth with the Almighty, instruct him? He that reproveth God, let him answer it* (*o*). When you murmur and repine under afflicting providences, this is a presuming to instruct God how to deal with you, and to reprove him, as if he were in the wrong. It is to fasten an error on the counsels of divine wisdom. Yea, there is implicit blasphemy in it, as if you had more wisdom and justice, to dispose of your lot, and to carve out your portion, than God hath: This is upon the matter the language of such a disposition, "Had I been on God's counsel, I had ordered this or "that better."

4. By unbelieving jealousies of God. When God changeth his dispensations toward you who are his children, and seems to frown upon you; or, when you change to the worse, when a tender and lively disposition is gone, and you have not such access to God as formerly: Then you begin to question his love, and are jealous that he hath cast you off, and that his heart is not toward you. This is to reproach him, as if he were changeable in his gracious counsels and purposes. When you are in a good temper, you think he loves you; but when it is not so, you cannot believe but he hates you. This is to charge him, that he is not *in one mind* (*p*), but now in one mind, and then in another.

Use 3. For exhortation: In several branches.

Exhort. 1. Make it your business to secure to yourselves a saving interest in God through Christ. All things are ordered, in God's eternal decree and counsel, for the good of his own people. Therefore become his people, and get him for your God, and then the eternal counsel of his will is for you.

When

(*n*) Jonah, iii. 10. (*o*) Job xl. 2. (*p*) Job xxiii. 13.

When God is yours, then all the promises are yours: And what are the promises, but declarations of God's eternal purposes of love, grace, and mercy, toward his people? When your interest in God is secured, you need not be afraid what shall be the events of providence concerning you and yours; all is laid down and ordered for the best in God's eternal counsel. O blessed are they for whom the eternal counsel of the divine will is engaged: And it is engaged for all his people, all that have joined themselves to God in a perpetual covenant through Christ. The promises of the covenant shew what is God's eternal will and pleasure concerning them; and nothing can hinder the accomplishment of them: For *his counsel shall stand, and he will do all his pleasure;* and *what his soul desireth, even that he doth* (*q*). Therefore come and take hold of God's covenant; close with Christ the blessed Mediator; and chuse God in him for your God: And then none can obstruct the good pleasure of his will concerning you. He will break through all impediments in his way, to bring about his eternal purposes of love and grace.

Exhort. 2. Study to know the counsel of God's will; what his eternal decrees and purposes are. But you may say, How can we know that? For *who hath known the mind of the Lord? or who hath been his counsellor* (*r*)? I answer, Indeed God's eternal decrees and counsels are great secrets, and it is intolerable boldness for us to pry into them, or attempt to know what God would not have us to know. We cannot have an absolute knowledge and discovery of his eternal counsel. Yet we may have some knowledge of it, even before the event. And, 1. We may know it, in so far as he hath been pleased to reveal it to us in his blessed word, by the promises and prophesies in the holy scriptures. 2. We may have some conjectures about his counsel, or know it in the general scope and drift of it, from such things as are preparative of the execution, and from his way and manner of dealing in former times. At least, 3. We may know it in so far as concerns our duty, and these things that are to be done by us. So it is said of the men of Issachar, that they *were men that had understanding of the times, to know what Israel ought to do* (*s*). Though we cannot absolutely know what God will do; yet we may know what we should do, with respect to what may be the counsel of his will, as to what shall fall out in our day. The people of God are his friends and familiars, to whom he imparts his secrets: *His secret*

(*q*) Isa. xlvi. 10. Job xxiii. 13. (*r*) Rom. xi. 34. (*s*) 1 Chron xii. 32.

cret is with the righteous (*t*). As the secrets of his word, so also of his providence. They are admitted to know his secret counsels and purposes in some measure. Hence the Lord says of Abraham, with respect to what he was to do to Sodom, *Shall I hide from Abraham that thing which I do* (*u*). He imparts to his people his mind and counsels, as men do to their friends. Sometimes they cannot shun to have strong impressions concerning such and such events. God sometimes begets strong instincts in their minds, whereby they are premonished of their duty, though they cannot certainly determine what shall be. They have no infallible persuasion of the event: Yet they know more of God's mind and counsel than other men do; and sometimes have great light, where others meet with gross darkness.

Well then, study to know God's counsel, so far as he hath revealed it in his word; and so far as he may be pleased to impart it to you, by secret instincts and impressions upon your minds. Labour to get upon his secrets. For this end, 1. Become the friends of God. Get a deep sense of your natural enmity against God; lay down the weapons of your rebellion; and embrace and close with Christ the blessed peace-maker, and employ him to bring you into favour and friendship with God. It is a part of friendship, to communicate secrets. Hence our blessed Lord says to his disciples, *Henceforth I call you not servants, for the servant knoweth not what his Lord doth: But I have called you friends; for all things that I have heard of my Father, I have made known unto you* (*x*). 2. Be much in the exercise of a holy fear of God. For *what man is he that feareth the Lord? Him shall he teach in the way that he shall chuse* (*y*). Reverence the majesty of God, and stand in awe of him. When you have a deep reverence of God upon your heart, so that you are afraid to offend him; and are glad to know his counsel, that you may not resist it, or be found standing out against it, but may be found in the way of your duty; then are you in the way to know much of his mind and counsel. 3. Study humility and meekness of spirit. For *the meek will he guide in judgment; the meek will he teach his way* (*z*). Proud and self-conceited persons, who are wise enough in their own eyes, and are full of the contrivances and devices of their own hearts, God will not impart his counsels to them. But such as are meek, and humble, and low in their own eyes, and

dare

(*t*) Prov. iii. 32.   (*u*) Gen. xviii. 17.   (*x*) John xv. 15.
(*y*) Psal. xxv. 12.   (*z*) Psal. xxv. 9.

dare not trust their own hearts, and are resolved to follow the divine conduct; such shall know much of his counsel, even as to future events. 4. Be much in God's company, and keep up constant communion with him. Such as do so, shall have secret intimations of his counsel. The bosom disciple had the privilege of being acquainted with Christ's secrets, and therefore was put upon it to enquire who should betray him. Says the prophet, *I will stand upon my watch, and set me upon the tower, and will watch to see what he will say unto me* (a). Saving graces and duties, in the exercise whereof communion with God is kept up, are the believer's watch-tower, from whence he may expect to have discoveries of the divine counsel. Get up to the mount of meditation, and be much in the mount with God in prayer; and then shall you have a clearer prospect of things at a distance than other men have.

SERMON LXXIX.

Exhort. 3. WHEN you know God's counsel, or have it any way imparted to you, own and close with it. Do not resist it or stand out against it. Whatever is owned by God, is sure to be established by him, and therefore should be owned by us. Said Laban and Bethuel about Rebekah, *The thing proceedeth from the Lord; we cannot speak unto thee bad or good* (a). And when Paul's friends perceived that it was of God that he would go up to Jerusalem, they said, *The will of the Lord be done* (b). And it was Gamaliel's counsel to the Jews, *If this counsel, or this work, be of men, it will come to nought: But if it be of God, ye cannot overthrow it, lest haply ye be found even to fight against God* (c). It is true, all desires and endeavours against the counsel and purpose of God are not unlawful, when his will and counsel is secret, and not revealed to us. It was in David's heart, to build an house for God: This was no sin; he *did well that it was in* his *heart* (d). Yet it was against the counsel of the divine will. But when any work is evidently of God, and he hath declared his counsel to establish it, we ought quietly to acquiesce therein. Upon this ground the Lord dissuades Rehoboam and the house of Judah from going against the ten tribes; *Ye shall not go up, nor fight against them:—for this thing is of me* (e). That is, it is from my counsel and providence. In such cases, the opposing

(a) Hab. ii. 1.
(a) Gen. xxiv. 50. (b) Acts xxi. 14. (c) Acts v. 38, 39.
(d) 1 Kings viii. 18. (e) 1 Kings xii. 24.

ing and refifting the counfel of God, is a great evil. For, 1. Such oppofition is vain. We cannot overthrow his counfel. It shall ftand in fpite of us, and all devils and men. 2. Such oppofition is finful. It is a fighting againft God, oppofing him, and ftanding out againft him. 3. It is dangerous. What danger muft there be in poor worms, fighting againft the great God, and entering the lifts with Omnipotency? I fay then, when God's counfel is imparted to you, own it, and clofe with it.

Yet this muft be underftood with great caution. We are not to miftake our own apprehenfions of what is like to come, as declarations of the counfel and purpofe of God. We may have ftrong apprehenfions of fome events, and yet it may be our indifpenfible duty to oppofe ourfelves to the accomplifhment of them. The reafon is, becaufe fuch apprehenfions are not always impreffions from God. His fecret will and counfel may be quite contrary to our prefent apprehenfions. Yet when the will and counfel of God is made evident to us, with refpect to any future event, as fometimes it may be, we are not to ftrive and ftruggle againft it, but to reverence the counfel of the divine will. In the Lord's prayer, we pray that his *will may be done;* his will of decree, as well as his will of command: and all our defires ought to be conceived with fubmiffion to his will and pleafure.

Again, we muft diftinguifh between man's devices and contrivances, and God's counfel in them. We are not always to own and clofe with the devices and contrivances of men, with refpect to any event, for thefe may be very wicked: But we are always to own and clofe with the counfel of God in them, when the fame is difcernible by us; becaufe though their devices and contrivances be wicked, yet God's counfel in them is good; therefore you fhould reverence it, and acquiefce in it. If we let God have his will, it will be fo much the better for us: But if we do not, yet he will have it whether we will or not.

Exhort. 4. Let us reverence the majefty of God in all events of providence, in all his difpenfations and adminiftrations. All is *after the counfel of his own will.* Nothing comes to pafs, but what God hath from all eternity determined and fet in order. Many times fuch things fall out as are crofs to our defires and inclinations: And in this cafe we are apt to cenfure and find fault, as if fuch things were not well ordered. But there are two things, which if duly confidered, tend to filence and quiet us under fuch difpenfations: As, 1. Nothing falls

falls out but according to the will and pleasure of God: For he *worketh all things after the counsel of his own will.* It was his eternal will and pleasure that such things should come to pass in time. This should quiet us, and strike us with holy reverence. Whatever his dispensations be, we should acquiesce in his will and pleasure: For it is God's prerogative, to dispose of all things according to his own will: *He doth according to his will in the army of heaven, and among the inhabitants of the earth* (*f*); *he giveth giveth kingdoms to whomsoever he will;* and he *may do what he will with his own* (*g*). His own will and pleasure is the supreme and satisfactory reason of all his administrations. In this our blessed Lord acquiesced; and so should we: *Even so, Father, for so it seemed good in thy sight* (*h*). 2. All events of providence are ordered in infinite wisdom: for he *worketh all things after the counsel of his own will.* It is not said, *after his will,* but *after the counsel of his will;* importing that things are decreed and ordered by him in great wisdom. The smallest events are ordered, not by the counsel of men, but by the counsel of God. All are the products of perfect wisdom, being wisely ordered for his own glory, and the good of his church and people. Therefore when our hearts rise against God's dispensations, we should recollect ourselves, and say, " Is not this the product of God's eternal counsel? And if " so, then it must be wisely ordered, for he *is wise in counsel,* " *and excellent in working.* Such and such things are fallen " out contrary to my desires and inclinations; I would have " had matters otherwise ordered: and I thought God might " be more glorified in my way; but now I see I was mistaken; " for such and such events had never been determined in the e- " ternal counsel of God's will, if they had not been more for " his glory. I am satisfied that there is infinite wisdom in " them, though I cannot see it, seeing they are ordered by " the infinitely wise God."

Upon these grounds, I say, we should reverence the majesty of God in all events of providence, when matters fall out otherwise than we would have them. Yet this is not to be so understood, as if we were not to be duly affected with sad dispensations. There are many events of providence with which we should be very deeply affected, and which should make a very deep impression upon our spirits. I give instance in these two. 1. We should be deeply afflicted, both for our own sins,

and

(*f*) Dan. iv. 35. (*g*) Dan iv. 17. Matth xx. 15. (*h*) Matth. xi. 27.

and for the sins of others among whom we live. This hath been the temper of the saints: They mourned for their own iniquities, and for the sins of a profane and wicked generation among whom they lived. It is true, God decreed to permit your sins, and the sins of others for his own glory; and they shall issue in his glory at last: Yet God is not beholden to your sins or theirs for any glory that he hath by them; seeing in their own nature, they are dishonourable to him, and strike against his glory. That they are made to issue in his glory at last, is the product of infinite wisdom, not of the irregular actions or intentions of men. Therefore it becomes us to mourn deeply, for the dishonour done to God, both by our own, and other mens sins. 2. We should be deeply afflicted for the miseries and distresses of the church of God. When the church is brought low, and the people of God are under persecution; or when the interests of Christ are in great danger: Such rebukes of providence should make a very deep impression on us, and be laid deeply to heart. The saints have been much afflicted when the church was in a sad case. The people of God under their captivity, *wept when they remembered Zion* (*i*). Jeremiah was deeply affected with the miseries of the church; as we read in his Lamentations. *Eli's heart trembled for the ark of God* (*k*). And when Jerusalem was laid waste, and the people of God were in great affliction, Nehemiah could not conceal his grief, even before the king (*l*). Certainly, when the church is in great distress, or the interests of Christ in great danger, such sad events of providence should leave a mighty impression upon our hearts. And that, (1.) As they are brought to pass by the lusts, malice and wickedness of men, whereby God is much dishonoured. (2.) As they are punishments of sin, and evidences of God's displeasure against his church and people. And, (3) In so far as they at present strike against God's declarative glory. For, though such sad events of providence are indeed products of God's wise counsel; yet in the mean time, they are matter of grief and sadness to us. That they shall issue at last in the glory of God and the good of his people, is indeed matter of faith, and will be matter of joy to all that love God, when they see it. But at present God's declarative glory suffers by them; and we must take things as they appear to us, seeing we are not able to look into the bottom of God's designs.

Vol. II. N°. 6.   S   But

(*i*) Psal. cxxxvii. 1.   (*k*) 1 Sam. iv. 13.   (*l*) Neh. i. 3, 4. and ii. 1, 2.

But though it be so, that we should be thus deeply affected with such sad events of providence that befal the church; yet we should be so far satisfied, as to reverence the infinitely wise God, in ordering such things in the eternal counsel of his will, being confident that he will promote and carry on his eternal designs by them, to wit, his own glory, and the good of his church and people. Let us not quarrel with God upon the account of any event, nor find fault with any of his dispensations; for all is well ordered in his eternal counsel. Therefore, that you may be helped to judge aright of such events of providence, and to reverence and adore God's wise counsel in them, I give these following directions.

1 Do not judge of God's providences by their outward aspect and appearance; else God may lose the glory of the work, and you the comfort. Do not judge of God's dispensations by what they seem to be, but by what they really are. His dispensations may have a very frowning aspect, when he designs nothing but love and mercy to his church and people: For, he loves to bring light out of darkness, to give the valley of Achor for a door of hope, to bring meat out of the eater, and sweetness out of the strong, and to bring about mercies and deliverances for his church by very improbable and contrary-like means. There is many times much more good in God's dispensations than what appears to us. His way of working is often under a vail of contrarieties: He brings something out of nothing, light out of darkness, and order out of confusion. His end is not to satisfy his peoples curiosity, but to try their faith. He knows well what he is doing about his church, when we know not: *I know the thoughts that I think towards you, saith the Lord, thoughts of peace, and not of evil, to give you an expected end* (*m*).

2. Distinguish between God's main work, and such events of providence as are but preparations to it. God's everlasting and wise counsels for the good of his church are brought to pass by degrees. When God brought the children of Israel into straits at the Red-Sea, they interpreted that as a design for their destruction, and censured the kindness of God toward them in bringing them out of Egypt. Yet that dispensation was but a preparation for their more glorious and comfortable deliverance. God trades his grapes in the wine-press; but it is but a preparation of them to afford a delicate wine. He He plows his church, that he may prepare her for fruitfulness. He hews his stones, to fit them for the building. He seems

some-

(*m*) Jer. xxix. 11.

sometimes to dig in the bowels of the church, when he is only preparing to lay the foundation for raising a glorious structure.

3. Do not look only to present providences, but to their ultimate end. The end both beautifies and crowns the work. And we must consider, not only the immediate end, but the more remote and ultimate end: For God, in his providences towards his church, hath his ends oftentimes at a great distance from us, so that they are not to be brought about in our days. God designed to bring the children of Israel into the land of Canaan; yet they must take the brick-kilns of Egypt, the Red-Sea, and the wilderness, in their way. Who would have imagined that the bondage they were brought under, and the great straits they were reduced to, could mean any good to them? Yet so it fell out: Their darkest dispensations had light in their latter end, and their greatest bondage led on to their more glorious liberty. As the wheels of a clock, so the wheels of providence, may seem to counter-work one another; yet they all tend to one blessed end. The wheel is still going forward, even when it seems to go quite backward. Therefore when, at any time, the public work of God seems to be going backward, and cross winds seem to turn the whole course; yet let not Zion's friends be discouraged: For though the lesser wheels seem never so cross and contrary in their motions, yet the great wheel is still moving right on to a blessed and happy end.

4. Do not draw your conclusions from single events of providence, but from the whole scheme. Providence is a draught of many pieces. When you view these pieces singly and apart, there seems to be great confusion; but view them together, and you will perceive admirable beauty. As the wise contrivance of a builder is not seen, till the several parts of the building are set together: So it is here. We can best judge of the wisdom of God's eternal counsel, by viewing the harmony of providence. The single threads of providence may seem very knotty and uneven, and so seem to give just occasion of censure: But how much will it raise our admiration, to see them all woven into a curious piece of work. Therefore, learn to wait patiently till God hath finished his work, before you draw your conclusions. We judge not of a picture, by the first draught, but by the last lines. When a man is drawing a picture, looking on the first draught, you will think it ugly: But if you could see the idea of it in the limner's mind, or did patiently wait till he finish his work, you would see it

to be a beautiful piece. So, when you look on God's works before they are finished, you are apt to pass a wrong judgment upon them: But if you could see the idea of them in the eternal counsel of his will, or had the patience to wait till he finish his work, you would then see an admirable beauty in it.

Exhort. 5. Reverence the will and pleasure of God in all duties, as well as in all events. God's laws and commands, enjoining our duty, are declarations of the eternal counsel of his will, not what shall be done by men, but what shall be their duty to do. This is what God hath determined and appointed in his eternal counsel. His commands are the decrees and edicts of Heaven concerning man's duty. Now, men are naturally very impatient of the yoke of duty, and cannot endure *what is commanded* (n), as is said of the Israelites. Men snuff at the commands of God, and have high reasonings against them. Particularly, many duties are hard and difficult, costly and dangerous, cross to our inclinations and carnal interests: And with respect to these, the hearts of men are apt to rise against God; " These are hard sayings; this " is an heavy yoke, who can bear it?" But remember that all God's laws and commands are the results of the eternal counsel of his will, whereby he determined to make such and such things your duties: So that there are two things here that should quiet and satisfy you, and engage you to a deep reverence. 1. It was the eternal will and pleasure of God, that such and such things should be made your duties: And his will is the supreme reason of all things; for he is our absolute Sovereign. Therefore, when God hath signified his will and pleasure, that should be argument and motive enough, though the duty be never so cross to your desires and carnal interests. And indeed the bare signification of the will of God, is enough to a gracious heart, so far as it is such. Hence it is used as the great argument to press obedience: *This is the will of God, even your sanctification :* And, *in every thing give thanks ; for this is the will of God in Christ Jesus concerning you* (o). Seeing it was his will and pleasure to make such and such a thing to be your duty, you should not stand disputing, nor enquiring into a reason, but set about it, though never so contrary to your own will, or to the will of other men, or to the custom and fashion of the world. Therefore quit your will to God, and resign yourselves to his will and pleasure in all things; and learn to do his will, because it is his will, though

no

(n) Heb. xii. 20.   (o) 1 Thess. iv. 3. and v. 18.

no profit or advantage should redound to you by it. 2. It was in infinite wisdom, that God determined to make such and such things your duties. His laws are the result of his wise counsel. They are framed by his wisdom, though enacted by his will: So that they are all *holy, and just, and good* (p). All he requires is for our own good and happiness. Therefore if a tender regard were had to the wise counsel of the divine will, carving out our way and duty, the world would be quite another thing than it is; the noise of groans and cursings would be no more heard in our streets, peace would be in all borders, joy and singing would found in all habitations. God's laws are framed in the eternal counsel of his will, for the good of particular persons, and the good of human societies. Nothing is enjoined but what is sweet, rational, and useful to men.

SERMON LXXX.

Exhort. 6. IN all your ways acknowledge God, and go to him for counsel. Whatever your devices and contrivances be, yet the eternal decree and counsel of God shall certainly be accomplished. Solomon tells us, *There are many devices in a man's heart: Nevertheless the counsel of the Lord, that shall stand* (a). Therefore learn to resolve with God, and to take him into consultation with you: For without him all your devices will come to nothing. All our devices and reckoning to which God gives no allowance, are but as a reckoning without a man's host, as we use to speak: For man proposes, but God disposes. But O, what a happiness is it, that you may have counsel from him, whose counsel shall stand, and have God determining and resolving for you. Therefore, away with all your solicitous and distracting cares and fears, and cast yourselves on God for his blessed conduct. *Be careful for nothing ; but in every thing by prayer and supplication with thanksgiving, let your requests be made known unto God* (b). He can best counsel you to that which will have blessed success. All events are in the hand of the Lord: Therefore that man that neglects God, and makes his own will his counsellor, will chuse a mischief to himself, instead of a comfort and blessing. God can direct you best: The disposal of all your actions is in his hand, and depends upon the pleasure of his will. O Lord, says the prophet, *I know that the way of man is*

(*p*) Rom. vii. 12.   (*a*) Prov. xix. 21.   (*b*) Phil. iv. 6.

not in himself; it is not in man that walketh to direct his steps (*c*).

Exhort. 7. Resign yourselves absolutely to the will and pleasure of God, in disposing of your outward lot and condition, and all your affairs and concerns. All that shall befal you, is already unalterably appointed and determined, in the eternal counsel of the divine will: And it is both your duty and happiness, who are the children of God, to refer yourselves to God's determination. Even a Pagan could say, † " He hath " a truly great and generous mind, who can resign himself to " God's disposal." You owe such a deep reverence and regard to his will and pleasure, that you ought to refer yourselves wholly to it. He is the potter, and ye are the clay: And he may do with his own what he pleases ‡. Therefore there should be such a holy indifferency upon your spirit, that you should be content to be put in any condition God sees meet. Again, he hath from eternity determined your lot in great wisdom. All is ordered in the counsel of his will for your good, who are his children, as well as for his own glory: And, being infinitely wise, he knows what is for your good infinitely better than you do yourselves. Therefore, unless you blaspheme God, and think him foolish or ignorant, you ought to submit your lot to his disposal, that he may cut and carve it, according to his will and pleasure. Again, his counsel shall stand, and he will do all his pleasure concerning you and your affairs, whether you will or not. Therefore you can gain nothing by your non-submission; you will only create much trouble and vexation to yourselves. But the sweet of your lives lies in refering all to his will. It is his condescension to ask your consent, and he craves it for your own good. Therefore, say with David, *Behold, here am I, let him do to me as seemeth good unto him* (*d*). I am content that God put me in any condition he pleases.

Exhort. 8. In managing your affairs and business, let all your purposes, resolutions, and undertakings, be with a reservation of the will and pleasure of God. So the apostle teacheth: *For that ye ought to say,* says he, *If the Lord will, we shall live, and do this, or that* (*e*). All your business is contrived already

---

(*c*) Jer. x. 23.

† *Hic est magnus animus, qui se Deo tradidit.*

Sen. de vit. beata. 15.

‡ *Permittes ipsis expendere numinibus, quid Conveniat nobis, rebuiq; sit utile nostris.* Juven.

(*d*) 2 Sam. xv. 26. (*e*) James iv. 15.

ready in the eternal counsel of his will. God hath not only a negative, but an affirmative vote in all things: Therefore be not peremptory in your resolutions, nor too confident of success; but refer all your undertakings to the will of God. You cannot tell what may be in the womb of his eternal counsel concerning your affairs. How soon may he check your carnal confidence and presumption? Though your enterprizes be managed with never so much wisdom and contrivance; yet a determination may be past in God's eternal counsel, that they shall not prosper; and it may be his will and pleasure to blast them, and nip them in the bud. Therefore, in all your purposes and undertakings, still reserve the will and pleasure of God; " If the Lord will, I will do so and so; if the Lord " will, I will accomplish such a design." We find that the saints frequently use such forms of speech: *But I will come to you shortly, if the Lord will;* and, *I trust to tarry a while with you, if the Lord permit* (*f*). And though it be not necessary always to make such an express reservation: Yet it is most necessary that there be a reservation of the divine will and pleasure, either implicit or express; and it were good to accustom ourselves to such a holy form of speech, to stir up reverence in ourselves, and to instruct others.

Exhort. 9. Trust in God, and leave yourselves on him, in the way of your duty. Nothing can come to pass but according to the counsel of his will: So that you need not fear what devils or men can do. It is a vain and foolish thing, to trust in creatures, or depend on them; for all creatures are like idols, *They cannot do evil, neither is it in them to do good* (*g*). All events are in the hand of the Lord. If you trust in creatures, you will surely meet with many disappointments. But God hath past a determination on all things in the counsel of his will: And his will is the weal of them that trust in him, as he hath declared in his word: And none can obstruct his will and pleasure; his eternal counsels for the good of his people shall not fail. Whatever impediments or *thorns* are set in his way, he can *go through them, and burn them together* (*h*). Therefore commit yourselves to him, and rest on him.

But trust him in the use of lawful means. Mind your duty, and refer the event to God's will and pleasure. You know not what his eternal will and pleasure is about the event: But he hath told you your duty, wherein you are to wait on him. He hath in deep wisdom kept his particular purposes secret, that

---

(*f*) 1 Cor. iv. 19. and xvi. 7.   (*g*) Jer. x. 5.   (*h*) Isa. xxvii. 4.

that you may walk according to an appointed rule, and use all lawful means for compassing your ends.

Exhort. 10. Improve this doctrine against the exorbitancies and over-boilings of your passions, under a frowning aspect of providences, or when sad events befal you. Such things are apt to irritate and inflame our passions, and to mar the quiet and composure of our minds. But there is that here, if duly improved, that may abundantly quiet, stay, and satisfy our souls; to wit, that nothing can befal us, but what God hath from all eternity determined in the counsel of his will. Particularly, improve this, 1. Against perplexing and disquieting fears, when you see any evil like to befal you, or hanging over your head. What need you fear, when nothing can come to pass, but what God hath determined in his eternal counsel, for his own glory and the good of his people? And what he hath determined shall come; so that your fears are in vain and to no purpose: All your fear and perplexity cannot hinder the execution of his counsels. 2. Against anxiety in the use of means. Why are you anxious about the event and success, when that is unalterably fixed and determined in God's eternal counsel? It should ease you of anxious thoughts and cares, and induce you to use lawful means for bringing about your good ends and purposes with composure of spirit, when you consider, that there is nothing you project to bring about, but God hath had a determinate will and counsel about it, whether it shall be brought about or not; and that his will and counsel cannot fail of being accomplished. 3. Against torturing reflections on yourselves or others, when sad events befal you; such as, "If this or that had not been done, or if this or that means had not been used, such a thing had not befallen me." Lord, said Martha, *If thou hadst been here, my brother had not died* (*i*). I speak not of sins which are the cause of our trouble, and should be thought on, and mourned for; but of other things that are the remote occasions of our trouble, and about which people often torture themselves with disquieting thoughts, blaming themselves or others for this or that. In this case, it may quiet us to consider that it was necessary such an event should be; God had determined it in the counsel of his will. 4. Against excessive grief and sorrow, impatience and murmuring, under what is afflicting and troublesome to us. This leads me to

Exhort. 11. Study patience, and quiet submission to the will and pleasure of God, under afflicting dispensations. *Affliction cometh*

(*i*) John xi. 21.

cometh not forth of the dust, neither doth trouble spring out of the ground (k). It cometh not by chance: There is a supreme divine hand that orders it. Whoever are the instruments of your trouble, there is a higher decree and determination to be regarded in it, than what is past by men, even the decree and counsel of God. The church in their prayer acknowledge, that what wicked men did against Christ, was that which *God's hand and counsel determined before to be done* (l): And the apostle Peter tells the Jews, that Christ was *delivered by the determinate counsel and foreknowledge of God* (m). The same is true also of all the afflictions you met with; they are nothing else but what God appointed and determined for you in the eternal counsel of his will. Hence the apostle says, *That no man should be moved by these afflictions: For yourselves know, that we are appointed thereunto* (n). Whatever afflictions you meet with, you were appointed unto them, and they appointed for you, in God's eternal decree: Therefore you should not be moved by them, to impatience, discontent, or murmuring. The kind of your affliction; all the bitter ingredients in your cup; the degree and measure of your trouble; the instruments of it; the time and duration thereof; all were appointed and determined unalterably in the counsel of the divine will.

There are three things here, which, if duly considered, may engage you to patience and humble submission, and quiet and still the risings of your spirits against God, under the smartest affliction.

1. It was the eternal will and pleasure of God that such an affliction should befal you. This should make you say, *The will of the Lord be done: It is the Lord, let him do what seemeth good unto him*. Being Sovereign Lord, he hath right to determine according to his will and pleasure, and is liable to no account. He hath supreme and absolute power and dominion, to dispose of you and all creatures according to his will, and to put you and them in what condition he pleaseth. *Behold he taketh away, who can hinder him? Who will say unto him, What doest thou* (o)? As the will of God revealed in his word should be the rule of our actions, so the will of God discovered in his works should be the rest and ease of all our irregular passions. Hence, even a heathen philosopher says *, " Why may not a man refuse to
" obey God in what he commands, as well as to submit to him
" in what he inflicts? And then what ground can there be
" for

(k) Job v. 6. (l) Acts iv. 28. (m) Acts ii. 23. (n) 1 Thess. iii. 3. (o) Job ix. 12. * Epictet. L. 4 c. 22.

"for any pretence to religion." Therefore when God hath declared his will by the event, you should silence all your murmurings and disputings, and, with Aaron, *Hold your peace* (*p*), how smart soever your affliction may be. When God's will is done, he is pleased; and should not that which pleases God, please you too? it should sweeten the bitterest cup, when you consider that it is God's will that you should drink it. It was once the saying of a court-flatterer, *That which pleaseth the king pleaseth me* *. It is no flattery to say so to God, but your indispensible duty.

2. God appointed and determined that such an affliction should befal you, not barely by his will, but by his wisdom; by *the counsel of his will*. It was in infinite wisdom that he ordered such an affliction for his glory and your good, if you have resigned yourselves to him through Christ And will you stand in the way of his glory? Should you not heartily acquiesce in what the infinite wisdom of God hath appointed, for glorifying his name, and promoting your spiritual and eternal happiness? Though you cannot see how such an affliction can be for his glory and your good, yet you are bound to believe it against sense and carnal reason, because he hath said it. *All things work together for good to them that love God* (*q*) He is infinitely wiser than you. You cannot descend into the depth of his wisdom and counsel. It was the saying of a heathen †, "That must needs be much more desirable, which is chosen "by the wisdom of God, than that which I chuse."

3. The counsel of God's will, whereby he appointed such an affliction for you, is unalterable: For, he *worketh all things after the counsel of his own will*. There is nothing in the counsel of his will, but what he worketh effectually and infallibly. *What his soul desireth, even that he doth* (*r*). Such an affliction being appointed for you, whether you submit or not, you cannot avoid it. You cannot make God alter his eternal counsels and purposes. He is mightier than you, to maintain his own purposes. Why then will you contend with God by your discontent and murmuring? Whatever his counsel is, shall stand, and cannot be recalled ‡. All your struggling against it is in vain: For, *if he cut off, and shut up, or gather together, who can hinder*

(*p*) Lev. x. 3.
* *Placet mihi quod, regi placet; harpulas apud.* Herod. Lib. 1.
(*q*) Rom. viii. 28. † Epictet. L. 4. C. 7.
(*r*) Job xxiii. 13.
‡ *Optimum est pati quod emendare non possis.* Sen. Epist. 107.

hinder him (*s*)? If he changed his purpofe, he would difgrace his nature; and fhall he do fo for you? Is it not better that you fhould fuffer, than that God fhould be impaired in any of his perfections? Suppofe you had your choice, could you wifh that he fhould alter his purpofes to gratify your humour and fancy, or that any of his eternal counfels fhould fail and not take effect? If his purpofe might fail in one thing, why not in another? And then how could you be perfuaded that his purpofe according to election fhall ftand? And if there were the leaft ground of doubt here, what would become of all your hope and comfort?

Well then, improve thefe confiderations, in order to your patience, and filent and quiet fubmiffion under affliction. This will make your affliction eafy; whereas your fpurning againft it, like a bullock unaccuftomed to the yoke, will make it heavy and troublefome †. O, what a fweet life will you have, even under heavy preffures of affliction, and what heavenly ferenity and tranquillity of mind will you enjoy, when you acquiefce in the good will and pleafure of God, and embrace every difpenfation, how fharp foever it may be, becaufe it is determined by the eternal counfel of his will?

Ufe 4. For comfort to the children of God. Is it fo that God *worketh all things after the counfel of his own will*, fo that nothing can fall out but what he hath determined in his eternal counfel, and whatever he hath determined in the counfel of his will fhall certainly come to pafs? O what matter of comfort is here to you whom he hath taken into covenant with him! And,

1. It is matter of comfort, that all events are in fo good a hand, in the hand of your God, who loves you, and ftands engaged for you in an everlafting covenant. O, how well is it for you that it is fo! It is he that hath appointed and cut out your lot and condition for you, and nothing is or can be in your lot but what he hath determined and appointed in the eternal counfel of his will; fo that you need not fear, nor perplex yourfelves with anxious thoughts. Whatever changes or revolutions there are or may be in the world, yet you may be affured that all fhall go well on your fide. The Lord gives commiffion, *Say ye to the righteous, that it fhall be well with him* (*t*), whatever way the world go. The preacher fpeaks with great affurance, *Surely I know that it fhall be well with them that fear God, who fear before him* (*u*). God's intereft in and relation to you, and his everlafting

---

(*s*) Job xi. 10.

† *Ducunt volentem fata, nolentem trahunt.*

(*t*) Ifa. iii. 10.   (*u*) Eccl. viii. 12.

verlasting love, give you ground to conclude, that all things concerning you are ordered for the best in the eternal counsel of his will; and that cannot fail.

2. From this doctrine you may be assured of the accomplishment of the promises, that not one word shall fail of all that the Lord hath promised unto you. Sometimes God's dispensations toward you seem to cross and contradict his promises; and in such cases you are apt to cry out with the psalmist, *Doth his promise fail for evermore* (x)? But God's promises cannot fail, seeing they are declarations of his eternal purposes of love and mercy, or of the eternal counsel of his will, which shall be infallibly accomplished. *What his soul desireth, even that he doth* (y). And what he hath promised, that he desireth. His counsel stands, therefore his promise cannot fail.

3. Here is matter of comfort against the subtle devices and contrivances of the enemies of the church. They are usually men of great parts and refined wits, and employ their wit in plotting and contriving the church's ruin. But all their devices and counsels against her, shall not be able to frustrate the eternal counsels of the divine will for her good. All their plots, devices, and contrivances, are over-matched by the infinitely wise God. As they have their devices and counsels, so God hath his: And his counsel shall stand and take place in all generations, in spite of all the devices and counsels of men. *There are many devices in a man's heart,* says Solomon, *nevertheless the counsel of the Lord, that shall stand* (z). God's counsel stands against many devices: One hint and intimation of the counsel of God, is able to nullify and make void all the projects and devices of men in the contrary, though never so many. *The kings and rulers of the earth may take counsel together against the Lord, and against his anointed;* they may consult, plot, devise, and determine what they please, against Christ and his interests; but all is to no purpose: *He that sitteth in the heavens shall laugh, the Lord shall have them in derision* (a). And the decree and counsel of God, for the stability and enlargement of Christ's kingdom, shall stand firm and stable, and be infallibly accomplished. This hath been verified in all ages hitherto. Many projects and designs have been on foot in the world against the church and people of God; yet the counsel and purpose of God hath stood notwithstanding. If mens devices be not according to the counsel of the divine will, they shall certainly evanish like smoke.

4. Here

(x) Psal. lxxvii. 8.   (y) Job xxiii. 13.   (z) Prov. xix. 21.
(a) Psal. ii. 2, 4, 7.

4. Here is matter of comfort amidst all the reelings and overturnings of time, and seeming confusions that are or may be in the world. We are apt many times to think that the world is out of course, and that all things reel about in confusion. But it is comfortable that all is set in a beautiful and comely order in God's eternal counsel; so that all events of Providence, whatever aspect they may have to us, are by God's wise counsel, made subservient to his great end and design, of promoting his own glory and the good of his church and people. Let us improve this great truth to establish our hearts in the most unstable times. All is clear above, how cloudy soever here below: All is calm in heaven, though tempestuous here on earth. There is no confusion or disorder in the counsel and purpose of God. *He is in one mind* (b) to glorify his name, gather, build up, and save his elect: This is his great purpose, to which all events are subservient, and which all the world cannot hinder.

(b) Job xxiii. 13.

DISCOURSE XIX.

Of the Unity of the Divine Essence.

SERMON LXXXI.

Deut. vi. 4. *Hear, O Israel, the Lord our God is one Lord.*

POLYTHEISM and Atheism, that is, the having of many gods, and the owning no God at all, are very near of kin, being births of the same womb, and fruits of the same madness. They that hold a multiplicity of gods, are equally atheists with them that own no God. Therefore the Gentiles are said to be *without God a*); or, as it is in the original, *atheists;* as being no less atheists in holding a multiplicity of gods, than if they had acknowledged no God at all. They that have not the one only God, have really no God, because they have not the true God.

I have spoken of the being and existence of God, and of some of his glorious attributes and perfections; and am now to

(a) Eph. ii. 12.

to speak, from this text, of the unity of the divine essence. Having shewed that God is, and what he is, I am now to shew that he is *one only*.

In this book Moses delivers to the children of Israel a repetition, or second edition, of the laws of God, with some additions, explications, and enlargements, and various exhortations to, and enforcements of the observation of them. This he did a little before his death. The motions of grace in good men are usually most quick, when they draw near their everlasting rest. Then it is usually that the pulse of their soul beats strongly. How diligent should we be in doing good, when we consider that our time is short? In this chapter we have an exposition of the first commandment, which is continued in some of the following chapters. In the first three verses we have a preface, wherein Moses exhorts and encourages the children of Israel to obedience and keeping up the practice of religion, when God should bring them into Canaan.

In my text, he asserts the unity of the divine essence, as the first truth to be believed. The Jews reckon this verse one of the choicest portions of holy scripture: Therefore they write it in their phylacteries; and read it in their houses every day, morning and evening, according to an established order among them. And they reckon themselves happy in so doing; for they have this saying among them, *Blessed are we, who every morning and evening say, Hear, O Israel,* &c. but much more blessed and happy are they, who daily consider and improve this text of scripture.

In it we have these two things:

1. A preface demanding attention—*Hear, O Israel,—Hear,* not with the ears only, but with the mind and heart also. Attend earnestly, and consider seriously, and believe and improve this great truth that I am now to deliver. Importing that this is a truth that requires our utmost attention. Therefore it is very observable, that in the original text, the last letter of the first word, and the last letter of the last word of this verse, are written extraordinarily great; and there is also a mark set in the margin: Both which are designed to excite and engage to attention. So that this here delivered is a truth to which we should give most earnest heed.

2. The truth here asserted—*The Lord our God is one Lord*—Where these two things are implied. 1. That the true God is JEHOVAH; that is, a Being infinitely perfect, and self-sufficient, who hath his being of himself, and gives a being to

all

all other things, especially to his promises. 2. That this JEHOVAH was their God, viz. by covenant. He was the God of all the Israelites, by external visible covenant; but the God of the truly godly among them, by special internal covenant. This is that which renders every thought of God sweet, when we have a saving interest in him as our God. That which is here expressed is, that this JEHOVAH, who was the God of Israel, is *one*. *The Lord our God is one Lord.* The great JEHOVAH is *one*, and *one only*. He *only is God, and there is no other but he* (b); as this text is explained by a learned scribe. It is the opinion of many worthy divines, that in this text we have a plain insinuation of a trinity of persons in the unity of the Godhead. For, the words in the original text run thus, *The Lord, our God, the Lord, is one.* So that the name of God is here thrice repeated, and yet all declared to be one. But though I nothing doubt that the Spirit of God hath here a respect to that great mystery of the Trinity; yet I conceive that these words are no convincing argument for the proof of it: Therefore we have great cause to bless God that this glorious mystery is more plainly revealed to us elsewhere in the holy scriptures.

The doctrine I propose is this,

The true and living God, the infinitely perfect, self-sufficient, and self-existing Being, is one only.

This is asserted in our Shorter Catechism, in answer to that question, *Are there more Gods than one?* The answer is, *There is but one only, the living and true God.*

In handling this doctrine, I shall,

1. *Premise some things for clearing the doctrine.*
2. *Confirm the truth thereof.*
3. *Make application.*

First, For clearing the doctrine, I shall shew, 1. That we speak here of the true and living God. 2. In what sense he is said to be one.

1. We speak here of the true and living God. Other gods there are very many. And, 1. Many are gods by unjust usurpation, as the devils, who are *the gods of this world;* and Antichrist, who *exalteth himself above all that is called God, or that*

(b) Mark xii. 32.

is *worshipped, so that he, as God, sitteth in the temple of God, shewing himself that he is God* (c). In the Romish church, he hath that blasphemous title given to him, *The Lord our God the Pope:* And they call him *a visible God,* and *their supreme God on earth.* But the true God is but *one.* 2. Many are gods in men's erroneous opinion and persuasion. Many have been falsely so reputed by men that deceived themselves in their own imaginations; as these deities whom the heathens worshipped. But really, and in truth, there is but one God. Hence the apostle says, *There be gods many, and lords many: But to us there is but one God* (d). 3. Many are gods improperly, and by participation. So magistrates are called *gods* (e), because they are God's substitutes and deputies on earth, by whom he governs and judges; and because they bear a stamp of his image upon them, in their glory and honour, authority and dominion over others. But there is but one God properly and originally, and who is so by nature.

But why is he called the true and living God? He is called the true God, in opposition to the false gods of the Gentiles. Hence the prophet says, *The Lord is the true God.—The gods that made not the heavens, &c. they are vanity, and the work of errors* (f). Our God is the true God, very God, God indeed, and not a false or feigned god: But the gods of the heathens are false gods, feigned deities, that have nothing of the divine nature in them; they are *no gods, but the work of men's hands, wood and stone* (g). Next, he is called the living God, in opposition to dead idols. Hence are these expressions, *Turn from these vanities, unto the living God;* and, *Ye turned to God from idols, to serve the living and true God* (h). Particularly, he is called the living God, 1. With respect to what he is in himself. He *hath life in himself* (i): That is, he hath it originally and primarily. And he lives and reigns for evermore. *He is the living God, and an everlasting King* (k). Yea, he is life essentially; *life* itself (l). 2. With respect to what he is to his creatures. He is the fountain of life to them: *With thee is the fountain of life* (m), says psalmist. In the original, it is in the plural number, *the fountain,* or *well of* LIVES: That is, of all kinds of life. He is the fountain of the natural life: *In him we live* (n). He is the fountain of the spiritual

(c) 2 Cor. iv. 4. 2 Thess. ii. 4. (d) 1 Cor. viii. 5, 6. (e) Psal. lxxxii. 6. (f) Jer. x. 10, 11, 15. (g) 2 Kings xix. 17, 18. (h) Acts xiv. 15. 1 Thess. i. 9. (i) John v. 26. (k) Jer x. 10. (l) John xiv. 6. (m) Psal. xxxvi. 9. (n) Acts xvii. 18.

life: *He quickens those who are dead in trespasses and sins* (o) And he is the fountain of eternal life in glory: *When Christ who is our life shall appear, then shall we also appear with him in glory* (p).

2. Let me shew you in what sense the true and living God is said to be one. For clearing this, notice these things. 1. God may be said to be one two ways. (1.) In opposition to mixture. That is most properly one, which is simple, without any mixture or composition. So, God is one, that is, he is a most pure and simple essence, altogether uncompounded. His essence and attributes are all one in him, though variously apprehended by us. (2.) In opposition to multitude: And so we understand it here. God is so one, that he is the only one, and there is none else. 2. When we say that God is one only, we do not mean that he is one personally; for there are three distinct persons in the Godhead: But that he is one essentially; one in nature, essence, and being. 3. We do not speak here of a specifical unity, as a certain Socinian expresses himself, who calls the Father and the Son one in kind and specie. But we speak of a numerical unity. Now, a thing may be said to be one in number two ways. (1.) Affirmatively; and so every individual creature may be said to be one in number. Thus, when we call a thing one, we still leave place for a second and third of the same kind, at least in our apprehension and conceit. No creature is so one, but we may conceive that there are or may be more. Though there be but one sun, yet he that made that one, may make as many more as he pleaseth. (2.) Exclusively. A thing is said to be one, when besides it there cannot be such another. † And so we say God is one, exclusively of any other. He is one only, so as it is impossible there should be another. He is not only one, but the only one, most one, of all things ‡ the onest, if that word may be used. He is most perfectly one, because he is the most perfect Being; so that there neither is nor can be more than one God.

Secondly, I proceed to confirm this truth, that the true and living God, the great JEHOVAH, is but one only; and I shall confirm it, 1. From scripture. 2. From the consent of nations. 3. From reason.

(o) Eph. ii. 1. (p) Col. iii. 4.

† Unum Deum, *non intelligendum est* unum numero *dici, sed universitate. id est, qui propterea unus dicitur, quod alius non sit.*
           Ruffus in Exposit. Symb.

‡ *Unissimus*, saith Bernard.

1. From scripture. God himself says so in his blessed word. And he can as soon cease to be God, as speak any thing not according to truth, either out of ignorance, or out of envy. And we may and must argue from the holy scriptures, because some that profess to own their divine authority, have yet upon the matter at least, introduced a plurality of Gods into the Christian faith; as the papists and Socinians; which I shall afterward make appear. The holy scriptures hold forth this truth of the unity of the divine essence three ways. Affirmatively, negatively, and exclusively. 1. Affirmatively; when it expresly affirms that God is *one*. As in my text; and these following: *In that day shall there be one Lord, and his name one. Have we not all one Father? Hath not one God created us? There is none good, but one, that is God. It is one God, who shall justify the circumcision by faith, &c. There is one God and Father of all. There is one God, and one Mediator* (*q*). 2. Negatively; when it simply denies all other gods but one; as in these texts: *The Lord he is God, there is none else besides him. See now, that I, even I am he, and there is no God with me. There is none holy as the Lord, for there is none beside thee. There is none like thee, neither is there any god beside thee. For who is God, save the Lord? or who is a rock, save our God? Before me there was no god formed, neither shall there be after me. I, even I am the Lord, and beside me there is no Saviour. Besides me there is no god. Is there a god besides me? Yea, there is no god, I know not any. I am the Lord, and there is none else; there is no god besides me. I am God, and there is none else; I am God, there is none like me. There is none other God but one* (*r*). 3. Exclusively; when it excludes all but this one God; as in these texts: *Thou art the God, even thou alone, of all the kingdoms of the earth That all kingdoms of the earth may know that thou art the Lord God, even thou only. Thou, even thou art Lord alone. That men may know, that thou whose name alone is JEHOVAH, art the most High over all the earth. Thou art God alone. This is life eternal, that they might know thee the only true God, and Jesus Christ whom thou hast sent* (*s*).

More particularly, 1. The holy scriptures require us to have no other God; that is, to set up no other in the room and place of God to ourselves. So the first commandment runs,

Thou

(*q*) Zech. xiv. 9. Mal. ii. 10. Matth. xix. 17. Rom. iii. 30. Eph. iv. 6. 1 Tim. ii. 5. (*r*) Deut. iv. 35. and xxxii. 29. 1 Sam. ii. 2. 2 Sam. vii. 22. Psal. xviii. 31. Isa. xliii. 01, 11. xliv. 6, 8. xlv. 5. and xlvi. 9. 1 Cor. viii. 4. (*s*) 2 Kings xix. 15, 19. Neh. ix. 6. Psal. lxxxiii. 18. and lxxxvi. 10. John xvii. 3.

Thou shalt have no other gods before me. And to the same purpose, God says by the prophet, *Thou shalt know no god but me* (*t*). If there were any more gods, it would be a great wrong not to own and acknowledge them; so that the very first commandment, which is the foundation of all the rest, would be most injurious and unlawful. He requires us to have no other God, because indeed there is no other; and he would not have us to set them up as gods, who indeed are no gods. 2. The holy scriptures ascribe to one God the creation of all things: As in divers of these texts already quoted, and also these following: *By the word of the Lord were the heavens made, and all the host of them by the breath of* HIS *mouth. Of old hast* THOU *laid the foundation of the earth: And the heavens are the work of* THY *hands* (*u*). And this is ascribed to him exclusively of any other. So it is said, that he *alone spreadeth out the heavens, and treadeth upon the waves of the sea* (*x*). And God himself tells us, *I am the Lord that maketh all things, that stretcheth forth the heavens alone, that spreadeth abroad the earth by myself* (*y*). And from this is inferred his divine eminency and excellency: As in that song, *Thou art worthy, O Lord, to receive glory, and honour, and power: For thou hast created all things, and for thy pleasure they are, and were created* (*z*). Hence also is that imprecation against all the idol gods of the heathen, *The gods that have not made the heavens and the earth, even they shall perish from the earth, and from under these heavens* (*a*). And it is very observable that these words are originally written, not in the Hebrew tongue, as the rest are, but in the Chaldean tongue; that the people of God under the Babylonish captivity might openly, plainly, and boldly profess the true God, in a language their enemies understood. It was a saying common among those Greeks that held one supreme Deity, *Let him that saith he is a god, make another world.* 3. The holy scriptures refer to one God, the preservation and government of all things; as in these following texts; *Thou, even thou art Lord alone, thou hast made heaven, the heaven of heavens, with all their host; the earth, and all things that are therein; and thou preservest them all. O Lord, thou preservest man and beast. By him all things consist. He upholds all things by the word of his power. His kingdom ruleth over all. He doth according to his will in the army of heaven, and among the inhabitants of the earth* (*b*). And when the holy Spirit is speaking

(*t*) Hof. xiii 4. (*u*) Psal. xxxiii. 6. and cii. 25. (*x*) Job ix. 6. (*y*) Isa. xliv. 24. (*z*) Rev. iv. 11.
(*a*) Jer. x 11. (*b*) Neh. ix. 6. Psal. xxxvi. 6. Col. i. 17. Heb. i. 3. Psal. ciii. 19. Dan. iv. 35.

ing of the divine providence in conducting the children of Israel through the wilderness, he says, *The Lord alone did lead them, and there was no strange god with him* (c). 4. They refer all works of grace to one God; as in these texts: *Who can forgive sins but God alone? I will strengthen thee, yea, I will help thee, yea. I will uphold thee with the right hand of my righteousness. When the poor and needy seek water and there is none, and their tongue faileth for thirst, I the Lord will hear them, I the God of Israel will not forsake them. I, even I, am he that blotteth out thy transgressions for mine own sake, and will not remember thy sins* (d). I might multiply texts of scripture to this purpose. All the promises run thus. They are all made by one only God, and therefore are expressed in the singular number, *I* will do this, and *I* will do that, for my people. 5. The holy scriptures enjoin religious worship to be performed only to one God. *I am the Lord, that is my name, and my glory will I not give to another, neither my praise to graven images. Thou shalt worship the Lord thy God, and him only shalt thou serve* (e). There is a story, that when the Roman Senate heard of the miracles that Christ did in Judea, they decerned divine worship to be given to him; but that Tiberius crossed it, when he heard that he would be worshipped alone. If there were more gods than one, we might serve and worship more than one: But this is expresly forbidden. God declares himself to be a jealous God, and that he cannot endure any co-partner in worship. 6. The holy scriptures hold forth the true God whom we worship to be incomparable; as in these texts; *There is none like me in all the earth. There is none like unto the God of Jeshurun. Who is like unto thee, O Lord, amongst the gods? who is like thee? Amongst the gods there is none like unto thee, O Lord. Who in the heavens can be compared unto the Lord? Who among the sons of the mighty can be likened unto the Lord? I am God, and there is none like me* (f). The most excellent beings in heaven and earth come infinitely short of him. They are not worthy to be mentioned in one day with him. *His name alone is excellent* (g).

But why doth the Spirit of God insist so much on this in the holy scriptures, that God is *one*, and *one only*; that he is *God alone*, and that there is *none else*, and that there is *none like him*?

(c) Deut. xxxii. 12. (d) Luke v. 21. Isa. xli 10, 17. and xliii. 25. (e) Isa. xlii. 8. Matth. iv. 10. (f) Exod. ix. 13. Deut. xxxiii. 26 Exod. xv. 11. Psal. lxxxvi. 8. and lxxxix. 6. Isa. xlvi. 9. (g) Psal. cxlviii. 13.

Of the Unity of the Divine Essence.

him? 1. God knows how prone we are naturally to set up others in the room and place of God to ourselves. 2. Many that profess to own the unity of the Deity, do not duly consider and improve this great truth. Therefore we are expressly required to attend to it and to lay it to heart: *Hear, O Israel, the Lord our God is one Lord.* And again, *Know therefore this day, and consider it in thine heart, that the Lord he is God in heaven above, and upon the earth beneath; there is none else* (h). 3. That we may hence learn to entertain high, reverend, and honourable thoughts of this one only God, and low and base thoughts of the most excellent beings in comparison of him, and be engaged to seek all our happiness in him alone.

SERMON LXXXII.

2. I Confirm the doctrine from the consent of nations. Not only Christians, but Jews, Mahometans, Pagans, all seem to agree in this, that there is but one supreme God. And though some of them have admitted a plurality of subordinate gods: Yet by accounting them to be subordinate, they have in effect denied them to be true gods; for a subordinate god is a contradiction, and really no god. Some historians tells us, that the devout priests among the Mahometans, five times every day ascend into the tops of the turrets of their temples, whence they proclaim with a loud voice, *There is no god but one God*. And although gods were multiplied among the Gentiles, according to men's own fancies, yet it was from the dotage and darkness of their spirits that they did so, as drunkards and madmen usually see things double. Besides, one Maximus, a heathen, writing to Augustine, gives this excuse for the polytheism of the Gentiles, to wit, † That they worshipped one supreme Essence, though under divers names; and that they had several deities that they might by so many several parcels adore the whole divine Essence. Seneca, also speaks much to the same purpose ‡, and Symachus, in a

learned

(h) Deut. iv. 39.

† *Equidem unum esse Deum summum a'q; Magnificum, quis tam Demens, tam Mente captus, neget esse certissimum? Hujus nos Virtutes per mundanum Opus diffusas multis Vocabulis invocamus, quoniam Nomen ejus cuncti proprium ignoramus.—Ita fit ut, dum ejus quasi quædam Membra cerptim variis Supplicationibus prosequimur, totum colere profecto videamur.* Inter Epist. August. N. 43.

† *Tot Appellationes ejus possunt esse quot Munera. Hunc et Liberum Patrem, et Herculem, ac Mercurium Nostri putant. Si hunc*

learned oration, wherein he craved of the emperors Valentinian and Theodosius a restitution of the Roman gods, affirms that they had respect only to one God, but had divers ways to bring them to that God; that they did not hold such things as they worshipped to be gods, but that in them they worshipped the true God. It is also observable, that the opinion of the plurality of gods among the heathen, prevailed only among the rude and vulgar sort, * who were deceived and led into it by certain lying and ridiculous fables. The wiser sort among them, when they spoke seriously, bore testimony to the unity of the Deity. Hence Plato, writing to his friend, says, "† Would you know when I am serious in writing? When I am serious, I begin with one God: But when I am in jest I begin with many." And both Socrates and Plato, in their description of God, ascribe unto him unity. Socrates, it is said, suffered death for maintaining this truth. The Platonics worshipped one supreme Essence, whom they called ‡ *The King*. The philosophers called God sometimes § *That Being*, or, *the only Being*; sometimes, ‖ *That one Thing*. Pythagoras' advice to his scholars was, *to search the Unity*. I might also make mention of Aristotle, Epictetus, Cicero, and divers others, who maintained the unity of the Godhead. From all which it appears, that the opinion of the plurality of gods prevailed only among the vulgar. Hence many think that the sect of philosophers among the heathens, who were called atheists, were not so called as if they thought or believed that there was no God, but because they opposed the vulgar opinion of the plurality of gods. And even the more superstitious Gentiles, who admitted a multiplicity of gods, owned one supreme God, whom they called ** *The Father of men and gods*. And Orpheus, who is said to be the first that put forth an edition of the names and kinds of their gods; yet afterward, being sensible of his folly, he, in a written discourse to his son Musæus and his other friends, recanted his wild errors,

and

Naturam Voces, Fatum, Fortunam: Omnia ejusdem Dei Nomina sunt, varie utentis sua potestate. Sen. L. 4. de Benef. c. 7.

* *Unus revera Deus est, qui Cœlum fabricavit et Terram —At nos Mortales, Versutia (sciz quorundam Hominum) decepti, Statuimus—Deorum Imagines—Et his Sacrificia & vanos Conventus tribuendo, hoc modo nos pios esse reputamus.* Sophocles.

† *Hinc discas scribam ego serio necne: Cum serio, ordior Epistolam ab uno Deo; Cum secus, a Pluribus.* Plato Epist. 13. ad Dionis.

‡ Ὁ Βασιλεύς.   § Τὸ ὄν.   ‖ Τὸ ἕν.

** *Pater Hominum Deorumq;*

and owned and acknowledged but one God †. So that nature hath a sense of this truth: As it shews that there is a God, so it shews that there is but *one only*.

3. I confirm this truth by reason. I formerly proved that there is a God: Therefore there must be but one. ‡ Either there is but one only God, or then it is impossible there can be any at all: For, there can be but one independent, infinite, omnipotent, and eternal Being. I might argue from all the divine attributes and perfections; but I shall mention only a few arguments.

Arg. 1. God is a Being absolutely necessary; as appears from the arguments adduced to prove that God is. They generally conclude in this, not only that God is, but that it is absolutely necessary he should be, and that he cannot but be. But so it is that there is but one Being absolutely necessary: For all the arguments that are adduced to prove the necessary existence of an infinitely perfect Being, do only infer the existence of one such Being. As for example, that it is necessary there should be some first cause; that is, an eternal, infinite, and independent Being, who hath his being of himself, and is the author of being to all other things: This argument doth only prove the necessary existence of one such cause; § for one such is sufficient for the production, preservation, and government of all things; therefore more are superfluous. There is no need of them. And seeing one only Being is absolutely necessary, it plainly follows that there must be one only God. Certainly, he that made the world, can preserve, govern, and guide the world without the assistance of any other god: For, if he needed any assistance, he were not God, an infinitely perfect and all-sufficient Being. And whatever power, wisdom, or other requisite perfections, can be imagined to be in many gods, for making, preserving and governing the world; all these are in one infinitely perfect Being: Therefore it is superfluous to feign many, seeing one is sufficient. From what is said, this at least must be granted, that it is possible there may be but one God: And if it be possible there may be but one, of necessity there must be but one; for we cannot imagine that to be God, which is possible not to be.

Arg. 2. From the divine eminency, dignity and excellency,

---

† Ἑῖς ἐςὶ Αὐτογενής, ἑνὸς ἔκγονα πάντα τέτυκται.
                                Orph. apud Clem. in Protrep.
‡ *Deus si unus non est, non est.* Tertul. contra Marc. L. 4.
§ Οὐκ ἀγαθὸν πολυκοιρανίη· εἷς κοίρανος ἔςω.

cy, God is absolutely the best and most excellent Being. When we conceive God, we thereby conceive a Being that is absolutely the best, infinitely excellent. But so it is, that there can be but one such. If we conceive more gods than one, we must conceive them, either to be worse than that one; and consequently no gods; or as good as he, and so none of them is God, because not one of them is absolutely the best, there being others as good as he. It adds greatly to the excellency of any thing, that it hath no peer or equal, that it is beyond compare: If you can find any thing of the same kind as good as it, this derogates from its excellency. So † it belongs to the excellency of God's being, that he is God alone, and hath no equal in worth and perfection. To imagine or feign other gods, is to derogate from his excellency, and consequently to make him no God. Therefore the Spirit of God insists so much upon this in the holy scriptures, that he is *God alone* (a); that he is *without compare* (b); and that there is *none like him* (c). His Being alone is excellent, because there is no such being as his. His name, *I AM*, speaks the incomparable nature of his Being. He is such a Being, that he alone is, and all other beings are no beings in comparison of him. *All the inhabitants of the earth are reputed as nothing* (d). *All nations before him are as nothing, and they are counted to him less than nothing and vanity* (e).

Arg. 3. From the divine independency. There can be but one independent Being, therefore but one only God. If we could conceive more gods than one, we must conceive either that they depend on that one, which is really to conceive them no gods; or that they do not depend on that one, and so that we make that one no God. Particularly, 1. There can be but one independent in Being. If there were more gods, either one of them would be the cause and author of being to the rest, and then that one would be the one only God; or none of them would be the cause and author of being to the rest; and so none

of

---

† *Deus cum summum magnum sit, recte veritas nostra pronunciavit, Deus si non unus est, non est—Porro Summum magnum unicum sit necesse est, ergo & Deus unicus erit non aliter Deus nisi summum magnum, nec aliter summum magnum nisi parem non habeat, nec aliter parem non habeas, nec aliter parem non habeas nisi unicus fuerit.*
Tertul. adv. Marcion. L. 1. C. 2.

(a) Psal. lxxxvi. 10. 2 Kings xix. 15, 19. Neh. ix. 6.
(b) Psal. lxxxix. 6. (c) Exod. ix. 14. Isa. xlvi. 9. Jer. x. 6, 7.
(d) Dan. iv. 35. (e) Isa. xl. 17.

of them would be God, beacufe none of them would be independent, or the fountain of being to all. 2. There can be but one independent in working. For if there were more independent beings, then in thefe things wherein they will and act freely, they might will and act contrary things, and fo oppofe and hinder one another; fo that, being equal in power, nothing would be done by either of them. Yea, though we should fuppofe a plurality of gods, agreeing in all things, yet feeing their mutual confent and agreement would be neceffary to every action, it plainly appears that each of them would neceffarily depend on the reft in his operations; and fo none of them would be God, becaufe not abfolutely independent.

Arg 4. From the infinitenefs of God. It is neceffarily included in the notion of God that he is infinite. But there can be but one infinite Being: For fuppofe there were two fupreme Beings, either one of them would include the other, and fo that which is included would be finite, and have fome dependence on the other in which it is; or one of them would exift feparately from the other, and fo none of them would be infinite, becaufe none of them would contain all things, nor fill all things. If there be one infinite Being, that is bounded or limited by no place, how can there be an infinite being exifting feparately from it.

Arg. 5. From the omnipotency of God. There can be but one Omnipotent. For, fuppofe two omnipotent beings, then the one is able to do whatfoever he will, and yet the other is able to refift and hinder him. If the one cannot hinder the other, then that one is not omnipotent; if he can hinder the other, then that other is not omnipotent. Again, we muft conceive two fuch beings, either as agreeing, and fo the one would be fuperfluous; or as difagreeing, and fo all would be brought to confufion, or nothing would be done; for that which one would do, the other would oppofe and hinder. The order and harmony of the world, the conftant and uniform government of all things, is a plain argument that there is but one only omnipotent Being.

Arg 6. There can be but one eternal Being; therefore but one God. An eternity of being admits not of plurality or multiplicity. It is God's prerogative and excellency, that he is the Firft of all beings. So is his eternity expreffed; *I the Lord the Firft, and with the Laft, I am he. I am Alpha and Omega, the Beginning and the End, the Firft and the Laft* (*f*).

(*f*) Ifa. xli. 4. Rev. xxii. 13.

God is the First, that is, he is before all things, absolutely the First. Now, if there could be two beings of eternal existence, none of them would be absolutely the first, and so none of them would be God. The first Being can be but one.

Arg 7. The supposition of a plurality of gods is destructive to all true religion. For if there were more than one God, we would be obliged to serve and worship more than one: But this is impossible for us to do, as will plainly appear, if we consider what divine worship and service is. Divine worship and service must be performed with the whole man. This is what the divine Eminency and Excellency doth require, that we love him with all our heart, soul, mind, and strength; and serve him, with all our heart; and that our whole man, time, strength, and all we have, be entirely devoted to him alone: But this cannot be done to a plurality of gods; for in serving and worshipping a plurality, our hearts, time, strength, &c. would be divided amongst them. To this purpose our blessed Lord argues, *No man can serve two masters: For either he will hate the one, and love the other; or else he will hold to the one, and despise the other. Ye cannot serve God and Mammon* (g). Mammon is thought to be an idol which the heathens reckoned to be the god of money or riches. Now, says our Lord, you cannot serve them both; if you would have the Lord for your God, and serve him, you must renounce Mammon. We cannot serve two gods or masters: if but one require our whole time and strength, we cannot serve the other.

Arg 8 If there might be any more gods than one, nothing would hinder, why there might not be one, or two, or three million of them. No argument can be adduced for a plurality of gods, suppose two or three, but what a man might, by parity of reason, make use of for never so many. Hence it is, that when men have once begun to fancy a plurality of gods, they have been endless in such fancies and imaginations. To this purpose is that charge against the Jews, who in this conformed themselves very much to the nations round about: *According to the number of thy cities are thy gods, O Judah* (h). And Varro reckons up three hundred gods whom the heathens worshipped. Yea, Hesiodus reckons three thousand of them †. And indeed, if once we begin to fancy more gods than one, where shall we make an end? So that the opinion or conception of a plurality of gods is most ridiculous and irrational.

Thirdly,

(g) Matth. vi. 24.   (h) Jer. ii. 28.
† Τρὶς μύριοι εἰσὶ Θεοί. Hesiod. in Theog.

Thirdly, I shall now apply this doctrine.

Use 1. For confutation. And,

First, It serves to confute the heathens and Pagans, who held and maintained a great plurality of gods whom they worshipped. It is true, they generally held that there was but one supreme God; yet they dishonoured and affronted him, by setting up others as gods, to whom they gave divine and religious worship and adoration. And it is very strange and amazing to consider, that they admitted into the number of their gods, not only mortal, yea, dead men, † but beasts also, and inanimate creatures, and the most mean and pitiful of them. As many worshipped the sun, moon and stars; so ‡ the Thebans worshipped sheep and weasels; the inhabitants of Mendes, a goat; the Thessalians, storks; the Syrophœnicians, doves; the Egyptians, dogs, cats, crocodiles, yea, leeks, onions, and garlic. Yea, many of the heathens deified and worshipped murderers, adulterers, thieves, drunkards, and other such pests of mankind.

But seeing the light of nature and reason teach that there is but one only God, whence then did the multiplicity of gods among the Gentiles arise? I answer, 1. From their ignorance, and vain imaginations of God. The apostle tells us, *They became vain in their imaginations, and their foolish heart was darkened—and changed the glory of the incorruptible God, into an image made like to corruptible man, and to birds, and four-footed beasts, and creeping things* (i). They indulged themselves in vain conceits of God. They thought his power and presence might reach one place, and not another: As the Syrians, who imagined that the Israelites worshipped such as were *gods of the hills, but not of the plain* (k). ‖ Men being pressed by manifold straits, necessities, and distresses, did look and seek for helpers on all hands, and so multiplied gods unto themselves, from a vain conceit that one supreme God was not sufficient for all their needs. 2. The variety and multitude of the attributes and works of God, might give occasion to men to think of a plurality of gods, and to attribute so many and great works and perfections, rather separately to many gods, than conjunctly to one. 3 God in his just judgment gave up the heathens to such gross and abominable

---

(i) Rom. i. 21, 23. (k) 1 Kings xx. 23.

† *Quicquid humus, pelagus, cœlum mirabile gignunt, id dixere deos, colles, freta, flumina, flammas.*   Prudent.

‡ Pomey's Pantheon, p. 5.

‖ *Fragilis et laboriosa mortalitas in partes ista digessit, infirmitatis suæ memor, ut portionibus quisq; coleret, quo maxime indigeret.*

                                              Plin. C. 2.

abominable idolatry, as a juſt puniſhment for their abuſe of nature's light in other things. The apoſtle ſeems to take notice of this in the text already quoted: *Becauſe*, ſays he, *that when they knew God, they glorified him not as God, neither were thankful, but became vain in their imaginations, and their fooliſh heart was darkened. Profeſſing themſelves to be wiſe, they became fools: and changed the glory of the incorruptible God* (*l*), &c. They had ſome knowledge of the divine excellencies and perfections, by the light of nature, and the works of creation: But they abuſed that knowledge, and did not worſhip and glorify God as became theſe his perfections; and they were puffed up with a conceit of their own wiſdom: And for their pride and abuſe of their knowledge, God gave them up to greater darkneſs and blindneſs of mind, ſo that the light of nature in them was much obſcured; hence they indulged their own conceits of God, and ſo fell into groſs and abominable idolatry.

More particularly, the heathens deified and worſhipped ſuch as had been great or famous men among them. And they were led to this, 1. By the inſolence of ſome powerful men; ſuch as divers of the Roman emperors, who affected to be adored, and eſteemed gods. Some of them were ſo impudent, that they would be adored even when alive, and had temples and altars conſecrated to them. 2. By a prepoſterous deſire to perpetuate the memory of extraordinary and uſeful men among them. Such men made themſelves firſt to be admired among the vulgar; and this admiration was by degrees turned into a profound reſpect, till at laſt, † to eternize their names, the people enrolled them among the number of their gods, and owned them as ſuch. 3. By vile flattery. For, flattering ſubjects, to gratify the pride, vanity, and ambition of their kings and princes, erected images of them in eminent and public places, and offered incenſe to them, as they did to their other gods. 4 Some feigned their anceſtors to be gods, and obtained them to be ſo reputed

(*l*) Rom. i. 21, 22, 23.

† *Unde igitur, ad homines opinio multorum deorum perſuaſione pervenit? Nimirum ij omnes, qui coluntur ut dij, homines fuerunt, & ijdem primi et maximi reges: Sed eos, aut ob virtutem, qua profuerunt hominum generi, divinis honoribus affectos eſſe poſt mortem; aut ob beneficia et juventa, quibus humanam vitam excoluerunt, immortalem memoriam conſecutos, quis ignorat.* Lactant. de Ira Dei.

Hic eſt vetuſtiſſimus referendi gratiam bene merentibus mos, ut tales numinibus adſcribantur, quippe & omnium aliorum deorum nomina, et quæ ſupra ſydera relata, ex hominum nata ſunt meritis. Plin.

reputed by people, that by this means they might gain the more reverence, respect, and authority, unto themselves.

Again, many of the heathens owned and worshipped the sun, moon, and stars, for their gods; being led to this by observing and admiring their magnitude and greatness, the rare and hidden matter and substance of them, their wonderful splendor and brightness, their swift and regular motion, and their various and excellent effects and influences on inferior bodies. Hence it was that these heralds and messengers of God were either mistaken for God himself, or reputed to have certain deities residing in them. Of this Job speaks; *If I beheld the sun when it shined, or the moon walking in brightness; and my heart hath been secretly enticed, or my mouth hath kissed my hand* (*m*).

Other things also were reckoned by them amongst the number of their gods, for their extraordinary virtues and qualities; as fire, water, winds, which the Persians worshipped: Or for their strength and bigness; as whales, crocodiles: Or for their usefulness to men; as sheep, dogs, cats, leeks, onions: Or for their power over the bodies of men; as fevers and other diseases.

I shall add no more on this head; only we may take occasion from what hath been said, to admire and praise the great goodness of God, in making the light of the glorious gospel to shine into this dark corner of the earth. Consider, 1. How deep we were sunk into the darkness of Pagan idolatry and superstition. Historians give account that we were a most barbarous nation, and that our fathers were most gross and abominable idolaters, and worshipped the most monstrous and mis-shapen idols. 2. Consider how many nations God hath been pleased to pass by, and what a lamentable case they are in, the devil himself being worshipped by some of them. 3. Let us consider, that the gospel came not into this nation by chance, nor by the counsels of men, nor by a stated course in nature, but by the special providence and care of God. It was not our pains or purses that procured it, nor our goodness that deserved it; but God sent it. O then, let us be thankful to God for so great a blessing, and express our thankfulness by a high esteem of the gospel, by blessing and praising God for it, and making a thankful improvement of it. This is the way to keep the gospel still among us, and to have all the counsels, projects, and contrivances of wicked men against the gospel turned into nothing.

SERMON

(*m*) Job xxxi. 26, 27.

SERMON LXXXIII.

Second, THIS doctrine serves to confute divers ancient heretics. Some observe that there are few of the ancient heretics that did not assert and own, directly or indirectly, a plurality of gods. Some of them, viz. the Marcionites and Manichees, held that there are two gods; one a good god, the author of all good, and the god of the Christians; the other an evil god, the author of all evil, and the god of the Jews: for they could not understand how things of so contrary a nature, as good and evil, could proceed from one and the same god. This heresy they borrowed from some ancient heathen philosophers, especially the Persians, who held that there are two gods; one, the principle of all good, which they resembled to light; the other, the principle of all evil, which they resembled to darkness. And Plutarch says, that among the Greeks, the good principle was called God, and the evil principle † the devil. But in the judgment of some ‡ this is a corruption of a much more antient tradition, concerning that old serpent the devil, who, by tempting our first parents, brought sin, and all the evil consequents of it, first into the world. In opposition to this heresy, as a learned gentleman observes §, that expression, *one God,* was inserted in all the most ancient creeds, whether Greek or Latin, making the first article run thus, *I believe in one God,* or *in the only God.*

Most true it is, that the devil, the prince of darkness, is the author of a great many evils in the world; and hence it is that the devil himself is worshipped by many of the Pagans, out of fear: But how absurd is it, to reckon a being in its own nature evil to be a god? And whereas it was pretended by the Manichees, that these two principles of good and evil are in themselves infinite; how then could they effect any thing? For both being infinitely wise and powerful, they would be an equal match to one another, and by their eternal opposition and equal conflict, tie up one another's hands, and so be able to do neither good nor evil. As for these evils that are in the world, they are either evils of sin, or evils of punishment. Evils of sin are of all other evils the worst: But being considered formally, they are only privations of moral goodness and rectitude; so that

---

† Δαίμων.
‡ Dr. Tillotson, late archbishop of Canterbury's Sermon of the Unity of the Divine Nature.
§ Sir Peter King's History of the Apostles' Creed, cap. 2.

that they can have no efficient cause, properly so called, but only a deficient cause, viz. the creature sinning. As for evils of punishment, it is evident, that the infinitely good God, who is the author of all good, is also the author of all afflicting evils. *Shall there be evil in a city, and the Lord hath not done it* (a). As he doth good to all, so he may, and sometimes doth, afflict men with various evils, to punish them for sin, to manifest his infinite holiness and hatred of sin, to give check to atheism, to reclaim sinners, and awaken them to repentance; and with respect to his own, that he may correct and chastise them for sin, cure them of many heart-evils, wean their hearts from the world, and make them weary of the world, and long to be in heaven. So that afflicting evils are sometimes useful and profitable, yea, necessary for us, in our present state. Therefore it was without any shew of reason that some have maintained that such evils could not proceed from a good God.

There were also other ancient heretics, called Tritheists, who parted the Godhead into three distinct essences, holding that the Father, Son, and Holy Ghost, are not only distinct persons, but have each of them a distinct essence; so that they did plainly profess that there are three gods. Before these there were a sort of heretics, called by some Triformians, who held that the Father, Son, and Holy Ghost differ from the divine essence as parts from the whole, making the Godhead to be compounded of three distinct parts, which parts are called Father, Son, and Holy Ghost: So that, in effect, they held that there are three gods. But it may be alledged, if there are three distinct divine Persons, are there not then three distinct Gods? I answer, no such thing will follow: For though there be three distinct persons, yet there are not three distinct natures or essences, but the same individual nature or essence; the like whereof is not to be found among all the creatures. In one and the same most simple divine essence, there are three distinct persons, who all partake of the same infinite essence, not by division, but by communication; so that the essence is not divided in the persons, nor yet the persons separated from the essence, but only so distinguished that the one is not the other. And although a finite singular nature cannot be communicated to more persons, but is terminated in one; yet the divine nature, being infinite, may be communicated to more.

Third, This doctrine serves for the confutation of the Papists, who, though they profess that there is but one only God, yet, in effect, set up other gods to themselves besides him. As the ancient

(a) Amos iii. 6.

ancient Pagans had their celeſtial and terreſtrial gods, ſo the Papiſts ſet up others as gods to themſelves, both in heaven and in earth.

1. They ſet up other gods to themſelves in heaven; as the angels, the virgin Mary, and other ſaints departed.

(1.) They ſet up angels as gods to themſelves, while they give unto them religious worſhip, ſuch worſhip as is due to God alone. But chiefly they worſhip the archangel Michael, and the reſt of the angels that † *ſtand before God*, and wait immediately upon him, as they expreſs themſelves. Theſe angels they call ‡, "Princes of the royal houſe of heaven, and preſi-"dents of all the churches." And of theſe they reckon ſeven by name, to whoſe honour and worſhip there is a famous temple built and conſecrated at Rome. And as they aſſign to every particular man and woman a tutelar angel, ſo they religiouſly worſhip theſe angels, and pray to them. What is this but to ſet them up as gods, in the room and place of God, unto themſelves?

(2.) They make a god, or goddeſs, to themſelves of the virgin Mary, while they aſcribe to her, ſupreme power: Yea, a right to command Chriſt. They call her *, "The queen of "heaven, the port of Paradiſe, the lady of the world, the pa-"troneſs of mankind, the moderatrix of the whole univerſe, "the mother of grace and mercy, the fountain of life, the light "of the church." All which are titles peculiar to God and Chriſt, or equal to ſuch. Again, they pray to her § to command her ſon to do what they deſire, which is to prefer her before Chriſt. And to the honour of the virgin Mary they celebrate feaſts, erect temples, monaſteries, altars, &c. and they dedicate to her ſhips, houſes, cities, colleges, yea, whole kingdoms. What is all this but to make her a god?

(3.) They make to themſelves gods of other ſaints departed, while they pray to them with all the rites and ſolemnities of a religious worſhip, and that for ſuch bleſſings as God alone can give; yea, for ſpiritual bleſſings, to purge them from their ſins, and to inſpire them with virtue ‖. They ſing hymns to their praiſe, ſay maſſes for their honour, conſecrate times and places for their worſhip, and profeſs to place their truſt and confidence
in

---

† *Angelos coram Deo aſſiſtentes.*
‡ *Principes auæ cœleſtis, eccleſiarum omnium præſides.*
* Offic. B. Virg. and Pſalter Marian. in Chemnit. Exam. pt. 3d.
§ *Jure matris impera Redemptori.*
‖ Chemnit. Exam. p. 136.

in them *. Is not all this to make gods of them, by ascribing to them omniscience, omnipresence, and omnipotence, which are the peculiar properties of God? And what a vast number are they whom they do thus religiously worship? and † divers of them never had any real being: and of others we have no certainty that they are in heaven; they may be among the damned for ought we know.

This popish worship of angels and saints, is a plain revival of the heathens' worshipping their demons and heroes. Their canonizing saints answers to the senate of Rome's Apotheosis, that is their enrolling deceased men among the number of their gods. And what is it that the papists have not a saint for, as well as the antient Pagans a god or a goddess? The Pagans had one Æsculapius for a god of physic; but the Papists have as many peculiar saints as there are diseases: They had Mercury for the god of tradesmen; but these have a saint almost for every trade. And whereas the Pagans had rural deities, so have the Papists rural saints. Such an exact conformity is there in the Romish church to the antient Pagans in their multiplicity of gods. This is also evident in their performing religious worship to the saints in the temples of the Pagan gods; as is notorious in their consecrating the Pantheon at Rome to the virgin Mary and all the saints, which was by the Pagans dedicated to Cybele and all the gods. And some of their own writers observe ‡, that this agreement with the Pagans was not by chance, but by imitation, and of design to allure and gain the Pagans to their religion and profession.

2. The Papists set up other gods to themselves on earth. And, 1. They make the Pope their god, in ascribing to him exorbitant titles and prerogatives; for they expressly call him, *their Lord God the Pope, the best and greatest, and supreme God on earth, a visible Deity;* and § they ascribe to him an extravagant power, and extravagant homages and services are done to his person in public solemnities. 2. They make the wafer or host in the sacrament a god to themselves. For, from their false hypothesis of its being transubstantiated into the very body of Christ, they adore and worship it as God, when it is lifted up by the priest, at the ringing of a little bell. And the host is reserved

---

* *See* Chemnit Exam. *and* Breviar Rom. *and* Whitby of Idol.
† Danger of Popery, page 4.
‡ Polid. Virg. de rerum Invent. in the Proem to the five last books, *and* Gregory the Great, Lib. 9. Epist. 71.
§ More's Mystery of Iniquity, Part I. Book II. C. 10.

reserved in a box, and carried in procession, and solemnly adored by all who see it. What abominable idolatry and prodigious madness is this, for men to adore and worship what they eat. 3. They make the cross their god; the cross on which Christ was crucified: For they pray to it, and that for spiritual blessings, and call it their only hope. So that they set up a piece of wood for their god. And under the name of the cross they understand, not only that particular tree on which Christ was crucified, but any cross made like it of whatsoever matter, yea, figures or representations of it. They ascribe divers supernatural effects to it, and boast of many miracles wrought by it. Hence they make a manifold use of the cross, and of the sign of the cross, ascribing to it a sanctifying, saving, delivering, and preserving power and virtue. And some of them † plead for the highest degree of divine worship to the cross. 4. They make gods to themselves of divers images. For though the learned among them pretend that they do not worship the images themselves, but only those that are represented by them: Yet this is not according to truth; for the Counsel of Trent ‖ decerns that due honour and veneration be given to images. And in the 2d Council of Nice it is repeated above twenty times, that *images of saints are to be adored* §. And they condemn them that say, they are to be *reverenced*, and not to be *adored*. And they attribute to divers images no less than a divine power, while they ascribe to them supernatural effects; such as, the averting of thunder and lightening, the expulsion of devils, the advocation of angels, and the protection of saints. ¶ And they pray expressly to the image of Veronica, " O ho-" ly picture, purge us from all sin within and without, and " bring us to that country where we may see the face of Christ." And it is plain, that much of their worship lies in their devotion to images: For they kneel before them, and sometimes creep to them; they offer oblations, light candles, and burn incense to them; they set them on eminent places for veneration; and they carry them in procession, for averting pests, or hurt to corns, and for other supernatural effects. 5. They make gods to themselves of manifold relics. For they boast and make a

shew

---

† Thom. pt. 3. Qu. 25. Art. 4. Bonavent. L 3. in Sentent. ad Dist. 9.

‖ Sess. 25.　　　§ Act 6.

¶ *See* Pontifical *in the* Consecration of the Image of the Blessed Virgin, *and in the* Consecration of the Image of St. John the Evangelist.

new of innumerable relics of Christ, with respect to his infancy, with respect to his riper age, with respect to his passion, and with respect to his exaltation: And of manifold relics of the Virgin Mary, of the apostles, of the martyrs, and of other saints departed; and these relics they religiously worship and adore.

Thus they make many gods unto themselves, celestial and terrestrial gods, angelical and human gods, gods of wood and stone, of gold and silver, the work of mens hands, a breaden god. Innumerable are the persons and things which they have set up in the room and place of God unto themselves: So that they have outstript the very pagans in their multiplicity of gods. And although they profess that there is but one only God, yet while they give that worship to others which is due to him alone, they in effect make many gods, and are guilty of the grossest idolatry. Their distinction of *Latria* and *Dulia*, is ridiculous, and makes nothing for them: For, as the common people know not the importance of it, so their learned men are much puzzled how to distinguish accurately between the two. And seeing they give that worship to others which is due to God only, it is no matter by what name they call it. And that which they call *Dulia*, and give to saints and angels, is in scripture appropriated to God alone, as may be obvious to them that understand the original text (*b*). And the apostle finds fault with the Galatians, that before their conversion, they *did service to them that were by nature no gods* (*c*). And the worship and service there condemned, as is clear from the original text, is the same which the papists give to saints and angels. So that no kind of religious worship, under any name whatsoever, is to be given to creatures, but to God alone. I add that some of the papists give that which they call *Latria*, or supreme religious worship, to other things besides God; as to the cross, and the host in the sacrament.

I shall conclude this head with a few practical inferences. And, 1. Let us bless God for our reformation from popery. This is a mercy never to be forgotten to all generations, and ought always to be remembered with praise and thanksgiving to God. 2. Let us detest and abhor popery, as for their gross and damnable corruptions in doctrine, and their horrid cruelty, so also for their abominable idolatry, particularly in setting up others as gods to themselves besides the true God. 3. Let us pity them that are under the darkness of popery, not only in the nations abroad, but even here at home. There are some

places

(*b*) Matth. iv. 10. (*c*) Gal. iv. 8.

places belonging to this land where the reformation from popery never yet had place, or but of late: And there are some other places where popery hath been on the growing hand, and gaining ground; so that many poor people are deluded, and led away to worship such things as are no gods. Let us pity them, and pray much for them. 4. Let us take heed that we ourselves be not deluded, or drawn away to popery, and particularly to join with them in their idolatrous worship. For this end, let us get and keep upon our hearts a deep sense of the great evil and danger of Romish idolatry: Let us make choice of the holy scriptures for the only rule of our worship, as well as of our faith: Let us take heed of self-conceit and self confidence, and exercise a humble and self-denied dependence on God through Christ, for the teaching and conduct of his Spirit, that he may lead, guide, and establish us, in the good ways of the Lord. 5. Let us manifest our zeal against popery on all proper occasions, and particularly in our zeal for the Protestant succession. Nothing can have a greater tendency to bring in popery, than promoting the interest of a popish pretender to the throne. Therefore let us manifest and shew our zeal for the succession to the throne in the Protestant line of the illustrious house of Hanover, as that we will stand by, and earnestly contend for, by all means proper to us in our place and station.

SERMON LXXXIV.

Fourth, THIS Doctrine serves to confute the Socinians, who though they impiously and blasphemously hold Christ to be a mere man, yet call him *true God*, and the *great God*, and own that religious worship is due to him. They deny that he is God by nature, but only by office and favour, and in a secondary and inferior manner. Hence they distinguish between an increated and created God, an independent and dependent God, a supreme and subordinate God. What is this but to introduce a plurality of gods into the Christian faith? And when they admit two gods, what reason can they give why there might not be a great many more. It is plain, * that they cannot acquit themselves from the charge of abominable idolatry, while they give divine worship to him whom they hold to be a mere creature,

---

*. *In idolatriam incides, quum dominum vere non fatearis, adoresque illum quem Deo Patri consubstantialem esse non credas, sed potius creaturam.* Cyril. Thesaur. L. 2. C. 1.

creature, and not God by nature: For the apostle describes idolatry to be, the giving *service*, or worship, to things which *by nature are no gods* (*a*).

Fifthly, This doctrine serves to confute a set of men who have extended the power and prerogative of kings and princes beyond measure. Some court-parasites and flatters have kept no bounds in their assertions even about the commanding power of the magistrate, as if we were bound to obey whatever he commands, without any trial or examination; and if the magistrate command what is unlawful, then, say they, he is answerable to God for commanding, but we are not chargeable with guilt for obeying. I have sometimes had occasion to hear with mine own ears much to this purpose from that sort of men: And it is very agreeable to what some have written on that head *. And in the late times of our sad defection, the estates of parliament in Scotland ascribed unto the king such an absolute authority as obliged the subjects to obedience without reserve †. And the people of God were reproached with disloyalty, and suffered grievous persecution, for their simple non-obedience to the iniquitous commands of the magistrate. What is all this, but

(*a*) Gal. iv. 8.

* In cases and disputes of public concernment, private men are not properly *sui juris*. They have no power over their own actions: They are not to be directed by their own judgments, or determined by their own wills, but by the commands and determinations of the public conscience. And if there be any sin in the command, he that imposed it shall answer for it, and not I whose whole duty it is to obey. The commands of authority will warrant my obedience; my obedience will hallow, or at least excuse my action, and so secure me from sin, if not from error.

Dr Parker's Preface to Bramhall's Vindication. Page 308.

† K James VII. Parl. 1. Sess. 1 Act. 2. The estates of parliament declare, that our kings were invested with absolute authority: and that they abhor and detest—all principles and positions which are contrary or derogatory to the king's sacred, supreme, absolute power and authority:—and that they hold themselves obliged—to assure all his enemies, who shall adventure on the disloyalty of disobeying his laws, or on the impiety of invading his rights,—that they firmly resolve to give their entire obedience to his majesty without reserve.

Nota. Most of the laws enacted in that parliament are declared impious and intolerable grievances, by the meeting of the estates, April 13, ann. 1689. And the foresaid act, except in so far as concerns the annexation of the excise to the crown, together with many other acts of that parliament, are rescinded, by K. William and Q. Mary, Parl. 1. Sess. 2. Act 28.

but to make a god of the magistrate, yea, to honour him above God? It is to give the magistrate an absolute, and God a limited obedience; to justle God out of the throne, and put the magistrate in his room; to set man upon the throne of God, and God at the footstool of man. It is a sacrilegious usurpation of God's prerogative: For it is his peculiar prerogative, that his will is the rule and measure of what is just and good. Certainly, whatever princes enjoin by their laws, is to be tried and examined by the holy scriptures: This examination and judgment of private discretion is what all Protestants generally plead for in divers controversies between the papists and us, and without which we must transform men into brutes †. And subjects do not hereby make themselves their prince's judges, but only judges of their own actions, in judging, so far as concerns themselves, whether the acts of obedience required be agreeable to the unerring rule of the word of God. And this is the more necessary, considering the *account* they must *give of themselves unto God* (*b*). Again, the ascribing an absolute and unlimited power to princes is horridly blasphemous, and gives great advantage to the papists in the controversy between them and us about the pope's infallibility.

To conclude this head, let us bless God, that the iniquitous laws and commands of princes are not our trial at this time. But if ever it shall be your lot, to live in such times and places of the world where this may be your trial, remember then that it is better to obey God than man (*c*). None can reward your obedience as God can do. Men may give you lands and estates, and places of profit and preferment; but they cannot give you a crown of glory that fadeth not away. None can punish your disobedience as God can do. Men may kill the body; but God can destroy both soul and body in hell. God can secure you against all the wrath and threats of men, for not obeying their iniquitous laws: But all the princes in the world cannot secure you against the wrath of God, when his law is broken.

Use 2. For instruction: In several particulars.

Instr. 1 Is the true and living God but one only? Then, what cause have we to bless the Lord, that we have the only true

---

† *Qui hoc judicium privatis eripiunt, homines in belluas plane transformant. Cum igitur dogma proponitur credendum, aut præceptum aliquid faciendum, quia credere & facere sunt actus mei, si me hominem rationis participem præstare velim, examinare opportet quicquid proponitur ad scientiam meam.* Daven. de Judice. Cap. 3.

(*b*) Rom. xiv. 12. (*c*) Acts v. 29.

true God clearly revealed and made known to us in his blessed word? How many in the world do this day sit in darkness, and know nothing of him? Though many of the heathens had a notion of the unity of God, yet they knew not who he was. Excellent to this purpose is that text: *This is life eternal, to know* THEE, *the only true God, and Jesus Christ whom thou hast sent* (d). O what cause have we to be thankful, that we have been born and brought up in such an age of the world, and in such a climate, where the only true God is clearly revealed to us? This is owing to the good providence of God, who *hath determined the times before appointed, and the bounds of* mens *habitation* (e). To have the knowledge of him who is the one only God, is a great blessing; especially if he hath savingly revealed himself to you. For this our blessed Saviour thanks the Father on the behalf of his people: *I thank thee, O Father, Lord of heaven and earth, that thou hast hid these things from the wise and prudent, and hast revealed them unto babes* (f). O, what cause have we to admire his grace and goodness to us, that having hid the knowledge of himself from many wise and learned men, he hath revealed himself to us!

Instr. 2. How miserable is their case, who have God for their enemy! He is the one only God; therefore, if he be against you, it matters not who be for you. When he is your enemy, none else can deliver you; for he is God, and there is none else. O, how miserable and helpless will you be, when he ariseth to execute his wrath? For there is no other god in heaven or earth, that can deliver you out of his hand.

Instr. 3. Is it so, that the true God is but one only? Then, they are happy who have him for their God. He is the one only God; therefore *if he be for* you, *who can be against* you (g)? Ye whose God the Lord is, have but one Master to please, and one Benefactor to seek unto. Better one than many. Make him your friend, and then your business is done, and your happiness secured. Many gods are not needful. To your happiness there needs no more but this one only God. There is enough in this one, so that you are happy enough in him alone. The more you content yourselves with this one only God, the happier you are. Better one fountain than a thousand cisterns; one all-sufficient God, than a thousand insufficient ones. He *stretched out the heavens alone, and spread abroad the earth by* himself (h); and there was no strange god with him. What a hand and

(d) John xvii. 3.   (e) Acts xvii. 26.   (f) Matth. xi. 25.
(g) Rom. viii. 31.   (h) Isa. xliv. 24.

and arm muſt he have, and how wiſe muſt he be, who made all theſe alone, having no help from any other? O, there is none like your God. *Among the gods there is none like* him. Other gods are but new upſtarts: But your God is *from everlaſting to everlaſting God* (i). They have no power to help their worſhippers: *They are vanity, and the work of errors* (k): But he hath all power in his hand. What can he not do for you? They are but dead idols; but he is the living God. All the nations uſed to boaſt of their gods; but none have ſuch a God to boaſt of as you have. He is too hard for all the gods of the nations, and can eaſily baffle them all. This is your happineſs who believe in Chriſt, that you are taken into covenant with this one only God.

Uſe 3. For reproof, to many carnal profeſſed Proteſtants, who, though in word they profeſs that God is one only, and give external worſhip to him alone, yet practically ſet up other things as gods unto themſelves beſides him. And indeed none are careleſs of getting a ſaving intereſt in the true God, but have other gods beſides him. There is no man but muſt have ſome god or other; ſomething on which he placeth his affection moſt, that he loves and reſpects above all other things, and that hath dominion over him. If the true God be not your God, you have doubtleſs ſomething elſe ſet up in his room. I am afraid it may be ſaid of many of you, that you *have ſet up* your *idols in* your *hearts* (l). As there is outward groſs idolatry, ſo there is inward heart idolatry. The firſt commandment implies as much: *Thou ſhalt have no other gods before me.* Theſe words, *before me*, amongſt other things, imply the ſpirituality of the command. You may have other gods before the Lord, though you have none before the world.

The great idol-god that the moſt part of profeſſed Chriſtians ſet up to themſelves is ſelf. A man's ſelf is naturally a god unto him. Hence it is that ſelf-denial is the principal and firſt leſſon in Chriſtianity. *If any man will come after me,* ſays Chriſt, *let him deny himſelf* (m). If we ſaw into the ſecrets of mens hearts, we would ſee the moſt part of men ſerving and worſhipping themſelves. And, 1. Many will be ſubject to none, but to their own will. Like theſe, who ſaid, *As for the word that thou haſt ſpoken unto us in the name of the Lord, we will not hearken unto thee. But we will certainly do whatſoever thing goeth forth out of our own mouth* (h). Men naturally affect a ſovereignty,

(i) Pſal. lxxxvi 8. Deut. xxxii. 17. Pſal. xc. 2. (k) Jer. x. 15. (l) Ezek. xiv. 3. (m) Matth. xvi. 24. (n) Jer. xliv. 16, 17.

reignty, and cannot endure that any other should lord it over them. That is practically their language, *Our lips are our own, who is lord over us (o)?* They would have the sovereign command of their own actions, and will not be controuled by another. Like those who gave this return to God's call to repentance: *There is no hope, but we will walk after our own devices* &c *(p)*. 2. Many have an immoderate and inordinate love unto themselves, which is predominant and prevalent in their souls. Their love to themselves shuts out love to God and their neighbour; and they prefer their own private interest to the public. 3. Many depend on themselves. Some depend on their own wisdom, as if that were sufficient to direct their way. Others depend on their own righteousness, as if it were sufficient to commend them to God, and bring them to heaven. 4. Many aim at themselves in all they do, and make themselves the end of their actions. They set up self at the end of every action, and justle out God, and refer all they do to their own profit, or their own honour and advancement. Thus self is suffered to usurp the rights of the Godhead, and is set up in the room and place of God.

Well then, when you will take your own course, and are obstinate for doing your own will, and walking in the ways of your own heart, and will not be controuled by admonitions and reproofs: Or, when you doat upon and over-love yourselves; or admire yourselves, because of your gifts, parts, and excellencies; and are careless how it go with the public, so your own interests prosper: Or, when you make your own bosom your oracle, and are confident of your own wisdom, as if you could do well enough without God: Or, when you trust to your own righteousness, and think to be saved by your own doing: Or, when you make use of religion to serve your own turn, and bring about your carnal ends; and put yourselves upon a profession of religion, from a prospect of some worldly advantages to be had by it; and aim at yourselves, your own profit or repute, in all your public actings and appearances for God: In all these and the like cases you make self your God.

More particularly, there are these three that the most part of men set up as gods unto themselves.

1. Many make the devil their god. The poor Indians worship him bodily. But you may readily think it strange, that I should say, that any within the church have the devil for their

---

(*o*) Psal. xii. 4.   (*p*) Jer. xviii. 11, 12.

their god. But the Jews might on as good ground think strange, when Christ told them that the devil was *the father* (*q*). All wicked men have the devil for their god and father. He is *the god of this world* (*r*); that is, of the unbelieving, unregenerate world. When you will do the devil's work, and hearken to his suggestions, and practically prefer them to the laws of God; then you make the devil your god, and set him up in God's room.

2. Many make the world their god. And here again there are, if I may so say, three lesser deities, profit, pleasure, and honour; or, as the apostle terms them, *The lust of the flesh, the lust of the eyes, and the pride of life* (*s*); called by some, *the unregenerate world's trinity*. 1. The covetous man makes his gold and money his god. Therefore *covetousness* is called *idolatry*; and *the covetous man is* called *an idolater* (*t*). When you set your hearts on worldly things, so that they wholly divert you from duty, or habitually distract your hearts in duty, and you spend your time and strength in the pursuit of them, then you make these things your gods †. 2. The voluptuous man makes his pleasures his gods. His *god is his belly*: And he *serves not the Lord Jesus Christ, but* his *own belly* (*u*). When you let loose the reins, and give up yourselves to sensual delights, and are *lovers of pleasures more than lovers of God* (*x*), then you make a god of pleasure. 3. The ambitious man makes his honour and reputation his god. This is what his heart is most set upon. *Honour me before the people* (*y*), said Saul. When you are ready to prostitute your soul and conscience, for worldly greatness and grandeur, or places of honour and preferment; or, all you do in religion is, that you may get a name, and maintain your reputation with your Christian neighbours: Then you make a god of your honour and repute.

3. The flesh, or the corruption of nature, is that which many set up as a god unto themselves. Therefore carnal men are said, *to walk after the flesh* (*z*). The flesh is the governing principle in them, and they are wholly carried away with the inclinations and desires of corrupt nature. When you give the flesh

---

(*q*) John viii. 44.   (*r*) 2 Cor. iv. 4.   (*s*) 1 John ii. 16.
(*t*) Col. iii. 5. Eph. v. 5.

† *Avarus aurum, Gulosus ventrem, Libidinosus Penem & Beelphegor colit. Lasciva mulier, quæ cum in Deliciis mortua est, adorat venereas voluptates.* Hieron. in Amos. C. 4.

(*u*) Phil. iii. 19. Rom. xvi. 18.   (*x*) 2 Tim. iii. 4.   (*y*) 1 Sam. xv. 34.   (*z*) Rom. viii. 1.

flesh its full liberty, and can deny yourselves in nothing, and cocker every fleshly appetite; and are careless whether God be pleased or displeased, so you may get the flesh pleased, then you make the flesh your god.

Thus we see how many things there are which even professed Protestants set up to themselves in the room and place of the true God. Many profess to own God, and that he is their God, yet they have other gods besides him. Many of you, if challenged for this, would instantly deny it, and that with an asseveration and aversation, God forbid that I should have any other God. Yet it is plain that there are other things on which you bestow your hearts and affections, or upon which you employ your time, strength, and parts, more than upon God. Therefore Satan hath bewitched you, and your own hearts have deceived you, when they persuade you, that you have no other god but the true God.

SERMON LXXXV.

IN prosecuting this purpose a little further, I shall, 1. Give some marks and characters whereby you may know what these things are that many set up unto themselves in the room and place of God. 2. I shall endeavour to hold forth to you the great evil of this.

First, The marks and characters are these following.

1. That is your god which you have a predominant and immoderate love unto. What is it that lies nearest your heart? If the world lie nearer; if a husband, or a wife, or a child lie nearer your heart than God doth, these are your gods. Whatever earthly thing it be, the enjoyment whereof affords you more delight than any thing else, or the want whereof grieves you excessively, even more than the want of communion with God, to be sure you make a god of it to yourselves; it hath too much room in your heart. Oh, how much of this is to be found amongst us!

2. That is your god that you are under the power of, so that you voluntarily subject your soul unto it, in a way of service and obedience: For, such a subjection of soul is a tacit acknowledgement of supremacy and sovereignty. Well then, consider what it is that you are at most pains for, or that getteth most of your time, strength, and labour, or that you set yourselves most to please. When you obey the devil, and do his work, and habitually and easily hearken unto his temptations and suggestions, then the divil is your god. When you obey the

flesh, and follow the dictates of your corrupt nature, and are set to do whatsoever your corrupt hearts bid you do; and your life, study, and labour, are employed in pleasing the flesh : Then the flesh is your god. When you consult flesh and blood whether you should obey God or nor, this is to authorize flesh and blood above God. Once more, when you yield obedience to the laws of men, in contradiction to the laws of God, and subject your soul and conscience to them; what is this but to set man upon the throne of God?

3. That is your god that you trust to and depend upon. For, trust and dependence is a tacit acknowledgement of a sufficiency in that which we depend upon. Well then, that which you place your hope and confidence in, as that which can do great things for you, and make you happy, and stand you in stead, expecting your happiness from worldly things, that is your God. This is what Job renounceth, *If I have made gold my hope; or have said to the fine gold, Thou art my confidence* (a). Again, when you put your trust and confidence in men or horses, in armies or navies, for safety and protection, victory and success; what is this but to put these things in the room and place of God? Further, that is your god which you depend upon, and have your recourse unto, in your straits and extremities, so that your heart is taken off from running to God, or relying on him. Solomon tells us, *The rich man's wealth, is his strong city* (b). If he abound in wealth and riches, he thinks he is well made up. If he be in danger, he trusts his money will redeem him : If dearth and famine come, he trusts his money will provide for him : If the pestilence come, he trusts his money will carry him to some other part of the world: If he fall into the hands of enemies, he trusts his money will be his ransom. Thus, many place their confidence in their riches, and so make a god of them. Others trust in their power and strength, or in their wisdom and policy : Which is plainly to make gods of these things.

4. That is your god which you make your chief and principal end and scope in what you do, and beyond which there is nothing you aim at. It is an honour peculiar to God alone, to be the chief and ultimate end and scope of all our actions. Well then, when you busy yourselves about the world, and are diligent in your lawful calling and employments, that you may have great wealth and outward abundance, and you aim at nothing beyond that, then wealth is your god. Again, when you eat and drink merely to gratify your sensual appetite,

(a) Job xxxi. 24.   (b) Prov. x. 15.

tite, and to fill your belly ; then your belly is your god. Once more, when you perform duties, or attend ordinances, or make public appearances for God and religion, that you may have glory and praise from men, then your credit and reputation is your god and idol.

5. That is your god which is the chief object of your delight and complacency. When your chief delight and contentment lieth in pleasing the flesh, and this gives you a joy and rest of mind, and choketh all delight in God; then the flesh is your god. Again, when the enjoyment of any worldly thing quiets your mind, and solaceth your soul, under the guilt of many wilful sins, and all your soul-dangers; then that worldly thing is your god. So it was with that rich man that sung a requiem to his soul; *Soul, thou hast much goods laid up for many years, take thine ease, eat, drink, and be merry* (c); when that peace, pleasure, and delight that you daily feed upon, is brought from the world, then the world is your god.

6. That is your god which is most the object of your fear. When you fear man more than God, this is to set up man above God. Now, it is a sign that you fear man more than God, when the fear of man proves a snare to you, by driving you to sin; as it did those who *did not confess Christ, left they should be put out of the synagogue* (d). So that men may be guilty of idolizing and making gods even of their very enemies whom they hate; when they fear them that can only kill the body, more than him that can destroy both soul and body.

7. To conclude: that is your god which alienates and estranges your heart from God. That which is so much in your mind, that God is justled out, and your thoughts are so much busied about it, that God is not in all your thoughts, or the thoughts of him are great strangers to you, that is your god. That which courts your heart continually, so that you have little or no heart for any thing that is good; that which leads and carries your heart, so that you are habitually diverted thereby when about duty, meditating, or praying, or reading, or hearing the word; that is your god.

From all this it appears, that there is much inward heart idolatry, though there be no open gross idolatry among us. Many of you set up idols and strange gods in your hearts, though you have none set up in your houses.

Second, I proceed to shew you the great evil of this inward heart-idolatry. 1. The sin is great. 2. The misery is great.

And

(c) Luke xii. 19.   (d) John xii. 42.

And what I am to say on these heads is applicable also to outward gross idolatry.

1. To set up any thing whatsoever in the room and place of God unto ourselves is a great sin. For,

(1.) It is a denying of God. Hence Job says, *If I have made gold my hope, or have said to the fine gold, thou art my confidence. If I rejoiced because my wealth was great, and because mine hand had gotten much, &c—I should have denied the God that is above* (e) These last words are applicable to all that goeth before. To make gold your hope and confidence, is as truly a denial of God, as the worshipping of the sun, moon and stars. For, seeing it is his prerogative to be God alone, therefore to set up any other for your god, is in effect to deny him. And seeing there is an utter inconsistency between the having the true God for your God, and the having of any other; therefore the setting up any other, is a renouncing and rejecting him from being your God. When you give that room in your heart, that love, or fear, or trust to any other, that is only due to God, then you have denied the God that is above.

(2.) It is a great dishonour to God. It is a great disparagement and indignity done to him, to prefer other things before him, or to love other things better than him: For nothing can come in competition with the great God, but what is infinitely below him. The combined excellencies of all the creatures, being laid in the balance with God, do not bear so great a proportion as a feather to a mountain. To forsake God for the world, or for a vile lust, is to leave a treasure for a trifle, a mountain of gold for a heap of dung, yea, all things for nothing. You look upon the Gaderenes as worse than swine, because they preferred their swine to Christ: And what better do many of you, who prefer mere trifles to the great God, yea, a soul-murdering lust before him †?

(3.) It is a robbing God of his sovereignty. As the setting up of another in the government, instead of the lawful prince, is rebellion and usurpation: So, to give to any other that homage of service and obedience, or that trust and confidence, which is only due to God, is to ascribe unto it that sovereignty which is proper to him alone. It is to justle him out of his throne, to take the crown off his head, to wrest his sceptre out

(e) Job xxxi. 24, 25. 28.

† *Idololatria Deo fraudem facit, honores illi suos denegans, & conferens aliis, ut fraudi etiam contumeliam conjungat.*

Tertull. Lib. de Idolol. c. 2.

out of his hand, to bestow it upon base things that are infinitely below him.

(4.) It is spiritual adultery in professors of the true religion. Hence the Lord says to his ancient people, *Plead with your mother, plead; for she is not my wife, neither am I her husband,* &c (*f*). As if he had said, She hath committed adultery by defiling herself with idols, and so hath broken her faith to me; therefore I will divorce her; she is not my wife. Hence also such as kept themselves from Romish idolatry are called *virgins* (*g*). This is applicable also to inward heart-idolatry; therefore such idolaters are called *adulterers* (*h*). They are chaste virgins to Christ, who keep their hearts for him, and do not willingly entertain other lovers. But when you set up idols in your hearts, and hug and embrace strange lovers, this is spiritual adultery: It is contrary to the marriage-covenant in which you virtually engaged by baptism.

(5.) It is a great affront to God. This is implied in the reason annexed to the first commandment: *Thou shalt have no other gods* BEFORE ME. You cannot set up to yourselves another god, but it is done in his sight and presence, and while he is looking on. Said king Ahasuerus of Haman, *Will he force the queen also before me?* So say I to you, will you affront God to his face, and set up another god while he is looking on? This is as if a wife would commit adultery even in her husband's presence.

(6.) It is the height of folly and madness: For these things that you set up as gods unto yourselves can never supply the room and place of a god unto you; they cannot help and deliver you, nor bless you and make you happy: Therefore it is great folly to make choice of them; especially considering that the great God offers himself to be a God to you upon very gracious terms. You who set up any other in the room and place of God, greatly prejudge yourselves by your own choice, in refusing him who is infinitely better. What madness is it to *forsake the fountain of living waters,* for *broken cisterns* (*i*). To forsake God, the fountain of all happiness, for broken cisterns that can hold nothing at all!

(7.) It is a practice worse than that of pagans. Hence the Lord chargeth the Jews with dealing worse with him than the heathens had done with their idols: *Pass over the isles of Chittim, and see; and send unto Kedar, and consider diligently; and see if there be such a thing. Hath a nation changed their gods, which*

are

(*f*) Hos. ii. 2. (*g*) Rev. xiv. 4.
(*h*) James iv. 4. (*i*) Jer. ii. 12, 13.

are yet no gods? But my people have changed their glory for that which doth not profit (k). The heathens do not change their gods, though they be but idols and false gods: Therefore it is unparallelled wickedness for any of you, who stand solemnly engaged that the Lord shall be your God, to change him, and that for mere vanities and vile lusts. Let heathens and pagans blush and be ashamed at such impiety!

2. Your misery is great, in setting up other things in the room and place of God unto yourselves. For,

(1.) These things cannot be a God to you; as I hinted already. It is plain that your vile lusts cannot be a God unto your souls; and it is as true, that the world and the things thereof cannot be so. Your worldly enjoyments cannot make you happy; they cannot bless, content, and satisfy your soul. No, no; they are all vain and empty in this respect. *Vanity of vanities, saith the Preacher; all is vanity* (l). And they are transitory and perishing things, that perish with the very using of them, and so cannot accompany you into eternity; therefore they can never be a God unto you. Though they have the room and place of a God, by your inordinate love to them, and that trust and confidence which you repose in them; yet they cannot act the part of a God to your soul. This will be evident to you in a day of distress: They cannot be a God to you then. What will you do when distress and trouble cometh upon you, and you shall be surrounded with troubles without, and filled with fears, griefs, and sorrows within; and God shall say to you, as to that people, *Go, and cry unto the gods which ye have chosen; let them deliver you in the time of your tribulation:* And, *where are thy gods which thou hast made thee? Let them arise, if they can save thee in the time of thy trouble* m)? These things that you set up in God's room, can neither deliver you from trouble, nor comfort you in trouble; nor save your soul from the wrath to come.

(2.) They shall be so far from being gods unto you, that they shall prove your tormentors. There is nothing that robs God of your heart, but will prove your tormentor sooner or later. When God awakens your conscience, and lets you see what a mad and foolish choice you have made; or, in a day of trouble, when you know not what to do, being destitute of friends and comforters; how will it gall you to the heart, and rack your soul with horrors of conscience, to think how you have slighted the great eternal God, and preferred base things
before

(k) Jer. ii 10, 11. (l) Eccl. i. 2. (m) Judges x. 14. Jer. ii. 28.

before him! I assure you, an awakened conscience is a sore place; and all the world cannot give you a plaister for it. And I add, that your choice of other things besides God will greatly aggravate your misery in hell. What do the damned in hell think of their choice, when all their good things are past? The folly of their choice is a great part of their misery and torment. Hence Abraham is brought in speaking to the rich glutton, *Remember that thou in thy lifetime receivedst thy good things, and likewise Lazarus evil things: But now he is comforted, and thou art tormented* (*n*). These things that you set up for gods to your soul, will but provide matter for the worm of an evil conscience to gnaw upon to all eternity.

(3.) Your setting up other things besides the Lord to be your god, will bring down the heavy wrath of God upon you: For, the Lord is a *jealous God*, and cannot endure that other things should rob him of his glory and honour. His jealousy implies two things, 1. His tenderness of his honour. His glory and honour is very dear to him; and he will not lose one tittle of it. *I am the Lord*, says he, *that is my name, and my glory will I not give to another, neither my praise to graven images* (*o*). As if he had said, I will not, and therefore see you to it that you do not, give away my glory. 2. His terribleness in case of his dishonour. Hence Moses says, *The Lord thy God is a consuming fire, even a jealous God* (*p*). *Jealousy*, saith Solomon, *is the rage of a man* (*q*); so the jealousy of God is the rage and fury of God. God will shew himself terrible to you who rob him of his glory, by setting up other things in his room. *Their sorrows shall be multiplied that hasten after other gods* (*r*). We have in scripture two remarkable instances that clear this. One is of Eli: Why did the Lord punish him so severely? What was his sin? It was this, he gave the honour of God unto his sons; as the Lord tells him, *Thou honourest thy sons above me* (*s*) The other is of Herod: He *made an oration unto* the people; whereupon *the people gave a shout, saying, It is the voice of a god, and not of a man. And immediately the angel of the Lord smote him, and he was eaten of worms* (*t*): Why? *Because he* accepted the applause, and *gave not God the glory*. Eli sinned in giving the honour of God unto his sons; and Herod in taking it to himself: But God taught them both how dear his glory was to him. If you rob God of his glory, by setting up other things as gods unto yourselves, he will make you know to your cost, that he is God, and that he alone is to be worshipped.

(*n*) Luke xvi. 25. (*o*) Isa xlii. 8. (*p*) Deut. iv. 24. (*q*) Prov. vi. 34. (*r*) Psal. xvi. 4. (*s*) 1 Sam. ii. 29. (*t*) Acts xii. 22. 23.

SERMON LXXXVI.

Use 4. FOR dehortation. O take heed of the sin of idolatry, in setting up other things in the room and place of God unto yourselves; and giving to them that worship, or these religious respects, that are due to God alone. Let me here warn you, both against outward gross idolatry, and against inward heart-idolatry.

First, Beware of outward gross idolatry, in having and worshipping other gods besides the true God with the outward man. From this the apostle dehorts us, *Little children, keep yourselves from idols* (a). Blessed be God, we are not at present in danger from temptations to Pagan and heathen idolatry. But I warn you especially to take heed of Romish idolatry, in worshipping saints and angels, and divers relics and images, and other things, to which the Papists give that worship which is due to God alone. To engage you to this, I propose these two considerations.

Consid. 1. There is great danger of being drawn away to Romish idolatry. Idolatry is a spreading evil. Men are naturally much inclined to it. How did it spread itself under the Old Testament, in all corners of the world, not only among the more barbarous and ignorant, but also the more polished and civilized nations. Judea only was free of it, and that only in some intervals of time between destroying judgments: For though they vomited up their idols, when they were under some sharp scourge; yet they usually licked them up again, when God visited them with peace and prosperity. Particularly, Romish idolatry is a very creeping thing, and steals and insinuates itself upon men insensibly. There are many plausible pretences and insinuations, whereby Romish emissaries easily impose upon simple and credulous souls. Hence it is that *Mystery* is said to be *written on the whore's forehead* (b). Romish idolatry did steal into the church by degrees, and under a disguise: And it is usually obtruded under the name and disguise of piety and devotion. Therefore Babylon is said to give *the wine of her fornication* in *a golden cup* (c). Wine is pleasant and and alluring in itself, but much more so, when given in a golden cup. The grossest idolatry of the church of Rome, as they cloke and palliate it, hath a glittering shew. It is gilded over with very plausible pretences, and many subtle distinctions are invented

---

(a) 1 John v. 21.   (b) Rev. xvii. 5.   (c) Rev. xvii. 4.

vented to make it go down the better: So that simple souls are apt to be much taken with it. And let none of you think that you are in no danger: For great is the power of delusion, especially when God in his just judgment gives up a people to it: And there are many things that might justly provoke God to give up this generation to be deluded into Romish idolatry: Such as, not keeping up a due detestation of it; much inward heart-idolatry amongst professors; a profane neglect of the worship of God in many; and in others, formality, hypocrisy, lukewarmness, and carnality in duties of worship, corrupting the worship of God with the inventions of men, &c.

Consid. 2. Idolatry is a very woful evil. For,

1. It is most hateful and abominable to God. Therefore it is called abominable idolatry. Serving other gods is that *abominable thing that God hates.* Hence the Lord complains, *I am broken with their whorish heart which hath departed from me, and with their eyes which go a whoring after their idols* (d). It is so hateful to God, that he would not communicate with idols in any thing. And, 1. He would not be called by the same name. Hence he says to Israel, *Thou shalt call me Ishi, and shalt call me no more Baali. For I will take away the names of Baalim out of her mouth, and they shall no more be remembered by their name* (e). The words *Baali* and *Ishi* both signify *a husband.* Only some observe that *Baali* signifies a husband under the notion of authority; and *Ishi* a husband under the notion of love: So that Baali, as well as Ishi, might be said of God, for any thing that is in the name itself. Yet because it was abused and given to idols, God would no more be called by that name. 2. He would not be worshipped in the same place with idols. Therefore, when Dagon was set up beside the ark, God threw it down again, and brake the neck of it. 3. He would not be worshipped with the same sacrifices. Hence the apostle says, *Ye cannot drink the cup of the Lord, and the cup of devils: Ye cannot be partakers of the Lord's table, and of the table of devils* (f). 4. He would not be served with the same priests. Therefore these priests that went back from the Lord, and became priests to idols, when the children of Israel went astray, were never admitted to serve him again in the priestly office, but only to attend upon, and minister unto the priests (g).

2. It exposeth to dreadful and terrible wrath. Idolatry is a sin that God cannot and will not bear with; because it robs him

---

(d) 1 Pet. iv. 3. Jer. xliv. 4. Exek. vi. 9. (e) Hof. ii. 16, 17. (f) 1 Cor. x. 21. (g) Ezek. xliv. 10.—14.

him of his glory, and is the greatest affront that can be offered unto him. The Lord our God is a jealous God. On this ground he diſſuades from idol-worſhip, *Thou ſhalt worſhip no other god; for the Lord, whoſe name is jealous, is a jealous God* (*h*). He is no leſs tender in the matters of his worſhip, than the huſband is of the honour of the marriage-bed. By this he is diſtinguiſhed from all falſe gods. They were not jealous, though their worſhippers went after other gods beſides them: But our God is a jealous God, and can admit no rival or copartner in his worſhip *I am the Lord,* ſays he, *that is my name, and my glory will I not give to another, neither my praiſe to graven images* (*i*). Hence it is that nothing doth more provoke God to wrath, than the ſin of idolatry. It makes his anger and *fury come up in his face;* and kindles *conſuming* wrath (*k*). This was the ſin that brought heavy judgments on God's ancient people. And for this, dreadful and terrible wrath is threatened and predicted to come on Romiſh Babylon: And pure and unmixed wrath is denounced againſt ſuch as join in communion with Papiſts in their idolatrous worſhip and other abominations: *If any man worſhip the beaſt and his image, and receive his mark in his forehead or in his hand: The ſame ſhall drink of the wine of the wrath of God, which is poured out without mixture into the cup of his indignation; and he ſhall be tormented with fire and brimſtone, in the preſence of the holy angels, and in the preſence of the Lamb* (*l*). So that there is a neceſſity of abſtaining from Romiſh idolatry upon pain of damnation, yea, of more than ordinary torments in hell. A cup of pure unmixed wrath will be the portion of ſuch as live and die in the communion of that idolatrous church. O what a deſperate religion muſt it be, that hath ſuch a dreadful condition in the expectation thereof!

Now, that you may be preſerved from idolatry, and particularly from Romiſh idolatry, I propoſe a few things by way of direction. 1. Keep up a high and honourable eſteem of God. Maintain high and exalting thoughts of him 2. Get a tender regard to his glory and honour. Let the glory of God be dear to you, above all that can be dear to you in the world. When his glory is dear to you, you will not dare to rob him of one tittle of it 3. Let all creatures be low and baſe in your eyes in compariſon of him. What are all the creatures before God, but *as nothing and leſs than nothing? Behold, he put no truſt in his ſervants, and his angels he charged with folly* (*m*).

What

(*h*) Exod. xxxiv. 14   (*i*) Iſa. xlii. 8.   (*k*) Ezek. xxxviii. 18. and xliii. 8.   (*l*) Rev. xiv. 9, 10.   (*m*) Iſa. xl. 17. Job. iv. 18.

What are either angels or saints, that they should be brought in to rival God in his worship, and to share of his glory? Their holiness waxeth pale and dim in his presence, and is but a shadow of his unspotted and infinite purity. 4. Keep up a just detestation and abhorrence of idolatry. God would have it so much abhorred by his people, that he discharged them to take the names of the heathen gods in their mouth: *Make no mention of the names of other gods*, says he, *neither let it be heard out of thy mouth* (n). The meaning is, that they should not mention their names without necessity, and not without detestation. Therefore, it were to be wished that, in Christian schools and colleges, the names and stories of the heathen deities were not so commonly and familiarly used, nor with such shew of respect, as they usually are. Certainly, *we have not so learned Christ*. We ought not to name them without abhorrence. This the psalmist resolved upon: *Their drink-offerings of blood will I not offer*, says he, *nor take up their names into my lips* (o). Not that he thought it simply unlawful to name them; but he would not speak of them without detestation. 5. Keep at a due distance from idolatry. Avoid all occasions of and temptations to it. And, (1) Take heed of countenancing Romish idolatry with your presence, by going to mass, &c. if an opportunity should offer. As this is dangerous to your own soul; so your example in this matter may have a mischievous influence. It tends to harden idolaters in their abominations, and gives great encouragement to them, and may be a stumbling-block to weak Christians; so that you would thereby bring down the guilt of other mens sins upon your own head. The countenancing such gross abominations is reckoned a consenting to them; and actors and consenters are reckoned equally guilty and punishable, especially before God. (2.) Beware of familiar society with idolaters. It is dangerous to converse familiarly with Papists, or to be found among them without necessity. God hath warned you of your danger; *Come out of her, my people, that ye be not partakers of her sins, and that ye receive not of her plagues* (p). And it is much more dangerous now, when God is ready to pour out the vials of his wrath upon Babylon. Judgments on great sinners oft-times sweep away those in their community. Particularly, take heed of associating yourselves to Papists by marriage. Marriage with idolaters proved a sad snare to the children of Israel: *They were mingled among the heathen, and learned their works;*

(n) Exod. xxiii. 13.   (o) Psal. xvi. 4.   (p) Rev. xviii. 4.

works; and they served their idols, which were a snare unto them (*q*). And the strange women that Solomon married, *turned away his heart after other gods* (*r*). Remember the apostle's exhortation, *Be ye not unequally yoked together with unbelievers: For what fellowship hath righteousness with unrighteousness? and what concord hath Christ with Belial? or what part hath he that believeth with an infidel? or what agreement hath the temple of God with idols* (*s*)? 6. Exercise much humble dependence on God through Christ, by faith and prayer, for grace and strength to hold out under whatever temptations you may meet with. Particularly, be much in prayer: And in prayer plead for the accomplishment of that promise; *The Lord will famish all the gods of the earth, and men shall worship him, every one from his place, even all the isles of the heathen* (*t*). Where the Lord promiseth, by judgments on idolaters, to blast the reputation of their idols, as not being able to help their worshippers, so that people should withdraw worship from them as useless things. The honour, worship, and service, that is given to idols, is as it were their meat; so that when God is made the only object of religious worship, then idols are famished. To the same purpose, plead the accomplishment of that promise, *And it shall come to pass in that day, saith the Lord of Hosts, that I will cut off the names of the idols out of the land; and they shall no more be remembered* (*u*). O be earnest with God in prayer, that he would famish all the idols of the nations; and particularly, that he would starve and abolish the idolatry of the church of Rome.

Second, Let me dissuade you from heart idolatry; the giving that honour and respect to other things with the inward man, which is due to God alone. Consider, 1. This is a most insinuating evil. Idols easily wind themselves into the heart. Men are not aware of it many times, when their hearts and affections go out inordinately or immoderately after other things besides God; especially, if they be lawful and allowed objects, such as, husband, wife, children, or the good things of the world. These things are apt to get too much room in our hearts, when we are not aware of it. Therefore we need take the more heed to ourselves. 2. It is most dishonourable to God. Such idols set up in the heart, rob him of his glory, spoil him of his sovereignty, and offer a great affront to his majesty, as I shewed already. What an affront and dishonour

(*q*) Psal. cvi. 35, 36. (*r*) 1 Kings. xi. 1, 4. (*s*) 2 Cor. vi. 14, 15, 16. (*t*) Zeph. ii. 11. (*u*) Zech. xiii. 2.

honour is it to the great God, to prefer other things before him, as if they were more worthy of your respect, and of your heart and affections than he is? 3. God's eye discovers the closest idolatry, not only in men's actions, but also in their hearts and affections. Hence the people of God take his omniscience to witness; *If we have forgotten the name of our God, or stretched out our hands to a strange god: Shall not God search this out? For he knoweth the secrets of the heart* (x). You have to do with a heart-searching God, unto whose eyes all things are naked and open; so that your heart cannot go a whoring, even for a little, after other things, but he sees it, and knows it: And he will surely call you to an account; and he will disprove all these excuses and pretences, whereby you seek to cloke and cover such a practice.

Take heed, therefore, of setting up idols in your hearts. All are in danger; but especially such of you as are in a wealthy outward condition. A rich and full condition in the world lies most exposed to the danger of heart-idolatry. Hence our Lord to says his disciples, *How hardly shall they that have riches enter into the kingdom of God?* And when they were astonished at what he said, he answered, *How hard is it for them that trust in riches to enter into the kingdom of God* (y)? First he says, *How hard is it for them that have riches:* and afterward, *How hard is it for them that trust in riches:* Plainly intimating, that it is hard for men to have riches, and not to trust in them. Therefore it was wise Agur's prayer, *Give me not riches*—*Lest I be full and deny thee, and say, Who is the Lord?* Such of you as are rich and live in outward plenty and prosperity, and have a great affluence of the good things of this life, are greatly in danger of giving to these things too much of that room in your hearts that is due to God alone. Therefore, watch against this. Maintain a constant holy jealousy of your own corrupt hearts, and watch over them, and keep them with all diligence. Be afraid, lest something or other rob God of your hearts and affections; or of that time, strength, and labour, that should be employed in his service, and for his glory and honour.

Use. 5. For exhortation; in several branches.

Exhort. 1. Let me exhort you to put away all strange gods, these idols that are set up in your hearts. There is much of this heart-idolatry to be found among us: So that I may exhort you in the words of Joshua, *Put away the strange gods which*

(x) Psal. xliv. 20, 21. (y) Mark x. 23, 24. (z) Prov. xxx. 8, 9.

which are among you (a). Whatever hath that room in your heart and affections, or these religious respects given to it, that are due to God alone, that is *a strange god*. Let all such strange gods be put away. For clearing this, know that some of these things that men set up in their hearts in the room and place of God, are in their own nature evil; and others are in their own nature good and lawful.

1. Some things are in their own nature evil; as the lusts and works of the flesh. These must be put away wholly and absolutely, without any reserve; as poisonous weeds are to be plucked up by the roots. The lusts of the flesh are not to be regulated, but extinguished; not moderated, but wholly abandoned: And that, in your vow, purpose and resolution; in your affections; in your earnest endeavours; and in the course of your life. The bent of your heart and affections must be against them; you must watch, and strive, and pray against them all, without any reservation; and they must be relinquished in the course of your conversation.

2. Other things are in their own nature good and lawful: As our near and dear relations; the comforts and conveniencies of the bodily life, profits, pleasures, and honours, meat and drink, sleep and recreation, credit and preferment. Now, when I call you to put away your strange gods, I do not call you to fall out with or forsake your dear relations, or to be strange to your own flesh: Nor do I call you to a voluntary poverty, to throw away your estates and earthly enjoyments, or to neglect your lawful callings: Nor do I call you to a total abstinence from lawful pleasures and delights; for, these being in themselves lawful, may be used, and being rightly used would be comforts to us in our pilgrimage. But when these things are immoderately loved, desired, and delighted in, so that they estrange and alienate your hearts from God; then they become strange gods to you. In this case, you must put them away, renounce and abandon them, so as they may be no more in the room and place of a god unto you. This is what Christ exhorts his spouse unto; *Come with me from Lebanon, my spouse, with me from Lebanon: Look from the top of Amana, from the top of Shenir and Hermon, from the lions dens, from the mountains of the leopards* (b). By the mountains here mentioned, we are to understand the most excellent and choice contentments and enjoyments in the world, which the men of the world take so much delight and pleasure in. You must come from them, and look from them; that is, forsake all

---

(a) Josh. xxiv. 23.   (b) Cant. iv. 8.

all the profits, pleasures, and honours of the world for Christ; quit them all, so as to get your hearts and affections lifted up above them: For what are they but lions dens, and mountains of leopards; that is, such things as the brutish men of the world hunt after, and take up their rest in, as their only happiness. Renounce the world, and all the enjoyments and comforts of it, so as not to seek your happiness in them; get your hearts weaned from them, so as you may be in a readiness to part with them upon the call of God. Be not the world's underlings; moderate your desires after, and cares about the world; study to manage your worldly business without prejudice to your immortal souls: And then you have renounced the world, and put away these strange gods.

SERMON LXXXVII.

LET me press this exhortation from these three considerations.

1. Consider what these things are that many of you idolize and set up in the room and place of God unto yourselves. They are either the lusts and works of the flesh, or things in themselves lawful. If they be the lusts and works of the flesh; such as abominable uncleanness, drunkenness and gluttony, chambering, and wantonness, wrath, malice, envy, and the like: O, how sad is it when these lie nearest your heart? Then you hug the devil in your bosom, and transform yourselves into very brutes. You may find some present pleasure in sin; but O, it will be bitter in the latter end. The pleasures of sin may go down sweetly, but they will come up again like gall and wormwood, when God awakens your consciences. But if these things you set up in God's room, be things in themselves lawful, such as riches, honour, and lawful pleasures; consider what empty things these are: They are all but vanities. Riches are so: They *certainly make themselves wings, they flee away as an eagle towards heaven* (a). Pleasures are so also; they are but *a thing of nought* (b). And honour and applause is a vain airy thing; a mere shadow, a wind and a breath. Yea, all things under the sun are vanity, and *vanity of vanities* (c). Solomon had more and longer experience in the enjoyment of these things than ever any other man had: Yet when he comes to draw up the total sum, it amounts to this, *All is vanity and vexation of spirit.*

2. Your

(a) Prov. xxiii. 5. (b) Amos vi. 13. (c) Eccl. i. 2.

2. Your putting away your idols and strange gods is necessary to right covenanting with God: For this is an express clause of the covenant, that the man who will covenant with God must forsake all his idols. *Forget also thine own people, and thy father's house* (d): And our blessed Lord says, *Whosoever he be of you, that forsaketh not all that he hath, he cannot be my disciple* (e). God will not covenant with you on any other terms. The covenant of grace is a marriage-covenant: And God will not be married to you, unless you be content to divorce all your former lovers; for he is a jealous God, and can endure no rival.

3. Your putting away your idols and strange gods will come to a happy account. For, 1. This is the way to honour God. It shews what esteem you put upon God, when you are content to quit even what is dearest to you for his sake, and count all things but loss and dung for him: And *them that honour him he will honour* (f). 2. It will be most acceptable and pleasing to God. When the children of Israel put away their strange gods, *God's soul was grieved for their miseries* (g). And God promiseth that upon their abandoning their idols, he would shower down all his blessings upon them. When your idols are divorced, the heart of God will be toward you, and his love and favour will multiply all kinds of blessings upon you, as your need and profit requires them. 3. When you are engaged in putting away your idols and strange gods, then surely there will be a bargain between God and you: For your renouncing these is a special fruit of divine grace, and is therefore a blessed token; and God never brings the heart so far on in consenting to the terms of the covenant, but he brings it further.

Well then, be persuaded to put away all your idols and strange gods: And for your direction in this matter, I propose these things. 1. Search out your idols. Though you see many of your idols, yet there may be other idols lurking secretly in your heart, that you see not. Be diligent in searching out these, and be earnest with God to discover them to you. 2. Lament and bewail the idolatry of your hearts, as the children of Israel did their outward gross idolatry: *We have sinned against thee*, say they, *both because we have forsaken our God, and also served Baalim* (h). Let it be matter of grief to you, that other things have been set up in God's room, and

---

(d) Psal. xlv. 10   (e) Luke xiv. 33.   (f) 1 Sam. ii. 30.
(g) Judges x. 15. Isa. xxx. 22, 23, 24.   (h) Judges x. 10.

and have juſtled him out of his throne. 3. Nouriſh good thoughts of God. O he *is good, and doth good* (*i*) The deep ſenſe of this would make you willing to quit even what is deareſt to you for his ſake. 4. Attend the ordinances diligently; eſpecially the preaching of the word: And be earneſt with God to join his power and efficacy with it, that it may divide between your ſoul and your idols. 5. Improve afflicting providences this way. Sometimes God is pleaſed to make your fellowſhip with your idols very bitter and unpleaſant unto you, by tryſting you with various diſappointments from ſuch things as your hearts doat upon: And you never atain to the right uſe of ſuch diſpenſations, but when you are thereby engaged to renounce your idols. 6. Under the deep ſenſe of your own inſufficiency addreſs yourſelves to God in prayer. It is above the power of nature to divorce a man from his idols. This is God's work. Therefore be earneſt with him to take this work in hand. Plead the accompliſhment of that promiſe, *Ephraim ſhall ſay, what have I to do any more with idols* (*k*). He ſhall ſay it, ſays the Lord; I will make him ſay and do it.

Exhort. 2. Is it ſo that the true and living God is but one? Then let us behave ourſelves worthily, and as it becomes, toward this one only God. Let us behave ourſelves toward him as God alone. In order hereunto there are ſeveral duties I ſhall exhort you unto.

Duty 1. Own the Lord JEHOVAH as God alone, as the one only God. That God who is one in three diſtinct Perſons, who hath revealed himſelf in Chriſt, and whom we profeſs to worſhip; own and acknowledge him to be God; as the people of Iſrael did, when they ſaw the fire come down, and conſume Elijah's ſacrifice; they cried out, *The Lord he is the God: the Lord, he is the God* (*l*). And own and acknowledge him as God alone, as Hezekiah did; *Thou art the God,* ſays he, *even thou alone, of all the kingdoms of the earth* (*m*). Give him the glory of being God alone, of his matchleſs and incomparable excellency, by owning and acknowledging that there is none like him in heaven or earth. *There is none like unto the God of Jeſhurun.* And, ſays the pſalmiſt, *Thou art God alone* (*n*). It is indeed one of the moſt awful ways of praiſing God, to acknowledge that there is none like him. Honour him as a non ſuch God. Own him as the only object of all religious worſhip and adoration. As the elders in their ſong,

Thou

(*i*) Pſal. cxix. 68.　(*k*) Hoſ. xiv. 8.　(*l*) 1 Kings xviii. 39.
(*m*) 2 Kings xix. 15.　(*n*) Deut. xxxiii. 26. Pſal. lxxxvi. 10.

Thou art worthy, O Lord, to receive glory, and honour, and power (o). And own him as the only founiain of all deliverance, salvation comfort, and happiness; as the psalmist, *Who is God save the Lord? or who is a rock save our God?* On this ground God exhorts his people to acknowledge none but him; *Thou shalt know no god but me; for there is no saviour besides me* (q). Own and acknowledge him as the God of all consolation, the God of all grace, the God of salvation, and the Father of lights and mercies.

Duty 2. Labour to get and entertain a high and reverend esteem of him as matchless and incomparable. O, let him be dear and precious to you. Indeed, you cannot esteem him according to his worth and dignity: Yet your estimation of him should know no measure. Esteem him above all that can be dear to you in heaven or earth; and say with the Psalmist, *Whom have I in heaven but thee? and there is none upon earth that I desire besides thee* (r). There ought to be such a transcendent esteem of God, as all other things may be lessened, in your estimation of them, and respect to them, in comparison of him. Count all things *but loss and dung* (s), for him. This esteem is necessary to draw in your hearts to God, and to keep your hearts to him and with him. And it is necessary to make you part with all things for him, and to put you upon an earnest pursuit after the enjoyment of him and communion with him. Therefore, to raise your esteem, study to know him as he hath revealed himself in his word: Cry for open eyes to see him: Be earnest with him to reveal and manifest himself to your soul; that you may see such glory and excellency, such fulness and all-sufficiency in him, as may raise your esteem of him, above all other beings whatsoever.

Duty 3. Let it be your great uptaking business to have this one only God for your God. This is required in the first commandment, *Thou shalt have no other gods before me.* Thou shalt have me and me only for thy God. Seeing there is but one only God, it greatly concerns you to look to it that he be your God.

I shall here propose, 1. A few things by way of motive, to excite and quicken you to a deep and serious concern this way. 2. Some directions what to do that you may have this one only God for your God.

First,

(o) Rev. iv. 11.   (p) Psal. xviii. 31.   (q) Hos. xiii. 4.
(r) Psal. lxxiii. 25.   (s) Phil. iii. 8.

First, To excite and quicken you to make it your great business to have this one only God for your God, consider,

1. You must of necessity have some God or other. You cannot be without one. You will still be bestowing your heart and love, your time and strength, upon one thing or other. Hence Elijah says to the people, *If the Lord be God, follow him: But if Baal, then follow him.* And Joshua, *Chuse you this day whom ye will serve* (*t*). We must of necessity chuse one or other. Man hath no sufficiency in himself; therefore his soul is still going out after some one thing or other, to fill and satisfy it. Men cannot want something in the room of a God.

2. There is no other God but the Lord. Nothing else besides the great JEHOVAH can be a God unto you. Nothing else can supply his room. Your best earthly comforts and enjoyments, though they may have the room and place of a God in your heart, yet cannot act the part of a God for you. They cannot make you happy, nor yield you solid heart's content and satisfaction. This appears from these two consideration. 1. Consider the nature of the soul. It is a spiritual and immaterial substance, endowed with noble faculties: Worldly things are far below it. Your noble soul is but abased, abused and vexed, and not employed or satisfied, when it is subjected to such inferior and base things. Hence the Lord expostulates with sinners, *Wherefore do ye spend money for that which is not bread? and your labour for that which satisfieth not* (*u*)? Worldly things are but *broken cisterns that can hold no water* (*x*): A man may have too much of them, and yet never enough to satisfy: They often cause lothing, but can never yield true heart's content; because they bear no proportion to the vast desires and capacities of the immortal soul 2. Consider your soul as it is now through the fall. It is full of sin: It is a filthy and polluted soul, a sick and diseased soul by sin. Hence it is that nothing can content and satisfy it, but what can cure it. As a sick man can take no pleasure in such things as formerly he delighted in, unless he be cured of his sickness: So here, worldly things cannot cure a sick and diseased soul, therefore they cannot content and satisfy it †. Your best earthly comforts cannot help you in the amazements and horrors of conscience, nor in the agonies

---

(*t*) 1 Kings xviii 21. Josh. xxiv. 15. (*u*) Isa. lv. 2. (*x*) Jer. ii. 13.

† *Mors iis terribilis est, quorum cum vita omnia extinguuntur.*
            Cic. Parad. 1

nies of death, nor in the horrors of eternity. So that nothing besides the Lord can be a God to your soul.

3. This one only God is sufficient. He is *God Almighty* (*y*). Orig. *God All-sufficient*. Having the Lord for your God, you need go no where else to make up your happiness and blessedness. ‖ There is enough in this one God to make you compleatly happy. He can suit all your faculties, and supply and answer all your necessities, and fill up and satisfy all the desires and capacities of your immortal soul. O, there is no want in him. All good is treasured up in him; so that you may be happy enough in him alone. He is the well of salvation, the Lord of life, the God of all consolation. You need no more but this one God. He can content and satisfy your soul to the full, even in the want of all other comforts. He can *perform all things for* you (*z*). He can do infinitely more for you than all the creatures in heaven and earth can do.

4. You may have this God for your God, if you be not wanting to yourselves. Blessed be he, he is content to be wholly yours on gracious terms. He requires you to take him for your God, *Thou shalt have no other gods before me*. It plainly implies this, *Thou shalt have me for thy God*. To the same purpose he speaks by the psalmist, *Hear, O my people, and I will testify unto thee; O Israel, if thou wilt hearken unto me. There shall no strange god be in thee: Neither shalt thou worship any strange god. I am the Lord thy God; open thy mouth wide, and I will fill it* (*a*). And he takes it grievously, when you refuse and reject his kind and gracious offers: Therefore it follows, *But my people would not hearken to my voice, and Israel would none of me. So I gave them up unto their own hearts' lust* — *O that my people had hearkened unto me, and Israel had walked in my ways!* And his willingness to become your God doth plainly appear from the whole design and contrivance of the gospel. Why did he provide a Mediator, and give him to the death for lost sinners? Why did he set up a second covenant after the breach of the first; but that he might, without any stain to his honour, become a God to a company of lost mankind?

5. When once you get this one only God for your God, you are made up for ever. *Happy is that* person *or people whose God is the Lord* (*b*). When God is yours, then all that he is, and all that he hath, are yours. O what a blessed bargain is this! Again, a covenant-interest in God can never be made void.

When

‖ *Satis solatii in uno Deo.*

(*y*) Gen. xvii. 1. (*z*) Psal. lvii. 2. (*a*) Psal. lxxxi. 8, 9, 10, 11, 12, 13. (*b*) Psal. cxliv. ult.

When God is once yours, he will always be yours: As the psalmist says, *This God is our God for ever and ever* (c). This appears from his love to his people, which is like himself, everlasting and unchangeable; and from the nature of the covenant of grace, which is everlasting, and stands fast for ever. Again, such as have a saving interest in God as their God, have ground of hope and comfort in the deepest distresses. On this ground the psalmist raises up his soul to hope in God; *Why art thou cast down, O my soul?—Hope thou in God; for—he is my God* (d). To conclude, it cannot be expressed what a happiness it is to have the Lord for our God. This will never be fully understood, till we come to heaven. Hence it is said, *God himself shall be with them, and be their God: And God shall wipe away all tears from their eyes* (e). When believers come to heaven, where they shall sigh and sorrow no more, then the *Lord shall be their God*; that is, then they shall fully reap the blessed fruits and advantages of a covenant-interest in God; and then they shall fully understand what it is to have the *Lord for their God*; and never till then.

6. If you do not take the Lord for your God, it will be one of the saddest ingredients in your misery, that ever you had him in your offer. Your slighting and rejecting his kind and gracious offers, as it will greatly aggravate your sin and guiltiness, so it will bring upon you double wrath and vengeance. In hell, it will be one of the most bitter ingredients in your misery, that God offered himself to you, and you would have none of him. Oh, it had been better for you, that you had been born and brought up among poor Indians and Pagans, who never had such rich offers made unto them; for, it will be more tolerable for *them* in the day of judgment, than it will be for *you* (f).

SERMON LXXXVIII.

Second, IN the next place, I propose some things by way of direction, what to do that you may have this one only God for your God.

1. I recommend to you serious deliberation and consideration. One great cause whence it is that God's gracious offers are so much slighted and despised, is want of serious consideration. Men are heedless, and careless of soul concerns, like fools

---

(c) Psal. xlviii. 14.   (d) Psal. xlii. 11.   (e) Rev. xxi. 3, 4. (f) Matth. xi. 22.

fools and madmen, or men out of their wits. Hence it is said of the Prodigal, *When he came to himself, he said. How many hired servants* (a), *&c.* He was beside himself before, like one not in his right wits. Oh sinners, that you would come to yourselves, and ponder seriously what concerns your precious souls. Ponder and weigh seriously your great misery while you are without God, and what a happiness it would be to have a saving interest in him.

2. Study the knowledge of God. Alas, he is an unknown God even to many that are called by his name; therefore they are careless whether he be their God or not. But if you knew him, you could not live without him. Therefore study to know him, as he hath revealed himself in his word, and in Christ; and be unsatisfied till you know him savingly. Diligently improve all means, ordinances, advantages and opportunities, for attaining the knowledge of God. Be diligent and attentive in reading and hearing the word, and attend the ordinance of catechising.

3. Renounce all other gods, as I formerly exhorted you. When the people of Israel professed to chuse the Lord for their God, Joshua exhorts them to *put away the strange gods that were among* them (b). Unless you part with your idols, the Lord will not be your God. Therefore say with Ephraim, *What have I do any more with idols* (c)? Your hearts must be taken off all other things, that you may look at God alone: And when he is looked at alone, his glory and beauty will so appear, that in your esteem, among all the gods there will be none like him.

4 Close with Christ by faith. God cannot be your God but in and through Christ. For, 1. He cannot be your God till you be reconciled to him, and of enemies become friends; and there can be no peace or reconciliation between an offended God and you, but through Christ the only peace-maker. Therefore, flee to Christ who hath made peace by the blood of his cross, and employ him to make peace between God and you. 2. He cannot be your God till you have a saving union with Christ. For he is first a God to Christ, and then to believers: And he is therefore a God to believers, because he is first a God to Christ. Hence our Lord says to Mary, *I ascend unto my Father, and your Father; and to my God, and your God* (d). Being first a God unto Christ the Mediator, he becometh also a

God

(a) Luke xv. 17. (b) Josh. xxiv. 23. (c) Hos. xiv. 8.
(d) John xx. 17.

God unto believers, by virtue of their union with him. Being myſtically one with Chriſt, they ſhare with him in all his intereſts and relations. Now, you cannot have a ſaving union with Chriſt, but by faith in him. Faith is the uniting grace. He *dwells in our hearts by faith* (e). Therefore under the deep ſenſe of your ſinful and loſt ſtate, betake yourſelves to Chriſt, and receive and cloſe with him: Conſent heartily to the gracious terms on which he is offered.

5. Make choice of the Lord for your God. He will not be your God againſt your will. This muſt be determined by your own choice. Therefore, as Joſhua ſays to the people, *Chuſe you this day whom ye will ſerve* (f). Chuſe him deliberately. Let all objections and difficulties be ſeriouſly pondered, that your choice of him may be the reſult of the deepeſt conſideration. Chuſe him abſolutely. There muſt be no ſecret reſerves, no conditions, in your choice of him, nor any place left for repentance. Chuſe him once for all, ſo as never to part with him, whatever inconveniencies may follow. Chuſe him wholly, in all that he is: Chuſe him Father, Son, and Holy Ghoſt, to be your God. Chuſe God the Father, to be your all-ſufficient and ſoul-ſatisfying portion: Chuſe God the Son, to be your Saviour and Redeemer, your King, Prieſt, and Prophet: And chuſe God the Holy Ghoſt, to be your Sanctifier, Guide, and Comforter; accounting it your happineſs to be ſanctified and governed by him, as well as comforted by him.

6. Yield and reſign yourſelves unto God to be his people (g). The Lord will not be your God, unleſs you will be his people. So the promiſe runs, *I will be your God, and ye ſhall be my people.* Therefore, make a ſolemn ſurrender and reſignation of yourſelves to God through Chriſt, to be a peculiar people to him. Give yourſelves to him, wholly, ſoul and body, without reſervation; for ever, without reverſion, no more to be you own, nor any others, but his. It muſt be the fixed purpoſe of your heart never to go back. Lord, I will be thine, and never more mine own.

7. Give yourſelves much to prayer. And, 1. Pray for an enlightened underſtanding, that you may come by a diſcovery of the matchleſs excellency of God, and of that fulneſs and all-ſufficiency that is in him. This is neceſſary to draw in your hearts to him. Pray for *the ſpirit of wiſdom and revelation in the knowledge of him* (h). Plead for the accompliſhment of that promiſe,

(e) Eph. iii. 17.   (f) Joſh. xxiv. 15.   (g) 2 Chron. xxx. 8.
(h) Eph. i. 17.

promise, *I will give them an heart to know me* (i). 2. Pray for an inclined heart. That God would frame your heart to chuse him, and draw in your heart to himself by the attractive power of his grace. Plead for the accomplishment of that promise, *They shall say, The Lord is my God* (k). I will make them say, and do it.

Duty 4. Is the Lord the one only God? Then give your whole heart to him. This is what he calls for; *My son, give me thine heart* (l). It is not said, give me a part, or a corner, but thine heart, thy whole heart. Many seem content to give God a part, but not the whole. Their hearts are divided between God and the world, between God and their idols. God hath, as it were, a corner in it, and the devil and sin hath all the rest. But God will have all, or nothing. Therefore he blames his ancient people for dividing their hearts; *Their heart is divided*, says he; *now shall they be found faulty* (m). God will have nothing to do with that heart that is divided between him and other lovers. He cannot endure any halting between him and idols. He will have no part of your heart reserved for any other, or for yourselves to dispose of at your pleasure. And indeed, all is too little for so great and so good a God as he is. Such is his incomparable excellency, that you cannot give him any thing too good for him. When you have given him the whole heart, the best you have, yet you do not give him according to the excellency of his nature. And why will you reserve any part of your heart for any other, when this one only God can fill all the corners of it? Indeed, you need no more but God, to satisfy, refresh, and delight your heart. *Open thy mouth wide*, says the Lord, *and I will fill it* (n). There is enough in him to make your heart run over. To conclude, when you profess to give God a part of your heart, but not the whole, you do, in effect, give him nothing at all: For that part which is reserved, and given to Satan, will in time draw the whole after it: It is a pledge that all shall fall to him at last. Well then, give your whole heart to this one only God. What an excellent antidote would this be against your many heart-evils. Ye that are serious Christians complain that you have bad hearts: But give them to God, and he will make them better. Your heart is an unsettled heart; but give it to God, and he will establish it by grace: It is a polluted unclean heart; but give it to God, and he will sanctify and cleanse it: It is a backsliding heart;

(i) Jer. xxiv. 7.   (k) Zech. xiii. 9.   (l) Prov. xxiii. 26.
(m) Hos. x. 2.   (n) Psal. lxxxi. 10.

heart; but give it to God, and he will take the custody of it into his own hand: It is an unruly heart; but give it God, and he will rule in it, and make the government of it the more easy to you.

Duty 5. Make the one only God the only object of all your religious worship and service. This is expressly required, *Thou shalt worship the Lord thy God, and him only shalt thou serve.* And again, *Thou shalt know no God but me* (*o*). Serve and worship him alone. He alone is worthy of it; as it is said in the Song of the Elders, *Thou art worthy, O Lord, to receive glory, and honour, and power* (*p*). He alone is the object of all religious worship. When the apostle John fell at the angel's feet to worship him, he rejected it by this argument, *See thou do it not: I am thy fellow-servant, and of thy brethren that have the testimony of Jesus: Worship God* (*q*). As if he had said, I am not God; and such worship is due to him alone. Hence, the worship of God is infered from the unity of his essence: *All nations whom thou hast made, shall come and worship before thee, O Lord, and shall glorify thy name: For thou art God alone* (*r*). Worship is due to him as being *God alone.* He alone hath these excellencies and perfections that are required in the object of religious worship, such as omniscience, omnipresence, omnipotence, supreme excellency, glory and majesty. Therefore let none share with him in this honour. He can endure no rival or competitor †. He *will not give his glory to another* (*s*).

Well then, serve and worship him alone. And serve and worship this one only God with *the whole heart,* with an entire heart. This is enjoined; *Serve the Lord thy God with all thy heart, and with all thy soul:* And, *only fear the Lord, and serve him in truth with all your heart* (*t*). Whatever service God requires, he will have it performed with the whole heart. This is one of the characters of such as are truly blessed, *they seek God with the whole heart* (*u*). Hence the psalmist prays, *Unite my heart to fear thy name* (*x*). In serving and worshipping God, all the powers and faculties of your soul should be united, that they may run in one channel. Study to serve him with the greatest fervour and vehemency of heart and affection, and with the full bent of your desires. To this purpose is that
exhortation,

---

† *Illa sublimitas non potest habere consortium, cum sola omnium teneat potestatem.* Cypr. de Vanit. Idol.

(*o*) Matth. iv. 10. Hos. xiij. 4. (*p*) Rev. iv. 11. (*q*) Rev. xix. 10. (*r*) Psal. lxxxvi. 9, 10. (*s*) Isa. xlii. 8. (*t*) Deut. x. 12, 1 Sam. xii. 24. (*u*) Psal. cxix. 2. (*x*) Psal. lxxxvi. 11.

exhortation, *Gird up the loins of your mind* (y). Gather in the strength of your soul to your work, that your whole heart and soul may be intent upon it.

I shall give instance particularly in some acts of worship and service that are due to this one only God.

First, Love him with all your heart. This is infered from the unity of the divine essence, in the verse following my text. *Hear, O Israel, the Lord our God is one Lord. And thou shalt love the Lord thy God with all thine heart, and with all thy soul, and with all thy might.* And this is called *the first and great commandment* of the law (z). Consider, 1. Love is but for one object: For this affection is much weakened and scattered when it is laid out on divers objects; as a river that is divided into divers channels. Indeed, the true object of love is but one, and that is God: For he is to be loved for himself, and other things for his sake. Love is meet for nothing but God: He alone deserves these heights and excesses that are in this affection †. You make gods of other things, when you love them without a subordination to God. 2. God alone doth most deserve your love, because he is most good. *He is good, and doth good* (a). Good is the object of love: but who so good as God is? He is all goodness in himself, and the original and fountain-cause of all goodness in the creatures. He is a bundle and heap of worth and perfection. All the scattered excellencies in the whole creation centre and meet in him: So that though every hair of your head were a man, and every soul there had a love equal to that of the angels, yet would not your love be enough for the loveliness of God. *He is altogether lovely* (b). There is nothing in him but what is amiable. 3. Love is the best thing you can bestow upon God. It is a gift in the giving whereof hypocrites cannot join with sincere Christians. There is nothing else but a hypocrite may give it as abundantly as the most upright in heart. They may give their eyes, their hands, their ears, their tongues, yea, their lives to God; but their love they cannot give. Love is the sum of all duties: Therefore all the duties of the first table are comprised in this, *Thou shalt love the Lord thy God.* Give to God what you will, if you do not give him your love, you give him in his esteem just nothing. Love is the marrow of all duties; the salt that seasons every spiritual sacrifice.

Well

(y) 1 Pet. i. 13   (z) Matth. xxii. 37, 38.
† *Minus Domine te amat, qui aliquid tecum amat, quod propter te non amat.* Aug. Lib. Confess.
(a) Psal. cxix. 68.   (b) Cant. v. 16.

Well then, set your love on God; and love him with all your heart; and let none else have such a love but himself. Do not say of any thing else, I love it with all my heart: For this favours of idolatry; supreme love is due to God alone. Therefore let the one only God be the one only in your dearest love. And, 1. Let your love to God be an ardent and fervent love. Labour to have your heart carried out after him with the greatest fervency and vehemency of affection. This is to love God with all your heart, and soul, and mind, and strength. There is no danger of excess here: We may easily over-love other things, but we cannot over-love God; yea, we always come short. Yet your love to God, if it be of the right stamp, will be an ardent and heart-burning love. 2. It must be a superlative love. You must love God above all other things, else you do not love him at all. He is the one only God; therefore none can challenge such a love from you as he can do. Indeed, you cannot love God so much as he deserves to be loved, nor so much as the angels and saints in heaven love him; and it may be that none of you love him so well as some eminent saints on earth have loved him: Yet you must love him more than any thing else is loved, else your love to him is not sincere. To the soul that loves him, he is like oil upon water, always uppermost. 3. It must be an entire love. He is one only; therefore your heart must be united in his love, and the whole stream of your affection must run toward him.

Second, Fear him alone. This also is inferred from the unity of the God-head, in one of the verses following my text: *Thou shalt fear the Lord thy God, and serve him* (*c*). God is the only object of religious fear. *Thou, even thou art to be feared* (*d*), says the psalmist. Fear none in comparison of him; and fear none in opposition to him: For, being God alone, he hath absolute, supreme, and uncontroulable power. Hence he demands the glory of his absolute sovereignty; *See now, that I, even I am he, and there is no god with me: I kill, and I make alive; I wound, and I heal: Neither is there any that can deliver out of my hand* (*e*). Fear him alone. 1. In opposition to great and powerful men. So our Lord exhorts, *Fear not them who kill the body, but are not able to kill the soul; but rather fear him who is able to destroy both soul and body in hell* (*f*): And the prophet: *Neither fear ye their fear, nor be afraid: Sanctify the Lord of hosts himself, and let him be your fear, and let him be your dread* (*g*).

We

(*c*) Deut. vi. 13.   (*d*) Psal. lxxvi. 7.   (*e*) Deut. xxxii. 39.
(*f*) Matth. x. 28.   (*g*) Isa. viii. 12, 13.

We vilify God, and defile his glory, when our fear of man ſtifles our faith in God. It is to value the power of the creature above the power of the Creator. Hence he ſays, *Who art thou that thou ſhouldeſt be afraid of a man that ſhall die?—and forgetteſt the Lord thy Maker* (*h*). Our inordinate fearing of man is an implicit forgetting of God. 2. In oppoſition to forged and feigned deities. This doctrine of the unity of the divine eſſence is uſeful to free the ſoul from the anxious fears of a falſe deity. Seeing he is God alone, fear none of the gods of the heathen. *I am the Lord your God*, ſays he, *fear not the gods of the Amorites in whoſe land ye dwell*: And, *Ye ſhall not fear other gods* (*i*).

Third, Truſt in him alone. Being God alone, he is the only fit object of truſt. It is ſpiritual whoredom, to doat upon the creature. It is a practical denial of God, and a ſetting up creatures in his room. Hence the Lord ſays to his ancient people who truſted in Egypt for help, *Now the Egytians are men, and not God* (*k*). Intimating that by their dependence on them, they advanced them from the ſtate of creatures, to that of almighty deities. Hence is that dreadful curſe, *Curſed be the man that truſteth in man, and maketh fleſh his arm, and whoſe heart departeth from the Lord* (*l*). Again, ſeeing God is one only, *truſt in* him *with all your heart* (*m*). Truſt in him wholly, entirely, and with full confidence: For, he hath all events in his hand. There is no god beſides him, to controul him, or cope with him. He hath uncontroulable authority and power, to diſpoſe of all creatures and events, ſo as to ſerve his own purpoſes by them: Therefore, *if he be for* you, *who can be againſt* you (*n*). He is God alone. His power is above all power, and his wiſdom above all wiſdom. There is none like him. Therefore, let us depend on him entirely. *He is a buckler to all thoſe that truſt in him: For who is God, ſave the Lord? Or, who is a rock, ſave our God* (*o*)? In all your ſtraits and difficulties, take heed that your heart do not ſecretly turn aſide to vain confidences. That man that cannot entirely truſt God, whether men be pleaſed or diſpleaſed, cannot long be true to him.

SERMON LXXXIX.

Fourth, HAVE your recourſe to God alone, in all your wants, ſtraits, and miſeries: For, there is none

---

(*h*) Iſa. li. 12, 13. (*i*) Judges vi. 10. 2 Kings xvii. 35, 37. (*k*) Iſa. xxxi. 3. (*l*) Jer. xvii. 5. (*m*) Prov. iii. 6. (*n*) Rom. viii. 31. (*o*) Pſal. xviii. 30, 31.

none else; none that can deliver from all evil, and enrich with all spiritual blessings, who can pardon sin, and save the sinner. *Besides* him *there is no Saviour* (a). You can go to no other with hope of success, if you neglect God: For he alone knows all your wants and miseries, and he alone is able to supply and relieve you. When you go to others, you go to them that are no gods. To run to the creatures, rather than to God, for the supply of your necessities, is a practical denial of him. Hence the Lord says to Ahaziah, *Is it not because there is not a God in Israel, that thou sendest to enquire of Baalzebub the god of Ekron* (b)? This was Asa's sin; *In his disease, he sought not to the Lord, but to the physicians* (c). Seeing the great JEHOVAH is God alone, seek every thing you need at his hand. The psalmist encouraged himself in his addresses to God from the consideration of his matchless being and singular unity: *Among the gods*, says he, *there is none like thee. For thou art great, and dost wondrous things: Thou art God alone* (d).

Fifthly, Subject your soul and conscience to him alone. Have no other Lord over your soul and conscience. Being God alone, he alone can give laws to the conscience. Hence it is said, *The Lord is our judge, the Lord is our Lawgiver, the Lord is our King* (e). The words being taken in a spiritual sense, are exclusive of all others: He is our only Judge, our only Lawgiver. *There is one Lawgiver*, says the apostle, *who is able to save, and to destroy* (f). God alone knows the conscience, and he alone can punish the conscience; therefore he alone can give laws to it immediately. God hath reserved to himself alone the sovereignty over the conscience; he hath subjected it to himself alone. To make conscience a slave to man, is to set man on the throne of God. Therefore let not the authority of the greatest on earth have place, to the prejudice of that obedience you owe to the one only God. It was the apostle's answer to the council, *Whether it be right in the sight of God, to hearken unto you more than unto God, judge ye* (g). That is not true loyalty to man, which leads you to be disloyal to the great God. Seeing he is God alone, and there is none like him among all the nations, let none have an obedience equal to him. All the obedience you are to give to man, is to be paid in obedience to God, and with an eye to his command:

(a) Isa. xliii. 11. (b) 2 Kings i. 6. (c) 2 Chron. xvi. 12. (d) Psal. lxxxvi. 8, 10. (e) Isa. xxxiii. 22. (f) James iv. 12. (g) Acts iv. 19.

mand: For it is the command of God that binds our conscience to obey the lawful commands of men †.

Particularly, subject your consciences to God alone in the matters of his worship, and do not yield to the impositions of men. To impose laws upon the conscience, which God hath not imposed, is to usurp God's prerogative, and affect a divine royalty, and is therefore the very spirit of Antichristianism; for it is the apostle Paul's character of Antichrist, that *he exalteth himself above all that is called God* (h): viz. By making himself absolute lord of the conscience. It it God's prerogative to be the only sovereign Lawgiver to his church. And he was always so tender of this part of his prerogative, that he would not have any thing made in the tabernacle or temple, but what himself had appointed. *And look*, says he to Moses, *that thou make them after their pattern, which was shewed thee in the Mount* (i). And afterward, though the power of appointing officers and ordinances in the church, was delegated to Christ, and was among the rest of the royalties given to him as Mediator; yet even he was to do nothing in this matter, without appointment and pattern, being, as Mediator, the Father's Servant. Hence it is said, that *he was faithful to him that appointed him* (k) Now, faithfulness in a trust implies a punctual observing instructions. And if even the blessed Mediator was to appoint no part of divine worship, but what he had instruction for; what unaccounaable boldness and presumption must it be, for any man, or any set of men, to arrogate to themselves a power of imposing their own, or other mens inventions in the worship of God, upon the consciences of the Lord's people? This is a bold ascent into the throne of God, by usurping a dominion over the conscience; and is to bring the consciences of the people of God under a woful bondage and slavery. Therefore *let us stand fast in the liberty wherewith Christ hath made us free* (l). We are bound to stand to the defence of it, with courage and confidence, and with the utmost of our power and ability, against all opposition, and upon all hazards whatsoever. Even among the heathens, as a learned author

---

† *Si aliquid jusserit Proconsul, aliud jubeat Imperator, nunquid dubitatur, Illo contempto illi esse serviendum? Ergo si aliud imperator, aliud jubeat Deus, quid judicatur? Major potestas Deus: Da Veniam, O Imperator.* Aug. de Verb. Domin. Matth. Serm. 6.

(h) 2 Thess. ii 4.   (i) Exod. xxv. 40.   (k) Heb. iii. 2.
(l) Gal. v. 1.

author observes †, it was a natural notion, not to receive a form of worship, but what had a stamp of a divine authority.

There are yet two duties more, to which I would exhort believers in Christ, from this doctrine. And so,

Duty 6. Is your God the only God? Then rest satisfied in him alone. Seek no where else to make up your happiness: And let no outward wants, straits or miseries, mar your happiness and contentment in the enjoyment of him. Even believers in Christ, often give way to discontent and murmuring, when their outward lot is not according to their mind. What is this but a practical denial of God's all-sufficiency, as if he that fills all things, were not enough to fill your heart? What would you be at? The one only God is yours; and cannot you be satisfied? Dear Christians, do not disgrace your God by a discontented spirit. Is the one only God yours? Then you have cause enough to rest content and satisfied, and to reckon yourselves happy in the enjoyment of him, whatever your outward lot be. Therefore rest satisfied with him alone.

For your help in this matter, take these directions. 1. Clear up your interest in God. Give all diligence to attain to clearness in this matter, that the one only God is your God. 2. Often review your happiness in him, as the psalmist: *The Lord is the portion of mine inheritance, and of my cup—The lines are fallen to me in pleasant places, and I have a goodly heritage* (m). He is your God, who is God alone, incomparable in worth and perfection. *There is none like unto the God of Jeshurun* (n). None can do for their favourites as God hath done and can do for you. There is enough in him to fill, satisfy, and delight your soul. Study what God is, and what there is laid up in him. Read over his glorious names; and walk through the blessed chambers of his presence, his glorious attributes; and see what treasures are laid up there for your soul. And then reflect upon your own interest in him, and say, Lo this God is my God; and all that he is, all that he hath, is mine. 3. Get much experience of God upon your own heart. Pant and long after him: Pursue after the enjoyment of him, and more near and intimate communion with him; after the light of his countenance, and refreshing experiences and manifestations of his love and grace. Get your hearts so filled with God, as

† Charnock's Discourse of the Knowledge of God.
(*m*) Psal xvi 5, 6.   (*n*) Deut. xxxiii. 26.

it may be no damp upon your spirit, to have nothing left you but God.

Duty 7. Is your God the one only God? Then cleave to him; as Barnabas exhorted the young converts at Antioch, *that with purpose of heart they would cleave unto the Lord* (*o*). He is God alone. There is nothing else to whom you can go, if you turn your back on him: As Peter said, *To whom shall we go, thou hast the words of eternal life* (*p*). This one only God is sufficient to your happiness, and all other things are but vanities. Therefore having chosen him for your God, O do not change; do not turn again to the pleasures of sin, and the vanities of the world. The constancy even of pagan nations, in adhering and cleaving to their false gods, will furnish matter of reproach against you, if you forsake the only true God. Hence the Lord pleads against that people, *Hath a nation changed their gods, which are yet no gods? But my people have changed their glory, for that which doth not profit* (*q*)? Change when you will, you will change for the worse. But cleaving to him is honourable to him: It is a practical acknowledgement of his excellency; you thereby proclaim to the world that there is none like him.

Exhort. 3. Is it so that the great JEHOVAH is one only? Then, let all that profess his name, study to maintain and promote unity among themselves, that they may be one as he is one. How earnestly doth Christ pray for this: *Keep through thine own name those whom thou hast given me, that they may be one as we are. That they all may be one, as thou Father art in me, and I in thee, that they also may be one in us, that the world may believe that thou hast sent me. And the glory which thou gavest me, I have given them, that they may be one, even as we are one* (*r*). The unity of the Godhead in the Trinity of Persons, is a strong argument to persuade Christians to unity among themselves: For there is nothing wherein we can resemble God more. Therefore the apostle urgeth Christians to *keep the unity of the Spirit in the bond of peace,* by this argument, that *there is one God and Father of all* (*s*). It concerns us to study a holy unity, as we would evidence ourselves to have this one God for our God and Father in Christ. What a shame is it for those that serve one God to be at odds among themselves? Our Master's work is hereby hindered and neglected.

Particularly,

(*o*) Acts xi. 23. (*p*) John vi. 68. (*q*) Jer. ii. 11. (*r*) John xvii. 11, 21, 22. (*s*) Eph. iv. 3, 6.

Particularly, let me, from this doctrine, press a threefold unity among Christians.

1. Union in opinion and judgment. Endeavour to be *of one mind, and to be perfectly joined together in the same mind, and in the same judgment* (t). It is true, different degrees of knowledge, even among the Lord's own people, cannot but occasion some differences of judgment in lesser things, till they come to heaven, where there will be perfect *unity in faith and knowledge* (u). Yet there is but one faith allowed by Christ even in lesser truths. Therefore the apostle presseth unity among Christians by this argument also, that *there is one faith* (x). There is but one way of religion and worship that God allows. Hence the promise runs, *And I will give them one heart and one way, that they may fear me for ever* (y). There is but one way that is agreeable to the pattern. Therefore when the flourishing state of the church under the New Testament is promised, it is said, *In that day shall there be one Lord, and his name one* (z). This therefore we should aim at and endeavour, so far as is possible, to be of one mind in the things of God: As it is said of the primitive Christians, that they *were of one heart, and of one soul* (a). *Of one heart*, that is, *of one mind*. It is certainly a most desirable blessing; and it would be the more easily attained, if people did lay aside their prejudices, passions, worldly interests, and selfish designs; and seek the truth impartially, on what side soever it lies; and in all matters of religion, eye and mind but one Lord.

2. Union in affection. So it is said of the primitive Christians, that they *were of one soul* (b); that is, there was such a sweet harmony of love and affection, as if all of them had but one soul. Christians should be *knit together in love* (c). And differences of judgment in lesser things should not hinder this. You should study to be of *one heart*, when you cannot be in every thing of *one mind* †. So, *Have compassion one of another; love as brethren* (d). When lesser debates are managed by Christians, with wrath and passion, and bitterness of spirit; and there are uncharitable contentions, animosities, and heart-burnings;

(t) 1 Pet. iii. 8. 1 Cor. i. 10. (u) Eph. iv. 13. (x) Eph. iv. 5. (y) Jer. xxxii. 39. (z) Zech. xiv. 9.
(a) Acts iv. 32. (b) Acts iv. 32. (c) Col ii. 2. (d) 1 Pet. iii. 8.

† It is noted by one of the Fathers, Christ's coat, indeed, had no seam; but the church's vesture was of divers colours: Whereupon he says, *In veste Varietas sit, scissura non sit.*
Lord Bacon, Essay 3.

burnings; this is a great dishonour to God, and disgrace to religion. It is matter of shame, when they who have one God for their Father, strive and contend after such a manner.

Hence Abraham says to Lot, *Let there be no strife between me and thee;—for we be brethren* (e). Joseph's brethren used it as a powerful motive to him to forgive their sin, that they were *the servants of the God of his father* (f)? They that serve one God, and one Master, should be one among themselves. *Have we not all one Father?* says the prophet, *hath not one God created us? Why do we deal treacherously every man against his brother* (g)? Unity in affection would keep the strong from despising the weak, and the weak from censuring and judging the strong. And O, how would this adorn the gospel, and commend religion, and render it amiable in the eyes of the world; *Behold, how good, and how pleasant it is, for brethren to dwell together in unity* (h)! What an honour was it to religion in Tertullian's time, when the heathens had this to say of the Christians, † *Behold how they love one another!*

3. Unity in practice, endeavours and actings. You should cleave to one another, and walk together, in all duties tending to your mutual edification; as it is said of the primitive Christians, *They continued stedfastly in the apostles doctrine, and fellowship, and in breaking of bread, and in prayers. And they, continuing daily with one accord in the temple, and breaking bread from house to house, did eat their meat with gladness and singleness of heart* (i). You should endeavour to *glorify God with one mouth;* and to be of *one way*, as well as *one heart* (k). Only remember, it must be an union in God's way, in the ways of truth and and holiness. For that unity that is made up by abating any thing of our zeal for God and his truths, is not unity, but a carnal compliance. But in the ways of truth and holiness, we should study to be as one man in our endeavours and actings. In the service of this one only God, we should be *knit together as one man.* (l). Having one God to serve, we should serve him with one consent. Where this is, it is a sign of thriving service: Therefore it is promised as a great blessing, *For then will I turn to the people of a pure language, that they may all call upon the name of the Lord, to serve him with one consent* (m): Or, *one shoulder*, as the word may be rendered. Join shoulder to shoulder,

---

(e) Gen. xiii 8. (f) Gen. l. 17. (g) Mal. ii. 10. (h) Psal. cxxxiii. 1. (i) Acts ii. 42, 46. (k) Rom. xv. 16. Jer. xxxii 39. (l) Judges xx. 11. (m) Zeph. iii. 19.
† *Vide ut invicem se diligant.* Tertull. Apol.

der, for promoting his service, and advancing his glory. Join together *as one man*, that you may *strive together*, by all holy and united endeavours, *for the faith of the gospel* (n).

Well then, let us study to maintain and promote unity among ourselves, and, with others of the Lord's people, that they and we may be one as God is one. And for this end, let us often propose to ourselves the unity of the Godhead in the trinity of persons; that we may be thereby quickened to study and endeavour some dark resemblance of him therein. And pray much for this holy unity. How earnestly did Christ pray for it (o)! O pray, that God would bless the ministers and members of this church with one heart and one way: That he would stamp an impress or dark image of his unity on our societies and assemblies: That as God is one, so we may be one in his service, and in advancing and promoting his glory. Plead the accomplishment of that promise, *In that day there shall be one Lord, and his name* (p). Plead it in its full extent. It is a promise of the enlargement of Christ's kingdom through the world in the latter days; and of the unity of his kingdom, in being subjected to one Lord, and following one way of doctrine and worship. Unity in the faith, and uniformity in religion and worship, is a blessing to be expected in Christ's kingdom now in the latter days. The full accomplishment of this promise seems to be reserved for the conversion and restoration of God's ancient people. Pray that the nations may cast off idolatry, and agree in worshipping one God, in one way of spiritual worship.

Use 6. For comfort to them that have a saving interest in God as their God. It is matter of great comfort to you who are the children of God, and in covenant with him, that your God is the one only God, God alone. This may comfort you, 1. With respect to yourselves in particular. 2. With respect to the church in general.

1. With respect to yourselves in particular. Every man is happy or miserable, as the god is whom he serves. But your God is the one only God. He who hath no superior, no equal or fellow, is thine. He that is, and there is none else, is thine. There is none like him in heaven or earth, *none like unto the God of Jeshurun* (q). Therefore, no people like his people: So it follows, *Happy art thou, O Israel, who is like unto thee?* And, says David in his prayer, *thou art great, O Lord God: for there is none like*

(n) Phil. i. 27.   (o) John xvii.   (p) Zech. xiv. 9.   (q) Deut. xxxiii. 26, 29.

like thee; neither is there any god besides thee.—And what one nation in the earth is like thy people, even like Israel (r)? Your God is God alone. None can stop the execution of his gracious purposes, or the accomplishment of the gracious promises he hath made to you. Your happiness is sure: You have his word for it who is the one only God.

2. With respect to the church in general. He who is the God of Zion is God alone. He is her God, who hath no equal in worth and perfection. He hath no equal to controul him, or cope with him. This may comfort you, 1. When enemies combine and make head against the church. Her God is the one only God; therefore she is safe, though all the powers of the earth were gathered together against her. All creatures, good and bad, are under his dominion. They are all in his hand. Whom need you fear? From whom is the church in danger? Hezekiah encouraged himself on this ground, in his address to God against Sennacherib: *O Lord God of Israel*, says he, *who dwellest between the cherubims,* THOU *art the God, even* THOU *alone, of all the kingdoms of the earth—Lord, bow down thine ear and hear* (s), &c. 2. When there is no human probability or likelihood of the accomplishment of what God hath promised to his church. He hath promised to make his Zion *a burdensome stone for all people;* to make *kings her nursing-fathers, and queens her nursing-mothers;* and that *the kingdoms of the world* shall *become the kingdoms of our Lord and of his Christ* (t). Now, though at present there is no human probability or likelihood of the accomplishment of these promises; yet it is comfortable, that he who hath promised is God alone, and therefore able to make good his word. Hence it is, that the people of God, are encouraged to expect promised mercies and blessings from the consideration of this: *Is there a God besides me,* says the Lord? *Yea, there is no God; I know not any* (u). Being God alone, none is able to overpower him, in his designs for the church's good.

(r) 2 Sam. vii 22, 23.   (s) 2 Kings xix. 15.   (t) Zech. xii. 3. Isa. xlix 23. Rev. xi. 15.   (u) *See* Isa. xliv. 6, 8. xlv. 5. and xlvi. 9, 10, 11.

DISCOURSE

DISCOURSE XX.

Of the Trinity of Persons in the Godhead.

SERMON XC.

1 John v. 7. *For there are three that bear record in heaven, the Father, the Word, and the Holy Ghost, and these three are one.*

IN the two preceding verses, the apostle had laid down this as a certain truth, that Jesus Christ is the Son of God; and that he came to redeem his people, from the guilt, filth, and power of sin, by his blood and spirit. And this being a fundamental article of the Christian religion, he proves it by the testimonies borne thereunto. 1. In general, by the Spirit, verse 6th, *It is the Spirit that beareth witness, because the Spirit is truth.* Whereby we are to understand the Spirit in the hearts of believers, witnessing to this great truth, by giving them gracious experiences and feelings of the justifying and sanctifying virtue of the blood and spirit of Christ. 2. More particularly, he proves this truth, viz. That Christ is the Son of God, and the Saviour of the world, by the testimony given to it by two ranks and orders of witnesses; one in heaven, in my text; and the other in earth, in the verse following. So that in these two verses, we have the whole testimony given to the truth of the Christian religion. As Christ's being the Son of God, and the Saviour of the world, is a truth of the greatest moment; so it is not easy to believe it, and to be firmly fixed in the faith of it: Therefore is this truth confirmed by so many witnesses.

In my text then, we have the first rank or order of witnesses; and they are here variously set forth unto us. As,

1. By their number—*There are three.* According to the law (a), the testimony of two human witnesses was a sufficient legal evidence to prove a thing to be true: But here are three divine witnesses, whose testimony must be infallibly true, seeing they are Truth itself.

2. By their work—They *bear record*, or *witness.* And what do they bear witness unto? Even to this great truth, that Jesus Christ is the Son of God and the Saviour of the world, as appears from the context.

3. By their place—*In heaven.* Which is not to be so understood

(a) Deut. xvii. 6.

stood as if heaven were the place where they bear record or witness; for the apostle's scope here is to shew, what ground we, who are on earth, have to believe that Jesus is the Son of God, which must be some testimony given to us on earth. Therefore *in heaven* must be connected with the word *three;* so that the words may be read thus, *There are three in heaven that bear record.* And the expression imports, 1. That these witnesses testify to us immediately from heaven. 2. That the glory and majesty of these witnesses doth chiefly shine in heaven. 3. That they testify to us in a glorious, heavenly, and majestic manner. And, 4. That their testimony is not heard and regarded, received and acknowledged, save only by them whose hearts and minds are lifted up to heaven.

4. By their names. Witnesses are usually expressed by name: So it is here; there is *the Father, the Word, and the Holy Ghost.*

The first witness is the Father. He bare record or witness to this truth, that Jesus is the Son of God. 1. By the scriptures of the Old Testament. 2. By an immediate and audible voice from heaven, in a great congregation of people, at Christ's baptism, saying, *This is my beloved Son, in whom I am well pleased* (b). And this testimony was renewed and confirmed at his transfiguration (c). 3. By the works and miracles which he gave Christ to finish, by communicating his nature and operation with him as God. So our Lord tells us, *The works which the Father hath given me to finish, the same works that I do, bear witness of me* (d).

The second witness is the Word; that is, the Son, the second person of the Godhead. He is called *the Word*, 1. In respect of his person and eternal generation. As words are begotten in our thoughts, and are the express image of them †: So is Christ begotten of the Father from all eternity (e), and *the express image of his person* (f). He is his perfect and essential image. 2. In respect of his office. As words reveal our will, and express our meaning; so Christ is the Word of the Father, as revealing and declaring him, and his mind and will, to the church in all ages: For *no man hath seen God at any time; the only begotten Son, who is in the bosom of the Father, he hath declared him* (g). 3. Because he is the chief subject of the written word.

For,

(b) Matth. iii. 17.   (c) Matth. xvii. 5.   (d) John v. 36.
(e) Psal. ii. 7.   (f) Heb. i. 3.   (g) John i. 18.

† Ὅς ἐστιν αὐτῦ λόγος ὁ ῥητὸς ἀλλ' ἐνεργής.

Ignat. Epist. ad Magnes.

For, as he is the great mercy promised to the fathers under the Old Testament; so he is the truth and substance of all the types and shadows under the law, and the marrow and kernel of the gospel.

But how is it that Christ is brought in as a witness to this truth, that he is the Son of God, seeing none can be a fit witness in his own cause? Our blessed Lord himself solves this objection; *Though I bear record of myself,* says he, *yet my record is true; for I know whence I came, and whither I go* (*h*). Our blessed Lord, being true God, the God of truth, is a witness above all exception, and is not to be bound by the rules prescribed to fallible and sinful men in such cases. And being the great Angel and Messenger of the Covenant, sent by the Father, he ought to have all credit in publishing his commission and instructions. And I add, that Christ as God, testified of himself incarnate, that he was the Son of God.

But how did he bear witness to this truth? 1. By declaring and affirming himself to be *the Son of God*; which he did frequently. 2. By proving this truth: Partly, by his whole doctrine; *never man spake like* him: Partly, by his works and miracles; *The same works that I do,* says he, *bear witness of me:* And partly, by his resurrection, whereby he was *declared to be the Son of God with power* (*i*).

The third witness is the Holy Ghost, or Spirit. He bare record or witness that Jesus is the Son of God, by descending upon him in the likeness of a dove at his baptism; by descending afterward upon his apostles and disciples; by inspiring the holy penmen with the doctrine of Christ; by commending the same to the world; and by sealing up this truth to the consciences of the Lord's people, who are therefore said to be *sealed with the holy Spirit of promise* (*k*).

5. By their unity—*And these three are one.* Not only one in consent of will and agreement, because they testify the same thing, as if they were one witness; but also one in essence; in which sense Christ says, *I and my Father are one* (*l*). And that this is the meaning here, appears from the variation of the phrase in the very next verse. Here he says, *These three are one;* but of the witnesses in earth, *these three agree in one.* Now, if the same thing were intended and signified in both places, why then is the phrase so suddenly changed? Concerning the

witnesses

(*h*) John viii. 14. (*i*) See John viii. 12, 14, 17, 18. and vii. 46. and v. 36. Rom. i. 4. (*k*) Matth. iii. 16. Acts ii. 2, 3. 2 Pet. i. 21. Eph. i. 13. (*l*) John x. 30.

witnesses in heaven he says, *These three are one:* But this could not be said of the witnesses in earth; therefore he comes as near it as the matter will allow, in saying, *These three agree in one.* Further, grant it were so, that the Father, the Word, and the Holy Ghost are here said to be one in consent of will and agreement; yet this doth here necessarily suppose their oneness in nature and essence: For whatever is not God, being mutable and fallible, its testimony cannot be said to be divine and one with God's, as this testimony is said to be, in the text and context.

This text thus explained is a very clear and express testimony to the Trinity of Persons in the Godhead. True it is, that this text is left out in divers ancient copies of the New Testament; and hence it is that it is omitted by some of the ancient fathers in their disputes against the Arians. But it is as true that many most ancient and best approved copies retain this text. Lucas Burgensis saith, that in thirty-five old copies, they found it wanting but in five. And it is quoted by many of the ancient fathers, as Cyprian, Tertullian, Athanasius, and others. Yea, in the council of Nice it was urged by Athanasius against the Arians, and no exception was then made against it. And this verse was constantly and solemnly read as a part of scripture, both in the Greek and Latin churches†. And it is found in all the printed copies except one. Yea, it is retained and expressed by the Socinians themselves, in their German version, printed at Racovia, A. D. 1630. And the series of the context, and scope of the place, necessarily require this verse: For the words following, *and there are three that bear record in earth,* cannot have a right construction, but upon supposition that there are three also that bear record in heaven, with which these three in earth are connected by the conjunctive particle *and.* Therefore, that this text is wanting in some ancient copies, must be ascribed, either to the carelessness of the transcribers; or, which is more probable, to the fraud and deceit of some heretics, who denied the Son to be one in essence with the Father. The deceit of heretics, and particularly of the Arians, in corrupting and mutilating the sacred text, by their sacrilegious hands, was frequently discovered and complained of. And indeed the Arians seem to have had too fair opportunities for so doing, when not only divers emperors were Arians, but Arianism was spread almost through all parts of the known world.

† Selden. de Syned. Lib. II. Cap. 4.

Of the Holy Trinity.

The doctrine I propose from these words, is this:

There are three distinct Persons in the Godhead, the Father, the Son, and the Holy Ghost, who are one in nature and essence.

For here the apostle names *the Father, the Word*, that is, *the Son*, and *the Holy Ghost*. And he speaks of them as three distinct witnesses; and consequently as three distinct persons: not human, or angelical, but divine persons; therefore their testimony is called *the witness of God* (m). And these three are here declared to be *one*, that is one in essence, as I have already cleared.

In prosecuting this weighty purpose, I shall,

1. *Premise some things to the consideration of this doctrine.*
2. *Endeavour in some measure to clear it, by explaining some terms necessary to be used in this matter.*
3. *Prove this great truth from the holy scriptures.*
4. *I shall speak of the distinction of the Persons, both from the divine essence, and among themselves.*
5. *I shall speak of their Unity.*
6. *And lastly, make application of the doctrine.*

First, Some things premised to the consideration of this doctrine.

These things I am to premise being of some weight and moment, and divers of them controverted between us and the adversaries of the true religion, I shall therefore insist a little upon them.

1. I premise, that the doctrine of the Trinity is a fundamental article of the Christian religion; so that the knowledge and belief thereof is absolutely necessary unto salvation, in those that are adult and come to the years of discretion. Indeed, some deny it to be so much as an article of faith, as the Socinians: Others, viz. the Arminians, deny it to be fundamental; that by this means they may gratify their brethren the Socinians, and be in case to receive them into their church-communion. But this is the engine of the devil, whereby he endeavours to subvert the truths of God: He first brings the weight and necessity of these truths into question, that men being by this means rendered secure, may be the more easily induced to part with them.

We grant that there are different degrees of the knowledge of

(m) Verse 19.

of this mystery; some have more, and others less. But we say that the doctrine of the holy Trinity is such a fundamental article of our faith, that they who are grossly ignorant of it cannot be in the way of salvation; and that so much clearness in the knowledge of this truth from the holy scriptures, is absolutely necessary, as may be a ground of faith in the thing itself.

Our blessed Lord placeth eternal life in the right knowledge of this mystery: *This is life eternal*, says he, *that they might know thee the only true God, and Jesus Christ whom thou hast sent* (n). There can be no hope of eternal life without the knowledge of the true God; and he who is one God in three distinct persons, is the only true God. Hence it is, that though the Gentiles knew there was an infinite supreme Being, yet because they were ignorant of a holy Trinity, they are said *not to know God*, and to be *without God* (orig. *atheists*) *in the world* (o). So that without the knowledge of the trinity of persons in the Godhead, the only true God cannot be taken up, believed in, and worshipped. Again, let it be considered, that on this article of our faith, other fundamental articles depend; such, particularly, as concern God's sending his Son to be the Saviour of the world, and Christ's incarnation and satisfaction. They that take away the mystery of the holy Trinity, take away the Godhead and personality of the blessed Mediator, and consequently enervate his satisfaction: So that the shaking this article of our faith, overturns the whole Christian religion, and the only way of salvation that God hath revealed in the holy scriptures. Further, such as are initiated by baptism, are commanded to be baptized, *in the name of the Father, and of the Son, and of the Holy Ghost* (p); that is, unto the belief, profession, and obedience of the holy Trinity. To this they are virtually engaged: To God in three persons they are virtually dedicated and consecrated. Therefore † adult persons were not admitted to baptism, till they had made profession of their faith in the holy Trinity. And ‡ it was the custom of the ancient church, to instruct those that were to be baptized, for the space of

---

(n) John xvii. 3.   (o) 1 Thess. iv. 5. Eph. ii 12.   (p) Matth. xxviii. 19.

† *Ad sacrum Lavacrum regenerationis venientes, confessi sic, credo in Deum Patrem Omnipotentem, & in Jesum Christum filium ejus unigenitum, & in Spiritum Sanctum.*
                Inter. Oper. Athanas. Tom. 2. Lib. 11. ad Theophil.

‡ Hieron. Epist. 61.

of forty days, in the doctrine of the Trinity. Undoubtedly, it must be fundamentally necessary to know in whose name we are baptized, to whom we are devoted, and whom we are engaged to serve, obey, and worship. And I add, that the doctrine of the holy Trinity was by the ancients sacredly received and owned as a fundamental article; as appears from the creed commonly called *The Apostles' Creed*, and from the Nicene and Athanasian Creeds, from the writings of the ancient fathers, and the decrees and canons of ancient councils. So that this is a doctrine you should especially be established in: It is necessary that you be well rooted and firmly fixed in the faith thereof; for if this foundation be removed, all true religion falls to the ground.

2. I premise this, that the Trinity of persons in the Godhead, is a glorious and incomprehensible mystery. This is and must be owned by all that acknowledge any mystery at all. It is expresly called *a mystery*. The apostle tells the Colossians, how solicitous he was that they might attain to the *acknowledgement of the mystery of God, and of the Father, and of Christ*. So that the doctrine of the holy Trinity is a mystery, a secret above the reach and capacity of human understandings, a depth that reason cannot fathom. Though it be not against reason, yet it is above it: It dazzles and overpowers the most piercing apprehension. So that it is a mystery, not only to the wise men of the world, but in its own nature. There is in it a light inaccessible, such as reason cannot look into. In it consists the most incomprehensible and sublime perfection of God. The whole gospel is a mystery. It is called *the mystery of faith;* and *the mystery of Christ;* and the apostle cries out, *And without controversy, great is the mystery of godliness, God was manifest in the flesh, justified in the Spirit* (*q*), *&c.* The whole gospel is full of mysteries. There is scarce any thing in divinity but is a mystery in itself, how common soever it may be in the apprehensions of men. There is a depth in gospel truths, which the more we search into, we find to be the more profound. But all mysteries are not of one measure; some are greater than others: And this mystery of the holy Trinity is the mystery of mysteries. The mystery of Christ's incarnation, death and resurrection, is a great mystery: But this of the holy Trinity is greater than it, and without controversy the greatest of all, being the beginning and end of them all. All divine mysteries have their rise here, and all of them return hither.

3. I

(*q*) 1 Tim. iii 9. Eph. iii. 4. 1 Tim. iii. 16.

3. I premise, That the doctrine of the holy Trinity cannot be demonstrated by reason, nor is it evident by the light of nature, else it would be no mystery: For divine mysteries are such secrets as the wit of man could never have found out. This is plainly such: We could never have attained the knowledge thereof without divine revelation. Of this mystery our Lord speaks; *No man knoweth the Son but the Father; neither knoweth any man the Father, save the Son, and he to whomsoever the Son will reveal him* (r).

Indeed if nature be considered as in Adam in the state of innocency, it seems to be plain and evident, that some clearness in the knowledge of this mystery was natural to him, in so far that he was created with the knowledge thereof. For, he was made after the image of God in knowledge; and it is the chief part of this knowledge, to know God; not only what he is, by having some general notions of a Deity: but also who he is, so as to be able to apply these general notions to him who is one God in three Persons; for he is the only true God. Hence we find express intimation of the blessed Trinity, or at least of a plurality of divine Persons, in man's creation; *Let us make man after our image* (s). And seeing God the Father, Son, and Holy Ghost, created man, he cannot be imagined to have been ignorant of the blessed Trinity, unless we say that he was ignorant of his Creator.

Yet now, after the fall, the doctrine of the Holy Trinity is such a mystery as no man could ever discover without divine revelation. To attempt the proof and demonstration thereof by natural reason, derogates both from the dignity of this glorious mystery, and from faith, in making adversaries apprehend that we rely on such reasons, and build our faith upon them. It is plain, that no argument can be brought from natural reason, that doth solidly conclude that there is one God in three distinct Persons. Hence it is that none of the pagan philosophers did ever, by their deepest search, discover this mystery. It is true, some passages expressing some notion of a Trinity in the Deity, occur in divers heathen authors; such as Orpheus, Trismegistus, the Sybills, Plato, and his followers. But such passages were either some general notions received by tradition from the Jews, or taken out of the scriptures themselves, and by these pagans misunderstood; for they dreamed of three distinct separate essences: Or else such passages were foisted into the writings of these Pagans, by the fraud and fallacy of some Christians, who counted it a piece of

(r) Matth. xi. 27.   (s) Gen. i. 26.

of zeal to lie for God. And the more clear such passages are, the more they are to be suspected: For, it cannot be imagined, that God would give a more clear revelation of this mystery to some heathens, than he did to his own people the Jews, to whom *were committed the oracles of God*.

From all which we conclude, that although the mystery of the Trinity may, in some sort, be illustrated by natural reason, yet it cannot be found out nor solidly demonstrated by it. The similes used by schoolmen and other divines in this matter, though they may a little gratify the fancy, yet they are utterly unsatisfactory; seeing there is no proportion at all between things finite and that which is infinite: And to me they seem rather to darken, than to illustrate this truth; therefore I intend to use none of them. This is a mystery proper to the holy scriptures. Other truths are revealed in nature; but this is a treasure peculiar to the church.

SERMON XCI.

4. I Premise, that the doctrine of the holy Trinity is plainly revealed in the holy scriptures. The papists, though they are found and orthodox in this article, yet deny that it is clearly and plainly revealed in the written word, and therefore have recourse here to their unwritten traditions: And this they do, that they may have occasion for charging the holy scriptures with obscurity and imperfection. But whatever secret there be in this glorious mystery of the Trinity, and though it be given us to *know* it only *in part*, and to *see* it but *as through a glass darkly;* yet so much is given us to know concerning it as is necessary unto salvation. Though the τὸ διότι, or τὸ πῶς, that is, the particular manner *how it is*, be inexpressible and incomprehensible; yet the τὸ ὅτι, *that it is*, is plainly revealed, more darkly in the Old Testament, but more clearly in the New; and what is more darkly revealed about it in some places of the New Testament, is more plainly revealed in other places. So far hath God revealed this mystery in his blessed word, as we both may and ought to attain to some distinctness therein; such distinctness as is held forth in the holy scriptures, the only rule and measure of faith. It is certainly the sin of many professors of Christianity, that they do not study this glorious mystery of mysteries.

5. I premise, that the proof and demonstration of this mystery is to be taken from the holy scriptures. This follows from what hath been said. It cannot be demonstrated by reason,

nor is it evident by the light of nature: Therefore whatever we are allowed to know concerning it, is to be learned only from the written word. We are to frame all our notions and conceptions of it, according to divine revelation, which is a sufficient ground of faith, even in these things which cannot be comprehended by reason: And in all our inquiries about it, we must hold to the word of God. This certainly is most safe, that we may not involve ourselves in unnecessary difficulties, or lose ourselves in an inextricable labyrinth, while we seek to be *wise above what is written*. So far as the holy scriptures lead us, we may go with safety: But where scripture-light fails, there we are to make a stand, and go no further, lest we dash our brains while we wander in the dark. Hence,

6. I premise, that this mystery is to be studied with much humble sobriety. It is to be adored and admired, and not curiously searched into. Many of the schoolmen have run to a woful excess here, and have taken an unwarrantable liberty in discoursing of this incomprehensible mystery. Men of presumptuous spirits, not being satisfied with the simple truth of God, and being curious to find satisfaction to their own reason, have with a daring boldness, searched by their vain reasonings into this incomprehensible mystery, which God hath compassed about with the divine darkness of inaccessible light. What is this but a daring to behold the infinite glory of God with eyes of flesh, and to seek to approach that light that is inaccessible, and would dazzle and blind the eyes of sinful mortals? Hence it is, that these schoolmen, of whom I speak, have miserably darkened this truth, by their curious and bold inquiries, and entered into an endless labyrinth of difficulties, out of which the thread of reason and dispute could never extricate them. A learned divine, as a worthy gentleman relates *, startled at their audacious vanity, saith, he reads the schoolmen about such things, as he hears men swear or take God's name in vain, even seldom, unwillingly, and with horror. We are therefore obliged, both in point of interest and duty, to search into this mystery with sober minds, lest we puzzle faith, while we would inform and satisfy reason. That saying among the ancients ought here especially to be remembered †, " There is " danger in speaking of God even the things that are true." And that of Bernard ‡, " It is rashness to search into these things,

---

* Polhil of Faith.
† *De Deo etiam vera dicere periculosum est.* Cypr.
‡ *Scrutari hæc Temeritas est, credere Pietas est, nosse vero Vita æterna est.*

"things, piety to believe them, and life eternal to know them."
And that of Augustine †, "No where do men err with greater
"danger." Errors here, are of very dangerous consequence with
respect to the whole of religion. Therefore in studying this
mystery, let us content and satisfy ourselves with the clear
knowledge and firm belief of the τὸ ὅτι, *that it is;* avoiding
all bold and curious into the διότι, or particular manner *how
it is.* The full uptaking of this mystery is peculiarly reserved
till the time when we shall see God as he is. *At that day,* says
our Lord, *ye shall know that I am in my Father, and you in me,
and I in you* (a). Therefore let us restrain curiosity, and adjourn
all these inquiries to which we can have no satisfaction from
divine revelation, till we come to heaven and see, which will
be the peculiar happiness of believers in Christ. *The secret
things belong unto the Lord our God: But those things which are
revealed belong unto us, and to our children for ever* (b). Upon
which last words, *unto us,* and *to our children,* the Hebrew hath
extraordinary pricks, to stir up to earnest attention to what
is spoken. To be *wise above what is written,* is sinful and dangerous folly; but to be *wise according to what is written,* is true
wisdom and sobriety. This sacred and profound mystery, in
regard of the manner how it is, is one of these secrets which
belong to God alone: For *no man knoweth the Son but the Father; neither knoweth any man the Father, save the Son, and he
to whomsoever the Son will reveal him* (c).

7. I premise, That the doctrine of the holy Trinity is of
great practical use in religion. Some Arminians reproach this
mystery as an useless speculation, of no use with reference to
Christian practice. But all divine truths are *according to godliness* (d): Much more this great and fundamental truth, which
is the spring and fountain of all true religion. The truth is,
the practice of all serious piety depends upon it. There can
be no true religion where the true God is not worshipped:
Nor do they worship the true God, but an idol or figment of
their own brain, who do not worship that God who is one
essence in three distinct Persons. Particularly, this doctrine
is of great use in prayer and other acts of immediate worship;
for in all these we address ourselves to the Father, through
Christ, by the Spirit; according to that of the apostle, *For
through him* (that is, Christ) *we both have an access by one Spirit
unto*

† *Nec periculosius alicubi erratur.* Aug. de Trin. L. 1. C. 3.
(a) John xiv. 20. (b) Deut. xxix, 29. (c) Matth. xi. 17.
(d) Tit. i. 1.

unto the Father (*e*). And though there were no other use to be made of this glorious mystery, but to restrain the curiosity of mens spirits, and keep them within the bounds of sobriety and faith, this were enough. O that we may all learn this from it, to get and entertain more awful and reverend apprehensions of that glorious and incomprehensible Majesty with with whom we have to do, and a more deep humbling sense of our darkness and ignorance before him.

Secondly, The truth of the doctrine cleared.

I proceed in the next place, to clear this truth, which I shall endeavour to do, in some measure, by explaining some terms that are commonly used in this matter.

Divines, in explaining this glorious mystery, use divers words and terms; which though they are not expresly contained in the holy scriptures, in so many letters and syllables; yet are most fit and proper to convey into the minds of men, the true and genuine meaning of what is revealed in the scriptures about this doctrine. The Antitrinitarians of old, and the Socinians, and divers Arminians of late, would have the use of all such words and terms to be utterly laid aside; pretending that they are unscriptural, new, and strange, and such as occasion contention and debate; but with a real design to overturn the doctrine itself. I confess it is the thing itself that we should especially be established in, and that from clear scripture; and if there were a consent and agreement in the thing itself, we should not wrangle needlesly about words. But seeing the adversaries of the true religion, have no other design in exclaiming against the terms used by divines in this matter, but that they may the more easily reject and overturn the mystery itself that is expressed by them; † and the terms themselves being very proper, and of great use in explaining this mystery, and for refuting adversaries; therefore the use of them ought still to be retained.

I shall not speak of all the terms or words used by divines in this matter. Only when we speak of a Trinity of Persons in the Godhead, three terms come to be explained. 1. What is meant

---

(*e*) Eph. ii. 18.

† *Scholasticæ semper moris est Disciplinæ, si quando Hæret eorum nova Doctrina exurgit, contra insolentes Quæstionum mutationes, rebus immutabiliter manentibus, nominum vocabula immutare.*

  Athan. Oper. Tom. 2. in Disp. cum Ario.

Ad inveniendum nova nomina fidem antiquam Significantia, coegit necessitas disputandi cum Hereticis. Thom. 1, Q. 29. Art. 3.

meant by Godhead. 2. What we are to underſtand by Perſon, and what is the uſe of that word here. 3. What is the import of the word Trinity.

1. By the Godhead is meant the divine nature or eſſence; So that theſe three, the Godhead, the divine nature, and the divine eſſence, are ſynonymous terms, words of the ſame import and ſignification. The word Godhead is ſcriptural. And the divine nature is expreſſed by words or terms equivalent to eſſence: As in that text, *From him who is, and who was, and who is to come*: And that name, I AM THAT I AM, denoteth the eſſence or being of God. And we have the divine nature expreſſed by the apoſtle Peter. And idols are differenced from the true God by this, that they are *by nature no gods* (*f*); which implies that the true God is God by nature, and conſequently God in reſpect of his eſſence: So that God may be conſidered eſſentially, or in reſpect of his eſſence.

2. What are we to underſtand by the word Perſon? and what is the uſe of that word here? and in what ſenſe do we ſay, that there are three diſtinct Perſons in the Godhead?

A perſon is generally defined to be an individual or ſingular being, ſubſiſting, rational, incommunicable, not ſuſtained by another, nor a part of another. 1. I ſay, it is an individual, or ſingular being; not a general eſſence or nature: So that mankind is not a perſon; but a particular or individual man is ſo. 2. It is a being ſubſiſting. So that accidents are not perſons. Subſiſtence denotes a manner of exiſtence proper to ſubſtances. A perſon muſt ſubſiſt and not exiſt only. 3. It is a rational being. We do not call a book, or a tree, or a beaſt, a perſon. 4. It is incommunicable: it cannot be communicated to another. So that the nature of man is not a perſon, becauſe it is communicable to every particular man. But every particular man is a perſon, becauſe that nature which he hath in particular, cannot be communicated to another. 5. A perſon is not ſuſtained by another. So that the human nature of Chriſt is not a perſon, becauſe it hath no ſubſiſtence in itſelf, but is ſuſtained by his Deity. 6. A perſon is not a part of another. Therefore the ſoul which is a part of a man is not a perſon. Thus I have ſhewed you what a perſon is, in things created; or what a created perſon is.

Now, the diſtinct ſubſiſtences in the Godhead are by divines called Perſons, by a ſimilitude taken from a created perſon, becauſe

---

(*f*) Acts xvii. 29. Rom. i. 20. Col. ii. 9. Rev. i. 4. Exod. iii. 14. 2 Pet. i. 4. Gal. iv. 8.

because created persons seem to have some dark resemblance of them: For as created persons are subsistences singular, intelligent, and incommunicable; so are the subsistences in the Godhead. So that there is some aptitude in this term Person to express the subsistences in the divine nature. We have no other word or term to express them by. The divine nature or essence being but one, and yet there being three, each whereof hath the whole Godhead in himself; one and yet three; there must be some words or terms to express this mystery: And these are the safest and fittest to express the same to our understanding; one in essence, and three in persons. These are the best that we can use in so deep a matter, for preventing the errors and mistakes of those, who would either multiply the essence, or abolish the Persons. Seeing there are three differences in the Deity, which the scripture speaks of by the names of Father, Son, and Holy Ghost, and speaks of them as we use to do of three distinct Persons; what reason can be given why we should abstain from using the word Person in this argument? And I add, that the use of this word, in explaining this mystery, is agreeable that text, where Christ is called *the express image of* the Father's *Person* (g). And the original word must necessarily be rendered Person, seeing it is used there to denote the peculiar subsistence of the Father, of which the Son is the express image. So that it is plain from that text, that the Father, considered as distinct from the Son, is a person; and that the Son, considered as distinct from the Father, and as the express image of his person, must be a person also. And what is said of the Father and the Son, must also be true of the Holy Ghost, who is God equal with both, yet different from them both, as they differ from each other, though not by the same incommunicable property.

But though it be very proper to use the word Person in explaining this glorious mystery; yet this word is not to be taken or urged here in the extreme rigour: But in applying this term by way of similitude unto God, we must always look to it that we remove from him all imperfection. We must therefore observe a vast difference between a created, and an increated Person. Three persons among men have three particular individual essences or natures: But all the increated Persons have the same individual essence. Hence it is said in my text, *There are three that bear record in heaven—and these three are one:* *One*, viz. in nature or essence, as I cleared when I explained the words. So that the asserting that there are three Persons

in

(g) Heb. i. 3.

in the Godhead, doth not infer any separation or division in the Godhead; for the persons in the Godhead are not separated or divided, but only distinguished, so as the one is not the other. Again, one created person hath not his in-being in another; but one increated person is in another. The Father is in the Son, and the Son in the Father, and both in the Holy Ghost, and the Holy Ghost in both. *I am in the Father*, says Christ, *and the Father in me* (*h*). And what is said of the Father and the Son, is true also of the Holy Ghost, who is God equal with both. To shut up this head, the word Person is used here, to shew that the Father, Son, and Holy Ghost, are not three acts, nor three offices, nor three attributes, nor three manifestations, nor three operations; but three distinct subsistences, distinguished from one another by their incommunicable properties. And we use the word Person rather than Subsistence, because it hath more in it, and expresseth more excellency than the word Subsistence: For it is proper to say, that a beast subsists; but it were absurd to say, that a beast is a person, because a person is an intelligent subsistence. From all that is said, it plainly appears, that the use of the word Person, in explaining this glorious mystery, is not to be stumbled at; especially if we add a fit epithet, and say, that the Father, Son, and Holy Ghost, are divine or increated Persons.

From what hath been delivered, we may have some notion of a divine Person, so far as we are capable to apprehend this mystery, viz. that it is the divine Essence subsisting in a special manner, upon the account of a special and incommunicable property. So, in the person of the Father, there is the divine Essence, subsisting in a special manner as the Father, on the account of his special and incommunicable property of begetting the Son. Or, a divine Person is † a mode or manner of subsistence in the divine Essence, distinct from others in the same individual Essence, by a peculiar and incommunicable property. So that created and increated persons differ in this, that every created person hath a particular and individual essence or nature of his own; but in the same individual divine Essence there are three distinct Persons. Again, created persons are separated or divided one from another; whereas among the divine Persons there is no separation or division, but only a distinction, each Person having his distinct personal property.

(*h*) John xiv. 10.
† *Subsistentia in essentia Dei, quæ ad alios relata, proprietate incommunicabili distinguitur.*
Calv. Inst. Lib. I. C. 13. s. 6. post Justinum & Damascenum.

perty. The divine Essence is so perfect and indivisible, that it is not capable of such a difference of persons as is among men: For in the divine nature or essence there can be no separate existence, seeing the essence and existence are the same in God; and necessary existence being an inseparable attribute of his essence, he can have no other existence than what is implied in his very essence. From all which it follows, that no other way of distinction can be conceived here, but by different modes of subsistence in the same individual divine essence.

Now, the different modes or manners of subsistence in the Godhead, are what the holy scripture plainly acquaints us with, the Father, the Son, and the Holy Ghost, as having mutual relation to each other. On these the distinct personalities are founded: For the Father is distinct from the Son, and the Son from the Father, and the Holy Ghost from both. And the relations being so different, that one cannot be confounded with the other; therefore that which results from the relation or mode of subsistence, being joined with the essence, is that which we call a Person. Hence it appears that the persons in the Godhead are not mere modes, or naked relations, but the Godhead subsisting under such different modes or relations. The divine essence is to be taken together with the mode to make a person: So that the notion of a person doth, besides the manner of subsistence, necessarily suppose the divine nature together with it; and a person is that which results from the divine nature and subsistence together.

3. What is the import of the word TRINITY? This word in its native signification, signifies the number of any three things: But by ecclesiastical custom it is applied by way of eminency to this mystery alone, and limited to signify the three persons in the Godhead. It is true, this word is not to be found in the holy scriptures in so many letters and syllables; yet there are words equivalent to it in signification, here in my text, *There are three that bear record in heaven.* This word is not to be so understood, as if the divine essence consisted of three persons as so many parts. Therefore ‖ we use the word Trinity, rather than Triplicity: For Triplicity denotes a thing compounded of three as so many parts, and so would infer a multiplication of the essence; but Trinity denotes three distinct subsistences in the same individual essence.

SERMON

‖ *Nec quoniam Trinitas est, ideo Triplex putandus est: Alioqui minor erit Pater solus, aut filius solus, quam simul Pater & filius.*
August. de Trin. Lib. VI. C. 7.

SERMON XCII.

Thirdly, **T**HE truth of the doctrine confirmed.

I go on to the third general head, viz. to prove the doctrine, that there are three distinct Persons in the Godhead.

This is a very weighty point, on which the whole of revealed religion doth depend, and which being shaken or overturned, the whole Christian religion falls to the ground; so that the people of God need to have their faith firmly established in the belief of this glorious mystery from clear scripture grounds; and so much the more that, in our time, and in this island, there are bold attempts made to revive the old Arian heresy, which, if God permit, may prevail to overthrow the faith of some, and to shake the faith of sincere Christians, by subtle and sophistical reasonings. For these reasons, I humbly judge it may not be unedifying, through the blessing of God, to insist a little in the proof of this great fundamental article, and that from the holy scriptures alone, it being a truth wholly supernatural.

The Socinians, who labour all they can to destroy the faith of this mystery, cry out against it as a new opinion, devised after the times of Christ and his apostles: Therefore I shall prove this great truth, from divers texts of scripture, 1. In the Old Testament. 2. In the New Testament.

1. From divers texts in the scriptures of the Old Testament.

This being a fundamental article, the knowledge and belief whereof is absolutely necessary unto salvation (as I formerly shewed) it must needs have been revealed and made known to the people of God under the Old Testament. And truly, if it had not been revealed to the Jews of old, the true God had not been known, believed in, and worshipped by them; seeing he is the only true God, who is one in essence, and three in persons. I confess that this glorious mystery was not so clearly revealed unto the Jews of old, as it is unto us in the New Testament; but more darkly, as the nature of the Old Testament dispensation, and the infant state of that church required: Yet was it so far revealed to them as was necessary unto salvation. This will be evident by considering the particular texts on which we build. I shall therefore, from the scriptures of the Old Testament, prove, 1. That in the Godhead, there is a plurality of Persons, that is, more persons than one. 2. That there are three distinct persons in the Godhead, neither more nor fewer.

1. I prove

1. I prove that there is a plurality of Perſons, that is, more perſons than one, in the Godhead; and that from two places of argument.

(1.) From ſuch places of ſcripture where the Lord ſpeaks of the Lord, or is diſtinguiſhed from the Lord. See ſome texts to this purpoſe. As, Gen. xix. 24. *Then the Lord rained upon Sodom and upon Gomorrah, brimſtone and fire from the Lord out of heaven.* That is, God the Son, who now appeared upon the earth in a human ſhape, which he frequently did as a prelude of his future incarnation, rained from God the Father in heaven; both concurring in this work, according to their order and manner of working. For, if the deſign of this expreſſion were only to ſignify, that this ſhower of fire and brimſtone proceeded from the immediate hand of God, it had been ſufficient to ſay, *the Lord rained out of heaven,* without adding *from the Lord.* Therefore it is certainly ſo emphatically expreſſed, *the Lord rained from the Lord,* to denote a plurality of perſons in the Godhead. Another text is, Pſal. xlv. 6, 7. *Thy throne, O God, is for ever and ever.—Thou loveſt righteouſneſs, and hateſt wickedneſs; therefore God, thy God, hath anointed thee with the oil of gladneſs above thy fellows.* The Jewiſh Talmud applieth this pſalm wholly to the Meſſiah. And that theſe words particularly are by way of apoſtrophe ſpoken to him, the ancient Jews granted; and their later doctors, though they impugn the doctrine of the holy Trinity, cannot deny it. And the apoſtle to the Hebrews expreſsly applies theſe words as ſpoken to Chriſt. Now, here is mention made of *God anointing,* and *God anointed; O God,—God, thy God, hath anointed thee* (*a*). A plain intimation of a plurality of divine perſons. The meaning is, God the Father furniſhed the human nature of Chriſt with theſe gifts of the Spirit, that were neceſſary to the diſcharge of his mediatory office. And the Father is here called Chriſt's God, not only in reſpect of his human nature, but alſo, ſay ſome †, in regard of his divine nature. As he is his Father, ſo he is his God, having communicated his nature to him by eternal generation: Whence the Son is called by the ancients, *God of God.* The Father is Chriſt's God alſo in reſpect of his mediatory office, and in regard of the eternal covenant between them about the redemption of elect ſinners. A third text to this purpoſe, is in Pſal. cx. 1. *The Lord ſaid unto my Lord, Sit thou at my right hand until I make thine enemies thy footſtool.* Our bleſſed Lord quotes this text in Matth. xxii. 43, 44. Where he proves that he to whom the Lord JEHOVAH

is

(*a*) Heb. i. 8, 9. † Owen in Loc.

is brought in speaking, must be more than a mere man, seeing David calls him *his Lord:* And seeing he is more than a mere man, he must needs be a divine person distinct from JEHOVAH. So that here also we have a plurality of divine persons; and the meaning is, *God the Father said to God the Son.* A fourth text is Prov. xxx. 4. —*What is his name, and what is his Son's name, if thou canst tell?* Where the Father and the Son are distinguished. And they must needs be divine persons that are here spoken of; because their name, that is, their nature and perfections, are unspeakable. Another text, to the same purpose, is in Hof. i. 6, 7. *And God said unto him,——I will have mercy upon the house of Judah, and will save them by the Lord their God.* Where two are mentioned; one that promiseth to save his people, and that is God; and another by whom he will save them, and he also is called, *the Lord their God.* Again, Dan. ix. 17. *O our God, hear the prayer of thy servant,—for the Lord's sake.* That is, for Christ's sake, for the sake of the blessed Messiah. He is here spoken of as a distinct person, and a divine person; for who else could obtain access in prayer to a holy God for guilty sinners, but he who is very God?

In all these texts, the Lord is distinguished from the Lord, not essentially, seeing there is but one God; therefore personally, or as one person is distinguished from another. One of two must be intimated thereby, either a plurality of divine natures or essences, which is contrary both to scripture and reason; or a plurality of divine persons.

(2.) That there is a plurality of persons in the Godhead, is evident from such places of scripture, where God speaks of or to himself in the plural number. And here I begin with that famous text about the creation of man. *And God said, Let us make man in our image, after our likeness* (*b*). Let *us,* in the plural number; and so are the following expressions used by God in the same work, OUR *image,* OUR *likeness.* The ancients unanimously agree, that a plurality of persons in the Deity is here revealed and intimated. Yea, the Council of Syrmium †, tho' Arianising in their Confession of Faith, yet denounceth an *anathema* unto any that shall deny these words, *Let us make man,* to be the words of the Father to the Son.

It is very observable, that in the whole preceding account of the work of creation, God is brought in speaking constantly in the singular number; *And God said, Let there be light; and God said, Let there be a firmament.* And although even in that word,

VOL. II. Nº. 7.   G g   *and*

(*b*) Gen. i. 26.   † Socrat. Lib. II. C. 25.

and *Elohim said*, there may be, according to some divines, a respect had to a plurality of persons in the unity of the divine essence, a noun in the plural number being joined with a verb in the singular number: Yet here, in verse 26th, the mystery of that is more clearly revealed, the manner of expression, constantly used before, being suddenly changed, and God brought in speaking in the plural number, *Let us make man in our image*. This cannot be imagined to be done without some peculiar reason. And both the Jews, and Socinians, and other Antitrinitarians are aware of this; but they are at an utter loss what reason to assign, and know not what to pitch upon. And indeed, without a supposition of a plurality of divine persons, no tolerable account can be given of the reason of this expression, by them that acknowledge the unity of the divine essence. For, whereas it is pretended that God speaks here of himself in the plural number, after the manner of kings and princes: I shall have occasion to shew the vanity of that pretence afterward. And it cannot be said, that God speaks these words to the angels, *Let us make man after our image*. For † man was not made after their image, but after the image of God alone; as is plain from the very next verse. *So God created man in his own image, in the image of God created he him.* Nor did God use the ministry of angels in the creation of man: For creation being a work of infinite power, they could not co-operate with God in it, nor contribute any thing thereunto; and being a pure act of infinite sovereignty, there was no use of any intermediate instrumental cause therein, as there is in the government of the world. And the holy scripture expresly denies that God took counsel with any besides himself in the work of creation (*c*).

I cannot here omit what an eminent learned writer observes ‖, that whereas God designed the manifestation only of his being and glorious perfections in other parts of the visible creation; he designed also the manifestation of himself, as subsisting in three distinct persons, in the creation of man. Hence it is that the first express mention of a plurality of persons in the divine essence, is in man's creation. And they are here brought in as consulting about it, after the manner of men, because

(*c*) Isa. xl. 13, 14.

† *Neque enim conservis ea consultationis dignitas competit; neque angeli creaurunt hominem; neque potest creatura unquam adæquari suo Creatori; homines autem perfecti æquales erunt angelis: Neque una est imago Dei & creaturarum.* Basil. M. Lib. 9. Hexaemeron.

‖ Owen in Heb. Vol. II. Exerc. 3.

because man was specially designed to the glory of the sacred Trinity, or to the glory of God as three in one. And hence it is also, that the holy scripture, speaking of man's Creator, doth often use the plural number. As in these texts: *Thy Maker is thine husband;* orig. *thy Makers is thine husbands;* and, *Let Israel rejoice in him that made him;* orig. *in his Makers;* and, *Remember now thy Creator;* orig. *thy Creators;* and, *where is God my Maker;* orig. *my Makers* (*d*). These texts plainly prove that he who made us is, in some sense, more than one; which cannot be otherwise understood, than of a plurality of persons in one divine essence. And hence it is that the Holy Ghost expresseth God's making man, sometimes in the singular number, to denote the unity of the divine essence; and sometimes in the plural number, to denote a plurality of persons in the same essence.

This text will be further illustrated, by comparing that in Gen. iii. 22. *And the Lord God said, Behold, the man is become as one of us.* Where the Holy Ghost explains the meaning of that place, *Let us make man in our image.* For clearing this, let it be considered, that when Satan tempted our first parents to eat of the forbidden fruit, he solicited them to it by this promise, *Ye shall be as Gods.* It should be rendered, *as God*, in the singular number: For the word is, *Ye shall be as Elohim*, which is the name whereby God is usually expressed in the preceding history of the creation. *And God said, Let there be light; and God said, Let there be a firmament; and God said, Let us make man.* The word in the original is, *and Elohim said.* So that when the devil promised to our first parents, *ye shall be as God*, as *Elohim*, certainly he understood no other but that God that said, *Let us make man.* Now these words, *Behold, man is become as one of us*, are a holy irony, or sarcasm, whereby God upbraids our first parents with the issue of their enterprize in compliance with the devil's temptation. As if he had said, " Behold " how happy man is by taking the devil's counsel; now he is " *become as one of us*, is he not? He is a brave man indeed." So that in this sarcasm, God had an eye to what the devil promised to our first parents, *Ye shall be as God*, as *Elohim:* And seeing the devil did thereby understand no other but that God that said, *Let us make man;* it is plain and evident, that these words, *as one of us*, can be understood of no other but God himself; and, being in the plural number, cannot be understood otherwise, than of a plurality of divine persons, by them that
own

(*d*) Isa. liv. 5. Psal. cxlix. 2. Eccl. xii. 1. Job xxxv. 9.

own the divine essence. It cannot be said, that God speaks this of himself and the angels, *man is become as one of us:* For, as not one word hath been as yet spoken concerning the angels; so it is a most absurd conceit to imagine, that the great God should associate the angels to himself in such a kind of equality as this expression intimates; nor did the devil promise to man, nor did man affect, a likeness to the angels, but to God himself. The truth is, no proper interpretation can be given of these words, so as to give no countenance to the opinion of a plurality of Gods, unless we suppose a plurality of persons in the Godhead.

A third text where God speaks of or to himself in the plural number is in Gen. xi. 6, 7. Where we read of God's confounding the language of the builders of Babel. This was an effect of the mighty power of God upon their minds and tongues, and no less miraculous than the gift of tongues bestowed on the apostles: But so it is, that this work is here ascribed to a plurality; *And the Lord said,—Go to, let us go down, and there confound their language.* It cannot be understood as spoken by the Lord unto the angels, as if he needed either their advice or their assistance; for there is not a word about the angels in the whole context, but only of the Lord JEHOVAH. Therefore God here speaks this to himself, or the Father to the Son and the Holy Ghost. And to God alone is this work appropriated in the following verses (8, 9.), *So the Lord scattered them abroad:* And, *The Lord did there confound the language of all the earth.*

Another text to the same purpose, is in Isa vi. 8. *And I heard the voice of the Lord, saying, Whom shall I send, and who will go for us?* The change of the number, *I* into *us*, is very remarkable: And both being meant of one and the same Lord, who speaks of himself both in the singular and in the plural number, there is here also a sufficient intimation of a plurality of persons in the same individual divine essence. Besides this, no satisfying reason can be given of this manner of expression.

It is pretended by adversaries, that in these texts, God speaks of himself in the plural number, after the manner of kings and princes, who use to say, WE *will and command,* or, *It is* OUR *will and pleasure.* But the vanity of this pretence will appear from these following considerations.

1*st*, The introduction of this stile among kings and princes, is of a much later date than the history of the creation, and comparatively modern; and what then was not, could not then be alluded unto. This stile or manner of speech, whereby

whereby kings and princes speak of themselves in the plural number, is not agreeable to the genius of the Hebrew tongue, as some observe; nor to the simplicity of the first ages of the world; nor to the custom of the Eastern monarchs; nor to the holy scripture: For, in the holy scriptures, kings and princes are brought in speaking of themselves always in the singular number (e): even in their decrees and orders, which now run in the plural number (f); yea, the most ambitious kings and princes speak so (g); and when speaking in their greatest glory and majesty (h). I might multiply texts to this purpose: And not one contrary instance can be produced in all the scripture. So that the stile now used amongst kings and princes is the invention and practice of later times, and that which nothing but use and custom hath given reverence and majesty unto: And it is a rash and presumptuous attempt, to thrust the use of a modern stile into the holy scriptures.

2*dly*, This stile used by kings and princes in later times, is rather humbling than exalting. They speak of themselves in the plural number, not to intimate their majesty and greatness, but rather their modesty and wariness, and that they may not seem to speak in their own name, but with the joint advice and suffrage of their counsellors and ministers of state. But God hath no counsellors, nor hath he need of any; for *who hath been his counsellor* (i)? And there is something peculiar in God's way of speaking of himself, that is no ways agreeable to the modern stile of kings and princes speaking of themselves; particularly in that expression, *Man is become as* ONE OF US (k).

3*dly*, In the holy scriptures, God doth generally speak of himself in the singular number; only some few places excepted, where the plural number is used to denoted a plurality of divine Persons, as I have already shewed. Now, if in these few places, God speaks of himself in the plural number after the manner of kings; why then doth he not always, or at least frequently, speak after this manner? And why did he not use this form of speech in that kingly act of promulgating the law from Mount Sinai? Certainly, if any thing required the kingly stile that is pretended, that wherein God discovered so much of his Majesty and Royalty did so: But so it is, that in
that

(*e*) Gen. xiv 21. and xx. 9 2 Sam. iii. 28. 1 Chron. xxi. 17. and xxix 14. 2 Chron. ii. 6. (*f*) 2 Chron. xxxvi 23. Ezra vi. 8. and vii 21. Dan. vi 26. (*g*) Exod. v. 2. Dan. ii. 35. iii 29. and iv. 4 (*h*) Dan. iv. 30. (*i*) Rom. xi. 34. (*k*) Gen. iii. 22.

that in that whole tranfaction with his ancient people, he fpeaks of himfelf conftantly in the fingular number.

SERMON XCIII.

2. I Shall prove, ftill from the fcriptures of the Old Teftament, that there are three diftinct Perfons in the Godhead. It is true, this myftery is not fo clearly revealed in the Old Teftament, as in the New. Yet even there, we have a difcovery of the Trinity of Perfons in the Godhead. 1. In the threefold repetition of the name of God, which occurs divers times in the fame place. 2. In the account that is given to us of fome of the great and wonderful works of God.

(1.) In the threefold repetition of the name of God, which occurs divers times in the fame place. I begin with the facerdotal Benediction *The Lord blefs thee, and keep thee. The Lord make his face fhine upon thee, and be gracious unto thee. The Lord lift up his countenance upon thee, and give thee peace* (a). Where the name JEHOVAH, the Lord, is three times repeated; and as learned critics obferve, each of them with a different accent in the original. The Jews themfelves think there is fome myftery in this; and certainly it can be no other than this, to denote threes diftinct Perfons, each of whom is JEHOVAH, as this is explained in the apoftolical benediction in the New Teftament (b). And then to thofe three Perfons, there is a threefold benefit afcribed; protection, to the Father; grace, mercy and pardon, to the Son, the Purchafer; and peace, to the Holy Ghoft, the Comforter. To the fame purpofe, in Jacob's bleffing his grand-children, there is mention made of God three times: *God, before whom my fathers, Abraham and Ifaac, did walk; the God who fed me all my life long unto this day; the Angel, who redeemed me from all evil, blefs the lads* (c.). By the Angel of whom he fpeaks, we cannot underftand a created angel, but the increated Angel and Meffenger of the covenant, the bleffed Meffiah, a divine Perfon, Jacob's Redeemer, and that *from all evil*, and confequently from the evil of fin; and whom Jacob here worfhippeth and prayeth to for the bleffing. To this alfo may be refered the fong of the feraphims, Ifa. vi. 5. *Holy, holy, holy is the Lord of Hofts* †. True it is, fuch

---

(a) Numb. vi. 24, 25, 26.   (b) 2 Cor. xiii. 14.   (c) Gen. xlviii 15, 16.

† "Ἅγιος Ἅγιος Ἅγιος λέγοντα (viz. τὰ ζῶα) τὰς τρεῖς ὑπος

such repetitions are often used in scripture, to denote the certainty of a thing; and so, this repetition may be used here, to signify that God is eminently and unquestionably holy. Yet, when we consider the whole context, and the light given thereunto by other texts, in the New Testament, where this place is quoted, it will plainly appear, that the repetition here used is designed to intimate a Trinity of Persons in the unity of the Godhead. For, in verse 8th, there is, as I formerly observed, an intimation of a plurality of Persons in JEHOVAH to whom this song is sung: And what is spoken here to the prophet by JEHOVAH, verses 9, 10. is elsewhere ascribed to the Son, and to the Holy Ghost (*d*). Another text to the same purpose, is that, *Hear, O Israel, the Lord our God is one Lord* (*e*). The words in the original run thus, *The Lord, our God, the Lord, is one*. Which seems to be a plain intimation of a Trinity of Persons in the unity of the divine Essence.

I confess these texts, considered in themselves, afford no convincing argument to prove a Trinity of Persons in the Godhead: Yet when we consider that there are more clear discoveries thereof, even in the Old Testament, I make no question, that the Spirit of God hath in these texts a respect to this glorious mystery.

(2.) We have a more clear discovery of a Trinity of Persons in the Godhead, in the accounts that are given of to us in the Old Testament of some of the great and wonderful works of God. I shall mention three of them. As,

First, In the historical account that is given to us of the creation of the world. We find that work ascribed to three distinct Persons, by comparing Gen. i. 1, 2, 3. with other texts in the Old Testament, illustrated by some in the New. *In the beginning God created the heaven and the earth —And the Spirit of God moved upon the face of the waters. And God said, Let there be light.* Where we have, 1. God creating. 2. The Spirit of God moving upon the face of the waters. Where, by the Spirit of God, we cannot understand the wind or air, as some pretend we should, seeing none of these were as yet created; but a distinct Person who concurred in the work of creation, even the Holy Ghost, to whom this work is elsewhere ascribed.

ασεις τελειας δεικνυντα εςιν, ως και εν τω λεγειν, Κυριος, την μιαν ουσιαν δηλουσιν. Athan. Tom. i. Edit. Paris. p. 155.

Sanctus hic est Pater, Sanctus hic est Filius; Sanctus hic est Spiritus Sanctus. Rabbi Simeon in L.

(*d*) John xii. 41. Acts xxviii. 25. (*e*) Deut. vi. 4.

ascribed. Job tells us, *By his Spirit he hath garnished the heavens:* And the psalmist says, *Thou sendest forth thy Spirit, they are created* (*f*). 3. Here also we have the Word, by whom all things were made. It is the observation of several worthy divines † on these words, *And God said;* that is, say they, he commanded, not by an act of his powerful will only, but chiefly by his substantial Word, the Son, to whom the work of creation is also ascribed (*g*). And some of these divines think he is called *the Word*, principally for this reason. They confirm this observation, by comparing what we have in Genesis i. with John i. 1, 2, 3. where the evangelist, alluding, say they, to what is said in the history of the creation, describes *the Word* of which Moses spake, as a Person eternally co-existing with the Father. *In the beginning was the Word, and the Word was with God, and the Word was God. The same was in the beginning with God—all things were made by him.* To this they think the psalmist alludes, when he says, *By the word of the Lord were the heavens made, and all the host of them, by the breath of his mouth* (*h*). And indeed this text seems to be more express to our purpose: For here we have distinct mention made of three concurring in the work of creation; The Lord JEHOVAH, the Father, the *Word of the Lord*, that is, his substantial and personal Word, the Son; and the *Breath of his mouth*, or, as the word may be rendered, the *Spirit of his mouth*, that is, the Holy Ghost, called elsewhere, *the Breath of the Almighty* (*i*). It seems that the ancient Jews did thus understand these texts of scripture: For it was of old the common faith of the Jewish Church, that all things were made and disposed by the *Word of God* as appears from their Targums, where the *Word of God* is often mentioned. And that by it they did not understand the word of his power, but a divine Person, appears from the personal operations that are there frequently ascribed to it; as, that the Word of God did this, or, said that, and thought, and went, which are actions proper to persons. And in Bereshit Rabbah, they say of these words, *The Spirit of God moved, &c. This is the Spirit of the King Messiah* (*k*).

Second, In the historical account that is given us of the redemption of Israel out of Egypt, their being conducted through the wilderness and brought into Canaan. God doth often challenge

---

(*f*) Job. xxvi. 13. Psal. cxliv. 30. (*g*) Col. i. 16, 17. Heb. i. 3. (*h*) Psal. xxxiii. 6. (*i*) Job xxxiii. 4. (*k*) Gen. i. 2.

† See Charnock's Discourse of the Knowledge of God in Christ. p. 493.

challenge that work to himself, as his own proper and peculiar work; particularly, in the preface to the Decalogue, *I am the Lord thy God, who have brought thee out of the land of Egypt, out of the house of bondage.* Yet we find that work ascribed to three distinct persons. 1. It is ascribed to the Father. Of this there is no question made; therefore I shall not insist upon it. 2. It is ascribed to the Son. Exod. iii. 2, 7, 8. *And the Angel of the Lord appeared unto him in a flame of fire out of the midst of a bush—And the Lord said--I am come down to deliver them out of the hand of the Egyptians.* Where, by the *Angel of the Lord*, we cannot understand a created angel; but the uncreated Angel of the covenant, the blessed Messiah, the Son of God; as appears from the whole context: For he is all along called God, or the Lord; and verse 6th, he calls himself *the God of Abraham, the God of Isaac, and the God of Jacob;* and we see, verse 10th, that it is he that gives Moses a commission to go to Pharaoh, and that in his own name. Another text to this purpose, is Exod. xxiii. 20, 21. *Behold, I send an Angel before thee to keep thee in the way, and to bring thee into the place which I have prepared. Beware of him, and obey his voice, provoke him not: For he will not pardon your transgressions: For my name is in him.* By this Angel we are still to understand the uncreated Angel of the covenant, a divine Person: For pardoning sin, which is God's prerogative, is ascribed to him; and the Lord says of him, *My name is in him.* He doth not say, *My name is* ON *him*, or *given to him*, but IN *him;* that is, my divine nature or essence is *in* him. 3. This work is ascribed also to the Holy Ghost. Isa. lxiii. 7, 9, 10. *I will mention the loving-kindnesses of the Lord, and the praises of the Lord, according to all that the Lord hath bestowed on us; and the great goodness toward the house of Israel, which he hath bestowed on them—In all their afflictions he was afflicted, and the Angel of his presence saved them: In his love and in his pity he redeemed them, and he bare them, and carried them all the days of old. But they rebelled, and vexed his holy Spirit,* &c. Where we read of three distinct Persons, to whom this work of bringing the children of Israel out of Egypt toward Canaan is ascribed; the Lord JEHOVAH, the *Angel of his presence,* and his *holy Spirit.* And here are distinct personal actions ascribed to them; to the Lord JEHOVAH, there is ascribed, loving-kindness, mercy and goodness, toward his people; to the Angel of his presence, there is ascribed, saving, redeeming, bearing and carrying them; and to his holy Spirit, his being vexed, turning to be their enemy, and fighting against them.

Third, In the prophetical account that is given us of our redemption by Chriſt. Our Lord Jeſus, the bleſſed Meſſiah, promiſed under the Old Teſtament, is often held forth as the true eternal God, to be ſent by the Father, and furniſhed by the Holy Ghoſt, for accompliſhing the work of redemption; whereby the myſtery of the ſacred Trinity is not obſcurely revealed. See to this purpoſe, Iſa. lxi. 1, 2. *The Spirit of the Lord God is upon me, becauſe the Lord hath anointed me to preach good tidings unto the meek; he hath ſent me to bind up the broken-hearted, to proclaim liberty to the captives, and the opening of the priſon to them that are bound.* Our bleſſed Lord applies this text to himſelf (*l*). And indeed ſuch works are here aſcribed to him as are proper to God alone, as *binding up the broken-hearted, proclaiming liberty to captive* ſinners, &c. God alone hath power to make theſe things effectual. And ſeeing, in this place, there is mention made of two divine Perſons, diſtinct from him, viz. the Lord JEHOVAH, and his Spirit, ſending, and anointing him; there is here a plain intimation of a Trinity of divine perſons. To the ſame purpoſe is that text, *And now the Lord God and his Spirit hath ſent me* (*m*). It is the Lord who is all along brought in ſpeaking; ſo that we have here, the Lord ſent, and the Lord God and his Spirit ſending him. See alſo Hag. ii. 4, 5.—*I am with you, ſaith the Lord of Hoſts; according to the word that I covenanted with you when ye came out of Egypt, ſo my Spirit remaineth among you.* Theſe words, *according to,* are not in the original text; ſo that theſe words may be read and rendered thus, *I am with you—with my word which I covenanted with you,—and my ſpirit remaining among you.* And by *the Word which he covenanted with* them, we are to underſtand his ſubſtantial Word, the bleſſed Meſſiah, whom he had promiſed to them.

Thus I have proved from the ſcriptures of the Old Teſtament, not only that there is a plurality of divine perſons, but alſo that there are three diſtinct Perſons in the Godhead. And although we have the help of New-Teſtament-light, in diſcovering what is more obſcurely revealed about this myſtery in the Old Teſtament: yet, ſeeing God was pleaſed to give ſuch a revelation of himſelf to the Jews of old, he did certainly accommodate that revelation ſo far to their capacity, as they might hence receive ſuch inſtruction concerning this myſtery as was neceſſary to their ſalvation. And ſeeing the later Jews have a vail of blindneſs upon their hearts in reading the Old
Teſtament,

(*l*) Luke iv. 18, &c.   (*m*) Iſa. xlviii. 16.

Testament, and are bewitched with a cursed hatred against Christ, it needs not seem strange that their eyes are shut against that light, which the Old Testament saints, not being blinded with any prejudice, did, by the help of the Spirit, behold with great comfort.

I proceed to prove this fundamental great truth.

II. From divers texts in the scriptures of the New Testament.

The truth is, there are few pages, if any, in the whole New Testament, wherein we have not some intimation of, or argument for, a plurality of divine Persons. Therefore I shall pass this, and prove that there are three distinct Persons in the Godhead, the Father, the Son, and the Holy Ghost. My text is a clear proof of this, as I formerly explained it. Moreover this truth is evident,

1. From Christ's baptism, Matth. iii. 16, 17. *And Jesus, when he was baptized, went up straightway out of the water: And lo, the heavens were opened unto him, and he saw the Spirit of God descending like a dove, and lighting upon him. And lo, a voice from heaven, saying, This is my beloved Son, in whom I am well pleased.* Where we have three Persons, the Father, the Son, and the Holy Spirit †. And they are here distinguished, 1. By certain signs and symbols whereby they were pleased to manifest themselves. The Father manifested himself by an audible voice, the Son was manifested in the human nature, and the Holy Ghost manifested himself in the shape of a dove. 2. By their distinct personal actions and operations. The Father spake with a voice from heaven, the Son ascended out of the waters of Jordan, and the Holy Ghost descended in a visible shape. So that here are three distinct Persons. And they are divine Persons. Concerning the Father, there is no question. And these words spoken of the Son, *This is my beloved Son, &c.* cannot be said of any mere creature. And by the Spirit of God, we cannot understand a naked quality, or some property of God, or some work and operation only; for assuming a visible shape, descending from heaven, lighting and resting on Christ, are actions proper to persons.

2. From the institution of baptism, Matth. xxviii. 19. *Go ye, therefore, and teach all nations, baptizing them in the name of the Father, and of the Son, and of the Holy Ghost.* Here also we have three distinct Persons mentioned: For, it is observable, that

---

† *Unde illud veterum, Abi Ariane ad Jordanem, & videbis Trinitatem.*

that, in the original text, the demonstrative article is thrice repeated, being prefixed to each of them; as if it were said, *baptizing them in the name of* THAT *Father, and of* THAT *Son, and of* THAT *Holy Ghost.* Certainly the repetition of the article wants not its peculiar emphasis. And as they are distinct Persons, so they are divine persons; for they are here so joined together, as that ministers are commanded to baptize, no less in the name of the Son, and of the Holy Ghost, than in the name of the Father. And which way soever we expound this phrase, *in the name;* whether thus, by the authority, and at the command and appointment of the Father, Son, and Holy Ghost; or thus, into the profession and obedience of the Father, Son, and Holy Ghost, dedicating the person baptized, to their worship and service: Either of these argues that they are divine Persons; for who hath authority to appoint ordinances and seals of the covenant, and whom are we to worship and serve, but God only? And † as the Father, Son, and Holy Ghost, are three distinct divine Persons; so they are one in nature and essence, and equal in authority and power: Therefore it is not said, *in the* NAMES of the Father, Son, and Holy Ghost; but, *in the* NAME, in the singular number. Considered personally, each hath a distinct name; Father, Son, and Holy Ghost: But considered essentially, they have but one name ‡, being one and the same God, undivided in essence and operation, and equal in authority and power.

3. From the apostolical benediction, 2 Cor. xiii. 14. *The grace of the Lord Jesus Christ, and the love of God, and the communion of the Holy Ghost, be with you all. Amen.* Here again three Persons are mentioned: For God is here to be taken personally, for the Father, who is most frequently called God in scripture, because he is the first Person in order, and the Fountain of the Deity in respect of communication; and because he is represented in scripture as sustaining and defending the majesty of the Deity in the business of our salvation. Now, from these three Persons, the apostle prayeth or wisheth for three blessings, which comprehend the whole business of salvation,

---

† *Quia dixit in nomine, evidenter unam Deitatem in Trinitate consistere declaravit: Et quod prosequutus est, Patris & Filii & Spiritus Sancti, per singula Nomina singulas Personas inesse distinxit.* Athanas. Oper. Tom. 2. Lib. 1. de unita Deitate Trin. ad Theoph.

‡ *Etsi sint tria Nomina personalia trium Personarum, est tamen unum Nomen essentiale.* Thom. Aquin. Part. 3. Qu. 66 Art. 5. ad 6.

salvation, according to the manner and order of working proper to each person. There is, *the love of God* the Father, in the design or purpose of salvation to an elect company; *the grace of Christ* the Son, in the purchase of it; and *the communion of the Holy Ghost*, in the application. Or thus, the love of the Father, in election; the grace of the Son, in redemption; and the communion of the Holy Ghost, in sanctification. These distinct personal operations, in the business of our salvation, cannot be ascribed to any that is not God: So that here also we have three distinct divine Persons.

4. From these places where there is express mention made of three, distinct from each other, and to whom such works or actions are ascribed, as are proper to God alone. See several texts to this purpose. And first, John xiv. 16, 17. *And I will pray the Father, and he shall give you another Comforter, that he may abide with you for ever. Even the Spirit of truth, whom the world cannot receive.* And compare with this, John xv. 26. *But when the Comforter is come, whom I will send unto you, from the Father, even the Spirit of truth, who proceedeth from the Father, he shall testify of me.* Here are three distinct persons mentioned. As the Father and the Son are two distinct persons: So the Holy Ghost, who is called the Comforter, and the Spirit of Truth, is a third person; for he is *sent*, and *cometh*, and *testifieth*, which are things proper to a person; and he is *another Comforter*, and so distinct from the Son, and *given* and *sent* by the Father, and so distinct from him. And as the Father is a divine person, so are the Son and the Holy Ghost divine persons, as appears from the texts quoted. 1. The Son is a divine person. For although, in the first text, he speaks of himself only as Mediator interceding with the Father to send the Spirit; yet he also sends the Spirit, no less than the Father doth, as we see in the other text. And although only the Holy Ghost's proceeding from the Father is expressed, yet his proceeding from the Son also is supposed in the Son's sending him. 2. The Holy Ghost is also a divine person; as is clear from the titles here given to him from his office and work in believers. He is the Comforter, who works comfort in believers, by applying Christ's purchase to them, and sealing the same to their hearts. And he is the Spirit of Truth, both in himself, and in his operations in believers. And his being sent by the Father and the Son, doth not argue any inequality or inferiority, seeing equals may send one another; it only points at the order of the divine persons in subsistence and operation. So that here we have three distinct persons, whereof

of each is God: And seeing there cannot be three Gods, nor any more than one, therefore all three must be one and the same God; and consequently, in the same individual divine essence, there are three distinct persons, the Father, the Son, and the Holy Ghost.

SERMON XCIV.

ANOTHER text to the same purpose, is in 1 Cor. xii. 4, 5, 6. *Now there are diversities of gifts, but the same Spirit. And there are differences of administrations, but the same Lord. And there are diversities of operations, but it is the same Spirit who worketh all in all.* Where the apostle is pressing the Corinthians to unity among themselves, notwithstanding of different gifts, offices, and administrations in the church; and that because all these come from one and the same God: But these are here ascribed, partly to the Holy Spirit; partly to the Lord Christ; and partly to God the Father, who is here and frequently else-where, called God, by way of eminency, for the reasons before expressed: Therefore the Father, Son, and Holy Spirit, are that one God; for none else can be the author of these gifts, offices and operations in the church, but God only.

A third text, is in Gal. iv. 4, 5, 6. *But when the fulness of the time was come, God sent forth his Son, made of a woman, made under the law, to redeem them that were under the Law, that we might receive the adoption of sons. And because ye are sons, God hath sent forth the Spirit of his Son, into your hearts, crying, Abba, Father.* Where again we have three distinct persons, the Father sending, the Son sent, and the Spirit of the Son, who is also said to be sent. And, 1 It appears from these verses, that the Son is a divine person distinct from the Father: For, as he is the Son of God in a way proper and peculiar to himself, his only-begotten Son; so he had a being and subsistence before his incarnation, seeing he could not be sent forth in the fulness of time, unless he had an existence before; and the dignity of his person is such, that he was fit to accomplish the work of redemption, and to purchase that great privilege of adoption for elect sinners; and the Holy Ghost proceedeth from him, no less than from the Father, being therefore called the Spirit of the Son. 2. It appears that the Holy Spirit also is a divine person distinct from the Father and the Son. As he is not a naked quality, or an operation and work only, but a person subsisting of himself; so he is not a mere creature, but a divine person, seeing he dwells in the hearts of believers, and furnishes
them

them for, and assists them in the duty of prayer: And he is distinct from the Father and the Son; for he is the Spirit of the Son, and sent by the Father.

A fourth text is in Eph. ii. 18. *Through him we both have an access by one Spirit unto the Father.* In the preceding verses the apostle is speaking of Christ; and then it follows, *For through him, &c.* Here also we have all the three persons. 1. The Father, to whom we have access. 2. The Son, through whom we have access, as the way, and the only Mediator, who hath procured for us access and liberty to approach unto God. 3. The Holy Spirit, by whom we have access, as our guide to lead us, by working saving graces in us, and actuating these graces, and helping our infirmities in duty. So that if it were asked, To whom do we pray? The answer is, To God as a father. But whence have we hopes of access to God in prayer? Through Christ the blessed Mediator. Who gives us an heart to come to God through Christ? The Holy Spirit.

A fifth text is in Eph. iii. 14, 15, 16, 17. *For this cause I bow my knees unto the Father of our Lord Jesus Christ, of whom the whole family in heaven and earth is named, that he would grant you, according to the riches of his glory, to be strengthened with might by his Spirit in the inner-man: That Christ may dwell in your hearts by faith.* Here again we have, 1. God the Father; who is described, (1.) From his relation to Christ, *the Father of our Lord Jesus Christ.* (2.) From his relation to the church, *of whom the whole family, &c.* 2. The Holy Spirit, called the Spirit of the Father, and who, residing in believers, is the author and giver of their spiritual strength. 3. Christ the Son, who dwells in the hearts of believers, that is, hath a near and intimate union with them. So that here such things are ascribed, not only to the Father, but also to the Son and Spirit, as are proper to persons, and to divine persons.

The last text I shall mention, is in Rev. i. 4, 5, 6. *Grace be unto you, and peace, from him who is, and who was, and who is to come; and from the seven Spirits who are before his throne; and from Jesus Christ, who is the faithful witness, and the first-begotten of the dead, and the Prince of the kings of the earth, &c.* Here again, 1. Three distinct persons are mentioned. (1.) The Father, who is described from his eternal being and existence, *who is, &c.* (2.) The Holy Spirit, called *the seven Spirits,* because of his manifold and various operations. (3.) The Son, Jesus Christ. 2. It appears that they are divine persons; that the Son and the Spirit are so, as well as the Father: For, as Christ the Son, hath such titles, epithets and works, attributed to him, as are

proper

proper to God alone; so the Spirit is put between the Father and the Son, as equal with both; and both Christ and the Spirit are named here, as senders of this epistle to the seven churches in Asia, and as objects of religious worship, from whom the apostle John wisheth grace and peace, which are blessings that God alone can give. And as they are distinct persons, and divine persons, so they must be one and the same God, because of the unity of the divine essence. I might adduce other texts for the proof of this doctrine, in the book of the Revelation, and especially in the epistles to the seven churches in Asia. In a word, there is not one of the epistles wherein we have not some proof of this great truth: For the Father is the sender of them all, as appears from Rev. i. 1. Christ the Son is he who immediately gives John a commission to write, as is evident from the titles he takes to himself in the preface to each epistle; and the Holy Ghost is mentioned in the conclusion of each epistle as a joint speaker, *He that hath an ear, let him hear what the Spirit saith unto the churches.*

Thus I have proved, from the holy scriptures, that there are three distinct persons in the Godhead, the Father, the Son, and the Holy Ghost, and that they are one in nature and essence. I add only one argument more from the holy scriptures; and it is this. There could be no redemption of lost elect sinners, without a plurality of persons in the Godhead. For, to our redemption a Mediator was necessary, to take up the difference, and make up the breach that sin had made between God and us: And none could be a fit Mediator between God and man but an infinite person. Our Mediator behoved to be God and man in one person, that he might be equally distant from, and equally drawing near to both parties, and equally affected to their interests. But how could God give such a Mediator, if the Godhead consisted only in one person? Again, our Redeemer behoved to be a person of infinite power, that he might be able to endure what he was to suffer, and especially to bear up under the weight of that wrath that was due to our sins; and that he might be able to overcome by suffering. And he behoved to be a person of infinite worth and dignity, that his sufferings might be of an infinite value, to make satisfaction for such an infinite evil as sin is, and to make a purchase of inestimable blessings. But how could this be, if there were not a plurality of persons in the Godhead? How could one and the same person make satisfaction to himself? The truth is, unless we suppose a plurality of persons in the unity of the

Godhead,

Godhead, our redemption can neither be understood nor believed.

Yea more, not only a plurality, but a Trinity of persons in the Godhead, is evident from the way of salvation laid down in the gospel. For, in effecting and bringing about the salvation of lost sinners, there are three distinct operations unquestionably divine, and proper to God alone, viz. The contrivance, the purchase, and the application of this salvation. These three operations, by their effects, demonstrate a Trinity of persons in the Godhead, no less than common providence doth the unity of the Deity. As none but an infinite Person could contrive our salvation, so there must be another infinite Person to purchase it, and a third infinite Person to apply it: For, as the contrivance of our salvation is an effect of infinite wisdom, so the purchase and application thereof are effects of infinite and omnipotent power. Our salvation is a work too worthy to be contrived by any but God, or to be transacted by any but his Son, or to be applied by any but his Spirit. So that unless there were three distinct persons in the Godhead, our salvation could never be accomplished or brought about. Therefore it is well observed by some divines, that God's end and design in the work of redemption, was not only to glorify the infinite perfections of his nature, but also to glorify the persons distinctly, according to their distinct acts and operations.

Well then, from what is said, it is plain and evident, that such as deny a Trinity of persons in the Godhead, overturn the only way of salvation, and render the salvation and redemption of lost elect sinners utterly impossible. Hence it is, that as no antitrinitarian ever had, so it is utterly impossible that they can have, any right and orthodox sentiments about man's redemption.

Fourthly, Of the distinction of the persons in the Godhead.

I proceed now to the fourth general head proposed, which is to speak of the distinction of the divine persons, 1. From the divine essence. And, 2. Among themselves. I shall endeavour to be plain, and, the Lord assisting, to speak agreeably to divine revelation.

1. Then, let me speak a little of the distinction of the persons from the divine essence. That they are distinguished from the essence, is plain and evident: For the essence is but one; but the persons are three. The essence is absolute, but the persons are relative. The essence is common to the three persons; but a person is incommunicable, the persons being distinguished by their incommunicable properties. The essence

is more extensive; but the persons are more contracted: For, although the divine essence be adequate to the three persons jointly considered, yet it is of larger extent and consideration than any one of them; because though each person hath the whole Godhead, yet not exclusively of the rest of the persons, to whom it is also communicable. Again, the essence is the principle of all external acts and operations toward the creature; for these being undivided, are the works of one and the same God, and so common to all the three persons: But the persons are the principle of all internal acts and operations of one person toward another; for the essence neither begetteth nor is begotten, neither breatheth nor is breathed; but the Father begetteth, the Son is begotten, and the Holy Ghost proceeds from both by spiration or breathing. So that it is manifest that the persons are distinguished from the divine essence.

But here it is questioned by divines, how they are distinguished; or, of what nature the distinction is that is between them. And herein divines are not of one mind. But this being an incomprehensible mystery, it were far more adviseable to wave a positive answer to such a question, and modestly to profess our own ignorance: For the truth is, all these kinds of distinction that are mentioned by divines and schoolmen in this matter, do sink far below the sublimity of this glorious mystery; and being taken from things created, can afford but a very faint shadow of it.

We can better answer the question negatively, than positively: That is, we can better tell how the persons are not distinguished from the essence, than how they are distinguished; better, of what kind the distinction is not, than of what kind it is. The persons then, are not distinguished from the divine essence, as individual or singular substances from their species: For the divine essence is itself most singular and individual; and the persons are not distinct substances or beings, as we shall hear afterward. Nor are the persons distinguished from the essence, as parts from the whole; for the divine essence is most simple and uncompounded. Nor are they distinguished really, as one thing or being differs from another; for this also would infer a composition in God †. As the essence is not divided in the persons; so neither are the persons separated from the essence, but only so distinguished as the one is not the other.

---

† *Nec hujus Trinitatis tertia Pars est unus, nec major Pars duo quam unus est ibi, nec majus aliquid sunt omnes quam singuli.*
Aug. contr. Maxim. Lib. III. C. 10.

ther. But though they are not distinguished really, in the sense I have already expressed; yet they are not distinguished only in our thoughts and conceptions, but the distinction is such as hath a foundation in things themselves. In this sense it is that some divines say, that the persons are distinguished really from the essence: They mean no more but this, that the distinction between them is founded in the divine nature, and not in our reason and conception: They are truly distinct, whether we think of it or not. Thus I have shewed how the persons are not distinguished from the essence: But to shew positively how they are distinguished, how great the distinction is, and of what nature it is, is above our capacity; it is inexpressible and inconceivable.

2. In the next place, I shall discourse to you of the distinction of the Persons among themselves.

We are here carefully to avoid two extremes, that have been the spring and original of gross heresies in the church. 1. On the one hand, we are carefully to avoid the error of Sabellius, who, in the third century, opposing himself to those who denied the Son to be co-equal and co-essential with the Father, did run into the other extreme, and would admit of no distinction, between the Father, Son, and Holy Ghost, save only in our conception, and in name and denomination: Holding that one and the same person hath different names and denominations given to him, because of different effects and operations; and therefore is called sometimes the Father, sometimes the Son, and sometimes the Holy Ghost; as the heathens gave different names to the sun, because of its different operations and effects. This is an abominable heresy: For it is plainly to hold that there is but one Person in the Godhead; and that Father, Son, and Holy Ghost, are but three several names given to the divine essence, because of its several manifestations or operations; and if no other difference were to be admitted between the Persons, then, such nominal persons might be multiplied to a very vast number, seeing God's operations and manifestations are various and manifold. 2. On the other hand, we are with equal care to avoid the error of the Tritheists, who maintained that the Father, Son, and Holy Ghost, are three Eternal Spirits essentially distinct one from another; and that the Father did communicate to the Son and Holy Ghost their distinct essences; so that they did in effect assert three Gods, one supreme, and the other two subordinate. But this error flies in the face even of nature itself.

Therefore, in opposition to both these extremes, we hold

and maintain, according to the holy scriptures, that the †Father, Son, and Holy Ghost, are three distinct Persons in the same individual divine essence. They are not divided, but only distinguished. Many things even in nature, are distinct, though they cannot be divided. So, the Father, Son, and Holy Ghost, neither are nor can be divided; where one is, there they are all: but they are distinguished so as the one is not the other. That they are three distinct Persons, I have already proved. Such distinct actions and operations are ascribed to them, as are only proper to distinct Persons. This is most evident in the incarnation; for neither the Father, nor the Holy Ghost, were incarnate, but the Son only. And my text is a clear proof of their distinct personalities: For here they are brought in as three distinct Witnesses, and consequently as three distinct Persons; for one and the same person, though he had a thousand names, cannot pass for more than one witness.

But here also, it is questioned by divines, How the Persons are distinguished; or, what is the nature of the distinction between them. I shall trouble you very little with philosophical terms of distinction. Only, as I said concerning the distinction of the Persons from the essence, so may I say here concerning their distinction among themselves; we can better tell negatively how they are not distinguished, than positevely how they are distinguished. The Persons then are not distinguished from one another, in our reason and conception only, but in themselves. The Father is a distinct person from the Son, and the Holy Ghost from both, whether we conceive so or not. Nor are the Persons distinguished essentially or substantially, as three distinct particular essences or substances: For, though there be three distinct Persons, yet there is but one and the same individual essence Hence divines say ‡, that in the Trinity there is *Alius & Alius*, that is, another and another; but not *Aliud & Aliud*, that is, another thing and another thing. The Father is another Person from the Son, and the Holy Ghost from both; yet they have the same individual essence.

---

† Ἐν τὰ τρία θεότητι, καὶ τὸ ἐν τρία ταῖς ἰδιότησιν, ἵνα μήτε τὸ ἐν Σαβελλιον ᾖ, μήτε τὰ τρία τῆς πονηρᾶς νυν διαιρέσεως. Greg. Nazianz. Orat. 37. νυν. i. e. *quæ nunc ab Arianis introducitur.*

‡ Ἐστὶ μὲν γὰρ ἄλλος καὶ ἄλλος, ἵνα μὴ τὰς ὑποστάσεις συγχέωμεν, οὐκ ἄλλο δὲ καὶ ἄλλο, ἐνγὰρ τὰ τρία καὶ ταυτὸν τῇ θεότητι. Greg. Nazianz. Orat. 51.

essence. Consequently, they are not distinguished as three Persons among men are; seeing every human person hath a distinct particular nature or essence of his own, but the divine nature or essence is wholly and entirely one and indivisible; so that the Persons are not separate or divided substances, as three individuals of the same kind are. The ground of the distinction is not the substance or essence, but the communication of it. Again, the persons are not distinguished from one another, as joint parts of the same divine essence: For, as this is repugnant to the simplicity of God; so, upon this supposition, none of the persons would be God, as not having the whole Godhead in himself. Nor is the distinction between the persons, a distinction of degree, state, or dignity; seeing all the persons are equal. But to express positively, how the persons are distinguished among themselves, or what is the nature of the distinction between them, is above our capacity, seeing the holy scripture is silent, and we have no example to match it in things created; which needs not seem strange, seeing God is an incomprehensible Being, beyond all compare. Or, we may say in general, the distinction between them is not natural, but supernatural.

SERMON XCV.

YET there are some things wherein the distinction of the divine persons among themselves is plainly discovered. As, 1. Their personal and incommunicable properties. 2. Their order of subsistence. And 3. Their order and manner of working. I shall therefore speak of each of these.

I. Of the personal and incommunicable properties of the three persons in the Godhead.

Each of the divine persons hath his distinct personal property, which is incommunicable to any of the other persons. What these are, our Larger Catechism acquaints us, in the answer to that question, "What are the personal properties "of the three persons in the Godhead?" The answer is, "It is "proper to the Father to beget the Son, and to the Son to be "begotten of the Father, and to the Holy Ghost to proceed from "both from all eternity." These properties do not establish unequal degrees among the persons, but design their different manner of subsistence, and so constitute the persons. They are the proper foundation of the distinction of the persons in the same undivided essence.

They are called personal properties; because each of them

is proper to a person, whereas the essential properties are common to all the three persons in the unity of the Godhead. And they are called incommunicable; because each of them is so proper to one person, that it is not common to any other, so that they constitute the incommunicability of the persons. Hence it appears that the active spiration or breathing of the Holy Ghost by the Father and the Son, seeing it is not proper to either person, but common to both, is not a personal property, and so doth not constitute a person. These properties are by some called relative properties, because they constitute the relative subsistences in the divine essence, Father, Son, and Holy Ghost. Hence it is, that innascibility, as the schoolmen term it, that is, *not to be begotten*, or *not to be of another*, though it be a property of the first person, yet not being a relative property, doth not constitute a person. And beside innascibility, being only a negative property, cannot constitute a person, which is a positive subsistence. It is founded on the positive properties of the Son, and Holy Ghost, and is only a denying these properties of the Father.

Others express the personal properties thus, paternity, filiation, and procession, or proceeding: But these relations do not constitute the persons, nor found their distinction; but rather suppose them to be constituted, and are declarative of the same. Hence they are by divines called Notions, because they notify or make known the distinction of the persons, and their order of subsistence.

Now, I say, these personal properties are the proper foundation of the distinction of the persons. Their distinction originally lies in this, that the Father begets the Son, and the Son is begotten of the Father, and the Holy Ghost proceeds from the Father and the Son. I shall speak a little to each of these, especially the two last.

I. It is the personal and incommunicable property of the Father to beget the Son. This the Father testifies of himself, *Thou art my Son, this day have I begotten thee* (a). Hence Athanasius calls the Father, † *the Fountain and Principle of the Son*. The name Father is a relative: And the proper foundation of this relation is generation; for he is Father in a far more proper sense than this title can be given to any other. And this is proper to the Father alone; he only begets, and is not begotten of any other. Hence he is said, by the ancient fathers, to be *unbegotten* *, which the schoolmen call innascibility: But

we

(a) Psal. ii. 7.

† Πηγὴ ϰ ἀρχὴ τῦ υἱῦ * Ἀγέννητος.

we may with equal reason add inspirability; for the Father doth not proceed from another any manner of way; he hath not the original of his personal subsistence from any other. Hence he is said to be of himself; which is not to be understood in respect of the divine essence; for so the Son and the Holy Ghost are that God who is of himself, as well as the Father; each of them hath the same individual divine essence which is of itself. But when the Father is said to be of himself, it is to be understood of the manner of his having the essence, or his manner of subsistence. He hath not the divine essence communicated to him from any other person. He hath his personal subsistence of and from himself. Hence he is said to *have life in himself*, and to have *given to the Son to have life in himself* (b). From what is said it appears, that the proper notion of the Father is this, he is a person subsisting eternally in the one individual essence of the Godhead, not communicated to him from any other, but communicating the same essence in which himself subsisteth, that it may subsist in a different manner.

II. It is the personal and incommunicable property of the Son, to be begotten of the Father. Hence he is called *the only begotten of the Father* (c): Because he is begotten by him in an eminent and singular manner, such as can agree to no other, viz. by an eternal communication of the divine essence, that it may subsist in a different manner: So that he hath the original of his personal subsistence from the Father. In this sense, he is called by the fathers in the Nicene council, in their creed, † *God of God, Light of Light, very God of very God.* And though these expressions may seem harsh, yet I may have occasion to shew more particularly in what sense they may be admitted. This is proper to the Son alone: He only is begotten. It is true, not only the Son, but the Holy Ghost also, proceeds from the Father; but the Son only proceeds by generation, and the Holy Ghost by spiration. The Father is the original of personal subsistence to both: He is the original of personal subsistence to the Son, by generation; and he, together with the Son, is the original of personal subsistence to the Holy Ghost, by spiration.

I shall here take occasion to discourse a little of the eternal generation of the Son. And, 1. I shall prove that the Son is begotten of the Father from all eternity. 2 I shall speak a little

(b) John v. 26.   (c) John i. 14.

† Θεὸς ἐκ θεν, φῶς ἐκ φωτὸς, θεὸς ἀληθινὸς ἐκ θεῦ ἀληθινν.

tle of the nature of this generation. And then, 3. I shall make some practical improvement of this head.

First, I prove from the holy scriptures that the Son, our Lord Jesus Christ, is begotten of the Father from all eternity. I shall insist a little on this, because it is blasphemously denied by the Socinians. And,

1. This is clear from Psal. ii. 7. *I will declare the decree, the Lord hath said unto me, Thou art my Son, this day have I begotten thee.* This is applied to Christ in several places in the New Testament (d). The word, *this day,* doth not denote a certain time when this generation began, but is used to express the eternity thereof. And that which is eternal is expressed by this term, to shew that all things past and to come, are present with God, in regard of his eternity. In eternity there is no succession, no yesterday, or to-morrow; but it is all as one continued day, or moment, without any succession or change. Therefore the generation of the Son, being eternal, is rightly designed by this term. And although in this and the following verses, we have a declaration of God's decree and appointment, concerning the advancement of Christ to his mediatory throne and kingdom: Yet, in this verse, the generation of the Son is not mentioned as a part of that decree, but as the foundation thereof; for, unless Christ had been the Son of God by an eternal generation, he could not have been our Mediator, nor could he have obtained a throne and kingdom, as such. And it appears, that Christ is here called the Son of God, in an eminent manner, such as the angels themselves cannot lay claim to, by comparing herewith that text, *Being made so much better than the angels, as he hath by inheritance obtained a more excellent name than they: For unto which of the angels said he at any time, Thou art my Son, this day have I begotten thee* (e). Where it is evident, that the generation here spoken of, is such as is proper and peculiar to the Lord Christ, and whereby he is extolled, not only above all men, but above the angels themselves. This eternal generation of the Son was solemnly declared and manifested by his resurrection. This is the apostle's scope, when he says, *And we declare unto you glad tidings, how that the promise which was made unto the fathers, God hath fulfilled the same unto us their children, in that he hath raised up Jesus again: as it is also written in the second Psalm, Thou art my Son, this day have I begotten thee* (f). He might well say, that this scripture
in

(d) Acts xiii. 32, 33. Heb. i. 4, 5. and v. 5.   (e) Heb. i. 4, 5.
(f) Acts xiii. 32, 33.

in Psal. ii. 7. was fulfilled by the raising Christ from the dead, because, by his resurrection, the truth thereof was so openly manifested and declared. So the same apostle tells us, he was *declared to be the Son of God with power, by the resurrection from the dead* (g).

2. From Prov. viii. 22,—30. *The Lord possessed me in the beginning of his way, before his works of old. I was set up from everlasting, from the beginning, or ever the earth was. When there were no depths, I was brought forth: When there were no fountains abounding with water. Before the mountains were settled; before the hills, was I brought forth.—When he prepared the heavens, I was there.—When he appointed the foundations of the earth: Then was I by him as one brought up with him; and I was daily his delight, rejoicing always before him.* By Wisdom, who is brought in speaking in this chapter, we are not to understand wisdom in general, or wisdom as it is a virtue or quality in man; for not one thing here mentioned is, in any tolerable sense, applicable thereunto. Nor are we to understand that essential attribute of the divine nature which is called wisdom; for the the things here spoken concerning Wisdom, can be no way verified in any of God's essential attributes. Therefore, by Wisdom here, we are to understand a subsisting person; for such things are attributed thereto, both in this and the next chapters, as are proper only to a person. And we can understand no other than a divine person; seeing he is here held forth to be eternal. None in the ancient church, no not the Arians themselves, did ever question, that by Wisdom here is understood the Son of God. And this is the more evident, because this is one of the names given to him in the New Testament: He is called the *Wisdom of God*, 1 Cor. i. 24. And the principal things here spoken of Wisdom, are expresly attributed elsewhere † unto the Son. Again, the Wisdom that speaks here is the same that speaks in Prov. i. 20, &c. And it is evident, that by Wisdom there, we must understand a divine person: For thus he speaks, verse 23d, *Turn you at my reproof, I will pour out my Spirit unto you, I will make known my words unto you. Because I have called, and ye refused, &c.* I say then, that by Wisdom, in Prov. viii. we must understand a divine person, e-

ven

(g) Rom. i. 4.

† *See and compare these places:* Prov. viii. 11. *with* Phil. iii. 8. Verse 15. *with* Rev. xix. 16. Verse 22. *with* John i. 1, 2, 3. Verses 23, 24. *with* Col. i. 15, 16, 17. Verse 30. *with* John i. 18. Verse 32. *with* Rev. xxii. 7, 14.

ven the Son, our Lord Jesus, the personal Wisdom of God. Now, what says he? *The Lord possessed me,* or *acquired,* or *obtained me.* But how? Certainly not otherwise than by true generation, in which respect he is said to be *brought forth,* or *begotten,* verses 24, 25. and to be *as one brought up with* the Father, verse 30. And that, not in time, but *from everlasting, before his works of old,* and *or ever the earth was,* verses 22, 23.

3. I argue from Mic. v. 2. *And thou, Bethlehem-Ephratah, though thou be little among the thousands of Judah, yet out of thee shall he come forth unto me, that is to be Ruler in Israel; whose goings forth have been from of old, from everlasting.* This text is applied to Christ in Matth. ii. 6. And that it must be understood of him, is evident, because he is here promised as the King and Ruler of his church: And in the following verses, there is ascribed to him, the calling of the Gentiles; and invincible power and majesty, in his providence, doctrine, and miracles; and an universal kingdom and government over Jews and Gentiles through the earth. Now, there is a twofold going forth here attributed to him. The first is external and visible, viz. his going forth from the city of Bethlehem, by being born of a virgin. This is a temporal generation, and is therefore spoken of as a thing to come, *He shall come forth unto me.* But lest any should look on him as a mere man, and as one that began to be at his incarnation, therefore a second going forth is mentioned, which is internal and eternal; *Whose goings forth have been from of old, from everlasting;* or, *from the days of eternity,* as it is in the original text. These words design his eternal generation, as being begotten of the Father from all eternity: For he could not *go forth* from the Father *from everlasting,* but by generation.

4. That the Lord Christ is begotten of the Father from all eternity, is clear from his being called the Son of God. He is often so called in scripture. The Father did solemnly proclaim him to be so by an audible voice from heaven, both at his baptism, and at his transfiguration (*h*). He is the Son of God in a most proper and singular manner, viz. by the Father's communicating to him the divine essence by eternal generation. This name, being given to Christ, is more excellent than any name given to the angels, though they also are called *the sons of God: For unto which of the angels said he at any time, Thou art my Son, this day have I begotten thee* (*i*). He is so the Son of God, as on that account he is equal with the Father. Therefore, when our blessed Lord told the Jews, *My Father worketh hitherto, and I work:* It is said, *The Jews sought the more to kill him,*
because

(*h*) Matth. iii. 17 and xvii. 3.   (*i*) Heb. i. 4, 5.

because he not only had broken the Sabbath, but said also, that God was his Father, making himself equal with God (*k*). Our blessed Lord's scope is plainly to shew, that he was undivided from the Father in working, and one in essence with him, and consequently not subject to the law of the Sabbath. The Jews concluded from this, that he made himself equal with God. And they did rightly conclude so; for he did not find fault with them for so doing, nor charge them with reproaching him; nor doth he clear any mistake in it, as certainly he would have done, if they had been in any. Therefore, what they conclude from his discourse, is plainly asserted by the apostle, in these words, He *thought it not robbery to be equal with God* (*l*). So that Christ's scope in John v. is plainly to shew, that he was the Son of God in such manner, that he was the same in substance with the Father, and equal with him in glory and dignity. Hence he is called by the apostle, THE *Son*, or THAT *Son*, by way of eminency: And Peter, in his confession, says, *Thou art Christ, the Son* (or *that Son*) *of the living God.* And he is called God's OWN *Son*, and his *only-begotten Son*, and his *beloved Son* (*m*). Therefore he must be the Son of God in a singular way, and such as is proper to himself, which can be no other than by eternal generation, and communication of the same individual essence ‡.

SERMON XCVI.

Second, I SHALL, in the next place, speak a little of the nature of the generation of the Son. Our blessed Lord himself doth in some measure explain it to us, so far as we are capable to apprehend this mystery, when he tells us, *As the Father hath life in himself, so hath he given to the Son to have life in himself* (*a*). So that, *to beget the Son,* is, *to give to the Son to have life in himself, as the Father hath life in himself;* which doth necessarily import a communication of the same individual essence. For, to *have life in himself,* is an essential attribute of God; that is, to have life independently, from and of himself, and to be the fountain of all life to the creature, is a perfection proper to God, inseparable from his nature, yea, the same with

his

(*k*) John v. 17, 18. (*l*) Phil ii. 6. (*m*) Heb. i. 8. Matt. xvi. 16. Rom. viii. 32. John i. 14, 18. Matth. iii. 17.

‡ Ὑιὸν ἀκούων μὴ καταχρηστικῶς ἀκοῦε μόνον, ἀλλὰ υἱὸν ἀληθῶς υἱὸν φυσικόν.

Cyril. Hierosol. Catech. 11.

(*a*) John v. 26.

essence: Therefore the Father cannot give it, unless he give the essence itself: And he cannot give the essence by way of alienation, for then he himself would cease to be God; nor by way of participation, seeing the divine essence is one and indivisible; therefore it must be by way of communication. So that the generation of the Son is, that eternal action of the the Father, whereby he did communicate to the Son, the same individual essence which he himself hath, that the Son might have it equally with himself.

Here it is questioned by divines, whether the divine essence be communicated, or only the manner of the essence, or its mode of subsistence. Some say, if the essence be communicated, how then is the Son † *God of himself*, having the Godhead communicated to him? Others say, if the essence be not communicated, then how can the Son be God? But I humbly apprehend that these two may be reconciled, by expressing ourselves thus, that there is a communication of the divine essence, not that it may exist, but that it may subsist after a different manner: So that the Father is to the Son the original of his personal subsistence in the divine essence; that is, the Son hath his subsistence, as the second person, from the Father. For, when we say that the divine essence is communicated by the Father to the Son, the plain meaning seems to be this, that it is from the Father that the divine essence subsists after such a manner; or, that it is from the Father, that there is such a another manner of subsistence in the same individual essence.

But here, some may enquire, How did the Father communicate the divine essence to the Son? Or, how did he beget the Son? What is the manner of this generation *? This indeed is a very curious question; for the thing is ineffable and inconceivable. It is impossible for us poor worms to understand or explain, wherein this generation consists. It is not natural, but supernatural, and wholly divine, and therefore incomprehensible by us. Yea †, it is incomprehensible even by the angels themselves. As God himself is incomprehensible, so is the manner of this generation. We may hereunto apply that in Isa. liii. 8. *Who shall declare his generation?* It seems to be for this reason that it is expressed in

† 'Αυτοθεος.

* *Quod Deus filium habeat, crede; Quomodo autem, ne sis curiosus; quaerens enim non invenies.* Cyril. Hieroso. Catech. 11.

† *Hic vox Silet, mens deficit, non tantum mea, sed etiam Angelorum.* Ambr. Lib. de fide Cap. 5.

in the plural number, *His goings forth have been from of old* (*b*): importing that Christ's eternal generation is superexcellent and incomprehensible: All excellencies, and infinitely more than we can conceive, are summed up in it. Hence an ancient faith ‡, "The Son is begotten ineffably and incomprehensibly." The manner of his generation is, as Justin saith §, "Ineffable and above our understanding, above our reason, and above our comprehension." There are insuperable difficulties even in natural generation. It will conquer our understandings, to comprehend even our own generation. Hence the preacher says, *Thou knowest not what is the way of the spirit, nor how the bones do grow in the womb of her that is with child* (*c*). Yea, we cannot exactly explain the generation even of the meanest things in nature: How skin, and flesh, and sinews, and veins, and bones, and entrails, and so many different organs, and members of so many various operations should arise out of so inconsiderable a matter; this is inexplicable by us. How much less can we explain the eternal generation of the Son of God?

This generation being altogether mysterious and incomprehensible, as to the manner of it, all curious searching and prying is to be avoided in this matter. It becomes us to reverence it with silence, and to reckon it much for us to learn that he is begotten ‖. The schoolmen, by inquiring and searching curiously into the manner of it, have wearied themselves in vain, and instead of bringing further light into this glorious mystery, have darkened it more, both to themselves and others. It is true, it is shadowed forth to us in the holy scriptures by divers similitudes, taken sometimes from the sun, from which the beams issue forth continually and inseparably, so that the sun is neither before them nor without them; sometimes from the mind, which by understanding itself, doth form in itself an image or idea of itself; sometimes from our words, which are begotten in our thoughts, and are the express image of them. The Spirit of God seems to allude to these things, when the Son is called *the brightness of his Father's glory, and the express image of his person*: And when he is called

Wisdom;

(*b*) Mic. v. 2.   (*c*) Eccl xi. 5.
‡ Ἐγεννήθη δὲ ἀνεκφράσως ᾗ ἀπερινοήτως.
                                    Author Expos. Fidei.
§ Ἄῤῥητος ᾗ ὑπὲρ νῦν, ὑπὲρ λογον, ᾗ ὑπὲρ καταληψιν.
‖ Θεῖ γέννησις σιοπῇ τιμάσθω μέγα σοι τὸ μαθεῖν ὅτι γεγέννηται.
                                    Greg. Nazian.

Wisdom; and *the Word* (d). But although some relief may be given, by such allusions, unto our weak understandings, in the contemplation of this glorious mystery, as to the τὸ ὅτι, that it is: prvoiding always, that in applying them to God, every thing of imperfection be removed: yet these things would be carefully adverted unto. 1. Such allusions are not designed by the Spirit of God, to explain to us the manner of the thing, viz. how the Son is begotten of the Father; this being wholly incomprehensible. Therefore great caution should be used, lest we carry such similitudes too far, and beyond what the Spirit of God intends by them. 2. The metaphors used, especially in Heb. i. 3. are so obscure and dark, as a learned commentator observes †, and the difficulty of discerning the true and genuine meaning of the Holy Ghost in them, is such, that the expressions there used, may well be reckoned amongst these places, which God in his infinite wisdom hath left in his blessed word, for taming our arrogance, and exercising our parts, diligence, and humble dependence on himself. 3 However the Spirit of God, in speaking of of the generation of the Son, may in some places use metaphorical expressions; yet we are not warranted hereby to take a liberty to use similitudes and metaphors of our own and other mens' devising. Therefore the curiosity of the schoolmen, in using various similitudes for expressing the way and manner of the generation of the Son, is intolerable boldness and arrogance; for all similitudes fall infinitely short in this incomprehensible mystery. The generation of Christ is a mystery so profound, that it is dangerous for us to search into this depth, further than we have light from the holy scriptures. Therefore let us be soberly wise in this matter. Let us rest satisfied in this, that we have the τὸ ὅτι, *that it is,* plainly revealed; leaving the τὸ διότι, or manner *how it is,* to God himself, who alone hath the perfect knowledge of himself. Excellent to this purpose is the advice of Ruffinus †; " Forbear to examine " narrowly, how the Father begat the Son, or to launch forth " curiously into this hidden depth, lest by much gazing upon
" the

(d) Heb. i. 3. Prov. viii, and ix. chap. 1 John v. 7. John i. 1.

† Owen in L.

‡ *Quomodo autem Deus Pater genuerit filium, nolo discutias, nec curiosius te ingeras in profundo Arcani, ne forte dum inaccessæ Lucis fulgorem pertinacius perscruteris, exiguum ipsum qui mortalibus divino munere concessus est, perdas Aspectum.* Ruffin. de Symb.

" the brightness of that inaccessible light, you lose that little
" sight which of God's free gift is granted to poor mortals."

But though these things be so, yet some things we may safely adventure upon, in a consistency with divine revelation, to distinguish the generation of the Son from temporal generations among men, and to prevent dangerous errors and mistakes, by explaining negatively what this generation is not. And let us endeavour to do this, with reverence and godly fear, looking up to the Father of lights for light from above.

It is not needful to insist upon the analogy between the eternal generation of the Son, and temporal generations among men. The most proper generation in things created, is the vital production of another in the same nature. A man begets a son; that is, he produceth another of the same nature with himself. There is a communication of the essence of the begetter to him that is begotten, whereby he that is begotten partakes of the same nature with him that begets. So here, in this eternal and ineffable generation, the Father communicates to the Son the same divine essence which he himself hath, so that the Son is of the same nature or essence with the Father. And as among men, the son bears some likeness or similitude of the father; so here, the eternal Son is the Father's express and perfect image and similitude, even *the express image of his person* (e). Yea, the generation of the Lord Christ is the most proper generation, a generation that is most properly so called: For generation being the production of the like in the similitude of nature; therefore, where there is the nearest identity of nature, there must be also the most proper generation: But here, the Father hath begotten a Son of the same individual nature or essence with himself. The generation of the Son must needs be far more proper than any temporal generation of the creature, because it is in a far more perfect manner, and the identity of nature is most perfect.

But though the generation of the Lord Christ be most truly and properly a generation; yet it is not of the same univocal nature with generation in creatures. As the nature of God is incomprehensible, so also is the nature of this generation. We may observe an infinite difference and disproportion between it and human generation, in these following particulars.

1. In human generation there is a communication of the same specifical essence: But in the generation of Christ there is a communication of the same individual essence; which must be so, because of the individual unity of the divine nature. Human

(e) Heb. i. 3.

man generation is by way of multiplication; a father begets a son, who hath a distinct individual nature or essence of his own: But the divine nature or essence is not capable of division or multiplication, so that he that is begotten hath the same individual nature with the Father. Hence it appears that there is no difference or inequality in the nature or essence, it being the same in both; only, the Son hath it by communication from the Father.

2. In human generation there is a communication only of a part of the parent: But the divine nature or essence, being spiritual and indivisible, there is in the generation of the Son a communication of the whole essence. We are not so to conceive of this mystery, as if the Son were a part of the essence or substance of the Father, and so of the same nature with him: For, the divine essence being incapable of any division or partition, if there be a communication of the essence, it must be of the whole essence; so that God is the Father of his Son, as Athanasius speaks † without any division of the substance. The divine essence is wholly and entirely communicated by the Father to the Son: And by communicating the whole essence, he communicated to him all essential properties.

3. In human generation, he that is begotten is not only distinct from him that begetteth, but separate from him. The reason is, because he that begets, begets without himself. But here, the eternal Father did not beget the Son without himself, but in the same individual essence ‡: So that, although the Son be a distinct person from the Father, yet is he not divided or separated from him. The essence is communicated * inseparably, say the ancient Fathers. Hence *the Word* is said to be *with God;* and the Son is said to be *in the Father*, and the *Father in* him (*e*). The Father hath begotten the Son in and of himself. So that although the Father communicate the whole divine essence to the Son, yet he hath the whole divine essence in himself. Hence an ancient father expresseth himself thus, " Thoug the person of the Son remain distinct from the per-

"son

---

† Ἄλλως ἐστὶν ἡ τῶν ἀνθρώπων γένεσις, καὶ ἄλλως ἐστὶν ὁ υἱὸς ἐκ τοῦ πατρός· τῶν μὲν γὰρ ἀνθρώπων τὰ γεννήματα μέρη πῶς τῶν γεννώντων εἰσίν—ὁ δὲ Θεὸς ἀμερὴς ὢν ἀμερίςως ἐστὶ ᾗ ἀπαθὴς τοῦ υἱοῦ πατήρ. Athan. Oper. Tom. 1. Epist. de Decret. Syn. Nicenæ.

‡ *Epiphanius docet ita aloquendum ut Filius dicatur* ἐκ οὐσίας *quasi extra patrem Genitus, ἀλλ᾽ ὁμοούσιος.* Epiphan. in ancor. § 6.

* Ἀμερίςως. (*e*) John i. 1. and xiv. 10.

"son of the Father, yet he subsists in that substance of which he is begotten, and nothing is taken off from the substance of the Father by his being begotten of it †."

4. Human generation is temporal; so that the father is in time before the son, and begets one younger than himself. But the generation of the Lord Christ is eternal. *The Lord possessed him in the beginning of his way, before his works of old:* He *was set up from everlasting, from the beginning, or ever the earth was: His goings forth have been from of old, from everlasting:* And, *in the beginning was the Word.* Hence he is called *the first-born of every creature* (*f*); that is, begotten before all the creatures. As the Father and Son are from everlasting God; so they are from everlasting, Father and Son. These relations and their personal properties are no less eternal than the divine essence. So that there is not here any priority in duration, as if the Father were elder than the Son, or the Son younger than the Father *: For the generation of the Son is the eternal act of the eternal Father, whereby he begets the Son co-existing eternally with himself, in the same individual essence. Hence it appears that the Son did not, by being begotten, pass from not being to being. As he was not before his generation: So he did not begin to be by his generation; but did always proceed from the Father, by an eternal and internal act, as the beams do constantly flow from the sun; though in a way more eminent, and inexpressible by us.

From what is said, it plainly appears, that although the generation of the Son be the most proper generation: Yet, being wholly supernatural, and quite different from all generations in the creatures, we are not to measure the one by the other, nor to argue from natural generation to that which is supernatural, nor to judge of this mystery by examples and instances from the creatures. But in using this similitude of natural generation, and applying the same to God, we are to remove from it whatever implies any imperfection, or any thing not becoming the majesty of God.

Two things I shall add further for clearing the nature of the generation of the Son. 1. It doth not import any inequality in the Son, nor priority of dignity in the Father. For, as I observed

---

† Hilar. de Trinit. Lib. IV. N. 6.

(*f*) Prov. viii. 22, 23. Mic. v. 2. John i. 1. Col. i. 15.

* Ἐιδὲ τὴν ἀπὸ χρόνου λαμβάνεις ἀρχὴν, καὶ ἄναρχος· ποιητὴς γὰρ χρόνων ὑχ ὑπὸ χρόνον. Greg. Nazianz. Orat. 39.

observed before, * in begetting the Son, there is a communication of the same individual essence to him, the dignity whereof being infinite, no greater can be imagined. Even human generation doth not import any inequality in the nature of the son, more than in the father: Much less doth the generation of the eternal Son imply any inequality of the Son with the Father. 2. The divine essence is neither the principle nor the term of this generation; but as the person of the Father is the principle, so the person of the Son is the term. The divine essence neither begets nor is begotten, else it would be multiplied, and so there would be not only three persons, but three Gods: But the person of the Father begets, and the person of the Son is begotten. True it is, that by generation the essence is communicated; for as the person of the Father is the principle that begets, so the divine essence, as subsisting in his person, is the principle by which this generation is performed: But generation, as it is by a person originally, so it terminates in a person; for, as I already observed, the essence is communicated to him that is begotten, not that it may exist, but that it may subsist after another manner. So, that the Son is from the Father by generation, not in respect of his essence, but in respect of his person. Hence it appears that the generation of the Son maketh nothing against his Godhead: For, he is God of himself, though not the Son of himself †. He hath no original of his deity, but only of his personal subsistence.

SERMON XCVII.

Third, I shall now make some application of this head. *Use* 1. We see here the infinite dignity and excellency of the person of our Mediator. He is the eternal and only begotten Son of God, God equal with the Father, and consequently a person of infinite worth and dignity. He is of equal dignity with the person of the Father, being the *Father's Fellow*, and one who *thought it not robbery to be equal with God* (a). Hence we may be assured of the infinite efficacy of his mediatory actions, and of the infinite value of his sufferings. The fulness of the satisfaction made by him, ariseth from

---

* *Illi dedit suam æqualitatem, quem non genuit inæqualem.*
August. Tract. 47. in Joan.

† 'Αυτοθεος, *sed non* 'Αυτουιος. F. Ham. disp. 7.
A se Deus, a patre Filius.

(a) Zech. xiii. 7. Phil. ii. 6.

from the dignity of the perſon ſatisfying. The head of a king is of more worth and value than the head of a common ſubject: So Chriſt's perſon, and conſequently the ſufferings of his perſon, were of more worth and value than the ſouls and bodies of all men. Therefore the ſcripture lays ſo much ſtreſs upon this, that it was *God that laid down his life, and ſhed his blood* for us; and that the blood which he ſhed was *the blood of the Son of God.* Hence it is called *his* OWN *blood,* as an evidence of its unſpeakable worth and value. It was the blood, not of a mere man, but of *the Son of God* (*b*). Though he ſuffered only in his human nature, yet the human nature, in ſuffering, being united to the divine nature in his perſon, therefore his ſufferings were the ſufferings of an infinite perſon. It was the ſame perſon who was *the brightneſs of his Father's glory, and the expreſs image of his perſon,* who did *by himſelf purge our ſins* (*c*). The ſufferings of great men are very eſtimable; O then, how eſtimable muſt the ſufferings of the great God be! On this account, his ſufferings, though temporal, did more than down-weigh the eternal ſufferings of a world of men. Well then, we may hence be fully perſuaded, that Chriſt, by his obedience and ſufferings, hath fully ſatisfied divine juſtice, and paid every farthing of the elect's debt: So that we may with full confidence and aſſurance, caſt ourſelves on this bleſſed Mediator, and reſt on his ſatisfaction as full and complete. We may ſafely venture our ſouls on this bottom.

Uſe 2. See here and admire the aſtoniſhing love of God in ſending Chriſt into the world for our ſake. This is held forth as the moſt ſignal manifeſtation of God's wonderful love: *God ſo loved the world, that he gave his only begotten Son,* &c. *And in this was manifeſted the love of God toward us, becauſe that God ſent his only begotten Son into the world, that we might live through him. Herein is love, not that we loved God, but that he loved us, and ſent his Son to be the propitiation for our ſins* (*d*). The admirable greatneſs of God's love in this matter, will appear from theſe conſiderations.

Conſid. 1. Who was ſent: His only begotten Son. If Chriſt had been a mere man, though born after another manner than other men, there had been no ſuch expreſſion of God's love in the way of our redemption. But herein the love of God ſhines radiantly,

(*b*) 1 John iii. 16. Acts xx. 28. 1 John i. 7. Rev. i. 5. Heb ix. 12. and xiii. 12. (*c*) Heb. i. 3. (*d*) John iii. 16. 1 John iv. 9, 10.

radiantly, that he whom God sent is his own eternal Son, God equal with the Father, an infinitely glorious person. We are so fond of our children that we cannot part with them for a little time; but though God had but one Son, yet he spared him not for our sake. So the apostle tells us, *He spared not his own Son, but delivered him up for us all* (*e*). O what admirable love was this? Says the Lord to Abraham, *Now I know that thou fearest God, seeing thou hast not withheld thy son, thine only son from me* (*f*). So here, by this we may know that God loves us, because he did not withhold his Son, his only Son from us. He would not send an angel or archangel; he would not entrust them with our salvation: But he sent his own Son. God hath nothing too near or dear to him for elect sinners. Consider, 1. How worthy Christ is in himself. He is very God, the only begotten of the Father, the King of kings, the Prince of the kings of the earth. A greater or more glorious person could not be sent or given for us. 2. How dear he was to the Father. He was his *own* Son, his *only-begotten* Son, his *beloved* Son, the *Son of his love*. He is called *his dear Son*. The Father loved him dearly: Therefore he is said to be *in his bosom*. He was *the Father's delight* from eternity (*g*). O the infinite complacency and contentment the Father had in him! We use to be very sparing of things that are dear to us, and loth to part with them: But though Christ was infinitely dear to the Father, yet he *spared him not* (*h*). O astonishing love!

Consid. 2. How he was sent: Not in outward pomp, glory and majesty, nor in the equipage of a prince; but in *the form of a servant*. His divine glory and majesty was vailed under the sinless infirmities of our nature. He *made himself of no reputation, and took upon him the form of a servant, and was made in the likeness of men* (*i*). Yea, he assumed our nature, not when it was innocent, but when it was in us guilty and polluted with sin: He came *in the likeness of sinful flesh* (*k*). Yea, he became viler than any of the sons of men, in respect of his mean, low, and afflicted condition. O admirable love, that, for our sake, the Lord of all things should be sent to be a servant! *The Son of man came not to be ministered unto, but to minister* (*l*).

Consid. 3. For whose sake he was sent. Was it for angels that sinned? No; God would shew them no such favour. Though the angelical nature be in itself far more excellent

than

(*e*) Rom. viii. 32. (*f*) Gen xxii. 12. (*g*) Col i. 13. John i. 18. Prov. viii. 30. (*h*) Rom. viii. 32. (*i*) Phil ii. 7. (*k*) Rom. viii. 3. (*l*) Matth. xx. 28.

than the human nature; yet God would not send his Son to be a Redeemer for angels, but for men. Was it for sinless and innocent men, and such as were in a state of friendship with God? No; but for sinners and enemies, such as were in arms against God, and had despised his authority, and cast off his sovereignty, and as much as in them lay stained his glory (*m*). Herein the supereminency of divine love was illustrious, that he would send his only-begotten Son into the world, for broken, bankrupt, dyvor sinners, such as were vile and abominable in his sight; rebels and enemies, who had forfeited all the blessings of their creation, and had made themselves liable to eternal wrath and vengeance. *God so loved the world,* when we had so sinned, and had sunk ourselves into a state of damnation.

Consid. 4. For what end God sent his Son: Even to suffer for us in our nature. To suffer what? All sorts of sinless miseries and at last the painful, shameful, and cursed death of the cross. O, how admirable is this, that the eternal Son of God should be sent, to hang upon a cross, as a public spectacle of shame, and to bleed to death, and that for such rebels as we are! This shews the greatness of God's love: *God commendeth his love toward us, that while we were yet sinners, Christ died for us* (*n*). If the Son of God had been sent into the world, only to view our vileness and misery, it had been another matter; but he was sent to die, and to die the worst of deaths. And what was this to the wrath of God which he suffered in his soul! As his body was abused and spit up, pierced and wounded, racked and tormented to death upon the cross; so his soul did lie under the lashes of sin-revenging justice, and was scorched in the hot furnace of his Father's wrath. O the immense and unmeasurable love of God that is manifest in all this! From this instance it is that we learn, that *God is love* (*o*).

Well then, when we consider what an one Christ is, the eternal and only-begotten Son of the Father, the great eternal God it greatly commends God's love toward us, that he should be sent into the world, to suffer and die for the redemption of such rebels and enemies as we are. Here is love without any parallel: such love, that all other love in comparison of it is as nothing. Herein the love of God is gone to the uttermost: *God so loved the world, that he gave his only begotten Son* (*p*) Here the love of God is screwed up to the highest pitch: *He* SO *loved;* this SO is unutterable and inconceivable. O what admirable

---

(*m*) Rom. v. 8, 10. 1 Pet. iii. 18. (*n*) Rom. v. 8. (*o*) 1 John iv. 8. (*p*) 1 John iv. 10 John iii. 16.

able love is here! Love let out upon a world of finners; and let out to fuch a degree, as to give a Son, and an only-begotten Son, that we might live through him†! Here is a mine fo rich, that no creature can count the value of it; a depth fo great, that no creature can fathom it. O the depth and height, the the length and breadth of this love! God fo loved the world— How much did he love it? Angels and men cannot tell you.

O then, dear Chriftians, admire the love of God in Chrift toward you. It is fo great that it could not be wound up to a higher ftrain. *Herein perceive we the love of God, becaufe he laid down his life for us* (q). *Herein*—as if we could perceive it in nothing elfe, becaufe we can perceive it in nothing comparatively to this. Here is the utmoft bound, if I may fpeak fo, of an infinite love. This love is fo great that it is myfterious and incomprehenfible. It *paffeth knowledge* (r). That God fhould lay out fuch a love on forlorn filthy clay, is the wonder of angels and men. Admire and praife this love. It is frequently extolled and admired by the faints in fcripture; and it will be admired and praifed by angels and faints to all eternity: Therefore fpend more of your time this way. This is an exercife both pleafant and profitable.

Ufe 3. From this doctrine we may take occafion to obferve and admire Chrift's great condefcenfion, in thefe two inftances. 1. In that he was content to be fent into the world for our falvation and redemption. Though he was the eternal and only-begotten Son of the Father, of the fame effence with him, and equal with him in glory and dignity; yet being fent by the Father, he came moft chearfully and readily, to do what was the Father's will for our redemption. Hence he is brought in fpeaking, *Then faid I, Lo, I come: In the volume of the book it is written of me. I delight to do thy will, O my God* (s). Though he was *in the form of God*, clothed with divine glory and majefty: Yet he *made himfelf of no reputation, and took upon him the form of a fervant;* he vailed his divine glory, by affuming our nature, with all the finlefs infirmities thereof: And *he humbled himfelf, and became obedient unto death, even the death of the crofs* (t). He voluntarily fubmitted himfelf to undergo whatever was neceffary for our redemption. What aftonifhing condefcenfion

---

† *Dilexit nos Deus dulciter, fapienter, fortiter: Dulciter, quia carnem induit; fapienter, quia culpam cavit; fortiter, quia mortem fubftinuit.* Bern. in Cantic.

(q) 1 John iii. 16. (r) Eph. iii. 19. (s) Pfal. xl. 7, 8. (t) Phil. ii. 6, 7, 8.

defcenfion was this, that he, who was very God, of equal dignity with the Father, fhould thus humble himfelf for vile worms! Can we, after all this, entertain any hard thoughts of Chrift? 2. In that he is pleafed to own believers in him for his brethren. The apoftle tells us, *He is not afhamed to call them brethren* (*u*). Though there be an infinite diftance between him and us; though he is God's own eternal and well-beloved Son, of infinite dignity, glory, and excellency; and though we are vile lothfome guilty creatures: Yet he is not afhamed to own us under fuch a nigh relation, to avouch us as his brethren. Indeed he is fo glorious, and we are fo vile and miferable, that he might juftly be afhamed of us, and lothe us; yet fuch is his condefcending love, that he is not afhamed to call us brethren. O how aftonifhing is this! If Mephibofheth thought it a great condefcenfion in David, to take fuch notice of him, though he was Jonathan's fon; what is it for the King of kings, to own us for brethren, in our vile and low condition! Chrift's condefcenfion, in thus overlooking the diftance between him and us, is not eafy to be believed, and therefore is eternally to be admired. What matter of comfort is here to you who are believers in Chrift! No vilenefs, mifery, or unworthinefs in you, fhall hinder him from owning and avouching you as his brethren. Yea, though your own relations defpife you; though the world hate, reproach, and perfecute you; though you fhould be efteemed as the off-fcourings of all things: yet the blefled Son of God is not afhamed of you, but will openly own you as his brethren, before angels and men.

Ufe 4. Make it your great bufinefs to get Chrift. Confider what a worthy one he is. Angels and men cannot count his worth *. He is a perfon of unfpeakable worth, of infinite dignity and excellency, being the eternal and only begotten Son of God, God equal with the Father. He is *fairer than the fons of men*. All the beauty of God is in Chrift; for he is *the brightnefs of his Father's glory, and the exprefs image of his perperfon* (*x*). O what a lovely and amiable one is Chrift! when God gives Chrift to you, he gives the richeft jewel in his cabinet, and as it were the laft mite of his treafure: He can give you nothing beyond this. This gift is as great as God himfelf, and as dear to God as himfelf. Chrift is a rich treafure: *The fulnefs of the Godhead dwelleth in him bodily:* And, *in him are hid*

all

(*u*) Heb. ii. 11. (*x*) Heb. i. 3.
* *Chriftus & Cælum non patiuntur Hyperbolem.*

all the treasures of wisdom and knowledge (y). When you get Christ, then you have all things in him; for *Christ is all* (z). He is a magazine and storehouse of all spiritual riches. There is enough in him to answer all your wants and wishes. Indeed you need no more but Christ to make you eternally happy. Being God equal with the Father, what is there that he cannot do for you? He is an able Saviour and Redeemer. He is strong and mighty, to conquer your spiritual enemies, and to master all opposition in your way to glory. *He is able to save them to the uttermost that come unto God by him* (a). To shut up all: Is Christ of such infinite dignity and worth, being the only begotten Son of the Father? Then once get Christ, and all the blessings and privileges of the covenant are sure to you; God will deny you nothing that is needful for you. *If God spared not his own Son, but delivered him up for us all; how much more will he not with him freely give us all things* (b)?

Well then, give yourselves no rest till Christ be yours. Such is his matchless excellency and worth, that † you should be ready to welcome death, even in the most formidable shape, so you may have Christ. Receive this great and unspeakable gift of God as he is offered in the gospel; close with him by faith. For this end, labour to get a deep sense of the absolute need you have of Christ; study his matchless and incomparable excellency and worth; and cry much for the drawing and conquering power of grace upon your heart.

Thus I have spoken of the personal and incommunicable properties of the Father and of the Son.

SERMON XCVIII.

III. IT is the personal and incommunicable property of the Holy Ghost, to proceed from the Father and the Son. This is not obscurely implied in that text, *But when the Comforter is come, whom I will send unto you from the Father, even the Spirit of truth, which proceedeth from the Father, he shall testify of me* (a). Where, though there be express mention made only of his proceeding from the Father; yet his proceeding from the Son is not thereby denied or excluded, but on the

contrary

(y) Col. ii. 9. with ii. 3. (z) Col. iii. 11.
(a) Heb. vii. 25. (b) Rom. viii. 32.

† Πῦρ ϰ̀ ϛαυρὸς, θηρίων τε συϛάσεις, σκορπισμοὶ ὀϛέων, συγκοπαὶ μελῶν, ἀλησμοὶ ὅλȣ τȣ σώματος, κακαὶ κολάσεις τȣ διαβόλȣ ἐπ' ἐμὲ ἐρχέσθωσαν· μόνον ἵνα Ἰησȣ͂ Χριϛȣ͂ ἐπιτύχω.

(a) John xv. 26. Ignat.-Epist. ad Rom.

contrary it is supposed in the Son's sending him. And his proceeding from the Father is rather expressed, because the Father is the original of personal subsistence, both to the Son and to the Holy Ghost. Now, this is proper to the Holy Ghost alone, to proceed from the Father and the Son: So that the true notion of the Holy Ghost is, that he is the third person subsisting eternally in the one infinite essence of the Godhead, as having the same essence communicated to him from the Father and the Son, by proceeding from them both.

For clearing this, observe that the term procession, in a larger sense, is applicable, both to the Son, and to the Holy Ghost. And the procession of both is twofold, temporal and eternal. 1. There is a temporal procession of the Son and Holy Ghost; which lieth in their coming forth from God about the work of our salvation. So, the Son did proceed from the Father, when he came forth from him by his incarnation, as the Father's great Ambassador to accomplish the work of of our redemption. Of this our Lord speaks; *Ye have believed that I came out from God. I came forth from the Father, and am come into the world: Again I leave the world and go to the Father* (b). Just so, the Holy Ghost proceeds from the Father and the Son, when he is sent by them to apply the redemption Christ hath purchased: *The Father will send him in my name*, says Christ: And again, *I will send him from the Father* (c). 2. There is an eternal procession of the Son and Holy Ghost; which lies in their having the divine essence eternally communicated to them. So, the Son proceeds from the Father, by eternal generation. Of this our blessed Lord speaks, *I proceeded forth and came from God: Neither came I of myself, but he sent me* (d). Or, as the original text hath it, *From God I proceeded forth, and am come.* The first clause points at his eternal procession by generation; and the latter, being in the present time, relates to his temporal procession, or his coming from God to accomplish the work of redemption. To the same purpose, he says elsewhere, *I am from him, viz* by eternal generation; *and he sent me*, (e), viz. with a commission and instructions as Mediator. Thus also, the Holy Ghost proceeds from the Father and the Son, by eternal spiration or breathing. Hence he is called *the Spirit of truth, which proceedeth from the Father* (f). So that the term procession, when applied particularly to the Holy Ghost, is to be understood more strictly, of his peculiar

---

(b) John xvi. 27, 28. (c) John xiv. 26. and xv. 26. (d) John viii. 42. (e) John vii. 29. (f) John xv. 26.

manner of proceeding, as diſtinct from the generation of the Son.

In diſcourſing on this ſubject, I ſhall ſpeak a little, 1. Of the principle of this proceſſion. 2. Of the nature of it. 3. Of the difference between it and the generation of the Son. And then, 4. I ſhall apply this head. Theſe are deep myſteries: Therefore, in ſpeaking and hearing of them, we need to entertain a deep reverence of the glorious majeſty of God, and much holy fear and trembling, leſt we ſpeak or think of God the thing that is not right; and there is need to guard againſt all curious ſearching and prying into what God hath not revealed: And this, through the divine aſſiſtance, I ſhall endeavour to do.

Firſt, As for the principle of this proceſſion, we ſay that the Holy Ghoſt proceeds eternally from the Father and the Son. That he proceeds from the Father, is uncontroverted among them that own a Trinity of perſons in the unity of the divine eſſence. It is plainly aſſerted by our bleſſed Lord; *Even the Spirit of truth*, ſays he, *which proceedeth from the Father* (g). Hence, he is called *the Spirit of the Father*, and *the Spirit of him that raiſed Jeſus from the dead* (h). But there is a famous controverſy long agitated between the Greek and Latin churches, or the eaſtern and weſtern churches, about the proceſſion of the Holy Ghoſt from the Son. About the year 381, the council of Conſtantinople, which was the ſecond general council, having condemned the Macedonian hereſy, and aſſerted the Deity of the Holy Ghoſt, did in their explication of the Nicene Creed, make theſe words a part of it *, that *the Holy Ghoſt proceeded from the Father*. And about the year 434, the Council of Epheſus, being the third general council, decreed that no addition ſhould be made to the Creed. Yet, about the end of the ſixth century, in the weſtern, or Latin church, this addition was made, † *and from the Son*. Long after this, in the ninth century, when the Greek and Latin churches fell a quarrelling with one another about juriſdiction, the eaſtern, or Greek church, did reproach the weſtern, or Latin church, with corrupting the ancient Creed by an addition of their own, contrary to the decree of a general council; and obſerving that the Latin church did thereby advance herſelf above other churches, as judge in matters of faith, they did thence take occaſion plainly to deny the proceſſion of the Holy Ghoſt from the Son. And here began that famous ſchiſm between

(g) John xv. 26. (h) Matth. x. 20. Rom. viii. 11.
* Τὸ ἐκ τοῦ πατρὸς ἐκπορευόμενον. † Filioq.

between the Greek and Latin churches, which was increafed by the Latin church, their urging an expreffion as a neceffary article of faith, which formerly was not done; and by the Greek church, their inferting in the Athanafian Creed the word *only* †. Both were blame-worthy in this matter; the Latin church, for adding to the Conftantinopolitan Creed, contrary to the decree of another general council; and the Greek church, for adding to the Athanafian Creed, and rejecting a doctrine agreeable to, and founded on the holy fcriptures, and owned by the more ancient fathers of the church. True it is, that the Greek church is on this ground unjuftly charged with herefy by the Latin church, feeing they own the Holy Ghoft to be a divine perfon diftinct from the Father and the Son, and of the fame fubftance with them, and that he is the Spirit of the fon, no lefs than of the Father: Yet it is an error in the Greek church, to deny the proceffion of the Holy Ghoft from the Son; for the fentence of the Latins, which is embraced by the reformed churches, viz. that the Holy Ghoft proceeds from the Son, no lefs than from the Father, is, as I faid, moft agreeable unto, and founded upon the holy fcriptures.

This may be confirmed by thefe arguments. 1. The Holy Ghoft is fent by the Son, no lefs than by the Father. *I will fend* him *unto you,* fays Chrift, *from the Father:* And, *If I depart, I will fend him* (that is, the Comforter, *unto you* (*i*). Now, his miffion by the Son neceffarily fuppofeth his eternal proceffion from the the Son; feeing the order of operation, in the Son's fending the Holy Ghoft from the Father, follows the order of fubfiftence among the divine perfons. The right of miffion arifeth from the communication of the Effence. Hence, the Father is never fent by the Son; nor is the Father or the Son ever fent by the Holy Ghoft; but as the Son is fent by the Father, becaufe he hath the divine effence communicated to him by the Father; fo the Holy Ghoft is fent both by the Father and by the Son, becaufe he hath the divine effence communicated to him by them both, and fo proceeds from them both. The Son having the fame right of miffion with the Father, hath alfo communicated the fame effence. 2. The Holy Ghoft is called *the Spirit of the Son,* and *the Spirit of* Chrift, no lefs than of the Father (*k*). Now, as he is called the Spirit of the Father, becaufe he proceeds from the Father; fo it muft be for the like reafon, that he is called the Spirit of the Son, viz. be-

---

† Ἀπὸ τῦ μόνυ πατρὸς Art. 7.

(*i*) John xv. 26. and xvi. 7. (*k*) Gal iv. 6. Rom. viii. 9. Phil. i. 19.

viz. because he proceeds from him, and that by spiration or breathing. 3. Whatever the holy Spirit hath, he hath it from the Son, no less than from the Father. Our Saviour tells us, *When the Spirit of truth is come—He shall not speak of himself; but whatsoever he shall hear, that shall he speak—He shall receive of mine, and shall shew it unto you* (*l*) All these precious truths, gifts and graces, which the holy Spirit communicates to believers, he hath them, not of himself only, but by communication from the Father and the Son; which necessarily imports a communication of the divine essence from the Father and the Son. For, as I said formerly, the order of operation follows the order of subsistence. As the Son works from the Father, because he hath his subsistence as a divine person from the Father; so the Holy Ghost works from the Son, as well as from the Father, because he hath his subsistence as a divine person from the Son, no less than from the Father. 4. We may argue from Rev. xxii. 1. *And he shewed me a pure river of water of life, clear as chrystal, proceeding out of the throne of God, and of the Lamb.* By the pure river of water of life, some divines understand the Holy Spirit, whose consolations and effects are often in scripture compared to *waters* and *rivers of waters*. Now, this is said to *proceed out of the throne of God, and of the Lamb:* which, according to these divines, imports the procession of the holy Spirit from the Father and the Son.

We see then, that we have good warrant from the holy scriptures for asserting, that the Holy Ghost proceeds eternally from the Father and the Son. It is true, some ancient creeds, in the first ages of the church, do only express the procession of the Holy Ghost from the Father, omitting these words, † *and from the Son*. But this was done, because at that time there was no controversy as yet moved concerning the procession of the Holy Ghost. Particularly, when the Council of Constantinople met, about the year 381, there was no other contest about the Holy Ghost, but whether he was truly God or not: Therefore the great design of that Council was to settle that truth, and make it a part of the Creed. But that the procession of the Holy Ghost from the Father and the Son, was a truth received and taught in the church long before the Greeks denied it, is evident from divers ancient writers. A popish writer ‡, who is orthodox in this point, produceth fifteen Greek, and as many Latin witnesses, to prove this.

But may it not be said, that the Holy Ghost proceeds from the

---

(*l*) John xvi. 13, 14.

† Filioq. ‡ Pellarm. de Christo Lib. 2. c. 22.

the Father BY the Son? This form of speech is used by ancient writers in the Greek church, as Basil, Theophilact, Damascen ‡, Cyril *, and others. And, at the Council of Florence, about the year 1439, an union was endeavoured between the Greek and Latin churches, by proposing this term of speech to be agreed unto, viz. "That the Holy Ghost did proceed "from the Father by the Son, eternally and essentially; as from "one and the same principle." This was subscribed by divers members of that council, both Greeks and Latins: But the Greeks did afterward resile from what they had subscribed.

However, seeing the Greek church makes no difference in the consubstantiality of the persons, therefore divers learned men think, that FROM *the Son*, and BY *the Son*, in the sense of the Greek church, was but a strife about words, or a difference in the manner of speech. And indeed the last expression may admit of an orthodox meaning. For, though we ought not to say or think that the Holy Ghost proceeds from the Father by the Son, as he were principally from the Father, and secondarily or less principally from the Son; seeing the spirative virtue and efficacy is one and the same in both: Yet, if we look to their manner of subsistence, in regard whereof the Father is the fountain of the Deity, and the original of personal subsistence to the Son, then the expression may be admitted, viz that the Holy Ghost proceeds from the Father BY the Son, in regard of the order and manner of procession; for the generation of the Son is first in order before the procession of the Holy Ghost, according to our manner of conceiving. And besides, the expression seems to agree to the order of operation among the divine persons; for the Father worketh all things by the Son: But though the expression may, in this sense, be admitted; yet we are not so to understand it, as if the Holy Ghost did proceed only from the Father, and not also from the Son. He doth so proceed by the Son, as he doth also proceed from him. And this we hold and maintain upon the scriptural grounds before laid down, according to what is said in our Larger Catechism, viz. That "the Holy Ghost proceeds from the Fa- "ther and the Son from all eternity:" Which is plainly asserted also in the Athanasian Creed, in these words, " † The Ho-
"ly

---

‡ *Spiritum Sanctum esse per filium, sed non a filio.*
Damascen, Lib. de Orthod. fide Cap. 11.

* Πνεῦμα ἅγιον ἐκ τῦ πατρὸς δι υἱῶ προσερχόμενον, πατρὶ ᾗ υἱῶ ὁμοούσιες. Cyril. Patriarch. Constant. de Homolog. fidei.

† Τὸ πνεῦμα τὸ ἅγιον ἀπὸ τυ πατρὸς ᾗ τυ υἱῦ, ἢ πεπεμμένον, ὕτε δεδημιυργημένον, ὕτε γεγεννημένον, ἀλλ' ἐκπορευτόν.

"ly Ghost is of the Father and of the Son, not made, nor created, nor begotten, but proceeding."

Second, In the next place, I shall speak a little of the nature of this procession. It is indeed an incomprehensible mystery, so that the way and manner of it is inexplicable by any creature, much more by us in this state of imperfection. Yet something we may adventure to say of the nature of it, agreeably to what God hath revealed. In general, the procession of the Holy Ghost is not a change from not being to being; nor a progress from that which is imperfect to that which is more perfect; nor a removing from one place to another. But we may have some notion of it from what our Lord saith: *As the Father hath life in himself, so hath he given to the Son to have life in himself* (*m*). As the Father gave to the Son, so did the Father and Son give to the Holy Ghost, to have life in himself; which necessarily implies their giving to him the divine essence itself: And they could not give the essence to him by way of alienation, nor by way of participation; therefore it must be by way of communication. Hence it appears, that much of what I spoke concerning the generation of the Son, is applicable to the procession of the Holy Ghost; seeing both agree in this, that there is a communication of the divine essence, both in the one, and in the other. Hence,

The procession of the Holy Ghost is, his having the same individual divine essence which the Father and the Son have, communicated to him in a peculiar way, from the Father and the Son, that it may subsist after a different manner. So that the Holy Ghost hath the original of his personal subsistence from the Father and the Son jointly. I said, that the divine essence is communicated to the Holy Ghost, in a peculiar way and manner: As it is communicated to the Son by generation; so it is communicated to the Holy Ghost by spiration, or breathing. Hence he is called the Spirit; not in regard of his essence, for so the Father and the Son are also a Spirit; but in regard of his personal subsistence. He is the Spirit, in a singular manner proper to himself, as having his personal subsistence by spiration, or breathing. Hence, he is often called *the Spirit of God*, and *the Spirit of the Lord*, and *the Breath of the Almighty*, and *the Breath* (orig. *Spirit*) *of the Lord's mouth* (*n*). And many divines think that our blessed Lord did symbolically signify so much, when being to give the Spirit to his disciples, *he breathed on them, and said, Receive ye the Holy Ghost* (*o*).

From

(*m*) John v. 26.   (*n*) Job xxxiii. 4. Psal. xxxiii. 6.
(*o*) John xx 22.

From what is said it appears, that this breathing the Holy Ghost by the Father and the Son, is, that eternal act of the Father and the Son, whereby, in an ineffable manner, they did jointly communicate to the Holy Ghost, the same individual divine essence which they themselves have, that the Holy Ghost might have it equally with themselves. Several things we may notice in this description. 1. I say, the breathing the Holy Ghost is an eternal act. For, the Holy Ghost, being a divine person, must needs be eternal: And consequently, his procession by spiration, whereby he hath his personal subsistence, must be eternal also. 2. I said, that the Father and the Son did communicate to the Holy Ghost the divine essence; not a part of the essence, but the whole; so that the Holy Ghost hath the whole divine essence in himself, no less than the Father and the Son have. 3. I said, that they did communicate to him the same individual divine essence which they themselves have: For the divine essence is most perfectly one, and indivisible, and wholly incapable of any separate existence. 4. I said, that the Father and the Son did jointly communicate the essence: So that † although the Father and the Son be distinct persons, yet in this communication they are not to be considered as distinct principles, but as one principle, both concurring thereunto by their joint virtue and efficacy, which is the same in both. 5. I said, that they did communicate the essence to the Holy Ghost in an ineffable manner: For ‡, as the manner of the generation of the Son, so also the manner of the procession of the Holy Ghost, is incomprehensible, and what we poor creatures cannot account for.

Third, I proceed to speak a little of the difference between the generation of the Son, and the procession of the Holy Ghost. It is most certain and evident that they do differ. For, 1. To be begotten and to proceed, design different manners of subsistence in the divine essence, and so constitute distinct persons. The Son only is begotten; therefore he is called *the only begotten of the Father* (*p*) : He hath no fellow or co-partner in

---

† *Pater & filius sunt duo spirantes, propter pluralitatem suppositorum; non autem duo spiratores, propter unam Spirationem.*
   Thom. Aquin. Part. 1. Quest. 36. Act 4. ad 7.

‡ Ἀκύεις γέννησιν, τὸ πῶς μὴ περιεργάζυ: ἀκύεις τὸ προϊὸν ἐκ τῦ πατρὸς, τὸ ὅπως μὴ πολυπραγμόνει.
        Greg. Nazian. Orat. 29.

(*p*) John i. 14.

in his generation: So † that the Holy Spirit hath not the relation of a Son to the Father by his procession, as the second person hath by his generation. Again, the holy Spirit only proceeds, viz. by spiration; so that the Son hath not the relation of a Spirit to the Father by his generation, as the Holy Ghost hath by his procession. 2. By generation the Son hath the original of his personal subsistence from the Father alone: But by procession the Holy Ghost hath the original of his personal subsistence, both from the Father, and from the Son. 3. As the Son is the second person in order, and the Holy Ghost the third; so generation is first in order before spiration, according to our manner of conceiving, though both be eternal. 4 † By generation the Son hath not only a different manner of subsistence in the divine essence, but also a right or property, in conjunction with the Father, of communicating the same essence, that it may subsist after a different manner: But the Holy Spirit, by procession, hath only a different manner of subsistence in the divine essence, but no property of communicating the same essence to another person.

From these things it plainly appears that there is a difference between generation and spiration. This is so manifest that it cannot be denied. But how they differ; that is, how the manner of communicating the divine essence to the Son by generation, differs from the manner of communicating the same essence to the Holy Ghost by spiration; what the formal difference is, and wherein it lies, is wholly mysterious and ineffable. As the manner of generation and procession, so consequently the difference between them, is incomprehensible. Therefore the ancient learned fathers were not ashamed to profess their ignorance in this matter. " ‡ There is is a dif-
" ference," saith Augustine, " between generation and pro-
" cession: But I know not how to distinguish them, because
" both are ineffable " And elsewhere he saith, " § To dif-
" tinguish between procession and generation, I know not ; I
" have

---

* Πνεῦμα ἅγιον ἀληθῶς τὸ πνεῦμα, προιὸν μὲν ἐκ πατρὸς ὑἱ- κῶς δὲ ὐδὲ γὰρ γεννητῶς ἀλλ' ἐκπορευτῶς. Greg. Nazian. Orat. 39.

† *Pater talem genuit filium, ut quemadmodum de se, ita de illo quoque procedat Spiritus.* S. August. Serm. 38.

‡ *Est differentia inter Generationem & Processionem; sed ego distinguere nescio, quia utrumque inenarrabile.*
Aug. lib. 3. Cont Maxim. Cap. 14.

§ *Distinguere inter Processionem & Generationem, nescio, non valeo, non sufficio.* ibid.

" have no skill, I am not able." And to the same purpose Damascen, " * We learn that there is a difference between " generation and procession: But what is the manner of the " difference, we know not." Therefore the boldness of the schoolmen in attempting to explain the difference between them is unaccountable. Some men, by aspiring to hidden wisdom in this matter, have exalted their own folly: For their notions do rather raise and augment difficulties than remove them, and involve the matter rather than explain it. Therefore it is much more safe, modestly to profess our ignorance, than curiously to pry into this incomprehensible mystery. It is certainly no better than madness, for men to let their wit go at liberty, and play the wanton, in the deep things of God. Hence an old father, being urged to assign a difference between generation and procession, gave this answer, " † Tell thou me what generation is, and I will tell thee what " procession is, that we both may be mad."

Fourth, In the last place, I shall make some application of this head. Is it so, that the holy Spirit proceeds from the Father and the Son from all eternity; that he is of the same substance with them, and every way equal with them? Then,

1. Let us admire the love of God, in giving his holy Spirit to such vile unworthy creatures as we are. It is the great and high dignity and prerogative of all believers in Christ, that the holy Spirit is given to dwell in them. *He dwelleth with you*, says our Lord, *and shall be in you* (*q*). And says the apostle, *He that raised up Christ from the dead, shall also quicken your mortal bodies, by his Spirit that dwelleth in you* (*r*). And, *know ye not—that the Spirit of God dwelleth in you* (*s*)? Hence their bodies are called *temples of the Holy Ghost* (*t*). He is present in them in a special and gracious way. He is first of all in Christ their head, and then in believers as his members. He is really in them, and united to them. Now, the gift of the Spirit must needs be a precious and inexpressible gift, considering the infinite dignity and excellency of his person: He is very God, equal with the Father and the Son. O what astonishing love is this, that he should be given to vile sinners, slaves to Satan,

and

---

* Ὅτι μὲν ἐστὶ διαφορὰ γεννήσεως μεμαθήκαμεν; Τίς δὲ τρόπος διαφορᾶς, μηδαμῶς. Damascen. de Orth. Fide Lib. 4. Cap. 10.

† Dic tu mihi quid sit Generatio, & ego dicam quid sit Processio, ut ambo insaniamus. Gregor. Nazianz.

(*q*) John xiv. 17. (*r*) Rom. viii. 11. (*s*) 1 Cor. iii. 16. (*t*) 1 Cor. vi. 9.

and enemies to God! That a habitation of lusts and devils should be made a temple for the Holy Ghost!

2. Make it your great work and business to get the Spirit, to have the Holy Ghost dwelling in you. Consider, 1. How necessary this is. That is plain language, *If any man have not the Spirit of Christ, he is none of his* (*u*). That is, he doth not belong to him; he hath no interest in him, and so can have no benefit from him. You are dead in your sins, till you get the Spirit. He is as necessary to the spiritual life, as the soul is to the natural life. Without the Spirit, you cannot perform duties aright: You cannot worship God in the Spirit, nor pray in the Spirit (*x*). Though you multiply duties, yet God regards them not, if you have not the Spirit. And without the Spirit neither ordinances nor providences can have any saving fruit. 2. Consider the unspeakable advantages of having the Spirit. When you get the Spirit, he will quicken you, and raise you up to a new life: He will renew and sanctify you, and make you vessels meet for God's use and service: He will unite you to Christ, and make you partakers of him and the glorious blessings of his purchase: He will mortify and subdue your corruptions, heal your spiritual diseases and distempers, quicken, actuate, and assist your graces, and help and assist you in all your duties. In a word, when you have the holy Spirit dwelling in you, he will be to you a Spirit of illumination, a Spirit of wisdom, a Spirit of life, a Spirit of power, a Spirit of holiness, and a Spirit of prayer. O, how unspeakable are the advantages of having the Spirit!

Well then, be earnest to get the Spirit. And for this end, 1. Pray much for the Spirit. For, *God gives the Spirit to them that ask him* (*y*). God's promise of the Spirit should encourage you to prayer. We have a promise of the Spirit, Ezek. xxxvi. 27. *And I will put my Spirit within you, &c.* but mark what follows, verse 37. *Thus saith the Lord God, I will yet for this be enquired of by the house of Israel, to do it for them.* So that, prayer is a mean God hath appointed for bringing forth the promise of the Spirit to a performance. Pray earnestly from a sense of your need, and be very importunate: And pray in the name of Christ, who hath purchased the Spirit; for the *Spirit* is *sent in his name* (*z*). 2. Wait for the Spirit in all the ways and means of God's appointment. Diligently attend the public ordinances, especially the preaching of the gospel; for that

(*u*) Rom. viii. 9.   (*x*) See Rom. viii. 26, 27.   (*y*) Luke xi. 13.   (*z*) John xiv. 26.

that is the chariot in which the Spirit rides triumphantly, when he makes his entrance into the soul: Therefore it is called *the ministration of the Spirit* (a). 3. Resign and give up yourselves to the Spirit. Give him the key of your whole soul, that he may come and dwell in it; of your understanding, will, and affections. Let no room be shut against him. He can fill and replenish the whole soul. Give up your whole man to him, that even your bodies may be the temples of the Holy Ghost. He will have all, or nothing. Resign yourselves to him, to be enlightened, instructed and taught by him ; to be sanctified, cleansed, and adorned by him ; to be led, ruled, guided, and conducted by him. You must be heartily willing and desirous that he do his whole work in you.

3. Ye who have the Spirit, be careful to keep and retain him with you. Considering his infinite dignity and excellency, and the unspeakable advantages of his presence with you, he is well worth the keeping. And there is great danger of losing the Spirit. Though God will never take away his Spirit totally nor finally from believers; yet he may be taken away in a great measure, not only with respect to common gifts, but also with respect to special grace. The Spirit may be provoked to withdraw much of his presence, not only with respect to comforting influences, but also with respect to quickening and strengthening influences. Therefore let it be your great care to keep the Spirit.

For this end, 1. Get and entertain a holy fear, lest God take his holy Spirit from you. I mean a fear of caution and diligence, such as may put you upon preventive means. There is great cause of fear, considering your own vileness and guiltiness, the infinite purity and holiness of God, and the dreadful examples of God's taking away his Spirit in a great measure, even from eminent saints. 2. Be diligent in using and employing the gifts and graces of the Spirit, for the glory of God, and your own and others spiritual good. 3. Be much in the daily exercise of faith and repentance. O, lie not under the guilt of known sins. Make it your employment every day to have breaches made up between God and you. 4. Carry right toward the Spirit. Take heed of quenching, grieving, vexing, or resisting him in any of his operations. Take heed of banishing away the Spirit, by pride, vanity, idleness, security, or other evils. Take heed of rejecting his invitations, slighting his motions, refusing his suggestions. The holy Spirit is very sensible of, and will not easily put up your miscarriages

(a) 2 Cor. iii. 8.

riages toward him. Therefore be careful to give him good entertainment. Obey the Spirit, and walk in the Spirit. Cherish his motions and breathings; obey his counsels; follow his conduct. Take heed of neglecting duties to which you are strongly moved by the Spirit, and of committing sins contrary to clear light and conviction. 5. Be much in prayer. Be earnest in deprecating God's taking his Spirit from you. Pray with the psalmist, *Take not thy holy Spirit from me* (*b*). Make this a part of your daily prayer.

SERMON XCIX.

THUS I have discoursed of the personal properties of the three persons in the Godhead, viz. That it is the personal property of the Father to beget the Son, and of the Son to be begotten of the Father, and of the Holy Ghost to proceed from the Father and the Son from all eternity: And have shewed that these personal properties are the proper foundation of the distinction of the persons. Now, from these personal properties there arise other two things, wherein the distinction of the persons among themselves is plainly evident. As, 1. Their different order of subsistence: And, 2. Their different manner of working. And so I proceed to speak to you,

II. Of the order of subsistence among the divine persons.

The persons in the Godhead are distinguished also by their different order of subsistence. This order of subsistence appears, from the processions and relations arising out of that infinite sea of being. The second person proceeds from the Father by generation, and so hath the relation of a Son to the Father. The third person proceeds from the Father and the Son by spiration, and so hath the relation of a Spirit to them both, being therefore called *the Spirit of the Father*, and *the Spirit of the Son* (*a*). So that the Father is from none, the Son is from the Father, and the Holy Ghost from both; to wit, in regard of their personal subsistence. Therefore, in the holy scriptures, the Father is held forth as the first person, having the original of his personal subsistence in himself, and not from another; the Son is held forth as the second person, having the original of his personal subsistence from the Father; and the Holy Ghost is held forth as the third person, having the original of his personal susistence from the Father and the Son.

But

(*b*) Psal. li. 11.   (*a*) Matth. x. 20. Gal. iv. 6.

But when we say that the Father is the first person, this adds no excellency to the Father, nor derogates any thing from the Son or the Holy Ghost. For, 1. † It is not a priority of time or duration; as if the Father were before the Son and the Holy Ghost: For all the persons are co-eternal, eternity being an essential perfection of the divine essence. Nor, 2. Is it a priority of dignity or excellency: For each person hath the whole Godhead in himself, and consequently infinite and supreme dignity and excellency, which is an essential attribute of the Godhead. Nor, 3. Is it a priority of causality; as if the Father were properly the cause of the Son and of the Holy Ghost: For this would import a dependence, as there is of the effect upon the cause; and so neither the Son nor the Holy Ghost would be God. Nor, 4. Is it a priority of nature; seeing there is the same individual nature in all the three persons. But when the Father is said to be the first person, the Son the second, and the Holy Ghost the third; this priority is only a priority of order, which only respects their personal subsistence: So that the Father is the first person, the Son the second, and the Holy Ghost the third, in order of substance: Hence it is said, *As the Father hath life in himself, so hath he given to the Son to have life in himself* (*b*). Though independent and inexpressible life is common to all the persons in the unity of the divine essence: Yet the Father is first in order in having it, and hath given it to the Son, and so also to the Holy Ghost, by communicating to them the divine essence. And this doth not argue any inequality or inferiority in the Son or Holy Ghost, seeing they have the same life infinitely, independently, and equally with the Father; for the Son hath it in himself, and so also the Holy Ghost hath it in himself, as well as the Father.

In regard of this order of personal subsistence, the Father is frequently first named in scripture: As in the institution of baptism, and in my text, and elsewhere (*c*). It is true, the Son is sometimes named before the Father (*d*); and the Holy Spirit is placed sometimes before the Father (*e*), and sometimes before the Son (*f*). But that may be done, to shew their equality in majesty, glory and dignity: Or we may say, that it is done, for reasons respecting the œconomy of our salvation, wherein

---

† Ἐν ταύτῃ τῇ Τριάδι οὐδὲν πρῶτον ἢ ὕστερον οὐδὲν μεῖζον ἢ ἐλαττον. Ἀλλ᾽ ὅλαι αἱ τρεῖς ὑποστάσεις συνδιαιωνίζουσαι ἑαυταῖς εἰσὶ καὶ ἴσαι.

Athan. Symb.

(*b*) John v. 26.   (*c*) Math. xxviii 19. Rom. i. 7. 1 Cor i. 3.
(*d*) 2 Cor. xiii. 14. Gal. i. 1.   (*e*) Eph. ii. 18.   (*f*) Rev. i. 4, 5.

wherein the several persons have, by their own voluntary condescension, distinct offices and operations ascribed to them, according to their different order of subsistence in the divine essence. But most frequently the Father is first named. This order of personal subsistence is also implied in the Son's being called *the express image of his Father's person, and the image of the invisible God* (g). So that the Father is, as it were, * the original type, and the Son his express image or † character: Now, the original type is before its image or character. Therefore divines ascribe a kind of eminency to the Father, not in regard of the divine essence, which is one and the same in all the three persons; but in regard of the manner of his subsistence, having his subsistence from none, and being the original of personal subsistence to the Son and Holy Ghost. Hence he is called by the ancient Fathers, ‡ *the Fountain of the Deity;* not absolutely, as to its existence; but respectively, as to its communication to the other persons. Therefore it is that the name GOD is so often, peculiarly, and by way of eminency, given to the Father in scripture (h).

III. Of the order and manner of working among the divine Persons.

The distinction of the divine persons among themselves is manifest also in their different manner of working; to wit, in their external works, which have the creature for their object.

Most true it is, that in these external works all the divine persons concur jointly: They belong to one person as well as another. Hence they are called essential works, because they are common to all the three persons in the unity of the divine essence. The Father, Son, and Spirit, being one in essence, § are undivided in operation and working. Hence our Lord saith, *My Father worketh hitherto, and I work.* The Father's work and his, are one and the same. And *what things soever the Father doth, these also doth the Son likewise* (i). Hence is that theological maxim ‖, " The external works of the holy Trini-" ty are undivided:" They are equally common to all the three persons. And they are so in a twofold respect. 1. With respect to the principle of operation. The operative virtue and efficacy, whereby these works are what they are, is essential, and

---

(g) Heb. i. 3. Col. i. 15.   (h) John i. 1, 2. Matth. xvi. 16. Heb. i. 1, 2. and elsewhere   (i) John v. 17, 19.

* Αρχιτυπος.   † Εκτυπωμα.   ‡ Πηγαῖα θεότης.

§ *Trinitas inseparabiliter operatur.* Aug. de Trint. L. 4. C. 21.

‖ *Opera Trinitatis ad extra sunt indivisa.*

and consequently one and the same, and common to all the three persons. Their will, power, and wisdom, are one and the same, undivided: And the same individual act is the act of all the persons. 2. With respect to the effect and work itself. There is not a different effect from the Father, which is not from the Son; nor from the Son, which is not from the Spirit: But they so concur in an united way, that what cometh from one, cometh from all *. So that all the persons are one immediate and perfect cause of every external work. Therefore in such works, † when only one person or two are named, the whole Trinity is to be understood. Hence it is that equal honour and glory is due from us to all the persons.

But though the external works of God are undivided, and common to all the persons; yet there is a difference in the manner of working. This different manner of working is that whereby each person worketh according to his distinct manner of subsistence. ‡ Their manner of working upon the creature is answerable to their manner of subsistence in the divine essence. This different manner of working is seen in these two: 1. In their order of operation. 2. In the termination of the action. I shall begin with the last, because I intend to insist upon the first.

First, In the termination of the action: When some divine action or operation terminates in one of the persons. So, at Christ's baptism (*k*), ‖ The voice that came from heaven was terminate in the person of the Father; the apparition in the shape of a dove, in the person of the Holy Ghost; and the manifestation in the flesh, in the person of the Son. Yet all these actions or operations, were effectively the actions of the whole Trinity. This is more plain and evident in the incarnation of the Son. All the persons did jointly concur therein, according to the order of working proper to each of them. As the Son did assume a human nature to be his own: So, the Holy Ghost was the immediate agent in framing his body, and uniting

---

* *Miro itaque eodemque utique divino modo, ab omnibus fiunt opera omnium, ab omnibus etiam singulorum.*
August. Lib contra Serm. Arian. Cap. 15.

† *Quando unus trium in aliquo Opere nominatur, universa operari Trinitas intelligitur.* August. Enchirid. Cap. 38.

‡ *Modus operandi sequitur modum Subsistendi.*

‖ *Vocem de Cælo super Filium post Baptismum Trinitas fecit: Et tamen non pertinet nisi ad Patrem.* Ambros. in Symb Apost. C. 9.

(*k*) Matth. iii.

ing the human to the divine. *The Holy Ghost shall come upon thee*, says the angel to Mary, *and the power of the Highest shall overshadow thee* (*l*). And the Father did contrive and order it: What the Spirit did, was according to the counsel and will of the Father: It was his work by the Spirit: *A body*, says Christ, *hast thou prepared me* (*m*). These are the words of the Son to the Father, to whom the preparation of Christ's body is assigned in a peculiar manner. So, that, † effectively, it was the work of all the persons: His body, or human nature, was prepared by the Father, wrought by the Holy Ghost, and assumed by the Son. Yet terminatively, it was the work of the Son only: For, neither the Father, nor the Holy Ghost, were incarnate, but only the Son; the human nature being assumed to subsist in his person alone.

Second, In their order of working. There is an order in the operation, as well as in the subsistence of the three persons. All the persons are equal, but their order of working is different. ‖ The Father worketh from himself, by the Son, and by the Holy Ghost: The Son worketh from the Father, by the Holy Ghost: The Holy Ghost worketh from the Father and the Son, by himself. This order of working follows the order of subsistence, and is agreeable thereunto: And it is declared in scripture by these expressions, of the Father's sending the Son, and of the Father and Son, their sending the Spirit. I shall therefore speak a little of the order of working proper to each person in the Godhead; and then observe some things concerning the same, for preventing mistakes and curbing vain curiosity.

1. Then, the Father being the original and fountain of the Deity, in respect of subsistence, is also the original and fountain of all divine works in respect of order. Hence all things are said to be of him: *To us*, says the apostle, *there is but one God, the Father, of whom are all things* (*n*). And all things are referred to him by the Son, as the original and first principle of action. *Verily, verily*, says he, *I say unto you, the Son can do nothing of himself, but what he seeth the Father do; for what things soever he doth, these also doth the Son likewise* (*o*). This place the ancient

---

† *Incarnationem verbi Trinitas fecit; et tamen non pertinet Incarnatio nisi ad Verbum.* Ambros. U. S.

‖ Ο Πατὴρ διὰ τȣ λόγȣ ἐν πνεύματι ἁγίῳ τὰ πάντα ποιεῖ.
 Oper. Tom. 1. Epist. 1. ad Serap.

(*l*) Luke i. 35.   (*m*) Heb. x. 5.   (*n*) 1 Cor. viii. 6.
(*o*) John v. 19.

ancient fathers underſtood of Chriſt, as the ſecond perſon, not as Mediator. The Father firſt ſets the copy, after which the Son writes: So that the order of working begins from the Father. Hence he is often called by the fathers, * *The Fountain of the Deity, and of operation.* Being the firſt perſon, in order of ſubſiſtence, he is alſo firſt in order of operation; and having communicated the divine eſſence to the Son and the Holy Ghoſt, he doth alſo, by them, communicate the effects of divine wiſdom, power, and goodneſs: So that he works by them both.

(1.) He works by the Son. All things are of the Father by the Son. So the apoſtle tells us, *There is but one God, the Father,* OF *whom are all things;—and one Lord Jeſus Chriſt,* BY *whom are all things* (*p*). Of the Father, as the fountain; and by the Son, as the medium. Hence the Father is ſaid to ſend the Son (*q*); not only as man, but as God; for the Holy Spirit, who hath only a divine nature, is ſaid to be ſent by the Father and the Son. All the effects of divine power, wiſdom, and goodneſs, are communicated to the creature, immediately by and through the perſon of the Son. I give inſtance of this in a few things. 1. In the work of creation. God the Father *created all things* BY *Jeſus Chriſt: All things were made* BY *him: And* BY *him God made the worlds* (*r*). All were made by him, as the power and wiſdom of the Father. So it is ſaid, *All things were created* BY *him, and* FOR *him* (*s*). Becauſe all were created for him, therefore all were created by him. Becauſe he was to be the head of the elect kingdom which God intended to eſtabliſh by him; therefore in the firſt creation, he was as the head of all God's works. 2. In upholding all things. BY *him all things conſiſt* (*t*). God ſupports the whole creation by his Son. By him it is kept from ſinking into its original nothing. With reſpect to this our Lord ſaith, *My Father worketh hitherto, and I work* (*u*). The care of continuing the creation is given and committed to the Son, as he that hath undertaken to retrieve and bring forth the glory of God in it, notwithſtanding of the great breach made upon it by ſin. 3. In the providential rule and diſpoſal of all things. This is done alſo in and by the Son: For *the Father judgeth no man, but hath committed all judgment unto the Son* (*x*). *All judgment*—That is, ſupreme

---

* *Fons Divinitatis & Operationis.*

(*p*) 1 Cor. viii. 6. (*q*) John v. 24, 30. and x. 36. Rom. viii. 3. Gal. iv. 4. (*r*) Eph. iii. 9. John i. 3. Heb. i. 2. (*s*) Col. i. 16. (*t*) Col. i. 17. (*u*) John v. 17. (*x*) John v. 22.

supreme dominion and sovereignty over all the creatures, and the government and administration of all things in heaven and earth; this is committed by the Father to the Son. It is not to be understood only of the dominion over all things given to him as Mediator for the good of the church; for Christ's scope there, is to prove his conjunction and equality with the Father: Therefore it is to be understood chiefly of his government and administration of all things, as God equal with the Father. This is committed to the Son by the Father, in communicating to him the same divine essence. The Father doth not any particular act of government without the Son, but exerts them all by him. It is by him that he exerteth his power and the efficacy of his providence, in ruling and governing the whole creation. Some judicious divines think that this is what is emblematically expressed in Ezekiel's vision (*y*), wherein the providence of God in ruling the whole creation, is represented by a chariot of cherubims; and the Son of God is represented in the form of a man, ruling and disposing of all things, and as the Almighty whose voice was heard among the wheels. 4. In all the gracious revelations and communications of himself and his will. It is the very substance and end of the gospel, to reveal the Father to us by and in the Son, and to declare that we can have no acquaintance or communion with the Father but through him. So the evangelist tells us, *No man hath seen God at any time: The only begotten Son, who is in the bosom of the Father, he hath declared him* (*z*). And our blessed Lord says, *Neither knoweth any man the Father, save the Son, and he to whomsoever the Son will reveal him* (*a*). And so it is also, as to all the communications of his Spirit and grace: All is by the Son; as, the Lord willing, I may shew afterward.

(2.) The Father works also by the Holy Ghost. So the psalmist tells us, *By the Word of the Lord were the heavens made; and all the host of them, by the Breath of his mouth* (*b*). Orig. *By the Spirit of his mouth*. And the apostle says, *God hath revealed them unto us* BY *his Spirit*: And, *He that raised up Christ from the dead, shall also quicken your mortal bodies,* BY *his Spirit that dwelleth in you* (*c*). So that the Father worketh by the Spirit. Hence he is said to *send the Spirit*: And the *Spirit* is called *the Power of the Highest* (*d*); that is, of the Father; because it is by him that the Father exerteth the divine power in all external works.

So

(*y*) Ezek. i. (*z*) John i. 18.
(*a*) Matth. xi. 27. (*b*) Psal xxxiii. 6. (*c*) 1 Cor. ii. 10. Rom. viii. 11. (*d*) John xiv. 26, 28. Luke i. 35.

So much for the order of working proper to the Father.

2. The Son, being the second person in order of subsistence, is also second in order of operation. Having his subsistence, as the second person, from the Father, he doth also work from him: And having, in conjunction with the Father, communicated the divine essence to the Holy Ghost, he doth also work by him, no less than the Father doth.

(1.) The Son works from the Father. As the Son is from the Father, in order of subsistence; so the actions of the Son are from the Father, in order of motion and direction: For *the Son can do nothing of himself, but what he seeth the Father do: For what things soever he doth, these also doth the Son likewise* (d). When it is said, that the *Son doth nothing of himself*, this doth not exclude his own proper power as God, but holds forth that, in order of working, he works from the Father; which is also intended, when he saith, *I can of mine own self do nothing* (e). This is further confirmed by that expression, that he *doth what he seeth the Father do:* Which is not to be so understood, as if the Son's work were posterior to the Father's, and done in imitation of his: But it is a borrowed expression suited to our capacity, pointing out that ineffable communication, whereby the Father communicates to the Son, his nature, will, wisdom and power; so that, as he is from the Father, in order of subsistence, so he works from him, in order of operation. Hence he is said to *come out from the Father* (f), and to *come in his Father's name* (g), and to *work in his Father's name* (h).

(2.) He works by the holy Spirit. So it is said, that in the days of Noah, *Christ went and preached by his Spirit to the spirits now in prison.* Hence he is said *to send the Spirit;* and the Spirit is said to glorify Christ (i), by communicating what he receives from him. Whatever the Spirit communicates to believers, he receives from Christ, and thereby glorifies him as the storehouse of his people.

3. The Holy Ghost, being the third person in order of subsistence, is also third in order of operation. Having his subsistence as the third person, from the Father and the Son, he doth also work from them. He works as sent by the Father and the Son. To this purpose our Lord speaks: *Howbeit, when he, the Spirit of truth, is come, he will guide you into all truth: For he shall not speak of himself, but whatsoever he shall hear, that shall he*

(d) John v 19. (e) Verse 30. (f) John xvi. 28. and xvii. 8. (g) John v. 43. (h) John x 25. (i) 1 Pet. iii 19. John xv. 26. and xvi. 7, 14.

he speak; and he will shew you things to come. He shall glorify me, for he shall receive of mine, and shall shew it unto you. All things that the Father hath are mine: Therefore said I, that he shall take of mine, and shall shew it unto you (k). The Spirit doth not speak of himself, but what he hears from others, viz. from the Father and the Son. All these precious truth, gifts and graces, which the Spirit communicates to believers, are communicated by him from the Father and the Son.

Ere I proceed, let me make some application.

Use 1. Let us improve what hath been said for confirming our faith about the distinction of the persons in the unity of the divine essence. For, we see that the Father hath an order of working that is not proper to the Son or Holy Ghost; and the Son hath an order of working that is not proper to the Father or Spirit; and the Holy Spirit hath an order of working that is not proper to the Father or the Son: So that the Son is a distinct person from the Father, and the Holy Ghost a distinct person from both.

Use 2. Let us admire this order of working amongst the divine persons. It is indeed a deep mystery, as to the way and manner how it is: Therefore it is a subject more fit for admiration, than for curious search and inquiry. Certainly it becomes us to curb and restrain our curiosity in the deep things of God.

Use 3. Give equal glory of all the external works of God to all the three persons, Father, Son, and Holy Ghost. For though they have a different order of working, yet they all concur in every external work. What cometh from one cometh from all. You have nothing from the Son, but what you have from the Father and Spirit; and you have nothing from the Spirit, but what you have from the Father and the Son. Therefore give equal glory of all external works, and particularly of all the mercies and blessings you receive and enjoy, to all the three persons, to Father, Son, and Holy Ghost.

SERMON C.

I COME, in the next place, to observe some things about this order of working among the divine persons, for preventing mistakes, and curbing vain curiosity. *Obs* 1. When the Father is said to work by the Son, and the Father and Son, by the Holy Ghost, this is not to be so understood, as if one person did work by another, as an intermediate cause, or a subordinate

---

(*k*) John xvi. 13, 14, 15.

subordinate instrument. For, † the operation of the Son is not diverse from the operation of the Father, nor is the operation of the Holy Ghost diverse from that of the Father and Son. The Father, Son, and Spirit, being one in essence, are also undivided in operation and working: And the distinction of a mediate and immediate cause hath place only there where there is a diversity of essences and operations. But one person is said to work by another as the principal efficient. The Father worketh by the Son, as his own eternal Word, Wisdom, and Power; and the Father and Son work by the Holy Ghost, as the Power of the Highest. So that one person's working by another, infers no subordination but their different order of subsistence and working. *Obs.* 2. This order of working amongst the divine persons, doth not derogate from the supreme dignity of the Son and Holy Ghost. Our blessed Lord makes a sufficient proviso for his own dignity, when he testifies, that *what things soever the Father doth, these also doth the Son likewise* (a). He doth the same things, and he doth them *likewise*, or *in like manner* ‡. As there is an unity in the works themselves, so also in the manner of them, the order of operation being observed. As the Son is joint with the Father in all external works; so he is equal with him in doing them, working them *even so* as the Father worketh them: For *as the Father raiseth up the dead, and quickeneth them: Even so the Son quickeneth whom he will* (b). He quickeneth them even so as the Father doth; and he quickeneth whom he will. He works by the same power and authority, and absolute freedom of will with the Father. The Son, in his working, is absolute, sovereign, and independent, as well as the Father. And as this order of working, doth not derogate from the supreme dignity of the Son; so, by parity of reason, it doth not in the least derogate from the supreme dignity of the Holy Ghost. *Obs.* 3. This order of working, as to the way and manner of it, is incomprehensible by our understanding. That the Father worketh by the Son, and the Father and Son by the Holy Ghost; that the Son worketh from the Father, and the Holy Ghost from both, is a truth plainly revealed; and the way and manner how this is, is certainly most excellent and glorious, and infinitely perfect: Yet it is wonderful and admirable. It is a deep mystery, to be admired

(a) John v. 19.   (b) John v 21.
* *Operatur Sancta Trinitas una simplici atque indivisa Operatione, ἀμερίστως, καὶ ἀδιαστάτως.* Forbes. Instr. Histor. Theol. L. 1. C. 10.
‡ ὁμοίως.

mired rather than searched; for we cannot *by searching find out God.*

But though the order of working amongst the divine persons, as to the way and manner of it, be incomprehensible: Yet, being a thing plainly revealed, as to the τὸ ὅτι, *that it is;* and some distinctness in our apprehensions thereof, being necessary to the right understanding of the holy scriptures; and it being our unquestionable duty, to study the knowledge of God, so far as he hath been pleased to reveal himself: Let us therefore take this matter a little further into our consideration.

This different order of working among the divine persons, may be discovered and observed, 1. In the same works. 2. In different works.

(1.) In the same works. Though there is a joint concurrence of the three persons in all external works; yet do they concur even in the same work, according to their manner and order of subsistence in the divine essence. So, the original of the action is ascribed to the Father; the manner of working, to the Son; and the efficacy of operation, to the Holy Ghost. Again, the original or principle of the action is ascribed to the Father, who worketh from himself, by the Son and the Holy Ghost. So, it is said by the apostle, 1 Cor. viii. 6. *There is one God, the Father, of whom are all things.* To the Son is ascribed the administration or dispensation of the action, from the Father, by the Holy Ghost *. To this purpose the apostle adds, *And one Lord Jesus Christ,* by *whom are all things.* To the Holy Ghost is ascribed the consummation of the action, which he effects from the Father and the Son. *But all these worketh that one and the self-same Spirit, dividing to every man severally as he will* (c.) In this sense one of the ancients † calls the Father the Author or Original ‡, the Son the Administrator or Worker §, and the Holy Ghost the consummator or perfecter ‖. Take this one instance. The work of creation belongs to all the three persons; they did all jointly concur therein:

(c) 1 Cor. xii. 11.

* Πᾶσα ἐνέργεια ἡ θεόθεν ἐπὶ τὴν κτίσιν διήκουσα ἐκ πατρὸς ἀφορμᾶται, ᾗ διὰ τοῦ υἱοῦ πρόεισι, ᾗ ἐν τῷ πνεύματι τῷ ἁγίῳ τελειοῦται.
     Greg. Nyss. Lib. ad Ablab.

† Greg. Nazianz. Orat. 24

‡ Αἴτιος. § Δημιουργός. ‖ Τελειοποιῶν.

Ὁ πατὴρ δι᾽ υἱοῦ λόγῳ ἐν τῷ πνεύματι κτίζει τὰ πάντα.
    Athan. Oper. Tom. 2. Epist. 1. ad Serap.

therein: Yet they did concur according to their different order of subsistence and operation. For, 1. The work of creation, in regard of authority and order, doth peculiarly belong unto the Father. *He spake, and it was done: he commanded, and it stood fast* (*d*). And the apostle John tells us, *The four and twenty elders fell down before him that sat on the throne, saying, Thou art worthy, O Lord, to receive glory, and honour, and power: For thou hast created all things, and for thy pleasure they are and were created* (*e*). By *him that sat upon the throne*, we are to understand the Father; for he is spoken of as distinct from the Lamb, who is said to be *in the midst of the throne and of the four beasts* (*f*). So that all things were created at the Father's command and order, and for accomplishing his will and pleasure. 2. The same work of creation, in regard of immediate operation, peculiarly belongs to the Son: For the Father *created all things* BY *Jesus Christ*; and *all things were made* BY *him* (*g*): BY him, as the Power and Wisdom of the Father. 3. The same work of creation, in regard of disposition and ornament, doth peculiarly belong to the Holy Ghost. So it is said, *The Spirit of God moved upon the face of the waters* (*h*), viz. To garnish and adorn the world, after the matter of it was formed: For, *By his Spirit he hath garnished the heavens* (*i*).

(2.) In different works. Though all the works of God concerning the creature are wrought equally and inseparably by all the three persons; yet each person hath that work peculiarly ascribed to him, wherein his manner and order of subsistence doth most eminently appear. I give instance of this, 1. In the works of nature. 2. In the works of grace.

1. In the works of nature. So, the creation of all things is ascribed to the Father; the preserving and sustaining all things, to the Son; and the replenishing and filling all things, to the Holy Ghost. 1. The creating all things, being the first work, is ascribed to the Father, who is the first person in order. Texts of scripture might be multiplied to this purpose. Hence the Father is called *Lord of heaven and earth* (*k*). And in the Creed, commonly called The Apostle's, he is called *Maker of heaven and earth*. 2. The preserving and sustaining all things, being the second work, is ascribed to the Son, who is the second person in order. So it is said, he *upholdeth all things by the word of his power* (*l*). The upholding the world, and preserving

(*d*) Psal. xxxiii. 9.   (*e*) Rev. iv. 10, 11.   (*f*) Rev. v. 6.
(*g*) Eph iii. 9 John i. 2.   (*h*) Gen. i. 2.   (*i*) Job xxvi. 13.
(*k*) Matth. xi. 25.   (*l*) Heb. i. 2.

serving it from a dissolution because of man's sin, is peculiarly ascribed to the Son, as head of the creation, he having undertaken to retrieve the glory of God in it. The blessed Son of God preserves and upholds the world, as a stage whereon the glorious perfections of God were to be displayed in the great work of redemption; as in the purchase, so also in the application of it. 3. The replenishing and filling all things, being the the third work, is ascribed to the Holy Ghost, who is the third person in order. Of filling the hearts of the elect with grace, I shall speak afterward. Now I speak of filling men with common gifts. This work is appropriated to the holy Spirit. It is he that fits men for rule and government. After Saul was anointed king, it is said, *God gave him another heart:* and, *The Spirit of God came upon him* (m). All the gifts that even wicked kings, princes, and judges have, to fit and qualify them for government and the administration of justice, are the common works of the Spirit. So also light and knowledge in arts and sciences. Though this be ascribed to the Son, of whom it is said, that he *lighteth every man that cometh into the world* (n): Yet it is so his work as it is done by the Spirit; for he works by the Spirit. Again, skill in common arts and employments is from the Spirit. Hence Bezaleel is said to be *filled with the Spirit of God in wisdom, and in understanding, and in knowledge, and in all manner of workmanship: To devise cunning works; to work in gold, and in silver, and in brass, &c.* (o). All the skill and art that men have in their lawful callings and employments; all mens natural and acquired parts, gifts, and endowments; *All these worketh that one and the self-same spirit* (o), for the common good of mankind, and the support of human society. So that, though all the divine persons be equal, and work inseparably in all external works; yet one operation is ascribed to the Father, another to the Son, and another to the Holy Ghost, in regard of order:

II. In the works of grace. Here I shall speak of the order of working proper to each person of the Deity in the business of our salvation, and of the distinct offices and operations ascribed to them therein, in the holy scriptures, according to their different manner and order of subsistence in the divine essence. This a most useful and profitable doctrine, and highly necessary in order to the right understanding of the admirable expressions used in the holy scriptures, especially in the New Testament,

---

(*m*) 1 Sam. x. 9. and xi. 6. (*n*) John i 9. (*o*) Exod. xxxi. 2, 4, 5. and xxxv. 31, 32, 33. (*p*) 1 Cor. xii. 11.

Testament, concerning the operations of the holy Trinity in the business of our redemption and salvation; and that we may know and understand how to act faith aright on the blessed persons, and how to address ourselves to them in our worship. Unless this doctrine be rightly understood, we cannot know, or give any satisfying account, how the Son could make satisfaction to divine justice, seeing he is one and the same God with the Father and the Holy Ghost; why the Father is most frequently called God, &c. Yea, without some competent knowledge of this doctrine, scarce one page in the New Testament can be rightly understood.

In the holy scriptures there are different operations ascribed to the several persons in the business of our salvation, according to their distinct manner and order of subsistence. The original or beginning of our salvation is from God the Father; the dispensation is by the Son; and the application is through the Holy Ghost. Hence, election is ascribed to the Father, redemption to the Son, and sanctification to the Holy Ghost. See some texts of scripture to this purpose. As, 1. Pet i. 2. *Elect according to the foreknowledge of God the Father, through sanctification of the Spirit unto obedience, and sprinkling of the blood of Jesus Christ.* Here, election, which is the fundamental cause of salvation, is ascribed to the Father; reconciliation to the Son, and sanctification to the Spirit, as the means by which the purpose of the Father's electing love is brought about. Next, Tit. iii. 4, 5, 6. *But after that the kindness and love of God, our Saviour, toward man appeared: not by works of righteousness which we have done, but according to his mercy, he saved us, by the washing of regeneration, and renewing of the Holy Ghost; which he shed on us abundantly, through Jesus Christ our Saviour.* God the Father, out of his love and kindness to lost elect sinners, sent his Son to purchase salvation for them; and this purchased salvation is applied by the Holy Ghost, in his renewing and changing our natures. Again, 2 Thess ii. 13, 14. *God hath from the beginning chosen you to salvation, through sanctification of the Spirit, and belief of the truth, whereunto he called you by our gospel, to the obtaining of the glory of our Lord Jesus Christ.* God the Father did, from all eternity, chuse some to salvation and eternal glory; the Son purchased this glory for them, called therefore *the glory of our Lord Jesus Christ;* and this purchase is applied through the sanctification of the Spirit. See also the Apostolical Benediction, 2 Cor. xiii. 14. *The grace of the Lord Jesus Christ, and the love of God, and the communion of the Holy Ghost, be with you all. Amen.* Where, 1. Love, as the fountain of all, is afcribed to the Father, who is here called God by way of eminency. The Father, being the firft perfon in order, is reprefented as the fountain of all fpiritual bleffings, out of love to loft finners, and as expreffing and exerting his love by the Son and Holy Ghoft; therefore the love of the Father is affigned as the caufe of all. *God fo loved the world, that he gave his only begotten Son. God loved us, and fent his Son to be the propitiation for our fins* (*q*). 2. Grace is afcribed to the Son, our Lord Jefus Chrift; becaufe what is intended by the Father, is brought about for us by the grace of the Redeemer; that is, by his gracious condefcenfion, in fubmitting himfelf to a mean and afflicted condition for our fake. This is called the grace of Chrift: *Ye know the grace of our Lord Jefus Chrift*, fays the apoftle, *that though he was rich, yet for your fakes he became poor, that ye through his poverty might be rich* (*r*). 3. We have here the communion of the Holy Ghoft: Original, *the communication*. This is afcribed to the Holy Ghoft, becaufe all is applied and communicated to us by him, in his renewing and changing our natures, working faith in us, and drawing us to Chrift, fanctifying us, and making us holy, &c. So then, what the Father intended to the elect, the Son purchafeth, and the Holy Ghoft applieth †. The Father is as the fountain of grace; the Son is as the conduit or pipe to convey it to us; and the Holy Ghoft is the immediate operator and worker of it. So that the divine perfons work to each other's hands: The Father maketh way for the Son's work, and the Son for the Spirit's work.

In this the wifdom of God doth moft clearly fhine forth unto us: For, this order of things is moft agreeable to the order of the divine perfons, and their manner of fubfiftence in the divine effence. It was not congruous that the Father fhould be our Redeemer; becaufe, being the firft perfon in order, he is reprefented as fupreme Judge to whom fatisfaction was to be made. It was not agreeable that the Father fhould appear before the tribunal of the Son; or that the Son fhould be in the place of the Judge, and the Father in the place of the criminal; or that the Father fhould be bruifed by the Son, as the Son was by the Father: And the Father being the firft perfon,

(*q*) John iii. 16. 1 John iv. 10.   (*r*) 2 Cor. viii. 9.

† Ἡ γὰρ διδομένη χάρις ᾗ δωρεά, ἐν τριάδι δίδοται παρὰ πατρὸς δι υἱοῦ ἐν πνεύματι ἁγίῳ. Athan. Oper Tom. 1. Epift. 1. ad Serap.

Dilectio Dei mifit nobis Salvatorem, cujus Gratia Salvati Sumus; ut poffideamus hanc Gratiam, Communicatio facit Spiritus.

Ambrof. in 2 Cor. xiii. 13.

son, could not be sent by the Son, as the Son was by the Father. The order of the persons in the blessed Trinity had then been inverted. In the next place, it was not agreeable that the Holy Ghost should be our Redeemer; that he should purchase redemption for us, and that the Son should apply that redemption: Because then the Spirit, who is third in order, had been second in operation; and the Son, who is second in order, had been third in operation. As the holy Spirit, proceeding from the Father and the Son, is the third person in order: So his proper operation must be in order after the operations of the Father and the Son. As election precedes redemption, so redemption precedes the application of it: And according to the order of these works, is the order of the operation of the three persons. Election, which is the first work, belongs to the Father, who is the first person in order: Redemption, which is the second work, belongs to the Son, who is the second person; and the application, being the third work, belongs to the Holy Ghost, who is the third person.

SERMON CI.

BUT this being a doctrine of great use, and necessary to the right understanding the holy scriptures, especially in what concerns our salvation and redemption; therefore let us view a little more particularly, the distinct offices and operations that the blessed persons have in the work of our redemption, by their own voluntary condescension, and their joint consent and agreement, according to the manner and order of subsistence proper to each person. And here I shall discourse a little of the works and operations ascribed, 1. To the Father. 2. To the Son, And, 3. To the Holy Ghost, in the business of our salvation.

First, The Father being the first person in order, is represented in Scripture, as sustaining and defending the Majesty, and maintaining the rights of the Deity, in the business of our salvation. Hence he is so often called God in scripture, and much more frequently than the Son or the Holy Ghost are. Yea, in the same verse wherein all the persons are mentioned, the Father is called God by way of eminency; as in the Apostolical Benediction (a). Therefore to the Father are attributed in scripture such works and operations as belong to the offices of Lawgiver, and supreme Judge and Governor. So the apostle tells us, *There is one Law-giver, who is able to save*

and

(a) 2 Cor. xiii. 14.

and to destroy (b). And the prophet says, *The Lord is our Judge, the Lord is our Lawgiver, the Lord is our King* (c). And the Father is called *Lord of heaven and earth* (d). To him it belongs, according to his order of subsistence, to avenge a broken law, to judge what satisfaction was fit for the violation of it, and to determine and order all things concerning the salvation of sinners according to his pleasure.

Particularly, these operations that are, in the holy scriptures, ascribed to the Father, in the business of our salvation, may be considered in a twofold respect.

1. With respect to his eternal purpose of salvation. And so, election is peculiarly ascribed to the Father; as in that text, *Blessed be the God and Father of our Lord Jesus Christ, who hath blessed us—according as he hath chosen us in him before the foundation of the world* (e). God the Father, from all eternity, elected from amongst the lost posterity of Adam, whom he pleased, to everlasting life. Therefore, all is referred by our Lord to his good pleasure. *I thank thee*, says he, *O Father, Lord of heaven and earth, because thou hast hid these things from the wise and prudent, and hast revealed them unto babes. Even so, Father, for so it seemed good in thy sight* (f). Consequently, all the means, for accomplishing the ends of election, are of the Father's appointment; and particularly, the redemption of lost elect sinners, by the death and sufferings of his own dear Son. Therefore it is said, that *he hath chosen us in Christ* (g). The Father did first, in order of nature, chuse Christ to the mediatory office, and as the chief Corner-Stone to bear up the whole building; whence he is called *God's Elect* (h): And then he chose a company of lost sinners to be saved by and through Christ; therefore he is said to *predestinate them to be conformed to the image of his Son* (i). Hence the Father is represented in scripture, as the grand Author and Contriver of redemption, who laid down the whole platform thereof in his eternal purpose, according to his own pleasure. *Being predestinated*, says the apostle, *according to the purpose of him, who worketh all things after the counsel of his own will* (k). It was the Father that appointed Christ the Son to the mediatory office, to assume our nature, and to give himself a sacrifice for us; and so set him up as a skreen between an injured Deity and an offending creature. All is referred to the will of the Father by our Saviour; *Then said I, Lo, I come—I delight to do thy will, O my God*. And

says

(b) James iv. 12. (c) Isa. xxxiii. 22. (d) Matth xi. 25. (e) Eph i. 3, 4. (f) Matth xi. 25, 26. (g) Eph. i. 4. (h) Isa. xlii. 1. (i) Rom. viii. 29. (k) Eph. i. 11.

says he elswhere, *I came not to do mine own will, but the will of him that sent me* (*l*)

From what is said, it appears, that all spiritual blessings do originally spring from the Father: All the eternal counsels, contrivances, and resolves about them, are acts of his free grace. Therefore all are said to be *the mystery of his will, according to his good pleasure, which he purposed in himself* (*m*). And the apostle distinguisheth the Father from the Son by this character; *There is is one God, the Father,* OF WHOM *are all things; and one Lord Jesus Christ,* BY WHOM *are all thing* (*n*). The Father is the first mover and contriver of all spiritual blessings for us: *Of him are all things.* Therefore the whole work of redemption is often, in the Old Testament, called *God's salvation;* and in the New Testament, *the will of the Father.*

2. With respect to the accomplishment of his eternal purpose, in the fulness of time. And so, the works and operations ascribed to the Father, according to his order of subsistence, in the business of our salvation, may be considered, 1. With respect to Christ. 2. With respect to the Spirit. And, 3. With respect to the elect.

(1.) With respect to Christ. And, 1. The Father sent him into the world. *Neither came I of myself,* says our Saviour, *but he sent me* (*o*). And the Father sent him forth on this very errand, to purchase redemption for lost elect sinners, *to redeem them that were under the law* (*p*) 2. The Father fitted him for the undertaking. (1.) By giving him a body or human nature to be a sacrifice. *A body hast thou prepared me* (*q*), says Christ. (2.) By the gifts and graces of the Spirit conferred upon his human nature above measure. For, *it pleased the Father that in him should all fulness dwell* (*r*). And it is said, *God giveth not the Spirit by measure unto him* (*s*). God the Father *anointed* God the Son, *with the oil of gladness,* that is, with the gifts and graces of the Spirit, *above his fellows* (*t*); that is, above all believers, who share of his unction, according to their measure. 3 The Father commissioned him to the work. Therefore he is said to be *sealed* (*u*), as having his commission under the great seal of Heaven. And Christ pleads his commission: *Father,* says he, *I have finished the work which thou gavest me to do* (*x*). The Father prescribed his work to him, and gave him power and authority to carry it on, and instructions

(*l*) Psal. xl. 7, 8. John vi. 38. (*m*) Eph. i. 9. (*n*) 1 Cor. viii. 6. (*o*) John viii. 42. (*p*) Gal iv 4, 5. (*q*) Heb. x. 5. (*r*) Col. i. 19. (*s*) John iii. 34. (*t*) Psal. xlv. 7. (*u*) John vi. 27. (*x*) John xvii. 4.

tions how to manage it. Therefore he is said to have been *faithful to him that appointed him* (*y*). 4. The Father demanded our debt of him, and inflicted upon him the punishment due to our sins. *He made him to be sin for us, who knew no sin: The Lord laid on him the iniquity of us all: And it pleased the Lord to bruise him; he put him to grief* (*z*). And the Father is brought in speaking, *Awake, O sword, against my Shepherd, and against the Man that is my fellow, saith the Lord of Hosts* (*a*). 5. The Father accepted him, and his sufferings as a full satisfaction to justice. Hence it is said that *Christ gave himself for us, an offering and a sacrifice to God for a sweet smelling savour* (*b*). God smelt a sweet favour from the death of Christ. It was pleasing to him, as a sacrifice for our sins. It was God that *justified* him (*c*). He stood in our stead, charged with the guilt of our sins, before the bar of divine justice; and having suffered the punishment due to them, the Father justified him, and absolved him from that legal and imputed guilt. All the fruits of Christ's death manifest how acceptable it was to God, but especially the pouring out of the Spirit after his ascension. 6. The Father raised him from the dead. *Whom God hath raised up*, says the apostle, *having loosed the pains of death* (*d*). And he raised him in such a manner as to manifest him to be his own Son; which the apostle intimates in these words, *He hath raised up Jesus again, as it is also written in the second Psalm, Thou art my Son, this day have I begotten thee* (*e*). The debt being fully paid, and the demands of justice fully answered, by the satisfaction of Christ; the Father, as supreme Judge, did let our Surety out of prison. Therefore he is said to be *taken from prison, and from judgment* (*f*). 7. The Father exalted and glorified him. This also is frequently ascribed to the Father in scripture: As in these texts: *Therefore being by the right hand of God exalted, and having received of the Father the promise of the Holy Ghost, &c. Him hath God exalted with his right hand, to be a Prince and a Saviour. Wherefore God also hath highly exalted him, and given him a name which is above every name; that at the name of Jesus every knee should bow. The Lord said unto my Lord, Sit thou at my right hand, until I make thine enemies thy footstool* (*g*).

(2.) With respect to the Spirit. And so, the Father sends the Spirit by and through the Son, to work upon the hearts of the elect, and make them partakers of the redemption Christ hath

(*y*) Heb. iii. 2. (*z*) 2 Cor. v. 21. Isa, liii. 6, 10.
(*a*) Zech. xiii. 7. (*b*) Eph. v. 2. (*c*) Isa. l. 8. (*d*) Acts ii. 24. (*e*) Acts xiii. 33. (*f*) Isa. liii. 8. (*g*) Acts ii. 33. and v. 31. Phil. ii. 9, 10. Psal. cx. 1.

hath purchased. *I will pray the Father,* says Christ, *and he shall give you another Comforter.* Again, *The Comforter, who is the Holy Ghost, whom the Father will send in my name* (*h*). And the apostle says, *Because ye are sons, God hath sent forth the Spirit of his Son into your hearts, crying, Abba, Father* (*i*). The Father sends the Spirit, to perform his whole office, in applying to the elect that redemption, which he hath contrived, and the Son hath purchased for them.

(3.) With respect to the elect. The Father confers all spiritual blessings upon them. Hence the apostle gives thanks to the Father: *Blessed be the God and Father of our Lord Jesus Christ, who hath blessed us with all spiritual blessings in heavenly places in Christ* (*k*). Particularly, effectual calling, justification, reconciliation, and adoption, are in scripture ascribed to the Father. 1. It is the Father that calls elect sinners effectually, and brings them into a state of grace. *God is faithful,* says the apostle, *by whom ye were called into the fellowship of his Son* (*l*). As in the first creation, he *called these things that be not, as though they were.*(*m*): So it is in the new creation. 2. It is the Father that justifies elect sinners upon their believing. Therefore he is said to be *the justifier of him that believeth in Jesus.* And, says the apostle, *Who shall lay any thing to the charge of God's elect? It is God that justifieth: Who is he that condemneth* (*n*)? It belongs to the Father, as supreme Judge, according to his order of subsistence, to absolve believing sinners from condemnation, and to receive them into favour, upon the account of the righteousness and satisfaction of the Lord Christ, imputed to them, and received by faith. 3. It is the Father that reconciles elect sinners unto himself. So the apostle tells us, *All things are of God, who hath reconciled us to himself by Jesus Christ;* and *God was in Christ reconciling the world unto himself* (*o*). This is true, both with respect to the purchase; *God was in Christ reconciling us to himself,* by his satisfaction and merit: And with respect to the application; *God is in Christ, reconciling us to himself,* by virtue of our union with him. 4. It is the Father that adopts elect sinners upon their believing, and receives them into his family. Hence the apostle says, *God sent forth his Son, made of a woman, made under the law; to redeem them that were under the law, that we might receive the adoption of sons* (*p*). Upon Christ's satisfaction, and our laying hold upon it by faith, we receive the benefit of adoption from the Father: He receives

(*h*) John xiv. 16, 26. (*i*) Gal. iv. 6. (*k*) Eph. i. 3. (*l*) 1 Cor. i. 9. (*m*) Rom. iv. 17. (*n*) Rom. iii. 26. and viii. 33, 34. (*o*) 2 Cor. v. 18, 19. (*p*) Gal. iv. 4, 5.

ceives us into his family, puts us into the room and place of children, and gives us a right to all the privileges of his children. For it is *of him* that *the whole family in heaven and earth is named* (q). He is first a Father to Christ, and then through him a Father to believers. Thus, we see that these blessings and benefits are ascribed to God the Father. And because we obtain all spiritual blessings, in the way of a free and gracious covenant; therefore it belongs to the Father, in order of operation, to make this covenant with us, and to bring us into the bond thereof: According to these promises, *I will make an everlasting covenant with you:* And, *I will bring you into the bond of the covenant* (r). And this he doth by drawing us to Christ: For, *no man can come to* Christ *except the Father draw him* (s).

Moreover, the Father being the first person in order, therefore the other persons work from him, and all their operations are referred to him as the fountain of them. *I can of mine own self do nothing*, says Christ, *as I hear, I judge.* And, *The Spirit—shall not speak of himself; but whatsoever he shall hear, that shall he speak* (t). Hence it is that even these operations that are more peculiar to the Son and Holy Ghost, according to their order of subsistence, are often also ascribed to the Father; because the other persons are sent by him, and work from him, and according to his will. So, redemption, which is the proper work of the Son, is sometimes ascribed to the Father. As in the Song of Zacharias; *Blessed be the Lord God of Israel*, says he, *for he hath visited and redeemed his people* (u). And, says the psalmist, *with the Lord there is mercy, and with him is plenteous redemption. And he shall redeem Israel from all his iniquities* (x). Again, regeneration and sanctification, which are the proper works of the Spirit, are also sometimes ascribed to the Father. *Of his own will begat he us*, says the apostle, *by the word of truth* (y) And the Lord tells his people, *I am the Lord, who sanctify you* (z) And, as all the eternal counsels and purposes about spiritual blessings, are ascribed to the Father; so the purchase of them is also from him: For the Father gave and sent the Son to make the purchase; so that in purchasing all spiritual blessings, the Son worketh from the Father. The Father is also the original author of the collation of these blessings on the elect. It is *the God and Father of our Lord Jesus Christ*, that *blesseth us with all spiritual blessings* (a). In the communication of them, the

(q) Eph. iii. 15.   (r) Isa. lv. 4. Ezek. xx. 37.   (s) John vi. 44.   (t) John v. 30. and xvi. 13.   (u) Luke i. 68.   (x) Psal. cxxx. 7, 8.   (y) James i. 18.   (z) Lev. xx. 8.
(a) Eph. i. 3.

the Father hath a particular hand. Hence the apostle tells us, *Of him are ye in Christ Jesus, who of God is made unto us wisdom, and righteousness, and sanctification, and redemption* (b). Take notice, that it is not only said, he *is made to us*, but he *is made* OF GOD *to us*. All spiritual blessings, in the collation of them, are acts of the free and rich grace of the Father: For, *we have redemption through Christ's blood, the forgiveness of sins, according to the riches of his grace*, and, we are *justified freely by his grace* (c).

Second, There are offices and operations peculiarly ascribed to the Son, in the business of our salvation. The Son being the second person in order, and as it were the middle person of the Deity, did voluntarily undertake the work and office of Mediator, Surety, and Redeemer. *There is one Mediator*, says the apostle, *between God and man, the man Christ Jesus*: And, *Jesus was made a Surety of a better testament:* And Job says, *I know that my Redeemer liveth* (d). Particularly, the Son's work in the business of our salvation, may be considered in a threefold respect.

1. With respect to the Father. He did voluntarily and chearfully subject himself to his Father's will, in taking upon him the charge of the elect, undertaking the work of their redemption, and substituting himself in their room and place, as their Surety, to answer for their debt. Hence he is brought in speaking, *Then said I, Lo, I come, in the volume of the book it is written of me. I delight to do thy will, O my God* (e). So also, in obedience to his Father's will, he came into the world, and took upon him our nature; he subjected himself to the law, answered both its demands, by obeying and suffering, satisfied divine justice, ratified and confirmed the covenant by his blood, and made a purchase of all spiritual and eternal blessings. All this he did in obedience to his Father's will: *I came down from heaven*, says he, *not to do mine own will, but the will of him that sent me* (f): And, *My meat is to do the will of him that sent me, and to finish his work* (g).

2. With respect to the Spirit. He purchased for his church and people, all the gifts and graces of the Spirit, especially those that are saving; and he purchased them into his own hand, so that the dispensation of them is committed to him, as the great Lord Treasurer and Steward of Heaven. See and compare Psal. lxviii. 18. with Eph. iv. 8. In the one place it

---

(b) 1 Cor. i. 30. (c) Eph. i. 7. Rom. iii. 24. (d) 1 Tim ii. 5. Heb. vii. 22. Job xix. 25. (e) Psal. xl 7, 8. (f) John vi. 38. (g) John iv. 34.

it is said, *He received gifts for men;* and in the other, *He gave gifts unto men.* Upon his ascension, he received the gifts of the Spirit, that he might give them unto men. Accordingly it is said, *Being by the right hand of God exalted, and having received of the Father the promise of the Holy Ghost, he shed forth* of the same upon his apostles and disciples (*h*). *All things are delivered to* him *of* the *Father* (*i*). All blessings are entrusted to him: So that he sendeth the Spirit for applying his whole purchase, for converting the elect, for sanctifying them, for conducting and guiding them to glory; and, in a word, to do his whole work. *I will send him,* says he, *unto you from the Father* (*k*). Hence the Spirit is said *to receive of Christ's, and give it unto* believers (*l*).

3. With respect to the elect. He gave himself a sacrifice to satisfy divine justice for them, and so expiated the guilt of their sins, and purchased grace and glory, and all covenant-blessings for them (*m*). He also applies all by his continual intercession and effectual operation, as a compleat and perfect Saviour; For *he is able to save them to the uttermost that come unto God by him, seeing he ever liveth to make intercession for them* (*n*). Only, when I say that he applies his whole purchase, it must be so understood as that he doth it by the Spirit: For, this is the order of working proper to him, he worketh by the Spirit. And so, he bestows all spiritual blessings on the elect. Hence the apostle says, *God having raised up his Son Jesus, sent him to bless you, in turning away every one of you from his iniquities* (*o*). And, *him hath God exalted with his right hand, to be a Prince and a Saviour, for to give repentance to Israel, and forgiveness of sins* (*p*). He reveals the Father to his people: For, *No man hath seen God at any time: The only-begotten Son, who is in the bosom of the Father, he hath declared him* (*q*). And he draws them to himself: *Other sheep I have,* says he, *which are not of this fold, them also I must bring, and they shall hear my voice* (*r*). And again, *If I be lifted up from the earth, I will draw all men unto me* (*s*). And it is his work by office, to prevent and make up breaches between God and his people; to maintain a mutual intercourse and correspondence, peace and friendship between him and them; and to keep up freedom of access to the Father: For, he is their constant agent and *Advocate with the Father, always appearing*

in

(*h*) Acts ii. 33.   (*i*) Matth. xi. 27.   (*k*) John xv. 26.
(*l*) John xvi. 14.   (*m*) Matth. xx. 28. Heb. i. 2. Tit. ii. 14.
Gal. iii. 13, 14.   (*n*) Heb. vii. 25.   (*o*) Acts iii. 26.   (*p*) Acts v. 51.   (*q*) John i. 18.   (*r*) John x. 16.   (*s*) John xii. 32.

in the presence of God for them (t). In a word, he doth in the behalf of his people, execute the offices of a Prophet, Priest, and King, of which I may not now speak particularly.

Only, ere I leave this, observe these two things about the Son's office and operation. *Obs.* 1. The works that Christ performed as Mediator, God-man, come under a different consideration from these external works that are merely divine. These last are common to all the three divine persons: But the mediatory works are not so. What the human nature contributed to the mediatory works is proper to Christ alone: But what the divine nature contributed to them is common to all the persons; though they are, in order of working, peculiarly ascribed to the Son, who being the second person in order of subsistence, is also second in order of operation. *Obs.* 2. Because the Spirit is sent by the Son, and works from him, therefore these operations that belong to the Spirit in the business of our salvation, according to his order of subsistence, are sometimes in the holy scriptures ascribed also to the Son. I mean these operations that concern the application of redemption; such as, sanctification. Though this, being the third work in order, doth belong to the Spirit, who is the third person in order; yet it is sometimes ascribed to the Son. As in that text, *Christ loved the church, and gave himself for it, that he might sanctify and cleanse it* (u). And he is said to have *suffered, that he might sanctify the people with his own blood* (x). The reason of this is, because the sanctifying spirit is sent by the Son, and works from him, and in his name.

Third, There are distinct offices and operations ascribed to the holy Spirit in the business of our salvation. The Holy Spirit being the third person in order, hath such offices and operations ascribed to him, as concern the application of that redemption, which is contrived and destinated by the Father, and purchased by the Son, for elect sinners. How this application is made by the Spirit, our Shorter Catechism gives account in these words, "The Spirit applieth to us the redemption purchased by Christ, by working faith in us, and thereby uniting us to Christ, in our effectual calling." It is the blessed Spirit that calls sinners effectually, and brings them to Christ, and persuades and enables them to believe on him, and so unites them to Christ, and makes them partakers of the redemption he hath purchased. Hence, the Spirit is called by
some

(t) 1 John ii. 1. Heb. ix. 24. (u) Eph. v. 25, 16. (x) Heb. xiii. 12.

some divines, *The Executor of Christ's Testament.* It is the work of the Spirit to perfect and consummate the eternal designs of God's love upon the hearts of the elect. In this sense, according to worthy divines, the Spirit is called the Comforter: *I will pray the Father, and he shall give you another Comforter* (y), Original, *another Advocate.* The Holy Spirit is the Advocate, Agent, and Procurator of the Holy Trinity, to agent and prosecute the cause of God upon the hearts of the elect, to effect their salvation, contrived by the Father, and purchased by the Son. The Son is one Advocate, and the Spirit is another Advocate. As Christ the Mediator agents the cause of his people with God; so the Spirit agents the cause of God upon the hearts of his people.

SERMON CII.

PARTICULARLY, the Spirit, in applying the redemption Christ hath purchased, acts the part, 1. Of a teacher. 2. Of a Sanctifier. 3. Of a guide and leader. 4. Of a comforter.

1. The Spirit acts the part of a teacher. *The Comforter,* says our Lord, *who is the Holy Ghost, shall teach you all things* (a). In order hereunto, he sends forth teachers. *The Holy Ghost said, Separate me Barnabas and Saul for the work whereunto I have called them* (b). He furnisheth them with necessary gifts and graces: Therefore they are said to be *filled with the Holy Ghost* (c). He assists them in the exercise of their gifts: What the apostle did in the exercise of his office, was *by the power of the Holy Ghost* (d). And he concurs with them whom he thus furnishes and assists, by a saving illumination of the minds of men. Hence, he is called *the Spirit of wisdom and revelation,* by whom *the eyes of the understanding* are *enlightened* (e). The Holy Spirit opens the eyes of the soul, and furnishes the mind with the saving knowledge of divine truths and mysteries. On all these accounts, he is called *the Spirit of truth,* and is said *to guide into all truth* (f). He reveals truths clearly, and bears them in with life and power upon the heart.

2. The Spirit acts the part of a Sanctifier. On this account he is called frequently, the HOLY *Spirit,* and the HOLY *Ghost,* and *the Spirit of holiness* (g). He convinceth elect sinners of their sin and misery. *When he is come,* says Christ, *he will reprove*
(or

(y) John xiv. 16
(a) John xiv. 26. (b) Acts xiii. 2. (c) Acts ii. 4. (d) Rom. xv. 19. (e) Eph. i. 17, 18. (f) John xvi. 13. (g) Rom. i. 4.

(or *convince*) *the world of sin* (*h*). Next, he enlightens their minds with the knowledge of Christ: Hence he is called *the Spirit of wisdom and revelation in the knowledge of God* (*i*). And then, he renews their wills; whence we read *of the renewing of the Holy Ghost* (*k*). He regenerates elect sinners; therefore they are said to be *born of the Spirit* (*l*). He quickens them to a new life, and is therefore called *the Spirit of life* (*m*). He works faith in the hearts of the elect, and persuades and enables them to believe; hence he is called *the Spirit of faith* (*n*). And he works all other graces in their hearts: Therefore the graces are called *the fruits of the Spirit;* and the holy Spirit is called *the Spirit of grace* (*o*). Then, in the further progress of sanctification, he carries on this work, by killing sin in believers, and weakening the power of it more and more: Therefore they are said, *by the Spirit* to *mortify the deeds of the body* (*p*). And he renews them more and more after the image of God, by kindling in them more light, and love, and zeal. He promotes their growth in grace, and progress in holiness. They are *filled with joy and peace, and abound in hope, through the power of the Holy Ghost* (*q*). He quickens grace, and excites it to a lively exercise, by his gracious breathings and influences, his *north and south wind, blowing upon* their *garden,* and *making the spices thereof to flow out.* He *helps their infirmities* in prayer and other duties (*r*). And at last, he perfects his own work at death, when sin shall be utterly abolished, and grace ripened into glory.

3. The Spirit acts the part of a guide and leader. Hence believers are said to be *led by the Spirit* (*s*): And the psalmist prays, *Thy Spirit is good: Lead me into the land of uprightness* (*t*). Sometimes believers are under such dark and perplexing providences, that they are apt to mistake their way; they are like blind men, or men that have lost their way, and know not what to do. In this case, it is the office of the Spirit, to clear up to them their way and duty. This the psalmist prays for; *Cause me to know the way wherein I should walk* (*u*). The holy Spirit *brings them by a way that they knew not, and leads them in paths that they have not known, and makes darkness light before them* (*x*). He makes them *hear a voice behind them, saying, This is the*

(*h*) John xvi. 8. (*i*) Eph. i. 17. (*k*) Tit. iii. 5. (*l*) John iii. 5, 6. (*m*) Rom. viii. 2 (*n*) 2 Cor iv. 13. (*o*) Gal. v 22. Zech xii. 10. (*p*) Rom. viii. 13. (*q*) Rom xv 13. (*r*) Cant iv. 16. Rom. viii. 26. (*s*) Rom. viii. 14. (*t*) Psal. cxliii 10 (*u*) Psal. cxliii. 8. (*x*) Isa. xlii. 16.

the way, walk ye in it, when they *turn to the right hand, and when* they *turn to the left* (*y*). He leads them also, by governing their inclinations, *making* them *to go in the path of* his *commandments* (*z*). To this purpose is that promise, *I will put my Spirit within you, and cause you to walk in my statutes, and ye shall keep my judgments and do them* (*a*). As he gives them sweet and seasonable counsel, so he inclines their hearts to follow it, and will not suffer them to wander out of the good way he hath set before them.

4. The Spirit acts the part of a comforter. Hence he is often called *the Comforter* (*b*). He comforts believers, not only by conferring upon them matter of comfort, precious promises and sweet mercies, grace and peace and pardon, which are the food and fewel of joy: But also by his testimony and witnessing work, witnessing to believers what matter of comfort he hath conferred upon them. And so he comforts them, by clearing up to them their graces, blessings and privileges. They *have received*—*the Spirit which is of God, that they might know the things that are freely given to* them *of God* (*c*). He assures them of their interest in God's everlasting love, and refresheth their hearts with the sweet sense thereof. For *the love of God is shed abroad in* their *hearts by the Holy Ghost* (*d*). And he testifies their adoption to them, *bearing witness with their spirit, that* they *are the children of God* (*e*). By all which he calms and chears the conscience, and *fills it with joy and peace in believing* (*f*).

Thus I have considered the distinct offices and operations, that are in scripture ascribed to the several divine persons in the business of our salvation, according to their different manner and order of subsistence in the divine essence. I only add two things by way of caution. 1. When any one of the persons is said to have his distinct office and operation in the business of our salvation, this is not to be understood exclusively of the rest of the persons; † for, as I have already cleared, all external divine works are undivided, and common to all
the

(*y*) Isa. xxx. 21.   (*z*) Psal. cxix. 35.
(*a*) Ezek. xxxvi. 27.   (*b*) John xiv. 16, 26. xv. 26. and xvi 7.
(*c*) 1 Cor. ii. 12.   (*d*) Rom. v. 5.   (*e*) Rom. viii. 16.   (*f*) Rom. xv. 13.

† Ἁγιάζει, ᾗ ζωοποιεῖ, ᾗ φωτίζει, ᾗ παρακαλεῖ, ᾗ πάντα τὰ τοιαῦτα ὁμοίως, ὁ πατὴρ, ᾗ ὁ υἱὸς, ᾗ τὸ πνεῦμα, τὸ ἅγιον.
Greg Nyss. Lib. de S. Trinit.

¹ *Trinitas enim non sibi reconciliavit, per hoc quod solum verbum Carnem ipsa Trinitas fecit.*   Fulgent, Lib. 2. ad Monimum. Cap. 11.

the persons. It doth only respect their different order and manner of working. 2. The ascribing such different offices and operations to the several persons in the business of our salvation, doth not argue or imply any essential inequality amongst the persons, or any essential dependence of one person upon another in their operations; but only their different manner and order of subsistence, and the Son's proceeding from the Father, and the Holy Ghost from both, in the same individual essence; so that one God in three distinct persons is the one perfect cause of our salvation.

I shall now make some application of this head.

Use 1. For instruction, in several particulars. And, 1. From what hath been said, we may be instructed about the distinction of the persons in the Godhead. The ineffable, but yet distinct, operations of the Father, Son, and Holy Ghost, in the business of our salvation, are an uncontroulable evidence of their distinct subsistences in the same individual divine essence. 2. We may hence be instructed about the greatness of the sin of unbelief. There is in it a manifest opposition to the holy Trinity in their distinct offices and operations in the business of our salvation. 3. We may see here, whence it is that the sin against the Holy Ghost is unpardonable. It is against the Spirit's operation, which is the last in the business of salvation. But of these I will have occasion to speak afterward, in the general application of this doctrine.

Use 2. Here is much matter of holy admiration. And,

1. Let us admire the infinite wisdom of God in the business of our salvation. Here is the wisdom of God in a mystery. There is an unsearchable depth of wisdom in the distinct operations of the Father, Son, and Holy Ghost, in the business of our salvation; in the Father's contriving and ordering it, and the Son's purchasing it, and the Holy Ghost's applying it. These things are ordered, in an infinitely wise manner, incomprehensible by us. But let us admire what we cannot comprehend. O how beautiful to admiration will the whole work appear when the whole methods of it come to be read in heaven in the original copy; when they shall be seen in the face, in the bosom of God, in fair and plain characters!

2. Let us admire the condescension of the great God; that all the divine persons should be at work for the salvation of such vile wretches as we are: That the Father should be employed in contriving, the Son in purchasing, and the Holy Ghost in applying this salvation. There was no necessity lying on the blessed persons to be thus concerned; it was their own

free

free love that engaged them. O what are we, that the thoughts of the blessed Trinity should have been taken up about us so long ago, even from everlasting! And that they should be still at work for our salvation, and concur to make such rebels happy! And that they should thus concur for the salvation of some of fallen mankind, and not for the salvation of fallen angels! O what matter of holy admiration there is here! This the glorious angels desire to pry into. Admiration is one of the great duties of heaven: And the ineffable concurrence of all the divine persons, in the business of the salvation of lost sinners, will be matter of admiration to angels and saints for evermore.

Use 3. Hence we have direction in the acting and exercise of faith. Though Christ as Mediator God-man be the immediate object of faith, it being through him that faith makes all its approaches to God: Yet Christ as God, and the other divine persons, are the ultimate object of faith. And we are to act faith on all the divine persons, according as they act their love and grace distinctly toward us in the work of our redemption. 1. Then close with and receive all the divine persons. Close with the Father, as the contriver of redemption: Cast yourselves on his everlasting love. Close with the Son, as the purchaser of redemption: Rest on his satisfaction and merit. Close with the Holy Ghost, as the applier of this redemption: Receive him as your Teacher, Sanctifier, Guide, and Comforter. In a word, cast yourselves on the eternal love of the Father, and the infinite merit of the Son, and the almighty power of the Spirit. 2 Resign and give up yourselves to all the divine persons. Resign yourselves to the Father, to be justified and adopted by him: Resign yourselves to the Son, in all his mediatory offices: And resign yourselves to the Spirit, to be enlightened and sanctified by him, and guided and conducted to glory.

Use 4. Hence we have direction in all our worship. As our salvation is, in order of working, from the Father, through the Son, by the Spirit: So in all our commerce with God, we are to come to the Father, through the Son, by the Holy Ghost. So the apostle speaks; *Through him*, that is through Christ, *we both have an access by one Spirit unto the Father* (g). In all our worship, we are to address ourselves to the Father, through the Son, by the Spirit. 1. We are to address ourselves to the Father. Therefore gospel worship is called *a worshipping the Father*; and *calling on the Father* (h): Not as excluding the rest of the persons; but in respect of order of subsistence and working.

2. It

(g) Eph. ii. 18.   (h) John iv. 23. 1 Pet. i. 17.

2. It muſt be through the Son. For it is through him that God brings about redemption for us; therefore it is through him we muſt addreſs ourſelves to the Father for the bleſſings of it. *No man cometh to the Father but by him* (i). It is through him that we have hopes of acceptance and ſucceſs. It is by the merit of the Son we have acceſs to the throne of the Father. It is as the Father of Chriſt that he communicates himſelf graciouſly to us. Hence it is that the apoſtle, in giving thanks to God for ſpiritual bleſſings, deſcribes him from his relation to Chriſt: *Bleſſed be the God and Father of our Lord Jeſus Chriſt, who hath bleſſed us* (k), &c. 3. We muſt addreſs ourſelves to the Father, *by the Spirit*. It is the Spirit that giveth us an heart to come to God by Chriſt. He makes us *cry, Abba, Father* (l) Therefore employ the Spirit, and reſt on him for his aſſiſtance, and the influence of his grace.

Uſe 5. Let me exhort you from what hath been ſaid, to a ſerious concern, and holy care and diligence, about your own ſalvation. We have from this doctrine both a preſſing motive, and a great encouragement to this.

1. Here is a preſſing motive to a ſerious concern about your own ſalvation. You have heard of the diſtinct operations of the Father, Son, and Holy Ghoſt, about the ſalvation of loſt ſinners: Will it not be ſad, if after all this, you never mind ſalvation in earneſt, but make light of it? Surely, it muſt be a buſineſs of great moment and importance, and a benefit of unſpeakable worth and value, about which all the divine perſons have ſuch a concern: Therefore it muſt be brutiſh dulneſs and ſtupidity, not to value this ſalvation. What a high eſteem ſhould you have of that work that hath ſuch agents concerned in it? All the perſons in the Godhead are at work about this ſalvation; and ſhould not you, who are the parties intereſted, be alſo employed about it? Seeing there is ſuch an admirable concurrence of the divine perſons in this buſineſs, O what will become of them by whom this benefit is undervalued and neglected! How terrible will their judgment be, and how unavoidable! *How ſhall we eſcape, if we neglect ſo great ſalvation* (m)! Indeed, there will be no poſſibility of eſcaping. O, what terrible vengeance will be their portion, who neglect that ſalvation, which is contrived by the Father, purchaſed by the Son, and applied by the Spirit to all the elect! A refuſal of this great ſalvation in the offers of it, puts a ſcorn on all the perſons in the Godhead. Therefore I beſeech you, in the words

(i) John xiv. 6. (k) Eph. i. 3. (l) Gal. iv. 6. (m) Heb. ii. 3.

of the apoſtle, *that ye receive not the grace of God in vain* (*n*) : That grace which the Father contrived for loſt ſinners; that grace which the Son laid down his life for; that grace which is with all affectionate earneſtneſs tendered to you in the bleſſed goſpel; that grace that is ſo ſuitable to your neceſſities, wants, and miſeries: Oh, will you deſpiſe this grace? God forbid. It was an act of infinite love in the Father, to contrive ſalvation for ſuch wretches as you are; and it was an act of matchleſs love in the Son to purchaſe it; and it is admirable condeſcenſion in the Holy Ghoſt to offer it to you, yea, to ſtrive with you by his inward motions to accept of it. Oh, ſhall all theſe gracious methods and operations of the bleſſed Trinity be fruſtrated? Will you after all this neglect ſo great a ſalvation? How then will you be able to look God in the face, when you appear before him in judgment?

2. Here alſo is great encouragement to be ſeriouſly concerned about your ſalvation. For,

(1.) We ſee that the heart of God is much ſet on the ſalvation of loſt ſinners; he hath a great good-will to it: For all the divine perſons are concerned about it. Therefore, let not ſenſible ſinners indulge hard thoughts of God. Away with all your jealouſies of him. What ground can there be for any hard reflections upon him, after ſuch manifeſtations of his earneſtneſs for the redemption and ſalvation of ſinners? Here are three divine perſons employed in it; the Father contrives it, the Son purchaſeth it, and the holy Spirit ſtands ready to apply it to every believing ſoul. The Father employed all his wiſdom and grace about it from everlaſting: The Son ſpared no pains to accompliſh it; as he freely offered himſelf to the work, ſo he never repented of the undertaking: And the holy Spirit continueth to ſtrive with you, though you have long ſtriven againſt him. Though you have ſmothered many convictions, ſtifled many motions of the Spirit, and grieved him many a day by your obſtinacy and diſobedience; yet he is very importunate to prevail with you.

(2.) It is a great encouragement that there are three divine perſons to effect and bring about your ſalvation. O, what may not be expected? There is a divine perſon, to pardon you, and receive you into favour; and another divine perſon to expiate your guilt, and to bring you into favour with God; and yet another divine perſon to overcome your obſtinacy and unbelief, to vanquiſh temptations, doubts and fears, and to draw you to Chriſt, that Chriſt may bring you to the Father:
And

(*n*) 2. Cor. vi. 1.

And there are precious ordinances in and by which the Spirit worketh. O what encouragement have you to be serious, and to wait on in the use of means.

Use 6. Let me exhort you who are the children of God, to give the whole glory of your salvation to God alone; for you see that the divine persons carry it on amongst themselves: And to give equal glory of your salvation and redemption to all the three persons; for each person concurs in his own way and order to promote it.

1. Give the Father the glory of his electing love: As our blessed Lord did, *I thank thee,* says he, *O Father, Lord of heaven and earth, because thou hast hid these things from the wise and prudent, and hast revealed them unto babes : Even so, Father, for so it seemed good in thy sight*—*The Father himself loveth you* (*o*). And his love is the original of your redemption: All springs from that. It was his love that gave Christ to and for you: *God so loved the world, that he gave his only begotten Son* (*p*). His love, his will, his good pleasure which he purposed in himself, are frequently, in scripture, proposed as the eternal springs of your salvation, and of all acts of grace leading towards it: Therefore his love and grace are continually to be admired and glorified. The apostle could not consider *the will of God and our Father* in this work, without interrupting his discourse by a doxology: *Who gave himself for our sins,* says he, *that he might deliver us from this present evil world, according to the will of God and our Father, to whom be glory for ever and ever, Amen* (*q*). Glorify the Father, for any gracious work in any of your hearts. *Giving thanks unto the Father,* says the apostle, *who hath made us meet to be partakers of the inheritance of the saints in light* (*r*): And, *Blessed be the God and Father of our Lord Jesus Christ,* says he, *who hath blessed us, &c* (*s*). Glorify him as the *Father of our Lord Jesus Christ*: For, though you have all immediately from Christ, yet Christ hath all from the Father. *All things that the Father hath,* says he, *are mine* (*t*).

2 Glorify the Son. The apostles in their epistles do often give glory to Christ: As in these texts; *Through Jesus Christ, to whom be glory for ever and ever, amen: Our Lord and Saviour Jesus Christ; to him be glory both now and for ever, amen: And, Unto him that loved us, and washed us from our sins in his own blood;—to him be glory and dominion, for ever and ever. Amen* (*u*).

Christ

(*o*) Matth. xi. 25, 26. John xvi 27. (*p*) John iii. 16. (*q*) Gal. i. 4, 5. (*r*) Col. i. 12. (*s*) Eph. i 3. (*t*) John xvi. 15. (*u*) Heb. xiii. 21. 2 Pet. iii. 18. Rev. i 5, 6.

Christ did voluntarily and chearfully undertake and accomplish the work of your redemption, as himself declares: *Then said I, Lo, I come—I delight to do thy will, O my God* (x). And indeed if he had not taken this work in hand, there had been a stop there, and you had perished for ever. All the saving blessings you receive and enjoy are the fruits of his satisfaction and merit. Your salvation cost him dear: It is the purchase of his blood. Therefore glorify him for his admirable grace and condescension. *Worthy is the Lamb that was slain, to receive power, and riches, and wisdom, and strength, and honour, and glory, and blessing* (y). And glorify him as the storehouse of all your blessings: All are put in his hand, and from him you receive them. *Of his fulness have all we received, and grace for grace* (z). Christ is equal with the Father, in participating the honour of your salvation: Therefore he must have equal honour and glory from you; *That all men should honour the Son, even as they honour the Father: he that honoureth not the Son, honoureth not the Father who hath sent him* (a). Hence it is that the Father and Son are joined together in the saints praises: *Blessing, honour, glory, and power, be unto him that sitteth upon the throne, and unto the Lamb, for ever and ever* (b).

3. Glorify the Holy Ghost, for he applies all to you. You slept securely in sin, till the Spirit awakened you. You were unable and unwilling to lay hold on Christ, till you were made able and willing by the Spirit. How often were you called and invited; but you refused and slighted all warnings and instructions; and many a precious opportunity was lost: But the holy Spirit overcame your evil by his goodness, and broke in upon your heart in such a powerful way as you could not withstand. And since your conversion, all the rich communications of gifts and graces you have been partakers of, are from the Spirit: If he had not supported and guided you continually, you had ruined and undone yourselves. Therefore glorify the blessed Spirit. You have all from him. *He shall receive of mine*, says Christ, *and shall shew it unto you* (c). All the grace and peace you have, all the saving light that is in your understandings, all the gracious inclinations in your wills, all the supernatural impressions that are in your affections; all are immediately from the Spirit. Therefore let your souls be raised to give him glory, by the motions of his grace which you feel in your own hearts; by the comfortable sense

he

(x) Psal. xl. 7, 8.   (y) Rev. v. 12.   (z) John i. 16.
(a) John v. 23.   (b) Rev. v. 13.   (c) John xvi. 14.

he begets in you of your adoption; and by the support and comfort you have from him in all your conflicts and distresses.

Use 7. For comfort to believers in Christ. Your salvation cannot possibly miscarry, seeing such agents are concerned in it. All the divine persons concur together, and are at work about it. There is the eternal love of the Father, and the all-sufficient merit of the Son, and the omnipotent operation of the Holy Ghost: And what cannot eternal love, and infinite merit, and almighty power, do for you? Therefore you may be encouraged to wait with comfort and confidence, for the progress and consummation of your begun salvation. What may you not expect, who have such infinitely wise and powerful agents engaged to do for you?

SERMON CIII.

Fifthly, OF the unity of the persons in the Godhead. I proceed now to speak of the unity or union of the divine persons. Their unity consists chiefly in this, that they are one in essence. Each person hath the whole divine essence in himself, yet the essence is undivided; so that the essence, absolutely considered, is common to all the three. This unity is plainly asserted in my text, *And these three are one:* For it cannot be understood of a oneness of will only, as I cleared when I explained these words. The same is asserted also by our blessed Lord, in these words, *I and my Father are one.* It is an essential unity of which he speaks: For his scope, as appears from the context, is to prove that his power was sufficient to preserve his sheep, because he was equal in power with the Father, being one in essence with him. And so did the Jews understand him, and took up stones to cast at him, *because,* say they, *thou makest thyself God.* And our blessed Lord doth not contradict them in this, nor charge them with any falsehood, or a mistake of his meaning; but on the contrary, confirms the truth of what they rightly apprehended to be his meaning, in his following answer (*a*). This unity of divine persons in the same individual essence is also intimated to us in that famous text about the creation of man, Gen. i. 26. *Let us make man after our image.* Where, as we have a plain intimation of a plurality of divine persons; so, † the community

of

(*a*) John x. 30, 31, 32, 34, &c.

† Πᾶς ἑτερότης οὐσίας ἐν τῇ Τριάδι ἐν ᾗ ταυτότης ἐνεργείας εὑρίσκεται. Basil. M. L. 5. adv. Eunom.

of operation infers a community of nature: And † when it is said *our image*, in the singular number, this shews the oneness of the essence common to all the persons. The same is evident also from our Lord's prayer, *Holy Father, keep through thine own name, those whom thou hast given me, that they may be one as we are. And the glory which thou gavest me, I have given them, that they may be one even as we are one* (*b*). The particle *as* in these verses, doth not denote an exact equality, as if the Father and Christ were one, no otherwise than Christ and believers are one: it denotes only some kind of similitude and resemblance. The mystical union between Christ and believers, bears some resemblance of the essential union between the Father and Christ. Christ and believers are one mystically, as the Father and the Son are one essentially. This essential unity of the divine persons is also evident from the institution of baptism, where baptism is commanded to be administered, not *in the* NAMES, but *in the* NAME *of the Father, Son, and Holy Ghost* (*c*): Because although, considered personally, they have distinct names; yet, considered essentially, they have but one name, being one in essence, and so one and the same God. And indeed, if they into whose name we are baptized, were not one in essence, then we would be by baptism engaged to the service, worship, and obedience, of more Gods than one, which were most blasphemous once to imagine.

Now, the persons their being one in essence, is not to be so understood, as if they were one specifically, as three men are; as if there were a specific divine nature, and the three persons as so many individuals. This some have imagined. But it cannot be so. 1. Because then the three divine persons would be three Gods, as three human persons are three men. 2. Such a specific divine nature is either a mere logical notion or act of the mind, without any real existence belonging to it as such; which is contrary to the very notion of God, which implies a necessary existence: Or, it must imply a divine nature, which is neither Father, Son, nor Holy Ghost, which were a most absurd notion. 3. The distinction of individuals under the same species, is a kind of division of the species: But the divine essence is most perfectly one, and uncapable of any kind of division, Therefore the divine persons must
have

---

† Ει δὲ μία τῆς Τριάδος ἡ εἰκών, μία τῶν τριῶν ὑποστάσεων ἡ φύσις. Τὸ γὰρ ταυτὸν τῆς οὐσίας ἡ τῆς εἰκόνος ἑνότης κηρύτ]ω.

Basil Seleuc. Orat 1.

(*b*) John xvii. 11, 22.   (*c*) Matth. xxviii 19.

have one individual essence. Though the persons be distinct, yet this doth not take away the unity of the essence, which is whole and entire, indivisible and inseparable, in all the three persons, though we cannot comprehend how. * As we must not confound the persons, so neither must we divide or separate the essence. Though the Father, Son, and Holy Ghost, be distinct persons; yet they are one God, and have the same individual nature or essence. " † The Father is God, and the Son " is God, and the Holy Ghost is God; yet there are not three " Gods, but one God." There are indeed three who are God; but they are one and the same God: For though the Son and Holy Ghost be distinct from the Father; yet they are not distinct Gods from him, but only distinct persons. As Augustine saith, "‡ They are capable of number, as to their " relation to each other; but not as to their essence, which is " but one." This is further confirmed from the unity of the Godhead: For, if each of the persons be God, and yet there can be but one God, then each of the persons must be the same one God, and there can be no division of the essence by the distinction of the persons. As an ancient father saith, " § The most perfect unity is to be conceived in the most sim- " ple and incomprehensible essence:" So that the divine nature is not capable of such division and separation as the human nature is. There is certainly an inconceivable difference, between an infinitely perfect Being, and such finite limited creatures as individuals among men are. When therefore we say that there are distinct persons in the Godhead, it must be understood in such a manner as is agreeable to the divine essence ‖; and seeing that it is not capable of division or separation, the persons must be in the same undivided essence. †† As

the

---

* Μήτε συγχέοντες τὰ πρόσωπα, μήτε τὴν οὐσίαν διαιροῦντες.
Athan. in Symb. Art. 2.
In Patre & Filio & Spiritu Sancto, unitatem Substantiæ accipimus, Personas confundere non audemus.
Fulgent. Lib. contra Object. Arianorum.

† Θεὸς ὁ πατὴρ, Θεὸς ὁ υἱὸς, Θεὸς ᾗ τὸ πνεῦμα τὸ ἅγιον ἀλλ' ὅμως ὁ τρεῖς Θεοὶ, ἀλλ' εἷς Θεός. Athan. in Symb. Art. 5.

‡ *Hoc solo numerum insinuant, quod ad invicem sunt, non quod ad se sunt.* August. de Trinit L. 5. C. 8.

§ Ἡ δὲ μονὰς ᾗ ἑνὰς τῆς ἁπλῆς ᾗ ἀπεριλήπτου οὐσίας ἐστὶ σημαντικόν.
Basil. T. 2. pag. 926.

‖ *Talia sunt prædicata qualia subjecta permiserint.* Boeth.

†† Τίς ἄρρητος ᾗ ἀκατανόητος ἐν τούτοις καταλαμβάνεται ᾗ ἡ

the unity of the essence doth not confound the persons; so neither doth the distinction of the persons imply any division of the essence: Because the distinction of the persons is not founded on these properties that are essential, which are incapable of being divided; but on these properties that are personal, and relative, and incommunicable, and cannot be confounded: So that there must be one undivided essence, and yet three distinct persons. The same individual essence or substance subsists distinctly and differently in each of the three persons, or under three different modes of sussistence: So that the Son and Holy Ghost are co-essential and consubstantial with the Father. There is one and the same indivisible substance in all three. This is what is asserted in our Shorter Catechism, *and these three are one God, the same in substance.* Each person hath not a distinct substance of his own, separate from the substance of the other persons; but the one substance of the Deity is the substance of each person: For there cannot possibly be one individual essence in three persons that have peculiar substances of their own.

The ancient church, in that famous Council of Nice, Ann. 325, to express this unity of the persons, used the word ὁμοούσιος, that is, of the same substance or essence: Whereupon great troubles did arise in the church of Christ, and continued for a long time. Yet the ancient church had good reasons for using that word, because it did most clearly express the sense of what is revealed in the holy scriptures, about the unity of the Father, Son, and Holy Ghost, in nature or essence; and was of great use to detect the fraud of the Arians. And hence it was that this word was had in such abomination with them that denied the holy Trinity, in so much that they named the orthodox Homousians. It is true ὁμοούσιος is a word that may be extended to individuals of the same kind; but † the ancient fathers did not use it in that sense, but to shew that divine persons are ‡ of one and the same individual substance

or

κοινωνία ᾗ ἡ διάκρισις οὔτε τῆς τῶν ὑποστάσεων διαφορᾶς τὸ τῆς φύσεως συνεχὲς διασπώσης οὔτε τῆς κατὰ τὴν οὐσίαν κοινότητος τὸ ἰδιάζον τῶν γνωρισμάτων ἀναχεούσης.

Greg. Nyssen. Lib. de Differ. Essen. & Hypost.

† Τὸ ὁμοούσιν ἀκούοντες μὴ εἰς τὰς ἀνθρωπίνας αἰσθήσεις πίπτοντες μέρισι μὲν, ᾗ διαιρέσεις τῆς θεότητος λογιζώμεθα· ἀλλ' ὡς ἐπὶ ἀσωμάτων διανοούμενοι τὴν ἑνότητα τῆς φύσεως τὴν ταυτότητα τοῦ φωτὸς μὴ διαιρῶμεν. Athan. Oper. Tom. i. Epist. de Decret. Synod. Nic.

‡ Μιᾶς ᾗ ταύτῃ οὐσίας.

or essence. And this was the doctrine of the ancient fathers. Athanasius frequently asserts the indivisible unity of the divine nature. He says, "† That the Trinity is so undivided and united in itself, that wherever the Father is, there is the Son and the Holy Ghost." And Basil plainly asserts, that " the Son hath the very same essence with the Father; —the Son subsisting as from the Father, but ‡ in the same undivided essence." So also Augustine saith §, that " the Father, Son, and Holy Ghost, are one in the same individual nature." And elsewhere he saith, that " the three persons are one God, ‖ on the account of the ineffable conjunction of the Deity." And in another place, he says, " † There is one God, on the account of the individual Deity; and there are three persons, on the account of their peculiar properties." I have quoted these passages from the ancient fathers, and might quote a great many more, to let you see, that in different ages of the church, God hath had his witnesses who have borne testimony to this great fundamental truth of a Trinity in unity. And the consideration of this may be very comfortable to the people of God, and a confirmation of their faith, in cleaving and adhering to the truth, in these dangerous times.

But here, some are bold to enquire, *How can these things be?* How can there be but one individual essence, and yet three distinct persons? How can one be three, and three one? I answer, The divine essence, being infinite, is incomprehensible by any finite understanding; so that reason is no competent judge, whether it can subsist in three distinct persons, or not. But we believe it, and are bound so to do, because God hath so revealed himself in his blessed word. And we do not believe contradictions, when we so believe: For although in one individual essence there can be but one person, where the essence or substance is finite and limited; yet this hath no place

† Ἡ ἁγία ᾖ μακαρία Τριὰς ἀδιαίρετος ᾖ ἡνωμένη πρὸς ἑαυτὴν ἐστι ᾖ λεγομένη Ἰν πατρὸς πρόεσι ᾖ ὁ τῦ/ε λόγος, ᾖ τὸ ἐν τω υἱῶ πνεῦμα. Athan. Oper. Tom 1. Epist. 1. ad Serap.

‡ Τὸ δὲ τῆς οὐσίας ταυτὸν. Basil. Tom. 1. pag. 604.

§ Contr. Maxim. L. 1.

‖ *Propter ineffabilem Conjunctionem Deitatis.*

De Agone Christ. C. 16.

† *Propter individuam Deitatem unus Deus est; et propter unius cujusq; Proprietatem tres personæ sunt.*

August. contr. Maxim. L. 3. C. 10.

in an infinite Being. It is the peculiar prerogative of the divine essence, that it is capable of subsisting in more persons than one: And this prerogative is founded on the infinite, and therefore incomprehensible perfection of the divine nature. True, it is necessary that every person have a substance to support its subsistence: But with this difference; in created beings, that substance which each person hath, is a proper separate substance of his own; but the divine Being, not being capable of separate and divided substances, therefore the persons must needs subsist in the same individual substance or essence. So that each of the divine persons hath the divine essence belonging to it; and a divine person is the divine nature or essence subsisting under such a mode, or in such a distinct manner. But the manner how the three persons subsist in the same individual divine essence, is above our comprehension. Therefore, as an ancient faith, " † It is a manifest ar-
"gument of infidelity, to say, touching God, how can this
" or that be?" It is certainly a curious and bold inquiry into divine mysteries. It is the genius of faith to put the seal to all that God saith, without so much as asking any hows or whys.

But though the union of the divine persons in the same individual essence, is an incomprehensible mystery, infinitely above and beyond our conception: Yet from what hath been said, we may gather these properties of this union, which may give us some notion of the nature of it. 1. It is a spiritual union. It is not natural, nor carnal and bodily, but spiritual. Hence some have called the holy Spirit, the indissoluble Bond of the Trinity. Particularly Bernard hath this passage, " ‡ The
" Spirit itself is that indissoluble Bond of the Trinity, by
" which, as the Father and the Son are one, so also are we
" one in them." 2. It is a most close, most perfect, and most absolute union: An essential union. There cannot be a greater unity. Nothing can be more one, than the Father, Son, and Spirit are one. 3. It is an unity that consists with order and distinction. The unity of the Trinity doth not take away the distinction of the persons, nor confound their order. They are one and yet three. They keep their distinct personalities, and distinct personal operations, and their different manner

and

† Σαφὴς ἔλεγχος ἀπιστίας, τὸ πῶς περὶ Θεοῦ λέγειν.
Author Exposit. Fidei.

‡ *Est enim Spiritus ipse indissolubile vinculum Trinitatis, per quem sicut pater & filius unum sunt, sic & nos unum sumus in ipsis.*
Bernard. in Oct. Pasc. Serm. 1.

and order of working. 4. It is an everlasting and inseparable union: For in the divine nature or essence there can be no change. It cannot be divided. As the blessed persons were always one, so there can never be a separation.

Thus I have shewed, that the Father, Son, and Holy Ghost, are one in essence. Now, from their unity in essence arise and follow, their equality and parity in all essential attributes; their essential in-being in one another; and their unity in love, will and operation.

1. Their equality and parity in all essential attributes. Where there is the same individual essence, there must needs be an equality and parity in the greatness of perfection. † The three persons have the same essence, eternally, equally, and perfectly; not one excels another; none is more or less God than another. Each person hath the same Godhead, wholly, and in perfection, and therefore equally. So it is said of Christ, he *thought it not robbery to be equal with God* (d). and from the context there, it is evident, that Christ's inequality in respect of office, doth not take away his equality with the Father, in respect of nature or essence: He *thought it not robbery to be equal with God; but made himself of no reputation, &c.* Though he be the Father's servant, and so inferior to the Father, as Mediator; being Mediator as God-man, according to both natures: Yet as he is God, he is every way equal with the Father. This is further evident from John v. where our blessed Lord having asserted that *God was his Father*, viz. in a peculiar way proper to himself, by eternal generation, and communication of the same essence; the Jews did thence conclude, that he *made himself equal with God* (e). And that they did rightly conclude so, is evident, because our Lord doth not charge them with calumny on that account, or with any mistake of his meaning: But on the contrary, proves and confirms his equality with God, from his conjunction in operation with the Father; and gives particular instances of this conjunction and equality (f). Again, the equality of the divine persons appears from this, that they are often spoken of as equal. They are often joined together: As in the institution of baptism (g); in their witnessing from heaven, in my text; in the apostolical Benediction; and in John's salutation to the seven churches of Asia (h), where they are spoken of as concurring in an united way to give grace and peace.

Their

† Vide dictum Athanasii. pag. 776.
(d) Phil. ii. 6. (e) John v. 17, 18 (f) John v. 19, 20, 21,—30. (g) Matth. xxviii. 19. (h) 2 Cor. xiii. 14. Rev. i. 4, 5:

Their equality is also implied and signified, by the Son's being named sometimes before the Father (*i*); and the Holy Ghost's being named, sometimes before the Father (*k*), and sometimes before the Son (*l*): which is done to shew, that though one person be before another in order of subsistence, yet they are all equal in all essential perfections.

Particularly, the divine persons are equal,

(1.) In essential independency: For, *as the Father hath life in himself, so hath he given to the Son to have life in himself* (*m*). The Son hath divine life in himself, as well as the Father, and he hath it so as the Father hath it; and consequently he hath it originally and independently: So that the Son is *God of himself* *, as well as the Father: And so also is the Holy Ghost. The plain reason is, because they have one and the same individual divine essence, which is of itself. The Son and Holy Ghost are from the Father, in regard of their personal subsistence, not in regard of the essence. They have no original of their Deity, but only of their personal subsistence.

(2.) They are equal in power. Hence our Lord says, *Neither shall any man pluck them* (that is, *my sheep) out of my hand. My Father who gave them me, is greater than all: and none is able to pluck them out of my Father's hand. I and my Father are one* (*n*). Where our Lord, speaking of the preservation of his sheep, joins his own power with the Father's in that work; and gives the reason why he did so, because the Father and he are one in essence, and therefore work by the same power.

(3.) They are equal in glory, majesty, and dignity. One person is not greater or more glorious than another. True it is, our Lord says, John xiv. 28. *My Father is greater than I*: But that is to be understood of him, † *as he was Man and Mediator*, and in his then present state of humiliation; for, considered as the Son, he is of equal glory and dignity with the Father. Hence it appears that Christ's exaltation as Mediator to great glory, power and dignity, is not at all inconsistent with that essential power, dignity and glory, which he hath in himself as God, and wherein he is equal with the Father. Therefore the Father and Son are not to be severed in worship, but *all men should honour the Son, even as they honour the Father,*

(*i*) 2 Cor. xiii. 14. Gal. i. 1.   (*k*) Eph. ii. 18.   (*l*) Rev. i. 4, 5.   (*m*) John v. 26.   (*n*) John x. 28, 29, 30.

* Ἀυτοθεος.

† Ἴσος τῷ πατρὶ κατα τὴν θεότητα, ἥττων τῦ πατρὸς κατα τὴν ἀνθρωπότητα. Athan. in Symb. Art. 11.

Father, John v. 23. And what I have said of the Son is true also of the Holy Ghost: He is equal in glory and dignity with the Father and Son. This was the judgment of the ancient church ‡. · Hence Athanasius says in his Creed *, "There is "one person of the Father, another of the Son, and another "of the Holy Ghost: But the Deity of the Father, Son, and "Holy Ghost, is all one, their glory equal, their majesty co-e-"ternal." And indeed, if the Son and Holy Ghost were not equal with the Father in power and glory, they could not be God: For, a subordinate Deity is truly none at all. Supreme power, glory and dignity, are essential perfections of the Godhead: He that hath them not, is not God.

(4.) Being equal in glory, they must needs be equal in wisdom, holiness, goodness, mercy, and other essential perfections. Seeing each person hath the whole divine essence in himself: Therefore all the essential attributes must be true of every person. Particularly, the divine essence being infinite and eternal; therefore, as the Father is infinite and eternal, so is the Son and the Holy Ghost: Yet there are not three infinites, nor three eternals, but one; as Athanasius saith in his Creed †. The reason is, because the essential properties do not belong to the persons, on the account of their personality, but on the account of the divine essence, which is one and the same in all three. As the nature of each person is infinite and eternal; so also is each person, because of that nature.

SERMON

‡ Patres Concilii Constan. OEcom. 2di, *aiunt Patris & Filii & Spiritus Sancti, esse ὁμότιμον τὴν ἀξίαν.*

Apud Theodoret. Hist. Eccles. L. 5. C. 9.

Basilius M. *ait* ἡ Τριὰς σεβάσμιος ἐςὶν ἐν μιᾷ ᾗ ἀϊδίῳ δόξῃ.

L. 5. Contr. Eunom. C 15.

Basil. Seleuc. *ait Patris, Filii & Spiritus Sancti* ἀμέρισος ἡ τιμὴ.

Orat. 30.

Greg. Nazianz. *ait Patrem, Filium, & Spiritum Sanctum, esse Tria* ὁμόδοξα. *Unum autem esse Essentia & Impartibilitate Adorationis,* τῷ ἀμερίςῳ τῆς προσκυνήσεως. Orat. 24. *et in* Orat. 44. *ait* μία σύνταξις, λατρεία μία, προσκύνησις, δύναμις, τελειότης, ἁγιασμός.

* "Ἄλλη γάρ ἐςιν ἡ τῦ πατρὸς ὑπόςασις, ἄλλη τῦ ὑῦ, ᾗ ἄλλη ἁγίυ πνεύματος. Ἀλλὰ πατρὸς ᾗ ὑῦ ᾗ ἁγίυ πνεύματος μία ἐςι θεότης, ἴσα δόξα, συναΐδιος ἡ μεγαλειότης. Athan. in Symb. Art. 3.

† Ἀϊώνιος ὁ πατὴρ, αἰώνιος ὁ ὑὸς, αἰώνιον ᾗ τὸ πνεῦμα τὸ ἅγιον. ᾗ ὅμως ὐ τρεῖς αἰώνιοι, ἀλλ' εἷς αἰώνιος. Athan. in Symb. Art. 4.

SERMON CIV.

2. FROM the unity of the persons in the same individual essence, ariseth their essential in-being in each other. All the persons being one in essence, and each person having the whole essence in himself, it follows that, in respect of the essence, one person is in another. This our Lord himself asserts; *The Father is in me,* says he, *and I in him.* And again, *Believest thou not, that I am in the Father, and the Father in me?* And yet again in that same chapter, *Believe me that I am in the Father, and the Father in me* (a). Whence it appears, that there is a mutual inexistence of one person in the other: And that this is a great mystery not to be taken up by sense and reason, but only by faith; for it is faith that is put to it, *Believest thou not, &c.* And this is a chief article of the Christian religion, necessary to be studied and believed by us; therefore our blessed Lord urgeth it again, *Believe me that I am, &c.* To clear this a little, so far as we are capable to apprehend such a mystery, let it be considered, that the persons are in each other, not as they are persons, or in or by their own personalities; but by the oneness of their nature and essential properties. The same nature and essential properties being in each of the persons, by virtue thereof the persons also are in one another. The expression implies their most perfect, intimate, and inseparable union, and their eternal co-existence with one another. This is expressed in that text, *And the Word was with God* (b). Where the name God is to be taken personally for the Father: And the expression imports, that the Son was from everlasting inseparably with the Father, being not only with, but in the Father, and the Father in him: So that † the Father is never without the Son, nor the Son without the Father; but where the one is there is the other. And the same is true also of the Holy Ghost.

This is that which divines call ‖ the *inhabitation* and *indwelling* of the persons in each other. By this the ancient fathers did not understand a local inexistence, as of bodies, as when water is in wine; for that would imply different substances: But
such

(a) John x. 38. and xiv. 10, 11. (b) John i. 1.

† *Ubicunque aliqua Persona Divina, ibi est tota Trinitas—Neq; adest una Persona sine aliis; sed Trinitas inseparabiliter adest, ubicunq; una aliqua Persona.* Ambros.

‖ Ἐμπεριχώρησις.

such an indivisible unity, that the one cannot be without the other. Such is the unity of the divine essence, that the Father dwelleth in the Son, and the Son in the Father, and both in the Holy Ghost, and the Holy Ghost in both; but without the least confusion of their personalities. The Son is begotten by the Father, yet is in the Father, and the Father in him. The Holy Ghost proceedeth from both, yet is in both, and both in him; all in each, and each in all, in an ineffable manner.

Here we see the true ground and reason of the truth of what our Lord saith to the Pharisees; *If ye had known me*, says he, *ye should have known my Father also* (c): And of what he saith to Thomas and Philip, *If ye had known me, ye should have known my Father also; and from henceforth ye know him, and have seen him. He that hath seen me, hath seen the Father* (d). The ground and reason is, because he is in the Father, and the Father in him †. Our Lord himself, in the next verse, assigns this as the ground of what he asserts, *Believest thou not, that I am in the Father, and the Father in me. The fulness of the* undivided essence of the *Godhead dwelt in Christ bodily*, Col ii. 9. So that whosoever took up his Deity, were thereby forthwith led to know the Deity of the Father. And here we may see and admire God's gracious condescension, that seeing his divine nature could not be comprehended or taken up by us, he was pleased to reveal and manifest himself in his own Son, the express image of his person, clothed with our flesh, that in this mirror we might see God.

3. From the unity of the divine persons in the same individual essence, ariseth their unity in love. Being one in essence, they must needs love one another with the highest love. So, it is said, *The Father loveth the Son, and hath given all things into his hand:* And, *the Father loveth the Son, and sheweth him all things that himself doth* (e). The Father loveth the Son, not only in the quality of Mediator, but as his Son. He is the object of the Father's eternal love, as being the substantial image of his person. Hence, he is called his *beloved Son*, and his *dear Son*. And he is said to be *in the besom of the Father* (f); a phrase that expresseth intimacy, and oneness in regard of familiarity and delight. And as the Father loveth the Son, so the Son loveth the Father, and both love the Holy Ghost, and the Holy

---

(c) John viii. 19. (d) John xiv. 7, 9. (e) John iii. 35. and v. 20. (f) Matth. iii. 17. Col. i 13. John i. 18.

† *Non ut ipse sit Pater qui Filius, sed quod a Patris similitudine in nullo prorsus discrepet Filius.* August. in Loc.

ly Ghost loves them both. But the Father's love to the Son is particularly insisted upon, for these reasons. 1. To commend the Father's love to sinners, in giving the Son of his love out of his bosom, to redeem them by his death. 2. To commend Christ's love, who being dear to the Father, would yet come out of his bosom to redeem a lost elect company. 3. To assure us that by coming to the Son we shall be beloved of the Father for his sake. And, 4. To shew how acceptable the Son's interposition as Mediator is to the Father.

Now, the blessed persons being one in essence, their love to one another is not merely voluntary, as their love to us is, but necessary: And it is matchless; never was there such love between parties, as there is between the Father, Son, and Holy Ghost. Hence it is that they mutually seek the glory of each other. The Father glorifies the Son: So he prays, *Father, glorify thy Son* (g). The Son glorifies the Father: Hence he says to his disciples, *Whatsoever ye shall ask the Father in my name, that I will do, that the Father may be glorified in the Son* (h). And the Spirit glorifies the Son: *He shall glorify me* (i), says Christ. They have also a mutual delight and complacency in each other from everlasting. Hence Christ is brought in speaking, *I was daily his delight, rejoicing always before him* (k). The Father had an infinite delight and complacency in the Son, and the Son in the Father, and both in the Spirit, and the Spirit in both; all in each, and each in all, ere ever the world was made. And in this mutual delight and complacency consists much of the ineffable blessedness of God; as I had occasion to shew when I spoke of God's blessedness.

4. From their unity in the same individual essence, ariseth their unity in will. Being one in essence, they are also one in will. They all will the same things. This is an unity perfectly holy: They are one in that which is holy and heavenly. This is evident in their joint concurrence in the business of our salvation: They are all employed in it, with one consent and will.

5. From * their unity in essence, ariseth their unity in operation. The Father, Son, and Spirit, being one in essence, therefore

---

(g) John xvii. 1.   (h) John xiv. 13.   (i) John xvi. 14.
(k) Prov. viii. 30.

* *Non Naturam secamus sed Unitatem Naturæ & Voluntatis & Operationis confitemur.* Ambr. in Symb. Apost. Cap. 3.
Una Voluntas Patris et Filii, et inseparabilis Operatio.
Aug. de Trinit. L. 2. C. 5.

therefore all external works, that is, such works as have the creature for their object, are undivided, and equally common to all the three persons. Though their order of working be different, according to their different order and manner of subsistence: Yet the works themselves are common; so that the Father, Son, and Holy Ghost, are one immediate and perfect cause of all external works. But of this I spoke formerly.

Having spoken of the unity of the divine persons, I shall now apply this head, in a threefold word of exhortation.

Use 1. Meditate on this glorious mystery. Your meditations of God should be answerable to the revelation he hath made of himself: And having clearly revealed this of himself, that he is three in one, and one in three, certainly your minds should be more employed about it. Therefore do not satisfy yourselves in meditating of the unity of his essence, and his infinite perfections; but let your minds be raised higher, to contemplate this glorious mystery of a Trinity in Unity. Men and angels were made for this glorious spectacle: And indeed your understanding cannot possibly be employed about a more noble and excellent object than this, the contemplation whereof will be no small part of the happiness of the glorified above. Particularly, how sweet may it be to you who are the children of God, to behold in this admirable unity of the divine persons an idea or exemplar of your union with Christ, and with one another in him? According to that passage in Christ's prayer, *That they all may be one, as thou Father art in me, and I in thee, that they also may be one in us.—And the glory which thou gavest me, I have given them: That they may be one, even as we are one* (*l*). The particle *as* doth not always denote an exact equality, but oft-times some kind of resemblance only; as in that text, *Be ye therefore merciful, as your Father also is merciful* (*m*). So here, *That they may be one, even* AS *we are one:* The expression imports, that in the mystical union between Christ and believers, there is a shadow, or some dark resemblance of the essential union between the three persons in the Godhead. It is true, the mystical union falls vastly short of the essential union; yet it cometh nearest to it. Particularly, as the essential union between the divine persons is a most close and intimate union; so is the union between Christ and believers, a very close and intimate one. As the essential union is expressed, by the mutual inexistence of one person in another; as *thou Father art in me, and I in thee:* So the mystical union is expressed, by the mutual inexistence

(*l*) John xvii. 21, 22.   (*m*) Luke vi. 36.

of Christ and believers; he is *in them*, and they are *in him*. We have both in that one text, *I am in my Father, and you in me, and I in you* (n). Where the mutual inexistence of the divine persons is first signified; and then immediately follows the mutual inexistence of Christ and believers: plainly shewing, that in the latter we have some dark resemblance of the former. Therefore, let believers in Christ solace and refresh themselves, by contemplating, in that ineffable union of the divine persons, an exemplar and idea of their glorious union with Christ, and with one another in him.

Use 2. Contemplate this glorious mystery with holy and humble adoration and admiration. There are three admirable unions. 1. The essential union of the three persons in the Godhead. Of this my text speaks, *These three are one*. And it is expresly called a mystery (o), we read of the mystery of God, and of the Father, and of Christ. 2. The hypostatical union of the divine and human natures in Christ's person. *And without controversy*, says the apostle, *great is the mystery of godliness; God was manifest in the flesh* (p). 3. The mystical union between Christ and believers. *We are members of his body*, says the apostle, *of his flesh, and of his bones* (q): And then it follows, *This is a great mystery*. Bernard, one of the ancients, hath observed, that all these unions may be seen in Christ †, " He hath "a Father, and Spirit, says he, with whom he is one substance; "he hath a human nature, with which he is one person; he "hath adhering believers, with whom he is one Spirit." All these unions are great mysteries; but the first is the greatest of all. It is the foundation of the other two. As the mystical union between Christ and believers, depends upon the hypostatical union of the two natures in his person; so the hypostatical union depends upon the essential union of the three divine persons: For unless there were a plurality of persons in the Godhead, how could one person be given to assume our nature? And unless the three persons were one in essence, how could our nature be united to the divine nature in the person of the Son? As without God-man, there would be no fit person for believers to be united unto; so without a holy Trinity

in

(n) John xiv. 20.   (o) Col. ii. 2.   (p) 1 Tim. iii. 16.
(q) Eph. v. 30, 32.

† *Christus habet in se Patrem, cum quo est una Substantia; habet assumptum Hominem cum quo est una Persona; habet adhærentem sibi fidelem Animam, cum qua est Spiritus unus.*

Bern. de Verb. Psal. 23. Fol. 415.

in Unity, there would be no God-man. I say then, this is a great mystery, three in one, and one in three. I may call it the fundamental mystery of the gospel: It is the foundation of all other gospel mysteries; they all depend upon it. Consequently, it is an incomprehensible mystery; therefore more fit for admiration than for curious search and enquiry. Let us then admire what we cannot comprehend. One contemplating this mystery, cries out, ‡ *O most bright and shining darkness*. Here is light that is inaccessible; light that dazzles the most piercing apprehension. Let us therefore contemplate this mystery with a silent and believing admiration. Let us, as one says, adore it with a humble piety, lest we puzzle faith, while we would inform and satisfy reason.

Use 3. Let believers study to imitate the sacred Trinity in their union. *Be ye followers of God, as dear children* (r): And particularly, follow him in this according to your capacity; labour to be one, as the Father and Christ are one. This our Lord prays for; *That they all may be one, as thou Father art in me, and I in thee, that they also may be one in us* (s) These are admirable expressions: And our blessed Lord useth them, to draw believers to a closer union with one another in him. Study such an union as may be some small resemblance of the mystery of the holy Trinity. Walk like these that are one, as the Father, Son, and Spirit are one. Live so as if you had but one essence and interest. It is true, each of you hath a peculiar individual essence and substance of your own: Yet study to live and walk like them that are one body; yea, like these that are led and actuated by one Spirit, and have the same Holy Spirit dwelling in you, that is also in Christ: For, *he that is joined unto the Lord, is one Spirit* (t). Particularly, study, 1. Unity in judgment. Endeavour to be *perfectly joined together, in the same mind, and in the same judgment* (u). Study, so much as is possible, to be of one mind in the things of God. 2. Unity in love. The primitive Christians were *of one heart, and of one soul* (x). There was such unity in love, as if they had but one Spirit. Whatever lesser differences and debates there may be in matters of religion, yet take heed of managing them with passion and bitterness. Away with all animosities and heart-burnings. Labour to be *knit together in love* (y). Rejoice in one another's graces; delight in the fellowship and society of one another; and seek one another's welfare, both temporal and spiritual.

3. Unity

‡ *O Luminosissima Tenebræ!*
(r) Eph. v. 1.   (s) John xvii. 21.   (t) 1 Cor. vi. 17.
(u) 1 Cor. i. 10.   (x) Acts iv. 32.   (y) Col. ii. 2.

3. Unity in will. Will and desire the same things. Let your desires be united for the glory of God, and the advancement of Christ's kingdom. Particularly, unite your desires in prayer. Hence, 4. Study unity in your operations and actings. Study to be united in the duties tending to your mutual edification, and in your endeavours to advance the kingdom and interests of Jesus Christ. Division tends to ruin: Therefore, it is the stratagem of Satan and his instruments, to divide the people of God. But holy unity will be our strength against the common adversary. Therefore take heed of all divided practices, especially in your actings and appearances for God.

That you may the more resemble a sacred Trinity in unity, 1. Let your union be an holy union. There is an union that is made up by unholy means, and for unholy ends: This is a wicked combination. Godly dissention is better than wicked agreement. It must be an union in God's way, in the ways of truth and holiness. 2. Let your union be such as is consistent with order. There are diversities of gifts and offices; and the unity of the church should not confound the order of it. When men keep not their due place, things are shamefully brought into confusion. Therefore, in uniting our endeavours to advance the kingdom of Christ, let us keep within the bounds and limits of our place and station. 3. Let it be a constant union: So firm that the gates of hell may not be able to break it. Let us cleave fast to one another in the Lord. What becomes of a member that is cut off from the body? Take heed of separating or withdrawing yourselves from the societies of the Lord's people. It is dangerous to stray from the shepherd's tents.

I might adduce many arguments to press this holy unity, if it were proper here to insist on this head. We know not what there may be upon the wheels of Providence; or what trials may be at hand: And there may be endeavours used to divide us; and our divisions will be our ruin. But remember that you are by the same Spirit, and by one faith, united to the same Christ, and through him to the same Father. By a holy union, you will resemble the blessed Trinity, according to your capacity: And this will be your glory. Hence our Lord says in his prayer, *And the glory which thou gavest me, I have given them; that they may be one, even as we are one* (z). By dissention and division, you do what you can to deprive yourselves of that glory gifted by Christ, to be one as the Father and he are one.

Such

(z) John xvii. 22.

Of the Unity of the Persons. 333

Such a holy unity will be a great ornament to the gospel, and commend religion to others, and have a gaining influence to bring them to the acknowledgement of Christ and his truths. Hence our Lord prays, *That they also may be one in us; that the world may believe that thou hast sent me* (a). And such an unity will bring all your gifts and graces into the common bank, and render them useful and beneficial for advancing the common cause of religion. Therefore, let us take heed of dissolving the bonds of union, by pride, or passion, or envy, or tenaciousness, and want of brotherly forbearance: For, if these, or either of them, prevail, a train of mischiefs will easily break in upon us. Let us *stand fast in one Spirit, with one mind, striving together for the faith of the gospel.* Let us *endeavour to keep the unity of the Spirit in the bond of peace* (b). For this end, let us keep close communion with God in Christ. Our Lord prays, *that they may be one* IN US (c); that is, by being in us, and holding communion with us. And pray much for this unity, as Christ did in John xvii.

SERMON CV.

Sixthly, THE general use and application of the doctrine.

Use 1. For refutation of all Antitrinitarians whatsoever. All that deny the distinction of the persons, or the individual unity of the divine essence; all that deny the Deity of Christ, or of the Holy Ghost, do consequently deny a Trinity of persons in the unity of the Godhead.

Very great opposition hath been made by Satan and his instruments in divers ages, against this sacred truth of a Trinity in unity: And it may not be unedifying, through the blessing of God, to give you some brief account thereof, together with some observations thereupon.

Satan began his opposition very early, even in the days of Christ's flesh. Indeed the ancient Jewish Rabbis embraced the doctrine of the Trinity, as Petrus Galatinus hath shewed. Hence the Cabbalists, have these words, " † The Father is " God, and the Son God, and the Holy Ghost God; three " in one, and one in three." Yet the Jews, in Christ's time, were so much degenerate from the Faith and worship of their forefathers, that they seem to have lost the doctrine of the

holy

(*a*) John xvii. 21. (*b*) Phil. i. 27. Eph. iv. 3. (*c*) John xvii. 21.
† *Pater Deus, Filius Deus, Spiritus Sanctus Deus; Tres in uno, unus in Tribus.*

Holy Trinity; at least so far, that when Christ asserted his Deity, they were mad against him, and accused him of blasphemy, in making himself equal with God (*a*). After the resurrection and ascension of Christ, there were so many and so convincing evidences and effects of his Deity, that the church did quietly possess this sacred truth, of a Trinity in unity, for a season. But it was not long till Satan began to play his game, and aiming at the utter ruin of the church, did assault this doctrinal foundation of it. And he made a twofold assault.

The first assault he made was against the distinction of the persons in the Godhead. For this end, he mustered up his forces in the four first ages of the church. The first we have account of, as set a-work by Satan, was Simon Magus, who, with his followers, denied the Trinity of persons, affirming that the Father, Son, and Holy Ghost, are but ‡ divers names under divers operations. But about 38 years after the ascension of Christ, Ebion and Cerinthus were most active in their opposition to the doctrine of the Deity of Christ, and therein of the Holy Trinity. Against them the apostle John wrote his gospel, by infallible divine inspiration. And, O, what cause have we to adore and praise the wisdom and care of divine Providence, in ordering matters so, that this opposition was made by them, while the apostle John was yet living! For, hence it is that in his gospel, we have such an infallible divine determination of that grand controversy about the Holy Trinity, for the confutation of adversaries, and the confirmation of the faith of believers in all succeeding ages.

Nevertheless, that restless enemy the devil, did not give over, but raised up many adversaries, from time to time, against this sacred mystery. For how much soever these adversaries differed from each other in other things; yet they all agreed in this, that there was no such thing as an holy Trinity in unity. In consequence whereof, 1. Some denied the Deity of Christ: As Artemon and Theodotus, about the year of our Lord 200. And after them Paulus Samosatenus, bishop of Antioch, a stout champion for the devil, about the year 269. Though he was a man intolerably proud, passionate and covetous; yet he wanted neither parts nor interest, and was supported by Zenobia, a princess of great spirit and courage, and of the Jewish persuasion. But the Christian bishops at that time ran together, says Eusebius, as against a wolf which designed to destroy the flock, and in a Council at Antioch,

---

(*a*) John v. 18. and x. 30, &c.
‡ *Diversa Nomina sub diversa Operatione.* Ireneus.

Antioch, Ann. 272. after all his arts and subterfuges, condemned his heresy; and in a second Synod at the same place, deposed him. But about 40 or 45 years after that, Arius, a presbyter of Alexandria, who denied the Son to be consubstantial and equal with the Father, raised a terrible storm in the church. For, though his doctrine was condemned as heresy, in that famous council of Nice, which was the first general council, about the year 325. Yet the flame increased, and much blood and persecution followed, by Constantius, Valens, and other Arian emperors, and governors. And never was there a persecution more cruel and barbarous, while it lasted. But this fiery storm, which continued about thirty-six years, was at last extinguished, and the church again triumphed, and truth prevailed, against the gates of hell. This terrible storm was not yet over, when Photinus, bishop of Syrmium, about the year 350, denied the Deity of Christ, and his pre-existence before his nativity of the Virgin Mary; and by his pleasant way of converse, and subtle way of disputing, drew away many. His doctrine was condemned, even by the Arians themselves, especially in the Council of Syrmium, Ann. 356. which both condemned and deposed him. And Socrates tells us, * that what was then done in that matter, was universally approved, not only then, but afterward. 2. Other denied the Deity of the Holy Ghost: As Macedonius, bishop of Constantinople, about the year 360. His followers were called Pneumatomachi, that is *fighters against the Holy Ghost*. His heresy was condemned in the second general Council held at Constantinople, about the year 380. 3. A third sort owned only a nominal Trinity, and denied the distinction of the persons: As Praxeas and Hermogenes, Ann. 171. And after them Noetus, Ann. 240. But chiefly Sabellius, a disciple of Noetus, made the greatest noise about this heresy, about the year 260. He was so active in spreading it, that from him it was called Sabellianism. This heresy was also condemned by the church: For Tertullian writes against Praxeas, and charges him with introducing a new opinion into the church; and Epiphanius tells us † that Noetus with his followers were cast out of the church's communion.

All this was during the first four centuries. In the two following centuries, we find no considerable opposition made to the doctrine of the Holy Trinity: So that the church seems to have had peaceable possession of that sacred treasure during that

* L. 2. C. 29. † Epiphan. Hæref. 57. N. 1.

that time. Theodoret who flourished in the 5th century, affirms, * that all these heresies against our Saviour's divinity, were wholly extinct in his time, so that there was not so much as any small remainder of them. But Satan had yet another game to play: And so

The second assault he made was against the individual unity of the divine essence. In order hereunto, he stirred up divers instruments, about the beginning of the 7th century: Particularly, one John Philoponus, a famous philosopher of Alexandria, held one common specific nature in God, and three individual natures; as it is among men: So that he allowed no individual unity in the divine nature, but what was in the several persons. Hence he was called the leader of the heresy of the Tritheists: And Isidore saith that the Tritheists owned three Gods, as well as three persons. About the same time one Conon and his followers held that there was one immutable divine essence, but that the three persons had each of them a proper distinct individual nature or substance of his own. It is true, these maintained that the three persons are but one God, and utterly rejected the charge of Tritheism: Yet they were chargeable with it, upon the matter, and in consequence to their doctrine; for, three particular distinct divine substances must be three Gods; and, as a learned man observes†, their opinion looks too like asserting that there are three Gods, and yet but one God.

From the beginning of the 7th century till the time of our happy reformation from popery, we read of no considerable opposition made to this sacred mystery of the holy Trinity. Satan finding himself disappointed of his design in the vigorous attempts he made against this doctrinal foundation of the church, in the first ages of the New Testament; the power and policy of hell were, in the following ages, turned against the superstructure, and cast the same into confusion by the assistance of the papacy; nothing almost remaining firm and stable, but this fundamental truth of a Trinity of persons in the unity of the Godhead.

But when the ruins of many generations, in the superstructure of the church's building, were again in some measure, reared up by the Reformation; Satan finding himself disappointed again, and his labour for so many generations in a great measure lost, he returned to his old work of attacking the foundation; so that divers persons, by his instigation, attempted

---

* Theodor. Hæref. L. 2. in Phot. † Bp. Stillingfleet.

tempted the ruin of the church, by reviving old buried heresies about the holy Trinity. I shall not mention all that have made attempts this way since the Reformation, but only some more remarkable. One Michael Servetus, a Spaniard, and a monster of men, revived the heresy of Sabellius, say some; of Arius, say others. He was burnt at Geneva, for his horrid blasphemies, Ann. 1555. About three years thereafter, one Valentinus Gentilis did, in Helvetia, revive the heresy of the Tritheists, asserting three eternal Spirits of different order and degree. He was condemned at Geneva, and beheaded at Bern, for his horrid blasphemies against the Son of God, and the glorious mystery of the Trinity. After him Faustus Socinus set himself to corrupt, yea, overturn, the whole Christian religion; he and his followers, the Socinians, denying Christ to be God by nature, and asserting that he is a mere man, and that the Holy Ghost is not so much as a person. They blaspheme this sacred mystery of the Trinity as a mere human fiction, and have racked their subtle wits to undermine this great truth. Many of the Arminians, though they have not dared plainly to deny this sacred mystery, yet deny the necessity of this article, and its being fundamental: And this they do in favour to the Socinians, whom they own as brethren, and admit into their church communion. Yea, some of them * come near to an agreement with the Socinians, while they deny the Son to be of the same substance or essence with the Father; and affirm that the Father is first, not only in order of subsistence, but also in power and dignity, and that the Son and Holy Ghost are subordinate to him. And consequently, they do, upon the matter, whatever they pretend, overturn this sacred mystery of the holy Trinity. The people also that are commonly called Quakers, deny the distinction of the persons in the unity of the Godhead †. But I shall not insist on this: Nor need I to add any thing about the Deists, who, denying all revealed religion, do also deny a Trinity in unity, and blaspheme this sacred mystery.

But from the account I have given of the opposition made by Satan and his instruments to this great truth, I observe these two things. *Obs.* 1. All these heresies, broached and revived in divers ages, do by the craft and subtility of Satan, conspire

---

* See Episcop. Lib. 4. Institut. Cap. 32 and 35. and Curcel. in Præfat. ad opera Episcopii.

† See Norton Tract. against the Quakers, pag. 6, 7, &c. And Stalham Revilers rebuked, part 1. Sect. 7.

conspire in the same iniquity. † Though they are many and various, and appear with a different face, and seem to look diverse ways; yet there is a manifest conjunction between them in their opposition to the holy Trinity. By one and all of them did Satan assault the very foundation of the church. These heresies do not really differ from one another, so much as at first view they seem to do. All conspire in opposing this chief truth. All agree in this, that there is no such thing as an holy Trinity in unity. *Obs.* 2. How restless Satan hath been in his opposition to this great truth. Though he hath been often baffled, yet that shameless adversary hath as often renewed his attempts with great vigour. And no wonder, for, (1.) This is a most fundamental truth. One calls it *fundamentum fundamentorum*, because all other fundamental truths of the gospel are built upon this; so that this being overturned, the whole fabric of the Christian religion falls to the ground. (2.) This opposition is what our blessed Lord plainly foretold. When his disciples had made that great confession of him, *Thou art Christ, the Son of the living God;* he thereupon gives them this charter of the church's stability, *Upon this Rock will I build my church, and the gates of hell shall not prevail against it* (*b*). Christ is the rock on which the church is built; and the relation the church hath to him as the Rock, consists in the faith of this confession, *Thou art Christ, the Son of the living God.* And this our blessed Lord promiseth to secure against all attempts from the gates of hell; whereby he plainly declares that great and vigorous opposition should be made thereunto, by the power and policy of hell: So that it needs not seem strange that it hath accordingly come to pass. Satan began his opposition very early, and did renew it in divers ages of the church. God had a holy and spotless hand of providence in ordering all this, for the trial of professors, and discovering the faith and constancy of his own, to the praise of his grace, and their own comfort: And the consideration hereof should prevent our stumbling. We need not then think it strange, that Satan hath renewed his opposition to this sacred mystery, in the age wherein we have lived. Many in Britain have been seduced to Socinianism, and have made it their business to draw away others from the truth. And divers books and pamphlet have been published, and

---

(*b*) Matth. xvi. 16, 18.

† *De Sabellio & Ario extant elegantes Sedulii versus.*
Iste fidem trinam, ast hic non amplectitur unam:
Ambo Errore pares, quanquam diversa sequantur.

and difperfed among people, wherein this glorious myftery of the Trinity is affaulted with an impudent and daring boldnefs, and blafphemed as a contradiction and pure nonfenfe. It may be juftly inquired, what could engage men in fuch oppofition to this facred myftery. And I think they are not miftaken who derive the fpring and fountain of this oppofition from Pelagianifm, which had not its firft rife from Pelagius, but is a natural evil. For when men once fet up an independent free-will, and make man the caufe of his own falvation, no wonder if they are led thereby to deny Chrift's powerful redemption, and the Spirit's effectual application; and in confequence thereof, to deny the Deity both of the one and of the other. And hence it is that the Arminians do fo much incline to Socinianifm. But one thing more I mention as the fpring of this oppofition, is the pride of reafon. Men's idolizing their own wit and reafon, hath been a fruitful mother of herefies in all ages. For, men that are proud of their own reafon defpife divine revelation, and will not acquiefce in the wifdom and truth of God, nor fubmit to receive, even upon a divine teftimony, what their reafon cannot comprehend. And God juftly gives up fuch men to damnable delufions; for, pride and felf-confidence are evils that God ever was, and ever will be an enemy unto.

I fhall not now infift in the refutation of thefe adverfaries, having already, in fome meafure, cleared this great truth, and confirmed it from the holy fcriptures. Only we may obferve a few things in general againft them. *Obf.* 1. What our adverfaries maintain in oppofition to this doctrine, are but old buried herefies, revived and raifed up out of their graves. Some of them boaft of things new, and that they have found out fuch things as never entered into the minds of other men. But they bring nothing new, only fome old herefies, in a new drefs of captious words and flanting expreffions. Their opinions are no other but old exploded errors. They have joined themfelves to thofe that rendered themfelves infamous from the firft foundation of Chriftianity: And all their attempt is, to give a new fpirit of life to the carcafe of old rotten herefies. *Obf.* 2. The doctrine of our adverfaries doth highly reflect on the honour of Chrift and his apoftles. For the expreffions ufed by Chrift and his apoftles in the New Teftament are fuch, as do either prove Chrift to be true God, and God by nature; or then are intended to make men believe that he is God, when he is not fo; feeing, to all fincere and honeft minds, they appear to have fuch a meaning. So that, if Chrift be a mere man, as

our

our adversaries say he is, then these expressions are intended to set up Christ, a mere man, to be God. And what impudent and daring boldness is this, to make our Saviour affect to be God, when, according to them, he knew himself to be a mere man; and to make the apostles set up the worship of a creature, when their design was to reclaim the world from the worship of all such as *by nature are no gods* (*c*). *Obs.* 3. Though our adversaries have a high pretence to reason, yet they do plainly act against reason, in giving the sense of these scriptures, which are adduced for proving the doctrine of the holy Trinity, and of the Deity of Christ: For, their interpretations are new, forced, inconsistent with the scope of the place, and the chief scope and tenor of the New Testament, and different from the general sense of the Christian world from the times of the apostles; and the senses they put on these texts are so dark and enigmatical, as turn almost the whole gospel into an allegory: So that their interpretations are most irrational. *Obs.* 4. Such as have denied the Deity of the Son and Holy Ghost, could never find where to fix, or what to call them. Concerning the Son, some said he was a phantasm or appearance, and that he had no real subsistence: Others held him to be a mere man: Others imagined him to be a made God, created before the world, but not of the same essence and substance with the Father: And others have had yet more monstrous imaginations about him. Concerning the Holy Ghost, some imagined him to be a created Spirit; some said he was the gospel; and others held that he was Christ; and now the Socinians conclude that he is a quality, or a work and operation. Such hovering about, and wandering in various uncertainties, is a necessary fruit and consequent of men's departing from their proper rest. Having once turned away from what is revealed concerning these divine persons, it needs not seem strange, that they cannot settle, or agree, who and what they are. *Obs.* 5. What hath been in later years advanced by our adversaries, is what the faith of the church hath triumphed over in all ages, and what truth and learning, under the care and conduct of the Lord Jesus, have often baffled. So that all the oppositions made in our age, are nothing but old baffled attempts of Satan. The Saints have still prevailed against them, and the truth hath had the victory in all ages. Hence I draw these two inferences. 1. Here is ground of hope, that all the opposition and attempts made in our day against the doctrine of the

(*c*) Gal. iv. 8.

the holy Trinity, shall prove ineffectual, and come to nothing. Our adversaries now shall assuredly meet with the like success in their attempts, that others have met with who have gone before them. Truth shall still triumph and prevail, and the faith of the saints be maintained, against the gates of hell. 2. Here is matter of comfort to trembling Christians, who have trembling apprehensions of their danger, when the winds of error and heresy break loose. The opposition and assaults you may meet with, are no other, but what the faith and patience of the Lord's people have been exercised with in former ages, and have through grace triumphed over. Yea, the saints have borne testimony to this great truth of a Trinity in Unity, even in times of hot persecution, especially by the Arians, and have sealed their testimony with their blood.

SERMON CVI.

IT remains now that I should answer some objections, that are raised by adversaries, against our doctrine of a Trinity of Persons in the Unity of the Godhead. But ere I proceed to this, I premise these two things. 1. We are not to let go, or part with the faith of the holy Trinity, though we could not answer all the objections that are urged against it: Because we have good ground and reason to believe it. It is that which God hath revealed; and it is the highest reason to believe what God hath said to be true. Now, it is a rule, even amongst philosophers, that when a man hath once embraced an opinion, upon just grounds and reasons, he ought not to desert it, merely because he cannot answer every objection against it. There are a great many things in nature, of the truth whereof we are well assured, and yet we cannot untie all the knots and intricacies about their natures, properties, and operations: How much more is it so in truths that are supernatural and mysterious? When the objections against an opinion or persuasion, are not of the same weight and importance, with the reasons and grounds on which we embraced it, it is the height of folly to let it go on the account thereof. I notice this, especially for the sake of the more ordinary sort of Christians. It is one thing to be assured of a truth, and another thing to be able to answer all the objections that are raised against it. If you will part with your faith in any truth, merely because you are not able to answer some objections against it, you may find yourselves at last disputed into Atheism. One thing you may be assured of, that every argument from reason against a truth

revealed

revealed in the holy scriptures, is a sophism, though it may be you cannot discover the fallacy. Yet, 2. It is of no small advantage to the interest of religion, to defend even the greatest mysteries of it against the objections of adversaries. Some, in handling these mysteries, reject all arguments drawn from reason, as judging it unnecessary to give them any answer, and sufficient that they have God's own word for what they believe or teach. I confess that the authority of divine revelation, is sufficient to warrant our belief of the holy Trinity, and other sacred mysteries, whatever objections lie against them: Yet to slight arguments drawn from reason against the mysteries of religion, and not to ward off the thrusts of adversaries, is to tempt them either to reject divine revelation, or to put perverse senses upon it †.

These things being premised, I go on to remove objections. Many things are objected by adversaries against our doctrine that I judge not proper to be insisted upon in this place. Therefore I shall only observe some things in general; and then answer an objection or two, whereby greatest noise hath been made: And in the last place, draw some practical inferences from the whole.

In general, I observe these things. 1. Many of their objections are mere cavils and empty sophisms; as many worthy and learned divines have made appear. 2. Many of their objections are not levelled against the doctrine itself, as it is revealed in the holy scriptures, but merely against the explications thereof that are used by divines. But this a most preposterous and irrational course: For it is the doctrine itself, as it is revealed and proposed in the holy scriptures, that is the principal object of our faith: And unless the doctrine itself be owned, it is most foolish and irrational to move or entertain any debate about the way and manner of expressing it; and all foolish debates and contests ought to be avoided, especially in such sacred mysteries. 3. In many of their objections they argue from things finite to that which is infinite, where the consequence is utterly false. There are divers philosophical principles or axioms, which being understood of things finite, for which they are calculated, are most true; but if transferred to an infinite Being, are most false. As for example, That he

that

---

† *Illi qui Argumenta a recta ratione petita violenter rejiciunt, eaq; solutione indigna pronunciant, modeste quidem agunt, sed pessime de Religione mereri videntur.* Bisterfield in Synopsi præfixa Libro cui Titulus, Mysterium Pietatis Defensum contr. Crell.

that begets, and he that is begotten, cannot have the same individual nature or essence; that what is singular and individual cannot be communicated to more; that the same individual nature cannot be in three distinct persons: These and the like axioms must be kept within their own sphere, and limited to finite beings; for, if applied to an infinite Being, they are false. The reason is, because there is no proportion between that which is finite, and that which is infinite †. The divine essence, being infinite, hath such prerogatives as are peculiar to it, and are no way applicable to finite beings.

More particularly, it is objected by adversaries, that our doctrine concerning the holy Trinity is contrary to reason: And of this they endeavour to give several instances. Yea, they blasphemously charge this sacred mystery with contradictions, and as a thing absurd, and contrary both to reason and to itself ‡.

To this I repone a few things by way of answer.

1. We grant that nothing ought to be admitted as a principle of faith, that is contradictory to the principles of right reason. We reject with abhorrence any thing urged upon us as an article of faith, where there is evident proof of such a contradiction: As in the case of Transubstantiation. The reason is, because there is a sweet harmony between truth and truth, between natural truth and revealed truth. God is the author of both; therefore, though they be different, yet they cannot be contrary or repugnant one to another. To admit any thing as a mystery of faith, that is repugnant to right reason, opens a door for filling the world with lies and delusions, under the colour of divine mysteries: And to admit that any article of our religion is against reason, is to gratify Atheists and Infidels, and to tempt men to look on all divine revelations as mere forgeries. Therefore, * when any thing is urged as a reason, against a truth revealed in the holy scriptures, how plausible and subtle soever it may seem to be, yet right reason it cannot be, but only an umbrage and shew of it. But full satisfaction hath been given by divines, with respect to what

is

---

† Ὀυκ ἔςι γὰρ ὡς ἄνθρωπος ὁ Θεὸς ἵνα καὶ ἀνθρώπινα περὶ αὐτῦ τις ἐρωτᾶν τολμήση. Athan. Oper. Tom. 2. Epist. ad Serap.

‡ See Hist. of the Unitar. p. 9. N. 7. and Answer to a Sermon about the Trinity, p. 4, 5, 8.

* *Si Ratio contra Divinarum Scripturarum Authoritatem redditur, quamlibet acuta sit, fallit veri Similitudine, nam vera esse non potest.* Augustin. Ep. 7. ad Marcell.

is alledged by adverfaries, to be abfurd or contradictory in this facred myftery of the Trinity; and all the arguments adduced by them, for the proof of what they alledge, have been fhamefully baffled: So that they have never been able to this day, to juftify their bold charge againft this facred myftery, nor ever will.

2. There may be feeming contradictions that really are not fo. Some things may feem contrary to reafon, that are not fo indeed. The reafon is plain, becaufe many times what is pretended to be reafon, and appears to be fo to this or that man, is not reafon, but a mere fhew of it. Who can hinder feeming contradictions, which do not arife from the repugnancy of things in themfelves, but from the fhallownefs of men's capacities? Who can help the weak underftandings of men? We muft therefore diftinguifh between reafon in the abftract, and confidered abfolutely, which is the reafon of things; and reafon in the concrete, that is, reafon as it is in this or that man, which is weak and fhallow, and very far fhort of a juft and full comprehenfion of the whole reafon of things. Accordingly we fay, that though we are to admit nothing contrary to the reafon of things, yet we may have good ground and warrant, to embrace many things that are contrary to fome men's reafon: And particularly, we heartily embrace the doctrine of the holy Trinity, upon the faith of divine revelation, how contrary foever it may be to the reafon of all the Socinians and other Antitrinitarians in the world. But,

3. Our adverfaries, who are fuch high pretenders to reafon, while they urge reafon as judge of this facred myftery, do in effect overturn fome of the moft fundamental principles of reafon. I give inftance in a few things. 1. It is a fundamental principle of reafon, that what is finite cannot comprehend that which is infinite: But this is overturned by our adverfaries, while they argue thus, It cannot be fo and fo in things finite, therefore it cannot be fo in an infinite Being. It is as much againft reafon as againft faith, for finite creatures to think to fathom an infinite Being. 2. It is a fundamental principle of reafon, that divine revelation is the ground of faith. We ought to believe what God hath revealed, and that becaufe he hath revealed it, without enquiring for other grounds of faith. Our adverfaries overturn this alfo, while they affert, that we muft believe nothing till our reafon be firft fatisfied about it. But if the God of truth hath faid or revealed it, we need no further witnefs. " Human words," fays one *, " want wit-
" nefs:

---

* Salvian.

"ness: But divine carry their own testimony in themselves." True it is, our reason must be satisfied that the thing is revealed: It is against reason to believe without grounds: Therefore we ought to search into the grounds of our faith, and to use the best and most reasonable ways for attaining to the true sense of revelation. But when once it is evident that a thing is revealed, it is highly reasonable that this should immediately command our assent; so that to suspend our belief in this case, on any account whatsoever, is a violation of the law of nature. No reason can be brought to prove any thing in the world more certainly true than this principle, *That I should believe God;* so that if I do not believe him, I offend against the most indisputable principle of reason, against that which nature dictates. Reason pleads that our faith in what God hath revealed must be absolute, without any salvos or limitations. The gospel must *captivate every thought* (orig. † *all the intellect*) *to the obedience of Christ* (d). But the Socinians add a salvo to their belief of the holy scriptures; they will believe them no further than they find them congruous to their own reason: Whereas it is the highest reason in the world, in things of pure revelation, to captivate our understandings to the authority of God, and to subject them to infinite truth in all that it speaks to us. "It is just," says a schoolman ‡, "and purely rational, "that our understanding be captivated, and subjected to the "supreme truth: Nor can the soul be right, unless the under- "standing assent to the supreme truth, for itself, and above "all" That is, without any salvos or exceptions at all. The authority being infallible, the belief should in all reason be absolute.

4. Reason is not judge competent of the doctrine of the holy Trinity, nor a fit measure to try it by: And that on a twofold account. 1. Because, reason since the fall, is sadly corrupted. And, 2. Because this doctrine is a mystery above reason.

(1.) I say, reason, since the fall, is sadly corrupted. Before the fall, it was a pure virgin light, without any spot in it; but, by the fall, it was deflowered and wofully corrupted. As the blemish in the eye is not the light, nor the rust in the gold the pure metal: So, many times that is pretended to be reason, which is but the rust and spiritual corruption of it. Particularly,

† πᾶν Νόημα. (d) 2 Cor. x. 5.
‡ *Justum est ut Intellectus noster captivetur & subjaceat summæ Veritati—Nec potest esse Anima recta, nisi Intellectus summæ Veritati propter se, & supra omnia, assentiat.* Ronand. L. 3. Dist. 23.

larly, reason in us, since the fall, is weak, and fallible, and blind, in the things of God. 1. It is weak. It is so, even in things natural. In diving into the natures, causes, and effects of things, it is driven to many a nonplus; for it sees them, rather in their investing accidents, than in their pure and naked essences. Yea, it cannot so much as dive into the nature of a common stone, and look on the naked essence thereof †. Further, can our reason span the heavens, or number these golden letters the stars, or enter into the treasures of the snow, or ride a circuit with the winds, or tell how the massy earth hangs upon nothing, or draw out an occult quality to an open view? Thousands of things there are in nature, which may make the wisest men cry out with the poor Pagan, ‡ *This one thing I know, that I know nothing.* How much more weak must our reason be in things supernatural, and known only by revelation? Shall such a weakling as this, that is dunced and puzzled with so many things in nature, usurp the chair, and and sit down to judge of sacred mysteries? What presumptuous arrogance is this! 2. Reason in us is fallible §. Reason is a fallible thing, considering the subject in which it is: For it is vitiated by lusts, biassed by interests, perverted by education, darken by passions, and enthralled by prejudices. Hence it is that all the errors and heresies which have swarmed in the church in all ages, have been the progeny of corrupt reason. None have erred more foully, or been more mistaken in their apprehensions about gospel truths, than the greatest scholars, men of reason, and men admired for their parts and learning. And shall such a fallible thing usurp the throne, and sit in judgment on revealed mysteries? How absurd is this! 3. Reason in us is blind in the things of God. *The spirit of a man knoweth the things of a man* (e); and so may by natural reason judge of natural things: *But the things of God knoweth no man but the Spirit of God.* So that we cannot know the things of God, without an inward revelation by the Spirit. Hence our Lord says to his disciples, *It is given unto you to know the mysteries of the kingdom of heaven:* And to Peter, *Flesh and blood hath not revealed it unto thee, but my Father who is in heaven* (f). So that it is not by the carnal reasonings of men, that we can come to the right knowledge of divine mysteries, but by inward revelation. And, see 1 Cor. ii. 14. where the apostle opposeth the

natural

---

† *Dic mihi quid est Lapiditas*, said a learned man.
‡ *Hoc unum Scio, quod nihil Scio.* Socrat.
§ *Humanum est errare.*
(e) 1 Cor. ii. 11.   (f) Matth. xiii. 11. and xvi. 17.

natural man to the spiritual man: So that by the natural man, we are to understand that man that hath only a rational soul, a soul endowed with reason, but void of grace. He *cannot receive* or *know the things of God*, and that because they *are spiritually discerned*. He can gather up a great many notions, and so know the things of God notionally; but he knows them not spiritually, and therefore not congruously to their spiritual nature. He sees them only in their shell and letter, not in the mystery. So that the light of reason is not a light congruous to the things of God, which cannot be spiritually discerned but by a supernatural light.

I say then, that reason being sadly corrupted by the fall, cannot be a judge competent of the doctrine of the holy Trinity. Even Adam in innocence was unfit to controul the doctrines of God, when the eye of his reason was clear; how much more unfit are we, when by the fall our reason is so weak and blind in the things of God? " Wouldest thou see a reason," saith Augustine, " for all that God saith? Look into thine own un-
" derstanding, and thou shalt find a reason why thou shouldest
" not seek a reason."

(2.) Because the doctrine of the holy Trinity is a mystery above reason. It is above reason in its purity, much more above it in its pollution. It is too bright for any human understanding, much more for a sinful understanding. Many things are above reason, which are not at all against it; as might be verified by manifold instances, even in things finite: And must it not be much more so in things divine and supernatural. Such are all the truths of the gospel; they are mysterious; they dazzle and overpower the most piercing apprehension: So that reason cannot make sense of them, unless faith be the interpreter. Therefore reason must not be suffered to go at large, but be kept in custody under divine mysteries. When reason leaves its own sphere of natural notions, and passes over to the supernatural region, and there falls a judging divine mysteries; it is no longer reason, but brutish folly. Carnal reason speaks as absurdly and foolishly in supernatural things, as a beast, if it could speak, would do in matters of reason. Particularly, this truth of a Trinity in Unity, is the great mystery of mysteries, and is in a transcendent excess infinitely above and beyond the capacity of angels and men. How bold and presumptuous then are they, who would measure the sacred Trinity in their shallow understanding, and because it will not lie in so narrow a room, cast it away as no article of faith, as a thing not consistent with reason? When reason thus exalts itself

self in the things of God, it sinks below itself into brutish irrationality. This mystery cannot be comprehended by reason, and therefore disdains to be discussed and tried by it. Being a mystery above nature's light, therefore the light of nature cannot oppose it. Being above reason, it cannot be refuted by reason. Hence the emperor Gratian † would not allow the Arians to dispute of God, and therefore by a special law forbade such disputations; because the mystery of the Trinity is a mystery of faith, far above the reach of human reason.

But here our adversaries make a mighty outcry: "If," say they, "the doctrine of the Trinity be a mystery above reason, then we cannot in reason be obliged to believe it." They say ‡, it is inconsistent with the nature of man, and with the wisdom and goodness of God, to require us to believe any such thing. And a certain Socinian lays down this for a rule, ∥ "That cannot be believed by faith, which cannot be comprehended by reason." Hence they reject all such mysteries of faith as are above reason, and deny that there is any thing so mysterious in the gospel.

But we have no ground to reject a doctrine, when it is offered as a matter of faith, merely on this account, that it is above our reason and comprehension. This is evident from these two things.

1. Because, even in things finite, we may be certain of the being of many things, though we cannot comprehend the nature and manner of them. It is ingenuously confessed by our adversaries themselves §, that we converse every day with very many things, none of which we comprehend. And the same thing is acknowledged by a learned author, with respect to both material and immaterial substances *. Now, if our knowledge even of these is so dark; if our understandings come so far short with respect to the nature and manner of many things, that we are most certain of the being of; how unreasonable must it be to reject a doctrine proposed to us as of divine revelation, because we cannot comprehend the manner of it, seeing the higher any being is, it is the more remote from our knowledge. If we cannot comprehend the common natures of things, how

much

---

† Mr. Ley's Discourse of Disputations concerning Matters of religion, Cap. 6.
‡ See Christian. not Myster. p. 28, 145.
∥ *Nihil credi potest quod a ratione capi & intelligi nequeat.*
§ Answ. to a Sermon about the Trinity, p. 5.
* Essay of human Understanding, B. 2. Ch. 23. sect. 31, 32.

much less can we comprehend an infinite Being? If we can be certain in reason of many things in nature, which we cannot comprehend, why should a point of faith be rejected on that account? If we may in things finite, why not in that which is infinite? What imaginable reason can there be for this?

2. Consider the infinite perfection of the divine nature. This is so far above our reach, that God may justly oblige us to believe things concerning himself, which we are not able to comprehend as to the manner of them. The very idea or conception of a supreme Being, implies its being infinite and incomprehensible. Now, if nothing must be believed but what we can comprehend, then even the being of God were to be rejected, because the manner of his being is incomprehensible. If a Trinity of persons in the Godhead must be rejected, because we cannot comprehend the manner of it, then we behoved to reject one God as well as three persons. I might give instance also in the several perfections of God, his eternity, omniscience, omnipresence, &c. all which are incomprehensible. We are satisfied in point of reason that God is eternal, omniscient, omnipresent, &c. yet we cannot have distinct adequate notions of these perfections. Even these that are called communicable attributes, such as wisdom, power, holiness, &c. though we may have a distinct and clear conception of them, as they are in themselves; yet as they are in God, they are infinite, and so above our comprehension. Now, if in these things that are known of God by nature's light, we may be certain that a thing is, though we cannot comprehend the manner of it; why may we not be so in things purely revealed? For there can be no reason to tie us up more strictly in point of revelation, than we are without it. From the whole it is evident, that it is no relevant objection against any thing offered as a matter of faith, that the manner of it is incomprehensible by us. As God is infinite and incomprehensible, so he can testify some things concerning himself, which cannot be comprehended by reason, and yet being revealed, are most worthy of our assent and belief, on the account of his infinite truth and veracity.

From what is said, it appears, that in articles of faith, we are to believe more than we are able to understand, faith supplying the defects of our understanding †. Therefore, that is an excellent

---

† Τὰ τῇ πίστει παραδιδόμενα, ἀπεριέργαστον ἔχει τὴν γνῶσιν.
Athan. Oper. Tom. 2. Epist. 2. ad Serap.

lent saying of Augustine, "*When the foundation of faith is laid in the heart, which helps the understanding, we are to embrace with it all that it can reach to: And where we can go no further, we must believe without doubting." The reason is, because there are some things revealed, of which we can entertain some notion in our minds, though there may be some things belonging to them which we cannot distinctly conceive. We believe the τὸ ὅτι, that they are, though we cannot conceive or comprehend the τὸ διότι, or the manner how they are. We believe that God is from all eternity, though there be something that our understanding cannot reach unto, viz. the manner how he is so. So here we believe the doctrine of the holy Trinity, though we cannot distinctly conceive the manner, how three should be one, and one three. Hence an ancient Father says, "† We ought to believe the eternal Deity of the holy Trinity, though it be incomprehensible by any human understanding." And a late learned divine expresseth himself thus, "‡ I believe the doctrine of the holy Trinity: Yet I confess withal, such is the weakness of my understanding, that I am utterly unable to look into the depth of so great a mystery, and cannot but cry out, as the apostle did in another case, ὢ βάθος, O the depth and unsearchableness!"

From what I have said on this head, I shall now draw some practical inferences, and that by way of exhortation.

1. Let us labour to get and entertain a deep humbling sense of the weakness and insufficiency of our own reason. We are indeed poor shallow creatures. Our finite weak reason is not able to wade into the depths of divine mysteries. Therefore study much humility and submission of mind: For, as these qualifications will greatly commend you to God, so they will notably prepare you for faith, and give check to all curious and bold inquiries into such a deep mystery as this is.

2. Let us deny our own reason. Even sanctified reason must be denied, so as not to idolize it, or set it up as judge of divine mysteries, which are so far above it. But reason, as

it

---

* *Nos ergo Fratres, fide precedente, quæ sanat Oculum Cordis nostri, quod intelligimus sine Obscuritate capiamus; quod non intelligimus, sine Dubitatione credamus.* August. in Job 12. 39.

† *Absque ullo Principio et Fine credenda est Sanctæ Trinitatis Divinitas, licet Humanæ sit Menti ipsa Comprehensione difficilis.*

Ambros. in Symb. Apost. c. 2.

‡ Dr. H. on the Creed, p. 20.

it is a false light, as it plays the serpent seducing from holy truths, as it laughs at divine mysteries above its comprehension, this especially must be denied. You must *become fools, that you may be wise* (g). Abraham having God's promise for a feed, *considered not his own body now dead, nor yet the deadness of Sarah's womb* (h). He did not play the critic on either: He laid by his critical enquiries, and was denied to his own apprehensions of things, that he might give glory to God, by believing. O take heed of pride and conceit of reason. Your carnal reason is a false light, and if trusted to, will easily lead you into error. Men that have given up themselves to the conduct of natural reason, have run a wild course. These sons of pride, who set up their own reason for their only rule and guide, have plunged themselves into many damnable errors. Hence an ancient observes, "†That they became masters of error, who would not be disciples of truth." Therefore.

3. Let us submit our reason to divine revelation. Reason is to be captivated in matters of faith. All these high reasonings that exalt themselves against the doctrine of faith, are to be *cast down* (i). Certainly it is the most rational thing in the world, to chide down your reason, and lay aside the confidence of your own understanding, that you may believe these things God hath revealed, though you cannot comprehend them. It is one great end of the gospel, to sacrifice our shallow reason on the altar of faith, that we may honour the truth of God, in believing the mysteries of the gospel, upon the bare report he hath made of them in his blessed word, which is a much surer foundation than reason can afford. Believe the doctrine of the holy Trinity, though you cannot comprehend it, because the God of truth hath revealed it. Let faith seal to God's veracity, but do not offer to measure the mystery. Believe the thing so to be, but do not pry into the way and manner how it is. Do not say, How can these things be? That is the voice of corrupt reason, not of faith. It is the genius of faith to subject the mind to the authority of God. Abraham, being called by God, *obeyed* and *went out* of his own country, though he *knew not whither he went* (k). So, you ought to follow the conduct of the holy scriptures, even in these things that are above

---

(g) 1 Cor. iii. 18.   (h) Rom. iv. 19.   (i) 2 Cor. x. 4, 5.   (k) Heb. xi. 8.

† *Ideo Magistri Erroris existunt, qui Veritatis Discipuli non fuere.*
                                              Leo primus. Epist. 10.

above your capacity. Consider what the scripture saith, and subject your understandings to the oracles of God.

SERMON CVII.

Use 2. FOR information or instruction, in several particulars.

Instr. 1. From this doctrine, we may be instructed about the truth of the Christian religion. For that must needs be the true religion, that owns such a revelation as is most for the glory of God, and is most congruous to the salvation of lost sinners: But such a revelation we own, when we teach that there are three distinct persons in the unity of the Godhead. 1. Our doctrine is much for the glory and honour of God: For hereby it is that he is distinguished from all false gods, that he is one in three, and three in one. The prophet cries out, *There is none like unto thee, O Lord* (a). True it is, the attributes and works of God distinguish him from all others: For there is none in heaven or earth, that is infinite, or eternal, or unchangeable, the Creator, preserver, and governor of all things, but God alone. Yet idolaters have imagined their false gods to be so. But it never entered into the heart of any idolater, to imagine his god to be one in three, and three in one; one in essence, and three in persons. This is such a mystery, as in the opinion of idolaters themselves, none of their idols can be like unto JEHOVAH. 2. Our doctrine about a Trinity of persons in the Godhead, is most congruous to the salvation of lost sinners. For, unless this doctrine be believed and rightly understood, we cannot possibly understand how the salvation of lost sinners could be brought about: For how could a valuable satisfaction be made to justice for such an infinite evil as sin is, save only by an infinite person? And how could one and the same person make satisfaction to himself? The truth is, such as deny a Trinity of persons in the Godhead, overturn the only way of salvation, and render the redemption of lost sinners utterly impossible.

Therefore our blessed Lord, being to ascend into heaven, did recommend the open profession of the holy Trinity to all his followers, and appointed the same to be sealed and testified by the public sacrament of baptism, every where, and to all generations †: *Go ye, therefore,* says he, *and teach all nations, baptizing*

(a) Jer. x. 6.

† Athanasius, speaking of the holy Trinity, says, αυτη της καθολικης εκκλησιας η πιστις· εν Τριαδι γαρ αυτ' εθεμελιωσε και ερριζωσεν

baptizing them in the name of the Father, and of the Son, and of the Holy Ghost. So that all that embraced the Christian religion, were to be entered into the church, not by a bare verbal profession, but by a solemn rite of baptism, and that in the name of the Father, Son, and Holy Ghost; that is, they were to be baptized into the faith of the sacred Trinity: And the administration of that ordinance was enjoined, as a most public and solemn profession of a Trinity in unity. Therefore, as a learned divine observes *, the ancient Jews did rightly conceive, that the doctrine of the Trinity was not now to be kept up as a secret mystery from the world, but that the Christian church was to be framed upon the belief of it. And so did the Christian church understand it from the very beginning. Hence it was, that † they instructed their Catechumens, as they called them, in the doctrine of the Trinity, for the space of forty days, before they were admitted to baptism. And they rejected the baptism of divers heretics, because they denied the doctrine of the holy Trinity. And it is the opinion of some learned men ‡, that the most ancient creeds went no further than the form of baptism, viz. to believe in God the Father, Son, and Holy Ghost; and that other articles were added as heresies gave occasion for them.

Instr. 2. From this doctrine of the holy Trinity, we may be instructed, of the candour and sincerity of Christians in all ages, in solemnly owning and professing the faith of this sacred mystery of the Trinity, and acknowledging it as the great foundation of all other articles of the Christian religion. For, what should move men of equal, if not of greater abilities than other men, to own and espouse a doctrine that is seemingly contradictory in itself, a doctrine that seems absurd to carnal reason, a doctrine that meets with so great opposition, and a doctrine that is contemned and derided by men that have a high claim to the exercise of reason: I say, what should move men of great parts and abilities, to own and espouse such a doctrine, and to own it as the most fundamental article of their religion, were it not that they find themselves indispensably obliged so to do, upon the faith of divine revelation? This certainly

---

ὁ κύριος, εἰρηκὼς τοῖς μαθηταῖς, πορευθέντες μαθητεύσατε πάντα τὰ ἔθνη, &c. Athan Oper. Tom. 2. Epist. 1. ad Serap.

* Bishop Stillingfleet in his Discourse in Vindication of the Doctrine of the Trinity, pag. 219

† Hieron. Epist. 61.

‡ Erasm. de Conf. paris. Tit. 2. Voss. de Symb. Dis. 1. N. 38.

tainly is an argument of great sincerity and integrity; especially considering that this doctrine hath been owned and professed by Christians, when it was much against their own worldly interest. Surely, the more that men are concerned to maintain and defend a doctrine that is much opposed and contemned, and that against their own interest, the greater evidence do they give that they are firmly persuaded of the truth of it. What could move the primitive Christians, such as Justin Martyr and others, who must be owned to have been men of great sense, in their apologies to the Pagan world for the Christian religion, to mention such a mysterious and dark point as that of the Trinity is? Would they hereby have exposed the Christian religion to be ridiculed by men of reason, if they had not been firmly persuaded, that this was a most necessary part of the Christian faith? Why did they not conceal it, and only represent to the heathen emperors the fair and plausible part of Christianity, which one would think might have done them better service? The true reason of all this is, they were men of great sincerity, and therefore neither would nor could conceal what they were assured by divine revelation to be a most fundamental point of the Christian religion.

I cannot here omit what is pleaded by our adversaries the late Socinians, viz. That the doctrine of the Trinity hath been received and supported in the Christian world by force and interest. This is what they plead. Here then it is granted, that men will readily judge according to the evidence of reason, when there is no bias of force or interest to sway them. But so it is that the doctrine of the holy Trinity, was maintained and owned by the Christian church, when the main force of imperial edicts was against Christianity itself. There was in the first ages of the Christian church a free and general consent in it, even when the people of God were under grievous persecution, and the world was full of prejudices against the Christian religion. Yea, this doctrine was owned and professed, with holy magnanimity and resolution, by the orthodox Christians, under the Arian persecution, than which none was ever more cruel and barbarous. And seeing this doctrine of the holy Trinity, hath been owned and professed by Christians, when it was so much against their own interest, it is a plain argument that they were firmly persuaded of the truth of it, and that they were engaged to own it by other arguments and motives than force or fear. Their integrity cannot in reason be suspected, when at the same time, they might have secured their worldly interest much better, by renouncing the

the truth. And it cannot be supposed that they were so void of sense, as to be fond of nonsense, as our adversaries blaspheme, when sense would have done them equal or better service.

Instr. 3. From this doctrine we may be instructed about the great evil of sin. It is committed against a holy Trinity, against three infinitely glorious persons. The more persons are offended, the offence is still the greater: But here three infinitely glorious persons are offended and dishonoured by sin. For the Deity being one and the same in all the three persons, therefore what is against one is against all. Particularly, as I had occasion formerly to shew, in the holy scriptures the three divine persons have distinct offices and operations ascribed to them in the business of our salvation. The Father is represented as sovereign Lawgiver, the Son as Redeemer, and the Holy Ghost as Sanctifier. Now, sin strikes against all three. 1. It strikes against the Father, as sovereign Lawgiver. Therefore it is called *a transgression of the law* (b). Every sin contemns the authority of the Lawgiver, and slights the law that forbids it. Hence Nathan says to David, *Wherefore hast thou despised the commandment of the Lord, to do evil in his sight* (c)? You despise the law, and go about to make it void, when you give way to sin. So the Psalmist speaks, *They have made void thy law* (d). Sin contradicts God's sovereignty, and seeks to justle him out of his throne. Though the sinner doth not intend this, yet he doth so virtually, and God will so account of it †. Sin, in its own nature, strikes against the sovereignty of God. Every sin is an act of disloyalty and rebellion: Open sin doth, as it were, proclaim rebellion and war against God, and secret sin is conspiracy against him. 2. Sin strikes against the Son as Redeemer. It strikes against his mediatory glory, and wounds him in his office: For he came to *put away sin*, and to *destroy the works of the devil* (e). Therefore every sin is a building again what Christ came to destroy. Sin would make void the end of Christ's death, and make his office of none effect. When you will sin, you seek to tie these cords the faster that Christ came to loose; and consequently you seek to put the blessed Redeemer to shame, by defeating the purpose of his death. Again, sin is a piercing of Christ. *They shall look upon me,* says he, *whom they have pierced* (f). It was sin that was

---

(b) 1 John iii. 4.   (c) 2 Sam. xii. 9.   (d) Psal. cxix. 126.
(e) Heb. ix. 26. 1 John iii. 8.   (f) Zech xii. 10.
† *Est finis Operis, licet non finis Operantis.*

was the meritorious cause of his sufferings: When you sin, you commit that which cost Christ dear, and made him bleed, and cry out, and expire upon a tormenting cross. Every act of sin is interpretatively a stab to the heart of the Son of God. 3. Sin strikes against the holy Spirit as Sanctifier. It tends to make void his personal operation. It is the proper work of the Spirit, to sanctify sinners, to mortify and subdue sin, to cleanse, wash, and purge the soul from sin. But sin opposeth the Spirit in this work. Hence we read of *vexing, resisting,* and *grieving the Spirit* (g).

More particularly, from this doctrine we may be instructed concerning the greatness of the sin of unbelief, not assenting to the doctrine of the gospel, and not receiving Christ upon the terms of the gospel. This is a more sensible opposition and contradiction to the holy Trinity, than any sin against the light of nature; because there is an evident discovery of the holy Trinity in the gospel. All the divine persons concur, and have a hand in the salvation of lost sinners: Therefore, to reject this salvation is a sin that strikes against all the persons. The Father sends the Son to purchase this salvation; the Son comes, and dies, to makes the purchase; and the holy Spirit offers to apply it. To neglect all this, as is done by unbelief, must be a sin of a high aggravation, being a manifest opposition to the holy Trinity in their distinct offices and operations in the business of our salvation. Further, unbelief is a sin against the highest testimony, the testimony of the greatest persons that ever were or can be: As in my text, *There are three that bear record in heaven, the Father, the Word, and the holy Ghost.* They bear record or witness to this great truth, that Christ is the Son of God, and the Saviour of the world, as is clear from the context. Therefore the refusing Christ, and rejecting the salvation that the gospel offers, is a rejecting this infallible testimony, a sin against the highest Witness. Again, unbelief is an envying the holy Trinity the honour of our salvation. For all the persons are engaged in the work of saving lost sinners. The Father is engaged, by chusing some to everlasting life, by contriving a way of salvation for them, and by sending his Son to make a purchase of that salvation. The Son is engaged, by undertaking the work, by coming into the world, and dying and suffering for that very end. The holy Spirit is engaged: For he offers to apply Christ's purchase; he enlightens the mind with the knowledge of Christ, and pleads and strives with

---

(g) Isa. lxiii. 10. Acts vii. 51. Eph. iv. 30.

with sinners to embrace him. But unbelief tends to make void all this: For if it did universally prevail, not one soul would be saved. So that no sin strikes more against the honour of the blessed Trinity, than the sin of unbelief. Particularly,

1. Unbelief strikes against the Father: For it was the Father that sent Christ, and sealed him, and gave him a commission to be the Saviour of the world. So that unbelief, the not receiving and closing with Christ, is a refusing and rejecting God's Ambassador, a tearing his commission, and despising God's authority in him. It is to God the Father the affront is offered. *He that despiseth me*, says Christ, *despiseth him that sent me* (*h*). Though unbelief be an enmity immediately against the person of Christ, yet it redounds to the Father, because Christ is HIS Christ, HIS Anointed. 1. It is a disparaging the wisdom of the Father, in contriving redemption, as if the contrivance were a piece of folly, and he had been busied from eternity about a thing of nought, and had done so much about Christ to no purpose. It is a rejecting the eternal counsels of infinite Wisdom (*i*). 2. It is a contempt of the love and grace of the Father, in giving and sending Christ to save lost sinners. In the Father's giving Christ, there is such a manifestation of divine love and grace, as may astonish all created understandings (*k*). But unbelief casts a vile reproach on all this, and puts a scorn upon it, as not worth the noticing. By unbelief sinners spurn against the beatings of the heart of God. 3. It is a blemishing his infinite truth and veracity. For, as *he that hath received his testimony, hath set to his seal, that God is true:* So, *he that believeth not God, hath made him a liar, because he believeth not the record that God gave of his Son* (*l*) Though God hath engaged his royal word, that Christ is an able and sufficient Saviour, that all that believe on him shall be saved through him, and that there is no salvation in any other: Yet unbelief gives him the lie, and reproaches him as an impostor, and so strips him of the glory of his nature It stamps upon him the character of the devil, who is called *the father of lies* (*m*). Yea, it charges him with perjury; seeing to his royal word he hath added his solemn oath for the encouragement of sensible sinners (*n*). 4. Unbelief tends to make void the Father's counsel for the salvation of lost sinners. It is a thwarting God in his chief end and design. Seeing the Father hath chosen a
company

(*h*) Luke x. 16.   (*i*) Luke vii. 30.   (*k*) John iii. 16.
(*l*) John iii. 33. 1 John v. 10.   (*m*) John viii. 44.   (*n*) Ezek. xxxiii. 11.

company of lost mankind, and contrived a way of salvation for them, and sent his Son to accomplish it; to reject this salvation is, as much as in you lies, to make void the end of God, to frustrate his design, to tread under-foot the whole scheme of his counsel, and to deprive him of all the glory he proposed to himself in the work of redemption. Hence it is said, *The Pharisees and lawyers rejected the counsel of God against themselves* (*o*). True it is, God's end and design cannot be frustrated, nor his counsel made void; *the counsel of the Lord standeth for ever*, and God shall attain his design in spite of unbelieving sinners: Yet this is the nature and tendency of unbelief; so that, if it should prevail in all the children of Adam, this would be the effect of it.

2. Unbelief strikes against the Son, the Lord Jesus Christ. For, 1. It is an undervaluing his precious blood. Unbelievers count the blood of Christ *an unholy thing* (*p*): That is, a common and inefficacious thing, unprofitable for their salvation. They reject it, and trample it under-foot. Unbelief hath in it a secret sentiment of the insufficiency of Christ's blood for the great end of redemption, as if it were of no more efficacy than the blood of bulls and goats. 2. It is a despising and slighting Christ's love; and denying all these choice affections which engaged him in the work of redemption. Unbelief is a fleeing in the face of that love which purchased redemption at so dear a rate, and is at so much pains to gain the hearts of sinners. 3. It is a disparaging the wisdom of Christ; as if he had engaged in a foolish undertaking, by shedding his blood, and laying down his life for things of no worth and value; or, by suffering so much for purchasing pardon and salvation, which might have been obtained at a cheaper rate without being beholden to him. 4. It is a great indignity done to his person. It is *a refusing him* (*q*). A rejecting him who is God equal with the Father, the centre of the Father's delight, and the joy of his heart from everlasting. Yea, he is rejected by unbelief with a great deal of undervaluing. It is said of them that refused the invitation to the marriage-supper of the king's son, that *they made light of it, and went away, one to his farm, and another to his merchandize* (*r*). Unbelief is a preferring mere trifles to this pearl of great price, yea, a soul-murdering lust above him. It is an unworthy usage of him; a treating him as a worm, and not a man. 5. It tends to deprive Christ of the

---

(*o*) Luke vii. 30.   (*p*) Heb. x. 29.   (*q*) Heb. xii. 25.
(*r*) Matth. xxii. 5.

the honour of his undertaking, and of the fruit of his soul-travail. Seeing he did undertake the work of redemption, and came into the world on this very errand, and laid down his life for a company of lost sinners; then, not to receive and close with him, is to render all that he hath done and suffered vain and fruitless. The salvation of lost sinners was the reward promised to Christ, and which he proposed to himself for his satisfaction. So it is said, *He shall see of the travail of his soul, and shall be satisfied* (*s*). But by unbelief sinners do what in them lies to disappoint Christ of the satisfaction he set his heart upon, to rob him of his reward, and to frustrate him of the end of his sufferings.

3. Unbelief strikes against the Holy Spirit. It is the great errand of the Holy Ghost to the world, to convince men of this sin. Hence our Lord says, *I will send him unto you And when he is come, he will reprove the world of sin, and of righteousness, and of judgment. Of sin, because they believe not on me* (*t*). Unbelief is the principal fort against which the Spirit plants his battery. By his common illumination, he bears witness to the excellency of Christ, and the truths of the gospel; but unbelief slights this witness. It is the proper work of the Spirit, to convince men of their sin and misery, and of the necessity and excellency of Christ and his righteousness, and to draw them to Christ: There are many touches and motions of the Spirit that have a material tendency this way; but unbelief crosseth them all. The Spirit presseth the truths of Christ upon the souls of sinners, and urgeth them to embrace him; there are inward calls and secret courtings of the Spirit, importunate knocks at the door of the heart: But unbelief maintains the fort of the heart against the Spirit, and puts bars in his way to hinder him to enter. It is *a resisting the Holy Ghost* (*u*). Indeed, in the work of conversion the Spirit works mightily and insuperably, and overcomes all resistance: Yet there is great resistance made to the Spirit in his common operations; and thereby the Spirit is often provoked to depart, and to leave sinners to their own obstinacy.

From all this it appears, that the sin of unbelief sets itself in a direct opposition to the holy Trinity, in their joint concurrence for carrying on the salvation of lost sinners. Therefore the wrath and vengeance that shall come upon unbelievers must be dreadful and terrible. As under the Old Testament the measures of the sanctuary were double to other measures,

so

(*s*) Isa. liii. 11. (*t*) John xvi. 7, 8, 9. (*u*) Acts vii. 51.

so gospel vengeance will be double vengeance. The apostle puts the question, *What shall the end be of them that obey not the gospel of God* (x)? Dreadful and terrible will it be. It is inexpressible and inconceivable. The most scorching receptacles in hell-fire are reserved for unbelievers. Not one drop of water will be allowed to temper that devouring flame, but it will be as sharp as justice armed with infinite power can make it. Therefore take heed of this sin of unbelief, the refusing and rejecting an offered Christ. As your sin in so doing is great, and of a deep aggravation; so, if you persist in it, your judgment will be unavoidable and intolerable.

SERMON CVIII.

Use 3. FOR reproof, to several sorts of persons.

Repr. 1. To such as are ignorant of this glorious mystery of a Trinity in Unity. I speak not of a partial ignorance; for even the most knowing Christians amongst us are ignorant in part, and come short of that measure of knowledge that is attainable, even in this life. But I speak of gross ignorance. Alas, too many professed Christians know no more of a trinity of persons in the Godhead, than if this mystery had never been revealed. And hence it is, that they do ignorantly bear in their minds gross errors and heresies, as appears frequently by their answers when they are examined on this article. Some do ignorantly slide into the heresy of the Tritheists, as if there were three Gods; and others into the heresy of the Socinians, as if the Father only were the true eternal God.

But such gross ignorance of this mystery is a sad evil. For, 1. It is inseparably attended with gross ignorance of the whole truths and mysteries of the gospel: Particularly of these that concern the person, natures, and offices of the Lord Jesus, and his incarnation and satisfaction; and of these that concern the Spirit's effectual application of the purchased redemption. 2. It is in the judgment of the Spirit of God, downright Atheism. The Gentiles are said, by the apostle, to be *without God* (a); orig. *Atheists.* And why doth he call them Atheists? Because they were without Christ. Though men acknowledge that there is but one God; yet if they do not know God in Christ, God in three persons, they are Atheists 3 Such ignorance spoils all your worship, and renders it vain and fruitless. Though you have a form of worship; yet if you be ignorant of the holy Trinity, that inscription which was upon

the

(x) 1 Pet. iv. 17.   (a) Eph. ii. 12.

the altar at Athens, may be set on all your worship, *To the unknown God*. 4 Such ignorance amongst us is wilful and affected. For this mystery of the Trinity, as to the το᾽ ῞οτι, that it is, is plainly revealed, and frequently taught and preached; so that people can have no excuse for their ignorance. None come to any ripeness of years, are ignorant of a trinity of persons in the Godhead, under such a clear gospel-light, but who are *willingly ignorant* (*b*). They please themselves in their ignorance of this mystery, and are at no pains to attain to the knowledge of it. Oh, what a prodigious sottishness possesses some people in the midst of multiplied means of knowledge! Says our Lord to Philip, *Have I been so long time with you, and yet hast thou not known me, Philip* (*c*)? Men's long enjoyment of the means of knowledge is a great aggravation of their ignorance. It is certainly matter of great shame, to be ignorant of the true God, under such plenty of the means of knowledge. Hence the apostle says, *Some have not the knowledge of God; I speak this to your shame* (*d*). 5. The gross ignorance of this mystery is damnable; seeing a competent knowledge of it is absolutely necessary to salvation. *This is life eternal*, says Christ, *that they might know thee the only true God, and Jesus Christ whom thou hast sent* (*e*). That God, who is one in three persons, is the only true God; and the right knowledge of him, is the beginning, progress, and perfection of eternal life. And if it be eternal life to know him, it must be eternal death to be ignorant of him. Not only the denial of the holy Trinity, but also the ignorance of it, is damnable. *The Lord Jesus shall be revealed from heaven, with his mighty angels, in flaming fire, taking vengeance on them that know not God* (*f*). And if there be vengeance even for heathens that know not God, how much more vengeance must be reserved for professing Christians, that are ignorant of God under such special advantages and means of knowledge.

Repr. 2. To such as do not worship a Trinity in Unity. There may be some of you who have some knowledge of a Trinity of Persons in the Godhead, who yet do not know how to use and improve your faith of a Trinity in your worship. You worship God, without any distinct reflections on the personal operations of the Father, Son, and Holy Ghost, in the business of salvation. You worship God no otherwise than heathens and Pagans worship him, as the Creator and Governor of the world.

(*b*) 2 Pet. iii. 5.   (*c*) John xiv. 9.   (*d*) 1 Cor. xv. 34.
(*e*) John xvii. 3.   (*f*) 2 Thess. i. 7, 8.

world. You believe as Christians, and worship as Pagans. Such worship is vain, and will neither please God nor profit you. For, God will be worshipped as three in one, and one in three; it is as such he hath revealed himself to be the only object of religious worship And without a due consideration and right improvement of the faith of this mystery in your worship, you can have no access to God in it: For there is *no coming to the Father, but by the Son* (g). And you cannot worship God but by the help of the Spirit: For it is by *the spirit of adoption, we cry Abba, Father:* And *the Spirit helpeth our infirmities* (h). So that you must worship God, through Christ, by the help of the Spirit. Therefore, they that do not improve their faith of a Trinity in their worship, lose all their labour in it.

Repr. 3. To such as have gross misapprehensions of the glorious Trinity, or of any of the divine persons. Some ignorant people are apt to apprehend the Father as an old man, and the Son as a young man; or that the Father hath a power and pre-eminence over and above the Son. And too many of the vulgar sort of Christians look on the Son, as more merciful, loving, and condescending to poor sinners, than either the Father or the Holy Ghost. They think of the Father as all wrath and justice, and hard to be reconciled; and of the Son as more gracious Particularly, convinced and sensible sinners are apt to entertain hard thoughts of God the Father, as if he were more strange to sinners, and could have no love to them, nor wish well to them, till the Son gain him to it. Yea, upon this mistake some serious souls are filled with continual jealousies and suspicions of the love of God. But such apprehensions of the divine persons strike against their oneness in nature and essence, and their equality in all essential attributes, and are contrary to what is plainly revealed concerning them in the holy scriptures. All the divine persons are so deeply interested in the salvation of lost sinners, that one cannot be thought to love or desire it more than another. Yea, the Father's love is represented as the spring of all; and Christ is the free gift of his eternal love (i). And the Holy Spirit is sent by the Father, as well as by the Son, to apply the purchased redemption. And the blessed Spirit hath of himself a great love to, and desire after the salvation of lost sinners. How earnestly doth he strive with them? How importunately doth he knock at the door of their hearts? And with what patience doth

---

(g) John xiv. 6.   (h) Rom. viii. 15, 26.   (i) John iii. 16.

doth he stand and wait, though he meet with manifold denials and repulses? So that these misapprehensions, which ignorant people are apt to have of the divine persons, are most contrary to plain revelation. I acknowledge that atheistical conceits and wrong apprehensions of the blessed Trinity, may sometimes arise in the minds even of such as are truly gracious: But they must not be entertained and cherished. You ought to strive and protest against them, and bewail them, and complain of them to God, and cry for help against them.

Repr. 4. To such as sin against and dishonour the holy Trinity, or any of the divine persons Seeing the Son is God, and the Holy Ghost is God, as well as the Father; therefore sins committed against them, are equally hainous with sins committed against the Father. Yea, the Deity being one and the same in all three, you cannot sin against one, but you sin against all. But though every sin be against all the three persons; yet in the holy scriptures there are several sins spoken of as committed against the several persons distinctly, in so far as they strike against their distinct personal offices and operations in the business of our salvation. I shall therefore speak a little of each sort.

1. Men sin against the Father as sovereign Lord and Lawgiver, by rebellion and disobedience. So it is said, *they rebelled and vexed his holy Spirit* (k): And, says the Lord, *They rebelled against me, and would not hearken unto me* (l). When you will not be ruled and governed by God, but set up your own will in contradiction to his; when you despise and violate his holy laws, and will not be subject to them, but prefer to them your own devices and imaginations: This strikes peculiarly against the person of the Father, as being against his personal office as supreme Lord and Lawgiver. We find this exemplified in that people, who when the Lord called them to *return from their evil ways,* answered, *There is no hope, but we will walk after our own devices, and we will every one do the imagination of his evil heart* (m). The truth is, God's dominion and sovereignty is not slighted by any creature in the lower world but man; man hath none to join him in his disobedience and rebellion against God, but the devils: And there are not so many rebellions committed by inferiors against their superiors, as there are committed against God. Wicked men shake off the yoke of God, and will be subject to none but their own will. That is interpretatively their language, *Let us break their bands asunder,*

and

(*k*) Isa. lxiii. 10.   (*l*) Ezek. xx. 8.   (*m*) Jer. xviii. 11, 12.

and cast away their cords from us (*n*). Yea, many are much more impatient of the yoke of God, than of the yoke of man; and prefer obedience to the iniquitous laws of men, before obedience to the holy and good laws of God. This is to set man upon the throne of God, and God at the footstool of man; and to own the authority of man as superior to that of God. But how base is it for vile sinful dust to lift up itself against the sovereign and glorious majesty of God? A majesty before whom the devils shake and tremble, and the glorious angels cover their faces.

2. There are sins committed against the Son, the Lord Jesus Christ, the second person of the Godhead. Men sin against him,

(1.) By unbelief, not receiving him on the terms of the gospel. This strikes immediately against the person of Christ, as I shewed formerly. *He came unto his own, and his own received him not* (*o*). When you reject this pearl of great price, and will not receive and close with a whole Christ as he is offered; this is to pour contempt upon the Son of God: It is a great indignity done to his person, as if he were not worth the having. This is interpretatively the language of such a practice, " My lusts and pleasures are better to me than Christ and all " his purchase; I see no beauty in him why I should desire " him."

(2.) Men sin against Christ, by despair. So did Judas; having betrayed his Master, he despaired and hanged himself. When under a deep sense of sin, you despair of mercy, and conclude that it will be in vain for you to think of believing or repenting; this is most dishonourable to the Lord Jesus. It is a practical denial, either of his sufficiency, or of his faithfulness and sincerity. Despairing thoughts imply a secret sentiment, that Christ is either not able or not willing to save great sinners.

(3.) Men sin against Christ, by professing him for by ends: As in the days of Christ's flesh, many followed him for the loaves (*p*); so, in times of public reformation, and when religion is in request, many profess Christ for carnal and worldly conveniencies. This is to love Christ for his clothes, rather than for his beauty. Yea, it is a great dishonour to Christ, to make him subservient to your own interests, and to make him and his religion a means to accomplish carnal purposes. There are no greater enemies to Christ than such as profess him for their own self-interest. The apostle tells us, that such *whose god*

(*n*) Psal. ii. 3.   (*o*) John i. 11.   (*p*) John vi. 26.

god is their belly, and *who mind earthly things, are enemies to the cross of Christ* (*q*). They raise prejudices against Christ and his way in the minds of other men.

(4.) Men sin against Christ, by living Pagan lives under a Christian name and profession. When any of you that profess Christ, and are called by his name, lead graceless and vicious lives; such of you are called Christians, to the dishonour of Christ, and the reproach of Christianity. You have Christ's livery upon your back, but the devil's work in your hand. You put on Christ's cloke, that you may sin the more securely; and call him Lord and Master, only to mock him.

(5.) Men sin against Christ, by despising and contemning his ordinances. This is a very common evil. Alas, how many in the time wherein we live, are guilty of a profane withdrawment from the public ordinances: Others pretend conscience in separating themselves from the public assemblies of the people of God: And many who attend public ordinances, do not duly prize and value them. This is a great dishonour to Christ. He hath instituted public ordinances for his own honour and glory, and for our good; that he may be glorified by our owning him, and making public profession of his name; and that, in the due use of these ordinances, we may have access to him and communion with him: Therefore, to slight and despise them, as many do, is to envy Christ the honour due unto his name, to trample on his authority, and to put a slight on communion with him, and the great salvation offered by him in the gospel. This is a hainous iniquity.

(6.) Men sin against Christ, by opposition to his kingdom and interests. Men in place and power are often set a-work by Satan against the precious interests of Christ. *The kings of the earth set themselves, and the rulers take counsel together, against the Lord, and against his anointed* (*r*). When the devil hath a design against the church, he finds out instruments fit for his purpose, who oppose themselves to the planting, spreading, and success of the gospel, and set themselves to overturn the precious interests of the kingdom of Christ. And this they do, sometimes by open force and violence, sometimes by craft and subtility, and oftentimes by both. Thus wicked men set themselves against Christ, especially in his kingly office: They *will not have this Man to reign over* them (*s*). As this opposition is plain and open rebellion against the Son of God; so, it will bring down heavy wrath upon the opposers: *But those mine enemies*, says he, *who would not that I should reign over them,*

(*q*) Phil. iii. 18, 19.   (*r*) Psal i. 2.   (*s*) Luke xix. 14.

them, bring hither, and slay them before me. *He shall break them with a rod of iron, and dash them in pieces like a potter's vessel* (*t*). Therefore, that is a necessary advice and caution, *Be wise, now therefore, O ye kings: Be instructed, ye judges of the earth.—Kiss the Son, lest he be angry, and ye perish from the way, when his wrath is kindled but a little* (*u*).

SERMON CIX.

(7.) MEN sin against Christ, by denying and forsaking him, and turning their back on his cause and interests in a day of trial. This is most dishonourable to him, and opens the mouths of wicked men against him, as if he were a bad master. How did the disciples, their forsaking Christ, expose him to the contempt and scorn of his enemies? *The high-priest asked Jesus of his disciples* (*a*): Probably, how many there were, and where they were now, and how it came that they had turned their back on him, and had left him to shift for himself. Forsaking Christ, and deserting his cause and gospel, because of trouble and persecution from men, will open the mouths of enemies to speak evil of him. And, O, how sad is it, to give such occasion to wicked men to blaspheme his worthy name? What dangers should you not run? What sufferings should you not be content to undergo, to salve the honour of the Lord Jesus? Again, to deny and forsake Christ in an hour of trial and temptation, argues a great contempt of him: It is a preferring base things, carnal ease and worldly conveniencies, before him, as if these things were better than he.

(8.) Men sin against Christ, by base cowardice, in not daring to make profession of him in times of danger. Christ will have an open acknowledgement from all his servants: Therefore they are said to be *marked in their foreheads* (*b*). It is a disgrace to Christ, when his people dissemble their religion, and their respect to his work and cause, for fear of men, or for sinister and by-ends and respects: As the children of Israel, who though they were convinced in their own consciences, yet did not dare to disown Baal (*c*), fearing the displeasure of the king who was then present. † Christ is dishonoured, yea, denied by a politic and time-serving neutrality. There are some times and seasons when Christ, by his providence

(*t*) Luke xix 27. Psal. ii. 9.   (*u*) Psal. ii. 10, 12.
(*a*) Jon xviii. 19   (*b*) Rev. vii. 3.   (*c*) 1 Kings xviii. 21.
† *Christum deserit, qui Christianum se non asserit.*

providence doth, as it were, cry to you, Who is on my side? And when he calls for an open acknowledgement, none of you who are called by his name ought to hide yourselves in a corner, or keep yourselves in a wary reservation. *He that is not with me, is against me* (d), says Christ. Many cry up moderation to the prejudice of holy zeal. Indeed, moderation, taken in a right sense, is very commendable and praise-worthy; but that moderation that cools our zeal for Christ, when we are called to appear and act for him, is a sinful and cursed moderation.

(9.) Men sin against Christ, by sinful silence, when his interests are in danger, and his royal prerogatives are invaded. It is true, there,is *a time to keep silence, and a time to speak ; and a wise man's heart discerneth both time and judgment* (e) : So that there is need of much wisdom from above, to discern the proper seasons of speaking and acting for Christ, else we may give great advantage to enemies, and bring a great deal of misery on the church ; according to that of the preacher, *Because to every purpose there is time and judgment, therefore the misery of man is great upon him* (f). But there needs also much holy courage and resolution, that we may lay hold upon and improve such proper seasons, though with apparent danger to our own persons : For when men have access and opportunity to speak for Christ, and will not, or dare not, they do thereby betray his cause and interests into the hands of enemies; and their silence may cost them dear, even with respect to their worldly interests. We may hereunto apply what Mordecai said to Esther, *If thou altogether holdest thy peace at this time,—thou and thy father's house shall be destroyed* (g).

3. There are sins committed against the holy Spirit the third person in the Godhead: Sins that respect his distinct personal office and operation in the business of our salvation. Men sin against the Spirit, 1. By quenching the Spirit. 2. By resisting the Spirit. 3. By grieving the Spirit. 4. By vexing the Spirit. 5. By lying to the Spirit. And, 6. By blaspheming the Spirit.

(1.) By quenching the Spirit. From this the apostle exhorts us, *Quench not the Spirit* (h). The expression is metaphorical, borrowed from fire, which is quenched or extinguished, either by casting on water, or by withdrawing fewel, or by

---

(d) Exod. xxxii. 26. Matth. xii. 13. (e) Eccl. iii. 7. and viii. 5. (f) Eccl. viii. 6. (g) Esther iv. 14. (h) 1 Thess. v. 19.

by smothering the fire that it may not get vent. So, the holy Spirit is as fire, with respect to his enlightening influences, and his holy motions and excitements to duty: And with respect to these, the Spirit is quenched by various means. As, 1. By sloth and negligence, in not using and improving his gifts and graces. Solomon describes the evil nature and ruinous effects of spiritual as well as natural sloth, in many places of his Proverbs. This is like extinguishing fire by withdrawing fewel. When you give way to carnal sloth and laziness in religion, so that duties are neglected, or performed in a careless, slight and formal manner; then you quench the Spirit. Gifts and graces grow by exercise, but decay and languish by sloth and negligence. *From him that hath not, shall be taken away even that which he hath* (i). That is, he that doth not use and employ his gifts well, shall lose them. 2. By not entertaining and improving the motions and breathings of the Spirit. When you find something within you moving and urging you to duty; but you neglect these motions, and hang off, and do not act under present impulses: Then you quench the Spirit. Oh, how many quench all good motions in their hearts by woful delays: They shift the present performance of duties, to which they are urged by the Spirit, and put them off till another season. So did Felix, when he fell a trembling at Paul's sermon; *Go thy way for this time*, says he, *when I have a convenient season, I will call for thee* (k). 3. By harbouring and entertaining known sins, sins against light. When you will go on in any sinful course, contrary to the light of your own conscience; this wastes, wounds, and violates the conscience, more than any other way of sinning; so that it is more unapt to do its office, and cannot check for sin, and spur up to duty, as it was wont to do. You extinguish the light of the Spirit in you, when you sin and rebel against it. 4. By restraining the Spirit. When you are ashamed of the Spirit, as if it were a disgrace to be accounted spiritual, or persons walking in the Spirit; then you do dishonour the blessed Spirit; as a servant dishonours his master, when he is ashamed to wear his livery. Such are threatened by our blessed Saviour. *Whosoever shall be ashamed of me and of my words, in this adulterous and sinful generation, of him also shall the Son of Man be ashamed, when he cometh in the glory of his Father with the holy angels* (l). When you dissemble, conceal, or hide your graces, and do not give vent unto your love to God and zeal for him,

lest

(i) Matth. xxv. 29.   (k) Acts xxiv. 25.   (l) Mark viii. 38.

left you should be taunted and scorned by wicked men; then you quench the Spirit. This is like the smothering of fire, and not giving it vent. 5. By being careless, slight, and formal, in the use of these means, whereby the gifts and graces of the Spirit are cherished and maintained, and kept in life and vigour; such as, prayer, reading and hearing the word, meditation, &c. The apostle exhorts Timothy, to *stir up the gift of God which* was *in* him (*m*). As men quench or extinguish fire, when they do not stir it up: So you quench the Spirit, when you do not stir up his gifts and graces in you, but are careless and formal in the use of quickening, and upstirring means.

(2.) Men sin against the Spirit, by resisting the Spirit. With this Stephen chargeth the council, when he tells them, *Ye do always resist the Holy Ghost* (*n*). But, how can the Spirit be resisted? Wicked men resist the common motions and operations of the Spirit, though the resistance of the elect among them be overpowered by the efficacy of grace. Yea, there is a spirit of resistance in the best, while sin dwells in them; but the stronger operation of the Spirit maketh this resistance to give place.

But how and by what means is the Spirit resisted? He may be resisted, 1. In others. 2. In ourselves.

First, He is resisted in others. 1. By an envious opposition to their gifts and graces. When, being displeased that others should outshine you, you set yourselves against the lustre of gifts or graces in them, and labour to cloud and darken them, by detractions, defamations, and other such courses: This is a hainous sin against the Spirit. You do hereby work against the blessed Spirit, and labour to weaken that which he cherisheth, and to destroy that which he hath built in the hearts of other men. 2. By rejecting the wholesome counsels of godly ministers and Christians. In this sense the Jews are said to *resist the Holy Ghost, as did also their fathers* (*o*): That is, they stood out against them that were moved and acted by the Holy Ghost, in calling them to repentance and faith in Christ. So also, because the Spirit spake by the prophets, therefore disobedience to them is called disobedience to the Spirit (*p*). When either ministers or private Christians are moved by the Spirit, to warn you of your danger by sin, and to counsel you to repent and flee to Christ, and yet you will not hearken; this is to resist the holy Spirit in them.

Vol. II. N°. 8.   A a a   *Second*,

(*m*) 2 Tim. i. 6.   (*n*) Acts vii. 51.
(*o*) Acts vii. 51.   (*p*) Neh. ix. 30.

Second, The Spirit is refisted in ourselves, 1. By neglecting these duties to which we are strongly moved. When the Spirit comes knocking at the door of your heart, and yet you will not open, but put off his calls by lazy excuses, as the spouse did (*q*); this is a great contempt of his goodness and condescension. When the Spirit, by inward pulsations and persuasions, would draw you to more holy walking; and yet you will not, but oppose and resist many importunate motions: This is a great indignity done to the blessed Spirit; you fight, and strive, and wrestle against him. 2. By committing sins against the light and direction, the checks, dissuasions, and rebukes of the Spirit. When the holy Spirit stands in your way, and yet you will break through, and elude the importunity of many warm convictions, and baffle many pangs and checks of conscience; when you will go on in sin, against the inward workings of the Spirit, and his counsels are rejected, and his rebukes contemned, and all cords are broken, and your corrupt heart like a prevailing stream bears down all before it: This is to harden your heart against the Spirit, as it is said of the children of Israel (*r*). 3. When men bear up themselves impudently and stubbornly in their transgressions, though often called and urged to repentance. When you refuse to be humbled for your sins, and will not mourn for them and bewail them, though you meet with many things in the way of divine providence, attended with inward workings of the Spirit, calling and urging you to it; then you resist and stand out against the Spirit. So the prophet tells us of that people; *They hold fast deceit; they refuse to return* (*s*). When, though the Spirit set your sins before you, and there are inward calls and touches of the Spirit urging you to humble yourselves, and to repent and reform; yet you are impudent and shameless, and go on stubbornly in your own ways: This is to be stout-hearted against the Spirit; and hereby you justify yourselves in the face of God, as if you had done no evil: like these obstinate sinners who said, *wherein shall we return? what have we spoken so much against thee* (*t*)?

(3.) Men sin against the Spirit, by grieving the Spirit. From this the apostle dehorts us, *Grieve not the holy Spirit of God* (*u*). But how can the Spirit be grieved, seeing he is not subject to passions, as we are? For clearing this, know that the Spirit may be considered two ways. 1. As he is in believers. And so

(*q*) Cant. v. (*r*) Neh. ix. 29. (*s*) Jer. viii. 5. (*t*) Mal. iii. 7, 13. (*u*) Eph. iv. 30.

so he is subject to passions: that is, the spiritual and renewed part in believers may be grieved and vexed; they may do that which grieves their own and others spirits. And though this spirit be human, yet in a sort it is divine: For, the renewed part in believers is the effect and work of the holy Spirit: Therefore, when the renewed part is grieved, we may say the Spirit is grieved. 2. As he is in himself. And so he cannot be grieved properly: For, the passions of grief, anger, sorrow, as implying some imperfection, are not in God. As God cannot properly repent; so he cannot properly be grieved. But the Spirit is said to be grieved improperly (*x*). (1). When we do that which is just cause of grief, and usually with men works grief, and is in itself apt to grieve the Spirit, if he were capable of it. (2.) When we do that which provokes the Spirit, to do such things as men that are grieved by others use to do, viz. to chide, rebuke, and withdraw, which among men are usual effects and signs of grief.

But by what means is the Spirit grieved? In general, when believers do things, whereby their peace, joy, and comfort, are overclouded. Particularly, 1 By more gross sins. Hence the apostle exhorts, *Let no corrupt communication proceed out of your mouth.—And grieve not the holy Spirit of God—Let all bitterness, and wrath, and anger, and clamour, and evil speaking, be put away from you, with all malice* (*y*). When believers commit such sins as are gross in their nature, and such as are called *the manifest fruits of the flesh*, and *the pollutions of the world* (*z*); they grieve the Spirit by these, more than by other sins: Because they have more strength against these than against sins that are more spiritual: And these being contrary even to nature itself, are more contrary to grace than other sins: And such sins are a disgrace to religion, and harden wicked men in sin, and set them further off from religion; so that they cross the Spirit, in his great work of turning men from sin. 2. The Spirit is grieved even by lesser sins, when they are attended with high aggravations. When you sin wilfully, or deliberately or upon a small temptation, or against great light, or against many mercies, or against solemn vows and covenant-engagements: Such aggravated iniquities, though not so gross in their own nature, are a great grief to the Spirit. 3. When believers do not duly value and esteem the graces and comforts of the Spirit, his influences, and ordinances. When the Sabbaths are not your delight, nor the word your treasure, nor the

(*x*) Numb. xxiii. 19 (*y*) Eph. iv. 29, 30, 31.
(*z*) Gal. v. 19. 2 Pet. ii. 20.

the promises your joy; when the consolations of God are small with you; when you do not accept the counsels and comforts of the Spirit gladly, nor keep them diligently; when you prefer other things to them, the counsels of the flesh to the counsels of the Spirit, and worldly conveniencies and satisfactions to his comforts: This is a great contempt of the Holy Spirit, and cannot but grieve him exceedingly.

SERMON CX.

(4.) MEN sin against the Spirit, by vexing the Spirit. So, it is said of the children of Israel in the wilderness, that *they rebelled and vexed* God's *holy Spirit* (a). But how can the Spirit be vexed? What I said before about grieving the Spirit, may be applied here. The Spirit cannot be vexed properly, seeing he is not subject to passions as we are. But he is said to be vexed improperly, when we do that which in itself is apt to vex him, if he were capable of it; and when we do that, which provokes the Spirit to do, what men vexed by others use to do, viz. to chide, rebuke, and withdraw.

But how and by what means is the Holy Spirit vexed? We may understand this, by considering how the children of Israel vexed him in the wilderness. And, 1. Men vex the Spirit, when they do frequently commit the same sins. So did that people: They fell often into the sin of murmuring. Hence the Lord says, They *have tempted me now these ten times:* That is, many times. *How oft did they provoke him in the wilderness* (b)? When you fall frequently and easily into the same sins, then you vex the Holy Spirit, even though the sins you fall into be not so hainous in their own nature. A smaller sin often reiterated, amounts to as much as a great transgression. 2. When men fall into sin after it hath been often confessed and bewailed. So did the children of Israel in the wilderness: They fell into the sin of murmuring, after they had often confessed their sin in that matter, and had often professed to be humbled for it. When you have often confessed your sin to God, and have often professed to be grieved for offending and dishonouring him by it, and yet will commit it again, then you vex the Holy Spirit. Such sins are double-dyed, and draw deep. This is one of the special aggravations of the sins of this land: We sin after frequent solemn fasting and humiliation; we continue to go on in the same sins, which we have often solemnly confessed,

---

(a) Isa. lxiii. 10.   (b) Numb. xiv. 22. Psal. lxxviii. 40.

fessed, and for which we have often made solemn profession of humiliation before God, on public fasting days. Especially you vex the Spirit, when, after mercy begged, and graciously received, you will again transgress: This is great rebellion. It was this made Solomon's sin of such a deep dye: So it is said, *The Lord was angry with Solomon, because his heart was turned from the Lord God of Israel, who had appeared unto him twice* (c). 3. When men fall into these sins for which they have often smarted. So did the children of Israel in the wilderness: Though they had been often reproved and punished for their murmuring, yet they turned to it again. Nehemiah takes notice of this as a special aggravation of their sin, that though they had suffered so many miseries, yet *they did evil again before the Lord* (d). When after you have suffered much for your sin, after many rebukes from the Spirit, and checks from conscience, and frowns from men, and stripes from God; yet you will return to it again: O, this is hainous, and vexes the Holy Spirit exceedingly.

(5.) Men sin against the Spirit, by lying to the Spirit. So did Ananias and Sapphira (e). It is true, their sin was special and peculiar, and very horrid; therefore they were punished with sudden death. But there are more ordinary cases wherein men lie to the Holy Spirit. Hypocrisy is a lying to the Spirit. So it is said of the children of Israel, *They remembered that God was their Rock, and the high God their Redeemer. Nevertheless they did flatter him with their mouth, and they lied unto him with their tongues* (f). When you have a fair outward profession of religion, and busy yourselves in external duties, and make a great shew of devotion; yet your hearts are not right with God: Then you lie to the Spirit. You seek to put a cheat upon him, and deal doubly and deceitfully with him, as if he could be imposed upon by fawning pretences, and could not dive into the secrets of your hearts. Again, when you seek to palliate and cloke your sins, that they may not be seen in their own colours, and think to justify them by fair pretences and excuses; then you lie to the Holy Spirit. This was Ephraim's sin, of which the Lord complains, *Ephraim compasseth me about with lies, and the house of Israel with deceit* (g).

(6.) Men sin against the Spirit, by blaspheming the Spirit. And this is done divers ways.

First, By charging our sins upon the Spirit. When men in

(c) 1 Kings xi 9. (d) Neh. ix. 28. (e) Acts v. 3.
(f) Psal. lxxviii. 35, 36. (g) Hos. xi. 12.

an error or delusion, boast that they are taught or led by the Spirit: When men, transported with fury, wrath, and passion, in some matter of religion, call it the zeal of the Spirit: When licentiousness is counted Christian liberty, or sullen sadness and legal dejection is called godly sorrow, or a presumptuous and false peace is named the comfort of the Spirit. In these and the like cases men blaspheme the Holy Spirit: For what is all this, but to father errors and delusions, wrath and passion, licentiousness, and other evils, upon the blessed Spirit? It is a great indignity done to the Holy Spirit, to father your filthy brats upon him: It is as if a subject did father his bastard upon the prince.

Second, Men blaspheme the Spirit, by reproaching him in his divine operations, and ascribing them to some other cause. Thus, the Pharisees are said to blaspheme the Holy Ghost, when they attributed to the devil, these miraculous operations which Christ wrought by the power and Spirit of God (*h*). This is frequently done with respect to the more ordinary effects and works of the Spirit. When the eminent and evident effects of the power and grace of the Spirit, are ascribed to some other cause; and these are called the effects and operations of the devil, which are indeed the effects and operations of the Holy Ghost: When men count mourning, melancholy; and the joys and comforts of the Spirit are called delusions: When the light, quickening and assistance which the saints have from the Holy Spirit, are counted dreams and fancies: When the communications of grace and mercy, peace and comfort, from the Spirit, are given out to have nothing of truth, reality, or power in them; and are branded, as either diabolical delusions, or fanatical misapprehensions: In all these cases, men blaspheme the blessed Spirit. This is called *a doing despite to the Spirit of grace* (*i*). Yet, alas, how much of this is there in the generation wherein we live? The special operations of the Holy Ghost are opposed by many, both by word and writing; yea, by some that bear the name and character of the ministers of Christ, though not of the communion of this church: And the gracious operations of the Spirit in the hearts of the Lord's people, are turned by profane men into matter of scoff, derision, and reproach. Especially, as the Holy Spirit is the Spirit of regeneration and supplication, he is the object of multiplied blasphemies.

Third, Men blaspheme the Spirit, when by an unholy conversation they give occasion to others to think or speak evil of the

(*h*) Matth. xii 31. (*i*) Heb. x. 29.

the Spirit. Hence the Lord says of the Jews, that were carried away captive to Babylon, *They profaned my holy name, when they said to them, These are the people of the Lord, and are gone forth out of his land* (k). When the Babylonians observed the vicious lives of the Jews, they took occasion thereform to blaspheme the name of their God, and turned the same into matter of reproach: These, said they, are people that call themselves the people of God, and are come out of the holy land; and behold how profane and vicious they are in their lives. When men that pretend to have the Spirit dwelling in them, to be led by the Spirit, and to live and walk in the Spirit, are loose in their conversation; this gives occasion to profane men to think or speak evil of the Spirit. And such as by their vicious lives give occasion to others to blaspheme the Holy Spirit, are themselves chargeable with these blasphemies.

Fourth, There is a special kind of blasphemy against the Holy Ghost, which is declared in the holy scriptures to be unpardonable. I shall speak a little of this, for the help and relief of some, whose consciences are awakened and afflicted under the sense of sin, and are ready, without ground, to conclude that they are guilty of the unpardonable sin against the Holy Ghost. See three or four texts of scripture, where this sin is spoken of. Matth. xii. Our blessed Lord had cured a man possessed with a devil: Then it follows, verse 24. *But when the Pharisees heard it, they said, This fellow doth not cast out devils but by Beelzebub the prince of the devils.* And of their sin our Lord says, verses 31, 32. *All manner of sin and blasphemy shall be forgiven unto men; but the blasphemy again the Holy Ghost shall not be forgiven unto men. And whosoever speaketh a word against the Son of Man, it shall be forgiven him: But whosoever speaketh against the Holy Ghost, it shall not be forgiven him, neither in this world, neither in the world to come.* Another text to the same purpose is in Mark iii. 22, 28, 29, 30. The third text is that in Heb. vi. 4, 5, 6. *For it is impossible for those who were once enlightened, and have tasted of the heavenly gift, and were made partakers of the Holy Ghost, and have tasted the good Word of God, and the powers of the world to come; if they shall fall away, to renew them again unto repentance, seeing they crucify to themselves the Son of God afresh, and put him to an open shame.* The last text I mention is in Heb. x. 26, 27, 28, 29. *For if we sin wilfully, after that we have received the knowledge of the truth, there remaineth no more sacrifice for sins, but a certain fearful looking for of judgment, and fiery indignation, which shall devour the adversaries. He that despised Moses' law,*

(k) Ezek. xxxvi. 20.

law, died without mercy, under two or three witnesses: Of how much sorer punishment, suppose ye, shall he be thought worthy, who hath troden under-foot the Son of God, and hath counted the blood of the covenant, wherewith he was sanctified, an unholy thing, and hath done despite unto the Spirit of grace. From these texts, compared together, take this description of that unpardonable sin against the Holy Ghost: It is an avowed, wilful, malicious, and despiteful, rejecting and opposing the truth of the gospel, and way of salvation by Christ, after it hath been singularly made out to a man, both in the truth and goodness thereof, by the inward operation of the Holy Ghost.

That I may explain this description a little, notice these two things in it: The object about which the sinful act is conversant, and the act of the party with reference to this object. 1. We have here the object about which the sinful act is conversant, the truth of the gospel, and way of salvation by Christ. Not this or that truth, but the chief and principal truth of the gospel, concerning the way of salvation, contrived by infinite wisdom for lost sinners through a crucified Christ. It was this the Pharisees opposed. And it appears from the other texts quoted (*l*), that the wrong done by this sin is done to the Son of God, and to the Holy Spirit, who is sent to bear witness to the truth of the gospel. Next, I said that the truth of the gospel is made out to the party by the Spirit of God (*m*) Hence, this sin is called the sin against the Holy Ghost. The man is enlightened by the Spirit with the knowledge of the truth of the gospel, and convinced of the truth, and hath had some superficial tastes of the goodness and sweetness of it (*n*). 2. We have here the act of the party with reference to this object: It is a rejecting and opposing the truth of the gospel. (1.) A rejecting it; a renouncing the truth, or refusing it, contrary to conviction: Which is, upon the matter, a blaspheming the Holy Spirit, who bears witness to this truth, as a liar or impostor. Upon this the party relinquisheth and turneth his back on that way: He *falls away*, or *maketh apostacy* (*o*). (2.) An opposing the truth of the gospel: Partly, by reproaching and blaspheming the truth, and railing against it; whence this sin is called *Blasphemy against the Holy Ghost* (*p*). Partly, by persecuting the truth, and the professors thereof, as the Pharisees persecuted Christ. Next, I said in the description, that this rejecting and opposing the truth, that maketh up the unpardonable sin, hath these properties.

(*l*) Matth. xii. Mark iii. (*m*) John xv. 26. (*n*) Heb. vi. 4, 5. (*o*) Heb. vi. 6. (*p*) Matth. xii. 31.

properties. It is avowed; not secret, but open, in the view of the world. It is wilful; not unadvised, or from force or constraint. It is malicious; not out of weakness, from force or fear; nor out of love to the world, or for any good end proposed: But out of heart-malice against God and Christ, and the advancement of his kingdom; and from hatred of and malice against the truth. And this malice bewrays itself in despite; *putting Christ to an open shame, and doing despite to the Spirit of grace:* And all this contrary to clear conviction. All these particulars are clear from the texts I have quoted.

This is that sin against the Holy Ghost, which shall never be forgiven (*q*). And it is unpardonable, not from any defect of mercy in God, or of merit in the blood of Christ; but because the nature of this sin is such that it excludes what is necessarily required in order to pardon, viz. faith and repentance: For, *it is impossible* that such sinners can be *renewed again to repentance* (*r*); and consequently it is impossible they can obtain pardon. But why is it impossible for such sinners to repent and believe? I answer, not from any defect of power in God to convert such sinners, and renew and change them by grace: But because the greatness and hainousness of this sin is such, that God hath decreed and determined never to give such sinners grace to repent and believe, but to give them up to final hardness of heart and obstinacy in sinning; wherein God acts congruously to his infinite wisdom, justice, and holiness, considering the order of working amongst the blessed Persons, and the distinct offices and operations ascribed to them in the business of salvation. If a man sin against the Father as sovereign Lawgiver, by violating his laws, he may obtain mercy and pardon by fleeing to the blood and satisfaction of the Son: If he sin against the Son, by unbelief and slighting the offers of him, he may, by the inward operation of the Spirit, be brought to a better mind, and engaged at last to have recourse to Christ whom formerly he slighted, and by him to the Father. But if a man do despite to the Spirit of grace, and maliciously reject and oppose his inward operations; there is no remedy remains for that man: For there is not another divine person to provide relief for him, and the operation of the blessed Spirit is the last in the business of salvation. As the case of a sick man is desperate, when he wilfully rejects all remedies by which he may be cured, and maliciously riseth up against the physician himself; so it is here. Christ's sacrifice alone is appointed

(*q*) Matth. xii. 31. (*r*) Heb. vi. 6.

pointed and designed for the expiation of sin; and it is the work of the Spirit alone, to renew and sanctify sinners, and to work in them faith and repentance: Therefore, when both Christ's sacrifice, and the Spirit's operation, are maliciously and despitefully rejected; there is no mean left whereby the sinner may obtain pardon, or be renewed to repentance. To this purpose the apostle speaks, *If we sin wilfully, after that we have received the knowledge of the truth, there remaineth no more sacrifice for sins* (s) As they have justly forfeited all their interest and benefit by the one sacrifice of Christ; so there is not in the counsel or purpose of God any other sacrifice remaining, to be offered for the expiation of their sin: So that there is no relief for them: Christ is offered no more, nor can there be any other sacrifice offered for ever. And to all this I may add, that Christ's death and sacrifice was never intended for the expiation of this sin; which also follows from what hath been said, and may be intended by the apostle in the foregoing expression.

From the description I have given of the unpardonable sin against the Holy Ghost, I draw these conclusions. 1. As none without the church, or grosly ignorant, can be guilty of this sin; so none of God's elect can possibly fall under the guilt of it. 2. It is most difficult, if possible, to determine who are guilty of this sin, so as to point out the persons particularly; because the internal acts of the souls of men, and the principles from which they act are hid from us, who have not that gift of discerning spirits which was in the church in the days of the apostles. 3. Men may be guilty of many and great sins against the Spirit, and yet not be guilty of this unpardonable sin. In a word, whatever sins you have committed, yet if you are grieved for them, or if you would gladly have mercy and pardon through the blood of Christ, then you are not guilty of this sin. Yea, if after conviction and illumination, you do not hate the only way of salvation by Christ; or do not against light oppose the thriving of his kingdom, out of malice and despite against him: Then you have no reason to charge yourself with this sin.

Yet, let me caution you against such sins as lead to this unpardonable sin; as, all these sins against the Spirit which I already spoke of, quenching, resisting, grieving, or vexing the Spirit, or lying to him, or blaspheming him any of these ways I have mentioned. O, it is dangerous to sin against light, by omitting duties, or committing sins, contrary to clear conviction

(s) Heb. x. 26.

tion: And it is dangerous to refift the Holy Ghoft in his inward motions and operations upon your hearts and confciences. For, 1. By fuch fins you will provoke the Holy Spirit to depart from you. And he may fo depart as never to return again; as he did from Saul. Yea, fuppofe thou art truly gracious, yet he may depart in a great meafure, and for a long time; as he did from David (*t*). 2. When the good Spirit is departed, an evil fpirit will come in his room. So it is faid of Saul, that *the Spirit of the Lord departed from him, and an evil fpirit from the Lord troubled him* (*u*). And that evil fpirit may bring with him feven fpirits worfe than himfelf, and enter in and take poffeffion of your foul; fo that your laft ftate may be worfe than the firft (*x*). And, 3. You may at laft be left to fall into that unpardonable fin againft the Holy Ghoft, the very thoughts whereof may juftly fill your foul with horror. Men firft begin to neglect the Spirit, and quench his motions and breathings; then they go on to refift him; then they grieve him by more grofs fins; and by repeating thefe frequently they vex him: And when once you are come to this height in finning, you are in the next degree to that unpardonable fin. Therefore, as you love your fouls, take heed unto yourfelves. When once you have provoked the Holy Spirit to depart from you, and an evil fpirit hath come in his room, what is there to hinder your going on with full career to the height of all wickednefs?

SERMON CXI.

Ufe 4. FOR exhortation. In feveral branches.

Exhort. 1. Study the knowledge of this great truth of a Trinity of Perfons in the Godhead. Alas, many, even among us, are ignorant of it, as I already fhewed you. Such perfons ought to apply themfelves diligently to ftudy the knowledge of this facred myftery. For exciting and quickening them to this, I propofe thefe things to their ferious confideration. 1. A competent meafure of the knowledge of this great truth is abfolute neceffary unto falvation. Our bleffed Lord placeth eternal life in it: *This is life eternal,* fays he, *that they might know thee the only true God, and Jefus Chrift whom thou haft fent* (*a*). Such as know not a Trinity in Unity, cannot poffibly inherit eternal life. This myftery is the foundation of all thofe

(*t*) Pfal. li. 11, 12. (*u*) 1 Sam. xvi. 14. (*x*) Matth. xii. 44, 45. (*a*) John xvii. 3.

those articles of faith that concern the dignity of Christ's person, the truth and fulness of his satisfaction, and the power and efficacy of the grace of the Spirit in regeneration and conversion: Therefore a competent knowledge thereof must needs be absolutely necessary. Again, without a competent knowledge of this truth, there can be no right worship; for, such as do not worship a Trinity in Unity, do not worship the true God, but an idol and figment of their own brain. 2. A competent knowledge of this great truth is attainable, even by those that are of vulgar capacities. For, though it be an unsearchable and incomprehensible mystery, as to the τὸ διοτι, or the manner how it is; yet as to the τὸ ὅτι, that it is, it is so plainly revealed, that not only the learned, but the unlearned, may in the due use of ordinary means, attain to a sufficient knowledge thereof. That God is one; that this one God is Father, Son, and Holy Ghost; that the Father is God, that the Son is God, and that the Holy Ghost is God; that these three are distinct from each other; that the Father is the Father of the Son, and the Son the Son of the Father, and the Holy Ghost the Spirit of the Father and the Son: These things, I say, are so plainly revealed in the holy scriptures, that the knowledge of them may easily and with little pains be attained, even by them that are but of ordinary capacities. Therefore such as will be at no pains to attain this necessary knowledge, are left without excuse, and lie open to terrible wrath 3. The knowledge of this mystery is most profitable: For hereby an excellent foundation is laid for attaining to the knowledge of other gospel mysteries: And the more clear and distinct our knowledge of this truth be, the knowledge of other gospel truths will be the more easy Again, the knowledge of this truth must needs be highly profitable, because it is not an useless speculation, as some adversaries blaspheme, but a practical principle, of great use with reference to Christian practice. It is of great use in the whole spiritual life, and especially in prayer, and other duties of worship, in which we address ourselves to the Father, through the Son, by the Holy Ghost (*b*).

Well then, study the knowledge of this great fundamental truth: And do not satisfy yourselves with a mere speculative and notional knowledge; but seek earnestly after a practical, saving, and heart-affecting knowledge of it, such as may engage your heart to the blessed Trinity, that you may chuse, love, fear, and adore the glorious divine Persons. For this end, get a deep affecting sense of your ignorance; be ashamed of it

under

(*b*) Eph. ii. 18.

under such a clear gospel-light; lament and bewail it; be diligent in the use of the means of knowledge; and in the use of them, look up to God for his blessing, and the inward teaching of his Spirit.

Exhort. 2. Believe this sacred mystery of a Trinity in unity. Labour for a firm assent to this great truth: And you that do believe it, labour to have your faith in it more and more confirmed and strengthened.

To excite and engage you to this, I propose a few things to your serious consideration.

1. To know this truth and yet not to believe it, is a greater sin than simply to be ignorant of it. Such as have some knowledge of this mystery, and yet do not yield a firm assent to the truth thereof, are in worse condition than they that are grosly ignorant of it, even under such a clear gospel-light. For, they that will not believe it, fly in the face of the infinite truth and veracity of God, and make him a liar, by not receiving the testimony he hath given of himself. And such as contradict and oppose this great truth, have no part in God, or Christ, or eternal life.

2. Unless you believe this mystery, you cannot believe other gospel truths: For they are all built upon this as the foundation, and depend on it. Unless you believe the doctrine of the Trinity, you cannot believe the incarnation of the Son of God; and unless you believe Christ's incarnation, and the infinite dignity of his person, you cannot believe the verity and fulness of his satisfaction; and unless you believe that he hath fully satisfied divine justice, you cannot answer the call of the gospel, by coming to him, and resting on his satisfaction, for pardon, and peace, and eternal life.

3. You know not how soon, nor how much, your faith may be tried in this matter. The winds of error and heresy are in a great measure let loose, in the age wherein we live; and they may be yet let loose in a greater measure. There are many things that may justly provoke God to this; want of love to the truth, abusing gospel-light, pride and self-conceit in professors of Christianity, mens having itching ears, and nauseating the simplicity of the truth; these things may provoke a holy God to let loose a Spirit of error and heresy amongst us: And, alas, horrid Atheism, and irreligion, and contempt of serious religion, seem to pave the way for it. In former ages the faith of the church hath been tried in this great article of our religion; and we in this age cannot plead exemption from trials of the like nature. Many books and pamphlets have been
published,

published, even in Britain, in opposition to this glorious mystery: and even in our own time, bold attempts are made to revive the old Arian heresy, in denying the eternal Deity of our Lord Jesus Christ, which tends quite to overturn the whole Christian religion.

4. Even men of great knowledge, learning, and parts, may be in great danger, if their faith come to be tried in this great fundamental truth. Let none of you think that there is no fear of you. The best among you may be sore put to it, if trials come. The power of error and delusion is very great: Hence we read of *strong delusion* (c). Gross errors and heresies may prevail and spread, even in pure times of the church, and many may be carried away with them. The heresy of Ebion and Cerinthus, in denying the Deity of Christ, and consequently the holy Trinity, seems to have prevailed too much, even when the apostle John was yet living, which gave occasion to the penning of his gospel. And how much did the Arian heresy spread in the church? Great multitudes, yea, eminent men, and many bishops of great note, yea, many eminently godly, were brought by the violence of persecution to condemn the truth: And the defection under it was so great, that almost all the world was become Arian †. Great is the power of error and delusion, especially when God in his just judgement gives up a people to it: even eminent Christians may be carried away with it. Therefore the best amongst you need be at pains, to be more established in the faith of this glorious mystery.

5. If once your faith be shaken in this great article, it cannot be stable in any other article of the Christian religion. If this article go, all the other articles of the Christian religion will go with it. Once shake this foundation, and the whole building totters: So that nothing may be left to you but the name of being Christians. Such as oppose and deny this glorious mystery, may talk bigly of the Christian religion, as some of them do: But, alas, what is all they say but an empty sound of words? Sad experience confirms this. What is become of the Christian religion this day amongst the Socinians? Ah, it is dwindled almost into nothing; so that they do not so much as deserve the name of being Christians.

Well then, let it be your serious concern, to have your mind brought up to a full assent to this great truth, of a holy Trinity

---

(c) 2 Thess. ii. 11.

† *In Alexandria una Scintilla fuit, sed quia non statim oppressa est, totum Orbem ejus flamma populata est.* Hieron.

ty in unity, and to have your faith in it more confirmed and strengthened. In order hereunto I give these directions.

1. First of all, settle yourselves in the firm belief of the divine authority of the holy scriptures, else you cannot regard any thing said there, about this glorious mystery, as the truth of God, nor will your reason and understanding submit to it as of divine revelation. Therefore meditate deeply and frequently, on the many undeniable arguments of the divine authority of the holy scriptures. As for example, "The hea-
"venliness of the matter; the efficacy of the doctrine upon
"the hearts and consciences of men; the majesty of the stile;
"the consent of all the parts; the scope of the whole, which
"is to give all glory to God; and the full discovery they
"make of the only way of man's salvation †." I say, meditate much on these and other arguments, for confirming your faith in the belief of the divine authority of the holy scriptures; else nothing said in them will be of any weight, to procure your assent to this great truth of a holy Trinity.

2. Labour to be well fixed in the plain revelation of this mystery, before you enter on any debate about the particular explication of it. Adversaries do most preposterously level their disputes and cavils, not against the first, but against the second. They pass over the plain scriptural revelation of this mystery, and rise up against the explanations used by divines for further edification: And some weak and unstable Christians, being entangled by their cavils and objections, while they were not yet firmly established in the faith of what is plainly revealed, and meeting with things too high, hard, and difficult for them, have been quite carried off their feet; and being thus prepossessed with prejudices, and their darkness increased, the plain revelation of this mystery in the holy scriptures became of no use to them. Therefore, let it be your first work to consult the holy oracles, that you may see what is plainly revealed about the mystery itself; and labour to have your faith firmly established therein, before you enter one way or other upon particular explications.

3. Lay aside the pride of your reason, when you come to view and consider what God hath said in the holy scriptures about this glorious mystery. Do not read or search the holy scriptures with a mind to dispute, or to examine what you find there by your own reason. It is highly rational to believe what God hath said, to be true, though you cannot comprehend what he saith, as to the manner how it is. And it is the height

of

† Confess. of Faith, Chap. 1. Art. 5.

of arrogance and presumption, to think to dispute with him, or to think of calling such a deep mystery as this is to account before your shallow understanding †. Therefore, when you are to enquire, what God saith in his word about this sacred mystery, resolve to come, not to dispute with your Maker, but to believe what he hath revealed. Lay aside the confidence of your own understanding, that you may acquiesce in the wisdom and truth of God. Your soul must be even *as a weaned child* (*d*), in this respect. When you have laid aside the pride of your reason, then are you prepared to receive the testimony of God, and never till then.

4. Submit your soul to the plain and obvious sense of scripture testimonies, and do not, as many, seek out evasions, and pretences for unbelief. Many look into the holy scriptures with prejudicated minds: They are full of prejudices against this sacred mystery of a Trinity in unity: and so looking into the holy scriptures, they force a sense upon them which they will not bear. They seek rather to frame and mould their sense of scripture to their erroneous minds, than to inform their minds and regulate their belief by the scripture. Therefore have a special regard to the plain and obvious sense of scripture, and lay yourselves open to receive and entertain, what is there plainly revealed about this sacred mystery, and submit your minds to the authority of God.

5. When that which God hath said and revealed about this mystery is clear to you, it must be immediately received and believed upon the testimony of God alone. Believe what God says of himself, with a willing and ready mind; and dispute no more, and search no more into the mystery, as if you could find it out unto perfection †. It is not necessary to your belief of a holy Trinity, that your reason be satisfied about it: If God hath said, or revealed it, that is enough; there is no need of any further witness. In this respect, we owe God an implicit faith, as well as an implicit obedience. To believe this mystery only in so far as you find it congruous to your reason, is, in plain terms, not to believe at all: And to believe a thing because you can comprehend it, is not faith in God, but trusting in your own heart; it is not a sealing to God's truth and veracity,

* Τὰ γὰρ πίστει παραδοθέντα ταῦτα οὐκ ἐν ἀνθρωπίνη σοφία ἀλλ' ἐν ἀκοῇ πίστεως διανοεῖσθαι πρέπει.

Athan. Oper. Tom. 1. Epist. 2. ad Serap.
† *Cui magis de Deo, quam Deo credam.* Ambr. Lib. 5. Ep. 31.
(*d*) Psal. cxxxi. 2.

veracity, but a subscribing to your own wit and sagacity. Hence a learned man says of the Socinians, that they have " * hands with eyes in them." They will trust God no further than they see him. And Augustine, when the Manichees would believe only what they themselves pleased, tells them, " † Ye believe yourselves rather than the gospel." Your faith is nothing, if it be not ultimately resolved into the alone testimony of God. And if you do not rest and quiet your conscience on the bare word of truth, but will call in the help of reason and disputation, you will find yourselves further from satisfaction of mind than before. Therefore receive the testimony of God, for itself. Believe that God is one in three, and three in one, because he himself hath said it, though you know not how it is, or how it may be. There is no fear of being deceived; for, though he lead the blind in a way that they know not, yet he cannot possibly lead them wrong.

6. When reason musters up objections against this glorious mystery, labour to silence it by what is revealed. Lead your reason captive to the obedience of faith (*e*). Silence it with this answer, *The Lord hath said it.* It is true, reason hath its own good use in our attaining to the true sense and meaning of the holy scriptures, and in drawing necessary consequences from them: But herein it is to wait as an handmaid on the holy oracles, as Hagar did on Sarah; if it do not submit itself to them, then, as an ancient father adviseth, ‡ *cast out this bond-woman.* We are rather to cast out reason, than to loss this holy mystery. When reason riseth up against it, fly into that sanctuary of the apostle Paul, *Who art thou, O man, that repliest against God* (*f*)? Think that thou art but a man, and that he is God; and that it is unaccountable arrogance to dispute the truth of what he hath revealed. Therefore, when your faith of this mystery is bottomed upon plain scripture testimony, hold it fast, and let it not go, though you cannot answer all the objections that are mustered up against it.

7. I earnestly recommend serious and fervent prayer. Deal earnestly with God for faith to believe this glorious mystery. This great truth of a Trinity of persons in the Godhead, being

Vol. II. Nº. 9. C c c above

(*e*) 2 Cor. x. 5.   (*f*) Rom. ix. 20.
  * *Manus oculatas.* Mares.
† *Qui in Evangelio, quod vultis, creditis; quod non vultis, non creditis; vobis potius quam Evangelio creditis.*
    August. Contr. Faust. Lib. 17. Cap. 3.
‡ *Ejice Ancillam.* Clem. Alexand. in Strem.

above reason, and wholly supernatural, and our intellectual and believing faculties being corrupted by sin, they cannot lift up themselves to this truth without the power of grace. A divine power is necessary to elevate the believing faculty to supernatural mysteries. Hence faith is called the *gift* and *work of God*. It is the product of divine power: And it is fulfilled and consummated by power. Hence the holy Spirit is called the *Spirit of faith* (g). Therefore be earnest with God that he would enlighten and elevate your soul to entertain this truth, and raise up your mind to believe this glorious mystery, which is so far above it. And you that do believe it, pray that your faith may be increased and strengthened. Make the prayer of the disciples your prayer, *Lord, increase our faith* (h). Plead that you may be settled and established in the belief of this great fundamental truth. *The God of all grace stablish, strengthen, settle you* (i).

8. Improve your own experiences for the confirmation of your faith. Believers in Christ have rich and glorious experiences of a sacred Trinity. Hence our Lord says to his disciples, *Ye know him,* (that is, *the Spirit of truth) for he dwelleth with you, and shall be in you:* And a little after he adds, *We* (that is, the Father and the Son) *will come unto him, and make our abode with him.* And again he expresseth himself thus, *I will manifest myself to him* (k). So that the abode of the Father, Son and Holy Ghost, in the heart of a believer, is in a glorious manifestative way, such as giveth an experience of their being there. So also the apostle tells us, *Truly our fellowship is with the Father, and with his Son Jesus Christ* (l). He saith not, *our fellowship is with God,* but *with the Father and his Son.* And he speaks of it as a thing he well knew and was assured of, *Truly our fellowship, &c.* So that believers have glorious manifestations of the blessed Trinity. Again, they have experimental proofs of a Trinity in gracious returns and answers to their prayers. You who are the children of God have been worshipping a Trinity in unity, it may be, these many years past; and have had many returns and answers from heaven to such prayers, in abundance of spiritual blessings: And some of you know it, and are assured of it: And herein you have experienced that there is a sacred Trinity. For, if there be not three distinct persons in the Godhead, your worship hath been idol-worship, false and vain worship; and to such worship
God

(g) Eph. ii. 8. John vi. 29. Eph. i. 19. 2 Thess. i. 11. 2 Cor. iv. 13. (h) Luke xvii. 5. (i) 1 Pet. v. 10. (k) John xiv. 17. 23, 21. (l) 1 John i. 3.

God would make no returns but these of wrath. Therefore every godly Christian that worships one God in three persons, and hath gracious returns and answers from heaven, hath so many experimental proofs of a sacred Trinity. Bring forth such experiences, and improve them for the confirmation of your faith.

9. Beware of making bold adventures on snares and temptations. Particularly, beware of reading such books as oppose and impugn the blessed Trinity; and of conversing familiarly with such men as scoff at and blaspheme this glorious mystery, such as Socinians, Deists, and other Antitrinitarians. True it is, some persons, such as ministers, and solid, judicious, and established Christians, may, and sometimes ought, to converse with such men, for their conviction and recovery; and read erroneous and heretical books, though but rarely, and with abhorrence, that they may be in case to confute them, and warn others against them. But take heed of venturing without a clear call, and of going vainly beyond your line; for this may, in the righteous judgment of God, prove a sad snare to you, and provoke him to give you up to that delusion, which you make yourselves so obnoxious unto.

10. Employ Christ much, and depend on him for the conduct of his Spirit, to lead you into all truth. This he hath promised; *I will send him to you*, says he: *And when he, the Spirit of truth, is come, he will guide you into all truth* (m). It is the Spirit of Christ alone that can clearly reveal this truth to you, and bear it in with life and power upon your heart, and engage you to embrace, submit, and cleave to it. Act faith on Christ for the promised Spirit for this end. Rest and rely on him for light to clear up this truth to you, and grace to believe it, and strength to abide by it, and hold it fast, whatever trials and temptations you may meet with.

SERMON CXII.

Exhort. 3. BELIEVE in the holy Trinity. This is that which we profess in our Creed, commonly called, The Apostles Creed, *I believe in God the Father Almighty—And in Jesus Christ his Son our only Lord—I believe in the Holy Ghost.* And to this purpose our Lord exhorts his disciples, *Ye believe in God, believe also in me* (a) Where the Father is called God, by way of eminency, for reasons formerly expressed. The Holy Ghost, though he be not mentioned, is not

here

(m) John xvi. 7, 13.   (a) John xiv. 1.

here excluded: For, in verses 16th and 17th, he hath such titles and epithets given to him, as do plainly shew him to be the object of faith jointly with the Father and the Son. He is called the Comforter, and the Spirit of truth; and as such we are to believe in him.

In prosecuting this purpose a little, I shall,

1. Shew you, more generally, what is implied in believing in the holy Trinity
2. Urge you to this by some arguments and motives.
3. Give some directions, with respect to the exercise of faith in the several divine persons.

First, Believing in the holy Trinity implies, not only a belief of this sacred mystery, that there is a holy Trinity; and a giving credit to the holy Trinity, by assenting to their testimony in the holy scriptures: But it implies also, and chiefly, consent of will, and recumbency. 1. Consent of will; receiving and closing with the Father, Son, and Holy Ghost. So is this term interpreted in that text, *But as many as received him, to them gave he power to become the sons of God, even to them that believe on his name* (b), where believing on Christ is called a receiving him. 2. Trust and recumbency. *Ye believe in God*, says our Saviour, *believe also in me* (c) Or, as some render the words, *Ye trust in God, trust also in me*. So, faith in Christ is expressed by trusting: As in that text, *In him shall the Gentiles trust;* and in that expression, *Who first trusted in Christ* (d). And believing and trusting are used as equipollent terms in scripture: As in that of the psalmist, *Because they believed not in God, and trusted not in his salvation* (e). And the faith of the spouse is expressed by *leaning on her Beloved* (f): Agreeable whereunto is that expression; *Let him trust in the name of the Lord, and stay himself upon his God* (g)

More particularly, believing in the holy Trinity implies, 1. An hearty acquiescing in the way laid down by the blessed Trinity, for bringing about the salvation of lost sinners. It is brought about by their joint counsel and operation, as I formerly shewed; each person having his distinct office and operation ascribed to him in the business of salvation, according to their eternal counsel, the Father contriving and ordering it, the Son purchasing it, and the Holy Ghost applying it.

(b) John i. 12.   (c) John xiv. 1.   (d) Matth. xii 21. Eph i. 12.   (e) Psal. lxxviii. 22.   (f) Cant. viii. 5.   (g) Isa. l. 10.

it. Now, there muſt be an approving and well-liking of this way, as an infinitely wiſe and glorious contrivance, being moſt congruous to infinite wiſdom, and moſt for the glory of God and our good. 2. A receiving and cloſing with all the divine Perſons. You muſt cloſe with them as your God and portion, being content to have all your happineſs in the Father, Son, and Holy Ghoſt. You muſt take this one God in three diſtinct perſons to be your God, and cloſe with them, as having their diſtinct offices and operations in the buſineſs of our ſalvation. 3 A committing and concrediting our whole ſalvation to the bleſſed Trinity. You muſt commit your ſouls, and all that is dear to you, to the Father, Son, and Holy Ghoſt. Caſt yourſelves upon them, depoſite your greateſt concerns in their hand, and venture your all upon them: As the apoſtle did; *I know,* ſays he, *whom I have believed, and I am perſuaded that he is able to keep that which I have committed unto him againſt that day* (h). 4. A reſting and relying on all the divine Perſons, for their executing the ſeveral offices, and performing the diſtinct operations, aſcribed to them in the buſineſs of our ſalvation. You muſt reſt with full confidence on God the Father, Son, and Holy Ghoſt, being firmly perſuaded that they all concur in promoting the ſalvation of believers.

Second, Let me preſs this great duty of believing in the holy Trinity, by ſome arguments and motives.

1. Conſider, that God, in all that he is, is made over to believers in the covenant of grace; according to that great promiſe of the covenant, *I will be their God* (i). In which promiſe God repreſents himſelf to the faith of his people, not only in the glorious perfections of his nature, but alſo in his perſonal relations. *I,* who am Father, Son, and Holy Ghoſt, *will be your God.* The Father is theirs, to love, juſtify, and adopt them; the Son is theirs, to ſave and redeem them; and the Holy Ghoſt is theirs, to ſanctify, teach, guide, and comfort them. *I will be their God:* As if he ſhould ſay, I am God, and whatever I am, I am wholly theirs: Theirs, in my perſonal relations, Father, Son, and Holy Ghoſt. After the ſame manner are we to underſtand other promiſes of this nature; as that, *Thou ſhalt not be for another, ſo will I alſo be for thee* (k). *I* who am Father, Son, and Holy Ghoſt, will be for thee. So that the whole ſacred Trinity are made over to believers in the covenant: Therefore they are the object of faith, and we muſt believe in them.

2. Conſider, that believers are united to the whole Trinity, as

(h) 2 Tim. i. 12. (i) Ezek. xi. 20. (k) Hoſ. iii. 3.

as appears from that passage in Christ's prayer, *As thou Father art in me, and I in thee, that they also may be one in us* (*l*): And from these words to his disciples, *And I will pray the Father, and he shall give you another Comforter, that he may abide with you for ever.—Ye know him, for he dwelleth with you, and shall be in you* (*m*). *We*, that is, the Father and the Son, *will come unto him, and make our abode with him* (*n*). So that God the Father, Son, and Holy Ghost, have their abode, and *dwell* in the hearts of believers (*o*). We are first united to Christ, and then through him to God; for there is *no coming to the Father but by him* (*p*). And there is no coming to Christ, nor to the Father through him, but by the Spirit. Union is the Spirit's personal operation: It is the Spirit that worketh faith in us, and thereby unites us to Christ, and through him to the Father. Hence it is that believers have communion with all the divine Persons. We read of *fellowship with the Father and with his Son; and of the communion of the Holy Ghost* (*q*). We are united to the Father, as the fountain of grace; to the Son, as the conduit-pipe through which it is conveyed; and to the Holy Spirit as the conveyer of all grace to us. Now, believers being united to all the divine Persons, they must needs be the object of faith. We must believe in them, in order to an union with them; for faith is the uniting grace. Here is a great encouragement to this duty; when you believe in the holy Trinity, all the Persons will come and take up their abode in your heart. O, how admirable is this! That the Father, Son, and Holy Ghost, three infinitely glorious persons, should come and dwell in the hearts of sinners! What blessed guests are these! Where they come, they do not come empty-handed; they bring their own entertainment, even all saving graces, along with them.

3. To this we all stand engaged by baptism. For we are baptized *in the name,* or *unto the name of the Father, and of the Son, and of the Holy Ghost* (*r*). In baptism we are dedicated and devoted to the blessed Trinity, to the Father, Son, and Holy Ghost. And baptism being a seal of the covenant, seals a mutual engagement between God and us. As the Father, Son, and Holy Ghost, engage to convey their love, grace, and power to us: So, we engage to take the Father for our Father in Christ; and the Son, for our Saviour and Redeemer; and the Holy Ghost, for our Sanctifier, Teacher, Guide, and Comforter.

(*l*) John xvii. 21. (*m*) John xiv. 16, 17, 23. (*n*) 1 John iv. 16. (*o*) Eph. iii 17. Rom. viii. 11 (*p*) John xiv. 6. (*q*) 1 John i. 3. 2 Cor. xiii. 14. (*r*) Matth. xxviii. 19.

forter. So that we stand engaged by our baptism, to believe in the holy Trinity.

4. You should believe in all the divine Persons, because they are all joint in the business of our salvation: They do all conspire and agree together therein. Whatever may be expected from the eternal love of the Father, or from the infinite merit of Christ, or from the almighty power of the Spirit, it is all offered to you in this gospel. When the Father, Son, and Holy Ghost, become the joint object of your faith, they will be joint in answering the expectations of it. *I and my Father are one* (s), says Christ. And so is the Holy Ghost one with the Father and the Son. But how are they one? As they are one in essence; so they are one in saving, preserving, and perfecting the elect: For it is spoken in relation to their keeping Christ's sheep, as appears from verse 28th. When you grasp a sacred Trinity by faith, they grasp one another's hands for your salvation. As they are one in power, so they are one in their care of the flock: As they are one in nature; so they are one in the work of redemption and salvation, and in all the grace that flows down to the elect. It is a great encouragement to humbled souls to believe, to consider the infinite latitude of the object of faith, as it closeth with all the divine Persons: For, you will find, in the Father, infinite love and free grace to accept of you in Christ; in the Son, eternal redemption, everlasting righteousness, and full satisfaction; in the Holy Ghost, infinite power and virtue for applying Christ's purchase; and in all the Persons, almighty power, for upholding and preserving the elect, till they are brought to glory.

5. As your believing in the holy Trinity will interest you in all the divine Persons; so when you have an interest in them, nothing can be wanting to your complete happiness. All the Persons stand engaged for it. When you believe in the holy Trinity, then you have the co-operation of all the Persons for your eternal salvation. O, what a complete object have you for your faith! What can be wanting? You have *the grace of the Lord Jesus Christ*, and *the love of God* the Father, *and the communion of the Holy Ghost with you* (t). And when you have the love of the Father, the grace of the Son, and the communion of the Spirit, you want nothing to your solid happiness. When you have the Father, Son, and Holy Ghost, you have all things necessary, in their cause and fountain: For all things come from the love of the Father, the grace of Christ, and the communion of the Holy Ghost. O, what a blessed privilege

(s) John x. 30.   (t) 2 Cor. xiii. 14.

is this! Love, and grace, and communion; eternal love, infinite merit, and effectual application. This is a mystery felt by the saints, as well as believed. When you believe in a sacred Trinity, you have the Father to love you, Christ to redeem you, and the Holy Spirit to apply all to you. So that your salvation standeth upon a sure bottom: The beginning is from the Father, the dispensation is from the Son, and the application from the Holy Ghost. The effects and fruits of the electing love of the Father, are procured by the merit of Christ, and conveyed by the power of the Holy Ghost. O, let us admire the mysterious way of our salvation.

Third, I proceed to give some directions, with respect to the exercise of faith in the several divine Persons. All the Persons must be taken in as the object of faith. For clearing this, consider that the true object of faith is God in Christ. As *God was in Christ reconciling the world to himself* (*u*), so God in Christ is the object of faith. Christ is the more immediate object, and God the ultimate object thereof. 1. Christ, as Mediator, is the immediate object of faith; as he who, by his sufferings in our nature, fully satisfied divine justice. Hence it is called, *faith in the Lord Jesus Christ*. It is only through him and his mediation that faith makes its approaches to God. Many boast of their faith and trust in God, who never think of Christ. But you have no warrant to trust in God without a Mediator. Such guilty creatures as we are, can have no access to an infinitely holy God, immediately, or without the intervention of a Mediator. He is the only *way* to the Father, and there is no coming *to the Father but by* him. It is *through him we have access to the Father* (*x*). So that the first and immediate address of our faith is to Christ as Mediator. 2. God, even the whole sacred Trinity, is the ultimate object of faith. Though Christ, as Mediator, be the immediate object of faith; yet Christ, as God, in conjunction with the other divine persons, is the ultimate object thereof. Faith centres ultimately in the Deity. Hence are these expressions: *Such trust have we through Christ to God-ward;* and, *who by him do believe in God* (*y*). For, although Christ's mediation be the ground of our access to God; yet nothing is or can be the formal reason of, or object terminating our faith, but only the Deity or divine nature, whose infinite excellency and perfection doth alone merit this at our hand. There and there only can faith ultimately rest.

Well

(*u*) 2 Cor. v. 19.   (*x*) John xiv. 6. Eph. ii. 18.   (*y*) 2 Cor. iii. 4, 1 Pet. i. 21.

Well then, through Christ's mediation believe in all the divine Persons. And,

1. Believe in God the Father. He is the object of faith, as reconciling the world to himself in and through Christ As our thanksgivings are to be directed to him, as *the God and Father of our Lord Jesus Christ* (z); so is our faith. Christ, as Mediator, is the Father's servant, his messenger and ambassador: And faith looks through the ambassador to the Prince that employs him, and through the servant to the Lord that sends him. Therefore your faith must mount up to the Father, as the fountain of salvation, by whose authority all was transacted. *He that believeth on me,* says Christ, *believeth not on me, but on him that sent me* (a). You do not rightly believe in Christ, if you do not believe in the Father that sent him. Christ is the ladder by which your faith must mount up, and clasp about the Ancient of Days. And it is great encouragement to poor humbled sinners, that there is no room for any hard thoughts of the Father, after so signal a discovery of himself in Christ. He is not a God of unquenchable wrath. Was he not most willing to have his justice satisfied, and his wrath appeased, when he took all the course that was possible for infinite wisdom to invent, and infinite love to propose? Did he make such provision from eternity for nothing? Would he provide a Mediator never to bestow him? This cannot be imagined.

Therefore let sensible and humbled sinners be encouraged to believe in God the Father. And, 1. Acquiesce heartily in his wise contrivance of salvation, and in his chusing, designing, and sending his Son, to be our Mediator and Redeemer. 2. Receive God the Father. Embrace and close with him as your Father in Christ, and your all-sufficient portion; and own him as your sovereign Lord and Lawgiver. 3. Yield and give up yourselves to him, to be justified, pardoned, and adopted by him. Resign yourselves to the Father, to be his children; and to be his subjects, to be ruled by his laws, and to live in his obedience. 4. Rest and rely on God the Father, for the gift of Christ, and all the blessings of his purchase. Cast yourselves on his everlasting love, and his rich and free grace. This is the beautiful gate at which you must lie, waiting for an alms of pardoning mercy.

2. Believe in the Son, the Lord Jesus Christ. The object of justifying faith, is not the promises of Christ, nor the benefits of

---

(z) Eph. i. 3. (a) John xii. 44.

of Chrift, but his perſon. By faith we are married to Chriſt: Now, when a woman is married, ſhe doth not marry the eſtate, but the man. An intereſt in Chriſt's benefits follows upon believing, as the eſtate follows the marriage. God gives firſt his perſon, and then his benefits; and we muſt believe in him as God gives him. Well then, 1. Receive the Lord Jeſus Chriſt, and cloſe with him as he is offered in the goſpel. Take him for your Saviour and Redeemer, the Lord and Huſband of your ſoul Receive him wholly, in all his mediatory offices, to be your Prophet, Prieſt, and King. You muſt not ſever his perſon from his offices, nor yet his offices one from another. All his offices are ſuited to your wants, neceſſities, and exigencies, ſo that there is nothing in Chriſt that you can ſpare. You muſt take him, not only for your Prieſt, to ſave you; but alſo for your King, to rule over you, and to give laws to you, being heartily content to ſerve him, as well as to be ſaved by him. Take Chriſt and his yoke, Chriſt and his croſs, as well as Chriſt and his crown; being firmly reſolved to be ruled by his laws, and to take up his croſs, and follow him through well and woe. Thus, receive a whole Chriſt. Again, receive him only, as your alone Saviour and Redeemer, renouncing your own righteouſneſs, and whatever elſe comes in competition with him. And receive him freely: You muſt come to him empty-handed, as undeſerving and ill-deſerving creatures, and be content to take him as a free-gift. 2. Make a ſolemn ſurrender and reſignation of yourſelves to Chriſt, to be wholly, fully, and for ever his. Give yourſelves to him wholly, ſoul and body, without reſervation; for ever without reſervation, no more to be your own, nor any others, but his. Reſign yourſelves to him, to be ruled and governed by him at his pleaſure: And reſign yourſelves, to be ſaved by him in his own way, by his merits, righteouſneſs, and ſatisfaction alone. Commit your ſouls to him; entruſt them to him, for pardon, peace, and eternal life; and put all your concerns into his hands. 3. Reſt and rely on the Lord Jeſus, for pardon and life, and all the fruits of his mediation. Leave yourſelves on his blood and righteouſneſs; and reſt on his ſatisfaction, as full and ſufficient and of infinite value. *Surely, ſhall one ſay, in the Lord have I righteouſneſs and ſtrength* (b). Though you doubt what the event may be, and know not what will come of it; yet reſolve to venture, and caſt yourſelves on Chriſt; *though he ſlay me, yet will I truſt in him*. And reſt on him alone, quitting confidence in any thing you have done or can do. And reſt on him with full

(b) Iſa. xlv. 24.

full confidence, as a complete and perfect Saviour, who *is able to save them to the uttermost that come unto God by him* (c).

3. Believe in the Holy Ghost. Being the same God with the Father and the Son, he is also the joint object of faith with them. Therefore, 1. Accept of and close with the Holy Spirit, as your Sanctifier, Teacher, Guide, and Comforter. It is not enough that you are willing to take him for your Comforter, to cheer your heart, and to fill you with joy and peace; but you must accept of him also for your Sanctifier, being heartily willing to be sanctified by him, as well as comforted by him. Close with him as the Spirit of grace and holiness, to renew your souls, to subdue your corruptions, to furnish your souls with grace, and to make you holy. Take him for your Teacher, resolving to wait for his instructions, in the ways and means of his appointment, viz. his word and ordinances. Take him also for your Guide. Be denied to your own wisdom, renounce the counsels of flesh and blood, and close with the Holy Spirit as your leader, taking his blessed word for your directory. 2. Resign and give up yourselves to the Holy Spirit. Give yourselves to him, to be sanctified by him in his own way, being unfeignedly desirous to be rid of all sin, how dear soever it hath been to you; and resolving firmly through grace, to obey his motions, and to avoid these sins which may grieve the Spirit, and provoke him to suspend his operations and comforts. Again, under the deep sense of your own blindness and ignorance, resign yourselves to the blessed Spirit, to be taught by him in his own way, laying your souls open for his enlightening influences. And under the deep sense of your insufficiency to direct your own way, commit yourselves to the conduct of the Spirit, that he may guide you continually till he bring you to glory. 3. Depend continually on the blessed Spirit. Rest and rely on his infinite power and virtue for the effectual application of Christ's purchase. Depend on him, for light in your darkness, direction in all your doubts and perplexities, and comfort in all your troubles outward and inward. But especially, rest on him for the sanctifying influences of his grace; grace to mortify and subdue sin; grace to quicken you to, and assist you in duty; strengthening and confirming grace; preserving, upholding, and persevering grace, that you may hold out unto the end.

I shall only add, that in acting faith on any of the Persons, you would carefully advert that you do not divide the divine essence in your thoughts. The divine essence being one and the same in all three, you cannot believe in one, but you believe

(c) Heb. vii. 25.

lieve in all. They are the joint object of faith. And as they are one in essence; so in all their external works they are one in operation, and one Person doth not work without the rest: For, though there be distinct offices and operations ascribed to them in the business of our salvation, yet that doth only respect their order and manner of working On these accounts, I say, when we believe in any one of the Persons, we believe in all three. Yet it is good to act faith on them distinctly, according as they act their love and grace distinctly toward us in the business of our salvation. Yet all this is to be understood with respect to the ultimate object of faith, and such external works and operations as are merely divine: For Christ's mediatory works come under a different consideration, as I formerly † observed; and it is through him as Mediator that we believe in the holy Trinity, as I have also cleared before ‡.

SERMON CXIII.

Exhort. 4. WORSHIP a Trinity in Unity. Make this one God in three distinct Persons the object of your worship. I shall here lay down some positions that may be of use for our instruction and direction in worshipping the blessed Trinity.

Posit. 1. All the Persons in the Godhead are the object of divine and religious worship: For all these attributes and excellencies that are requisite in the object of religious worship, such as, supreme glory and majesty, omnipresence, omniscience, omnipotence, &c. all these are essential, and common to all the Persons. They are common to the Son; for *in* him *dwells the fulness of the Godhead bodily* (*a*). He is omnipotent, *the Almighty;* and *the Lord God Almighty;* and *doth whatsoever the Father doth* (*b*). He is omnipresent: He is with all his servants and people, though in different parts of the world, in their administration and participation of gospel-ordinances. It is his promise, *Where two or three are gathered together in my name, there am I in the midst of them:* And, *Lo, I am with you alway, even unto the end of the world* (*c*). He is omniscient: He *knoweth all things;* and *searcheth the reins and heart* (*d*). They are also common to the Holy Ghost. He is omnipotent; For he is *the Power of the Highest,* and *quickens the dead* (*e*). He is omnipresent:

---

† Page 307.   ‡ Page 392.

(*a*) Col. ii. 9.   (*b*) Rev i. 8 xi. 17 John v. 19.   (*c*) Matth. xviii. 20. and xxviii. 20.   (*d*) John xxi. 17. Rev. ii 23.   (*e*) Luke i. 35. Rom. viii. 11.

present: Hence the Psalmist says, *Whither shall I go from thy Spirit, &c*: And he is omniscient; for, he *searcheth all things, even the deep things of God* (*f*).

From what is said it appears, that the divine attributes which are the grounds of religious worship, are common to all the persons in the Godhead. Accordingly we find that, in the holy scriptures, religious worship is ascribed to the Son and Holy Ghost, no less than to the Father. 1. It is ascribed to the Son. As in these texts: *Kiss ye the Son. All men should honour the Son, even as they honour the Father. God hath highly exalted him, and given him a name which is above every name: That at the name of Jesus every knee should bow, &c. Let all the angels of God worship him* (*g*). And we are baptized in his name. And believers are often described by this, that *they call on the name of the Lord Jesus* (*h*). 2. It is ascribed also to the Holy Ghost: For, we are also baptized in his name: And grace and peace, and other spiritual blessings, which God alone can give, are wished or prayed for, from the Holy Ghost, no less than from the Father and Son: As in the Apostolical Benediction, and in John's salutation to the seven churches of Asia (*i*). And although the worshipping the Holy Ghost is more rarely spoken of in scripture: Yet that is not done, as if he were not to be worshipped together with the Father and the Son; but because of his personal office and operation in the business of our salvation, which answers to the order of subsistence and working amongst the divine persons. It is the holy Spirit who excites and quickens us to prayer, and gives us an heart to come to God through Christ. He makes us *cry, Abba, Father* (*k*). Therefore he is more frequently spoken of in scripture, as the Author and principle of our worship, than as the object of it.

Posit. 2. We may direct our worship to any one of the divine persons. This follows from what hath been said: If all the persons are the object of divine worship, then may we direct our worship to any one of them. And,

1. We may direct our worship to the Father. In this we have our blessed Lord for a pattern, in John xviith, and elsewhere. And the saints in scripture do often direct their prayers and praises to the Father: As the apostle, *Blessed be the God and Father of our Lord Jesus Christ*, says he, *who hath blessed us with all spiritual blessings*: And, *I bow my knees unto the Father*

(*f*) Psal. cxxxix. 7. 1 Cor. ii. 10. (*g*) Psal. ii. 12. John v. 22. Phil. ii. 9, 10. Heb. i. 6. (*h*) Acts ix. 14. 1 Cor. i. 2. (*i*) 2 Cor. xiii. 14. Rev. i. 4. (*k*) Gal. iv. 6.

Father of our Lord Jesus Christ: And again, *Giving thanks unto the Father, who hath made us meet, &c.* And we read of *calling on the Father*, and *worshipping the Father* (*l*).

2. We may direct our worship to the Son. The psalmist addresseth himself to the Messiah, our Lord Jesus, in these words; *Gird thy sword upon thy thigh, O most Mighty; with thy glory and majesty. And in thy majesty ride prosperously, because of truth, and meekness, and righteousness* (*m*). And it is said of Stephen, that he *called on God, saying, Lord Jesus, receive my Spirit* (*n*). But, in directing our worship to the Son, notice these things. 1. Christ being God and man in one person, and Mediator according to both natures; therefore it is the person of the Mediator, yea, the Man Christ, that is the object of our worship. For, though he is not to be worshipped as Mediator, nor as man: Yet that person who is Mediator, and who is man, is to be worshipped; seeing the person is one, though the natures are distinct. Yet, 2. This worship is given to the Mediator, only as he is God, and because he is God: For it is only as God that he hath these attributes and perfections that are requisite in the object of religious worship. 3. Though he is not to be worshipped as Mediator, as if his mediation were the formal reason of his adorability: Yet, in our worship, he may and ought to be considered as Mediator. For, his mediation being the only ground of our access to and acceptance with God, in any part of our worship, it may and ought to be considered by us, to encourage and embolden our hearts in approaching to God, to raise our confidence, and to warm our hearts with love and thankfulness. 4. In directing our worship to the Son, there is still a respect to be had to his mediation, as the ground of our access, no less than when we direct our worship to the Father. For, as there is but one God whom we worship; so there is but one Mediator, without whom there is no access to this one God (*o*).

3. We may direct our worship to the Holy Ghost: For, the holy Spirit being the same God with the Father and the Son; therefore he may be expressly prayed unto, as well as the Father and the Son: Though this be not so usual in scripture, for the reason already assigned.

Posit. 3 Though there be three distinct divine persons, and all are to be worshipped; yet there are not three distinct objects of worship, but one. Ignorant people, when they hear that

---

(*l*) Eph. i. 3. and iii. 14. Col i. 12. 1 Pet. i 17. John iv. 21, 23. (*m*) Psal. xlv. 3, 4. (*n*) Acts vii. 29. (*o*) 1 Tim. ii. 5.

that there are three persons to be worshipped, are apt straightway to divide their worship, and to imagine a Trinity of Gods. But all the persons are one and the same object of worship, seeing they are one and the same God. Though there be three distinct persons, yet there is but one divine essence; and the Son and Holy Ghost being the same God with the Father, are also the same object of worship. And further, the divine essential attributes, which are the grounds on which we adore God, are common to all the persons. The Father is omnipotent and omnipresent; and so is the Son and the Holy Ghost: Yet there are not three omnipotents or omnipresents, but one omnipotent and omnipresent God. The Deity being the formal object of worship, therefore in worshipping the persons, respect must be had to their essential attributes; and these being common to all the three, it plainly follows that they are not distinct objects, but the same object of worship. This is also evident from what our Lord says, *And whatsoever ye shall ask in my name, that I will do, that the Father may be glorified in the Son* (*p*). Where we see that Christ is joint with the Father in hearing and answering prayers; and consequently he is jointly prayed to with the Father. The like is true also of the Holy Ghost.

From this position, we may draw these inferences for our information and direction. 1. Whatever person we name in in our addresses to God, yet in every act of worship all the persons are worshipped. For, whatever person be named, he is God, and the same God with the other two: Therefore, if we worship him as God, we also worship the other two with him. Seeing the Son and Holy Ghost are the same God, and the same object of worship with the Father; † therefore they are worshipped by the same act of worship by which the Father is worshipped. Whatever person you name, you must not so fix your heart on one as to exclude the rest, else your prayer is sin. 2. It follows also, that there is no necessity of naming all the persons in your worship. You may direct you prayers to any one person, but with a due care of worshipping all in that one, remembering it is the same God, Father, Son, and Holy Ghost, that is worshipped. Hence, 3. When any one

(*p*) John xiv. 13.

† Μία προσκύνησις ή πατρος, ϰ ἐνανθρωπησαντος ϋϋ, ϰ ἁγίω πνευματος. Cyrill. Alexandr. Lib. de recta Fide Cap. 32.

Ἡ τε ἑνὸς προσκύνησις, των τριων ἐςι προσκύνησις, δια το ἐν τοις τρισιν ὁμότιμον της ἀξίας ϰ της θεότητος.

Gregor. Nazianz. Orat. 37.

one of the perſons is named, you muſt not think that he who is not named is leſs worſhipped; but in one act, we worſhip that one God, who is Father, Son, and Holy Ghoſt. 4. It is alſo evident from what hath been ſaid, that the naming, now one, and then another of the perſons, maketh no difference in the object of worſhip: For it is ſtill the ſame one God that is worſhipped, whatever perſon is named. Yet it is ſafeſt not to alter the denomination of the perſon in the ſame prayer, eſpecially before others; leſt thereby we give occaſion to them to foſter divided conceptions of the object of worſhip. 5. In our worſhip, ſuch expreſſions ſhould be forborn as tend to obſcure the unity of the object worſhipped. Some will pray to the Mediator to perform ſuch works and duties as peculiarly belong to his mediatory office; as to intercede or plead for them: But it is ſafeſt to forbear ſuch expreſſions, becauſe they diſpoſe men to think that praying to the Mediator is not the ſame with praying to God, and that the Mediator is of leſs glory and majeſty than the Father, and the Father leſs affectionate and tender towards ſinners than the Son.

Poſit 4. Though we may direct our worſhip to any one of the divine perſons; yet, in worſhipping the ſacred Trinity, it is moſt congruous, that a regard be had to their order of working, and the diſtinct offices and operations aſcribed to them in the buſineſs of our ſalvation. Now, in the buſineſs of ſalvation, the Father, being the firſt perſon in order, is repreſented as ſuſtaining and defending the majeſty of the Deity, and acting the part of ſupreme Judge and Governor; the Son acts the part of a Mediator, and procures for us acceſs to God in our worſhip; and the Holy Spirit acts the part of a Sanctifier, and as ſuch excites and quickens us to duty, and aſſiſts and helps us in duty: So that, it is by the ſanctifying Spirit that we are to addreſs ourſelves through Chriſt unto the Father. And ſeeing all ſpiritual bleſſings are originally from the love of the Father, through the grace and merit of the Son, by the communication of the Holy Ghoſt (*q*); therefore in ſeeking theſe bleſſings, we are to addreſs ourſelves to the Father, through Chriſt, by the Spirit. To this purpoſe is that expreſſion, *Through him we both have an acceſs by one Spirit unto the Father* (*r*). Accordingly we find that the ſaints in ſcripture uſually direct their worſhip to the Father, not as excluding the reſt of the perſons, but in reſpect of order of ſubſiſtence and working. And ſo did the ancient church. Hence Athanaſius hath this

Doxology,

(*q*) 2 Cor. xiii. 14.   (*r*) Eph. ii. 18.

Doxology, "† Through whom (that is, Jesus Christ) be glory "and power to the Father in the Holy Ghost." Well then, though the whole sacred Trinity be the object of worship, yet with a regard to the order of their working, and distinct personal operations in the business of our salvation, you are to direct your requests to the Father, resting on Christ for access, and looking to the Holy Spirit for help and assistance.

Again, it is congruous to the order of working amongst the divine persons, and to the distinct offices and operations ascribed to them in the business of our salvation, that if at any time you direct your requests to the Son, or to the Holy Ghost, it should be for such blessings and benefits as belong to their distinct personal offices. So the apostle prays for *love* from the Father, *grace* from the Son, and *communion* from the Holy Ghost (*s*). And in the holy scriptures, where petitions are directed to the Son, it is for such things as some way belong to his mediatory office (*t*). And so we may plead with him, to guide and govern his church, to pour out the Spirit, to to gift ministers, &c. And so also, when petitions respect the furnishing persons with gifts and graces, the sanctifying the soul, the enlightening the mind, the increasing and strengthening grace, &c. These being the works of the Spirit, and such as belong to his personal operation, such petitions may be directed to him. But it seems to be more congruous to the order of working among the persons, to pray that God would do such things by his Spirit. As the psalmist, *Uphold me with thy free Spirit;* and, *Thy Spirit is good; lead me into the land of uprightness* (*u*).

These things may be of use for your direction in your worship. But ere I leave this head, I must speak a little to a grave and weighty case. It may be matter of exercise to some serious souls among you, that you know not how to apprehend this one God in three distinct persons, when you are going about worship. Your thoughts fall into such confusion and disorder, and are so unstable, that you are sometimes sore disquieted.

I confess this is a great depth, not to be curiously pryed into: Yet I shall endeavour, the Lord assisting, to speak a little, agreeably to what God hath revealed, for the relief and direction

---

† Δι' ὗ (Ἰησῦ χριςῦ) τῳ πατρὶ ἡ δόξα ᾧ τὸ κράτος ἐν πνευματι ἁγίῳ. Athan Orat. 1, Contr Arian.

(*s*) 2 Cor. xiii. 14. (*t*) Psal. xlv. 3, &c. (*u*) Psal li. 11. and cxliii. 10.

tion of exercised Christians. To have some right conceptions of that glorious God whom you worship, is doubtless so necessary, that without this all your worship is profane and irreligious. Yet this is so great a depth, that it is dangerous for you to wade into it, lest by going too far you lose yourselves, and know not how to come out again. The path being narrow, your thoughts had need to walk the more warily. There are some things I shall warn you to beware of, and other things I shall positively recommend to you.

1. Some things I warn you to beware of in your worship. And, 1. Beware of poring too curiously upon the object worshipped, as if you could comprehend the mystery of a sacred Trinity, or understand the manner how God is one in three, and three in one. Aiming at this doth often disquiet and perplex the minds of serious Christians. Therefore take heed of descending to particular conceptions and notions of the Trinity of persons, or puzzling yourselves about conceiving one in three, and three in one. Remember, you cannot look upon God immediately, at least in this life. 2. Beware of forming in your minds representations, or shapes of a Trinity of persons in the unity of the Godhead. Men are naturally prone to fashion God in their minds in such and such a form. But it is most dishonourable to him, to set up any picture of him, so much as in your minds; for, God is purely spiritual: Therefore all such imaginations are with horror to be abandoned. Let your heart adore a spiritual Majesty, whom you cannot comprehend, and yet know to be, one in three, and three in one. 3. Beware of dividing the object of your worship, or separating the blessed persons, so much as in your thought and imagination; as if the Father were a distinct object of worship from the Son, or the Son from the Father, or the Holy Ghost from both. For, all the persons being one and the same God, are also one and the same object of worship, as I have already cleared.

2. There are some things which I positively recommend to you. And, 1. In all your worship come to God with the solid faith of this mystery of a Trinity in unity; and with real, thorough and deep impressions of the general truth, as it is clearly revealed in the holy scriptures. And labour to come with a deep conviction, that you are worshipping that one glorious God, whatever person be named. 2. Bound all your curiosity within the compass of these expressions, names, titles, attributes, whereby God hath manifested himself to us in his blessed word. When Moses desired to see God's glory, the

Lord

shewed him his *goodness*, by proclaiming his attributes before him (*x*). Thereby teaching us to conceive of God, as he hath manifested himself in his word by certain attributes which describe his nature. It is safest to rest here, without diving immediately into his essence: For, these must be the most solid notions of God that he himself hath taught us. 3. In your worship come to God admiring and adoring what you can have no particular and distinct conception of. Even the glorious angels admire and adore a sacred Trinity in their worship. The *seraphims cover their faces* with their wings, when they cry *Holy, holy, holy, is the Lord of Hosts* (*y*); importing that the holy Trinity is too mysterious and too bright an object, even for their understandings. 4. Labour to have such apprehensions of this glorious mystery, as may beget humility, holy awe and reverence, and such other affections and qualifications as true worshippers ought to have; and pore no farther on the object worshipped, than may serve to transform your heart into a likeness to him. It should be much more your exercise, to have becoming effects upon your own hearts, than to pore on this mystery: For, it is far better to have the heart filled with fear and reverence, than to have the head filled with imaginations. The real and practical honour of the blessed Trinity is best. Then do you honour a holy Trinity in unity, not when you conceive of the Mystery, but when you make a religious and practical use of it. Therefore hold you with what is practical, and do not give yourselves to what doth indispose and disquiet you. Yet, 5. Sometimes in your worship revive the thoughts of this glorious mystery, so it may be without distracting or perplexing your minds with any curious prying into the manner of it. Think that you are praying to that one glorious God, who is Father, Son, and Holy Ghost. Remember it is him you worship, and labour to stay your mind upon one God in three persons, and seek after no more. I am afraid that even knowing Christians do often fail and mistake here. In our worship, our minds are either reduced to such a simple unity, that we think upon one of the persons alone; or they are distracted and divided into such a plurality, that we worship, in a manner, three Gods in one †. Now it is a great practical mystery,

---

(*x*) Exod. xxxiii. and xxxiv. (*y*) Isa. vi. 2, 3.

† Ἡ τριας σεβασμιος ἐςιν ἐν μία ᾗ ἀιδίῳ δόξη, τὴν αὐτὴν ᾗ μίαν μόνην θιότητα πανταχῦ περιφέρυσα, ἄρρητος, ἄσχισος, ἀδιαιρετος.
Basil. M. L. 5. contr. Eunom. C. 15.
Nullis Fraudibus aut propriis aut alienis decipitur, qui Deum unum

mystery, to hold the right and middle way. Excellent to this purpose is that of Nazianzen; "† I cannot, says he, think up-on one, but by and by I am compassed about with the brightness of three: And I cannot distinguish three, but I am suddenly driven back into one." In your worship learn so to conceive of God, that while you worship one God, you may adore that sacred and blessed Trinity; and while you worship that holy Trinity, you may straightway be reduced to an unity. And learn so to conceive of God, as all the persons may have equal honour from you, seeing they are one object of worship. For this end be earnest for divine direction and assistance. Under the deep sense of your own weakness and insufficiency, depend on the blessed Spirit, whose work it is, by office, to help the infirmities of believers in all their worship.

SERMON CXIV.

Exhort. 5. SEEK earnestly after fellowship and communion with the holy Trinity. That there is such a thing is plain and evident from the holy scriptures. We read of fellowship with the Father and the Son. *Truly,* says the apostle, *our fellowship is with the Father, and with his Son Jesus Christ* (a), TRULY—as if he had said, this I am speaking of, is no fancy, but what hath a great reality in it. The carnal world look on communion with God as a fancy, as the heathens groundlessly pretended to a secresy with their gods: But believers have experience of the truth and reality of it. *Truly our fellowship is with the Father, and with his* SON. The Holy Ghost is not here excluded, though he be not particularly mentioned: But when the Father and the Son are named, he also is understood; for, he is the Spirit of the Father and the Son, by whom they communicate all spiritual good things to the elect; so that he is the more immediate Author of all gracious communications. Hence we read of *the communion of the Holy Ghost* (b). We have fellowship with the Father and the Son, but it is by the Holy Ghost. So that this
communion

---

sic colit, ut in Trinitate noverit nec personas confundere, nec substantiam separare. Fulgent. Lib. contr. Arianos

† Ὀυ φθάνω τὸ ἓν νοῆσαι, ϰ τοῖς τρισὶ περιλάμπομαι, ὐ φθάνω τα τρία διελεῖν, ϰ εἰς τὸ ἓν αναφέρομαι.

Greg. Nazianz. Orat. 40.

(a) 1 John i. 3.   (b) 2 Cor xiii. 14.

communion is with all the divine Persons. The reason is, because by the mystical union believers are united to the whole sacred Trinity. We are by faith first united to Christ, and then through him we are united to God: And union is the ground of communion. And indeed we can have no communion with any of the divine Persons, unless we have communion with them all. We can have no communion with the Father, without the Son; for, *no man cometh to the Father but by* him (*c*). And we can have no communion with the Son, without the Father; for, *no man can come unto* him, *except the Father draw him* (*d*). And we can have no communion with the Father and the Son, without the Spirit; for the Holy Spirit, being the third person in order, is, as I said, the more immediate author of all gracious communications.

In prosecuting this purpose a little, I shall,

1. *Shew, in some measure, what this communion with the blessed Trinity is.*
2. *Propose some motives to quicken and engage you to seek after it.*
3. *Give some directions what to do that you may attain to it.*

First, I shall endeavour to shew, in some measure, what this communion with the blessed Trinity is. It is indeed a very mysterious thing; and to speak of it fully, would require far more acquaintance with it, than is to be found amongst us in this imperfect state. It is taught only in the holy scriptures. We have no discoveries of it in the dim book of nature: For, though the heathens talked of a kind of converse and communion with their gods; yet, to bring in and make use of their notions in this place, would but darken your apprehensions of this glorious mystery. Therefore all our inquiries here must be bounded within the compass of the written word.

There is a twofold communion with the blessed Trinity, habitual, and actual.

1. There is an habitual communion, which all believers in Christ enjoy habitually, constantly, and equally. I may call it a state of communion; for, from it all acts of communion do flow, and upon it they do depend. This habitual communion hath these things in it. 1. A communion of natures. The Son of God assumed our nature, being *made in the likeness of sinful flesh* (*e*); so that our nature is taken into a personal union with

---

(*c*) John xiv. 6.   (*d*) John vi. 44.   (*e*) Rom. viii. 3.

with the Godhead. On the other hand, believers are made *partakers of the divine nature* (*f*). As he became the Son of Man, so are they made the sons of God. He had a mother on earth, and they have a Father in heaven. 2. A complication of interests. On the one hand, the whole sacred Trinity is made over to believers in the covenant, as I formerly † shewed. Yea, a whole God is made over to them, not only in his personal relations, but also in all his essential attributes that are common to all the Persons. The power, wisdom, goodness, mercy, faithfulness, &c. of God the Father, Son and Holy Ghost, are made over to them in the covenant. And God not only maketh over himself to them, but with himself all things. *All things are yours,* says the apostle; *whether Paul, or Apollos, or Cephas, or the world, or life, or death, or things present, or things to come; all are yours* (*g*). On the other hand, believers are resigned and given up to the blessed Trinity, according to that exhortation, *Yield yourselves unto God* (*h*). So, the Macedonians *gave their ownselves to the Lord* (*i*). Yea, not only believers themselves, but also all that they have, even to the lowest interest and enjoyment, is consecrated to God; according to that prophecy, *In that day shall there be upon the bells of the horses,* HOLINESS UNTO THE LORD, *and the pots in the Lord's house shall be like the bowls before the altar Yea, every pot in Jerusalem and in Judah shall be Holiness unto the Lord of hosts* (*k*). So that God in all that he is and hath, is the believer's; and the believer in all that he is and hath, sin excepted, is God's. 3. A communication of spiritual blessings, benefits, and privileges; such as regeneration, justification, adoption, sanctification, pardon of sin, peace with and access to God. All blessings and benefits that are absolutely necessary, necessary to the being of a Christian, are communicated to every believer. And we may here notice a fellowship between Christ and us in spiritual privileges. All spiritual privileges are first Christ's, and then the believer's. As he is the Son of God by nature, so are believers the sons of God by grace. God is his God and Father, and he is their God and Father also. Christ is God's *fellow;* and believers are Christ's *fellows*. Christ *is the heir of all things;* and believers are *joint heirs with Christ* (*l*). Again, believers have communion with Christ in his offices. Is he a King and a Priest? So are they. Is he a Prophet?

† Page 389.

(*f*) 2 Pet. i. 4. (*g*) 1 Cor. iii 21, 22, 23. (*h*) Rom. vi. 13. (*i*) 2 Cor. viii. 5. (*k*) Zech. xiv. 20, 21. (*l*) Eph. i 3. John xx. 17. Zech. xiii. 7. Psal. xlv. 7. Heb. i. 3. Rom. viii. 17.

Prophet? So are they. They have, not only the real advantage and benefit of Christ's offices, but there is something derived and communicated to them (*m*). As he was anointed with the gifts and grace of the Spirit, so are they anointed through him. They *have an unction from the Holy One.* Hence they are called *God's anointed* (*n*). 4. A communication of influences, viz. such influences as are necessary and constant. For, besides arbitrary influences, which fall under the head of actual communion, there are necessary influences of grace which are constantly communicated to all believers: Such as, influences to maintain the spiritual life; for, *he holdeth our soul in life* (*o*): Influences to promote their growth in grace, in less or more, one way or other, upward or downward; so, the apostle tells us, that *all the body having nourishment ministered from the Head, and knit together, increaseth with the increase of God* (*p*): And influences to uphold them under and against temptations, that they may not utterly fall and perish in their way to glory: The psalmist seals unto this: *Nevertheless,* says he, *I am continually with thee; thou holdest me by my right hand.* They are *kept by the power of God* (*q*).

2. There is an actual communion, which lies in that familiar intercourse that passeth between the blessed Trinity and the souls of believers: And that, 1. In set and solemn duties and ordinances. 2. In a course of holiness.

(1.) There is actual communion in set and solemn duties and ordinances. And here we must carefully distinguish between God's part and the believer's part. On the one hand, there are duties and services on the part of believers, whereby they hold communion with God: Such as, prayer and praise, reading and hearing the word, meditation, partaking of the sacrament. In these and the like duties, the souls of believers go out towards God, in the exercise of faith, love, and other graces. Hence it is that duties of worship are called our *drawing nigh God;* and our *visiting him* (*r*). On the other hand, there are communications of grace and blessings on God's part, whereby he holds communion with his people. Hence he is said to *meet his people* in duties and ordinances (*s*). When the saints go up to meet God, he comes down to give them a meeting. They *draw near to God, and he draws near* to them (*t*).

Duties

(*m*) Rev. i. 6. Psal. cv. 15.   (*n*) Psal. xlv. 7. 1 John ii. 20. Psal. cv. 15.   (*o*) Psal. lxvi. 9.   (*p*) Col. ii. 19.   (*q*) Psal. lxxiii. 23. 1 Pet. i. 5.   (*r*) Lev. x. 3. Isa. xxvi. 16.   (*s*) Isa. lxiv. 5. (*t*) James iv. 8.

Duties go up, and bleſſings come down. Ordinances are like Jacob's ladder, reaching from heaven to earth, by which God deſcends, and ſouls aſcend; God comes down, and hearts go up. O the ſweet viſits of love that are there! There are ſometimes ſuch ſhowers of divine bleſſings, ſuch influences of the Spirit of grace, ſuch openings of goſpel myſteries, ſuch ſheddings abroad of divine love, ſuch a preſence and glory in the ordinances, that believers are ready to cry out, *Surely God is in this place; O it is good to be here; it is good for me to draw near unto God.*

(2.) There is actual communion in a courſe of holineſs. *If we walk in the light, as he is in the light, then have we fellowſhip one with another* (*u*). There is a communion with God in holy walking: Hence it is ſaid, *Can two walk together, except they be agreed* (*x*)? God and the believer walk together like two intimate friends: And this is no mute or ſilent walk, but ſuch as is managed by gracious intercourſes between God and them. Therefore Enoch's communion with God is expreſſed by this, that he *walked with God* (*y*). Believers walk in the fear of the Lord, ſtudying to pleaſe him in all things, watching over and keeping their hearts with all diligence; and God keepeth up a ſecret correſpondence with their ſouls by his Spirit.

Thus I have ſhewed, in ſome meaſure, what this communion is. And that believers have this communion with the whole ſacred Trinity, will further appear, if we conſider, that, upon the one hand, all theſe duties and ſervices whereby they hold communion with God, are offered up to the Father, through the mediation of the Son, by the aſſiſtance of the Holy Ghoſt, as I cleared before. On the other hand, all theſe bleſſings and benefits, and influences of grace, that are communicated on God's part, come from the whole ſacred Trinity. Hence it is that grace and peace are wiſhed and prayed for from the Father and the Son; yea, from the whole ſacred Trinity (*z*). So that all ſpiritual bleſſings, all influences and communications of grace, are from the Father, originally, by command and order; from the Son, by merit and purchaſe; and from the Holy Ghoſt, by immediate communication.

Second, In the next place, I ſhall propoſe a few things by way of motive, to excite and quicken you to ſeek after this communion with the bleſſed Trinity. And, 1. This communion is moſt neceſſary, yea, abſolutely neceſſary. It is neceſſary as
the

(*u*) 1 John i. 7. (*x*) Amos iii. 3. (*y*) Gen v. 24. (*z*) Rom. i. 7. 1 Cor. i. 3. 2 Cor. i. 2. Rev. i. 4, 5.

the end and design of Christ's death; for he *suffered, that he might bring us to God* (a). He came to restore peace and intercourse between God and elect sinners. *The chastisement of our peace was upon him* (b). So that if you are strangers to this communion, you have no interest in the death of Christ, nor any saving benefit by it. It is necessary as that which we are called unto by the gospel: *God is faithful,* says the apostle, *by whom ye were called unto the fellowship of his Son* (c); which includes the outward as well as the inward call: So that you come short of, and, what in you lies, frustrate the design of the gospel, if you do not seek communion with God. Again, it is necessary as the end and design of gospel-ordinances: Hence the psalmist longed so much after the public ordinances, that he might *see the power and glory of God* there, and that he might *behold the beauty of the Lord* (d). Particularly, this communion is the end and design of the preaching and hearing the word: So the apostle tells us, *That which we have seen and heard, declare we unto you, that ye also may have fellowship with us: And truly our fellowship is with the Father, and with his Son Jesus Christ* (e). And it is the end of the sacraments, especially of the Lord's supper: Therefore that sacrament is called *the communion* (f). It is necessary also in order to your communion with the holy Trinity in glory. You must be *made meet to be partakers of the inheritance of the saints in light* (g): And you are not meet for communion with God in glory, unless you get communion with him here in grace; for, what should they do with the presence of God in heaven, who are careless of his company on earth? 2. This communion is very honourable. Consider with whom this communion is enjoyed, even with three infinitely glorious persons. It is reckoned an high honour to have fellowship with kings and princes; but how much more honourable is it, to have fellowship with God, the Father, Son, and Holy Ghost? For poor vile creatures to be advanced to the friendship and fellowship of the infinitely glorious God; to be his intimates and familiars: O, what an honour is this! 3. This communion is most sweet and pleasant. O, the pleasure that it yields, where it is felt and sensible! The soul in such a case, is ready to cry out, *The lines are fallen to me in pleasant places* (h). Communion with God is a little heaven given us here on earth. How pleasant is it to believers

to

(a) 1 Pet. iii. 18. (b) Isa. liii. 6. (c) 1 Cor. i. 9. (d) Psal. lxiii. 2. and xxvii. 4. (e) 1 John i. 3. (f) 1 Cor. x. 16. (g) Col. i. 12. (h) Psal. xvi. 5.

to be in God's company, to converse familiarly with him! This is so sweet, that it is able to make every thing sweet. It will make duties and ordinances sweet to you. It will sweeten every condition of life to you. It will sweeten all providences, even those that are most cross and afflicting, whether with respect to your own case or the church's. How cross soever God's dispensations may be, yet intimate communion with a sacred Trinity will yield a sweetness to you under them all. 4. This communion is most profitable. It hath a fructifying virtue; it will make your soul fat and flourishing. It hath an assimilating virtue: It will make you like God, and *change you more and more into his image* (*i*). It will promote humility: When Isaiah saw the glory of God, how did he sink into nothing in his own thoughts! *Wo is me,* says he, *for I am undone, because I am a man of unclean lips,—— for mine eyes have seen the King, the Lord of hosts* (*k*). It will breed contempt of the world; as it did in the psalmist, *Lord,* says he, *lift thou up the light of thy countenance upon us: Thou hast put gladness in my heart, more than in the time that their corn and their wine abounded* (*l*). It will cause great delight in duties and ordinances, which are the means of this communion, and will beget a great longing after them (*m*). 5. Herein lies man's excellency above the beasts, that he is capable of so high an elevation as to have fellowship and communion with the holy Trinity; and that God hath breathed into him a rational soul, that hath such vast and unlimited desires as can be satisfied with no less. Therefore, unless you seek communion with God, you do not act the part of men. You degrade yourselves, and debase and abuse a noble soul, in not acting according to the excellency of your natures. You act like beasts, and not like men.

Third, In the last place, I shall give a few directions what to do that you may attain to this high privilege of communion with the blessed Trinity. 1. Get a deep sense of your natural distance and estrangement from God by reason of sin. Ye that are yet in your sins are *far off,* and *strangers to God from the womb* (*n*). Labour to have the sense of this deep upon your hearts. 2. Renounce all iniquity. God can have no fellowship with you while you hold communion with your sins: For, *what fellowship hath righteousness with unrighteousness, and what communion hath light with darkness* (*o*)? He will have nothing

to

(*i*) 2 Cor. iii. 18. (*k*) Isa vi. 5. (*l*) Psal. iv. 6, 7. (*m*) Psal. lxiii. 1, 2. (*n*) Eph. ii. 12. Psal. lviii. 3. (*o*) 2 Cor. vi. 14.

to do, in a way of special grace, with you who will not part with your sins. He will not be of your communion. He will not *take you by the hand*, as the word may be rendered in Job viii. 20. Therefore renounce and abandon all your sins. Say, with Ephraim, *What have I to do any more with idols* (p)? 3. Get your peace made with God: For how *can two walk together, except they be agreed* (q)? Get God's friendship, if you would have his fellowship Therefore, *as if God did beseech you by us, we pray you in Christ's stead, be ye reconciled to God* (r). Embrace the offers of peace. Consent heartily to the gracious terms on which it is offered to you. Lay down the weapons of your rebellion against God; embrace Christ the blessed peace-maker; and resign yourselves to God through him. 4. Get a saving union with Christ, and with the whole sacred Trinity through him, and that by faith and believing, as I formerly exhorted you. Union is the ground of communion. 5. Wait on God in duties and ordinances; such as prayer, reading and hearing the word, meditation: For these are the means both of attaining to, and maintaining communion with God. The means are God's way: When you are diligent in the use of them, you are in God's way for a blessing; For he *meets him that rejoiceth and worketh righteousness, these that remember* him *in his ways* (s). *Blessed is he that heareth me,* says Christ, *watching daily at my gates, &c* (t) Though God be not obliged, yet it is the usual practice of his free grace, to meet with seeking sinners.

SERMON CXV.

TO conclude this exhortation, in seeking communion with God in duties and ordinances, I recommend these three things to you who are believers in Christ. 1. Set about cleansing and purifying work. *Let us draw near with a true heart, in full assurance of faith, having our hearts sprinkled from an evil conscience, and our bodies washed with pure water* (a). There ought to be a special purgation before worship. Hence the psalmist says, *I will wash mine hands in innocency; so will I compass thine altar, O Lord* (b). 2. Stir up such graces as serve to fit you for communion with God; such as, faith, love, longing desires after God, holy fear and reverence, humility, and

(p) Hof. xiv. 8.   (q) Amos iii. 3.   (r) 2 Cor. v. 20.
(s) Isa. lxiv. 5.   (t) Prov. viii. 34.
        (a) Heb. x. 22.   (b) Psal. xxvi. 6.

and brokenness of heart for sin. There ought to be a special excitation of grace, when you are to seek communion with God in his ordinances. Therefore stir up the grace of God that is in you. 3. See that you come to God by Christ. There is no access to him but through the blessed Mediator. *Through him we have access to the Father* (c). When you seek communion with God, bring Christ along with you in the arms of faith, that he may bring you in to God: For this is his work by office; he *suffered, that he might bring us to God* (d). Christ is our mercy-seat where God will meet with us (e).

Exhort. 6. Study this glorious mystery of a Trinity of persons in the Godhead. I formerly exhorted such as are ignorant to seek after a competent measure of the knowledge of this great truth: Now, I exhort you to labour to grow in the knowledge of it, so far as God hath revealed it.

For exciting and quickening you to this, consider these two things. 1. You are greatly obliged to study this mystery. Why else hath God revealed it? It is certainly our duty to study to know God, so far as he hath been pleased to reveal himself in his blessed word. Not to study this mystery, is a high reflection on the infinite wisdom of God, in giving us such a revelation of himself: And it is a great contempt of his goodness, especially considering, that it is more clearly revealed now under the New Testament, than it was under the Old; so that now we may *behold the glory of God with open face* (f), in comparison of what the saints did of old. Certainly, God expects a suitable improvement of this great advantage: *To whomsoever much is given, of him shall be much required* (g). Though the glorious angels know much of God, yet they still desire to know more (h): Especially, they study the knowledge of the blessed Trinity, in their order of working, and distinct personal operations in the business of our salvation: And are not we far more concerned than they? 2. This is a study both pleasant and profitable. (1.) It is a pleasant study. All knowledge is pleasant to the soul; and the pleasure is always proportionable to the excellency of the object. But here is the most excellent object, an infinitely glorious and blessed Trinity. In the serious study of this mystery, gracious souls meet with rich experiences of a soul-refreshing sweetness. Men take pleasure in studying mysteries, things hid from vulgar understandings: But here is one eminently such; a sacred secret;

(c) Eph. ii. 18. (d) 1 Pet. iii. 18. (e) Exod. xxv. 22.
(f) 2 Cor. iii. 18. (g) Luke xii. 48. (h) 1 Pet. i. 12.

secret; the myſtery of myſteries, that tranſcends the reach of of all created underſtandings. (2.) It is a profitable ſtudy. An increaſe in the knowledge of this myſtery is a great bleſſing. The apoſtle prays for it as ſuch to the believing Coloſſians, even that they might attain to the *riches of the full aſſurance of underſtanding, to the acknowledgement of the myſtery of God, and of the Father, and of Chriſt* (*i*). The more knowledge you have of this myſtery, your knowlege of other goſpel truths and myſteries, which are founded thereupon, will be the more clear and diſtinct. This is a practical principle, of great uſe and influence with reference to Chriſtian practice, particularly with reſpect to faith and worſhip, as I have formerly cleared. There is nothing to be ſtudied here, but what may, at one time or other, be matter of inſtruction, direction, or conſolation to you.

Well then, ſtudy this glorious myſtery: And ſtudy it, 1. With awful and reverend apprehenſions of the glorious majeſty of God, and of his infinite and incomprehenſible nature, as that which is to be humbly adored according to the revelation he hath made of himſelf. 2. With a deep humbling ſenſe of your own darkneſs, blindneſs, and ignorance. It is fit that the foundation ſhould be laid deep, when the building is ſo high. Wiſe Agur is, in his own eyes, brutiſh in knowledge, when he thinks of the incomprehenſible majeſty of God (*k*). How blind are you, even in things natural? How much more blind in the deep things of God? 3. With a deep ſenſe of the great great weight and importance of this doctrine Study it, not as a matter of an ordinary controverſy in religion, but as that wherein the ſalvation of your precious ſouls is directly and immediately concerned. 4 Study this myſtery with much humble ſobriety Take heed of all curious ſearching and prying into this depth. There is in all men a natural deſire after knowledge, eſpecially of things ſecret and myſterious. Hence it is that many deſpiſe and nauſeate what is plainly revealed, and catch after what is ſecret, and the clear and diſtinct knowledge whereof God hath reſerved unto himſelf. Such is the unbridled licenſe of the minds of men, that they will ſearch into that which God hath compaſſed about with a divine darkneſs of inacceſſable light: and will ſeek for ſatisfaction to their own reaſon, by wading into theſe depths that no created underſtanding can fathom. This is a woful evil: It is daring boldneſs. And ſuch labour is not only loſt, but highly prejudicial: Men often loſe what they have, by catching at what is too remote

(*i*) Col. ii. 2.   (*k*) Prov. xxx. ii, 3.

mote from them. Therefore, study this mystery with humble sobriety. Do not think to satisfy reason by studying what others have written on it. Do not search and enquire curiously into that which God hath not revealed. Many schoolmen have taken an unwarrantable liberty here. But the doctrine of the sacred Trinity is such a deep mystery, that it is certainly a high presumption to undertake to explain the manner of it, and a piece of manifest tyranny to impose the belief of such pretended explications upon the consciences of men. Scripture revelation is so large and deep, that there is enough there to take up your time and study, though you do not dive into things too deep for you.

But what shall we do, that we may grow in the right knowledge of this great mystery? I give these directions. 1. Labour to get your understanding faculty more enlarged. The scales fall off from our eyes by degrees; and some things are too bright for the soul at the first opening of its weak eyes. Therefore seek to have your eyes more opened, and your sight more cleared. Pray with the psalmist, *Open thou mine eyes, that I may behold wondrous things out of thy law* (*l*). 2. Deny your carnal reason. Till then, you can never entertain any right thoughts of this glorious mystery. The knowledge thereof is not to be attained by the strength of reason and natural parts. It is not the most piercing wit that profits most in this study. Yea, carnal reason laughs at divine mysteries which are above its comprehension. Therefore, put out your lamp, that it may be lighted by the Spirit. 3. Regard the holy scriptures as the proper measure and rule of this mystery. It is there only that it is revealed. Who could have apprehended a sacred Trinity, without the scripture? This is the holy balance that weighs it, the divine light that discovers it. Therefore, though you are to use the best helps for understanding the scriptures; yet labour to fetch all your knowledge of this mystery from them alone. Seek not to be wise *above that which is written* (*m*). Beware of abstruse speculations, and vain airy notions. 4. Labour to see the glory of the blessed Trinity shining in the face of Christ: For *in him dwells the fulness of the Godhead bodily;* and he is *the brightness* of the Father's *glory, and the express image of his person* (*n*). 5. Employ Christ. It is he that must reveal this mystery to you: For, *No man hath seen God at any time; the only begotten Son, who is in the bosom of the Father, he hath declared him. Neither knoweth any man the Father,*

(*l*) Psal. cxix. 18.   (*m*) 1 Cor. iv. 6.   (*n*) Col. ii. 9. Heb. i. 3.

Father, save the Son, and he to whomsoever the Son will reveal him (o). This is Christ's work by office. He is our Prophet and teacher; *The true Light which lighteth every man that cometh into the world* (p). Put him upon the exercise of his office. Look to him for much of the enlightening work of his Spirit. Go to him for eye-salve, to make you more quick-sighted in the things of God (q). 6. Give yourselves much to prayer. It must be *given you* to know this mystery (r). What you know aright of it, must be by the revelation of the holy Spirit. It is he that must *teach you all things*, and *lead you into all truth*. Therefore seek to be taught by the Spirit, who *searcheth the deep things of God*. Pray that *in his light* you may *see light* (s). 7. Do not satisfy yourselves with a mere speculative knowledge of this mystery. It hath a respect both to the understanding, and to the heart and life: To the understanding it is a mystery of faith; to heart and life, a mystery of godliness. These must not be separated. We must *hold the mystery of faith in a pure conscience* (t). A speculative knowledge is very fair, but barren; it may make you good scholars, but not good Christians; orthodox, but not gracious. Therefore seek after such a knowledge of a Trinity in unity, as may deeply affect your heart, and influence your life and practice. This is to be *taught, as the truth is in Jesus* (u). Let your great end in studying this mystery be practice, and not the satisfying of curiosity, or the perfecting of your understanding. Study to know a holy Trinity of persons, that you may believe in them, and worship them, and seek communion with them; and that you may love, fear, and adore, that glorious incomprehensible Majesty, who is one in in three, and three in one.

Exhort. 7. Give equal glory and honour to all the persons of the Godhead. 1. Give glory to them. The blessed angels glorify them: The seraphims cried one unto another, and said, *Holy, holy, holy is the Lord of hosts* (x): And why should not we glorify them? The divine persons also glorify one another, as I had occasion to shew when I spoke of the glory of God: And they are in this a blessed pattern for our imitation. 2. Give equal glory and honour to them. *All men should honour the Son, even as they honour the Father* (y). Many professors of Christianity practically err here; Some think altogether of God

(o) John i. 18. Matth. xi. 27. (p) John i. 9. (q) Psal xxxiv. Rev. iii. 18. (r) Matth. xiii. 11. (s) John xiv. 26. and xvi. 13. 1 Cor. ii. 10. Psal. xxxvi. 9. (t) 1 Tim. iii. 9. (u) Eph. iv. 21. (x) Isa. vi. 3. (y) John v 23.

God the Father; others honour the Son, but neglect the Father; and the most part neglect to glorify the holy Spirit. But you practically deny a Trinity in unity, if you derogate the least iota of glory from any of the three persons. They are equal in glory. The Father is not more God, than the Son, or the Holy Ghost. Though there be a priority of order, yet not of dignity and excellency. Therefore they must have equal glory from you. Give the glory of all divine excellencies and perfections to all the divine persons. Let them have the same glory of believing, adoration and worship. Give them the glory of all the good you do. Give them the glory of every excellent work, especially of a work of grace in any of your hearts. For they all concur in this work, as is clear from Cant. i. 11. where Christ promiseth to make his bride beautiful; *We will make thee borders of gold, with studs of silver.* In verse 9th, he was speaking in the singular number, *I have compared thee*, &c. But here the singular number is suddenly changed into the plural, We *will make*, &c. *We*, the blessed Trinity, Father, Son, and Holy Ghost. So that a work of grace is common to all the persons of the Godhead. The graces of the believer are pieces of their workmanship! So that the glory is due to one as well as another. Again, give the glory of your salvation to all the persons; for they all concur and conspire together here. Here the glory of the holy Trinity shines; the Father contriving and ordering, the Son purchasing, and the Holy Ghost applying this salvation. Even the glorious angels give glory to the sacred Trinity, saving sinners by their admirable joint counsel: *The heavenly host praised God, saying, Glory to God in the highest, and on earth peace, good-will towards men* (z). And we are more obliged and concerned than they. The Godhead being one and the same in all the three persons, they are equal in all essential attributes: Therefore equal glory is due to them.

Hence it was customary in the ancient church, to sing songs and hymns to the blessed Trinity. And divers doxologies have been used in the most solemn acts of religious worship. In some doxologies we will find only one person named: Sometimes the Father (*a*), and sometimes the Son (*b*). But though only one person be named, yet all the persons are understood *. Sometimes such doxologies are directed to God, as comprehending

---

(z) Luke ii. 13.

(a) Gal. i. 5. 1 Pet. v. 11. (c) Heb. xii. 21. 2 Pet. iii. 18. Rev. i. 6. * See Page 287.

hending all the persons (c). Sometimes all the persons are named distinctly, especially when heresies did arise and spread in the church. And here again, sometimes, and in some churches, all the persons were named as the object. Such was that of Augustine *, "To the Father, and the Son, and the Holy Ghost, "which Trinity is one God, be honour and glory for ever." Such doxologies were also used by divers others. Particularly, Dionysius Alexandrinus † hath this, "To God the Father, "and his Son, the Lord Jesus Christ, with the holy Spirit, "be glory and power for ever and ever. Amen." And this is the more considerable, because he joins with it, praising God in the same voice with those who have gone before us. Sometimes again, we find all the persons named in doxologies, with a regard to their order of subsistence and working; such as, *Glory be to the Father, by the Son, in the Holy Ghost.* Hence Athanasius hath this doxology ‡ "Through whom," viz. Jesus Christ, " to the Father, be glory and power, in the Holy Ghost." But the Arians abused this form of expression, and took advantage from it to infer a dissimilitude in the Son and Holy Ghost, to the Father; and to make the Son the instrument of the Father, and the Holy Ghost only to relate to time and place: And held that the Son was to be honoured only in subordination to the Father, and the Holy Ghost as inferior to both §. Therefore the doxology most universally used in the Christian church was that, ‖ *Glory to the Father, to the Son, and to the Holy Ghost.* And it was used in the church, especially against the Arian heresy, with this addition, ¶ *As it was in the beginning, so now and for ever. Amen.*

SERMON CXVI.

HERE a question is moved, whether this doxology ought to be sung in the public congregation after the singing of the psalm. The question is not about saying or singing doxologies,

---

(c) Rom. xi. 36. 2 Tim. iv. 18. Jude 25.

* Patri, Filio, & Spiritui Sancto, quæ Trinitas unus est Deus, honor & Gloria in seculum.

† Epist. 2. ad Dionys Roman.   ‡ See pag 401.

§ Bishop Stillingfleet's Vindication of the Doctrine of the Trinity, pag 201, 202.

‖ Gloria Patri & Filio & Spiritui Sancto.

¶ Sicut erat in principio, & nunc & semper, & in secula Seculorum. Amen.

doxologies, simply, to the blessed Trinity; for this is indeed a necessary duty, and is the practice of this church. We say doxologies, that is, we give and ascribe glory and praise to the blessed Trinity, in several expressions in our prayers, and particularly in the conclusion of them. And we sing doxologies to the blessed Trinity, when we sing psalms to the praise and glory of God. And though sometimes only one person is named, yet the other persons are also understood, as I have formerly cleared. But the question is about the use of such a form of doxology, and in such a manner.

That we may be the more distinct and clear in our answer, we must distinguish between what is lawful, and what is necessary, and what is expedient. A thing may be lawful in itself, that is neither necessary, nor expedient. Accordingly we say, 1. The use of the doxology is not necessary. It is indeed necessary that we give glory and praise to the Father, Son, and Holy Ghost: But the use of such a form of doxology, and in such a manner, is not necessary, neither by scripture precept, nor example. Therefore the use of it ought not to be imposed: This is utterly unlawful; for it entrencheth upon our Christian liberty, and is a manifest usurpation of authority over the conscience, which is the prerogative of God alone. Yet, 2. The use of the doxology is not in itself unlawful. I dare not condemn the simple use of it as sinful, especially in such churches where it hath always been in use and practice, and is used without offence. Providing always, that it be not used in a superstitious manner, and have no religious necessity put upon it, by either imposing or using it as necessary. But, 3. Though the use of the doxology be in itself lawful, yet the use of it, particularly in this church, is not expedient; and that on a twofold account. (1.) Because several worthy divines are against the use of songs or hymns of an human composure, though agreeable to scripture, in the public worship of God. I am not now to produce their reasons for it; nor is it necessary here to determine whether their reasons and grounds be valid and satisfying, or not. Only seeing some worthy and godly divines are against the use of such hymns in public worship, therefore the use of them is not expedient, seeing they could not be used without offence. But so it is, that the doxology we now speak of, though very ancient and agreeable to the holy scriptures, is yet but of a human composure. (2.) Because the doxology hath been and is much abused. For a religious necessity hath been put upon it, and it hath been used in a superstitious manner, in the times of the late Prelacy, and

still

still is so by those that own and adhere to that way. Who can account for their practice, who after the singing of a scripture psalm, rise up and stand at the singing of the doxology, as if greater reverence were due to a hymn of a human composure, than to psalms and hymns indited by the Spirit of God? Whatever reason there might be for such a practice in the ancient church, yet that cannot be pleaded now, when Arianism, blessed be God, is exploded †. Further, the singing the doxology is gone yet into a greater abuse, in the Romish church, where it is used most superstitiously, and the use of it enjoined as necessary, except at and about the time of the passion, and for some time after the sacrament; at which times the forbearance of it is made no less necessary. Now, the doxology being so much abused, therefore it is not expedient to use it. ‡ The use of it tends to harden Papists and others in their abuse and superstition, and is thereby become offensive to tender consciences; and therefore ought to be forborn. Indeed if the singing the doxology were a necessary duty, then it ought not to be forborn, whoever abuse it: But, as I said, it is not necessary, neither by scripture precept nor example. Now, when a thing not necessary, but only in its own nature lawful and indifferent, doth, by reason of circumstances, become offensive and inexpedient, then the use and practice of it is utterly unlawful; according to what the apostle saith, *All things are lawful unto me, but all things are not expedient: All things are lawful for me, but I will not be brought under the power of any:* And, *all things are lawful for me, but all things are not expedient: All things are lawful for me, but all things edify not* (a). Things only lawful in their own nature, are never lawful in the use, when they are inexpedient.

These are the grounds upon which we judge the singing of the doxology ought to be forborn. And upon such grounds it

---

† *Consentiunt omnes, receptam in Ecclesiis Orthodoxis fuisse hanc Formulam, ut consonam Doctrinæ Nicæni Concilii, contra Arianos.*
     Forbes. Instruct. Hist. Theol. L. 1. c. 22.

‡ *Docuerunt Apostoli, in indifferentibus faciendis vel omittendis, duo extrema esse cavenda; hinc quidem Scandalum infirmorum, inde pervicaciam falsorum fratrum. Si enim usu rerum mediarum videamus vel illos offendi, h. e. in fide labefactari: vel istos in falsa opinione obfirmari; omittendæ potius sunt, quia tunc per accidens fiunt illicitæ.* Pareus.

Extraneorum nobis est habenda ratio, ne dum eis obsequimur, ipsos in Superstitione confirmemus. Beza.

   (a) 1 Cor. vi. 12. and x. 23.

it was that this church agreed with the famous assembly of divines at Westminster, to lay aside the use of the doxology, for uniformity in the worship of God.

Exhort. 8. Beware of sinning against God. Here is a strong argument to dissuade from sin, that there are three distinct persons in the Godhead. The weight of the argument lies in these particulars. 1. All the divine persons are offended and dishonoured by sin. Every act of sin is against three infinitely glorious persons, as I hinted formerly. 2. All the persons are witnesses to every sin you commit. You cannot sin, but there are three infinitely glorious persons looking on. 3. All the persons will be witnesses against sinners in the great day. They will then bring all forth to the light; so that all your shifts and pretences will avail you nothing. 4. All the persons will jointly concur in taking vengeance for sin. For, as they are one in essence, so also in will and power. Every sin unrepented of lays you open to the wrath and vengeance of three infinitely glorious and powerful persons. The divine persons glorify one another, and consequently will avenge the wrongs and indignities done to each other.

Exhort. 9. Improve this great truth of a Trinity of persons in the Godhead, for confirming and strengthening your faith, in the belief of whatever God hath revealed, and particularly of the doctrine of the gospel. The truth of the gospel is confirmed by a threefold testimony, even by the testimomy of three divine witnesses of infallible truth and veracity; *For there are three that bear record in heaven, the Father, the Word, and the Holy Ghost; and these three are one.* To the same purpose is Christ's argument, proving against the Scribes and Pharisees, the truth of what he had spoken concerning himself; *It is also written in your law,* says he, *that the testimony of two men is true. I am one that bear witness of myself; and the Father that sent me, beareth witness of me* (*b*). Here, in my text, are three heavenly Witnesses beyond all exception; and three that are one in essence, and consequently so much the more one in their bearing record and witness; and they are here expressed by name, the Father, the Word, and the Holy Ghost. But what do they bear witness or testimony unto? They bear witness to the truth of the gospel, and particularly to that great truth, that Christ is the Son of God, and the Saviour of the world, as appears from the context. Out of the mouth of two such witnesses this truth might be established; but for superabundance, behold there are three. And that which they

(*q*) John viii. 17, 18.

they testify and bear witness unto, is the ground-work of a Christian's hope and consolation, that Christ *is the Son of God, and the Saviour of the world:* That he is a complete and perfect Saviour, being very God; so that he is *able to save them to the uttermost that come unto God by him.* Here is great encouragement to poor sensible sinners to come to Christ. God the Father, Son, and Holy Ghost, all agree in this, that Christ is a safe refuge for distressed and pursued sinners to flee unto, a strong plank for ship-broken men, a firm and sure foundation to build our salvation upon. Therefore such of you as find yourselves in a lost state, may come to Christ with confidence and hope, and lay the weight of your salvation upon his death and sufferings, with assurance to find rest and peace in him: For he is such an one in whom faith may triumph over sin and Satan, and hell and death. And it is great ground of encouragement and comfort to you that believe in Christ, that your Redeemer is strong and mighty, and that none can pluck you out of his hand.

Use 5. For exhortation, more particularly to believers in Christ. Indeed what I have already delivered is to be improved by them also, for their instruction, direction, and upstirring to duty. But I would apply myself a little more particularly to you that believe in Christ, and have the saving knowledge of, and a saving interest in the blessed Trinity. From this doctrine let me exhort such of you to the following duties.

Duty 1. Bless God for the knowledge of this mystery of a Trinity of Persons in the Godhead. Consider, 1. You had been eternally undone without the knowledge of it; this truth being fundamental to all other gospel-truths and mysteries. 2. You could never have known it but by divine revelation. For, it is a great mystery, wholly above nature. So that nature's light could never discover it to you. 3. God was not obliged to give this revelation of himself to you, more than he was to many others in the world to whom he hath denied it. You were no better than they; yea, it may be, worse, in natural and moral respects.

Well then, bless God for the knowledge of this mystery. Particularly, bless him for these three things. 1. That he hath revealed it to you in his blessed word. 2. That he hath revealed it more plainly and clearly in the New Testament, and that it hath been your lot to live in New-Testament times. 3. That you have it inwardly revealed to you by the Holy Spirit, so that you have the saving and practical knowledge thereof. *We speak the wisdom of God in a mystery,* says the apostle,

postle, *even the hidden wisdom.—Which none of the princes of this world knew—But God hath revealed the same unto us by his Spirit* (c).

For exciting and quickening you to bless and magnify the name of the Lord, more especially for the saving revelation of this mystery, consider, 1. How many and whom God hath passed by; even the far greater part of the world. Now, that God should pass by so many great, and wise, and learned men, and reveal himself savingly to the like of you; O, what a wonder of free grace is here! May you not cry out with the apostle, *Lord, how is it that thou wilt manifest thyself unto us, and not unto the world* (d)? Some of you are but babes in comparison of others; yet God hath revealed that to you, which the wisest in the world never knew. Therefore give thanks to the Father, as your Saviour did: *I thank thee, O Father,* says he, *Lord of heaven and earth, because thou hast hid these things from the wise and prudent, and hast revealed them unto babes* (e) 2. Consider the grace and mercy that is shewed unto you in this matter. The saving knowledge of a sacred Trinity is a special gift of God, and a greater evidence of his favour and friendship than if he had given you all the world. It is a distinguishing blessing: *It is given unto you to know the mysteries of the kingdom of heaven, but to others it is not given* (f). God hath given rich treasures of gold and silver to them, to whom he hath not given his blessing. All the treasures in the world cannot equal it. If Christ were here in person, he would bless you on this very account, as he did Peter: *Blessed art thou, Simon Bar-jona; for flesh and blood hath not revealed it unto thee, but my Father who is in heaven* (g).

Duty 2. Labour to get and entertain a bewailing sense of your ignorance of this mystery; there is even in the best and most knowing Christians much remaining ignorance of the Holy Trinity. All that you know of God is inconceivably less than what you are ignorant of. All that know God savingly, go mourning to their graves over their ignorance of him. Agur was one of the wisest and best men in his age; yet he cries out, *Surely I am more brutish than any man, and have not the understanding of a man. I neither learned wisdom, nor have the knowledge of the holy* (h). And this he spoke with reference to any knowledge he had of a sacred Trinity, as appears from verse 4th. *What is his name, or what is his Son's name, if thou canst tell?* Such as know God best are most sensible that they know

(c) 1 Cor. ii. 7, 8, 10. (d) John xiv. 22. (e) Matth. xi. 25.
(f) Matth xiii. 11. (g) Matth. xvi. 17. (h) Prov. xxx. 2, 3.

know but very little of him. Two things are to be lamented. 1. That you know so little of a sacred Trinity, even in comparison of what you might have known, and of what others have attained to who had no greater advantages than you have had. 2. That by reason of your remaining darkness and blindness, you are capable to know and understand so little of this mystery. Indeed it would be one blessed improvement of this doctrine, if we were thereby brought under a humbling and bewailing sense of our darkness, blindness, and ignorance. In this life our eyes are like the eyes of an owl before the sun: We are not able to bear the splendor and brightness of the glory of this mystery.

Duty 3. Be much in the contemplation of this sacred Mystery of a Trinity in unity. This is an exercise both pleasant and profitable, and will be your work and employment in heaven, where you shall see God *face to face*. Only avoid curiosity, and let your contemplations of this mystery be confined within the compass of divine revelation. There is enough there to employ your thoughts; and other contemplations are sinful and vain, and confound and disquiet the soul. Especially, contemplate the blessed Trinity of persons, in their distinct personal offices and operations in the business of your salvation. O what sweetness and pleasure may this yield unto you? To contemplate the love of the Father in your election, the grace of the Son in your redemption, and the communion of the Holy Ghost in your sanctification: To consider how it pleased God the Father, from all eternity, to set his love upon you, and to chuse you to grace and glory; and how it pleased the Son to undertake your redemption from everlasting, and to accomplish it in the fulness of time; and how it pleased the holy Spirit to renew you by grace, to draw you to Christ, and so to bring about the eternal design of the Father's love upon your heart. O think deeply on these things: And never leave thinking, till your hearts be deeply affected, till they be warmed with love to the blessed persons, and filled with raised admirations of their love and grace toward you.

Duty 4. Admire and adore this glorious mystery. Your wit is too shallow for this bottomless depth, how God is one in three, and three in one. It is enough for you, to know that it is, though you know not how it is. God were not infinitely great, if he were not greater than your understanding. Therefore adore this mystery with a humble faith, and do not search into it by the bold inquiries of reason. Certainly, humble believing is much more eligible than proud and vain curiosity;

osity; and there is much more profoundness in the sobriety of faith, than in the depths of human wisdom and learning. Admire also this glorious mystery. It is admired by the glorious angels, and will be admired by you in the mansions of glory: So that admiration is one of the duties of heaven, and therefore must needs have a great deal of sweetness and pleasure in it.

SERMON CXVII.

Duty 5. LABOUR to live by faith in the blessed Trinity. It is not enough that you believe in the divine persons at first closing with them, as I formerly exhorted; but you must also be much in the renewed actings and exercise of faith in them. To this our Lord exhorts his disciples: *Ye believe in God, believe also in me* (a). The first clause may be read imperatively as well as the latter, *Believe in God, believe also in me.* They had believed in God and Christ formerly: But now he exhorts them to set faith a-work in the renewed actings and exercise thereof. Study to live by faith in Christ, and through him, as a Mediator, in all the divine persons. I might enlarge on this subject; but I forbear, having already insisted so much in the application of this doctrine, beyond what I designed.

Only, to enforce this great duty, consider, that faith in the sacred Trinity is of excellent use, to calm present fears, and to arm the soul against future troubles. Our blessed Lord prescribed it to his disciples for this end: *Let not your heart be troubled,* says he, *ye believe in God, believe also in me* (b). Faith in the blessed Trinity is the grand remedy and antidote against perplexing heart-troubles, and desponding and disquieting fears: *Be not afraid,* says our Lord, *only believe* (c). This is the ballast that can keep your soul steady in a stormy sea. And that, 1. When you are under perplexing trouble and disquieting fears as to your own soul's case. Remember that God the Father, Son, and Holy Ghost, stand engaged to promote and perfect your salvation. Therefore rest and rely with full confidence and assurance on the everlasting love of the Father, the infinite merit of the Son, and the almighty power of the Holy Ghost. 2. When you are under perplexing trouble and disquieting fears with reference to the case of the church. When subtle enemies raise stirs and commotions to shake a happy settlement,

---

(a) John xiv. 1.　(b) John xiv. 1.　(c) Mark v. 36.

settlement, and trouble the waters that they may fish in them, we are often full of fears about the issue. When the church is brought low, or great dangers threaten the interest of Christ, which is our present case, there are usually great commotions in the minds of good men. As it was with Christ's disciples: They had a fond conceit of attaining some earthly grandeur by Christ; but matters going cross to their expectation, their hearts were filled with perplexing trouble. So it is oft-times with the people of God: They are too carnal in their expectations, looking for peace and prosperity and good days; and disappointments of such carnal expectations breed much disquieting trouble. Again, misinterpreting God's dispensations in his way of dealing with his church, and judging by sense and present appearance. From these and the like causes it is, that we are often full of disquieting fears, and our hearts sink within us, when God's dispensations toward his church have a frowning aspect. Now, what is the cure? I assure you, it is not a proper cure in such cases, to feed ourselves with carnal hopes. But Christ refers us to the sovereign cure, even to faith. Faith in the blessed Trinity is an excellent remedy and antidote against our disquieting fears.

Let us consider, that a whole sacred Trinity is engaged in delivering, preserving, and establishing the church, and in maintaining and supporting the precious interests of the kingdom of Christ. And, 1. The church is under the Father's care. He hath settled Christ upon his throne. *Yet have I set my King*, says he, *upon my holy hill of Zion* (*d*). And he hath insured to him by promise the perpetuity of his kingdom: That *his name shall endure for ever, and be continued as long as the sun.* That *his seed shall endure for ever, and his throne as the days of heaven* (*e*). And he hath engaged to promote the Mediator's interest, to defend and protect him in his government against all the storms and powers of hell, and to subdue and bring down all his enemies: That he *shall laugh* at them, and *have them in derision, and vex them in his sore displeasure;* and that Christ *shall break them with a rod of iron,* and *dash them in pieces like a potter's vessel:* That he *will beat down his enemies before his face, and plague them that hate him:* That he will *make his enemies his footstool, send the rod of his strength out of Zion,* and *strike through kings in the day of his wrath* (*f*). 2. The church is under the Son's care. To him as Mediator the care and preser-

(*d*) Psal. ii. 6. (*e*) Psal. lxxii. 17. and lxxxix. 29. (*f*) Psal. ii. 4, 5, 9. lxxxix. 23. and cx. 1, 2, 5.

vation of the church peculiarly belongeth. The church is given to him as his house and kingdom. *The government is laid on his shoulders* (g). He hath power given him over all the seed of the serpent, *over all flesh:* And he is made the *head of principalities and powers.* Yea, *all power in heaven and earth is given unto* him, to be exercised by him, for the good of the church (h). Particularly, (1.) He is a prophet, to provide against the subtilty of hereticks, by restoring, preserving, and establishing the purity of doctrine and worship. (2.) He is a priest, and that *for ever;* and *a priest upon his throne* (i): And he is so, that he may look to the reparations of his temple; and that he may intercede for his church, as he did for Judah and Jerusalem under the Babylonish captivity (k). He makes intercession for blunting the weapons of enemies, defeating their wicked designs, and turning their counsels to foolishness; and for pouring out the Spirit, to fit and qualify instruments for work and service to him, and to assist them therein (l). And it is a thousand times more comfortable, that he is an advocate in heaven, than if he were a king visibly on earth. (3.) He is a king to govern, protect and defend his church; and to beat up the quarters of hell, till he hath utterly ruined all their force, and established his Zion beyond the fears of any tottering (m). And he is a king of such power, that his throne can never be overturned or shaken by his enemies (n). 3. The church is under the Spirit's care. He stands engaged with the Father and the Son, in building, defending, and delivering the church. Christ hath *received of the Father, the promise of the Spirit* (o): And accordingly he pours out the Spirit on his church and people. And when the Spirit is poured out, when his gifts and graces are bestowed in a plentiful measure, this ushers in happy days to the church, and revives her withered and decayed state. When *the Spirit* is *poured upon us from on high,* then *the wilderness becomes a fruitful field, and the fruitful field* is *counted for a forest* (p). Hence, when the flourishing state of the church is promised, God promiseth to pour out the Spirit (q). It is the Spirit's work by office, to furnish men with gifts and graces, for the defence, deliverance, and increase of the church. He can be a Spirit of government in magistrates, and a Spirit of fire in ministers, for the church's interest,

(g) Isa. ix. 6. (h) John xvii. 2. Col. ii. 10. Matth. xxviii. 18. (i) Psal. cx. 4. Zech. vi. 13. (k) Zech. i. 12. (l) See Zech. iii. 4. &c. (m) Psal. ii. 6, 9. (n) Psal. lxxxix. 29. (o) Acts ii. 33. (p) Isa. xxxii. 14, 15. (q) Isa. xliv. 3. Joel ii. 28.

interest. Thus, the Lord stirred up the spirit of Zerubbabel, of Joshua, and of all the remnant of the people, to come and work in building the temple (*r*). When his time comes for delivering and building his church, he can call a Cyrus to be instrumental in it. And he will not want his Ezras and Nehemiahs to build the walls of his Jerusalem. He can fill them with wisdom and zeal, and assist them in spite of adversaries. He can inspire men with holy courage and resolution, to appear and act for the church, and make them overcome all impediments and bars in their way. This the Lord promised as a great encouragement; *According to the word that I covenanted with you when ye came out of Egypt, so my Spirit remaineth among you: Fear ye not* (*s*). And when enemies make violent irruptions upon the church, and threaten her ruin, he can raise up others to defend her against their fury and violence: *When the enemy shall come in like a flood, the Spirit of the Lord shall lift up a standard against him* (*t*). And sometimes he chuseth to deliver his church when human likelihoods and probabilities fail, by his own immediate operation, without any external force and power: *Not by might, nor by power, but by my Spirit, saith the Lord of hosts* (*u*). And lastly, it is the Spirit's work to make the ordinances of the gospel effectual, and to fill them with life and power (*x*).

We see then, that all the divine persons are one in their care of the church. There is no danger so dreadful or imminent, but they can prevent it; no misery so deep, but they can deliver out of it; no enemies so strong or subtle, but they can vanquish or outwit them. Therefore, let us not give way to perplexing heart trouble, or to sinking and desponding fears. *Let not your heart be troubled, neither let it be afraid* (*y*). Our fears and troubles are for want of faith: *Why are ye fearful*, says our Lord, *O ye of little faith* (*z*). Peter's feet did not begin to sink till his faith failed (*a*). Let us believe in the holy Trinity. Let us commit the care of all the concerns of the church, and of the precious interests of Christ, to God, the Father, Son, and Holy Ghost; and let us depend upon their love and care. We have here a triple prop to our faith, which should give us triple strength in believing. We have the Father, Son, and Spirit to trust in. Do but shut the eye of sense, and open the eye of faith, and you shall see great ground

(*r*) Hag. i. 14.   (*s*) Hag. ii. 5.   (*t*) Isa. lix. 19.   (*u*) Zech. iv. 6.   (*x*) 1 Thess. i. 5.   (*y*) John xiv. 27.   (*z*) Matth. viii. 26.   (*a*) Matth. xiv. 31.

ground of encouragement and comfort: You shall see the church under the care and protection of three infinitely glorious and powerful persons. Faith will carry off your heart from things seen to things unseen, from things present to things to come, from the creature to God. Therefore, let us set faith a-work, and cast anchor within the vail, waiting for and expecting relief from heaven.

Duty 6. Let Believers in Christ long to be dissolved, and to be with God in glory, where the mystery of the sacred Trinity shall be much more clearly revealed. There is still some darkness upon the face of this deep: But you shall have a more perfect knowledge thereof when you come to heaven †: As our blessed Lord hath told us, John xiv. 20. *At that day ye shall know, that I am in my Father, and you in me, and I in you.* True it is, that even in heaven, you cannot have a comprehensive knowledge of this glorious mystery: Yet it shall be no small part of your happiness above, that you shall contemplate it in another manner than you can do now. For, 1. That sight and discovery which you shall have of the blessed Trinity in heaven, will be more full, clear, and perfect, than any thing that can be attained in this life. While *here we know but in part* (*b*). O, how small a portion of him is known in the earth! Hence faith is sometimes opposed to vision (*c*). The sight of faith is no sight, in comparison of that of immediate vision. *Now we see through a glass, darkly, but then face to face* (*d*). Consider, (1.) In heaven your understanding shall be more enlarged, and a clearer light put into it. A holy Trinity in unity troubleth the present weakness of reason: But your knowledge shall be more complete, when the vail shall fall off from your heart, and the scales from your eyes, so that you shall behold without weakness and winking. (2.) There shall be a more full discovery of the object. In heaven you shall see God *face to face*: and *see him as he is* (*e*). You shall see him in his trinity. This glorious mystery shall then be unfolded. I say not, that you shall see into the bottom of it; for that is above the capacity of any creature: But there is certainly something within the curtain, that will outshine all that we can possibly conceive

---

† *Tripliciter in æterna illa & perfecta Beatitudine fruemur Deo: Videntes eum in omnibus Creaturis; habentes eum in nobis ipsis; Et quid his omnibus ineffabiliter jucundius sit atque beatius, ipsam quoque cognoscentes semetipsam Trinitatem.* Bern. in Serm.

(*b*) 1 Cor. xiii. 12.   (*c*) 2 Cor. v. 7.   (*d*) 1 Cor. xiii. 12.
(*e*) 1 Cor. xiii. 12. 1 John iii. 2.

conceive now. In heaven this glorious object shall be discovered and manifested, in a far more excellent way and manner, than it is at present to the eye of faith: And that discovery shall be fully adequate to the most enlarged capacities of the glorified saints. 2. That sight and discovery of the holy Trinity which the saints shall have in heaven, will be most sweet and pleasant. It is a trouble to weak eyes to behold a bright shining object: But when the object is beautiful, and the eye lively and vigorous, there is the more pleasure in the act of vision. So here, O what pleasure and delight will there be in contemplating this glorious object, a sacred Trinity, when there shall be no turbulent affections to confound the eye of the soul? 3. It will be an appropriating vision. When the glorified saints shall behold a Trinity in Unity, this will be the language of every look, *This one glorious God, Father, Son and Holy Ghost, is my God*. The owner of a house, and a stranger walking by, will look upon it with a very different aspect. The glorified saints shall behold a sacred Trinity as their own. 4. It will be such a sight and discovery as will save the expence of study. The soul will then see more at one view in a moment, than now it can see in a lifetime. So that there will be no need of diligent search and earnest study. We shall then attain to the knowledge of the blessed Trinity, without labour and difficulty. Well then, dear Christians, long earnestly for your heavenly state. O *when shall the day break and the shadows flee away!* When once you come to see God face to face, how joyfully will you join in that triumphant song; *Holy, holy, holy is the Lord of hosts*: And, *Holy, holy, holy Lord God Almighty, who was, and is, and is to come* (*f*). O long for that happy day when your clay tabernacle shall be dissolved, and you shall enter into the immediate presence of God, and see a sacred Trinity unvailed. Though there were nothing else to allure you to a longing desire after your final dissolution, this were enough.

Use 6. For comfort, To you who believe on the name of Christ, and so are interested in a whole sacred Trinity as your own. From this doctrine there arise many grounds of comfort and consolation to you. As,

1. Your portion is great and glorious: For all the persons of the Godhead, and whatever they can do, are made over to you by covenant, God the Father, Son, and Holy Ghost, are wholly yours. The Father is yours to love you. *The Father himself loveth you* (*g*), says Christ. The Son is yours, to redeem and save

---

(*f*) Isa. vi. 3. Rev. iv. 8.   (*g*) John xvi. 27.

save you. You may say, *My beloved is mine, and I am his* (*h*). And the Holy Ghost is yours, to dwell in you, to work in you, and to lead and guide you to glory. *Ye are the temple of God, and the Spirit of God dwelleth in you* (*i*).

2. Your sincere prayers are heard and accepted: For you have a gracious and merciful Father to go to. *Is Ephraim my dear Son?* says the Lord; *Is he a pleasant child?—My bowels are troubled for him* (*k*). You have the Son to introduce and bring you in to the Father. *Christ suffered that he might bring us to God* (*l*). And you have the Holy Ghost to quicken you to prayer, and to help your infirmities in it: For *God hath sent forth the Spirit of his Son into your hearts, crying, Abba, Father: Likewise the Spirit helpeth your infirmities* (*m*).

3. It is matter of comfort in all your afflictions and dangers, that you belong to the sacred Trinity, to Father, Son, and Holy Ghost. Their name was called on you in baptism; to them you were solemnly dedicated and devoted; and this you have ratified by your own voluntary resignation: So that you are objects of their watchful and tender care, and may be assured that it shall be well with you, whatever way the world go. How confident was the apostle Paul of the care of God in a time of great danger, when he could say, *God, whose I am, and whom I serve* (*n*). Further, you have the gracious presence of the whole blessed Trinity in your troubles and distresses. You have *the God and Father of our Lord Jesus Christ, the Father of mercies, and the God of all comfort,* to *comfort* you *in all* your *tribulations* (*o*). And the blessed Son of God lays to heart all your sorrows and distresses, and is ready to relieve you under them. He is *a merciful High Priest* (*p*): And the exercise of his tender compassion is excited and provoked by the experience he himself had of the like miseries in the days of his flesh (*q*). And you have the Holy Spirit to support and comfort you under affliction. *I will give you another Comforter,* says Christ, *that he may abide with you for ever* (*r*).

4. Your final perseverance and eternal salvation is sure and certain. Your salvation cannot miscarry, having such infinitely wise and powerful agents engaged to promote and perfect it. As you have one person of the Godhead to agent your cause with God, and to keep all right between him and you, by his

constant

(*h*) Cant. ii. 16.   (*i*) 1 Cor. iii. 16.   (*k*) Jer. xxxi. 20.
(*l*) 1 Pet. iii. 18.   (*m*) Gal. iv. 6. Rom. viii. 26.   (*n*) Acts xxvii. 23.   (*o*) 2 Cor. i. 3, 4.   (*p*) Heb. ii. 7.   (*q*) Heb. iv. 15.
(*r*) John xiv. 16.

constant intercession: So you have another person to agent the cause of God on your heart, to overcome your obstinacy and unbelief, to vanquish temptations, doubts, and fears, and to settle you in hope and comfort. All the persons join their hand and counsel for your safety. Hence it is that our Saviour says, *Neither shall any man pluck them* (that is, my sheep) *out of my hand.—And none is able to pluck them out of my Father's hand* (*s*). So, none can pluck them out of the Spirit's hand. And they all concur in carrying on a work of grace toward perfection. To this purpose is that expression, *We will make thee borders of gold, with studs of silver* (*t*). It is a promise to increase and perfect the believer's comeliness and beauty: And it is in the plural number, *we*. All the Person have a joint design in promoting the salvation of the elect. The perfecting a work of grace is a great work, and above your power: Yet fear not; a whole sacred Trinity hath undertaken it, and shall make it out to you. So that your perseverance, and the perfecting a work of grace in you, is infallibly sure and certain. When you consider the distinct offices and operations of the divine persons in the business of your salvation; and withal consider that each person is God: O, how comfortable is this! Not only one infinitely wise and powerful Person, but three, are employed in securing your salvation and eternal happiness. *To this one God, Father, Son, and Holy Ghost, be glory for ever.* Amen.

(*s*) John x. 28, 29.   (*t*) Cant. i. 11.

DISCOURSE XXI.

Of beholding the Glory of God in the Glass of the Gospel.

SERMON CXVIII.

2 Cor. iii. 18. *But we all, with open face, beholding, as in a glass, the Glory of the Lord, &c.*

SERIOUS Christians, especially on such occasions as this, long earnestly to see the glory of God in the sanctuary (*a*). And it is great ground of encouragement, that we have to do with

(*a*) Psal. lxiii. 2.

with a God who delights in manifesting his glory to such as long for it †. If we could believe, nothing would be able to obstruct our enjoyment of so great a blessing. Hence our Lord says to Martha, *Said I not unto thee, that if thou wouldest believe, thou shouldest see the glory of God* (b)?

In this and the preceding verses, the apostle is holding forth the great clearness of the gospel-dispensation beyond that of the law. There is a dark vail of ignorance on the hearts of all men by nature. This is common to the Jews under the law, with us under the gospel. But the Jews under the law were also under a vail of types and ceremonies, of prophecies and promises concerning Christ, so that they had but a dim sight of the glory of God. But that *vail is done away in Christ*, so that now believers *behold the glory of God with open face*. There is a twofold sight of the divine glory: The sight of immediate vision, proper to the saints in heaven; and the sight of mediate vision, or of faith, proper to the saints on earth. Of this last the apostle here speaketh.

What may be necessary for further clearing and explaining the words, will fall in while I open up the doctrine, which is this.

> Observ. *It is the peculiar privilege of believers in Christ, even in this life, that they have a clear, though imperfect sight of the glory of God, in the glass of gospel-ordinances.*

In handling this doctrine, I shall speak a little,

1. Of the object of this vision.
2. Of the nature of it.
3. Of the persons privileged with it. And then,
4. I shall apply the doctrine.

First, The object of this vision is *the glory of the Lord*. But what glory of the Lord is here to be understood?

Negatively, not his essential glory: For that cannot be seen, even by the eyes of the mind, at least in this life. When Moses did plead with God, *I beseech thee, shew me thy glory;* God answered, *Thou canst not see my face: For there shall no man see me, and live* (c). Moses saw only his back-parts, some imperfect image and representation of his glory. God's essence cannot be seen: For *no man hath seen God at any time.* He dwells in the

---

(b) John xi. 40.   (c) Exod. xxxiii. 20.

† This Sermon was preached immediately before the sacrament, being an action-sermon.

the light which no man can approach unto: *No man hath seen, nor can see him* (*d*). In this life, God hides his glory from us. He holdeth back the face of his throne (*e*): He will not suffer the bright lustre of his glory to appear, but *spreadeth a cloud upon it.* All that the best see here is but the *backparts* of his glory; some glimpses of it. We see but the *similitude of the Lord.* The most glorious manifestations in this life, are but *the appearance of the likeness of his glory* (*f*). And it is the great mercy and goodness of God to us that it is so: For, such is our weakness, that we are not able to bear the clear discoveries and superexcellent brightness of his glory. The very glimpses of it astonish, and leave us for dead: As we see in the apostle John: *His countenance*, says he, *was as the sun shineth in his strength. And when I saw him, I fell at his feet as dead* (*g*). The saints must die, before they can bear the weight of that glory, which consists in seeing God *face to face.*

Positively, The glory of the Lord, which is the object of that vision that the saints have in this life, is his declarative or manifestative glory; his glory in the manifestations and discoveries he is pleased to give of it. Now, God hath manifested his glory even in the works of creation and providence. But the clearest manifestation that ever he gave of his glory, is in the Mediator Christ; and that is the object of this vision. So the apostle determines in the very next chapter after my text: *God, who commanded the light to shine out of darkness, hath shined in our hearts, to give the light of the knowledge of the glory of God, in the face of Jesus Christ* (*h*). So that, it is the glory of God, as discovered in the face of Christ, that is, in his person as God-man, that is the object of this vision. He is *God manifested in the flesh* (*i*). Hence our Lord says, *He that hath seen me, hath seen the Father* (*k*). He that sees Christ spiritually, by faith, sees the Father; because the majesty and glory of God shine in Christ as an exact image. The glory of God being infinite and incomprehensible, such is our weakness, that it would dazzle and stupify us. As we cannot with our bodily eyes behold the sun, without being oppressed by its lustre: Far less can we with the eyes of our mind, look on the glory of God, without being overwhelmed by that dazzling light wherewith he clothes himself as with a garment. Therefore, God hath, in Christ as incarnate, contemperated his glorious perfections to our faith, love,

(*d*) John i. 18. 1 John iv. 12. 1 Tim. vi. 16. (*e*) Job xxvi. 9. (*f*) Exod. xxxiii. 23. Numb. xii. 8. Ezek. i. 28. (*g*) Rev. i. 16, 17. (*h*) 2 Cor. iv. 6. (*i*) 1 Tim. iii. 16. (*k*) John xiv. 9.

love, and contemplation; for they all shine forth in him. The glory of God is, as it were, refracted by Christ, and tempered to our weakness; so that instead of being overwhelmed by the glory, we may, by beholding it, be *changed into the same image* (*l*).

Particularly, in Christ we have the fullest, clearest, and most delightful manifestation of the glory of God, that ever was, or ever shall be, in this life.

1. In Christ we have the fullest manifestation of the divine glory. God hath manifested the glory of his infinite wisdom, power, and goodness, in the works of creation and common providence: But the glory of divine love, grace and mercy, had lain under a thick vail undiscovered, without a Redeemer. Again, in the creatures, the glory of divine wisdom is more illustrious in one; the glory of his power is more illustrious in another; the glory of his goodness is more illustrious in a third: But the glory of all the divine attributes is seen in Christ. They all centre in him. He is a stage on which they all act their parts. In him shines, the glory of divine wisdom, in contriving redemption. Here is manifold and hidden wisdom, even *the wisdom of God in a mystery*. The glory of his power, in Christ's incarnation, birth, miracles, support under his sufferings, and glorious resurrection. The glory of his love and grace, in giving his only begotten Son to and for such vile wretches as we are. The glory of his infinite justice, holiness and hatred of sin, in punishing the sins of the elect in the person of his dear Son. The glory of his truth and faithfulness, in accomplishing all the Old-Testament types, prophecies, and promises concerning Christ. So that all the divine perfections shine in *the face of Christ*. If you would see the glory of all the attributes of God, do but by the eye of faith look Christ in the face, and there you shall find the express characters of all that glory.

Further, in Christ we have a manifestation, not only of the glorious perfections of the divine nature, but also of a trinity of persons in the Godhead: For *in him dwells the fulness of the Godhead bodily;* and he is *the brightness of* the Father's *glory, and the express image of his person* (*m*). Therefore some divines do well observe that God's end and design in the work of redemption, was not only to glorify the infinite perfections of his nature, but also to glorify the persons distinctly, according to the distinct acts and operations ascribed to them in the business of our salvation. Here we have the Father contriving and ordering our redemption, the Son purchasing it, and the Holy Ghost applying

(*l*) 2 Cor. iii. 18.   (*m*) Col. ii. 9. Heb. i. 3.

applying it. The original is from God the Father, the dispensation is through the Son, and the application is by the Holy Ghost. Particularly, the mystery of the Trinity was manifested, 1. In Christ's mission. The Father gave him his commission. He *came not of* himself, but the *Father sent* him. *Him hath God the Father sealed.* The Holy Spirit fitted him for the undertaking with necessary gifts and graces. Hence Christ is brought in speaking, *The Spirit of the Lord God is upon me, because he hath anointed me* (m), &c. Where we have the Son sent, and the LORD JEHOVAH and his Spirit anointing and sending. And to the same purpose is that text, *The Lord God and his Spirit hath sent me* (n). 2. In his incarnation. Herein all the Persons did jointly concur, according to the order of working proper to each of them. The Father did contrive and order it: Therefore Christ assigns the preparation of his body to him in a peculiar manner: *A body hast thou prepared me* (o) The Holy Spirit was the immediate agent in framing his body, and in uniting the human nature to the divine: Hence the angel says to Mary, *The Holy Ghost shall come upon thee, and the Power of the Highest shall overshadow thee* (p). And the Son was he that assumed that human nature to be his own. So that his body, or human nature, was prepared by the Father, wrought by the Holy Ghost, and assumed by the Son. 3. In his baptism. As the Son was manifested in the human nature, and ascended out of the waters of Jordan (q): So the Father manifested himself by an immediate and audible voice from heaven; and the Holy Ghost, by descending on Christ in the shape of a dove. 4. In his death and sufferings. So it is said, *Christ through the eternal Spirit offered himself without spot to God* (r). Where we have, (1.) Who offered himself? Christ, the *Son of God.* (2.) To whom offered he himself? *To God.* The divine nature is here to be considered as peculiarly subsisting in the person of the Father. (3.) By whom offered he himself? *By the eternal Spirit*, not as an inferior instrument, but as the principal efficient cause. It was the Spirit that wrought in him that fervent zeal and love, that carried him through his sufferings, and rendered his obedience therein acceptable to God.

2. In Christ we have the clearest manifestation of the glory of God. That which we have in his works is but dim in comparison.

(m) John viii. 42. and vi. 27. Psal. xlv. 6. John iii. 34. Isa. lxi. 2. (n) Isa. xlviii. 16. (o) Heb. x. 5. (p) Luke i. 35. (q) Matth. iii. 16, 17. (r) Heb. ix. 14.

parifon. In the bleffed Mediator we have the moſt bright and perfpicuous reprefentation of the glory of God that ever was given. Hence, he is called *the brightnefs of glory* (*s*); or the radiancy and fparkling of God's glory, the very fplendor and refulgency of it. In Chriſt his glory is to be feen in a moſt illuſtrious manner. Hence Chriſt is called *the image of God* (*t*). The attributes of God are fo illuſtrious in Chriſt, that we cannot deliberately view and confider him, but we are prefently informed of the incomprehenfible glory of the Deity.

3. In Chriſt we have the moſt delightful manifeſtation of the glory of God. O, it is a pleafant manifeſtation that we have in him! Therefore it is called *the beauty of the Lord* (*u*). Out of Chriſt he is a confuming fire: But in Chriſt, he is a lovely object. In Chriſt he is manifeſted and feen in the glory of his grace, with his arms open to embrace finners. And thefe attributes that feemed to look with an ill afpect on one another, are in Chriſt mixed together with inexpreffible fweetnefs, and confpiring together for the welfare of believers: Juſtice making our iniquities to meet on him, that they might not lie on us; and wrath paffing by us, and feizing on him. In Chriſt we fee wrath appeafed, and juſtice fatisfied, and mercy rejoicing, as it were, over judgment. So that the attributes of God all meet in Chriſt, in their glory and fweetnefs; and combine together, in finging one and the fame note for the happinefs of believers. And how delightful is the manifeſtation we have of a facred Trinity in our Mediator! Here it is that believers may fee the Father contriving all fpiritual bleffings for them, the Son purchafing them, and the holy Ghoſt applying or conferring them. Here they may with delight contemplate the love of the Father, in giving his dear Son; the grace of the Son, in giving himfelf for them; and the communion of the Holy Ghoſt, in communicating to them the bleffed fruits of Chriſt's purchafe (*x*).

From what is faid, it is plain and evident, that in Chriſt we have the moſt excellent manifeſtation of the glory of God, that ever was fince the world began, or ever will be while the world ſtands. And this is the object of that vifion which the faints have in this life. And, O! is it not a glorious object? What a happinefs muſt it be to have open eyes to behold this glory?

Second, I proceed to fpeak of the nature of this vifion. Here let us confider, 1. The act of vifion. 2. The manner of it.

1. The

(*s*) Heb. i. 3. (*t*) Col. i. 15. 2 Cor. iv. 4. (*u*) Pfal. xxvii. 4. (*x*) 2 Cor. xiii. 14.

1. The act of vision—*We behold it*, says he. What kind of sight is this?

Negatively, 1. It is plain, that it is not a sight with the eyes of the body. For Christ, in whom the glory of God shines forth to us, is now removed out of our sight. And even when he was on earth in the days of his flesh, the divine glory shining forth in him, was not seen with the eyes of the body, but by the eye of faith. 2. It is not a sight by common illumination: For, even natural men may see much of the divine glory, not only in the works of God, but in the glass of the gospel, by the help of a common illumination. Hence we read of some that are *once enlightened*, but do afterward *fall* totally and finally *away* (*a*). 3. It is not a sight by prophetic manifestation. The prophets and servants of God of old had sometimes a special elevation of mind, whereby they had a glorious sight of God; as Jacob, Moses, Isaiah. God did in some resemblance shew them his glory, so far as they were capable of it, which did wonderfully affect them. But this was extraordinary; so that believers now are not warranted to seek or expect it.

Positively, That sight which believers have of the glory of God in the face of Christ, is spiritual and supernatural. It is a sight by a gracious illumination; a sight by faith. So, it is said of Moses, that he *saw him who is invisible* (*b*). He saw him by the eye of faith, who is invisible to the eyes of the body. Hence it is that faith is often expressed in scripture by seeing and looking (*c*). The resemblance between it and bodily sight stands in these things. 1. In bodily sight there is a seeing faculty. A blind man cannot see at noon-day. So, faith is the eye of the soul. By the grace of conversion, the dark vail is taken off the heart, and the eye of faith opened. This is called *the enlightening the eyes of the understanding;* and *the opening of the understanding* (*d*). By faith we have as powerful apprehensions of the glory of God in the face of Christ, as if we saw it with bodily eyes. 2. In bodily sight there is a medium or midds to render the object conspicuous. The sharpest sight cannot see in the dark. There must be light to discover objects. So, the glory of God in the face of Christ, is seen only by the light of his own Spirit. *In thy light, we shall see light* (*e*), says the psalmist. By the Spirit a divine light is sprung up in the soul. This is called God's *shining into the heart* (*f*). 3. In bodily

(*a*) Heb. vi. (*b*) Heb. xi. 27. (*c*) Zech. xii 10. Isa. xlv. 22. John i. 14. (*d*) Eph. i. 18. Luke xxiv. 45. (*e*) Psal. xxxvi. 9. (*f*) 2 Cor. iv. 6.

bodily fight there is an approximation or nearness, of the object to the eye. We cannot see things at too great a distance. Now, faith approximates the object, and brings it near hand: Therefore it is called *the evidence of things not seen* (g). Faith brings Christ near to the soul; so that the glory of God shining in his blessed face, is present to the eye of faith.

2. We have the manner of this vision. We behold it, says the apostle, *as in a glass;* and yet we behold it, *with open face.*

We behold it, *as in a glass.* There are divers things which are as glasses wherein we may see the glory of the Lord; the glass of the creatures, the glass of providence, and the glass of human learning: But the glory of God, as it shines in the face of Christ, is to be seen, only in the glass of the gospel and gospel ordinances. It is true, believers have sometimes a delightful view of the glory of God in the face of Christ, even in private duties; such as meditation, reading the word, prayer, &c. But the clearest, fullest, and sweetest views, are ordinarily in the glass of public ordinances. It is *in God's temple* that *every one speaks of his glory.* The saints long after the ordinances for this end, that they may *see his power and glory* (h). Therefore gospel ordinances are, according to some †, represented by a *sea of glass,* in regard of the transparency thereof, so that the glory of the Lord is clearly seen. There is indeed a satisfying and delightful sight of his glory to be had in public ordinances. Only they must be pure ordinances. The more pure and clear and fine the looking-glass be, we see the image in it so much the better: These ordinances in which you would see the glory of God in *the face of Christ,* had need be free from the mixture of any human inventions.

Especially the sacrament of the Lord's supper is as a clear glass wherein we may see his glory. A crucified Christ is there represented as in a glass (i). The sacrament is an image of Christ crucified, the picture that he hath left of himself. Looking on him by faith in that ordinance, we may have a delightful view of the glory of God in his blessed face.

More particularly, that expression, that *we behold the glory of the Lord* AS IN A GLASS, imports, that it is but an imperfect sight that we have of his glory in this life; and that in these three respects. 1. Because it is but mediate. When we see a thing in a glass, the object is not immediately presented to our eye, but only by the conveyance of the looking-glass.
Such

---

† Charnock's Disc. of the Knowledge of God in Christ.

(g) Heb. xi. 1. (h) Psal. xxix. 9. and lxiii. 1, 2. Rev. xv. 2. (i) Gal. iii. 1.

Such is our sight of the glory of God in this life: We see only some broken beams of his glory; some glimpses of it, scattered here and there, in this ordinance, and in that ordinance. 2. Because it is but weak. When we would view a thing in a looking-glass, we do not see the thing itself, but only some idea and representation of it; and that representation is but weak and languishing. So, our sight of the glory of God in this life, is but weak, and dark, and cloudy. Hence we are said to *see but as through a glass*, DARKLY (*k*). O what poor manifestations of the glory of God have the best of the saints in this life, in comparison of what they shall have in the life to come? 3. Because it is but transient. A sight of a thing in a looking-glass is but a transient and vanishing thing (*l*): One direct view of an object is much more satisfying than many views of it in a looking-glass. So, any sight we have of the glory of God in this life, is but transient and vanishing †. The believer stays not long in the mount. These views believers have of the divine glory quicken their appetite after more, but never give full satisfaction.

But though we behold the glory of the Lord *as in a glass*, yet we behold it *with open face*, that is, clearly and distinctly. That sight which we have of the glory of the Lord in the glass of ordinances, though it be imperfect, yet it is clear and distinct: And that, both comparatively, and also simply and in itself considered. 1. Comparatively to what the Jews had under the law. Under the Old Testament the glory of God was wrapt up in a cloud of legal sacrifices and dark prophecies; so that the Jews could discern it but dimly. But under the New-Testament we have more clear discoveries of the divine glory: For, prophecies are now accomplished, and the dim glass of legal ceremonies is broken. Christ the Body being now come, these dark shadows are done away: So that now, we behold the glory of God *with open face*. With reference to the saints in glory, we behold it but *as in a glass*: But with reference to the Jews, we behold it *with open face.* 2. Simply, and in itself considered. We have distinct views of the perfections of God in their affecting glory, shining into the heart. So the apostle tells us; *God hath shined in our hearts, to give us the light of the knowledge of the glory of God in the face of Jesus Christ* (*m*). The divine light that breaks into the heart, doth so enlighten it, that there is a clear spiritual sight of the glory

---

(*k*) 1 Cor. xiii. 12.   (*l*) James i. 23. 24.   (*m*) 2 Cor. iv. 6.
† *Rara hora, brevis mora.*

glory of the Lord. The sight of faith is so clear and distinct, that there can be nothing beyond it in this world. It can be superseded only by the light of glory. And I add, that it is so clear that it is unutterable. The saints themselves cannot make language of it. It is better felt than expressed. Who can conceive what transport of soul the saints sometimes feel, when they behold the glory of God in the face of Christ? It is as impossible to make you who are strangers fully understand this, as it is to make a man understand the heat of the fire who never felt it.

Third, I go on to speak of the persons privileged with this vision—ALL WE. We believers, whether ministers or private Christians. So that this is the privilege of believers in Christ, and of such only.

1. It is the privilege of believers in Christ, that they have a clear, though imperfect view of the glory of the Lord in the glass of gospel ordinances. This is promised to them: *Thine eyes shall see the King in his beauty* (n). And it is for this end they desire and long after the ordinances, that they may *behold the beauty of the Lord* (o). And they are prompted to this by their former experience: *My soul thirsteth for thee*, says the psalmist, *my flesh longeth for thee—To see thy power and thy glory, so as I have seen thee in the sanctuary* (p). They have formerly seen his glory in the sanctuary, and they would gladly see it again.

But when is it that believers have saving discoveries of the glory of God in the face of Christ? God hath not limited himself to any particular time; and it were high presumption for us to limit him. But there are some special times and seasons, wherein most usually they have more clear discoveries and views of his glory, than at other times. As, 1. At first conversion. Hence the Spouse exhorts the daughters of Zion, *Go forth, O ye daughters of Zion, and behold King Solomon with the crown wherewith his mother crowned him, in the day of his espousals, and in the day of the gladness of his heart* (q). In the day of espousals they get a glorious sight of him. This is that which engageth their hearts to him. They *see the Son, and believe on him* (r). They usually get more engaging and refreshing views of his glory then, than at other times; because then they are engaging with new difficulties, and new conflicts with the powers of darkness, which they were never acquainted with before. 2. Before some sharp trial. Hence the apostle tells

the

(n) Isa. xxxiii. 17.   (o) Psal. xxvii. 4.   (p) Psal. lxiii. 1, 2. (q) Cant. iii. 11.   (r) John vi. 40.

the believing Hebrews, that *after* they *were illuminated*, they *endured a great fight of afflictions* (*s*) Peter, James, and John, were to be witnesses to Christ's agony, and to meet with other sharp trials; therefore, before that, they were taken up into the Mount with Christ, where they were witnesses to his transfiguration, and saw his glory (*t*). The Lord dealeth thus with his people, to prepare them for, and to support and strengthen them under trials. 3. Under great trials and afflictions. Stephen, the first gospel martyr, *looking up, saw the glory of God* (*u*). Mount Calvary is often made a mount Tabor to believers, where they see the Lord in his glory. Thus, God comforts and supports his people in their tribulations. 4. When God is calling them to difficult and dangerous services. God called Moses to bring the children of Israel out of Egypt, a work wherein he was to meet with great difficulties, and a work of great danger, having to do with a powerful and angry king: Yet it is said, he *feared not the wrath of the king; for he endured as seeing him who is invisible* (*x*) This enabled him to go on with an undaunted courage and fortitude. 5. At the sacrament. The sacrament of the supper is a visible image of a crucified Saviour; there believers look on him by faith, and see the glory of the Lord in his blessed face. It is there they have been sometimes carried up into the mount, and have had such refreshing views of the glory of God, that they have been ready to cry out, *O, it is good to be here.*

But why doth the Lord grant unto his people such refreshing discoveries and views of his glory in the glass of gospel ordinances? 1. To wean their hearts from the world. There is such a bewitching beauty in worldly things, that they would steal away their hearts from God: But a sight of his glory darkens all the glory of the world. This made the apostle say, *Yea, doubtless, I count all things but loss, for the excellency of the knowledge of Christ Jesus my Lord, for whom I have suffered the loss of all things, and do count them but dung that I may win Christ* (*y*). 2. To engage their hearts more to God through Christ. Hereby he outbids Satan and the world that rival with him for the hearts and affections of his people. A saving sight of his glory is a most engaging thing: It raiseth him high in their esteem. 3. To advance and promote their conformity to him. As Moses's face shined, when he had been in the mount with God; so a sight of the divine glory hath a most assimilating virtue; be-

(*s*) Heb x. 32. (*t*) Matth. xvii. (*u*) Acts vii. 55. (*x*) Heb. xi. 27. (*y*) Phil. iii. 8.

lievers are thereby changed into the same image (z). 4. To commend the ordinances to them: To raise their esteem of them, and to engage them to diligence in the use of them. It renders the ordinances beautiful and amiable. Hence the psalmist cries out, *How amiable are thy tabernacles, O Lord God of Hosts? For a day in thy courts is better than a thousand* (a). 5. To confirm and strengthen their faith and hope in the belief and expectation of the glory to come. God hath promised to his people the happiness of immediate vision, that they shall see him *face to face*, and *behold his glory* (b): And to keep up their hopes, he gives some views of his glory now, as a foretaste and first-fruits, a pawn and pledge of the blessedness to come.

2. This is the privilege of believers only. Such of you as are strangers to Christ, and live and go on in sin, and are not renewed by grace, cannot have any saving discoveries of the glory of God, while you so remain. 1. Because you want a spiritual visive faculty. Sin blinds your minds This is the beam in your eye, and the dark vail on your heart. 2. You are under the power of Satan: And he *blinds your minds, lest the light of the glorious gospel of Christ should shine unto them* (c). 3. God will not shew his glory to such as you are. Saving disceveries and manifestations of God are acts and effects of the dearest love; *I will love him,* says Christ, *and manifest myself to him* (d). And God can have no love to, or delight in you, while you live in sin; nor can there be any friendly communion between him and you. 4. There is in you an utter averseness to a sight of his glory. Men naturally look on God under some dreadful notion, and therefore flee from his glory and brightness. Doth not your countenance fall at any lively appearance of God? And can you think that God, will manifest his glory to such as are averse to behold it?

Fourth, In the last place, I proceed to the application of this doctrine.

Use 1. For instruction, in several particulars. 1. See here the astonishing grace and condescension of the great God, that he will shew his glory to such as we are. O, who and what are we, vile sinful dust, that God will shew so great favour and kindness to such wretches! What can move God to this, seeing he is infinitely glorious, so that we can add nothing to him? Surely nothing could move him, but his own free grace. He will manifest his glory to such vile and unworthy creatures,

because

(z) 2 Cor. iii. 18. (a) Psal. lxxxiv. 1, 10. (b) Rev. xxii. 4. John xvii. 24. (c) Acts xxvi. 18. 2 Cor. iv. 4. (d) John xiv. 21.

becaufe it pleafeth him. Here is aftonifhing goodnefs, and grace paft finding out. 2. See here, how much we are obliged to the blefled Mediator. That the Son of God would become man, and fuffer and die, that we might have a delightful view of the glory of God in his blefled face: O, blefled be he for evermore. Had it not been for him, we had never been able to look on God without terror. 3. See here, what a blefling it is to enjoy the ordinances, and pure ordinances. Thefe are as pure glaffes wherein the glory of God is to be feen. The gofpel and ordinances thereof are the blefling and glory of Scotland: If thefe go, we may take up a lamentation, that the glory is departed from our Ifrael; and if our true glory go, it matters not though wealth and outward glory ftay behind. 4. See here, why the faints prize the ordinances highly, long for them earneftly, and attend them diligently; are at much coft and pains about them, and loth to part with them. Carnal men wonder what the faints mean, in making fo much ado about the ordinances, and in flocking to fermons and communions. But the true reafon is, becaufe they would behold the glory of God in the face of Chrift, and the ordinances are as glaffes wherein his glory is to be feen.

Ufe 2. For reproof, to them that flight and neglect the precious ordinances. Alas, many in this generation are guilty of a profane withdrawment from them. Others abfent themfelves upon very trivial occafions. A fmall matter proves a hindrance, where there is no love to God, nor defire after him, and the faving difcoveries and manifeftations of his glory. The great evil of this appears from what hath been faid. And, 1. The fin is great: For feeing God hath appointed ordinances for this end, that in them as glaffes we may fee his glory; therefore to neglect them, is to put a flight on this precious privilege, and to pour contempt on God's gracious condefcenfion, as if a fight of his glory were not worth the having. 2. The lofs and mifery is great. For, feeing all the fight we have of the divine glory in this life, is but mediate, in the glafs of ordinances; therefore fuch as neglect the ordinances, cannot expect any faving fight of the glory of God: And unlefs you fee his glory here in the glafs of ordinances, you can never fee him *face to face*.

Ufe 3. Is it fo, that the ordinances are the glaffes wherein the glory of God is to be feen? Then let me from this commend gofpel ordinances to you. They are precious on this very account. They are the means of the fulleft and cleareft manifeftations of the divine glory on this fide of heaven. God

hath

hath appointed them for this end, that in them we may behold his glory: And he hath not apointed them in vain. The experience of the faints can bear witnefs to the truth of this: And I doubt not there are fome hearing me whofe experience can feal the truth of it. You have fometimes been at the Lord's table, and have had fweet and refrefhing difcoveries of the glory of God in the face of a crucified Chrift reprefented to you in that great ordinance. Well then, let this commend the ordinances to you. And, 1. Efteem them highly. O let them be dear and precious to you above all earthly comforts. You fhould be ready to cry out with the pfalmift, *How amiable are thy tabernacles: One day in thy courts is better than a thoufand* (c). 2. Long after them earneftly: as the pfalmift; *My foul longeth, yea, even fainteth for the courts of the Lord* (d). 3. Attend them diligently. Bleffed are they that watch and wait at the pofts of Wifdom's doors. It is *in his temple* that *every one fpeaks of his glory* (e). You fhould be glad when an opportunity of waiting on God in his ordinances cometh in your way. *I was glad*, fays the pfalmift, *when they faid unto me, Let us go up unto the houfe of the Lord* (f). 4. Improve them fruitfully. Purfue the great end and defign of them, viz Saving manifeftations of the glory of God in the face of Chrift. Profane men care neither for ordinances, nor for God in ordinances: Hypocrites fatisfy themfelves with bare ordinances: But your end fhould be to fee the glory and beauty of the Lord in thefe glaffes; and you fhould purfue this end with holy vigour and earneftnefs. For this end, I recommend thefe two things to you. (1.) Be diligent in fecret duties. Ufually, they have the cleareft manifeftations, of the glory of God in the public ordinances, who are moft diligent in private duties. The experience of ferious Chriftians will confirm the truth of this. When you have been moft diligent and fervent in wreftling with God in fecret, you have had the fweeteft manifeftations in public. (2.) Cherifh the motions of the Spirit of God. Sometimes there is a work on your affections in the ufe of the ordinances; fome convictions of fin, and fome motions to duty. In this cafe, be careful to join iffue with the Spirit of God. O, take heed of grieving, vexing, quenching, or refifting the Spirit; for this will coft you dear. Jefus Chrift, who is good at the opening of hearts, is as good at the judicial fhutting of them: And he that is neareft to be drawn to God, and yet is never drawn,

will

(c) Pfal lxxxiv. 1, 10 (d) Pfal. lxxxiv. 2. (e) Prov. viii. 34. Pfal. xxix. 9. (f) Pfal. cxxii. 1.

will sink deepest in hell. O, do not quench the motions of the Spirit, lest God give you up to greater blindness and hardness.

Use 4. For exhortation. Make it your great business to get a sight of the glory of God in the face of Christ, in the glass of ordinances; especially in the clear glass of the sacrament of the Lord's supper. The sacrament is a glass that Christ left with his spouse, when he went to heaven, wherein she may see his face. *Do this in remembrance of me.* So also, *Do this to put me in remembrance of you.* So may the words also be understood. In the sacrament there are sweet interviews and reciprocal glances between Christ and his spouse. He looks on her with a gracious eye, and she looks on him by the eye of faith. Now, as in the glass of the sacrament, we may see the face of Christ; so in the *face* of Christ we may see the *glory* of God (g). Here a crucified Christ is represented; and your business is to look upon him by faith, that in his face you may see the glory of God.

But it may be objected, Did you not say just now, that this is the privilege of believers only, that they have saving discoveries of the glory of God? I answer, Indeed believers only have a right to such discoveries; they alone can lay claim to them and plead for them, on the account of their nigh relation to God, and their interest in the promises. Yet God is sometimes freely gracious unto sinners, and grants to them a saving manifestation of his glory, though as yet they have no right to it. Yea, it is amongst the first gracious works of the Spirit, upon the heart of a sinner, to discover to the soul the glory and beauty of God, as it shines in the face of Christ. It is this that draws in the sinners heart unto God. Again, when I exhort you to make it your business to see the glory of God in the face of Christ, I exhort you to believe that you may see his glory. As the first sight of his glory engageth the heart to believe in him; so the renewed acts and exercise of faith and believing, usher in further discoveries and manifestations of his glory.

Therefore I invite you all to seek after a sight of the glory of God in this great ordinance of the supper. We are to hold up this glass to you to-day; and I invite you to come and look upon a crucified Christ therein represented, that you may see the glory of God radiantly shining forth in him. And, 1. Behold the glory of divine wisdom, in contriving redemption for a company of lost sinners, through a crucified Christ: So that death is made the way to life, and shame the way to glory, and the cross the way to the crown. 2. Behold the glory of infinite

---

(g) 2 Cor. iv. 6.

nite love and grace, in giving his only begotten Son to and for rebels and enemies. *God so loved the world, that he gave his only begotten Son (h), &c.* O, what astonishing love is here! Even love and grace past finding out. 3. Behold the glory of divine power, (1.) In Christ's incarnation. That is an admirable expression, *The Word was made flesh, and dwelt among us (i).* Two natures, the divine and human, in themselves infinitely distant, met together in a personal conjunction: This was a greater manifestation of the glory of God's power than the creation of the world. (2.) In supporting the human nature of Christ under the great weight of divine wrath, even all that wrath that was due to all the sins of all the elect; such a load of wrath as would have sunk ten thousand worlds of angels and men. 4. Behold the glory of divine justice. Christ having substituted himself in our room and place, justice could not and would not spare him. *He spared not his own Son, but delivered him up for us all (k).* God would not abate him one farthing of the elect's debt, though he was infinitely dear to him, and his delight from everlasting. 5. Behold the glory of God's unspotted purity and holiness. Never was there such a demonstration of God's infinite holiness and hatred of sin, as in the death and sufferings of his own Son. Behold the glory of God's holiness, vindicating the honour of his law, by sheathing his sword in the bowels of his dear Son.

I say then, come and behold the glory of the Lord in this bright glass. To excite and quicken you to this, I propose a few considerations.

Consid. 1. This is a most necessary blessing. Without this your hearts can never be engaged unto God. Till you see the glory of God, your hearts will never come off from other things besides him; nor will you ever be persuaded to seek your happiness in him, and to pursue after the enjoyment of him. And unless you see his glory here in the glass of ordinances, you shall never see his glory in heaven: For, in heaven the sight of faith will be heightened to that of immediate vision. Your acquaintance with God must begin here in this life. We have the first glimpses of heaven here on earth. Again, a sight of his glory is necessary as the end of all the ordinances, and particularly of the Lord's supper. If you are come here on a right design, this is your errand, to see the glory of God in the face of a crucified Christ.

Consid. 2. A saving sight of the glory of God is a very great

and

(h) John iii. 16.   (i) John i. 14.   (k) Rom. viii. 32.

and ineſtimable bleſſing. For, 1. This is the great requeſt of the ſaints. How much was Moſes's heart ſet on this? *I beſeech thee*, ſays he, *ſhew me thy glory* (*l*). And though he obtained no more but a ſight of his back-parts, yet he was highly honoured by it. 2. It is for this end that the ſaints have ſuch an earneſt deſire after the ordinances, that they may *behold the beauty of the Lord*, and *ſee his power and his glory* (*m*). It is this that renders the ordinances ſo dear and precious to them. 3. A ſight of God's glory here is heaven anticipated. It will be the happineſs of the glorified ſaints to behold his glory immediately, and not by reflection as from a looking-glaſs: Therefore, a ſight of his glory now, though in the glaſs of ordinances, is heaven begun. This bleſſing would ſet you in the very ſuburbs of glory. 4. Conſider the excellent effects of this ſight. (1.) It is a heart-weaning ſight. A ſight of his glory would wean your heart and affections from the world, and all earthly delights and contentments. His glory being manifeſted darkens all other glory, and makes the ſame diſappear (2.) It is a heart-engaging ſight. It will ſo engage your heart to God, that you will count all things but loſs and dung for him; and if you had ten thouſand hearts, you would count them all too little for God. (3.) It is a transforming ſight. A ſight of his glory will transform your ſoul into a likeneſs to him, and ſtamp a divine beauty upon it. It will *change* you *into the ſame image* (*n*). (4.) It is an humbling ſight. It will humble you, and lay you low in the duſt at the feet of God. How did Iſaiah ſink into nothing in his own thoughts, when he ſaw the glory of the Lord (*o*)? (5.) It is an heart-affecting ſight. It will warm your heart and affections toward God and Chriſt. When you ſee his glory, you cannot chuſe but love him, and have ardent deſires after the enjoyment of him, and near communion with him. (6.) It is a pleaſant and delightſome ſight. Glorious objects are very pleaſant to the eye that is able to behold them: But what is all created glory but as a dark ſhadow to the glory of God? Therefore the beholding it cannot but yield an inexpreſſible pleaſure to the ſoul. (7.) It is a ſatisfying ſight. O, what contentment and ſatisfaction of ſoul is there, in beholding the glory and beauty of the Lord. In other things, the eye is never ſatisfied with ſeeing; but there is an infiniteneſs in the majeſty of God, to ſatisfy the panting ſoul, and to give a full reply to all its cravings.

To conclude this, A ſight of the glory of God in the face of
Chriſt

(*l*) Exod. xxxiii. 18.   (*m*) Pſal. xxvii. 4. and lxiii. 2.
(*n*) 2 Cor. iii. 18.   (*o*) Iſa. vi. 5.

Chrift, would make this a bleffed communion-day. It would excite and quicken your facramental graces to a lively exercife. When you fee the glory of God in the face of Chrift, how will this draw out your faith, and enflame your love, and quicken your defires, and enliven your holy joy? When you fee his glory, O what humility will there be under the fenfe of your own vilenefs? What holy admiration of his tranfcendent glory and condefcending grace? And what deep reverence of his glorious majefty? And all thefe are moft proper for the facrament. The lively exercife of thefe graces will make it a happy communion-day. Indeed a faving fight of his glory would make it one of the beft days that ever you had all your lives; fo that you would be ready to cry out, *This is the day the Lord hath made; we will rejoice and be glad in it* (*p*).

Confid. 3. A fight of the glory of God in the face of Chrift is an attainable bleffing. Bleffed be God, it is that which may be win at by fuch vile finners as we are. It was the very end of Chrift's incarnation, death, and fufferings, that poor finners might have delightful views of the glory of God in his bleffed face. And all the ordinances are appointed for this end: And furely, he hath not appointed them in vain. God hath promifed this bleffing: *Thine eyes fhall fee the King in his beauty* (*q*). And fome have attained it. Some have had fuch refrefhing and fatisfying difcoveries of the glory of God in the glafs of gofpel-ordinances, as have made them cry out, *Bleffed are they that dwell in thy houfe: One day in thy courts is better than a thoufand.*

But now, it may be enquired, What fhall we do, that we may get a fight of the glory of God in the face of a crucified Chrift, in the glafs of ordinances, and particularly in the facrament? Take thefe directions. 1. Labour to get the vail taken off your heart: The vail of darknefs and ignorance. This vail is on the hearts of all men by nature, and muft be removed by the Spirit of God, elfe we cannot with open face behold the glory of the Lord. Lament and mourn over the darknefs of your mind, and be earneft for the lively light of the Spirit. 2. Get your hearts purged from filthinefs. It is the *pure in heart that fhall fee God* (*r*). He muft have a clear eye who would behold a bright object. Particularly, get your hearts purged from corrupt affections, fenfuality, earthlinefs, pride, hypocrify, and unbelief: For thefe exceedingly mar and obftruct a fight of the glory of God in the glafs of ordinances.

(*p*) Pfal. xviii. 24. (*q*) Ifa. xxxiii. 17. (*r*) Matth. v. 8.

nances. Therefore *wash your hearts from wickedness* (s). Be earnest for the cleansing virtue of Christ's blood, and the sanctifying power of his Spirit. 3. Stir up yourselves. Every lazy looking on a crucified Christ in the sacrament will not serve the turn. There needs the greatest intenseness of heart, and consideration of mind. Therefore rouse up yourselves, and set seriously and earnestly to work. 4. Labour to have faith in exercise. Faith is the eye of the soul: And as it is not enough to have eyes, but they must be opened, else we cannot see objects that are presented to us; so, it is not the having, but the using of faith, that will give you a saving sight of the glory of God. Therefore set faith a-work: Open the eye of faith. 5. I recommend deep meditation. By it we enter within the vail to see the glory of the Lord: Meditate on the death and sufferings of Christ represented to you in the sacrament: And meditate on the infinite wisdom, love, and grace of God, that sparkle in the face of a crucified Christ: And let your meditations be deep and ponderous: Think till your hearts be affected. 6. Study much humility. God delights to manifest his glory to humble souls. *Though the Lord be high, yet hath he respect unto the lowly* (t). Be low in your own eyes, and cast yourselves down at God's feet. He doth oft-times hide his glory from his people, to humble them, and to prepare them for glorious manifestations. 7. Come to the table in much love to God and Christ. The more you love him, you may expect the sweeter manifestations. *He that loveth me,* says Christ, *I will love him, and will manifest myself to him* (u). O, there is no love lost that is laid out upon him: But how often do you lose your love, in laying it out elsewhere? 8. Stir up ardent and longing desires after a sight of his glory: As the psalmist; *My soul thirsteth for thee, my flesh longeth for thee——To see thy power and thy glory* (x). God hath promised to satisfy longing souls. Such ardent desires and longings are the birth of his own Spirit; therefore he will have a special regard unto them. 9. I recommend ejaculatory prayers. Even when at the table, dart up holy desires to God in the name of Christ. " O that God " would shine into my heart! Lord, open my blind eyes: O, " shew me thy glory: Draw by the vail: O, for one glimpse " of his beauty: Lord, increase my faith." 10. See that you employ Christ much. You cannot have a saving sight of the glory of God but by and through Christ: *For no man hath seen*

(s) Jer. iv. 14.   (t) Psal. cxxxviii. 6.   (u) John xiv. 21.
(x) Psal. lxiii. 1, 2.

God at any time: *The only begotten Son, who is in the bosom of the Father, he hath declared him* (y). Moses himself did not see the glory of God but by Christ. We read, that while the *glory* of God passed by, God put him in the *cleft of a rock* (z); which some think was a figure of Christ. Would you see the glory of God? Get into the cleft of the Rock Jesus Christ. Go to him for *eye-salve* to anoint your eyes that you may see (a): And employ him to discover the glory of God to you. 11. When you have done all, yet do not limit the Lord, neither as to the manner or degree of manifestation, nor as to the time thereof. If God will give you but one glimpse of his glory, it will be admirable condescension. And if you get such a sight of his glory as melts your heart with sorrow for sin, and enflames your heart with love to God; be content, and be thankful, though you get not such a discovery as ravishes your heart with joy. And then, do not limit him as to the time. The times and seasons of manifestation are in his own hand. He may chuse to manifest his glory at what times he pleaseth. Therefore wait on in the way of your duty. *Blessed are all they that wait for him* (b).

(y) John i. 18.   (z) Exod. xxxiii. 22.   (a) Rev. iii. 18. (b) Isa. xxx. 18.

DISCOURSE XXII.
Of Propagating the Knowledge of God †.

SERMON CXIX.

Isa. xi. 9. ———*For the earth shall be full of the Knowledge of the Lord, as the waters cover the sea.*

ALL the deliverances that God wrought for his church and people of old, were types and pledges of their spiritual deliverance by Christ. Therefore it is customary with the prophets, to take occasion from temporal deliverances, to discourse of that great and spiritual deliverance of the church by the promised Messiah. Accordingly, our prophet having, in the preceding chapter, foretold and promised deliverance to

the

† This Sermon and the following were preached on occasion of the public intimation of a contribution for propagating Christian knowledge.

the Jews from the Assyrians their enemies; he doth, in this chapter, take occasion from this, for the further comfort of the people of God, to speak unto them of their spiritual deliverance by the Messiah. And having discoursed of his pedigree and outward condition, of his transcendent excellencies and endowments, and of his faithful employment and exercise of them in the righteous administration of his government, in the first five verses: He doth, in the next place, shew what would be the blessed effect of Christ's gracious government upon the souls of his subjects; and that, 1. *Positively*, viz. That by the grace of Christ accompanying the gospel, such a blessed change should be wrought upon the hearts of people, as if they were transformed from beasts into men. This is set down in divers metaphorical expressions, verses 6, 7, 8. The meaning whereof is, that men of fierce and ungovernable dispositions, should be so changed by the grace of Christ, that they should become humble, gentle, and tractable. 2. This is expressed, *negatively*, in the first clause of the 9th verse, *They shall not hurt nor destroy in all my holy mountain:* That is, in my church. Wherever the gospel comes and prevails, men shall be innocent and harmless, comparatively to what hath been formerly. Then the ground and reason of all this is subjoined, in my text; whence shall such a blessed change arise and proceed? *For the earth shall be full, &c.* As if he should say, All that barbarity and inhumanity, and fierceness and ruggedness of temper, that is through the nations, is a fruit of their woful ignorance of God: But the time comes, in the days of the Messiah, when he shall set up his kingdom, that the knowledge of my name shall be spread far and near; and this shall have blessed effects upon the hearts and lives of people.

So that my text is a promise of the spreading of the knowledge of God through the earth. And in it we may notice these two things.

1. The thing spoken of—*The knowledge of the Lord:* The right knowledge of God, as he hath revealed himself in his word and gospel. It is the saving and practical knowledge of God that is chiefly here intended; and the speculative knowledge of him, as introductive thereunto.

2. What is promised with reference to this, viz. That *the earth shall be full of* it: By *the earth*, we are, by a metonymy, to understand the inhabitants of the earth. *They shall be full of the knowledge of the Lord.* 1. In regard of the measure and degree of this knowledge. Under the gospel, men shall be full of the knowledge of God, comparatively to what the saints were

were under the Old Testament. 2. In regard of extent: The knowledge of God shall be propagated through the nations; so that men of all nations, and of all ranks and qualities, and not a few such, shall partake of it. And this is amplified by a comparison, *As the waters cover the sea:* That is, the channel of the sea, by a metonymy. The meaning is, the earth shall be filled with the knowledge of God, as the channel of the sea is filled with water: The knowledge of God shall be spread over the earth, as the water is spread over the channel.

The doctrine that ariseth from these words, is this:

The propagating and spreading of the knowledge of God through the earth, is a great blessing, reserved for, and belonging unto, the times of the gospel.

For, it is promised here as a great blessing, and the spring and fountain of other blessings under the government of the Messiah: And it is promised as a New-Testament blessing. We have a text parallel to this in Habakkuk ii. 14. *For the earth shall be filled with the knowledge of the glory of the Lord, as the waters cover the sea.*

In handling this doctrine, I shall shew,

1. *What knowledge of God is here to be understood.*
2. *That the filling of the earth with the knowledge of God, is a very great and desirable blessing.*
3. *That this is a blessing reserved for, and belonging unto the times of the gospel. And then,*
4. *I shall apply the doctrine.*

First, What knowledge of God is here to be understood? For clearing this, let us consider, 1. The object of this knowledge. 2. The knowledge itself.

1. Consider the object of this knowledge; and that is, God. Now, God is not to be considered here absolutely, but in relation to some special manifestation of himself. There is a knowledge of God as God, by the light of nature: But this is not here intended; nor can it be the subject of any gracious promise, seeing it is common to all men. But God is to be here considered as revealed in Christ: So that the knowledge here intended is a knowledge of God in Christ; of God, as he hath revealed himself and his mind and will in the holy scriptures: A knowledge of him who is one God in three persons; for he is the only true God. Excellent to this purpose is that text;

text, *This is life eternal, that they might know thee the only true God, and Jesus Christ whom thou hast sent* (a). If we imagine a God out of a Trinity, we fancy an idol to ourselves.

2. Consider the knowledge itself, of what nature and kind it is. It is not a knowledge merely speculative or notional that is here intended; for such a knowledge is insufficient to transform the hearts of men, and to produce such a blessed change as is here spoken of in the context. But the knowledge of God here intended, is a saving and practical knowledge of him; such a knowledge as is a fruit of divine teaching, and the effect of an internal gracious illumination, when God *shines into the heart* (b). When not only there are some notions of God pictured in the brain, but the image of God is formed in the heart: Such a knowledge whereby the mind is renewed, being accompanied with faith and love in the heart. Such a knowledge of God as affects the heart, and influenceth the life and practice: Such a knowledge as changeth and reformeth the heart and life. This is that knowledge of God that is principally and ultimately here intended. Yet a speculative knowledge of God is not excluded, but included as introductive to the former: For, without the speculative knowledge of God, a man cannot have the saving knowledge of him. A speculative knowledge there may be, without a saving knowledge; but a saving there cannot be, without a speculative: As a foundation may be without a superstructure, but a superstructure there cannot be without a foundation. Well then, the knowledge of God here spoken of, is a speculative knowledge, as the foundation; and a practical and saving knowledge, as the superstructure.

Second, I am in the next place to shew, that the filling of the earth with the knowledge of God is a very great and desirable blessing. When knowledge increaseth, and spreadeth far and near through the world, O what a desirable blessing is this? This will plainly appear from these two things.

1. *The filling of the earth with the knowledge of God is a proper remedy of the sad and lamentable effects of that woful ignorance of God that at this day overspreads the earth.*
2. *It is a special mean for advancing and enlarging the kingdom of Christ through the nations.*

1. The filling of the earth with the knowledge of God is a proper remedy of the sad and lamentable effects of that woful
ignorance

(a) John xvii. 2. (b) 2 Cor. iv. 6.

ignorance of God that at this day overspreads the earth. For clearing this, consider these three things.

(1.) The far greater part of the earth is at this day under woful ignorance of God. The far greater part is without the church, and consequently under the darkness of ignorance. It was man's glory in his primitive state that he was endowed with the saving knowledge of God. But the first blot that sin made was upon Adam's understanding; and from him there is a darkness transmitted to the understandings of all men by nature: So that there is not a man that by nature understands God. Every man is born with a vail upon his heart, with darkness, and blindness in his understanding (c). And this continues to be the condition of all those that are without the church, and destitute of the blessing of divine revelation. Hence the times of Gentilism, are called the *times of ignorance:* And the Gentiles are said *not to know God;* and to be *without God;* and to *sit in darkness:* And the Pagan nations are called *the dark places of the* earth (d).

(2.) This woful ignorance of God that the far greater part of the nations is under, is the source and fountain of many sad and lamentable evils, both of sin and misery. 1. Hence spring many evils of sin. The apostle shews that the idolatry of the Gentiles did arise from their *vain imaginations of God,* and the *darkness of their foolish hearts* (e). All the idolatry that hath been, and is this day in the world, springs from ignorance and misapprehensions of God. Again, this woful ignorance is the cause of all the other wickedness that abounds through the nations. It is ignorance that fashions men to lust. Men *give themselves over to lasciviousness, to work all uncleanness with greediness, because of the blindness of their hearts* (f). Where ignorance of God is, it opens the very flood-gates of sin, so that wickedness breaks out like a torrent. The prophet says, *There is no knowledge of God in the land :* And then it follows, *By swearing, and lying, and killing, and stealing, and committing adultery, they break out, and blood toucheth blood* (g). Thus it is at this day in these nations that are destitute of the knowledge of God; O, what gross idolatry, inhumanity, barbarity, and other wickedness, is to be found among them! 2. Ignorance of God is attended with many evils of misery. Such as are under the darkness of ignorance, are in *the region and shadow of death* (h).

They

(c) Eph. iv. 18. (d) Acts xvii. 30. Gal. iv. 8. Eph. ii. 12. Matth. iv. 16. Psal lxxiv. 21. (e) Rom. i. 21, 22, 23. (f) 1 Pet. i. 14. Eph. iv. 18, 19. (g) Hos. iv. 1, 2. (h) Matth. iv. 16.

They *know not whither they are going* (i). Satan makes a prey of them; they are under his power; for he is *the ruler of the darkness of this world* (k) The darkness of the mind, and the power of Satan, are much the same thing. *To turn them from darkness to light*, says the Lord, *and from the power of Satan unto God* (l). He can lead any where those that want eyes to see their way. Oh, how miserable is the state and condition of these nations that know not God! The only way of salvation is hid from them; so that they are in the path way to hell: For, *Christ will be revealed from heaven, in flaming fire, to take vengeance on them that know not God* (m).

(3) The spreading and propagating the knowledge of God through the earth, is a proper remedy of all these evils. When *the earth shall be filled with the knowledge of the Lord:* this will produce a blessed change in the hearts and lives of men: Then *the wolf shall dwell with the lamb, &c.* Men of fierce, rugged, and cruel dispositions, shall be subdued and meekened by grace, and reclaimed from their inhumanity and barbarity; as we see in the context. Satan's kingdom is a *kingdom of darkness:* The light of knowledge is an utter enemy to it. The knowledge of God opens the secrets of Satan's kingdom, and reveals the mystery of his goverement. It is the breaking out of the light of the glory of God in the gospel, that makes *Satan fall from heaven like lightening* (n). In the primitive times of Christianity, when the knowledge of God in Christ was spread abroad by the gospel in the Gentile world; then Dagon gave way to the ark; down came all the altars, images, and superstitions of the Gentiles, and the whole frame of idolatry erected by Satan was demolished: So that scarce any part of the world doth now acknowledge a multiplicity of gods; and the names of Jupiter, Apollo, &c. are wholly buried among these nations that formerly adored them. And the spreading of the knowledge of God through the earth this day, would be a blessed means of reforming the gross idolatry that yet remains, and of reclaiming people from their other wickedness. When the light of the knowledge of God breaks in upon the heart, it is not only informing, but reforming; it reforms the heart and life. Such as learn Christ aright, and are *taught of God, put off the old man* with his *lusts* (o). They do not know God aright, who live and go on in sin. Yea, even the speculative knowledge of God in Christ, is oft-times effectual in reforming and cleansing

(i) John xii. 35.   (k) Eph. ii. 12.   (l) Acts xxvi. 18. (m) 2 Thess. i. 7, 8.   (n) Luke x. 18.   (o) Eph. iv. 20, 21, 22. 1 John iii. 6.

cleansing mens external conversation, and reclaiming them from gross sins. Some carnal men, though they are void of grace, do yet *escape the pollutions of the world, through the knowledge of the Lord and Saviour Jesus Christ* (*p*).

2. The filling the earth with the knowledge of God is a special means of advancing and enlarging the kingdom of Christ through the nations. For clearing this, consider these three things.

(1.) It is God's great aim and purpose, after the ascension of Christ, to advance the kingdom of the Lord Jesus. This is clear from that text, *The Lord said unto my Lord, Sit thou at my right hand, until I make thine enemies thy footstool* (*q*). Christ being set down at the right hand of God, it is the design and purpose of God to promote the interest of his kingdom, over the bellies of all his enemies, and to make them a footstool, whereby he may step up into his triumphant and glorious throne. This is emblematically set forth by the apostle John: *And behold, says he, a white horse, and he that sat on him had a bow, and a crown was given unto him, and he went forth conquering and to conquer* (*r*). A *white horse*, a *bow*, and a *crown*; altogether, emblems of victory and triumph and growing success. Hereby is represented the great success of the gospel, soon after Christ's ascension. And the rider on this horse, though he then began to conquer, hath not yet altogether given over, though for a time he seem to make a stop: For when the world shall be recovered from Antichristian darkness, we shall again find him mounted on the white horse of the gospel, and *on his head many crowns* (*s*), in token of manifold victories and triumphs over his enemies. So that, Christ having the grant of a kingdom over the nations, his design is to conquer, and carry all fair before him.

(2.) Christ's kingdom cannot be advanced and enlarged through the nations, unless there be a spreading of the knowledge of his name. This is necessary in order to it. People must hear of Christ, and know him, ere they can believe on his name, and subject themselves to his gracious government. Such as do not know him *see no beauty in him*, and therefore cannot *desire him* (*t*). Without the knowledge of God in Christ there can be no true religion. There is no right worship without it. Worship is the fruit of knowledge. Hence it is said, *The Egyptians shall know the Lord in that day, and shall do sacrifice and oblation* (*u*). Without the knowledge of God in Christ,

we

(*p*) 2 Pet. ii. 20. (*q*) Psal. cx. 1. (*r*) Rev. vi. 2. (*s*) Rev. xix. 11, 12. (*t*) Isa. liii. 2. (*u*) Isa. xix. 21.

we cannot serve him. Hence David exhorts Solomon, *know thou the God of thy fathers, and serve him* (x). We must first know him and then serve him. Without the knowledge of God in Christ, we cannot love, or desire, or delight in him: For, love presupposeth some knowledge of the object loved. Without the knowledge of him, the heart can never be gained to him. We read of *the key of knowledge* (y). Where this key is, the heart is fast locked upon Christ. And it cannot otherwise be: For the understanding is the leading faculty of the soul; therefore it must first be enlightened. The illumination of the mind is first, and then the inclinations of the will follow: For, God in his gracious operations, though he crosses corrupt nature, yet never crosseth the natural order of the faculties of the soul, but *draws with the cords of a man;* that is, by means proportioned and suited to the principles of his nature. Now, it is as proper for a man to be drawn by the light of knowledge, as for sparks of fire to flee upward.

(3.) The filling of the earth with the knowledge of God, is a special means for advancing and enlarging the kingdom of Christ. As Satan's kingdom is a kingdom of darkness, so Christ's kingdom is a kingdom of light: It is exceedingly promoted by the light of knowledge. When the knowledge of Christ's name is spread abroad, *his name is as ointment poured forth:* O how fragrant is it! It allures souls to love and prize him, and to count all things but loss and dung for him. The right knowledge of Christ engageth the heart to close with him: For *they that know* his *name, will put their trust in* him (z). When the knowledge of God in Christ was spread abroad by the gospel in the primitive times, it had, in a short time, wonderful success, in all parts of the known world, in conquering and subduing the nations to Christ. Though the instruments employed therein were outwardly mean and contemptible, though the doctrine itself was against corrupt nature, and the powers of the world against it, though the world was leavened with prejudices, and prepossessed with many false religions; yet the knowledge of Christ being propagated, did prevail for bringing in the nations to him; so that even this remote nation, which was inaccessible to the Roman armies, was yet made subject to Christ; and, as Tertullian speaks, *Christians were to be found in all places,—every where, but where their religion forbade them to be, in the idols temples.* If the knowledge of Christ were this day propagated through the earth, O what a mighty enlargement

---

(x) 1 Chron. xxviii. 9.   (y) Luke xi. 52.   (z) Psal. ix. 10.

largement of his kingdom would there be? The pfalmift fpeaks as a type of Chrift, *A people whom I have not known shall serve me: As soon as they hear of me, they shall obey me* (a).

Third, Let me fhew you, in the third place, that the filling of the earth with the knowledge of God, is a bleffing referved for, and belonging unto the times of the gofpel. And,

1. A fulnefs of this knowledge, in comparifon of what the Jews had under the law, a larger meafure and degree of it, is a New Teftament bleffing. This was promifed: *Behold the days come, faith the Lord, that I will make a new covenant* (whereby I underftand, the covenant of grace under the new difpenfation thereof) *with the houfe of Ifrael, and with the houfe of Judah —— And they shall teach no more every man his neighbour, and every man his brother, saying, Know the Lord; for they shall all know me, from the leaft of them, unto the greateft of them* (b). And it was foretold, that in the times of the gofpel, knowledge fhould *be increafed* (c). Hence New Teftament faints are faid to be *filled with all knowledge;* and *enriched in all knowledge:* And the apoftle prays for the Coloffians, that they might be *filled with knowledge in all wifdom and fpiritual underftanding* (d). Under the New Teftament the Spirit is more abundantly poured out. This is that which Chrift promifed as a fruit of his afcenfion, and which foon after his afcenfion began to be accomplifhed (e). There was a knowledge of God under the Old Teftament; but it was hid under types, and wrapt up in vails, till Chrift, who *was in the bofom of the Father,* came to reveal his name, and to bring *life and immortality to light by the gofpel.* It was but little that the faints then could attain to in the knowledge of God, *God having provided fome better things for us, that they without us fhould not be made perfeƈt* (f). They faw but very dimly: But now the glafs of legal ceremonies being broken, *we do with open face behold as in a glafs the glory of the Lord* (g). In comparifon of the faints in heaven, we *behold* but *as in a glafs;* but in comparifon of the Jews of old, we *behold with open face.*

2. The fpreading of the knowledge of God through the earth, the extent of it generally through the nations, is a New Teftament bleffing. This appears from the prophecies and promifes under the Old Teftament. There are many promifes of the enlargement of Chrift's kingdom; particularly

---

(*a*) Pfal. xviii. 43, 44. (*b*) Jer. xxxi. 31, 34. (*c*) Dan xii. 4. (*d*) Rom. xv. 14. 1 Cor. i. 5. Col. i. 9. (*e*) Luke xxiv. 49. Acts ii. 33. (*f*) Heb. xi. 40. (*g*) 2 Cor. iii. 18.

cularly in the xi. xlix. liv. lx. lxv. and lxvi. chapters of Isaiah. Especially, see Isaiah xi. 10, 11, 12. xliii. 5, 6. xlix. 6, 12. liv. 3. lv. 5. and lx. 2, 3, 9. From which texts, it is plain and evident, that in the times of the New Testament, the knowledge of God in Christ should be spread abroad, and fill the earth; so that the nations should join themselves to the church, and visibly own Christ, and subject themselves to him. Particularly, the knowledge of God is promised to the Gentiles, as the foundation of all true religion: *And the Egyptians*, says the prophet, *shall know the Lord in that day, and shall do sacrifice and oblation* (*h*). And Christ is promised as *a light to the Gentiles* (*i*). And our blessed Lord foretold, that *the gospel* should *be preached in all the world for a witness unto all nations* (*k*). True it is, these promises and prophecies were in part accomplished in the first times of the New Testament: Yet we have ground to expect a more full accomplishment of them, when the Jews shall be converted and brought in; as is evident from that excellent and clear prophecy in the xith chapter of the epistle to the Romans. And after the fall of Romish Babylon, *the kingdoms of the world shall become the kingdoms of the Lord and of his Christ* (*l*).

Thus I have shewed you, that the filling the earth with the knowledge of God, is a blessing reserved for the times of the New Testament. And it was necessary that it should be so, for the honour of Christ, who being ascended and set down on the right hand of the Majesty on high, poureth out the Spirit abundantly, as an undoubted evidence and token of the reality and fulness of his satisfaction, and of his glorious exaltation thereupon. Hence it is said, *The Holy Ghost was not yet given, because that Jesus was not yet glorified* (*m*). As the pre-eminence, fu'ly and ultimately to reveal God, was reserved for Christ, who came out of *the bosom of the Father:* So, the spreading of the knowledge of his name through the earth, was reserved for his peculiar glory. Hence is that promise made to Christ, *Behold, thou shalt call a nation thou knowest not, and nations that knew not thee, shall run unto thee, because of the Lord thy God; for he hath glorified thee* (*n*). Where, the reason rendered for the nations running to Christ, is God's glorifying him. The coming in of the nations to Christ redounds to his honour, and is part of that glory which the Father promised to him in the covenant of redemption.

SER-

(*h*) Isa. xix. 21. (*i*) Isa. xlii. 5, 6. Isa. xlix. 6. (*k*) Matth. xxiv. 14. (*l*) Rev. xi. 15. (*m*) John vii. 39. (*n*) Isa. lv. 5.

SERMON CXX.

Fourth, I PROCEED to the application of this doctrine.

Use 1. For instruction. Is it so that the filling the earth with the knowledge of God is a great blessing reserved for and belonging unto the times of the gospel? Then we may be hence instructed in these two things.

Instr. 1. It hence follows, that ignorance of God and Christ, especially in gospel times, is a sad and woful evil. Most certain it is, that mens ignorance of God and of Jesus Christ, under such plenty of the means of knowledge, is not invincible, but wilful and affected. Every man, now under the gospel, may be greater in point of knowledge than John the baptist (*a*): Because now we have many means, helps, advantages and opportunities, for attaining the knowledge of God, above and beyond others. The poor Pagans have no other teacher, but the dim book of nature. And although the Jews under the Old Testament had far better and more clear instruction, yet God was more obscurely revealed to them than he is to us. The glory of God was then wrapt up in clouds of sacrifices, ceremonies, and other shadows; but it shines to us *in the face of Jesus Christ.* Gospel-light now is like *the light of seven days,* in comparison of what it was under the Old Testament. Therefore it is matter of great shame to be ignorant of God now under such special means and opportunities of knowledge: For such ignorance is an argument, either of great negligence and slothfulness in the use of means, or of great dulness and incapacity. People's ignorance now is more inexcusable, and will render their judgment the more intolerable. Though the heathens had no more but the dim light of nature, yet because *they liked not to retain God in their knowledge,* therefore God *gave them over to a reprobate mind* (*b*). What then do they deserve who will not embrace or retain the knowledge of God by a clear gospel light

Instr. 2. It follows from this doctrine, that it is matter of sad regret and lamentation, that in these gospel times, the far greater part of the world is under woful ignorance of God. Oh, how many nations at this day, *sit in darkness, and in the region and shadow of death?*

But seeing the filling of the earth with the knowledge of God is a blessing belonging to the times of the New Testament, whence is it that so many nations now are destitute of the knowledge

---

(*a*) Matth. xi. 11.   (*b*) Rom. i. 28.

knowledge of God? I shall assign some causes of this. As, 1. Such as have the knowledge of God, have not been duly concerned to propagate it. Oh, what a woful indifferency is there among professors of the true religion in the generation wherein we live? What unconcernedness about the interests of the kingdom of Christ, and the salvation of the immortal souls of men? Many professors, if they can carry on and advance their trade with poor Pagans and infidels, are careless what become of their precious souls. If we can enrich ourselves with their carnal things, we are careless of making them partakers of our spiritual things. There have been designs and projects set a-foot for advancing trade with the Indians; but we have not been single and sincere in our designs to propagate the knowledge of God among them, therefore our other designs have not prospered. 2. Many professors of religion obstruct the entertainment of the gospel and of gospel-light, in infidel and popish countries, by their scandalous and vicious lives. Too many professors of Christianity, who have occasion to travel to such places of the world as are overspread with Pagan or Romish darkness, walk quite contrary to the principles of their holy religion, and thereby are a great reproach to it. To this purpose Nehemiah says to that people, *Ought ye not to walk in the fear of our God, because of the reproach of the heathen* (c)? Alas, many, instead of adorning, disgrace the gospel, and bring a foul stain and blot upon it, and create strong prejudices in the minds of poor Pagans against the true religion. It is very evident, that the prejudices that are this day through the world against the true religion, are mostly occasioned by the scandalous lives of professors. 3. There is a sad neglect of the duty of prayer. Though it be the purpose and promise of God, to fill the earth with the knowledge of his name; yet prayer is a necessary mean on our part, for bringing forth the gracious purposes and promises of God to a performance. Therefore after the making of divers promises, the Lord adds, *I will yet for this be enquired of by the house of Israel, to do it for them* (d). But, alas, is not the duty of prayer sadly neglected, and especially prayer, for the coming of the kingdom of Christ, and the propagating the knowledge of his name? 4. Undue methods have been taken by such as professed to propagate the knowledge of God, and to travel for the conversion of poor infidels. I shall not speak of the undue methods that have been taken by some professed Protestants: But as to the Papists, it is notour, that the hateful covetousness, and the barbarous and monstrous cruelties

(c) Neh. v. 9. (d) Ezek. xxxvi. 37.

cruelties of the Spaniards in the West-Indies, did beget strong and rooted prejudices in that poor people, against the God and religion of the Christians. 5. It seems that God's time for filling the earth with the knowledge of his name was not yet come. *The vision is for an appointed time; but in the end it will speak and not lie; though it tarry, wait for it* (e). Every divine dispensation hath its prefixed period. Not only the blessing, but the timing of the blessing is in God's hand. Therefore, all such as would faithfully promote the interest of the kingdom of Christ, must wait his time, and tarry his leisure. Because we know not the particular time, we must wait for it in the way of our duty, and in the due use of all proper means. And to this we have a twofold encouragement. 1. Though we cannot absolutely determine about times and seasons, yet it is probable from the holy scriptures, that the time is at hand, when *the earth shall be filled with the knowledge of the Lord; and the kingdoms of the world shall become the kingdoms of our Lord and of his Christ.* 2. When God's time is come, he will master all difficulties, and make all opposition to give way.

Use 2. For reproof. To them that oppose the propagating of the knowledge of God. It cannot be denied that the Papists are very diligent in propagating their religion: Like the Pharisees, they compass sea and land to make proselytes. But how do they this? Do they it by instructing the poor Pagans in the knowledge of God, and of the principles of the Christian religion, from the holy scriptures? And were they ever at any pains to have the holy scriptures translated into their vulgar tongues, that the poor people, by reading them, might learn the knowledge of God? No, no: This was never their way: Such methods would mar all their designs; the poor Indians would then become Protestants, and not Papists. Therefore they still keep them in ignorance, by denying the holy scriptures to them, and withholding from them the knowledge of most necessary points in religion; and poison them with gross and damnable errors and heresies instead of feeding them with the truths of God; and will not have their eyes open, save only to what they are pleased to teach them for promoting their own ends and designs. And in these countries where popery hath reigned for many ages, they do what in them lies to take away the key of knowledge, by restraining people from reading the holy scriptures in their own vulgar tongue, and crying up ignorance as the mother of devotion; and will have people to believe whatever is imposed upon them by the bare authority

(e) Hab. ii. 3.

rity of their priests, and nothing else: Whereby they are liable to that dreadful wo and curse, which our Lord denounced against the Lawyers, amongst the Jews; *Wo unto you Lawyers! for ye have taken away the key of knowledge: Ye entered not in yourselves, and them that were entering in ye hindered* (*f*).

But I heartily wish that too many professed Protestants did not set themselves to discourage laudable endeavours for propagating the knowledge of God through the earth. I confess we should look carefully to the propagating thereof at home, in the first place; seeing this is that which we are obliged unto by bonds of nature, and which divine Providence doth more immediately invite us unto. But why should our endeavours this way be confined to our own nation? Certainly our zeal for God should be more large and extensive. I cannot now speak of the various means, by which some men oppose themselves to the present glorious design of propagating Christian knowledge; only I heartily wish that such as set themselves to discourage such pious endeavours, would examine from what principle they act; if it be not from a principle of hateful covetousness and love of the world; and if they be not sadly defective in zeal for, love to, and desire after, the enlargement of the kingdom of Christ, and the salvation of the immortal souls of men.

Use 3. For exhortation. Is it so, that the filling the earth with the knowledge of God, is one of the great blessings of New-Testament times? Then, let me from this exhort you to these duties.

First, Such of you as are ignorant, would make it your business to attain to the knowledge of God in Christ. You live in gospel-times, and under plenty of the means of knowledge, and in a land where gospel-light is as the light of seven days: So that your ignorance is both shameful and inexcusable. Therefore, study the knowledge of God, as he hath revealed himself in Christ. Be diligent in the use of the means of knowledge, particularly in reading and hearing the word, in learning your Catechism, and in attending diets for catechising, when you have opportunity. And do not please yourselves with a speculative or notional knowledge of God, but seek after practical and saving knowledge. Be earnest with God in prayer, that he would *shine in your heart, to give you the light of the knowledge of the glory of God into the face of Jesus Christ*(*g*).

Second, Bless God and be thankful; and that, for these blessings. 1. Bless him for propagating the knowledge of himself

in

(*f*) Luke xi. 52.   (*g*) 2 Cor. iv. 6.

in gospel times, and that the knowledge of his name is not under such a confinement as under the Old Testament, when the means of knowledge were confined to one nation. 2. Bless him that he hath spread the knowledge of his name so far as to this remote corner of the earth. Historians testify what woful barbarity, inhumanity, and monstrous idolatry, prevailed in this nation, before God sent the light of the glorious gospel into it. 3. Bless him that it hath been your lot to be born and brought up in gospel times; and in such a nation, where the light of the glorious gospel shines so clearly; and in such a part of the nation as this, rather than in some other part, where people live in barbarity and ignorance. 4. Bless him that he hath filled you with the knowledge of his name. I hope, there are some of you of whom it may be said, as the apostle says of the believing Romans, you are *filled with all knowledge* (h): O bless God for this. The name of Christ should be to you *like ointment poured forth* (i). You should rejoice in its fragrancy, and bless God for the sweet savour of it. I may say to you, as our blessed Lord said to his disciples, *Blessed are your eyes, for they see; and your ears, for they hear. For verily, I say unto you, that many prophets and righteous men* (Luke adds, *many kings*) *have desired to see these things which ye see, and have not seen them; and to hear these things which ye hear, and have not heard them* (k). 5. Bless God that he hath given such ground of hope, that the knowledge of his name shall be yet further spread abroad through the earth; so that we look for blessed *days of the Son of Man*. All these are great blessings, for which we cannot be sufficiently thankful.

Third, Study to grow in the knowledge of God, that you may be filled with the knowledge of his name. Be always making progress, that you may *go on unto perfection* (l); and that your knowledge may be as *the shining light, that shineth more and more unto the perfect day* (m). The glorious angels, though they know much of God, yet they still desire to know more: *Which things*, says the apostle, *the angels desire to look into* (n). O, let us study to imitate them, in our search and enquiry into gospel truths and mysteries.

Fourth, Make it your business to propagate the knowledge of God in Christ through the earth: To have the light of knowledge spread abroad.

All

(h) Rom. xv. 14.   (i) Cant. i. 3.   (k) Matth. xiii. 16, 17.
Luke x. 24.   (l) Heb. vi. 1.   (m) Prov. iv. 18.
(n) 1 Pet. i. 12.

All are bound to this. We ought to be agents and factors for the kingdom of Christ. In and by baptism you were enlisted as soldiers under Christ's banner: and therefore ought to be valiant for his kingdom and interests. Where true grace is, it will incline the heart to this: For, as fire turns all that is near it into fire, so grace is very communicative of itself. If your knowledge of God be saving and practical, you will be zealously concerned to propagate it.

To excite and quicken us to this, let us take a serious view of the sad and lamentable case that the far greater part of the world is in at this day. The most of the nations are destitute of the knowledge of God. A dismal night of ignorance and barbarism is stretched over them; so that Satan doth easily make a prey of them. And in divers parts of the Christian world, where popery reigns and prevails, people are kept in ignorance, and perish in ignorance, having both their eyes put out. The poor people are miserably deluded by many churchmen, who themselves know better things. And how sad is the state of divers parts of this land, especially in the Highlands and Islands. In some places there hath been these years past a great growth of popery: In other places the reformation from popery never yet took place, or but of later years. And in divers places, parishes are of such a vast extent, that the legal provision of one school in a parish, can suffice for the education of very few of the children. And even here among ourselves, though divers hospitals are erected for the instruction and education of children, to the lasting glory and honour of the founders; yet many poor children that want means are sadly neglected; so that, being bred up in ignorance, they become openly vicious, and run into many disorders, such as stealing and robbing, so that they are not only unprofitable, but the very pests of the commonwealth. And, seeing these things are so, zeal for God and Christ, and pity and compassion toward so many thousands, abroad and at home, as are this day perishing in ignorance, should prompt every one of us to the use of all due means, for propagating the knowledge of God, that the kingdom of Christ may be advanced, and the eternal salvation of immortal souls promoted.

And here is a great encouragement to this, that we live in gospel times; and the filling of the earth with the knowledge of God, is a blessing reserved for the times of the gospel: So that there is great ground of hope, that your honest and earnest endeavours this way shall not want blessed success. There are mighty props to support and bear up our faith and hope in this matter.

matter. As, 1. God's decree and purpose to propagate the knowledge of his name, and to enlarge the kingdom of Christ through the nations. This is evident from the prophecies and promises under the Old Testament, which I already quoted. In endeavouring to propagate the knowledge of God, we join issue with him, and are workers together with him, by seeking to advance that which his decree hath established, and his heart is set upon. The decree and purpose of God engageth his power: And when he shall take to himself his great power, he will easily break through all impediments, and master all opposition. 2. Christ's intercession. *Ask of me,* says the Father to Christ, *and I will give thee the Heathen for thine inheritance, and the uttermost parts of the earth for thy possession* (o). Christ is this day interceding at the right hand of God for the spreading of the knowledge of his name, that the nations may be subdued, and brought under subjection to him. And his intercession is powerful and prevalent. This is a mighty encouragement to all that are agents and factors for the kingdom of Christ: He pleads for them: He is their Advocate and Intercessor at the Father's right hand, to direct their motions, to pardon their failings, to accept of their services, to prosper their endeavours, and to remove all impediments out of the way. 3. Christ hath all power put in his hand for advancing his kingdom and interests: *All power,* says he, *is given unto me in heaven and in earth. Go ye therefore, and teach all nations* (p). It is not the devil, that governs the world, but Christ. This is a great encouragement to them that are confederate with Christ for promoting his interests. He hath the government of angels, devils and men; and all events are in his hand. So that we have great encouragement, to use all proper means, for propagating the knowledge of God through the earth.

But what means are proper to private Christians for this end? You should propagate the knowledge of God,

1. By prayer. Hence the psalmist says, *Prayer also shall be made for him continually* (q): That is, Christ's subjects shall pray for the enlargement and prosperity of his kingdom. Great is the power of fervent prayer. When the disciples had joined together in prayer for the kingdom of Christ, it is said, *The place was shaken where they were assembled together, and they were all filled with the Holy Ghost* (r). Christ's kingdom is not advanced by external force, but by inward power and virtue. *Not by might, nor by power, but by my Spirit, saith the Lord of Hosts* (s).

(o) Psal. ii. 8. (p) Matth. xxviii. 18, 19.
(q) Psal. lxxii. 15. (r) Acts xiv. 31. (s) Zech. iv. 6.

Therefore, he hath taught us to pray, *Thy kingdom come.* Some observe, that it is one of the Jewish maxims, that *the prayer in which no mention is made of the kingdom of God, is no prayer.* Most certain it is, that if we are unconcerned for the kingdom of Christ, our prayers are as good as none, not acceptable to God.

2. By an exemplary holy conversation. This is necessary to promote the entertainment of the gospel among poor infidels, to remove prejudices, and to commend religion to their consciences (*t*). Let me recommend this especially to you who may have occasion in divine Providence, to travel to infidel or popish countries. Make it your business to live and walk like the gospel, and be exemplary in holiness and righteousness. This will put a majesty and splendor upon the true religion, and draw the hearts of men to a love and liking of it, and prepare them for further discoveries and manifestations of God and Christ.

3. By all other suitable endeavours: And particularly, by contributing liberally and chearfully some proportionable part of your earthly substance for promoting so good a work. The laudable examples of others should provoke us to an imitation of them. I cannot but take notice, that about the time of our late happy revolution, some worthy persons in England † did, upon their own proper charges, cause print the Bible in the Irish language, and sent a great quantity of them to be distributed among the people in the Highlands of Scotland, which was faithfully done under the direction of the General Assemblies of this church; and of later years, other worthy persons in England did contribute liberally for buying a great many libraries, which were sent to this land, and set up in divers places, especially in the North, Highlands, and Islands: All on this design, to propagate the knowledge of God: And it is notour, that there are famous societies for propagating Christian knowledge, both in England and Holland. And now also, through the good providence of God, there is a society erected in this land, by her Majesty's letters patent, for propagating Christian knowledge; and by authority and commission from her, there is a nomination made of the members of that society: And some are appointed to receive collections, and take subscriptions, from such whom the Lord shall be pleased to move to make a free-will-offering, for promoting and carrying on this pious design. The design, in general, is, to propagate the knowledge of God in Christ in this land, and in popish and infidel parts of the world. As for particular methods and means,

the

(*t*) 1 Pet. ii. 12. † The Hon. Robert Boyle, Esq; and others.

the society is to have these under their serious and deliberate consideration. Only, I presume so far as to acquaint you, that the instruction and education of poor children in this part of Britain, and especially in the Highlands and Islands, where there is most need; and the instructing of people that live in ignorance, both at home, and abroad in infidel and popish countries, if the fund amount to a sufficient provision; this is what is designed by the said society.

To quicken you to a chearful liberality upon this occasion, consider, 1. The work is very great, as is obvious to any considering person; and therefore will require a very great stock, that the yearly interest thereof may be able to answer the exigencies of so great a work. So that the nature of the work requires a bountiful donation from such of you to whom God hath given the good things of this life. 2. The design is truly pious and glorious. It is for the glory of God, the honour of the Mediator, the advancement of his kingdom, and promoting the eternal salvation of the immortal souls of men. And can you employ your charity on a more noble and worthy design? I add, that this design hath a manifest tendency to the good of the commonwealth: For, hereby a proper remedy is to be applied, for curing and preventing manifold disorders and vices destructive of human society, which at this day, abound among them that are bred up in barbarity and ignorance; and hereby many, whose ignorance renders them very unprofitable, may be rendered useful and serviceable for the public good. 3. There is great ground of hope that this glorious design shall prosper, through the blessing of God. As others have had great success in such a design elsewhere, particularly in England and Holland, which is a great encouragement to us: So, blessed be God, the management of this work, is put in such hands, concerning whom there is great ground of hope and confidence, that through the divine conduct and assistance, they will manage it with diligence and faithfulness. And many have already contributed largely toward this design; and it is hoped that God will incline others to follow their good example. 4 The success of this design will come to a blessed and happy account. It will be matter of praise to the blessed name of God, and matter of joy to all that love him, both in this and in future generations. The success of it will redound to the lasting honour of the liberal contributors, whose memory will, by a public record, be preserved precious to the generations to come. And the success of it will be the glory of Scotland. We know not how far God may honour this land, to propagate the knowledge of his name through the earth, though our first work is to begin at home.

Well then, let me intreat you to contribute liberally for so good a work. This is the way to honour God with your substance, and to bring a blessing on what you have. So doth Solon tell us, *Honour the Lord with thy substance, and with the first-fruits of all thine increase: So shall thy barns be filled with plenty, and thy presses shall burst out with new wine* (*s*). What you give for promoting so good a work, with an eye to the glory of God, is *lent to the Lord*, and his truth and faithfulness is laid in pawn, that *he will repay it* (*t*); And he hath many ways to do it. But if you draw in your hand, when Providence gives such a fair invitation to lay out for him, this may bring a curse upon yourselves, and upon all that you have: For *he that giveth unto the poor, shall not lack: But he that hideth his eyes, shall have many a curse* (*u*). Many a curse from the poor, and many a curse, saith a learned interpreter, from God himself. Niggard sparing is like to bring a moth upon your estate. *There is that scattereth, and yet increaseth*, says Solomon; *and there is that withholdeth more than is meet, but it tendeth to poverty* (*x*). Such of you to whom God hath given riches and wealth, or a competent portion of the good things of this life, are not absolute owners, but stewards of what you have, and must one day *give an account of your stewardship* (*y*). You are trustees for God. That portion you have of worldly things is a talent entrusted to you, to be employed, not only for your own and your families maintenance, but also for the glory of God and the good of others, especial their spiritual and eternal good. Now, the glory of God, and the eternal salvation of the precious souls of men, are deeply interested in this glorious design. And on this account, I may confidently say, you never had, and I think, never can have, a more glorious opportunity of *honouring the Lord with your substance*, and of *making to yourselves friends of the Mammon of unrighteousness;* never a more glorious opportunity of making your wealth and means forthcoming for the glory of God, and the good of immortal souls. Therefore, bless God who puts such an opportunity in your hand, and lay hold upon and improve it. And such of you as have riches and wealth, should reckon it your great honour, that God in his good providence hath so ordered your lot, that you can be useful for promoting such a pious and glorious design, by such means as the poor are not capable to use †. There have been designs and projects set a-foot for advancing

(*s*) Prov. iii. 9, 10. (*t*) Prov. xix. 17. (*u*) Prov. xxviii. 27. (*x*) Prov. xi. 24. (*y*) Luke xvi. 2. † *Nihil habet fortuna magna majus quam ut possit, & natura bona melius quam ut velit benefacere quam plurimus.* Cic. Orat. pro Rege. Deiotaro.

advancing trade, and there may be more: But I am perſuaded that ſuch deſigns will ſucced the better, when in conjunction with them, we ſincerely ſtudy to promote this deſign of propagating our holy religion.

I have inſiſted the more on this ſubject, becauſe of that averſeneſs I perceived in ſome to contribute any thing for ſuch a pious and charitable uſe. O take heed of making a ſhift to quiet your conſcience in the ſhameful neglect of this duty. Take heed of a narrow ſelfiſh ſpirit. And beware of vain reaſoning againſt this work and deſign, or your own contributing to it. Give according to your ability: And ſtudy, as much as you can, to proportion what you give to the great weight and importance of what you are called to promote. I beſeech you do not ſpare, when divine Providence calls you to ſpend. You that are rich ought to be very bountiful and liberal. God in his good providence offers you this occaſion and opportunity as a ſeed-time; and an harveſt will come in his own time: And *he that ſoweth ſparingly, ſhall reap ſparingly; and he that ſoweth bountifully, ſhall reap bountifully* (z). Pray much for a free and liberal heart; that God would make you as willing as he hath made you able. The Macedonians were *willing to their power, yea, and beyond their power* (a). And what you give, give chearfully, and with good will; *freely* and not *grudgingly;* for God *loveth a chearful giver* (b). And give with a right aim at the glory of God, and the good of ſouls (c). And follow what you give with your prayers. Pray that it may be *a ſacrifice acceptable and well pleaſing to God* (d). Pray for the ſucceſs of this deſign: That God would incline the hearts of many to a chearful liberality for promoting ſo good a work: And that he would favour the Society to which the management of this great truſt is committed, with his gracious conduct and aſſiſtance; that it may be brought to ſuch a happy account, as may be matter of praiſe to his glorious name, in this and ſucceeding generations. And ſo I conclude with that hearty thankſgiving and prayer, wherewith David ſeems to have ſhut up his life: *Bleſſed be the Lord God, the God of Iſrael, who only doth wondrous things. And bleſſed be his glorious name for ever, and let the whole earth be filled with his glory. Amen and amen* (e).

(z) 2 Cor. ix 6.   (a) 2 Cor. viii. 3.   (b) 2 Cor. ix 7.
(c) 1 Cor x. 31.   (d) Phil. iv. 18.   (e) Pſal. lxxii. 18, 19.

F I N I S.

CONTENTS.

DISCOURSE XV. Of Making the Glory of God our Chief End. From 1 Cor. x. 31.

MAKING the glory of God our chief end, what it is, and implies, 6. It ought to be our chief end, 1. In all our actions, 2. In all conditions of life, 7. Why it should be so, 10. Such as have other ends they chiefly aim at, reproved, 12. Mens aiming at themselves, wherein discovered, ibid. Evidences of it, 13. The great evil thereof, 15. Making the glory of God our chief and ultimate end, pressed, 16. Directions given, 17.

DISCOURSE XVI. Of Making it our great Employment and Business to Glorify God. From 1 Cor. vi. 19, 20.

What it is to glorify God, explained negatively and positively, 20. It is done inwardly and outwardly, ibid. That we are his, and not our own, a strong argument to engage us to it, 25. We are God's by a manifold right, 26. That God is so little glorified, lamented, 28. Whence it comes to pass, 29. Making it our great business to glorify God, pressed, 32. The employing all our talents and advantages this way, urged, ibid. How magistrates are to glorify God, 33. And private Christians, 37. The duty pressed, 38. Directions given, 41.

DISCOURSE XVII. Of God's Blessedness. From Psal. cxix. 12.

God is blessed 43. Blessedness in general, what it is, 45. God's blessedness in himself, what it is and implies, 46. He is incomparable in it, 49. He is the fountain of all blessedness in his creatures, 50. How he communicates himself as an infinitely blessed Being, both mediately in this life, and immediately in the life to come, ibid. He is the object of our blessedness, 51. Divers truths hence inferred, ibid. To enjoy God, what it implies, 54. Seeking to disturb his infinite blessedness, is madness, 55. Seeking blessedness and happiness in sinful pleasures or in earthly comforts, the evil of it, 56. Seeking to be blessed in the enjoyment of God, urged, ibid. Directions given, 58. God to be gone to for all needful blessings, 60. What blessings we are to seek from him, especially in preparing for the sacrament, 61. Earnestness for such blessings, urged, 63. Directions given, 64. Believers in Christ urged to several duties from this doctrine, 65. They should seek to be more blessed in a more full enjoyment of God, 67. Directions for this end, 68. An increase of spiritual blessings to be sought from God, 69. How to improve gospel ordinances, and particularly the sacrament of the Supper for this end, 70.

DISCOURSE XVIII. Of the Decrees of God. From Eph. i. 11.

God hath decreed all things that come to pass, 73. The general nature of the divine decrees, and in what sense they are attributed to God, 75. The extent of his decree, 79. The decree about the futurition of sin, considered, and cleared of several difficulties, with practical uses, 84. His decree about the fixed and unmoveable term of the lives of men, cleared and confirmed, with practical uses, 91. His decree is eternal, most wise, most free, unchangeable, absolute and independent, effectual, one and simple: Each of these cleared and proved, with practical uses, 101 The end of his decree, his own glory, 121. God's foreknowledge of all things to come, hence inferred, 123 How the divine decrees are abused, contemned, reproached and affronted, 125. The knowledge of God's decree and counsel to be studied, and how far, 132. His counsel to be owned and closed with, 134. His will and pleasure to be reverenced in all events, 135. And in all duties, 140. God to be gone unto for counsel in all our ways, 141. Resignation to his will and pleasure, patience and submission under affliction, and other duties, pressed, 142. Comfort to the children of God, 147.

DISCOURSE XIX. Of the Unity of the Divine Essence.

From Deut. vi. 4.

In what sense God is said to be one, 153. That God is one only, proved from scripture, the consent of nations, and reason, ibid. Of the multiplicity of the Pagan gods, 163. Divers ancient heresies confuted, 166. The Popish idolatry against the first commandment, 167. The Socinians, and divers others, confuted, 172. Divers inferences from this doctrine, 174. Many do practically set up other things to themselves in the room and place of God, 176. The great idolgod is self, ibid. How we may know what it is we set up as a god unto ourselves, besides the true God, 179. The evil thereof discovered, 181. Outward gross idolatry, and inward heart-idolatry to be avoided, 186. Putting away all strange gods, the idols of the heart, pressed, 191. Directions given, 194. We should behave ourselves worthily and as it becomes, toward this one only God, and how, 195. To get him for our God, urged, 197 Directions given, 199 He ought to be the only object of our religious worship and service, 203. Instance hereof given in several acts of worship, 204. The soul and conscience to be subjected to him alone, particularly in the matters of his worship, 207. A threefold unity among Christians pressed, that we may be one as God is one, 210. Comfort to them whose God he is, 213.

DISCOURSE XX. Of the Trinity of Persons in the Godhead. From 1 John v. 7.

Divers things premised, 219. The use of some words and terms not scriptural, vindicated, 226. What is meant by Godhead, Person, and Trinity, 227. A plurality, yea, a Trinity of divine persons, proved from the scriptures both of the Old and New Testament, 231. The distinction of the persons from the divine Essence, considered, 249. The distinction of the persons among themselves, 251. The nature of this distinction incomprehensible, 252. Wherein it is discovered, 253. The personal and incommunicable properties of the three persons, what they are, and how called by divines, ibid. The eternal generation of the Son, proved, 256. The nature of it, 259. It is mysterious and incomprehensible, 260. The scripture similitudes whereby it is shadowed forth, considered, 262. The vast difference and disproportion between it and human generation, 263. God's admirable love in sending his Son, and Christ's admirable condescension in coming for our redemption, 267. In what sense the term procession is applied to the Holy Ghost, 273. He proceeds eternally from the Father and Son, 274. The nature of his procession, 278. Of the difference between it and the generation of the Son, 279. We should labour to get and keep the Spirit, 282.

The

The different order of subsistence among the divine persons, 284. Their order and manner of working, 286. All external works common to them, ibid. The order of working proper to each of them, considered and explained, 288. Observations thereupon, 292. The different order of working discovered, in the same works, and in different works, both of nature and grace, 294 The offices and operations ascribed to the Father, to the Son, and to the Holy Ghost, in the business of our salvation, distinctly considered, 299. We should be seriously concerned about our own salvation, 313. The glory of it to be given to all the divine persons, 315. That they are one in essence, proved, 317. This is an incomprehensible mystery, 321. Properties of their union, 322. This mystery to be meditated on, and contemplated with humble adoration and admiration, 329. The holy Trinity to be imitated in their unity according to our capacity, 331.

In the general application, an historical account of the opposition made to this doctrine in all ages, with observations thereupon, 333. Some things premised to the answers to particular objections, 341. The objection taken from its alledged contrariety to reason, answered, 343. The objection, that we cannot be obliged in reason to believe what is above reason, answered, 348. Several inferences by way of instruction, 352. Unbelief strikes against all the divine persons, 357. Gross ignorance of this mystery, a sad evil, 360. Divers sorts of persons reproved, 361. Sins against the Father, against the Son, and against the Spirit, 363. The unpardonable sin against the Holy Ghost, inquired into, 375. The study of the knowledge of this doctrine, pressed, 379. The firm belief of it urged, and directions given, 381. Believing in the holy Trinity, what it implies, 388. Motives to press it, and directions with reference to it, 389. We should worship a Trinty in unity, 396. Several positions for our instruction and direction in this matter, ibid. How to conceive of this mystery in our worship, 402. Communion with the holy Trinity, what it is, 404. To seek it, urged by motives, and directions given, 408. This mystery to be studied, and how, 412. Directions given, 414. Equal glory and honour to be given to all the divine persons, 415. Doxologies customary in the ancient church, 416. About singing the doxology, 417. That there are three persons in the Godhead, a strong argument to dissuade from sin, 420. This great truth to be improved for confirming our faith in the belief of other gospel truths, ibid. Duties of believers from this doctrine, 421. Living by faith in the holy Trinity, urged with reference to our own and the church's case, 424 Comfort to believers in Christ, 430

DISCOURSE XXI. Of Beholding the Glory of God in the Glass of the Gospel. From 2 Cor. iii. 18.

The object of this vision, God's declarative glory, 432. The fullest, clearest, and most delightful manifestation thereof is in Christ, 434. The nature and manner of this vision, 436. It is the privilege of believers only, 440. Inferences from this for our instruction, 442. It should commend gospel ordinances to us, 443. A sight of the divine glory, in the face of Christ, to be sought after in the glass of gospel ordinances, especially that of the Lord's Supper, 445. Considerations to press this, 446. Directions given, 448.

DISCOURSE XXII. Of Propagating the Knowledge of God. From Isa. xi. 9.

The saving and practical knowledge of God in Christ is here intended, 452. The filling of the earth with this knowledge, a great blessing, 453. It is a blessing reserved for, and belonging unto the times of the gospel, 458. The great ignorance of God that is now in the far greater part of the world, a sad evil, 460. Causes thereof, 461. Such as oppose the propagating the knowledge of God, reproved, 462. Several duties pressed, 463. The propagating the knowledge of God in Christ through the earth, 464 Pressed by motives, 465. By what means it is to be done, 466. The contributing a proportionable part of our earthly substance for this end, seriously pressed, 467.

INDEX.

A.

Application of redemption ascribed to the Spirit, 297
Apprehensions, wrong of God, the evil of them, 362
Atheists the greatest enemies to mankind, 53

B

Believing, in the holy Trinity, our duty, 387. What is implied in it, 388. Motives to press it, 389. Directions with respect to the exercise of faith in the several divine Persons, 392. In the Father what it implies, 393. In the Son what it implies, 394. In the Holy Ghost what it implies, 395
Blaspheming the Spirit——It is done several ways, 374
Blessedness——That it is one of the divine excellencies, 43. In general what it includes, 45. In what sense it is attributed to God, 44. Of God in himself, what it implies, 46. Properties of it, 49 God is the fountain of blessedness to his creatures, 50 He communicates his blessedness, mediately in this life, immediately in that which is to come, ibid. He is the object of our blessedness, 51. True blessedness and happiness, wherein it consists, 54 It is attainable by us, 53. Seeking to disturb God's infinite blessedness is madness, 55. The evil of seeking blessedness in other things besides God, 56. To seek to be blessed in the enjoyment of God, pressed, ib. Directions for this, 58. Believers should seek to be more blessed in a more full enjoyment of God, 67
Blessing God, what it implies, 66

Blessings, temporal, may be sought from God, 60. Spiritual most excellent, 63. To be chiefly sought, 61. What these blessings are, ibid Motives to seek them, 63. Directions how to obtain them, 64. An increase of spiritual blessings to be sought after, 69.
Brethren——Christ's great condescension in owning believers as such, 271

C

Censuring God's decrees or administrations, the evil of it, 102, 129
Chance——nothing to be ascribed to mere chance, 75
Charity, for pious uses pressed, 468
Christ——the dignity and excellency of his person, 266. His great condescension in coming into the world, 270. Motives to get Christ, 271
Church——her distresses should deeply affect our hearts, 137. How to judge aright of sad events of Providence that befal her, 138. A whole sacred Trinity engaged in delivering and preserving her, 425
Cleaving to God urged, 210.
Comfort doth the Spirit, and how, 310
Communion with God in ordinances, motives to seek it, 68 Directions, ibid. With the holy Trinity, that there is such a thing, 404. Wherein it consists, 405. Habitual and actual, ibid. Motives to seek after it, 408. Directions for attaining to it, 410
Condescension of God to be admired, 311

Conscience

INDEX.

Conscience to be subjected to God alone, 207

Counsel—opposing and resisting God's counsel, condemned, 119, 127. God's counsel to be owned and closed with, 134

Creation—how the three divine persons concur in it, 295. How ascribed to the Father, ibid. Our creation an argument to engage us to glorify God, 26

Cross—Romish idolatry in worshipping it, 170

D

Decree—That God hath decreed whatsoever comes to pass, proved, 73. In what sense decree is attributed to God, 75. Variously expressed in scripture, 76. Two things usually distinguished in it, ibid. What is implied in it, ibid. It is the original spring and pattern of all things that come to pass, 77 The extent of it, 79. It extends to all possible connections between possible things, 80. The decrees of creation and providence considered, 81. God's decree, effective and permissive, what they are, 86. His decree is eternal, most wise, most free, absolute and independent, immutable, effectual, one and simple. Each of these cleared and confirmed, with practical uses, 101. The supreme and ultimate end of it his own glory, 121. How it is abused, contemned, reproached and affronted, 125. We should study to know it, and how far, 132. Directions in order to this, 133. A ground of comfort to believers in Christ, 147.

Decree about the permission of sin. *See Permit sin.*

Denying Christ, the evil of it, 366

Despair of salvation condemned, 364.

Discontent, a great evil, 131

Dishonouring God by sin lamented, 28

Dominion of God is universal, 83

Doxologies customary in the ancient church, 416. About singing the doxology, 417

E

Election peculiarly ascribed to the Father, 297, 300.

Enjoyment of God sufficient to our happiness, 57. God's enjoyment of himself, what it implies, 48

Esteem, high of God, pressed, 196

F

Faith—Christ is the immediate object, God the ultimate object thereof, 392. Living by faith in the holy Trinity pressed with reference to our own and the church's case, 424

Father God—Sins against him, 363. His personal property, 254. The order and manner of working proper to him, 288 Sinners apt to entertain wrong apprehensions of him, 362

Fear due to God alone, 205

Foreknowledge God hath of all things that come to pass, 123. How far the people of God may in an ordinary way foreknow future events, 132

Forsaking Christ a great evil, 366

Free agent God is, 106

G

Generation eternal of the Son proved, 255. The nature of it, 259. The manner of it incomprehensible, 260. Scripture

ture similitudes, whereby it is shadowed forth, considered, 262. A vast difference between it and human generation, 263.

Glasses in which we see God in this life, 437

Glory—what it is to make God's glory our chief end, 6. Why we should do it, 10. Wherein, or in what things, ibid. Motives to it, 16. Directions, 17. How far we are to intend the glory of God in every action, 9. It is the end of all his works, 11. The end of his decrees, 121. Sin not to be committed that God may have glory by it, 89.

Glorify—what it is to glorify God, explained negatively and positively, 20. That we are not our own but his, a strong argument to engage us to it, 25. That God is so little glorified, lamented, 28. Motives to improve all our talents this way, 32. Whence it is that men are not more active herein, 29. We ought to glorify God both in our public, and in our private stations, 33. Motives to press this, 38. Directions for this end, 41

God—his enjoyment of himself, what it is and implies, 48. To get an interest in him as our God, urged, 131, 197. Directions in order to it, 199. Why called the true and living God, 152. In what sense he is said to be one, 153 That God is one only, proved from scripture, the consent of nations, and reason, 154. Why this is so much insisted on in scripture, 156. God a Being absolutely necessary, 159. There are many gods, in what sense, 152. The multiplicity of the Pagan gods, 163. Whence it arose, ibid. The heresy of the Manichees, in asserting two Gods, confuted, 166. Many within the church practically set up other gods to themselves, 176. How we may know what we set up as gods unto ourselves besides the true God, 179. The sin and misery of so doing, 182. The happiness of such as have God for their God, 175. Unity of the Godhead comfortable to them that have an interest in God, 213. God to be owned as God alone, and how, 195. Putting away all strange gods, heart-idols, pressed from divers considerations, 191. Directions for this, 194

Godhead——what is meant by it, 227.

Gospel—God's great goodness in sending it to this nation, 165

Government of the world, the wisdom of God manifest in it, 104

Grace——divine grace to be admired, 109

Guide—how the Spirit doth believers, 309

H

Heart to be wholly given to God, 202

Holiness glorifies God, 23

I

I AM—the import of this name, 120

Ideas divine, the nature of them, 78

Idolatry of the papists against the first command manifold, 168. Outward gross idolatry, and particularly Romish idolatry,

INDEX.

latry, to be avoided, 186. A spreading evil, ibid. How to keep ourselves from it, 188. Heart-idolatry, arguments to dissuade from it, 190

Idols—what things men are apt to set up as idols in their heart, 177, 191

Jealousy of God, what it implies, 185

Jealousies of God, the evil of them, 131

Ignorance of God the fountain and spring of many evils of sin and misery, 454

Image-worship of papists, 170

Independent God is in being and working, 160. In his decrees and purposes, 113

Interests of Christ, opposition to them a great evil, 365

K

Kingdom of Christ, opposition to it a great evil, 365. A whole sacred Trinity engaged in maintaining and supporting the interests thereof, 425. The knowledge of God a special mean for advancing and enlarging it, 456. The advancing it is God's great aim and purpose, ibid

Kings, such as ascribe to them an absolute commanding power, to which obedience is due without reserve, condemned, 173

Knowledge of God, as a covenant-blessing, what it is, 452. Gross ignorance of God, a woful evil, 460 The filling the earth with the knowledge of God, a great and desirable blessing, 453. This is a blessing reserved for, and belonging to the times of the gospel, 458. Whence it is that so many nations are now destitute of it, 460 The propagating of it opposed by many, especially the Papists, 462. To make it our business to propagate it through the earth, urged by motives, 465. By what means this is to be done, 466. Contributing a proportionable part of our worldly substance for this end, pressed, 467

L

Life—the fixed and unmoveable term of our life decreed by God —the truth cleared and confirmed with practical uses, 91

Living God—why so called, 152

Longing for the happiness above, urged, 428

Love to God, with all the heart, pressed, 205. Properties of it, ibid.

Love of God, to be admired and praised, 109. His love in sending Christ, how admirable, 267

Lying to the Spirit, what it is, 373

M

Magistrates, their duty in suppressing atheism and profaneness, 35. What they ought to do for promoting the glory of God, 34. Election of fit persons for the magistracy, urged, ibid

Mary, virgin,—the popish idolatry in worshipping her, 168

Means—separating the end from them, condemned, 125

Mediator—if Christ is to be worshipped as Mediator, 398

Mind of God to be studied by us, 132

Murmuring under affliction, the evil of it, 131

O

Ordinances—the evil of despising them, 365, 443. A great blessing

blessing to enjoy them, 442. Prizing and attending them, urged, 444

P

Patience toward God under affliction, urged, 145

Perfect, God is absolutely, 46

Permit—God decreed to permit sin, 84. Why he did so, 85. Our doctrine doth not make God the author of sin, 88. Obj. This doctrine lays us under a necessity of sinning, Ans. 87. Caution against the abuse of this doctrine, 88

Perseverance of saints, how it is secured, 430

Person, what we are to understand by it in the mystery of the holy Trinity, and the use of that word vindicated, 227. What a person is in general, ibid

Persons in the Godhead are distinguished from the divine essence, 249. The nature of the distinction incomprehensible, 250 Distinguished among themselves, 251. The nature of this also incomprehensible, 252. Wherein this doctrine is discovered, 253. Of their order of subsistence, 284. All external works common to them, 286. Their different order and manner of working, ibid. Observations upon it, 292. Their different order of working discovered, 1. In the same works. 2. In different works, both of nature and grace, 294. The offices and operations ascribed to each of them in the business of our salvation, distinctly considered, 297, 300 The wisdom and condescension of God to be admired therein, 311. That they are one in essence, proved, 317. Not one specifically, 318. Their equality in all essential attributes, 323. Their essential in-being in each other, 326. One in love, will, and operation, 327. Equal glory and honour to be given to them, 324, 415.

Pope——papists make a god of him, 169

Procession—in what sense this term is applied to the Holy Ghost, 273. He proceeds from the Father and the Son, proved, 274. The nature of this procession, 278. Of the difference between it and the generation of the Son, 279

Professing Christ for by-ends, a great evil, 364. Relinquishing our profession in times of danger, a great evil, 366

Properties personal of the Divine Persons, what they are, and how called by divines, 254

Providence—God to be reverenced in all his ways of providence, 122, 135. Rules for right judging of cross providences that befal us or the church, 138

Purposes of God, matter of comfort to believers, 147

Q.

Quenching the Spirit, how it is done, 367

R.

Reason to be led captive to the obedience of faith, 350, 385, 383. To be submitted to divine revelation, 351 No competent judge of revealed truths, 345. Greatly corrupted since the fall, ibid. Pride of it to be laid aside in reading the holy scriptures, 383. Nothing contradictory

tradictory to the principles of it, ought to be admitted as a principle of faith, 343. Some of the fundamental principles of it overturned by adversaries to divine mysteries, 344. That a doctrine is above it, is no sufficient ground to reject it, 348

Redemption by Christ, originally from the Father, 279, 299. Lays a great obligation on us to serve and glorify God and Christ, 27

Resignation to God's disposal of our lot and condition, urged, 142

Resisting the Spirit, in what sense to be understood, 369. How he is resisted, ibid

Revelation of God to us, a great blessing, 175

Reverence of God, urged, 105. God to be reverenced in all his dispensations, 122, 135

Riches, men apt to idolize them, 178, 191

Right God hath to us manifold, 25

S.

Saints departed, the Romish idolatry in worshipping them, 169

Salvation, our own, a serious concern about it, pressed, 313. Equal glory of it to be given to all the divine Persons, 315

Sanctification—the worker of it the Spirit, 308

Satisfied we should be with God alone, 209

Seeing God in this life, 432. The object of this vision, not his essential but declarative glory, ibid. It is his glory as discovered to us in the face of Christ, 433. In Christ we have the fullest, clearest, and most delightful manifestation of divine glory, 434. The nature of this vision, 436. It is by faith, 437. The resemblance between it and bodily sight, ib. Beholding God's glory, as in a glass, what it implies, 438. How we behold it with open face, 439. This vision the privilege of believers in Christ, 440 Special times and seasons when God grants it, ibid. Why he grants it, 441. The privilege of believers only, 442. A sight of God's glory in the glass of ordinances, a necessary, excellent and attainable blessing, 446. Directions in order to it, 445, 448

Seeing God in glory will far exceed what we have on earth, 428

Self the great idol of most part of professed Christians, 12, 176. Mens aiming at it, wherein it is discovered, 12. The evil of it, 15

Silence sinful condemned, 367

Sin, the great evil of it, 355. Arguments to dissuade from it, 420. It strikes against all the divine persons, 355. Sins against the Father, 363. Sins against the Son, 364 Sins against the Holy Ghost, 367

Sin unpardonable against the Holy Ghost, what it is, 375. Whence it is unpardonable, 377. Sins that tend to it, 378

Son of God, sins against him, 364. His personal property, 255. In what sense Christ is called the Son of God, 259. The order of working proper to him, 291

Spirit of God—God's love in giving him admirable, 281. The order of working proper to him, 291. He is the Treacher, Sanctifier, Guide and Comforter of his people, 308. Sins against

gainſt him, 367. Motives to get the Spirit, 282. Directions how to get him, ibid. We ſhould be careful to retain and keep him, 283. Directions for this end, ibid.

Submiſſion to God in afflicting providences, 144

Succeſs—boaſting of it without a regard to the will and pleaſure of God, condemned, 128.

Suffering for God glorifies him, 25

Supper of the Lord,—a glaſs wherein the glory of God is to be ſeen, 438, 445. To ſeek after a ſight of God's glory there, motives, 446. Directions in order to this, 448. What bleſſings we are to ſeek after, by way of preparation, 61. Directions how to improve that ordinance for increaſe in grace, 70

T.

Teacher the Spirit of God is, 308

Terms, in handling divine truths, the uſe of ſome, not ſcriptural, vindicated, 226

Time—ſuch as live as if they were abſolute maſters of their own time, reproved, 96. Motives to improve time, 98. Directions for this end, 99

Trinity Holy——the doctrine thereof fundamental, 219. A glorious and incomprehenſible myſtery, 221. Is not demonſtrable by reaſon, nor evident by nature's light, 222. Plainly revealed, 223. The proof thereof to be taken from ſcripture only, ibid. To be ſtudied with humble ſobriety, 224. The doctrine of great practical uſe in religion, 225. The uſe of ſome words and terms therein, not ſcriptural, vindicated, 226. The import of the word Trinity, 230. The myſtery revealed under the Old Teſtament, 231. The objection, That God ſpeaks of himſelf in the plural number after the manner of kings and princes, anſwered, 236. Proof of a holy Trinity from divers texts in the Old and New Teſtament, 231. An argument from our redemption and the way of ſalvation God hath revealed, 248. An hiſtorical account of the oppoſition made to this doctrine in all ages, 333. Whence it is that ſuch oppoſition hath been made to it, 338. Some obſervations againſt adverſaries and their heretical doctrine, 339. Some things premiſed to the conſideration of objectors againſt it, 341. Some objections anſwered, 343. It is a myſtery above reaſon, 347. The truth of the Chriſtian religion, and the candour and ſincerity of primitive Chriſtians inferred from this doctrine, 352, 353. Groſs ignorance of it, a ſad evil, 360. Groſs miſapprehenſions of it a great evil, 362. Motives to ſtudy the knowledge of it, 379. Motives to get a firm belief of it, 381. Directions how to attain this, 383. Believers have experiences of a holy Trinity, 387. The ſerious ſtudy of this myſtery urged from ſeveral conſiderations, 412. How to be ſtudied, 413. Directions what to do that we may grow in the right knowledge of it, 414. This doctrine improved to diſſuade from ſin, 420. To be improved for confirming our

our faith in the belief of other revealed truths, ibid. Believers urged to several duties from this doctrine, 421. The knowledge of it matter of thankfulness to God, ibid. Our ignorance of it to be lamented, 422. To be seriously contemplated, ibid. To be admired and adored, 423. It will be contemplated in heaven in a far more excellent manner than now, 428. Grounds of comfort to believers from this doctrine, 429. The holy Trinity manifested to us in Christ, 434.

Tritheists, their heresy confuted, 167

True God, why he is so called, 152

Trusting in God, grounds of it, 143. God alone to be trusted in, 206

U, V

Vexed, how the Spirit can be, 372. By what means he is vexed, ibid

Unbelief, its opposition and contradiction to the holy Trinity, 356. It strikes against all the divine Persons, 357. Unbelieving jealousies of God the evil of them, 131

Unity of the divine Persons an incomprehensible mystery, 321 Properties of their union, 322. To be meditated upon, 329. To be adored and admired, 330 An idea or exemplar of believers union with Christ and with one another, 329

Unions admirable there are three, 330

United believers are to the whole Trinity, 390

Unity among Christians in judgement, affection and practice, pressed, 211. Believers should imitate the sacred Trinity in their unity, 331

W.

Will of God—his will and pleasure the supreme cause of all things, 107. To be reverenced in all events, 135. And in all duties, 140

Wisdom of God manifest in creation, government and redemption, 104. To be seriously contemplated in the discoveries made of it, urged by motives, 105. His wisdom in his decrees and purposes, considered, 103

Word, why Christ is so called, 216

Worldly things cannot make us happy, 197

Worship of God—therein we are to take laws from God alone, 208. Religious worship due to God alone, 203. All the divine persons are the object of it, 396. The distinction of *Latria* and *Dulia*, confuted, 171. Directions with reference to the object of our worship, 396. Our worship may be directed to any of the divine persons, 397. All three are but one object of worship, 399. In worshipping the Holy Trinity, a due regard to be had to their order of working, and the œconomy of salvation, 312, 400. How to conceive of the mystery of the Trinity in our worship, 402

PLACES OF SCRIPTURE

EXPLAINED IN VOLUME SECOND.

These marked † are the texts of the several Discourses.

Book	Chap.	Verse.	Page.	Book.	Chap	Verse	page.	Book	Chap	Verse.	Page
Gen.	1.	1, 2, 3.	239	Jer.	10.	11.	155	Acts	4.	32.	211
—	2.	240, 295		Ezek.	36.	20.	375		7.	51.	369
	3.	22.	235	Dan.	9.	17.	233		13.	32, 33.	256
	2.	6, 7.	236	Hof.	1.	6, 7.	ibid		27.	31.	96
	19.	24.	232		2.	16, 17.	187	Rom.	4.	19.	351
	29.	3, 4.	61		—	21, 22.	51		8.	13.	114, 116
	48.	15, 16.	236	Micah	5.	2.	258, 261	1 Cor.	2.	10.	48
Exod.	3.	2, 7, 8,	241	Zeph.	2.	2.	78		—	11.	346
	—	14	120		—	11.	190		6.	19, 20.	†19
	12.	41.	117		3.	9.	112		8.	6.	288, 301
	18.	21.	34	Hag.	2.	4, 5.	242		10.	31.	S.
	23.	13.	189	Zech	14.	9.	213		12.	4, 5, 6.	246
	—	20, 21.	241	Matth.	3.	16, 17.	143		15.	28.	51
	32.	10, 11.	14		4.	6.	125	2 Cor.	3.	18.	431
	—	22.	450		6.	24.	162		5.	18, 19.	303
Lev.	10.	3.	146		16.	16, 18.	338		10.	4, 5	345, 351
Numb.	6.	24, 25, 26.	238		28.	19.	220, 243		13.	14.	61, 244,
Deut.	6.	4.	†149				318				297
	29.	29.	225	Luke	1	35.	290	Gal.	4.	4, 5, 6.	246
1 Sam.	3.	14.	36		7.	30.	127		—	8.	171
	23.	12.	80	John	1.	1.	316	Eph.	1.	4	300
2 Kings	13.	19.	ibid		—	14	255, 279		—	11.	†71
1 Chron.	4.	10.	60		5.	17.	286		2.	12.	149
Job	7.	1.	91		—	17, 18.	259		—	18	247, 312
	23.	13, 14.	113, 119				321		3.	14—17	147
Pfalm	2.	7.	256		—	19.	286, 288		4.	30.	370
	16.	4.	53				291, 293	Philip.	2.	6.	323
	15.	5.	189		—	21.	293	Col.	1.	17.	289
	—	11.	48		—	22.	289	1 Theff.	3.	3.	145
	21.	3.	8		—	26.	259, 278		5.	19.	367
	27.	4.	436				285, 324	1 Tim.	1.	11.	43, 57
	33.	6.	240		—	30.	291	Titus	3.	4, 5, 6	297
	45.	6, 7.	232, 301		7.	29.	273	Heb.	1.	3.	228, 261
	110.	1.	232		—	39.	459		—	4, 5.	256
	119.	12.	†42		10.	30.	317		2.	11.	275
Prov.	3.	32.	133		14	1.	387 424		9.	14.	435
	8.	22—30.	257		—	7, 9.	327		10.	26.	378
	19.	21.	148		—	10, 11.	316		—	29.	358, 374
	30.	4.	233		—	16.	308	1 Pet.	1.	2.	297
Eccl.	9.	11.	75		—	16, 17.	245	1 John	1.	3.	386, 404
Cant.	1.	11.	416, 431		—	20.	225, 330		5.	7.	†215
	4.	8.	192		—	28.	324	Rev.	1.	4, 5, 6.	247
Ifa.	5.	19.	127		15.	26.	245, 272		4.	10, 11.	295
	6.	5.	238		16.	13, 14	276,		6.	2.	456
	—	8.	236				291		7.	3.	366
	11.	9.	†450		17.	11.	318		15.	2.	438
	49.	16.	242		—	21.	331		17.	4, 5.	186
	55.	5.	459		—	21, 22.	329		19.	12.	456
	61.	1, 2.	242		—	22.	318, 332		21.	3, 4	189
	63.	7, 9, 10.	141		18.	19.	366		—	6.	45
	—	10.	371		20.	22.	278				

www.ingramcontent.com/pod-product-compliance
Lightning Source LLC
Chambersburg PA
CBHW051848300426
44117CB00006B/306